DYING AND GRIEVING

Lifespan and Family Perspectives

DYING AND GRIEVING

Lifespan and Family Perspectives

Alicia Skinner Cook

Colorado State University

Kevin Ann Oltjenbruns

Colorado State University

Holt, Rinehart and Winston, Inc.

New York   Chicago   San Francisco   Philadelphia
Montreal   Toronto   London   Sydney   Tokyo

Cover design by Caliber Design Planning, Inc.

Library of Congress Cataloging-in-Publication Data

Cook, Alicia Skinner.
    Dying and grieving : lifespan and family perspectives / Alicia
Skinner Cook, Kevin Ann Oltjenbruns.
      p. cm.
    Includes index.
    ISBN 0030005124
    1. Death—Psychological aspects.   2. Bereavement—Psychological
aspects. 3. Grief. 4. Developmental psychology. 5. Family—
Psychological aspects. I. Oltjenbruns, Kevin. II. Title.
    BF789.D4C66 1989   88-26662
    155.9'37—dc19   CIP

ISBN 0-03-000512-4

Printed in the United States of America
9 0 1 2   039   9 8 7 6 5 4 3 2 1

Copyright Acknowledgments: Figure 3-3, reproduced from *Genograms in Family
Assessment* by Monica McGoldrick and Randy Gerson, by permission of W. W.
Norton & Company, Inc. Copyright © 1985 by Monica McGoldrick and Randy
Gerson.

Photo Credits: Cover, Dennis Stock/Magnum Photos; page 13, © Albert Noyes
Cook; page 51, © Elliott Erwitt/Magnum Photos; page 62, © Werner Voight/
S.I.P.A.; page 113, © Albert Noyes Cook; page 148, courtesy of The National
Cancer Institute; page 159, courtesy of Johns Hopkins Childrens Center; page
191, © Bill Ballenberg; page 230, Taro Yamasaki/PEOPLE Weekly/© 1987 Time
Inc.; page 242, © Mary Ellen Mark/Archive Pictures, Inc.; page 282, Barry Staser/
PEOPLE Weekly/© 1987 Time Inc.; page 288, courtesy of Poudre Valley
Hospital; page 298, © 1982 Chuck Fishman/Woodfin Camp & Associates; page
299, Bettmann Newsphotos; page 335, Ergun Cagatay/LIFE Magazine/© 1982
Time Inc.; page 342, © Eugene Richards/Magnum Photos; page 348, Blair
Godbout; page 391, John Sunderland; page 411, P. S. Davis; page 446, © Eugene
Richards/Magnum Photos.

To Marky "P." Hanson—for she taught so many to live fully

To our students—for they have enriched our lives

Preface

Death is a highly personal experience. It touches the core of our feelings and emotions as human beings. It brings us face-to-face with issues of life and living and leads us to question our values and priorities. Death as an imminent reality, death as the given destiny of all living things, and death as an abstraction all serve to bring critical questions to the forefront and help us define what is important in our lives. Confrontation with death on an emotional, intellectual, or physical level can be a process of growth.

Death is a family event. It occurs within the context of relationships and deep attachments. Families experience significant transformations when their systems are affected by the loss of one of their members. Understanding this process enables us to more effectively help families avoid negative outcomes as they adapt to the loss. By building on existing strengths and traditions, families can use their experiences with death to build closer bonds and enrich their family life.

The larger, societal context of death modifies the way it will be experienced by individuals and families. All societies have developed ways of interpreting and symbolizing death. Cultural attitudes and beliefs about death affect our personal views, beginning in childhood and continuing throughout adulthood. Expressions of grief and rituals surrounding loss are also strongly influenced or determined by the social milieu. In this volume, we discuss this material from a perspective that assumes social change. While providing a historical view, the text also examines recent modern developments and identifies issues related to death, dying, and grief that our society will be grappling with in the future.

We have attempted to provide a text that is firmly grounded in theory, strong in content, and thought provoking. We also think that a book of this nature must address the reader's own emotional reactions to the subject matter. We invite you to use this book to examine your own feelings and issues related to death, dying, and grief.

Uniqueness of the Text

Death is a natural part of life. Individuals typically encounter death and loss as they progress through their lives. Developmental theory suggests that the age at which an experience occurs is an important determinant of how it will be understood, adapted to, and resolved. This theory serves as a foundation and organizing framework for the text. An in-depth look at a variety of topics related to death, dying, and grief are provided as they pertain to particular developmental stages.

Individuals do not deal with death in isolation. Rather, they are influenced by the dynamic interactions with others in their family systems. The family and its individual members, in turn, are affected by larger systems, such as medical establishments, educational institutions, religious groups, human service organizations, legal systems, and the media. This systems approach is an additional unique feature of this text.

Sections entitled "Personal Accounts" follow each chapter. Each personal account is written by an individual who demonstrates personal insights into grief and loss—the kind of knowledge that comes from facing death oneself, suffering the loss of a loved one, or confronting the personal issues of death in a professional role. While originally conceived of as a way to supplement the scholarly material in the text and as a tool to remind students that we are talking about real people in real situations, the voices that are heard in these sections, in some sense, "say it all."

Learning aids are provided throughout the text to facilitate acquisition, understanding, and retention of the material. Chapter summaries and glossaries identify major points and important terms. Lists of suggested readings and related resources provide direction for those wanting to learn more about particular areas. Questions and activities at the end of each chapter provide an opportunity to probe further and ask deeper questions related to the subject matter. They also encourage students to explore their feelings, attitudes, and beliefs regarding a variety of topics and issues related to death, dying, and grief and provide an experiential component to the learning process.

An *instructor's manual* that contains a large number of true-false, multiple-choice, short answer, and essay test questions is also available. The questions test the student's understanding of the material, while allowing for differences in instructor preferences in evaluation. A variety of other valuable teaching materials are also included in the instructor's manual. Discussion questions, suggestions for journal entries, and case study proejcts are provided with instructions for effective use. These materials have been pilot-tested in a death, dying, and grief course at Colorado State University over the past decade and have been modified based on student feedback.

The text and auxiliary materials are appropriate for upper-division university courses on death, dying, and grief. Written from a multidisciplinary perspective, this text can be used effectively in programs in human development and family studies, psychology, social work, sociology, and other human service fields. Medical schools and nursing schools that emphasize the psychosocial aspects of caregiving will also find the book well suited to their students. The material in the text can be beneficial in other programs, such as pastoral counseling and mortuary science, that must prepare students for dealing with death and dying on an on-going basis. In addition, professionals currently working in the field will find the book to be a valuable resource and useful in staff development.

Acknowledgments

Many individuals have given time, energy, expertise, and emotional support during the preparation of this manuscript. In addition to providing tangible and needed assistance, their unselfish contributions provided consistent reminders to us of the importance of writing this text. Their enthusiasm and commitment to the project helped sustain us through our years of hard work. Among those who provided invaluable assistance in the preparation of the manuscript were Gail Bishop, Meg DeWeese, Peggy Ely, Dorothea Fritz, Rod Hannum, Rosemary Holland, Jill Kreutzer, Randy Larkins, Jackie Lindsay, Peggy Milano, Mike Nelson, Ken Oltjenbruns, and Tamina Toray. We also want to extend a special thank you to all the students who have worked with us over the years as teaching assistants. Their willingness to pilot-test materials, give constructive feedback, and ask critical questions has added a special energy to our work. We hope they will share our feelings of accomplishment. In addition, the reviewers involved at various stages of manuscript preparation have provided the objectivity and expertise needed for refinement and expansion. We thank the following reviewers for their careful reading and helpful comments: Sandor B. Brent, Wayne State University; James E. Johnson, Penn State; Mark W. Speece, Wayne State University; L. Eugene Thomas, University of Connecticut; Sylvia Zaki, Rhode Island College; Elaine E. Holder, California Polytechnic State University; T. L. Brink, College of Notre Dame; Marion Perlmutter, University of Minnesota; Robert J. Fitzsimmons, Central Connecticut State University; Billy C. Roland, East Texas State University; Victor M. Agruso, Drury College; Jeanne E. Cunningham, Glendale Community College. We would also like to express appreciation to the editors at Holt, Rinehart and Winston who patiently worked with us in this process. Nedah Abbott, Susan Arellano, Susan Driscoll, Brian Ellerback, Heidi Udell, Sonia DiVittorio, and Jeanne Ford each provided support in a variety of ways. Finally, we want to acknowledge the individuals who have allowed us to include their personal accounts in our text. They have shared some of their most private thoughts and feelings with you. We truly applaud their courage.

Each of us as individual authors would also like to sincerely thank the other for having made the task of writing this book not only a fulfilling one but an enjoyable one as well. Our friendship and mutual respect has grown as a result of this endeavor.

Alicia Skinner Cook

Kevin Ann Oltjenbruns

Contents

Preface   vii

PART I

Foundations of a Holistic Developmental Model   1

CHAPTER 1

The Dying Individual   3

Needs and Concerns of the Dying   5

Physical Needs and Concerns 6 • Emotional Needs and Concerns 9
• Social Needs and Concerns 12 • Psychological Needs and
Concerns 16 • Spiritual Needs and Concerns 18

Factors Affecting the Dying Process   21

Dying Trajectories 21 • Developmental Stages 23 • Ethnic/Cultural
Background 24

Historical Perspectives Related to Dying   25

Changes in Primary Causes of Death 25 • Change in the Arena of
Death 26

Recent Social Trends Related to Dying   27

Death with Dignity 28 • Living Will 29 • Hospice Care 30 •
Patients' Bill of Rights 34

Summary   34

*Personal Account—"An Experience in Listening: A Volunteer's
Memories" by Jean Hay 36*

C H A P T E R 2

Grief and Loss   46

Theories of Attachment and Loss   47

Freud's Theory 47 • Bowlby's Theory 48

Normal Grief Response   49

Manifestations of Grief 49 • Grief Work 53 • Duration and Intensity of Grief 54

Variables Related to the Bereaved: Factors Affecting Intensity and Duration of Grief   55

Sex 55 • Age 57 • Personality Characteristics 58 • Cultural Background 58

Variables Related to the Deceased: Factors Affecting Intensity and Duration of Grief   59

Relationship of Deceased to Bereaved 59 • Age of the Deceased 60 • Perceived Similarity to the Deceased 60

Variables Related to the Death Event: Factors Affecting Intensity and Duration of Grief   61

Suddenness of the Death 61 • Preventability of the Death 63

Additional Factors Affecting Intensity and Duration of Grief   68

Availability of Social Support 68 • Bereavement Overload 69

Helping Strategies   69

Give Permission to Grieve 69 • Encourage Expression of Grief 70 • Support an Acceptance of All Aspects of the Loss 70 • Listen to the Bereaved 70 • Share Information about the Grief Process 71 • Assist in Practical and Concrete Ways 71

Pathological Grief   72

Positive Outcomes of Grief   74

Summary   74

Personal Account—"In the Center of the Night: Journey Through Bereavement" by Jayne Blankenship   75

C H A P T E R 3

The Bereaved Family   90

Family Systems Theory   91

Developmental Stages of Families   93

Death as a Family Crisis   96

Variables Affecting the Family's Ability to Cope   96

Concurrent Stressors 97 • Family Resources 100 • Family's Perception of the Event 100

Adaptation of the Family Unit   101

Positive Outcomes 101 • Negative Outcomes 102

Intervention with the Family System   106

Family Tasks Involved in Coping   106

Maintain Open Communication 107 • Reassign Roles 107 • Provide Support to Other Family Members 109 • Modify Relationships with Social Networks 109

Intergenerational Issues Related to Death   110

Family Rituals Related to Death   112

Prefuneral Rituals 113 • Funerals and Memorial Services 113 • Postfuneral Rituals 114

Summary   114

Personal Account—"The Longest Day" by Pam Landon   115

P A R T I I

Developmental Perspectives on Dying and Grieving

131

C H A P T E R 4

Early Childhood Years   133

Physical Development   134

Skill Development 134 • Body Integrity 134

Cognitive Development   135

Background on Piaget's Theory 135 • Characteristics of Preoperational Thought 136 • Young Children's Understanding of the Concept of Death 138 • Young Children's Understanding of the Concept of Illness 140

Psychosocial Development   141

Toddlerhood: Autonomy versus Shame and Doubt 141 • Preschool Years: Initiative versus Guilt 143

Additional Needs of Dying Children   145

Trust 145 • Minimal Separation 146 • Normalization 147

Parents of Dying Children   149

Stressors on Parents 149 • Parent's Grief after Death of a Child 150

Children as Grievers   153

Therapeutic Interventions for Dying and Grieving Children 156

Child-life Programs 156 • Play Therapy 160 • Art Therapy 161 • Bibliotherapy 162

Summary   163

Personal Account—"Conversations with Ariane" by Nicholas Putnam 165

CHAPTER 5

School-Age Years 184

Physical Development 185

Cognitive Development 185

Characteristics of Concrete Operational Thought 185 • School-age Child's Concept of Death 188 • School-aged Child's Concept of Illness 189

Psychosocial Development 189

The Culture of Childhood 189 • Erikson's Crisis: Industry versus Inferiority 191

Additional Needs of Dying School-Age Children 192

Pain Management 193 • Continued School Attendance 194 • Continued Peer Interaction 195

Children as Survivors 196

Death of a Parent 196 • Death of a Sibling 200

Summary 204

Personal Account—"The Death of a Classmate: A Teacher's Experience Dealing with Tragedy in the Classroom" by Beth J. Evans 204

CHAPTER 6

Adolescence 215

Death-related Experiences of Adolescents 216

Adolescents' Understanding of Death 218

Formal Operational Thought 218 • Adolescent Egocentrism 223

Needs of the Adolescent with a Life-threatening Illness 224

Privacy 225 • Positive Body Image 226 • Expression of Individuality 228 • Independence and Control 232 • Peer Interaction 236

Helping Adolescents Cope with Life-threatening Illnesses
239

The Grieving Adolescent   241

Adolescent Manifestations of Grief 241 • Coping with Loss during
Adolescence 243

Adolescent Suicide   247

Causes of Suicide 247 • Suicide Prevention, Intervention, and
Postvention 249

Summary   252

*Personal Account—"The Absence of the Dead" by Mary Winfrey
Trautmann* 253

CHAPTER 7

Young Adulthood   268

Major Causes of Death during Young Adulthood   269

Needs of Young Adults with Life-threatening Illnesses   270

Developing Intimate Relationships 270 • Expressing Their Sexuality
272 • Receiving Realistic Support of Goals and Future Plans 275

Acquired Immune Deficiency Syndrome (AIDS)   279

Grief of AIDS Victims 281 • Grief of AIDS Survivors 283 • Ethical
Issues Related to AIDS 284

The Grief of Young Parents   285

Miscarriage 286 • Stillbirth and Death of a Newborn 287 • Sudden
Infant Death Syndrome 289 • Abortion 290

Death and War   291

Personal Consequences of Combat 292 • Healing the Emotional
Wounds 296

Writing during Bereavement   301

Summary 302

Personal Account—"Story of a First-Born" by Wende Kernan Bowie
303

CHAPTER 8

Middle Adulthood 327

Major Causes of Death during Middle Adulthood 328

Needs of the Dying at Midlife 330

Reevaluating One's Life 330 • Continuing Roles 331 • Putting
Affairs in Order 332

Coping with Life-threatening Illness: Considerations of the
Specific Disease Process 332

Heart Disease 333 • Cancer 337 • Amyotrophic Lateral Sclerosis
346

Losses during Midlife 354

Loss of a Spouse 354 • Loss of a Former Spouse: Grief after Divorce
360 • Loss of a Parent 362

Summary 365

Personal Account—"The Courage to Face Death" by Cecil Neth 366

CHAPTER 9

Late Adulthood 381

Developmental Themes of Late Adulthood 382

Major Causes of Death among the Elderly 383

Needs of the Dying Elderly 384

Maintaining a Sense of Self 385 • Participating in Decisions
Regarding Their Lives 386 • Being Reassured That Their Lives Still
Have Value 388 • Receiving Appropriate and Adequate Health Care
Services 389

Quality of Life Issues   391

Suicide and the Elderly   394

The Elderly as Grievers   400

Disability and Loss 400 • Widowhood: Loss of a Spouse 401 • Loss of an Adult Child 406 • Grandparents as Grievers 408 • Loss of a Pet 410

Summary   413

Personal Account—"Allowing the Debilitated to Die: Facing Our Ethical Choices" by David Hilfiker, M.D. 414

PART III

Implications for Caregivers   431

CHAPTER 10

Needs of Professionals Who Work with the Dying and Grieving   433

Concerns of Professionals   434

Personal Grief Reactions 434 • Work-related Stress 441

Coping Mechanisms   445

Individual Strategies 446 • Agency and Institutional Support 449

Professional Training Programs   452

Preparing Professionals to Cope with Death, Dying, and Grief 452 • Preparing Professionals for Multidisciplinary Work 454

Caring for the Dying: An Opportunity for Growth   455

Summary   456

Personal Account—"The Working through of Patients' Suicides by Four Therapists" by Susan Kolodny, Renee L. Binder, Abbot A. Bronstein, and Robert L. Friend 457

Subject Index   477

Author Index   484

P A R T   I

Foundations of a Holistic Developmental Model

1

The Dying Individual

Needs and Concerns of the Dying 5

Physical 6
Emotional 9
Social 12
Psychological 16
Spiritual 18

Factors Affecting the Dying Process 21

Dying Trajectories 21
Developmental Stages 23
Ethnic/Cultural Background 24

Historical Perspectives Related to Dying 25

Primary Causes of Death 25
Arena of Death 26

Recent Social Trends Related to Dying 27

Death with Dignity 28
Living Will 29
Hospice Care 30
Patients' Bill of Rights 34

Summary 34

"**A** dying individual is a living individual." That statement reflects a fundamental premise of this book. Just as healthy people have a variety of needs, so do the dying. Rebok and Hoyer (1979) note that "all deaths involve a complex interplay of cognitive, social, and biological processes" (p. 191). Like healthy persons, dying individuals are affected by particular developmental trends and thus reflect the needs and interests and capabilities that vary with each life stage.

A second major premise of this book is that death is a natural part of the lifespan. Although life expectancies have been extended significantly in the past century, death cannot be avoided. Even though many people in this country are isolated from the dying process as a result of the institutionalization (in hospitals or nursing homes) of most dying persons, we cannot be protected from the deaths of persons we love or from the ensuing grief.

A third basic premise of the book is that attitudes such as respect and empathy exhibited toward dying persons can be as important in helping them deal with their impending deaths as the functional skills (for example, giving medication) used in their care. Dying persons should be treated as human beings who deserve respect and concern and not simply as physical entities that are malfunctioning.

A fourth major premise is that attention must be paid both to the persons who are dying and to the social units of which they are a part. The entire family is affected by the death of one of its members. Thus, we need to be concerned not only with the grief responses of individuals but also with the changes in the family system as a whole while it strives to adjust to the death of one of its members.

A final premise of the book is the understanding that a holistic approach to meeting the needs of the dying individual and his or her family is valuable to all concerned. It is much too simplistic and unrealistic to assume that the needs of the dying are only physical. Although the decision to pursue curative measures or provide palliative (comfort) care together with decisions as to how to provide that care are crucial issues for the dying and their families, many other concerns are also paramount. In addition to physical concerns, emotional, social, psychological, and spiritual concerns must also be recognized as important. Support should be given to the dying in order to meet each of these categories of needs (Rebok & Hoyer, 1979). This approach is known as a *holistic perspective.*

Currently, interdisciplinary teams (doctors, nurses, child-life specialists, medical social workers, psychologists, ministers, nutritionists, among others) work together in a variety of health care settings. Their collaborative efforts emphasize the importance of providing holistic care. Members of the team share insights and information derived from training in their own

4

disciplines and help to create a treatment plan that is more comprehensive and effective than one determined by a single individual.

Needs and Concerns of the Dying

Before beginning a discussion of the needs and concerns of the dying, it is important to understand that the dying process is unique to each individual. Although we can discuss commonly experienced components of the dying process, it is inappropriate to assume that what is said here is true of every dying person. This section is intended to provide insight, not dictate a "right" way to die. We will examine important issues in the physical, emotional, social, psychological, and spiritual realms (see Figure 1.1).

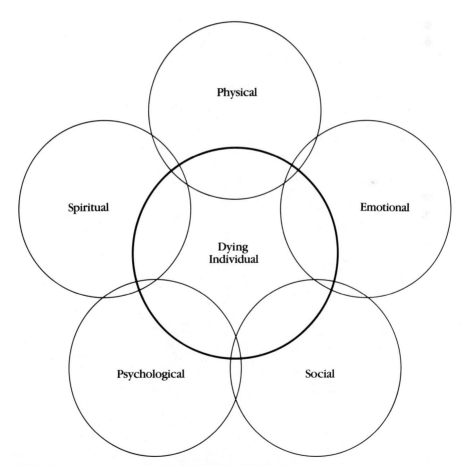

Figure 1.1   *Holistic Perspective of the Dying Process*

Physical Needs and Concerns

The realm of human existence that most immediately comes to mind when discussing death is the physical. Although many topics could be examined in this section (including disease entities, treatment modes, and nutritional issues), we shall limit our discussion to two primary areas: pain and body image. These two topics were chosen because they illustrate the close relationship between physical concerns and those of a social, emotional, and psychological nature.

Pain. Pain is the most commonly experienced symptom of terminally ill patients (Levy, 1988). In order that the dying may be assured of as high a quality of life as possible, many would argue that pain must be controlled (Saunders, 1978). Lack (cited in Dupee, 1982) has summarized the crucial elements of an effective pain control program: "(1) identification of etiology, (2) prevention of pain before it appears, and (3) selection of an analgesic regimen that allows the patient to self-administer drugs, maintain alertness, and live as normally as possible" (pp. 240–241). Levy (1988) noted that pain control may be based on one of the following basic approaches: modification of the source of the pain, interference with the transmission of the pain to the central nervous system, or altering the perception of the pain.

The cause of the pain must be known before appropriate therapeutic methods can be implemented. In our recent history, the most common treatment modality has been drug therapy. Currently, increasing attention is being given to alternative methods, including biofeedback, hypnosis, relaxation and imagery techniques, and acupuncture, among others. Regardless of the philosophy underlying the control of pain, pain management should be personalized.

Saunders (1978) has argued that it is not sufficient to simply alleviate pain once it is experienced, but rather it is important, if at all possible, to prevent the pain from ever occurring. Alleviation of pain implies that it has been experienced but relieved, while prevention implies that the physical suffering has been avoided altogether.

The goal of medication should be such that the dosage is sufficient to cross the pain relief threshold but not of such a quantity or of such a type that the medication causes the patient to become sedated. Freedom from pain while in a conscious and alert state allows dying persons to retain control over as much of their lives as possible and to have opportunities to complete their *unfinished business* prior to death (Bader, 1972). Kübler-Ross (1969) first used this term to refer to the need to draw closure to many facets of one's life. This may include, for example, apologizing for a long-past argument or arranging alternative care for one's surviving children. Not only do the dying need to "finish their business," but so do the grieving. One child, anticipating his mother's death, needed to let her know how much he cared about her:

> When my mom first had that g–tube in I just needed to tell her that I was going to miss her and said I'm going to miss you when you're gone and I know my family didn't want me to do it. But the minute it came out of my mouth I just felt so much better. But if she had died before I said that, I don't think I would have had that feeling. (Horne & Fagan, 1983, p. 16)

Many health practitioners, including proponents of the hospice philosophy (discussed in more detail later in this chapter), believe that medication should be self-administered (Magno, 1981; Saunders, 1978). Self-regulation of drugs allows the dying to retain a sense of control. Self-administration also minimizes their fear that their pain will be exacerbated if an upcoming dosage is not given in time. The patient does not need to become dependent on others to administer the drug or on predetermined timetables. If the medication can be self-regulated, the dying can participate in the appropriate modification of the dosage under the guidance of a physician. Although some individuals question the efficacy of a self-administration program, fears that the dying would abuse this opportunity have not been borne out. Coyle (1985) believes that addiction is not a concern when a patient has a terminal illness. In fact, most patients report a tendency to use fewer drugs when they know drugs are readily available if needed.

Although pain is typically regarded as physical in nature, it also has emotional and psychological components. For some persons, fear of pain heightens a sense of anxiety which, in turn, magnifies the sensation of pain or other physical stress (Magno, 1981; Rosel, 1978). Additionally, there can be a type of emotional pain that comes from the interpretation of what the pain means or from resultant changes in life-style. For example, patients may interpret pain as punishment for some transgression and feel guilty for past acts. Others may experience pain that is incapacitating to a point where they can no longer walk and, as a result, feel depressed due to a loss of independence. This, in turn, can contribute to a sense of inferiority or shame (Schoenberg & Senescu, 1970).

Body Image. *Body image* is defined as the "interpersonal experience of the person's feelings and attitudes towards one's body and the way he organizes these experiences" (Norris, 1970, p. 42). In order to create one's sense of body image, individuals examine their physical characteristics and use criteria from the cultural milieu to pass judgment on their own physical being. To some degree, the outcome of this process of passing judgment ultimately influences their psychological state.

An individual's body image may change over time as physical maturation progresses and physical skills develop. For example, adolescents must integrate body changes (height, development of primary and secondary sex characteristics, and so forth) into the image they already have of themselves. The ultimate outcome of that image in terms of "goodness" or "badness" is closely related to what messages are communicated by the culture in terms of what is attractive, valuable, or even enviable. For example, most Americans regard a particular range of height and weight, strength, and athletic prowess in males as positive characteristics. Women, on the other hand, are often judged on the basis of such features as face, figure, and hair.

A terminal illness may affect a previous sense of body image as a result of such changes as loss of weight, body parts, or body functions. For example, in a culture that values a female's figure and hair, a woman who loses a breast as a result of a mastectomy and her hair to the subsequent chemotherapy may have a very difficult time dealing with those losses and convincing herself that others find her attractive or valuable. A woman who has had a hysterectomy must deal with the fact that she will be unable to bear children and needs to reconcile that inability with her definition of womanhood or femininity. A woman who is so weak that she can no longer perform many of the tasks that she was once proud of doing may need to deal with a feeling that her body has betrayed her.

Both physical and psychological support must be given to the dying in order to deal with these changes. For example, a woman who has had a breast removed may be fitted with a natural looking prosthesis. A woman who has lost her hair after chemotherapy may wear an attractive wig if she so desires. Psychological support can be given by talking to her about how she is perceiving her body's changes and how she is feeling about them. She can be reassured, either by words or by physical closeness, that she is still attractive. Open communication, together with caring physical contact and comfort, are powerful tools in overcoming potential negative changes in body image.

The body's ability to function appropriately is referred to as *body integrity*. Dying individuals may face the gradual loss of body function. Viney (1984) studied 484 persons who were severely ill and found that a threat to one's body integrity did affect an individual's emotional state and was manifest in feelings of sadness, anger, helplessness, and hopelessness. Caregivers should attempt to help the dying individual understand the physical changes and deal with the ensuing emotions.

Emotional Needs and Concerns

Elisabeth Kübler-Ross has challenged professionals and nonprofessionals alike to be sensitive to the needs of the dying. In her classic book entitled *On Death and Dying*, Kübler-Ross (1969) delineated five stages to describe the dying person's progression toward acceptance of his or her impending death. Those stages are summarized here.

1. *Denial:* This stage is typically the initial reaction to the diagnosis of a terminal illness. It is characterized by the statement "No, not me, it cannot be true." Denial is the initial defense mechanism used to deal with news of impending death, but it is rather quickly replaced by partial acceptance.
2. *Anger:* This stage involves feelings of anger, rage, envy, and resentment as the dying person attempts to answer the question, "Why me?"
3. *Bargaining:* This stage involves an attempt to postpone the inevitable by asking that death be delayed in return for such things as "a life in the service of the church" or similar promises.
4. *Depression:* This stage is marked by two types of depression. The first is *reactive depression*, resulting from losses that are experienced as a part of the illness. For example, a woman may become depressed after the loss of her breast due to a mastectomy. The second type is *preparatory depression*, which anticipates impending losses such as separation from family.
5. *Acceptance:* This stage is marked by "a degree of quiet expectation . . . not a resigned and hopeless 'giving up' " (pp.112–113). The individual no longer actively struggles to survive.

It is recognized that Kübler-Ross has made a major contribution to the field of *thanatology*, which is the study of death, dying, and grief. Concerns have arisen, however, regarding the inappropriate application of her work by others. Many people have treated her theory as if it were a prescription, outlining steps to the "right way to die," rather than as a description of what she regarded to be true after observing hundreds of terminally ill patients. Kübler-Ross herself has argued against persons' attempting to force the dying into a mold based on her theory and, in essence, demanding that they make rapid progress through the first four stages in order to accept their fate. Additionally, Kübler-Ross's theory has been criticized because it does not take into account characteristics inherent in the dying individual (such as sex, age, previous life experiences, ethnicity, coping strategies, or nature of the illness) or concern itself with such factors as cultural environment or interrelationships with significant others (Kasten-baum, 1981).

The acceptance of the knowledge that one is dying is not necessarily universal, nor is it the culmination of a sequential series of emotional experiences. Rather, dying individuals experience a mix of emotions at any point in time, and those emotions may peak, diminish, and then recur. Shneidman (1978) noted that as he has worked with dying persons, he has seen "the wide panoply of human emotions—few in some people, dozens in others—experienced in a variety of orderings, re-orderings, and arrangements" (p. 206).

Rather than advocating a stage theory, Pattison (1977) describes three common clinical phases of the dying process. These are depicted in Figure 1.2.

1. The first phase is the *acute crisis phase*, which is triggered by the crisis of knowing that death is approaching. This phase is marked by great anxiety and sense of threat to one's self.

2. The second phase is the *chronic living-dying phase*. This stage is usually the longest and is typified by a variety of fears as well as grief for the many losses that are experienced as a part of the dying process.

3. The final phase is known as the *terminal phase* and is characterized by an increased withdrawal into one's self and an increased sense of acceptance of the anticipated death.

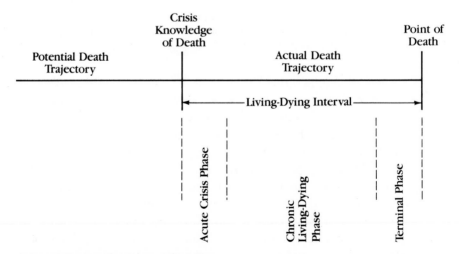

Figure 1.2   *Phases of the Dying Process*

Source: E. M. Pattison (1977), *The Experience of Dying*, Englewood Cliffs, NJ: Prentice-Hall, p. 44. Reprinted by permission.

Although this framework is helpful in understanding the changing emotional state of the dying, Pattison notes that the insights presented are not necessarily relevant to all dying persons and that it is crucial to respond to each person as an individual.

Much has been written about the emotional facets of the dying process. To a great extent, those descriptions primarily deal with what Pattison has described as the chronic living-dying phase. Many of the emotional responses to dying reflect a variety of fears. Others are manifestations of grief in response to the many losses that are a part of the dying process.

Fears.   Dying individuals often experience a wide variety of fears, including fear of pain or suffering, fear of isolation or abandonment, fear of extinction, fear of rejection, fear of the unknown, fear of indignity, and fear of an inability to fulfill one's responsibilities (Callari, 1986; Kastenbaum & Aisenberg, 1972; McGrory, 1978). Sometimes fears may clearly be recognized as such and confronted openly. Many times, however, the feelings that are present may not be clearly perceived or openly acknowledged as fears. Instead, these fears may be expressed indirectly. For example, individuals who are afraid of being isolated may not openly acknowledge that feeling but may still find it very difficult to allow visitors to leave.

Not only do dying persons experience a multitude of fears, so do family and friends, who are often afraid of not knowing what to do or say. Survivors may fear a life alone without their loved one and the changes that illness and death precipitate. Health professionals may fear a sense of failure when their patients die. Open communication among all persons in the system allows them to become more sensitive to the presence of fears and to be of mutual support to one another in alleviating their concerns.

Grief.   Grief is a natural response to loss. Although we will examine this reaction in more depth as it relates to survivors in Chapter 2, we must also understand that the dying themselves experience grief. The dying grieve in anticipation of the death event itself and the end of life. They also may grieve as a result of the many losses that can be intrinsic to the dying process. Dying persons often grieve over the many physical losses that they might experience (such as loss of prior energy level or loss of hair). Additionally, they are likely to experience many other losses that may not be readily visible but that elicit deep emotion. For example, dying individuals give up their dreams for the future. They may also lose a sense of control over their health status or body functioning (Rosel, 1978). Persons who are dying often face a loss of independence and, as a result, a loss of self-esteem, as others insist on performing tasks or making decisions for them. Another loss occurs as the dying become cognizant of family and friends withdrawing from them physically and/or socially.

The grief resulting from these many losses is characterized by a multiplicity of thoughts and feelings. Anger, guilt, remorse, anxiety, depression, rebellion, and aggression are among its common manifestations (Feigenberg & Shneidman, 1979). The dying need an opportunity to express their emotions in a supportive environment. When faced with so many losses, individuals have a right to grieve and a need to know that they are neither weak nor abnormal for doing so.

Positive Emotions.   Although many people assume there are no positive consequences to learning that death is imminent, Zinker and Hallenbeck (1965) would argue otherwise. Crises, such as impending death, allow the dying an opportunity to strive for "growth, self-actualization, and fuller being" (p. 349). In their review of pertinent literature, Zinker and Fink (1966) found that many people regarded knowledge of impending death as an impetus for the dying to achieve positive outcomes, such as growing emotionally in the face of adversity, strengthening emotional bonds with others, developing insights about the world, and positively evaluating their past lives. In a supportive environment, the dying can achieve dignity and demonstrate courage which can "counterbalance depression, anxiety, and fear" (Olin, 1972, p. 570).

Social Needs and Concerns

In order for the dying to deal effectively with their fears and to come to terms with their own grief, they need to know that others still care about them. As indicated earlier, a primary fear of the dying is a fear of loneliness or abandonment (Dupee, 1982). This fear may be exacerbated by many common reactions that others have toward the dying. These reactions have historically included the following: a failure to disclose the truth regarding the diagnosis of a terminal illness (Glaser & Strauss, 1965), a refusal to deal openly and honestly with death-related issues and feelings (Kastenbaum & Aisenberg, 1972), and physical and emotional withdrawal from dying persons (Charmaz, 1980).

Disclosure of Diagnosis.   In a Gallup Poll sampling of 1500 persons representative of the adult population of the United States, 82 to 92 percent of each subsample would want to be told if they had a fatal illness (Blumenfield, Levy, & Kaufman, 1978). Those subsamples were based on the following variables: sex, race, education, age, income, occupation, com-

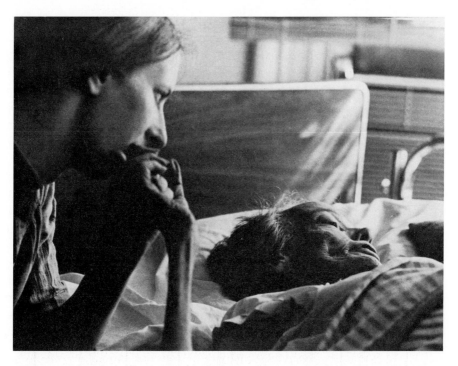

Photo 1.1   *Close, caring comfort deters a sense of isolation in dying individuals.*

munity size, and geographic region. Although the vast majority of persons would want to be informed of the fact if they were to have a terminal illness, this type of disclosure has not always taken place. These researchers noted that the majority of studies carried out prior to 1970 found that physicians did not favor telling patients about the severity of their illness. Health professionals sometimes hesitate to disclose the truth regarding the diagnosis for a number of reasons: (1) the patient does not want to be told, (2) the patient knows and does not need to be told, or (3) the patient will give up hope if he or she is told (Annas, 1974). It should be noted that these are perceptions only, not statements of fact.

There is evidence in more recent years that physicians and medical students are much more likely to directly disclose that a patient is dying than they have been in the past. Eggerman and Dustin (1985) collected data from 103 medical students and 15 family physicians. In response to the question "What is your feeling about telling a patient that he/she is terminally ill," 93 percent of the medical students and all of the physicians felt that patients have a right to know the truth about their illness if they request the information, and all but 2 percent of the medical students would tell their own patients. These data reflect a changing trend in sharing with a patient a prognosis of likely death. Many professionals believe that most persons know they are dying whether or not they are directly told (Rosel, 1978). Dying individuals gain this insight through (1) overheard statements, (2) changes in behavior of others toward them, (3) changes in the medical care routines, (4) changes in physical location of health care, (5) self-diagnosis by reading books or charts, (6) signals from the body and changes in physical status, and/or (7) altered responses by others toward discussing the future (Kalish, 1970). As people gather information to confirm their suspicions that they are seriously ill, they are in a state described by Weisman (1972) as *middle knowledge.* "Somewhere between open knowledge of death and its utter repudiation is an area of uncertainty called middle knowledge" (p. 65).

Communication Patterns.   In their classic study entitled *Awareness of Dying,* Glaser and Strauss (1965) examined the communication patterns between dying persons and those interacting with them. They identified four *awareness contexts,* defined as "what each interacting person knows of the patient's defined status, along with his recognition of others' awareness of his own definition" (p. 10):

1. *Closed awareness:* The patient does not know he or she is dying even though medical personnel and family members know it.
2. *Suspected awareness:* The patient does not know but only suspects, with varying degrees of certainty, that he or she is dying. The medical staff and family do know the patient is terminally ill.
3. *Mutual pretense:* The patient, medical personnel, and family know the patient is dying but there is tacit agreement to act as if this were not the case.
4. *Open awareness:* The patient, medical personnel, and family recognize and openly acknowledge that the patient is dying.

Today, even though more patients are directly being told by doctors they are going to die, the interactions with family and friends still often reflect patterns related to Glaser and Strauss's mutual pretense context. These interactions can be characterized as a *conspiracy of silence,* which is a mutual pact to avoid issues of consequence as they relate to the death and to focus only on the mundane (for example, the weather). This avoidance is not based on malice, but rather is an attempt to avoid painful or frightening interactions. It is unfortunate, however, that what is done with good intent may actually increase fears or feelings of abandonment. The dying are put into an *emotional quarantine* in which others do not allow them to share their true feelings, but rather force them to participate in formalities and to exchange platitudes (Weisman, 1972).

Many currently used avoidance strategies are similar to those described by Kastenbaum and Aisenberg (1972):

Reassurance: "You are doing so well now."
Denial: "You don't mean that; you are not going to die."
Changing the subject: "Let's think of something more cheerful."
Fatalism: "We are all going to die someday."

As difficult as it may be for all involved, open communication about the impending death can allow for mutual support, ameliorate fears of loneliness and abandonment, and allow the opportunity to finish business. It is *not* appropriate, however, to force the dying to participate in a discussion when they are unwilling or unable to do so. The dying should be allowed to determine the focus and set the pace of the dialogue (Evans, Esbenson, & Jaffe, 1981; Hinton, 1980).

Withdrawal.   Charmaz (1980) describes three major contributors to the withdrawal that is frequently experienced by the dying and those in their social environment. First, there may be certain environmental conditions present that make it difficult for previous patterns of interaction to continue. For example, the patient may be in a hospital that is many miles away from family and friends. Circumstances such as these can act as a wedge between the patient and significant others, interfering with regular contact and meaningful support. The second source of isolation is withdrawal by the dying person. This situation may be caused by such factors as discomfort, pain, lapses into unconsciousness, a variety of fears, and so forth. Third, there is often a social avoidance of the dying, which may be the most significant contributor to the dying person's isolation. Society may withdraw because of fear of death, uncertainty as to how to interact with the dying, and/or a feeling that the patient is becoming a burden (see Figure 1.3). *Sociological death* or *social death* are terms used to signify a withdrawal pattern that is of extreme magnitude.

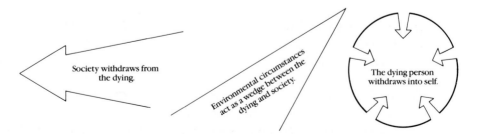

Figure 1.3   *Contributors to the Withdrawal Process*

Closely related to Charmaz's idea that environmental factors contribute to the withdrawal between the dying and their friends and family is the concept of a *change in a shared reality.* People often base a relationship on shared interests and activities. Once these can no longer be shared, the relationship weakens or terminates. For example, work colleagues may socialize outside of the work environment, but even then the focal point of much conversation is related to the job (tasks, deadlines, other colleagues). When dying persons are forced to leave their jobs, they may then find they have little or nothing in common with certain former coworkers. Thus, a pattern of withdrawal may result.

Because the dying must bring closure to more and more facets of their lives, it is only natural that as time passes they would need to gradually terminate certain relationships. There is neither sufficient time nor physical and psychological energy to continue all relationships to the same degree as before the onset of the terminal illness. The "emotional distancing" that results from withdrawal is not founded in ill will, but rather is a common coping mechanism (Evans et al., 1981).

Dissynchrony between dying persons and their loved ones, as they struggle to deal with the impending death, may place additional stress on relationships and cause more rapid withdrawal to take place. Christ (1983) defines *dissynchrony* as "an unevenness at different points in time in specific cognitive appraisal or affective states" (p. 61). One person in a given relationship, for example, may need to express and discuss feelings while the other may need some emotional distance and therefore refuse to talk.

Psychological Needs and Concerns

Psychological needs and concerns of the dying are many and varied. It is difficult, if not impossible, to totally separate psychological issues from those discussed earlier in this chapter. Issues that will be examined in this section are a sense of control, contribution to others, and a review of one's life.

Control and Independence.   Many individuals with life-threatening illnesses have reported that retaining some sense of control in their lives is crucial to their emotional well-being. Human beings desire this control from a very young age. For example, a toddler who loudly says "No!" to almost every request or who refuses all offers of help by a well-meaning adult is, in essence, communicating both a strong desire and a need to be in control of the situation. The need for control in some aspects of their lives can be crucial to dying persons in their attempts to retain a positive self-concept, since there is so much that they can no longer control. For example, individuals who are dying cannot indefinitely postpone death and continue to live. Body functioning may have deteriorated to such a point that they are no longer able to walk or swallow or control bladder function. The dying cannot prevent others from emotionally distancing themselves due to being frightened or unsure of what to say or do.

Since there is so much that the dying cannot control, it is crucial to permit control where it is possible. For instance, they should be allowed to participate in decisions regarding their own health care (such as deciding whether to continue seeking a cure or opt for palliative measures only, providing input regarding where they prefer to die, or refusing medications that sedate them). In order to make decisions that are personally appropriate, dying individuals need information about their diagnosis and prognosis, available therapies, and other pertinent facts. This information must be presented in clear terminology that is understandable to the patient. Explanations often need to be repeated because it is difficult to assimilate all relevant information at one time.

Closely related to the desire to retain a sense of control is the desire to remain as independent as possible. Dying individuals often prefer to perform tasks for themselves rather than depend on someone else for assistance. This may even be the case when there is a struggle to complete the task. For example, a dying adolescent may prefer to take an hour and a half to painstakingly bathe and dress herself rather than depend on her older sister or mother for help, even though it would take much less time.

Contribution to Others.   Even when given the opportunity to retain as great a degree of control as possible, the dying may still not be capable of doing many things for themselves and may have to depend on others to perform certain tasks. As a result, the dying may begin to question whether they are a burden to others and whether their lives have any value. In order to counteract a potential sense of worthlessness, the dying should be allowed the opportunity to contribute to the well-being of others. They may choose to do this in a variety of ways, depending to a great extent on such factors as energy level, presence of pain, and time remaining until death. For example, the dying may choose to mend clothes for their children, give directions on the care of the garden, or verbalize part of the family's history so that it might be recorded. All of these types of activities can enhance the dying individual's sense of self-worth.

Review of One's Life.   Most human beings want to know that their lives have been meaningful. The conclusion as to whether this goal has been accomplished is a very personal one; it is related to earlier involvement in various activities, past accomplishments, quality of relationships, and much more. Dying individuals strive to find an answer to the question "Was my life worthwhile?" To help answer this question, they engage in a process of life review.

Reminiscing is an important tool in promoting the life review and also in breaking out of the conspiracy of silence described earlier. It allows the dying to bring to mind important memories and share them with others. Reminiscing can confirm to the dying that others remember the roles they played and value the contributions they made. Although presented here in the context of impending death, the life review process is important in the lives of non–terminally ill persons who are facing death as a natural consequence of age. It may be a particularly important task, however, for those who are unable to live to their late adulthood years.

Spiritual Needs and Concerns

Spirituality includes the inspirational and existential aspects of our existence. It facilitates the integration of self into a larger universal scheme (Mauritzen, 1988). Many persons' sense of spirituality becomes magnified as death approaches (Ley & Corless, 1988).

The spiritual aspects of life and death are important to many people in our society, yet they are often disregarded by professional caregivers. Dr. Cicely Saunders, a leader in the hospice movement, has emphasized that spiritual needs of the dying must be acknowledged as part of a holistic approach (Rando, 1984). Personal philosophies, moral values, and religious belief systems are especially important to individuals facing death, and they need to be respected and supported by caregivers. The belief that individuals are part of a larger whole can provide much comfort to the dying (Morgan, 1988).

Meaning. Many believe that a primary component of our spiritual dimension is a search for meaning—meaning of life *and* death. Inner peace is promoted when answers to these fundamental questions are found. Doka (1983) has identified the following three major spiritual needs of dying individuals that relate to our human need for meaningfulness:

1. *The need to find meaning in one's life:* The dying often search for the ultimate significance of life—a search that extends beyond the acceptance of death. Existential issues are inevitably faced as one approaches death. The inability to discover or reaffirm meaning can

create a deep sense of spiritual pain. Answers do not necessarily have to be found in a religious context. However, religious belief systems give many individuals new purpose in life or help sustain previously developed values.

2. *The need to die an appropriate death:* "Appropriate" is defined as being consistent with one's self-identity. Dying individuals need an opportunity to interpret their own death within a framework that is congruent with their values and life-style. In a study in which physicians, nurses, and hospital chaplains were interviewed, Augustine and Kalish (1975) found "meaning" to be one of the three most important factors contributing to an appropriate death—meaning not only in one's past life but in one's remaining life and death as well. In many cases, individuals may also be making choices regarding the manner in which they will die. As they make difficult decisions concerning what is appropriate for them, the dying may request spiritual guidance or sanctions from spiritual leaders.

3. *The need to transcend death:* A sense of transcendence can come from many avenues. In a religious context, it is often viewed in terms of reassurance of immortality. Transcendence can also be achieved through the knowledge that future generations will follow or through the belief of the dying that their deeds will outlive them.

Hope.   Spiritual concerns often relate to the concept of hope. Kübler-Ross (1969) describes hope as a powerful dynamic force throughout the dying process. Richards (1980) has added that hope is a quality of being rather than a rational expectation. Regardless of the dying person's nearness to death, hope can still be maintained. Because of this human quality, caregivers can help sustain hope and give comfort to the dying. Possibilities for increasing hope are also present. According to Fairchild (1980):

> The enlargement of hope is even possible in the situation of the fatally ill person, but we must ask, "Hope for what?" For long-range survival, no. For an end to agony, perhaps. For a richer life now, yes. For a life after death? Christians are confident of that. Hope, even in terminal illness, can be enlarged. (p. 121)

As dying individuals cope with fear, uncertainty, loss of control, and disappointment, hope can offer much comfort.

Spiritual Beliefs.   Caregivers need to develop insight into the power of spiritual beliefs for helping many individuals cope with the process of dying. Millison (1988) recommends the following strategies for those working with the terminally ill:

1. Understand that growth in the spiritual realm presents opportunities

for development and healing that may not be present in other facets of one's life.

2. Be aware of your own spirituality, whether from a religious or non-religious origin.

3. Do not impose your own spiritual values on dying individuals.

4. Be supportive of the patients' sense of spirituality even if you do not personally share a particular belief.

Freund (1977) has noted that many caregivers have developed a reluctance to involve the clergy with the terminally ill, fearing that they will focus on encouraging confessions or conversions from the dying patient. For many, the traditional expressions of their faith such as prayer, the sacraments, and visits from the clergy give them great comfort. Hoy (1983) advises chaplains to "meet people where they are" when assessing the spiritual or religious needs of the dying. Individuals reach their last days from a wide variety of backgrounds, beliefs, and spiritual experiences. Hoy also has said that "the needs of those who profess no formal religious roots are no less real than those who do" (p. 185), and Pumphrey (1977) urges sensitivity to ways different individuals may want their needs met and to whom they may prefer to turn for spiritual support. Pat formulas cannot be given to the dying; spiritual needs will vary somewhat for each individual.

Numerous barriers may prevent individuals from meeting their spiritual needs and exploring spiritual issues. Caregivers and clergy may be intolerant of patients' belief systems, and they may fail to recognize and respect beliefs that differ from their own. This attitude can be both confusing and distressful to individuals anticipating death. Even if caregivers accept the dying person's spiritual orientation, they may feel uncomfortable discussing particular issues (such as the meaning of one's death) because they feel that exploration of these issues may be too painful for the dying person. Other obstacles that may block the expression of spiritual beliefs and the exploration of pressing spiritual questions during this time include limited privacy for discussing spiritual concerns, medical procedures that reduce the individual's ability to think clearly and express thoughts, and restricted access to spiritual counselors and religious leaders (Attig, 1983).

In some cases, spiritual concerns may cause severe distress. Peteet (1985), in a study of 50 hospital cancer patients, found that over half had concerns involving spiritual issues and about one-third were actively struggling with these problems. While he emphasized that religious issues can take different forms in different individuals, Peteet reported that most of the problems identified by patients in his study related to (1) loss of religious support (for example, a trusted minister leaves the patient's church); (2) pressure to adopt a different religious position (a wife urges her spouse to adopt her religious convictions); (3) unusual religious beliefs (a young woman in her final stages of cancer believes that she has been chosen to be a missionary and therefore expects to fully recover); (4) conflict between religious views and views of illness (a dying individual may feel unresolved anger toward God and be unable to reconcile his feelings with his religious beliefs, or the person may feel that the illness is due somehow to his past sins); and (5) preoccupation with the meaning of life and illness (an intense focusing on religion and spiritual questions in an attempt to understand what is happening).

In summary, professional caregivers should be aware of the spiritual needs of the dying as well as the obstacles that prevent them from being met. Staff members working with the dying also need to be well informed about diverse religious traditions surrounding death and their importance to particular patients and their families. The spiritual needs of the dying are rooted in their family, religious, and cultural systems (Dawson, 1986; Lamm, 1969).

Factors Affecting the Dying Process

The needs and concerns discussed earlier in this chapter are common components of the dying process but should not be regarded as universal. Even though there are many similarities among dying persons, there are many differences as well. Many factors affect the dying process and contribute to this variability, including dying trajectories, developmental stages, and ethnic or cultural background (see Figure 1.4).

Dying Trajectories

The certainty or uncertainty that a particular physical condition will end in death influences the emotional and psychological state of the individual, as does the time frame within which one is expected to die. Using these dimensions of certainty and time, Glaser and Strauss (1968) describe four *death trajectories:*

1. *Certain death at a known time:* for example, liver cancer
2. *Certain death at an unknown time:* for example, cystic fibrosis
3. *Uncertain death but at a known time of resolution:* for example, advanced heart disease with outcome dependent on the success of surgery

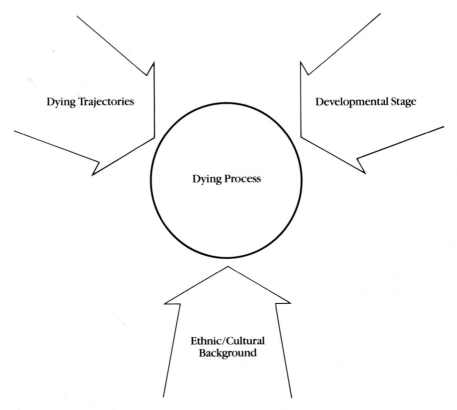

Figure 1.4 *Selected Factors Affecting the Dying Process*

4. *Uncertain death and unknown time of resolution:* for example, multiple sclerosis

Glaser and Strauss stress that the "dying trajectories are perceived courses of dying rather than actual courses" (1968, p. 6). One may *expect* to die within a particular time frame, but death may not occur within it. It is the expectation, rather than the fact, that influences the adjustment process of the dying and also others' interaction patterns with them. In addition, Pattison (1978) explains that trajectories with uncertain time frames are ultimately more difficult to deal with than those with certain time frames because of the ambiguity involved.

The four trajectories described by Glaser and Strauss do not appropriately describe all types of deaths. For example, many deaths are sudden and unexpected (such as accidents, suicide, or natural disasters). Because these types of trajectories have their effect on the survivor rather than on the deceased, they will be discussed in Chapter 2 as they relate to the bereavement process.

Developmental Stages

A study of human developmental processes reveals that individuals' needs and abilities change over time as a result of growth, maturation, and learning. *Development* is defined as "orderly and sequential changes that occur with the passage of time as an organism moves from conception to death. It includes those processes that are biologically programmed within the organism. It also includes those processes by which the organism is changed or transformed through interaction with the environment" (Vander Zanden, 1985, p. 4). We must realize, then, that there are stage-specific characteristics that influence the dying person's behavioral manifestations, focus and intensity of fears, desires for particular types of control, ability to understand information about the illness, and particular issues that need to be resolved prior to death.

In order to give insight into the importance of meeting normal developmental needs and of understanding normal developmental characteristics, Erikson's (1963) theory of psychosocial development and Piaget's (1963) theory of cognitive development will be used as a foundation for discussion of developmental issues in subsequent chapters.

Erikson's Theory.   Erikson (1963) hypothesized that an individual normally deals with a series of eight psychosocial stages or crises during the course of his or her lifespan. Each of these stages may potentially be resolved in either a positive or negative direction. The outcome of each crisis is closely tied to the type of environment or social support that is available to an individual facing a particular crisis.

Each of these crises will be discussed in more detail in the upcoming stage-related chapters. They are identified in Table 1.1. Attention will be paid to factors intrinsic to the dying process that may encourage a negative resolution to a particular crisis unless specific care is given to support a positive outcome.

Piaget's Theory.   Piaget (1963) has indicated that children think in a qualitatively different fashion than do adults. He theorized that their thinking matures over time and progresses through a number of stages (see Table 1.1). A child's capacity to reason has a direct relationship to the way in which we can most effectively provide information to a child who is

Table 1.1
Stages of Development: Erikson's and Piaget's Theories

Approximate Age Span	Erikson's Psychosocial Stages	Piaget's Cognitive Stages
Birth to 18 months	Trust versus Mistrust	Sensorimotor Period
18 months to 3 years	Autonomy versus Shame and Doubt	Preoperational Stage
3 years to 7 years	Initiative versus Guilt	
7 years to 11+	Industry versus Inferiority	Concrete Operational Stage
Adolescence	Identity versus Role Confusion	Formal Operational Stage
Young Adulthood	Intimacy versus Isolation	
Middle Adulthood	Generativity versus Stagnation	
Late Adulthood	Integrity versus Despair	

dying or who is grieving the death of another. This relationship will be described in more detail in upcoming chapters.

Ethnic/Cultural Background

Cultural variables have an effect on dying persons' beliefs about death, their coping strategies, manifestation of feelings, and much more. Fulton (1976) defined the death-related *culture complex* as "the rites, customs, and beliefs surrounding death" (p. 158). Similarly, Gruman (1978) describes *death system* by explaining that "each cultural era has a distinctive network of suppositions, norms, and symbols that are functionally effective in the routinized, communal management of death and dying" (p. 203).

Variations in practices and beliefs are evident when comparing death systems in various cultures. These systems may also vary from one subgroup to another within the same country. In their comprehensive study of ethnic groups in the United States, Kalish and Reynolds (1976) found many differences among Anglo-Americans, Black Americans, Japanese Americans, and Mexican Americans. They found variations in attitudes, values, expectations, experiences, and customs as evidenced by responses to a series of interview questions. For example, differences were found in how openly thoughts and emotions can be comfortably shared with others.

Membership in a particular cultural group not only has an impact on such attitudes and customs, it can also have an effect on the sensation or expression of pain (Wolff & Langley, 1977; Zborowski, 1952). Persons with a strong German heritage, for example, typically do not openly address personal feelings. Some cultural groups, such as Native Americans, regard pain as a sign of weakness and, therefore, socially unacceptable if displayed openly. Older Japanese Americans often try to mask their pain— even if in agony. This is done in order to avoid distressing others (Kalish & Reynolds, 1976).

Bates (1987) presents a biocultural model to explain why the perception of pain varies from culture to culture. Based on an extensive review of the research literature, she theorizes that

> social learning theory is instrumental in the development of meanings for and attitudes towards pain. Learned values and attitudes affect one's memories of prior pain experiences. Each of these is a factor which, according to the gate-control theory, may influence psychophysiological functioning, as well as behavior, when individuals are exposed to potentially painful stimuli. Therefore, it is likely that cultural group experiences influence the psychophysiological processes responsible for pain threshold and perception of pain severity, as well as pain response. (p. 48)

Given the many differences among and within cultural groups, it becomes evident that health professionals, family, and friends must be sensitive to a range of needs, thoughts, and emotions. Assumptions as to how people cope with death and dying cannot be based on either cultural stereotypes or universal statements.

Historical Perspectives Related to Dying

Changes in Primary Causes of Death

During the early 1900s, the majority of persons in the United States died of communicable diseases such as influenza, tuberculosis, diphtheria, and gastroenteritis. Since the turn of the century, however, we have seen a marked change over time in the contribution of these infectious diseases to the mortality rates in this country. In 1900, the category of influenza and pneumonia was the primary cause of death (see Table 1.2); in 1987, it ranked fifth (see Table 1.3). Tuberculosis, gastroenteritis, and diphtheria were also primary causes (ranked in the top 10) in 1900. By the late 1960s, however, these three diseases collectively contributed to less than 1 percent of all deaths in the United States. Other communicable diseases brought under control during this century include what had been com-

Table 1.2
The Ten Leading Causes of Death in the United States in 1900

Rank	Cause of Death	% All Deaths
	All causes	100.0
1	Influenza and pneumonia	11.8
2	Tuberculosis (all forms)	11.3
3	Gastroenteritis	8.3
4	Diseases of the heart	8.0
5	Vascular lesions affecting the central nervous system	6.2
6	Chronic nephritis	4.7
7	All accidents	4.2
8	Malignant neoplasms (cancer)	3.7
9	Diseases of early infancy	3.6
10	Diphtheria	2.3

SOURCE: National Center for Health Statistics (1983), *Monthly Vital Statistics Report,* Vol. 31, No. 13, p. 52. Washington, DC: United States Department of Health and Human Services.

mon lethal diseases of childhood—whooping cough, scarlet fever, measles, and rheumatic fever.

A number of factors contributed to bringing these diseases under control. Widespread immunization has essentially eradicated particular illnesses (such as smallpox). Availability of better nutrition has minimized susceptibility to certain diseases, and improved sanitation procedures have decreased the likelihood of rapid spread of an illness. Increased availability of "wonder drugs" such as penicillin has helped many survive what otherwise would have been a deadly illness.

As communicable diseases have been brought under control, they no longer are the primary causes of death. On the other hand, there has been an increase in the contribution of *chronic degenerative diseases* (those that primarily occur in later life and are thought to be related to the aging process) to the mortality rates (Lerner, 1980). Currently, the leading causes of death are diseases of the heart and malignant neoplasms (see Table 1.3).

Change in the Arena of Death

Prior to the early 1900s, almost all people died in their own homes. Medical facilities as we know them were essentially nonexistent. If a person was dying, the doctor (when one was available) went to the individual's home. Care depended on unsophisticated implements and utilized relatively few pharmaceutical agents. As medicine became increasingly dependent on technologies that were essentially nontransportable, the very sick and the dying moved into hospitals in order to take advantage of medical advances (for example, kidney dialysis machines and respirators). Doctors were no longer able to provide the same caliber of care in an individual's own home. By 1949, 49.5 percent of all deaths in the United States occurred in an institution. By 1958, that percentage had increased to 60.9 percent (Lerner, 1980). Currently, approximately 80 percent of all persons die in an institution.

As the arena of death shifted for the greater proportion of our population—from home to institution—family members and friends had fewer and fewer opportunities to interact with the dying. There is good reason to believe that this was a major contribution to society's discomfort in interacting with the dying and the resultant withdrawal or avoidance patterns.

Recent Social Trends Related to Dying

A number of recent social phenomena reflect a growing awareness that dying individuals have a multiplicity of needs and rights. These social

Table 1.3
The Ten Leading Causes of Death in the United States in 1987

Rank	Cause of Death	% All Deaths
	All causes	100.0
1	Diseases of the heart	36.4
2	Malignant neoplasms (cancer)	21.3
3	Cerebrovascular diseases (stroke)	7.5
4	Chronic obstructive pulmonary diseases and allied conditions	4.0
5	Pneumonia and influenza	3.9
6	Accidents and adverse effects	3.4
7	Diabetes mellitus	1.7
8	Suicide	1.5
9	Chronic liver diseases and cirrhosis	1.2
10	Atherosclerosis	1.1

SOURCE: National Center for Health Statistics (1987), *Monthly Vital Statistics Report,* Vol. 36, No. 3, pp. 8–9. Washington, DC: United States Department of Health and Human Services.

developments include the belief in a right to die with dignity, the signing of living wills that communicate one's wishes regarding the use of extraordinary measures to prolong life, the rapidly growing hospice movement, and the recognition of patients' rights.

Death with Dignity

Medical technology has increasingly become a double-edged sword. There is no question but that improvements in medical care have contributed to a greatly lengthened lifespan for the general population. There is a risk, however, that, for some, the technology does not contribute to a better quality of life but rather to what some refer to as prolonged dying. There is a time when death would be inevitable were it not for the prolonged use of life-support strategies.

With the advent of many technological advances, concern has arisen that we can sustain biological existence without ensuring that the extended life is of high quality. Loss of one's humanity to the dictates of modern technology can negate the opportunity to die with dignity.

> We must assure that technology's tremendous benefits do not prolong life at the expense of personhood and individuality. We must give serious attention to the ethical and moral problems associated with the unthinking treatment of people without due consideration to the consequences. We must somehow untie the emotional, legal, and ethical knots that bind us down and keep us from a fresh, vigorous rethinking of the dilemmas of modern medicine and modern dying. We must also reconsider routines, policies, procedures, and attitudes based on matters of mere efficiency and technological convenience and reinstitute those humane and human ceremonies, attitudes, and concerns that permit people to retain their dignity and sense of personal worth even during the process of dying. (Thompson, 1984, p. 229)

A variety of conditions, however, can contribute to a *death with dignity*. A sense of control, individuality, and self-worth contribute to the possibility of a dignified death. Compatibility between one's own desires surrounding the process of death and the reality of the situation also contributes to a sense of dignity (Martocchio, 1986).

Intense media coverage of such cases as the following illustrate the public's interest in a variety of issues related to death with dignity and the right to make choices regarding treatment and intervention.

> *Chad Green:* a child with acute lymphocytic leukemia whose parents refused chemotherapy and went into exile in Mexico in order to seek alternative treatment.

Karen Ann Quinlan: a young woman in a state of irreversible coma whose family decided to take her off a respirator and won the legal right to do so.

Barney Clark and William Schroeder: the first two recipients of artificial hearts.

Baby Doe: a newborn infant with severe congenital abnormalities whose parents wanted to deny life-sustaining care.

Hector Rodas: a quadraplegic who won a court case demanding that the hospital terminate his feedings so that he might die.

The widespread attention given to each of these individuals (and many others) focused on a variety of ethical dilemmas including the following: (1) Is it imperative that families take advantage of available technology—technology that may sustain life but does not guarantee its quality? (2) Who has the right to determine which is ultimately more important—the quality of life or length of life? (3) Who is financially responsible for the extremely high cost of using modern medical interventions? These are but a few of the bioethical issues which our society faces today. As medical technologies develop, we must deal with the ethical dilemmas which often go hand-in-hand with our ever-expanding opportunities.

Living Will

Many individuals have concluded that extraordinary medical measures disallow what they personally define as a death with dignity. A growing number of these people have communicated their desire that measures not be taken to prolong their lives when there is no reasonable expectation of recovery. Many have expressed their wishes by signing what is known as a *living will.* A sample of this type of document is found in Figure 1.5.

There are many reasons why an individual may choose to sign a living will, including the following (Bok, 1976): (1) to allow an individual to retain some control over what happens at the end of his or her life, even if the individual is then no longer competent to make personal choices or to see that they are carried out, (2) to enable individuals to make choices for terminal care while they are still healthy and at a time when there is no doubt of their mental competence, and (3) to alleviate some of the guilt and anxiety on the part of relatives and health professionals who will later attempt to determine what type of life-supporting measures are appropriate.

In 1977, California became the first state to pass legislation to protect

To my family, my physician, my lawyer, my clergyman
To any medical facility in whose care I happen to be
To any individual who may become responsible for my health, welfare
*   or affairs*

   Death is as much a reality as birth, growth, maturity and old age—it is the one certainty of life. If the time comes when I, _____ can no longer take part in decisions for my own future, let this statement stand as an expression of my wishes while I am still of sound mind.
   If the situation should arise in which there is no reasonable expectation of my recovery from physical or mental disability, I request that I be allowed to die and not be kept alive by artificial means or "heroic measures." I do not fear death itself as much as the indignities of deterioration, dependence, and hopeless pain. I therefore ask that medication be mercifully administered to me to alleviate suffering even though this may hasten the moment of death.
   This request is made after careful consideration. I hope you who care for me will feel morally bound to follow its mandate. I recognize that this appears to place a heavy responsibility upon you, but it is with the intention of relieving you of such responsibility and of placing it upon myself in accordance with my strong convictions that this statement is made.

Signed _____

Date _____

Witness _____   Witness _____

Copies of this request have been given to ———————————————

————————————————

Figure 1.5 *The Living Will*

Source: Concern for Dying, 250 West 57th Street, New York, NY 10107.

physicians from legal action if they comply with patients' desires expressed in a living will. Since that time, many other states have passed similar right-to-die or natural death laws.

Hospice Care

The word *hospice* originally referred to a way station for weary travelers. More recently, it is the term used for a particular type of care provided to dying individuals and their families. The 1974 creation of Hospice of Connecticut in New Haven, modeled after St. Christopher's Hospice of London, marked the beginning of a rapidly expanding social movement in the United States. Since then, volunteer groups in hundreds of communities have engaged in a grass roots movement to humanize the dying process which, over the course of the twentieth century, had become a medical event destined to occur in a hospital rather than a uniquely personal event taking place in one's own home. In most home-based hospice programs, family caregivers are given support by professionals (under the guidance of the hospice medical director). Trained lay volunteers assist by performing daily tasks such as preparing meals or cleaning house, giving back-up relief to the primary family caregivers, and providing emotional support for grieving family members. Dying persons and their families are offered physical, emotional, social, psychological, and spiritual care. Two fundamental tenets of hospice care are that (1) the family and patient remain in control of their own decisions, and (2) physical pain must be alleviated to the extent possible so that the patient is comfortable enough to focus on other important issues.

NHO Guidelines.　The National Hospice Organization (NHO) serves as a regulatory body in the United States to ensure that organizations that call themselves "hospices" follow fundamental guidelines (National Hospice Organization, 1987). According to these guidelines, *hospice care* must:

1. Include both the patient and the family as the unit of care
2. Be provided by an interdisciplinary team that includes the patient and family
3. Be directed by a qualified physician
4. Focus on social, psychological, emotional, and spiritual needs in addition to medical needs
5. Include bereavement follow-up services for the family
6. Be available 24 hours per day, 7 days a week
7. Involve volunteer assistance
8. Provide palliative care (that is, comfort care rather than curative care)

Other crucial facets of the hospice philosophy include the belief that dying persons are living persons. As such, hospices strive to maximize the quality of remaining life by meeting the needs of the whole person while allowing the patient and family to retain as much autonomy in their decision making as possible. Hospice is a philosophy, not a singular type of facility. Services may be delivered at home, in a freestanding structure, or in a unit of a long-term care facility (Corr & Corr, 1983).

Contributors to Success.   Many factors have contributed to the rapid acceptance of the hospice philosophy (Ferrell, 1985; Millet, 1983; Paradis, 1985; Tehan, 1982). These are summarized here.

1. Provision of care either at home or in a home-like inpatient setting ensures a humanizing alternative to the increasing depersonalization that has become a part of our medical experience. The focus of hospice care is to provide personal comfort and promote dignity rather than to cure a disease; therefore, the dying individual is regarded as a "person" rather than a "patient." Because the primary caregiver does not have responsibility for a large number of other patients, he or she can spend more time learning how to meet the idiosyncratic needs or desires of the dying individual. For example, a family member who knows the patient well may realize that banana milkshakes have always been a favorite food and, therefore, be able to encourage a much-needed increase in caloric intake by preparing that preferred beverage. In another situation, the primary caregiver may be aware of how very important completion of a quilt is to the dying individual, so that she might give it to her only granddaughter as a wedding gift. Hospice volunteers might then be able to give the assistance necessary to finish the project while letting the dying grandmother do as much of the remaining work on the quilt as she is able to do and wants to do.

2. Most people derive a great deal of comfort and security from a sense of familiarity. As a result, many individuals prefer to die in their own homes. There they are surrounded by their own belongings and are accustomed to the sights, smells, and sounds in the environment. Dying persons can more easily remain in the mainstream of family life by being at home and by spending time in the rooms that are the usual site of daily routines. For example, many families may put a hospital bed in the living room or family room so that conversation and activity may include the patient. This involvement can help counterbalance the common fear of abandonment and isolation.

Although life changes dramatically for a family caring for a loved one, all can derive comfort from continuation of daily routines. Again, a sense of comfort can be derived from this involvement in the familiar. The family can gather, as they have in the past, to watch television, play a game, or look through a scrapbook. There is a focus on living rather than on dying. Leloudis and Pole (1985, p. 31) quoted one hospice patient's son as saying: "We're compressing a great deal of life into a very short time. To have as much of the real life available as possible, which the home environment provides, was a paramount consideration."

3. Although dying persons and their family members cannot control the course of the disease itself, they can retain control over many facets of their lives. The hospice philosophy encourages patients and families to determine what is best for themselves. Once they are given complete information and are made aware of their options, they are the ones who make decisions.

Hospice families, including the dying member, decide what type of support they desire from hospice staff. One family may desire, for example, to have volunteers come to the home to give spiritual support and request daily medical attention from a nurse. Another family may ask that a volunteer do the grocery shopping and care for the children for several afternoons a week. Hospice families may choose among various palliative medical treatments, depending on their unique situation. For example, many choose a self-regulated regimen of medication taken orally. If unable to swallow their medication, others would prefer rectal suppositories over shots.

Dying individuals and their families often work together to plan events following the impending death. Will there be a funeral or will there be a memorial service? Will the body be buried or cremated? Who will be the pallbearers? Other decisions revolve around such crucial issues as who will be responsible for the surviving children. Will the house be sold to minimize later financial obligations?

The decisions facing hospice families are many. By being allowed to make various decisions, these families are able to retain some sense of control even though they are powerless to prevent the death itself. Retaining control in some arenas contributes to the family's comfort and sense of self-worth.

4. *Family members experience a therapeutic outcome from directly contributing to their loved one's care.* Kirschling (1986, p. 124) notes, for example, that the majority of spouses caring for a dying husband or wife cited a number of very important needs, including (1) to be with the dying person, (2) to be helpful to the dying person, (3) to receive assurance of the dying person's comfort, (4) to be informed of the dying person's condition, (5) to be informed of the impending death, (6) to ventilate emotions, (7) to gain support from other family members, and (8) to derive acceptance, support, and comfort from health care professionals. Kirschling also reported that families regarded hospice care as meeting these needs more often than other types of care.

In order to help family members feel more secure in their interactions with the dying, we need to provide education as to how they might perform certain functions. For example, many caregivers report needing to learn how to help the patient ambulate and how to provide palliative care.

Unfortunately, many family members in the past have acquired these skills through trial and error. Hospice staff, however, currently regard that type of education as an important part of their mission.

5. *Given the increased expense of advanced medical technology, hospital room and board, and malpractice insurance, traditional health care costs are spiraling. Hospice services are typically considerably less expensive than other types of care.* Estimates of hospice costs indicate that they may be as little as one-sixth of the cost of hospitalization (Corless, 1988).

The hospice philosophy also guarantees that no one will be denied care if he or she is unable to pay. Sliding fee scales for service are common. Hospices that are appropriately certified may receive reimbursements from Medicare and Medicaid; many private insurance companies also include a hospice benefit.

Patients' Bill of Rights

As concern grows over providing quality holistic care to dying persons, many health care facilities have formalized their philosophy by adopting a *patients' bill of rights* such as the one in Figure 1.6. Additionally, some facilities have hired personnel to act as advocates for the sick and dying (patient advocates, medical social workers, and child-life specialists, among others). These staff members ensure that patients understand their medical procedures, give them the opportunity to ask questions, and encourage them to participate in the decision-making process.

Summary

Death is a natural part of the human experience. Dying persons, as living persons, have many needs and concerns that are similar to those of healthy persons. Other needs are unique to the fact that the individuals are dying. Using a holistic perspective, caregivers should give support for physical, emotional, social, psychological, and spiritual needs. Although there are many similarities in the way in which individuals face their own deaths, there is no single "right way" to die. A number of factors affect the dying process, including the expected time frame in which the death will occur, the age and related developmental stage of the dying individual, and his or her cultural background.

Since the early 1900s, we have seen marked changes in the primary causes of death, life expectancy rates, and arena of death. With the advent of increasingly sophisticated medical technology, there has been a grow-

I have the right to be treated as a living human being until I die.

I have the right to maintain a sense of hopefulness, however changing its focus may be.

I have the right to be cared for by those who can maintain a sense of hopefulness, however changing this might be.

I have the right to express my feelings and emotions about my approaching death in my own way.

I have the right to participate in decisions concerning my care.

I have the right to expect continuing medical and nursing attention even though "cure" goals must be changed to "comfort" goals.

I have the right not to die alone.

I have the right to be free from pain.

I have the right to have my questions answered honestly.

I have the right to have help from and for my family in accepting my death.

I have the right not to be deceived.

I have the right to die in peace and dignity.

I have the right to retain my individuality and not be judged for my decisions which may be contrary to beliefs of others.

I have the right to discuss and enlarge my religious and/or spiritual experiences, whatever these may mean to others.

I have the right to expect that the sanctity of the human body will be respected after death.

I have the right to be cared for by caring, sensitive, knowledgeable people who will attempt to understand my needs and will be able to gain some satisfaction in helping me face my death.

Figure 1.6   *Patients' Bill of Rights*

Source: This Bill of Rights was created in 1971 during a workshop on "The Terminally Ill Patient and the Helping Person," in Lansing, Michigan, sponsored by the Southwestern Michigan Inservice Education Council and conducted by Amelia J. Barbus, Associate Professor of Nursing, Wayne State University, Detroit.

ing awareness that we need to balance that mechanization with human care and concern. As an example, recent trends in our society reflect the belief that a person has a right to die with dignity. These trends include the spread of hospices across the country and also an increased number of people signing living wills.

ᴄᴢᴏ *Personal Account*

Jean Hay shares many important insights derived from her personal experience as a hospice volunteer. Dying and grieving persons often do not directly express their fears, their needs, and their wants in so many words. They do, however, express them through many nonverbal cues. You can "hear" them—but only if you listen very carefully.

An Experience in Listening: A Volunteer's Memories

Jean Hay

This article was written in memory of Jacqueline Genest.

With stars in your eyes and confidence in your motives and abilities, you start the training to be a hospice volunteer. During the training you share personal experiences, view films of hospice care that bring tears to your eyes, hear a panel of clergy outline the varied types of funeral rituals and a nurse lecture on the effects of various medications. *Then,* there is the all important session on *listening.*

After the personal interview with the Director of Volunteers, and armed with your folder full of pertinent information, a certificate of completion, and your hospice volunteer badge, you are now a full-fledged hospice volunteer. Then the day arrives when the director says, "I have just the right patient for you." You reply, "Oh, great!" Is she *listening?* Does she hear the tremor in your voice, feel the lump in your throat, sense the perspiring palms? The theory is now to become practice.

Together, you go to meet your patient—this person who has this thing in her that will no longer allow her to function in her usual way. This person is facing death, but must also learn to live in a different manner until that ultimate experience comes.

You meet a woman, who from her bed says, "I'm not going to need you very long because I'm going to get well soon and then we can go out to lunch." You look into her eyes and hear the denial, fear and great sadness, if you're *listening!*

You go at your prescribed time and do the agreed upon things. For a time she resists the need for you to come into her home to cook a meal, help with her shower, and grocery shop. She is fighting the disease, so she is fighting the need for you to be there. As the weakness and pain increase, and the loneliness from being set apart surrounds her, she looks forward to your visit. Her beautiful expressive eyes light up for you. Slowly, all the

From *The American Journal of Hospice Care,* May/June 1985, pp. 45–46. Reprinted by permission.

fear, disappointment, sadness and anger comes out, if you're *listening*. All of this isn't just in the words spoken, but in the silences between the words.

A young teenager flounces into the room noisily dropping her books on the table and griping loudly as she slams cupboard doors. There is no loving greeting for the sick mother, but rather barely a glance. All is anger and fear because this person is no longer the mother she knows and wants. Anger and fear of the unknown when her mother is gone. There is normal youthful resentment because this dreadful disease, which is eating up the family's financial resources, is curtailing her social life. Underlying all of this anger is her grief, which she cannot recognize and for which she has no other means of expression. It's all there. Are you *listening*?

The man comes home from work gaunt, weary, near exhaustion from the months of watching his beloved decline from moment to moment. He speaks of the problems of the daily care and the financial considerations. Suddenly, his eyes fill with tears and he sobs softly. You hold his hand and let him cry. Don't speak now; no platitudes please. Just touch and listen to his grief. There is panic in his voice and such a deep hurt in his eyes. You can hear his cry for help, for love, for understanding—if you're *listening*.

The dear friend comes in with homemade bran muffins, the only food her friend enjoys now. At first there is a businesslike discussion of the situation and slowly the front breaks down and her grief is revealed. She speaks of her concern for her friend's pain and the husband's panic. But also, if you're *listening*, she is crying for understanding and help. She wants understanding because of the frustration and, perhaps, guilt she feels because it is beyond her emotional capacity to care for her friend. It is almost unbearable to look at or touch her friend in this condition. She wants help because of her uncertainty as to the role she should assume at this time, and fear of what her role might be after her friend is gone.

Albert Schweitzer said, 'we are all so much together and yet we are dying of loneliness.' We spend years together in families and in friendly relationships and yet never really listen to each other. We are so busy clinging to our facades, the personalities we've developed over the years that hide the real us. That personality is our shield for so long we are afraid to drop it even when the fight is over. Only in that moment when we drop all pretenses and allow ourselves to just *be*, do we really *listen*.

Today, I spent seven hours with my hospice friend. We touched, kissed, hugged, and did those things necessary for her physical care, but we talked very little. We've passed that phase now and we speak with our eyes, our touching, and just quietly being together. In the afternoon, I sat beside her reading as she drifted in and out of sleep. She would open her eyes, and we would smile. Then she would drift off again and I would continue reading. At one point, she looked up with sad, moist eyes, and I silently held her for a while in my arms.

There is that communication that transcends the spoken word and reaches into the depths of the soul. Today, it was as if we were in a vacuum, a cocoon, a space out of this physical world, where the vibrations of the spoken word should have broken the fragility of the moment and destroyed the special understanding we shared—a rare, wondrous, and mystic experience.

Addendum

Today at 3:15 P.M. my friend died with her family and friends at her bedside. She had been comatose for several days, and in the last five hours, as her lungs filled, her labored breathing could be heard throughout the house.

The angry young teenager rarely left her mother's bedside. She cried, held her mother's hand, told her of her love, that she was the best mother anyone could have. She changed the cloth on her mother's brow, helped the nurses turn her, and powdered her perspiring body to make her comfortable. The angry facade was gone and she was able to express that love and grief she had been hiding.

The dear friend, who doubted her emotional capacity and questioned the role she should play, became a "Rock of Gibraltar" for the whole family. She spent all of her waking hours in the home. Not only did she look at her friend, but loved and caressed her. Although she had thought it would be impossible, she was at the bedside when her friend breathed that last dear breath. She may still be uncertain of the future role, but I believe she has found an inner source of strength that will carry her through this uncertainty.

The husband's words of love and release were the last my friend heard, "Darling, I love you so much, we all love you so much that we want you released from this suffering. Please, just let go, sweetheart." Within two minutes of that loving, selfless plea, my friend gave up the long terrible fight. Although the hurt is still in the husband's eyes, the strain of the past months has left his face and body, and he is at peace because he knows his beloved is at peace.

There were five people at the bedside that day. The other two I had not met before the last week. One was an older daughter living outside the home, who had come home lovingly to help care for her mother. A "wisp of a girl," who in her own grief gave her utmost to support her sister and her father. The other, the husband's business partner and the spouse of the dear friend, putting aside his own feelings of loss, gave his strength and love to his wife and the bereaved family. With his business acumen he was able to relieve the husband of all details attendant to a death in the home.

I don't know how much or how little I did for my hospice patient; I only know what she did for me. I was privileged to be associated intimately with a grand lady. In her most agonizing moments, her thoughts and concerns were of other people. She never failed to say "thank you," even for the most painful shot or treatment. Her last words to me, after I had moved her left leg to relieve the pressure of the mass, were "thank you."

I salute you, dear hospice friend, you have enriched my life and I am a better person for having touched yours. Namaste*

Questions and Activities

1. Why is listening such a valuable communication tool? Think of an incident in your own experience where you wished you had *listened* more during a particular interaction. What would you have learned if you had listened more?

2. Why is touch such a valuable communication tool when working with the dying?

3. Plan a 2-hour training session for people who plan to work with dying or grieving persons. The focus of your session is to enhance the trainees' communication skills while working with these groups.

4. Why is it difficult to be honest in our communications with the dying? Are there particular stages of the dying process when you believe it is more difficult to communicate with the dying?

5. If dying persons and/or their families are to make decisions regarding life-support systems or other medical technologies, what type of information should be provided? How should that information be provided? By whom?

Glossary

Awareness Contexts: Knowledge each person has regarding a patient's defined status, together with recognition of what the other person thinks.

Body Image: Interpersonal experience of the person's feelings and attitudes toward his or her own body and the way these experiences are organized.

Body Integrity: The body's ability to function appropriately.

Conspiracy of Silence: Mutual pact to avoid issues of consequence as they relate to death and to focus only on the mundane.

Culture Complex: A cultural group's rites, customs, and beliefs surrounding death.

---

*A Hindu greeting: "I respect the place in you where the entire universe resides. I respect that place in you where, if you are in that place in you, and I am in that place in me, there is only one of us."

Death Trajectory: Course of dying based on certainty of death from a particular cause and expected time of death. It is a perceived course of dying as compared to an actual course.

Dissynchrony: Differences between individuals in their grief experience related to a particular loss and the time needed to resolve the loss.

Emotional Quarantine: Situation in which others do not allow the dying to share their true feelings, but rather force them to participate in formalities and exchange platitudes.

Etiology: Cause of a disease.

Holistic Perspective: Acknowledgment of all aspects of the person (physical, emotional, social, psychological, and spiritual).

Hospice Care: A philosophy of care provided to dying individuals and their families that emphasizes death with dignity.

Living Will: Document designed to let individuals communicate their wishes regarding use of various life-support measures if there is no reasonable expectation of their recovery.

Middle Knowledge: Uncertainty as to whether one is actually going to die.

Palliative Care: Palliation, derived from the Greek word for "to lessen or mitigate," is therapy directed toward minimizing symptoms rather than curing the disease.

Sociological Death: Society's withdrawal, to an extreme degree, from the dying.

Thanatology: Study of death, dying, and grief.

Suggested Readings

Aries, P. (1981). *The hour of our death.* New York: Knopf.

> A historical treatment of attitudes toward death in Western culture from earliest Christian times until the present day. Comprehensive in coverage with interesting illustrations.

Corr, C. A., & Corr, D. M. (1983). *Hospice care: Principles and practice.* New York: Springer.

> Perspectives on hospice care are provided by professionals in the fields of nursing, medicine, pharmacology, physical therapy, occupational therapy, social work, psychotherapy, and religion. This book is a comprehensive resource that contains the latest developments in the field.

Kübler-Ross, E., & Warshaw, M. (1978). *To live until we say good-bye.* Englewood Cliffs, NJ: Prentice-Hall.

Kübler-Ross discusses her work with dying patients and their families. Photographs and intimate narrative sensitively portray children and adults in their final stages of life.

Winslade, W. J., & Ross, J. W. (1986). *Choosing life or death.* New York: Free Press.

An excellent book on legal and policy perspectives that includes detailed sections on issues related to kidney dialysis and health care financing.

Resources

Association for Death Education and Counseling
638 Prospect Avenue
Hartford, Connecticut 06105
(203) 232-4825

Concern for Dying
250 West 57th Street, Room 831
New York, New York 10107
(212) 246-6962

The Hastings Center
255 Elm Street
Briarcliff Manor, New York 10510
(914) 762-8500

National Hospice Organization
1901 North Fort Myer Drive
Suite 307
Arlington, Virginia 22209
(703) 243-5900

References

Annas, G. (1974). Rights of the terminally ill patient. *Journal of Nursing Administration, 4,* 40–43.

Attig, T. (1983). Respecting the dying and the bereaved as believers. *Newsletter of the Forum for Death Education and Counseling, 6,* 10–11.

Augustine, M. J., & Kalish, R. A. (1975). Religion, transcendence, and appropriate death. *Journal of Transpersonal Psychology, 7,* 1–13.

Bader, M. A. (1972). Personalizing the management of pain for the terminally ill patient. *Journal of Thanatology, 2*(3), 757–766.

Bates, M. S. (1987). Ethnicity and pain: A biocultural model. *Social Science Medicine, 24*(1), 47–50.

Blumenfield, M., Levy, N. B., & Kaufman, D. (1978). The wish to be informed of a fatal illness. *Omega, 9*(4), 323–326.

Bok, S. (1976). Personal directions for the care at the end of life. *The New England Journal of Medicine, 295,* 367–368.

Callari, E. S. (1986). *A gentle death: Personal caregiving to the terminally ill.* Greensboro, NC: Tudor.

Charmaz, K. (1980). *The social reality of death.* Menlo Park, CA: Addison-Wesley.

Christ, G. H. (1983). A psychosocial assessment framework for cancer patients and their families. *Health and Social Work, 8*(1), 57–64.

Corless, I. B. (1988). Settings for terminal care. *Omega, 18*(4), 319–340.

Corr, C. A., & Corr, D. M. (1983). *Hospice care: Principles and practice.* New York: Springer.

Coyle, N. (1985). Two issues in the management of pain in advanced cancer patients: Model of pain and pain relief versus fear of addiction. *The American Journal of Hospice Care, 2*(4), 31–34.

Dawson, P. S. (1986). Hospice: The spiritual dimension. In J. M. Zimmerman (Ed.), *Hospice: Complete care for the terminally ill* (pp. 179 – 196). Baltimore, MD: Urban & Schwarzenberg.

Doka, K. J. (1983). The spiritual needs of the dying patient. *Newsletter for the Forum for Death Education and Counseling, 6,* 2–3.

Dupee, R. M. (1982). Hospice—Compassionate, comprehensive approach to terminal care. *Postgraduate Medicine, 72*(3), 239–245.

Eggerman, S., & Dustin, D. (1985). Death orientation and communication with the terminally ill. *Omega, 16*(3), 255–265.

Erikson, E. (1963). *Childhood and society* (2d ed.). New York: Norton.

Evans, M. A., Esbenson, M., & Jaffe, C. (1981). Expect the unexpected when you care for a dying patient. *Nursing, 11,* pp. 55–56.

Fairchild, R. (1980). *Finding hope again: A pastor's guide to counseling the depressed.* New York: Harper & Row.

Feigenberg, L., & Shneidman, E. S. (1979). Clinical thanatology and psychotherapy: Some reflections on caring for the dying person. *Omega, 10*(1), 1–8.

Ferrell, B. R. (1985). Cancer deaths and bereavement outcomes. *The American Journal of Hospice Care, 2*(4), 18–23.

Freund, J. (1977). When should the clergyman be called? In E. R. Prichard, J. Collard, B. A. Orcutt, A. H. Kutscher, I. Seeland, & N. Lefkowitz (Eds.), *Social work with the dying patient and family* (pp. 208–215). New York: Columbia University Press.

Fulton, R. (1976). The sacred and the secular: Attitudes of the American public toward death, funerals, and funeral directors. In R. Fulton (Ed.), *Death and identity* (rev. ed.)(pp. 158–172). Bowie, MD: Charles Press.

Glaser, B. G., & Strauss, A. L. (1965). *Awareness of dying.* Chicago: Aldine.

Glaser, B. G., & Strauss, A. L. (1968). *Time for dying.* Chicago: Aldine.

Gruman, G. J. (1978). Ethics of death and dying: Historical perspective. *Omega, 9*(3), 203–237.

Hinton, J. (1980). Speaking of death with the dying. In E. Shneidman (Ed.), *Death: Current perspectives* (2d ed.) (pp. 187–196). Palo Alto, CA: Mayfield.

Horne, R., & Fagan, M. (1983). *Summary: Focus group discussions.* Skokie, IL: Les Turner ALS Foundation.

Hoy, T. (1983). Hospice chaplaincy in the caregiving team. In C. A. Corr & D. M. Corr (Eds.), *Hospice care: Principles and practice* (pp. 177–196). New York: Springer.

Kalish, R. A. (1970). The onset of the dying process. *Omega, 1,* 57–69.

Kalish, R., & Reynolds, D. (1976). *Death and ethnicity: A psychocultural study.* Los Angeles: Univeristy of Southern California Press.

Kastenbaum, R. J. (1981). *Death, society, and human experience* (2d ed.). St. Louis: C. V. Mosby.

Kastenbaum, R. J., & Aisenberg, R. (1972). *The psychology of death.* New York: Springer.

Kirschling, J. M. (1986). The experience of terminal illness on adult family members. *The Hospice Journal, 2*(1), 121–138.

Kübler-Ross, E. (1969). *On death and dying.* New York: Macmillan.

Lamm, M. (1969). *The Jewish way in death and mourning.* New York: Jonathan David.

Leloudis, D., & Pole, L. (1985). Reasons for choosing hospice care: How patients and primary caregivers make their selection. *The American Journal of Hospice Care, 2*(6), 30–34.

Lerner, M. (1980). When, why, and where people die. In E. S. Shneidman (Ed.), *Death: Current perspectives* (pp. 87–106). Palo Alto, CA: Mayfield.

Levy, M. H. (1988). Pain control research in the terminally ill. *Omega, 18*(4), 265–275.

Ley, D. C., & Corless, I. B. (1988). Spirituality and hospice care. *Death Studies, 12*(2), 101–110.

Magno, J. B. (1981, April). Hospice: Caring when curing fails. *The Internist,* 7–9.

Martocchio, B. C. (1986). Agendas for quality of life. *The Hospice Journal, 2*(1), 11–21.

Mauritzen, J. (1988). Pastoral care for the dying and bereaved. *Death Studies, 12*(2), 111–122.

McGrory, A. (1978). *A well model approach to the care of the dying client.* New York: McGraw-Hill.

Millet, N. (1983). Hospice: A new horizon for social work. In C. A. Corr & D. M. Corr (Eds.), *Hospice care: Principles and practice* (pp. 135–147). New York: Springer.

Millison, M. B. (1988). Spirituality and the caregiver: Developing an underutilized facet of care. *The American Journal of Hospice Care 5*(2), 37–44.

Morgan, J. D. (1988). Death and bereavement: Spiritual, ethical, and pastoral issues. *Death Studies, 12*(2), 85–89.

National Hospice Organization (1987). *Meeting the challenge for a special kind of caring: Standards of a hospice program of care recommended by the National Hospice Organization.* Arlington, VA: Author.

Norris, C. (1970). The professional nurse and body image. In C. Carlson (Ed.), *Behavioral concepts and nursing intervention*. Philadelphia, PA: Lippincott.

Olin, H. S. (1972). Failure and fulfillment: Education in the use of psychoactive drugs in the dying patient. *Journal of Thantology, 2,* 567–573.

Paradis, L. F. (1985). The development of hospice in America: A social movement organizes. In L. F. Paradis (Ed.), *Hospice handbook: A guide for managers and planners* (pp. 3–24). Rockville, MD: Aspen Systems.

Pattison, E. M. (1977). *The experience of dying*. Englewood Cliffs, NJ: Prentice-Hall.

Pattison, E. M. (1978). The living-dying process. In C. A. Garfield (Ed.), *Psychosocial care of the dying patient* (pp. 133–168). New York: McGraw-Hill.

Peteet, J. R. (1985). Religious issues presented by cancer patients seen in psychiatric consultation. *Journal of Psychosocial Oncology, 3*(1), 53–66.

Piaget, J. (1963). *The origins of intelligence in children*. New York: International Universities Press.

Pumphrey, J. (1977). Recognizing your patient's spiritual needs. *Nursing, 9,* 64–70.

Rando, T. A. (1984). *Grief, dying, and death: Clinical interventions for caregivers.* Champaign, IL: Research Press.

Rebok, G. W., & Hoyer, W. J. (1979). Clients nearing death: Behavioral treatment perspectives. *Omega, 10*(3), 191–201.

Richards, V. (1980). Death and cancer. In E. S. Shneidman (Ed.), *Death: Current perspectives* (pp. 322–330). Palo Alto, CA: Mayfield.

Rosel, N. (1978). Toward a social theory of dying. *Omega, 9*(1), 49–55.

Saunders, C. (1978). Terminal care. In C. A. Garfield (Ed.), *Psychosocial care of the dying patient* (pp. 22–33). New York: McGraw Hill.

Schoenberg, B., & Senescu, R. A. (1970). The patient's reaction to fatal illness. In B. Schoenberg, A. Carr, D. Peretz, & A. Kutscher (Eds.), *Loss and grief: Psychosocial management in medical practice* (pp. 221–237). New York: Columbia University Press.

Shneidman, E. S. (1978). Some aspects of psychotherapy with dying persons. In C. A. Garfield (Ed.), *Psychosocial care of the dying patient* (pp. 201–218). New York: McGraw-Hill.

Tehan, C. (1982). Hospice in an existing home care agency. *Family and Community Health, 5*(3), 11–20.

Thompson, L. M. (1984). Cultural and institutional restrictions on dying styles in a technological society. *Death Education, 8,* 223–229.

Vander Zanden, J. W. (1985). *Human development* (3d ed.) New York: Alfred A. Knopf.

Viney, L. L. (1984). Loss of life and loss of bodily integrity: Two different sources of threat for people who are ill. *Omega, 15*(3), 207–222.

Weisman, A. D. (1972). *On dying and denying*. New York: Behavioral Publications.

Wolff, B. B., & Langley, S. (1977). Cultural factors and the response to pain. In D. Landy (Ed.), *Culture, disease, and healing: Studies in medical anthropology* (pp. 313–319). New York: Macmillan.

Zborowski, M. (1952). Cultural components in responses to pain. *Journal of Social Issues, 8*, 16–30.

Zinker, J. C., & Fink, S. L. (1966). The possibility of psychological growth in a dying person. *Journal of General Psychology, 74*, 185–199.

Zinker, J. C., & Hallenbeck, C. E. (1965). Notes on loss, crisis, and growth. *Journal of General Psychology, 73*, 347–354.

2

Grief and Loss

Theories of Attachment and Loss 47

Freud's Theory 47
Bowlby's theory 48

Normal Grief Response 49

Manifestations of Grief 49
Grief Work 53
Duration and Intensity of Grief 54

Variables Related to the Bereaved 55

Sex 55
Age 57
Personality Characteristics 58
Cultural Background 58

Variables Related to the Deceased 59

Relationship of Deceased to Bereaved 59
Age of the Deceased 60
Perceived Similarity to the Deceased 60

Variables Related to the Death Event 61

Suddenness of the Death 61
Preventability of the Death 63

Additional Factors Affecting Intensity and Duration of Grief 68

Availability of Social Support 68
Bereavement Overload 69

Helping Strategies 69

Permission to Grieve 69
Expression of Grief 70
Acceptance 70
Listen to the Bereaved 70
Share Information 71
Practical Assistance 71

Pathological Grief 72

Positive Outcomes of Grief 74

Summary 74

An important focus of this book is the bereaved individual. The grief process is not understood by a large part of society and, as a result, many grieving persons do not receive the type of suppport that is most helpful to them.

Although there are differences in the formal definitions of the words "bereavement," "grief," and "mourning" (Pine, 1976), the words are often used interchangeably.

> *Bereavement* is the state of being that results from a significant loss (for example, due to death).

> *Grief* refers to the outcome of being bereaved. A variety of reactions— somatic, intrapsychic, and behavioral—constitute the grief response.

> *Mourning* connotes the social prescription for the way in which we are expected to display our grief (for example, wearing black or holding a wake).

While the focus of this text is on loss related to death, it is important to keep in mind that individuals experience grief after many different types of losses: (1) divorce (Froiland & Hozman, 1977; Hurley, 1987; Wallerstein & Kelly, 1976); (2) loss of a body part (Schoenberg & Carr, 1970); (3) loss of body function (Cameron, 1987; Newman & Paris, 1987; Winkler, 1987); (4) birth of a handicapped child (Davis, 1987; Parks, 1977; Wright, 1976); (5) loss of a job (Jones, 1979; Murray, 1987); (6) relinquishment of a child for adoption (Berman & Bufferd, 1986). These are only a few examples that illustrate that loss is pervasive in our lives. The grief resulting from these various losses in many ways parallels the emotional reactions triggered by a death. Each type of loss, however, also·involves unique factors.

Theories of Attachment and Loss

There are many different theoretical perspectives that provide insight into the grief process. Those posited by Freud (1917) and Bowlby (1980) were selected for two reasons: They frequently were used as the theoretical framework for the research cited throughout this book, and they also closely relate to the tasks of mourning presented later in this chapter.

Freud's Theory

According to Freudian theory, a major task facing individuals who have experienced the loss of a loved one is to withdraw the libido that was formerly invested in the relationship with the individual who has died. *Libido* refers to the energy of love and pleasure. Freud noted that the withdrawal of the libido is done over an extended period of time and at the expense of a great deal of cathectic energy. *Cathexis* is defined as the investment of psychic energy in, or emotional significance of, an object. In order to detach the emotional energy that had linked the survivor to the person who has died, Freud (1917) believed that "the memories and hopes which bound the libido to the object are brought up and hyper-cathected, and the detachment of the libido is accomplished. . . . when the work of mourning is completed the ego becomes free and uninhibited again" (p. 154). *Hypercathexis* refers to an extreme amount of psychic energy being invested in an object. Freud implies, therefore, that before persons can let go of a love object, they must, first of all, invest all the more energy in thinking about the person who has died. This is reflected by the preoccupation with the deceased that is a normal part of the grief process and is a precursor to the detachment of energy that ultimately takes place.

Bowlby's Theory

Bowlby's (1980) framework for understanding separation and loss is closely linked to his theory of attachment. Bowlby explains that humans have an instinctive need to form strong attachments to others. Separation, whether through death or other causes, elicits a variety of behaviors (such as clinging, crying, angry outbursts, or protest), indicating that an attachment bond did exist. While Freud hypothesized that involvement in the grief process necessitated the breaking of emotional ties with the deceased, Bowlby argues that the initial phases of the grief process involve a yearning for the lost person and an effort to reestablish ties. He describes the overall grief experience as progressing through four phases:

1. *Numbing*: This phase involves an inability to truly understand the loss and is reflected in such statements as "I can't believe it" or "I am in a dream."
2. *Yearning* or *searching*: This phase involves the bereaved individual's desire to recover the person who is now gone. Survivors may be preoccupied with the deceased. For example, a glimpse of a stranger may trigger the thought that their loved one is still alive.
3. *Disorganization* or *despair*: This phase is marked by despair, depression, and apathy, as the survivors discard old patterns of thinking, feeling, and acting.
4. *Reorganization*: This phase involves many strong emotions. It is a

time when survivors must redefine their sense of identity and their situation. They must attempt to fill unaccustomed roles and acquire new skills.

Grief is a multifaceted response. These phases are marked by a wide variety of thoughts, emotions, and behaviors.

Normal Grief Response

Upon hearing the news that a loved one has died, an immediate reaction is typically described as a sense of shock, numbness, or denial (Kavanaugh, 1972; Kübler-Ross, 1969). Shortly thereafter, the reality that the death has severed an important bond triggers an acute grief reaction, which gradually subsides as individuals reorganize their lives and accept the death. This process has been described by many authorities as proceeding through a series of stages. Even though authors use slightly different terminology, their basic structures are quite similar.

Bugen (1979) has raised a number of concerns regarding these stage theories. He argues that (1) the stages portrayed are not necessarily sequential—individuals may experience emotions in an order other than that posed by a particular stage framework and may experience symptoms from more than one stage at a time. (2) There are no clear-cut beginning or ending points for particular stages; rather, they blend dynamically. (3) The stage theories do not adequately reflect the uniqueness of an individual's grief. Persons may not experience all of the feelings described but may experience many others instead.

Manifestations of Grief

Grief is a "complex, evolving process with multiple dimensions" (Jacobs, Kosten, Kasl, Ostfeld, Berkman, Charpentier, 1987, p. 41). Looking at grief as a constellation of a wide variety of manifestations that are unique to a given individual in their combination, intensity, and duration provides an alternative to describing grief as a series of stages (Brasted & Callahan, 1984). In the following sections a variety of somatic, intrapsychic, and behavioral manifestations of grief are briefly described (see Figure 2.1). They will be discussed in more detail throughout the rest of the book in a variety of contexts, including the manner of death (for example, suicide), age of the bereaved, and type of relationship that was severed. The

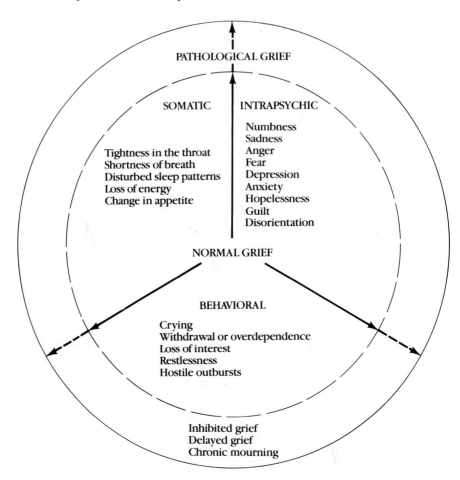

Figure 2.1 *Examples of Manifestations of Grief*

reactions noted are common components of grief but are *not* universal. The intensity of any given manifestation is expected to lessen over time if the individual is grieving in a normal rather than a pathological manner. Pathological grief is discussed later in this chapter.

Somatic Manifestations.   Lindemann (1944) was one of the first to clinically observe a large number of bereaved individuals. Many of the symptoms described by Lindemann were physical in nature. He noted that *somatic* distress such as a "feeling of tightness in the throat, choking with a shortness of breath, need for sighing, an empty feeling in the abdomen, and a lack of muscular power" (p. 142) is extremely common.

Photo 2.1   *Grief is a powerful human emotion for which most individuals are unprepared.*

More recently, researchers have corroborated Lindemann's findings that grief has a decidedly physical component. In addition to the somatic manifestations identified in Lindemann's classic study, disturbed sleep patterns, loss of strength and energy, change in appetite, and a tendency to be easily fatigued are also reported to be common symptoms of bereavement (Battin, Gerber, Wiener, & Arkin, 1977). Clayton, Desmarais, and Winokur (1968) found that physical symptoms such as headaches, blurred vision, difficulty breathing, abdominal pain, constipation, urinary frequency, and/or dysmenorrhea are reported by some grieving individuals.

Intrapsychic Manifestations.   The grief process involves a multiplicity of emotional and psychological reactions to the loss. Researchers have determined that the following *intrapsychic manifestations* are frequent components of grief: numbness, sadness, fear, depression, anger, loneliness, worry, worthlessness, guilt, anxiety, hopelessness, helplessness, discontentment, and self-pity (Clayton, 1975; Miles & Demi, 1984; Parkes, 1975).

Changes in thought processes are also common intrapsychic manifestations of grief (Malinak, Hoyt, & Patterson, 1979). For example, bereaved individuals have often reported being confused, disoriented, and unable to concentrate or attend to detail. Another psychological component of grief has been described as being a "hallucination." In this situation a particular sensory stimulus brings back such a vivid memory that, for a split second, the survivor believes the deceased is still alive. These sensory stimuli may be such things as a car door slamming in front of the house at the time when a widow's husband would normally come home from work or a child walking down the sidewalk wearing a dress very similar to one worn frequently by the parent's dead child.

Some bereaved individuals report that their thoughts are filled with memories of the deceased. They can think of little else other than the events leading up to the death or their previous interaction with the deceased (Lindemann, 1944). In its extreme, preoccupation with the deceased has been described as an "obsessional review" (Glick, Weiss, & Parkes, 1974).

For many individuals, feelings and thought patterns described as normal intrapsychic symptoms of grief are very different in either occurrence or intensity from anything they have experienced previously. As a result, many may question their sanity and may even fear that they are going crazy. In this case, appropriate reassurance must be given to the bereaved that this is not so. It can be helpful to the bereaved to be reassured that, as distressing as these thoughts and emotions are, they are normal manifestations of grief and that they will gradually diminish over time.

Behavioral Manifestations. Common behavioral manifestations include crying, withdrawal from others, overdependence on others, inability to perform daily tasks, restlessness, loss of interest in work or leisure-time activities, and hostile outbursts (Ball, 1977; Simos, 1979). Crying is a behavior that readily comes to mind when thinking of the grief process. It is a natural response for many to the sadness and depression being experienced. There are factors, however, that may encourage or inhibit a crying response. These factors include the sex and/or cultural background of the bereaved. Both are discussed later in this chapter.

Other behavioral manifestations relate to patterns of interaction with other survivors. Some grieving individuals choose to isolate themselves by withdrawing from persons in their social network. Withdrawal may be related to a variety of beliefs, such as "No one cares about me"; "No one can possibly understand the emotional pain I am experiencing"; "Others, too, may die and leave me, so it is wiser not to get involved"; "I am worthless and others will leave"; or "My grief is my own private affair." In contrast, some bereaved individuals become overly dependent on others. This dependence may be an outgrowth of a sense of helplessness that essentially paralyzes individuals for a period of time and prohibits them from performing tasks or making decisions on their own.

Hostile outbursts may be the result of the anger that is common to grief. The hostility may be aimed at family members, friends, or a particular individual or a more diffuse group, such as medical professionals or drunk drivers, whom the bereaved somehow holds responsible for the death. The pent-up emotional energy may be vented through explosive words or actions, such as striking out or throwing objects.

Inability to concentrate on daily tasks and loss of interest in work or leisure activities are indicative of the physical, emotional, and psychological energy being expended to deal with the loss itself and to reorganize patterns of living without the deceased. As time passes, survivors may gradually reinvest energy in a wide variety of activities.

Grief Work

Freud (1917) referred to grief as an absorbing process involving work. Many others have subsequently used the phrase *grief work*. As described by Lindemann (1944), grief work is "emancipation from the bondage to the deceased, readjustment to the environment in which the deceased is missing, and the formation of new relationships" (p. 143). Grief work progresses through a number of steps that involve a change in one's self-concept, aspirations, goals, and relationships with the external world. Coping with grief is an experience that is physically, emotionally, and psychologically draining. Grief is an individual's way of regaining balance and of restoring a sense of equilibrium in one's life. Worden (1982) believes that grief work involves four tasks: (1) to accept the reality of the loss, (2) to experience the pain of grief, (3) to adjust to an environment in which the deceased is missing, (4) to withdraw emotional energy and reinvest it in another relationship.

The first task, to accept the reality of the loss, demands that the bereaved break through the initial reaction of denial and accept the fact that the loved one has died. Although each individual's experience of grief is unique, the loss of a person to whom one is attached is expected to cause pain. Sometimes the bereaved refuses to feel this pain by cutting off his or her feelings and avoiding painful thoughts or reminders of the deceased. Avoidance of the pain during the time shortly following the death may cause repercussions at a later date.

Depending on the role the deceased played in their lives, survivors may have a relatively easy or a much more difficult time adjusting to an environment in which the deceased is missing. The bereaved may be forced to develop new skills or find other persons to fulfill some of the lost roles. Worden's description of adjustment to an environment in which the deceased is missing directly parallels Bowlby's fourth phase of reorganization. Worden describes the fourth task of grief work as withdrawing emotional energy and reinvesting it in another relationship. Accomplishment of this task is essentially the same as the detachment process that Freud explains as being fundamental to mourning.

Duration and Intensity of Grief

Although there is no absolute agreement as to how long the normal period of bereavement may extend, many experts (Hardt, 1978; Marris, 1986; Raphael, 1983) agree that it is likely to be significantly longer than the 4 to 6 weeks first stated by Lindemann (1944) as adequate time for recovery. While the most intense or acute feelings typically begin to diminish within 6 months to 1 or 2 years, many people experience continuing grief-related feelings for a much longer time. This is not regarded as abnormal unless there is such intensity after an extended period of time that the survivors cannot adjust to the loss in a way that allows them to reorganize their lives and function effectively in the real world. *Acute grief* refers to the period when the somatic, intrapsychic, and behavioral reactions are most intense. Emotional and physical resources are the most drained during this period. Although the grief work may continue well beyond the acute stage, the intensity of emotion and constant preoccupation with the loss gradually diminish.

Certain factors may periodically increase the intensity of the grief reaction even after it has largely abated. Due to the memories they trigger, certain days of the year may cause the bereaved to once again experience painful emotions and preoccupation with the deceased. These *anniversary reactions* are often precipitated by special days such as wedding anniversaries, birthdays, anniversaries of the date of death, Christmas, Passover or Thanksgiving. Feelings of grief may also be magnified by environmental cues such as hearing the deceased's favorite song on the radio, smelling her favorite perfume, or seeing his favorite flower. As time passes and as grief work continues successfully, these reminders of the loved one who has died often no longer precipitate bitter or painful memories, but rather happy or peaceful ones.

Variables Related to the Bereaved: Factors Affecting Intensity and Duration of Grief

The sex, age, personality characteristics (including coping mechanisms), and cultural backround of bereaved individuals influence the manifestations of grief and affect the intensity and duration of these manifestations (see Figure 2.2).

Sex

A number of researchers have studied the differential manifestations of conjugal bereavement between men and women. Parkes and Brown (1972) found that women experienced more health problems after the death of their spouses than did men. Sanders (1979) also found that widows have more physical problems than widowers after the death of their partners. In contrast to Parkes and Brown's and Sanders's studies, Gerber, Rusalem, Hannon, Battin, and Arkin (1975) differentiated between their widowed subjects based on the length of their spouse's fatal chronic illness. Bereaved males and females did not differ significantly in their health status if the chronic illness of their spouse was less than 6 months. If the terminal illness of their spouse was greater than 6 months, however, differences were noted. Men indicated more health problems than did women. Contradictions between these studies may be due to a number of factors, including the variability in age of the subjects, death situations, and methods used to gather data.

In addition to dissimilar somatic responses, Sanders (1979) found other

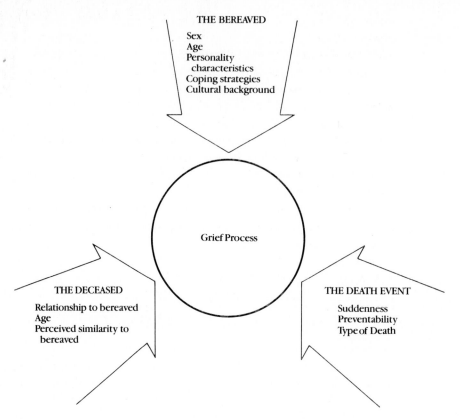

Figure 2.2   *Primary Factors Affecting the Grief Process*

differences between men and women grieving the death of their spouses. Women exhibited significantly more death anxiety. This research also indicated that men are more prone to denial while women are more prone to anger, social isolation, depersonalization, sleep disturbance, and loss of appetite.

Glick et al. (1974) studied widows and widowers during their first year of bereavement. Although men's and women's grief reactions did not differ substantially, their interpretation of the loss was dissimilar. Men indicated that they felt "dismembered" while women reported a sense of "abandonment."

A number of studies have examined the difference between mothers' and fathers' reactions to the death of a child. Peppers and Knapp (1980) found that mothers typically have a more extreme grief reaction than fathers to loss of a newborn child. Cook (1983) reported that fathers felt responsible for supporting other grieving family members and, as a result, did not feel they could openly share their grief with others. She also found that the sex of the parent was a significant factor in the difficulty experienced when dealing with first-year holidays such as Christmas, Passover, and Thanksgiving, as well as the anniversary of the death and the child's birthday. Mothers had a much more difficult time coping than fathers.

Even though men and women may, to some extent, have different somatic, intrapsychic, and behavioral manifestations of their grief, there is no indication that overall adjustment to bereavement varies significantly. Parkes (1975) studied the outcome following bereavement of widows and widowers. There were no significant differences between the number of men and women who achieved a "good outcome" as compared to a "poor outcome."

As thanatologists continue to research sex differences in response to loss, important questions remain unanswered. For example, are there intrinsic differences in the way men and women react to loss? To what extent are observed differences in the manifestations of grief due to innate differences between men and women and to what extent are they the result of gender prescriptions? Do differences between the grief reactions of men and women become greater in certain situations?

Age

The age of the bereaved is a variable that has an impact on the symptomatology of grief and also on the coping mechanisms available to the individual who is dealing with a loss. Though studies thus far have used different methodologies to determine bereavement outcomes for various age groups, some general trends have been identified. As noted in Chapter 1, Piaget's theory of cognitive development and Erikson's theory of psychosocial development are important for understanding the needs of the dying. These theories are also relevant to understanding the variation of grief responses across the lifespan. Raphael (1980) has noted that developmental conflicts currently being dealt with by the survivor will have an impact on the mourning process. Discussion of these issues, as they relate to particular age groups, is presented in Chapters 4–9.

Young children perceive death somewhat differently than do adults and only gradually learn that death is irreversible and universal, that dead persons are not able to function as living people, and that all individuals will die some day (Speece & Brent, 1984). At this point, however, there is no firm agreement by all researchers as to the age at which the separate components of the concept of death are acquired. A number of research studies focusing on a variety of questions related to concept acquisition are reviewed in Chapter 4.

Adults should not assume that because children perceive death differently they do not grieve. They do, in fact, grieve, but manifest their grief somewhat differently (Jewett, 1982; Krupnick, 1984; Wolfelt, 1983). Specific aspects of children's grief are discussed in Chapters 4 and 5.

A review of the research examining the effect of age on bereavement indicates not only differences between children and adults, but also differences among persons in various stages of adulthood. For example, the death of a spouse has more severe consequences for younger women than for older women (Gorer, 1965; Maddison & Viola, 1968). Sanders (1980) found that younger widows initially experienced greater intensities of grief, but at 18 months this trend reversed itself, with older spouses showing more intense reactions. Further explanation of adult-related differences in bereavement reactions is included in Chapters 7–9.

Personality Characteristics

The vulnerability of individuals who experience losses varies considerably depending on their personality. A person who is by nature highly dependent on others is likely to experience a more severe loss than an individual who has limited capacity to become involved with others.

Parkes and Brown (1972) studied various factors affecting the grief reactions that followed the death of a spouse. They reported that personality factors greatly influence the magnitude of grief. For example, previous severe depression of the bereaved indicated that there was more likely to be a poor outcome following the bereavement. Parkes and Brown explained that *poor outcome* meant reactions such as acquiring symptoms resembling those suffered by the deceased, extreme self-blame, or overactivity without a goal, among others. In addition, Gut (1974) reported that a variety of personality characteristics influence the individual's subjective experience of grief. For example, a low tolerance for frustration and anxiety may intensify the chances of a poor outcome of grief or lengthen the bereavement period.

Cultural Background

Charmaz (1980) has argued that what is typically viewed as an individualized and personal grief response must also be examined within the context of the culture in which persons live. Our cultural heritage helps to define prescriptions for what is regarded as appropriate expression of emotion and appropriate behavior subsequent to a loss. These prescriptions are a part of our early socialization as well as later social dictates (Kalish & Reynolds, 1976).

Rituals, such as wakes or funerals, are culturally determined activities that promote a recognition of the death and allow a particular degree of emotional release. For example, persons attending a funeral service in a Protestant church whose congregation is largely Black are often allowed an opportunity to experience unrestrained emotional catharsis in a community setting, whereas persons attending an Anglo-Protestant service often are not (Charmaz, 1980). Krupp and Kligfield (1962) have raised a concern that the deritualization of life that has occurred within the United States, coupled with the cultural mandate that mourning should be done privately, causes increased difficulty for persons attempting to deal with loss.

Kleinman, Kaplan, and Weiss (1984) caution people against stereotyping individuals simply because they are a part of a particular cultural or ethnic background. This is particularly inappropriate in a pluralistic society such as America where, over time, clearly defined cultural expectations have become blurred. First-generation immigrants may face a particularly difficult period of grief in that they may not have brought with them the "traditional resources for carrying out culturally expected bereavement practices" (p. 206), and, at the same time, it is not personally acceptable or comfortable for them to engage in mainstream bereavement practices.

In his review of relevant literature, Eisenbruch (1984a, 1984b) raised a variety of questions related to cross-cultural aspects of bereavement that need further study. Those questions include, among others: (1) Do individuals in all societies share similar private and public experiences of grief? (2) What is the relationship between an individual's private grief and his or her public mourning? (3) How widespread and useful are the positive factors, such as group support, in facilitating successful resolution of the grieving process? (4) How effective are the mourning practices of various ethnic groups in preventing pathological outcomes for these groups? Answers to questions such as these will provide continuing insight regarding cultural influences on grief.

Variables Related to the Deceased: Factors Affecting Intensity and Duration of Grief

Relationship of Deceased to Bereaved

The death of a person who held a peripheral role in the survivor's life is likely to trigger a less intense grief reaction than one who held a central role (Reilly, 1978; Rubin, 1985). Bugen (1979) has noted that the central-ity of the relationship may be determined by either a behavioral commit-ment or an emotional commitment. A behavioral commitment is related to the role that the deceased played in the bereaved's life and vice versa. For example, if the deceased husband was very dependent on his surviving wife to meet his daily needs, the bereaved widow may feel a great void in her life, not only because of her emotional commitment to her husband, but also because of the many hours in her day that she no longer fills with tasks performed to take care of him. In this case, the death of her husband created a role loss as well as an object loss. *Object loss* refers to the loss of a loved one. *Role loss* is defined as the loss of one's position or status in society (Flesch, 1975).

When attempting to gain insight regarding the nature of the severed relationship and its effect on the grief response, one must look beyond the centrality of the relationship in behavioral terms to the quality of the rela-tionship and its centrality in emotional terms (Fulton, 1970). The death of someone who was regarded as an intimate, a confidant, and a major source of support has a much greater impact than the death of someone who may have spent much time with the survivor but was never emotionally close.

Age of the Deceased

Freese (1977) explained that the age of the person who has died often has an impact on those who are grieving. He states that the "most traumatic of all is the death of a child, or of the parent of a child." Many will react to the death of an aged person as being appropriate because he or she was able to lead a full and long life, but feel that the death of a child is some-how premature or unjustified.

If the person who died was of similar age to the bereaved, the grieving individual often asks questions such as "Why did that person die and not me?" "How much longer do I have to live?" Concerns related to these types of quesions have an effect on the bereavement process.

Perceived Similarity to the Deceased

Though relatively little research has been done in this area, there is some indication that if the bereaved perceive themselves to be similar to the deceased, they may experience more grief than persons who perceive lit-tle similarity. Barnes (1978) has noted that children whose same-sex par-ent has died often view themselves as particularly vulnerable to death.

These children may need special help differentiating themselves from the deceased. Children whose siblings have died may also feel vulnerable because of the perceived similarity due to age.

Variables Related to the Death Event: Factors Affecting Intensity and Duration of Grief

Suddenness of the Death

The suddenness of the death has been found to be related to the grief experienced by many survivors. Sudden death intensifies the initial shock of the bereaved and, since there was no opportunity to prepare for the loss, all of the grief work must be done after the death (Bowlby, 1980). For example, thousands of individuals die each year due to heart attacks. If there had been no previous indication of heart problems, the survivors must face a totally unexpected death.

From the time a life-threatening illness is diagnosed, the dying individual, together with family members and friends, often begins to grieve. They grieve in anticipation of the emotional pain and also for the changes that the death will bring. They grieve the many losses that are a part of the dying process itself. This type of grief is known as *anticipatory grief.* If the death is an expected one, as is the case in death due to a terminal illness, part of the grief work may be done prior to the death. This, then, may serve as a mitigating factor in the intensity and duration of the grief experience once the death has occurred (Gerber et al., 1975). Additionally, the grief may be somewhat ameliorated by having had the opportunity to say good-bye to the person who is dying and to draw closure on a variety of concerns. There may be fewer regrets and less guilt as a result. If the illness has been a debilitating or a painful one, survivors may even feel a sense of relief when death does come (Chester, Jerardi, & Weger, 1980).

Many persons who have an opportunity to engage in anticipatory grief do have less intense reactions and complete their grief work earlier as compared to survivors of a sudden death. This, however, is not always the case. Exceptions seem to be those situations when the illness is a lengthy one (Schwab, Chalmers, Conroy, Farris, & Markush, 1975). These researchers found a negative impact on many of the survivors who anticipated the death of a loved one for longer than 6 months.

Sanders (1982) found both qualitative and quantitative differences in the grief response of survivors of short-term chronic deaths (STC) compared to long-term chronic deaths (LTC). The LTC survivors exhibited a

Photo 2.2   *Large-scale disasters are typically sudden and allow no opportunity for anticipatory grief among the many who are left to mourn.*

greater sense of isolation, rumination, loss of vigor, and loss of emotional control when compared to the STC survivors. The most debilitating factor was the higher degree of social isolation. Sanders explained this by noting that the care of the individual was so all-encompassing, there was little time or energy to continue previous levels of interaction. As a result, support systems diminished. In the case of shorter term illnesses, friends and relatives had not yet drifted away.

The value of anticipatory grief may be diminished in a situation of protracted illness because emotional and physical resources of the bereaved have been taxed to the limit prior to the death (Gerber et al., 1975). Additionally, Maddison and Walker (1967) have hypothesized that survivors who acted as primary caregiver for the dying over an extended period of time must deal not only with the death of a loved one, but also with the loss of this additional role and function.

Preventability of the Death

Bugen (1979) has argued that the question of preventability is an important influence on bereavement outcome. He explains that *preventability* is "the general belief that the factors contributing to the death might have been avoided" (p. 36). Whether or not the accident could have, in fact, been avoided is not really the issue. For example, if the survivor perceives that he or she may have contributed to the death or could have prevented the death, feelings of guilt increase. The belief that someone else is responsible elicits anger toward that person. Types of death that are generally regarded as having been preventable are death by homicide, suicide, or accident. On occasion, natural deaths are also thought to have been preventable. Some individuals feel that they may have been able to prevent a death . . . "If only I had taken Dad to the doctor last week." The perception of preventability can affect the grief reaction, regardless of whether the death actually could have been prevented.

Homicide.   Each year, thousands of family members and friends must deal with grief that has been intensified by the nature of the death itself. Due to the violent nature of homicide, the suddenness of the death, a variety of unanswered questions, and a belief that the death was preventable, the grief triggered by murder is often more intense and of longer duration than many other types of grief reactions. Problems become magnified by the survivors who also often feel stigmatized by the nature of the death. This may interfere with the availability of a sensitive support network to help the bereaved come to terms with the death. In addition, feelings of frustration or anger at not being allowed to grieve in privacy may be provoked by widespread media coverage.

Burgess (1975) explains that survivors of homicide experience somatic symptoms similar to those discussed earlier: insomnia, chest pains, palpitations, and headaches. Many of the intrapsychic and behavioral manifestations of grief precipitated by a murder necessitate additional discussion because they are frequently more intense than for a death due to natural causes. Others are unique to this type of death situation.

Recall that anger is a common component of grief. When a loved one has been murdered, bereaved individuals are likely to initially experience intense anger and rage directed at the murderer. Later, they may exhibit anger at the criminal court system if they deem that justice, as they see it, has not been served (Schmidt, 1986) or if they feel that the system has treated them insensitively. Guilt, too, is a typical component of grief but may be exacerbated if the survivors feel that they could or should have somehow protected the victim. Preoccupation with the deceased and the death event is common to grief resulting from any death, but the preoccupation may be more intense and more painful after a murder. Images that are prevalent both in conscious thoughts and in dreams often focus on "the terror and helplessness of the victim" (Rynearson, 1984, p. 1452). There is great concern regarding the trauma associated with the mode of killing and the suffering endured. Additionally, survivors may experience intrusive thoughts of wanting to kill the murderer as retribution for the crime.

Some behavioral manifestations of grief are unique to bereavement caused by murder. Survivors often experience a pervasive fear that then causes heightened anticipation and protective avoidance of violence as well as hypervigilance and frequent startle reactions. For example, the bereaved may restrict their activities in order to remain in familiar surroundings and to avoid strangers. Many survivors desire to seek retribution and spend many hours providing information to the investigative–judicial system or, in some cases, pursuing independent investigations. Some survivors initiate or support legislative action to demand harsher punishment for convicted murderers or to promote gun control. Others may advocate changes in the legal system that would ensure such activities as consistent communication with the family regarding the status of the case (Getzel & Masters, 1984). It is important that a search for retribution does not become a substitution for the necessary grief work and the ultimate acceptance of the death.

Suicide.   Like homicide survivors, persons who grieve as a result of the suicide of a loved one experience emotions that are somewhat different than those triggered by death due to natural causes. Rando (1984) has noted that survivors face such difficult problems that they themselves are oftentimes called "victims."

Anger and guilt are frequent components of a grief reaction. These emotions, however, are greatly intensified when associated with a suicide (Buksbazen, 1976; Demi, 1984; Schuyler, 1973). There is often extreme anger at the individual who committed suicide because that person is regarded as having willfully chosen death, which then precipitated the resulting pain, disorganization, and loneliness. Bolton (1986) shares a comment by one father whose daughter commited suicide: "Suicide is not a solitary act. A beloved person thinks that she is killing herself, but she also kills a part of us" (p. 202).

Additionally, survivors are frequently angry at themselves for not having predicted the possibility of the suicide and, thereby, prevented it. They may also be angry for not having helped the deceased to be sufficiently happy or satisfied with life such that suicide would not have even been considered. These survivors often feel at least somewhat responsible for the death and as a result may feel extremely guilty (Hatton & Valente, 1981). Although these survivors may desperately wish they had been able to prevent the suicide, they need help in understanding that they could not ultimately be held responsible for the other person's act.

Family members and friends may also experience a great deal of shame following the suicide (Rando, 1984). Although the survivors did not commit the actual suicide, they may feel that society is blaming them for the final act of their loved one. Many survivors do report that they feel stigmatized by others (Hauser, 1987; Solomon, 1983). Survivors may also feel shame if they, or others, believe suicide is a criminal act, a sin, or a sign of weakness or madness (Kastenbaum, 1981).

The stigma associated with a suicide often diminishes the availability of support that is crucial to a healthy and timely resolution of grief. Individuals who would normally be helpful during other periods marked by grief often engage in a conspiracy of silence because they feel very awkward and don't know what to say after the suicide. Calhoun, Abernathy, and Selby (1986) studied societal reactions to various types of deaths: suicidal, natural, and accidental. They found that many regarded interacting with survivors of a suicide as an aversive situation and would choose to avoid the family rather than risk saying or doing something that might be deemed inappropriate. In some instances, others may blame the survivor for not having "prevented the death" and choose to withhold comfort. This magnifies an already heavy emotional burden.

Survivors often doubt their own lovableness or sense of self-worth. These doubts can arise as a result of feeling totally rejected by the person who committed suicide. Questions arise regarding the quality of the relationship that had previously existed with that individual who committed suicide. In order to counteract some of the feelings that are particularly difficult after a suicide (such as shame and guilt), some survivors refuse to believe their loved one deliberately killed himself or herself. Instead, these survivors may insist that the death was caused by an accident (Worden, 1982).

Parents of children who have committed suicide face additional difficulties during their period of mourning. Parents often feel alienated from their surviving children, which increases their level of stress. They often have heightened fears that their other children may also commit suicide. The parents become overly concerned when they discipline or punish their children and wonder if it will trigger suicide by them also. Parental fears may be magnified as they question their own capabilities of being effective parents; they think that if they had been good parents, the suicide would not have occurred.

The normal preoccupation with the death is often heightened for suicide survivors, as it is for homicide survivors. They may become obsessed with the idea that they could have prevented the death and mentally rehearse the role of rescuer time and time again. Additionally, they engage in an ongoing search for answers to such questions as "What caused the suicide?" or "Could I have prevented it?" Although there are usually no clear-cut answers to such questions, survivors may continue to search for explanations (Dunn & Morrish-Vidners, 1987).

An important point to keep in mind is that an unsuccessful suicide attempt may also trigger many of the reactions previously discussed. Shame, guilt, blame, and stigma are among the reactions of families and friends whose loved one has attempted suicide (Ginn, Range, & Hailey, 1988).

Accident.   To date, very little attention has been paid to the relationship between accidental death and bereavement. Calhoun, Selby, and Abernathy (1984) and Sheshkin and Wallace (1976) did contrast grief due to death by accidental causes to death by suicide and natural causes. Sheshkin and Wallace discovered that widows whose husbands died by accidents were less likely to be blamed for the death and took less of a personal risk when telling others how their spouses had died than did survivors of suicide. Calhoun et al. (1984) found that survivors of accidental deaths could expect more sympathy from others than if the death had been due to either suicide or natural causes. Additionally, participants in the study by Calhoun et al. were asked to rate the amount of difficulty they expected persons would have in coping with four types of death (murder, suicide, accident, natural causes). They responded that natural causes would be the least difficult, followed by accidents, then suicide and murder. There was no significant difference between suicide and murder but all other pairs did reflect significant differences.

Lord (1987) studied 292 adults who had experienced the death of a family member as a result of an auto accident caused by a drunk driver. Her participants described a number of responses from others that were regarded as unhelpful shortly after the accident: Medical staff often lacked empathy and did not supply adequate information; police were not sensitive to families' needs when notifying them of the accident; the presence of too many people disallowed an opportunity for privacy. Other responses regarded as inappropriate or difficult during the weeks following the accidental death were: inappropriate comments regarding money or insurance by persons outside the family; lack of responsiveness by the police or district attorney's office; frustration with the legal system.

Doyle (1980) pointed out a number of factors that are related to the grief of survivors of accidental deaths. These factors include the manner in which the survivors were notified of the death, the physical condition of the body, media coverage of the accident, and involvement in lawsuits or insurance negotiations. Thus, we might expect the following circumstances to have the lowest risk of complicating bereavement: (1) compassionate notification of the death, (2) minimal disfigurement of the body, (3) minimal media coverage that does not focus on the sensational aspects of the accident, and (4) absence of need for either litigation or confrontation with insurance companies. It is crucial that law enforcement officers or rescue personnel show compassion when they notify family members that their loved ones have been killed in an accident (Hall, 1982). Clark (1981) explains that police officers can give psychological support both at the time of notification and later if further investigation of the accident is necessary.

Foeckler, Garrard, Williams, Thomas, and Jones (1978) studied drivers involved in fatal car accidents and found that "grief may be experienced by the driver for the act he has committed or been involved in" (p. 175), whether or not the driver knew the person who was killed. The drivers studied reported feelings of sadness, guilt, shame, anger, rage, depression, fear, confusion, and anxiety. Some drivers also felt cognitive dissonance when trying to cope with the idea that they (a good person) had killed another (a bad act). These researchers found that the social support of others was considered to be, by far, the most important help received by the drivers. Blame for the accident and the resulting lack of understanding and support were the most negative factors hindering resolution of the crisis.

Chesser (1981) also studied individuals who were coping with accidentally having killed another person. She found that if the survivors knew the person who had died, dealing with the death was even more complicated. They had to deal not only with their feelings of responsibility for the accident, but also with their own feelings of grief.

Additional Factors Affecting Intensity and Duration of Grief

Availability of Social Support

The availability of support from family and friends is an important resource to bereaved individuals and can serve as a helpful mediating variable in promoting a positive outcome to the grief experience (Andrews, Tennant, & Hewson, 1978; Vachon et al., 1982). Maddison and Walker (1967) found that many of the widows they studied who were judged to have had a "bad outcome" to their grief reported that they were not given understanding and support by relatives and friends. In Parkes's (1975) study, the widows and widowers who had a poor outcome also expressed a feeling that no one understood or cared about them.

Malinak et al. (1979) asked their subjects what they found helpful during their period of bereavement. The existence of a social support system was reported as being the most valuable. Malinak and his colleagues noted that "absence of such a system may portend difficulties" (p. 1155). Brasted and Callahan (1984) have noted that, for most bereaved individuals, "their natural support system and perhaps time will be the most effective therapy" (p. 541).

Vachon, Lyall, Rogers, Freedman-Leftofsky, and Freeman (1980) and Parkes and Weiss (1983) found that positive outcome of bereavement was correlated to long-term availability of social support. Unfortunately, extended support is often lacking (Peretz, 1970). Instead, our society often engages in a conspiracy of silence with the bereaved, similar to the avoidance technique used with the dying.

Individuals do not offer continued support to the grieving for many reasons. Often, individuals do not offer help because they do not know what to do or say and, as a result, choose to say or do nothing. Unfortunately, this lack of acknowledgment of the death and ensuing grief may be misinterpreted as a lack of caring or concern, rather than avoidance due to discomfort. Additionally, many people in our society do not understand the extended duration of the grief process. Lacking this knowledge, they do not recognize the need to offer support beyond the immediacy of the death.

Bereavement Overload

A factor that can complicate what would otherwise be a normal grief reaction is related to the number of other losses a person has recently experienced. Some individuals may be faced with what seems to be a high number of significant losses in a fairly short period of time. An example is a 45-year-old man whose mother died of cancer and whose son was killed in a motorcycle accident within the space of 6 months. In the following 8 months, he lost his job and was divorced. Each of these events, in and of itself, might be regarded as a significant loss. The fact that this individual suffered four such losses within the course of 14 months would make him susceptible to what is known as *bereavement overload.* Kastenbaum (1969) first used this term to reflect the situation of elderly persons who, because of their longevity, experience many losses. Bereavement overload indicates that a person is in a physically and/or emotionally weakened state due to a multiplicity of losses that leave little time between them for resolving the earlier grief.

Helping Strategies

Bereaved individuals need an opportunity to express their feelings in a supportive environment. This section includes a brief discussion of strategies that concerned individuals can use to help others who are grieving.

Give Permission to Grieve

In our society, many messages are given that indicate that one should not grieve for more than a very short time. This is partially due to a misunderstanding regarding the duration of a normal grief process and also to discomfort many people feel in the presence of individuals who are grieving. It can be very helpful, therefore, to communicate to the bereaved that it is normal, healthy, and permissible to grieve (Heikkinen, 1979; Rando, 1984). Giving permission to grieve can be initiated by such statements as "I know it must be very hard for you right now" or "I miss her, too." Open-ended invitations, such as "If you ever need a shoulder to cry on" or "If you ever need to talk," indicate to grieving persons that you recognize their right to grieve in addition to indicating your willingness to support them in the process.

Encourage Expression of Grief

As described earlier, the grief process can involve a variety of emotions. If the bereaved are encouraged to identify and express their emotions, they are more likely to ultimately become reconciled to their loss instead of inhibiting their grief or prematurely aborting it (Frears & Schneider, 1981; Lattanzi & Hale, 1984). The form of expression for grief-related emotions will vary from individual to individual. For example, some may verbalize their anger to friends, others may write about it in a journal, and others may release it through physical activity.

It is not appropriate or helpful to encourage (or demand) that the grieving "Keep a stiff upper lip" or "Look on the bright side." These messages, whether given directly or indirectly, may cause the bereaved additional pain by making them think others do not recognize their loss and the legitimacy of their emotional pain.

Support an Acceptance of All Aspects of the Loss

The bereaved must ultimately come to realize that a loss has occurred and also come to understand what that loss means to them (Lattanzi, 1982). It can be helpful to the bereaved to talk about the deceased as he or she was during life as well as to discuss the death event itself. Loss is multifaceted. Because the deceased often played a number of roles in the survivor's life, a variety of losses must be recognized and reconciled. For example, a child whose mother or father has died must recognize and deal with such varied role losses as comforter, breadwinner, storyteller, cook, nurse, and teacher, among others. Although other persons may contribute to fulfilling these roles, the death of a parent will involve the loss of that individual's contribution to need fulfillment. Each of these multiple losses can be discussed as the bereaved not only recognizes each loss, but also ultimately accepts each of them.

Listen to the Bereaved

Often people seem to feel that they must have the "right words to say" to the bereaved in order to be helpful and supportive. Experience has taught

most counselors and thanatologists, however, that there is no magic formula that will diminish the pain precipitated by the loss. Instead of hoping
for magic potions, the bereaved simply seem to want people to show that
they care. This can be done by being in close proximity to the bereaved
and by being available to listen (Hay, 1985; Rinear, 1975). Many persons
who are grieving indicate a need to share their story with others. They
need to tell and retell anecdotes about the deceased, details of the dying
process and death event, and thoughts and feelings related to life without
their loved one.

Share Information about the Grief Process

Many individuals who are unaware of the normal manifestations of grief
can find some comfort in knowing that their pain is normal and that their
experience of such thought-disordered symptoms as disorientation or
preoccupation with the deceased does not mean they are "going crazy."
It can be therapeutic, then, to provide information regarding common facets of grief (Lattanzi, 1982). Insights can be shared in such a way that the
bereaved can understand that they are not abnormal for experiencing what
they do and also that even though their grief may parallel that of others, it
is unique to them. Understanding that an individual's grief experience is
unique allows the bereaved to understand that there is no "right way to
grieve." It also comforts them to know that they are not "bad" if they are
not grieving in the same way as others. This knowledge can help alleviate
a sense of guilt that may be precipitated by others telling them how they
"should" grieve (Greenblatt, 1978).

Bereaved individuals also need information about the duration of grief.
They need to know that the pain does not disappear immediately after the
funeral, but, in fact, typically lasts for an extended period of time. Without
this knowledge, many believe that there is something abnormal in their
ongoing grief. This is particularly true in a society where comments such
as the following are quite common: "Oh, come on now! Your husband
died a month ago! He would not want you to still be so sad!"

Assist in Practical and Concrete Ways

Well-meaning persons often tell the bereaved to let them know if "there
is anything I can do for you." Rando (1984) stresses the need for people
to be more specific and concrete in their offers to help. Grief is such a
draining experience that the bereaved may have neither the energy nor

the insight to determine what others might do for them. Specific offers of assistance such as "I plan to bring a meal over" or "I would like to take the children to the park next week" put much less responsibility on the bereaved and, as a result, may more easily alleviate their burden.

Pathological Grief

The focus of the chapter thus far has been on normal grief reactions. Although many manifestations associated with grief are regarded as painful and physically taxing, they are most often an indication that grief work is progressing. It is difficult to definitively separate a pathological grief reaction from a normal one. The demarcation is essentially determined by the intensity or duration of particular symptoms rather than by the presence of a constellation of manifestations entirely different from the normal grief response. Demi and Miles (1987) asked 22 experts in the field of thanatology to identify those terms they felt best described grief that "fell outside of the normal range." Descriptors most commonly identified were "pathological, unresolved, self-destructive, dysfunctional, and prolonged" (p. 404). Behaviors, characteristics, or symptoms that were regarded as being outside of the parameters of normal grief were "violence directed toward others, inability to remember or talk about deceased, self-destructive behavior, loss of contact with reality" (p. 405). Other grief reactions that are considered to be pathological or abnormal include inhibited grief, delayed grief, chronic grief, memorialization, idealization, and identification with the deceased.

After the death of a loved one, some persons may not experience any of the common symptoms of bereavement to any significant degree. Some of these individuals may have truly come to terms with the loss and simply not have experienced any intense grief reaction after the death. Others, however, may be engaged in either an inhibited grief reaction or a delayed grief reaction. Individuals who have *inhibited* their *grief* show a prolonged absence of acknowledged grieving (Bowlby, 1980). These persons often pride themselves on their self-control and refuse to allow themselves to feel the emotional pain of the loss. For example, although the normal symptoms do not develop, the grief manifests itself through a variety of physical symptoms such as headaches, chronic indigestion, or ulcers.

Delayed grief, in contrast to inhibited grief, finds direct expression but occurs some time after the death. During the time when persons normally grieve and deal with their pain, persons with delayed grief have no thoughts or feelings that would indicate a loss has occurred. Subsequently, however, a different loss may trigger a magnified grief reaction that is really tied to an earlier one. For example, a woman who never mourned her mother's death 5 years earlier became emotionally and physically immobilized when her pet cat of 3 months was run over and killed. She admitted that she had loved her parent so much that, at the time of her death, she had simply refused to think about her mother's being gone and would not allow her sorrow to consume her. The sudden death of her cat, however, brought these thoughts and feelings to the surface.

Bowlby (1980) has described another variation of the normal grief response, *chronic mourning*, in which the manifestations of grief are unusually intense and last well beyond what is regarded as the normal grief period of 1 to 3 years. The bereaved continue in such an acute stage of grief that they cannot plan for the future or reorganize their lives. Aiken (1985) has indicated that one symptom of chronic grief is *mummification* of the deceased. This is a phenomenon whereby the bereaved attempts to leave things just as they were when the deceased was alive. *Memorialization* takes place when survivors insist on doing such things as putting fresh flowers by the deceased's sports trophies each day for years (DuVaul & Zisook, 1976).

Survivors who recall only positive characteristics of the deceased are participating in a process called *idealization* (Gut, 1974). Carried to its extreme, it is destructive. Idealization of the deceased may cause hardship for other people if the survivor continually compares them to the person who has died and finds them sorely lacking. Idealization may prevent the survivor from wanting to invest in other relationships, thinking "perfection" can be attained only once.

Identification with the deceased has occurred when the survivor manifests symptoms, problems, or behavioral characteristics that are the same as those of the deceased prior to death. Survivors who have not successfully completed the grieving process may keep "the lost one 'alive' by acquiring the symptoms that the deceased person manifested prior to death or by developing a problem that was a significant part of the character of the deceased person" (Stephenson, 1985, p. 154). Malinak et al. (1979) described one of their subjects who had survived her father's death as walking with his stride since the time he died.

It should be stressed that some idealization of or identification with the deceased may be a part of a normal grief response. Such reactions are only categorized as pathological when they consistently prohibit the survivor's resolution of grief over time. A parent who cannot love a surviving child because the deceased sibling was "perfect" is reacting abnormally. A surviving son who cannot pursue his own greatly preferred vocational choice because he feels he must become an architect like his deceased father is also experiencing an abnormal grief response.

Positive Outcomes of Grief

The literature dealing with the grief process focuses almost exclusively on manifestations and the struggle for resolution. Only a few authors have stressed that grief may have a positive aspect as well.

Malinak et al. (1979) interviewed 14 adults whose parents had died during the last 2 years. Approximately half of those individuals reported that, even though the death of their parent had been very painful, they realized that they had experienced a beneficial outcome as well. Individuals reported such benefits as "an increased sense of strength and self-reliance, a greater caring for friends and loved ones, and a more general quickening to life and deepening of their appreciation of existence" (p. 1155). Another positive outcome reported was placing value on the present rather than investing so heavily in what the future might bring.

Benoliel (1985) notes that the experience of a significant loss can encourage a search for meaning in one's life. For example, some find meaning in translating their experience into a creative modality such as music, poetry, or artwork. Others find meaning by enhancing relationships with persons around them.

Summary

Grief is a natural reaction to the experience of loss. This chapter focuses specifically on grief reactions related to the death of a loved one. Although each individual's grief is unique, there are many common somatic, behavioral, and intrapsychic manifestations. The intensity and duration of a person's grief reaction is affected by a variety of factors, including variables related to the bereaved individual, the deceased individual, the death event itself, availability of social support, and other recent losses. There are a number of strategies that can effectively be used to help those who are grieving deal with their loss. While grief involves emotional pain, bereavement also provides an opportunity for individuals to develop in postive ways and offers a new and expanded perspective on the meaning of life. In some situations, however, survivors do not cope with their loss in ways regarded as normal and healthy but rather exhibit a pathological response. Professional intervention is recommended in these circumstances.

◯ *Personal Account*

Jayne Blankenship's husband, Harvey, died of leukemia at the age of 30. They had been together 9½ years. She shares with us her personal experience of grief—her thoughts, her feelings, her reactions. Ms. Blankenship's diary traces her life through the seasons of the three years after her husband's death. The segment of the book included here reflects her grief at a point in time 3 months after Harvey's death.

In the Center of the Night: Journey Through Bereavement

Jayne Blankenship

I have little appetite anymore, but find myself eating compulsively, or rather drinking, especially before I leave the house. I'm not actually hungry, but I'm afraid I will be, afraid I won't be able to stand that little extra discomfort for even an hour if I am caught away from food. Repeatedly I open the refrigerator but then can't find anything appetizing. The food is there, but it never appeals. I find myself drinking milk, again and again, to fill the emptiness.

I tried to eat some raisin bran just now before I came upstairs, but it hurts to chew. I have a canker sore under my tongue, which makes me think of the enormous mouth ulcers Harvey had last fall from the drug Cytosar (he called it "the Czar")—or was it Vincristine ("the Count")—and how he couldn't talk. How did he eat? Why can't I remember? Why didn't they feed him intravenously? One day the sores fell off, a couple of hours apart. They were the size of quarters—gray and ugly. That was the day he started peeing blood. Emptying the urinal, I found it and told the nurse but not him. The next day he kicked the thing over, full, and blood spread all over the room and he was frightened and yelled at me for not telling him, and he was right. I was ashamed. But he was carrying so much anxiety that week, having learned he'd entered Blast Crisis, I just couldn't. He recovered though, after Fogle said no one expected he'd ever leave the hospital again. They were all waiting for cerebral hemorrhage because of the dropped platelets. The nurses shook their heads as we left—broad, broad smiles. It didn't surprise me. Our love was there, and his beautiful determination.

Those miraculous recoveries built false hopes, prevented me from recognizing the genuine onset of his dying. Oh, God, if only I could have seen it coming. If only I had spent that last night with him. I had stayed over before, in fear, but when it really counted, I was blind. I failed him.

From *In the center of the night: Journey through bereavement* (New York: G. P. Putnam's Sons, 1984), pp. 53–60. Reprinted by permission of Candida Donadio & Associates.

I am trying to get back into the world again, but it is very hard. Even when I wear sunglasses and pull my hair over my cheeks so less of me can be seen, I still feel dangerously exposed. I went back to chorus rehearsals for the first time tonight, but found I couldn't sing. I spent the whole evening fighting back tears, fumbling in my purse for Kleenex. I am grateful to these people—the purity of their voices at the Memorial Service stunned. The loud straight tone, coming suddenly from the balcony behind us, carved away the muscle of our resistance, laying bare the clean white bone of grief. But it is hard to be in public, even with them.

I am deeply troubled that I still cannot envision Harvey's face. Have I perhaps put our life together into a soft cocoon because it is too intense to deal with now? Or have I lost it utterly—will it just get worse? Some days there are tiny windows into it, for a second or two. But in general I have lost my memory. I can't even recall where Jordan and I slept in Kansas City when we went for his burial. It must have been at Harriet's, not Sharlene's, but there's no bed there for Jordan. Did they borrow a crib? I just can't remember. It's blocked. I do remember waking in the night, panicky, short of breath, stagefright waves in my stomach continuous for more than an hour. The light came from the right of the foot of the bed. Couch in Sharlene's den? I remember too, my compulsion to take a bath while the Havra Kadisha people were preparing his body for burial. I wanted to be bathing him by myself, holding him, caring for him. An urgency to soothe, to share, to absorb the pain of it. Or was it guilt? Was it because something in my head said, "If he had only felt more loved, he would have wanted to live, could have beaten the cancer"? Was I washing away my failure to keep him alive? Maybe it was just a means of postponing the finality of his burial. I kept everyone waiting, black limousine running, while I washed.

More and more I notice myself doing things that he would have done even when they are things I'd never do myself. Tennis (if only he could see me learning to play tennis), buying matzoh and gefilte fish, saying Kaddish (the Judaism was his, not mine. Why can't I shake this?), renewing his magazine subscriptions, using his shaving cream, wearing his pajamas and robe at night and his jeans in the day, saying things twice the way he did. Why am I doing this? Is it that I love him so much I want to *be* him? God! Maybe that's why I can't see his face. Because I am turning into him! I am really scared.

It startles me to look at pages I have written, even just grocery lists. I am constantly misspelling words. Freudian slips, substitutions, repeated syllables, phonic spellings everywhere. They shock me, show I'm more undone than even I would judge. And the others—my friends—they infuriate me. Everyone seems to find me perfectly normal and capable. They don't even notice when I forget, mid-sentence, what it was I meant to say.

My inner life is a shambles. Thinking muddled. Loss of structure, of will.

Entire psyche rotates, still, around Harvey—only his human force is not here to balance mine. Incessant depletion—strength sucked into a black hole. Directionless floundering. My work is disrupted too—a smaller, but genuine problem. The women's exhibit I put together, focus of eight months' concentration, ended for me with the opening the week before he died, momentum lost once it was framed and hung. The show has moved on now and is creating a stir in the Ætna Building in Hartford, the first place it has visited that is not accustomed to fine-art photography. Half the audience there is outraged by simple nudity (why do they seize on those few images?), and the others are threatened because the same figures aren't centerfold material. Hard to believe. Only a few have responded to the simple humanity in the photographs—women's portrayals of birth, work, friends, aging. I should feel good that it has generated corporate controversy—definitely a plus for the movement—but I am too fragile to feel anything but hurt that they don't admire it as they did in New London or Kingston. I am too tired to defend my efforts, and not really interested anymore.

Grant money for morning child care ended when the show opened, too. The financial aspect is meaningless because Jordan needs me now, not a sitter, but full-time mothering is devastating for me. I cannot complete a single thought. Constant interruptions. Wait. Endure. I hate this feeling. No purpose. Even the disease gave a framework—afternoons and evenings at the hospital, doctors' office visits, trips for immunotherapy, secrecy, driving Harvey to work, drugs, transfusions, seizures, Philip, friendships with nurses, and a constant girding for the unspeakable distant event. Now all I do is "babysit," and I'm incapable even of doing that well. I couldn't be teaching this semester if I had to. I cannot think or organize or care. My arms and legs are leaden. Every simple gesture saps me—getting out of bed, pouring milk on cereal, folding a towel, listening to Jordan, turning the steering wheel, writing a check. Nothing can be accomplished automatically anymore. How many years will this last? Forever? I have no enthusiasm for photographs—my own or others'—for teaching, for anything I know.

I wonder if it would be any different to go through this in a community where I had lived for a long time, where my own genuine deep friends—Sonia, Claire—were close by, and family, and family friends, and former teachers and ministers. Could it make a difference? Could anything soothe a hurt like this?

I am furious! Someone stole our red and purple geometric towels from the laundromat. I left them tossing in a dryer separate from the whites while I went to the hardware store and the market. Then I came home and unloaded the groceries. When I went back to the laundromat, the dryer door was standing open—just one purple washcloth left inside.

I could hardly restrain myself until I got home. I lugged the baskets in together, the full one nested inside the empty, half threw them into the office—clean clothes spilling out onto the rug—and slammed the door behind me. I leaned against it, clenching my teeth and fists and starting to growl. Then I lunged forward onto the stairs up to the kitchen and pounded them as hard and fast as I could with both fists. I kicked out backward, too, like a horse, against the door, not caring if I broke it down.

Those towels were special, damn it! We bought them for our crazy red bathroom in New York, for our first apartment. We always had red and purple anemones in there to match, under the silly framed picture of Mayor Lindsay. Damn! Damn! Damn! Haven't we been victimized enough? My husband died, World! Doesn't that earn us some kind of exemption?

Oh well, it's over now. I bruised the bone in my heel. Can't put any pressure on it. The limp makes me laugh. Sort of.

Today is the 18th of May—the three-month anniversary of Harvey's death. I am obsessed with the fact that I used the last of his shaving cream today. Nine and a half years of red-and-white-striped Barbasol cans—over. That can seemed to keep him closer in time—like the shiva candle, which I kept burning for weeks. As long as it held foam, as long as the candle burned, it couldn't have been very long since he was here. Why did it have to run out on the 18th? The 18th of March and April were hard too. Will this day of the month ever resume a normal face?

A special dream last night, like the early ones.

I am having dinner with friends but interrupt the meal because there's a documentary on TV about how my class at the Ecole Française made films. I am wild with hope to see Harvey, because he was in the last one. The color TV seems to enchant me. I enter into the program physically, like going through the looking glass. Harvey and I find each other in a gleaming snow-covered landscape, a limitless Sahara of snow. No cold, no coats, no trees or features on the drifts. Only the yellow clarity of love. A warm, clinging, wordless embrace—on and on—without a future, without a past. The feel of his neck and back and face and hair in my hands brings a peace beyond anything I have known.

And then I woke up. I was lying on my stomach. The deception slipped away, and the nausea of truth flattened me onto the sheet. To wake up was to be told he had died all over again.

I took a piece of beef out of the refrigerator tonight and set it on the counter. Jordan looked at it and asked, "Is Daddy's body like that now?"

Harvey's life insurance money came today. I stood in the hall with the unopened envelope in my hand. The world would have me be grateful. Do they call a piece of paper a fair trade? A piece of paper for Harvey's warm flesh and smile and compassion and intelligence? Do they call this compensation for his fear and suffering? For suffocating alone at night, drowning in the fluid of his own lungs? For not getting to watch his son grow up? For losing every star and snowflake, leaf and friend on this planet? I tore the end off the envelope and pulled out the check: $20,000. I felt like spitting on it. It could have been twenty million and I would have felt the same. It's as if they consider our not having to worry now about finances some sort of consolation.

I went back into our room, put the check on my dresser, and knelt down to finish sorting through the third drawer of Harvey's bureau—I've been doing one drawer each month. The Social Security doesn't make me angry like this, except that no one let us know about it before he died. He must have worried about what would happen to Jordan and me. The doctors had to have known, the lawyer. Why didn't anyone tell us? I suppose they thought we knew already. The monthly payments are adequate really, not much less than all three of us used to live on after doctor bills. But the insurance money makes me sick.

I couldn't make any more decisions, so I took the one box of things I thought might mean something to Jordan when he is 10 or 12—his father's crepe-soled shoes and favorite tie, his denim jacket, trench coat, Norwegian sweater, wallet—down to the basement and carried the carton of things for the chorus thrift shop out and put them in the back of the car, leaving the rest for another day. Then I pulled a sweater over Jordan's head, put him in his car seat and drove to Westerly and dropped them off.

Now I am home again. The need to cry is acute. Oh, the tears come and my face contorts, but I can't let go or sob. And I need to, I crave the release. It started out all right at the very first, but Jordan got so upset, repeatedly, when he saw me weeping that I developed a kind of inhibition. One day he even threw his blanket over my head. The orgasmic dreams I experienced the first two months are apparently gone now, too. I am a taut coil of grief-tension.

This morning it was raining again, and the grief was pressing out on my skull so hard I was afraid the bone might crack. A sound too violent for others to withstand was going to bellow up out of me. Desperate for privacy, I tried to get a sitter. I called six or eight people, straining to be casual, "I know it sounds silly, but I need to take a walk." No one was free. I began to get frantic. It was hard to get my breath. It felt like I was trapped under water, pinned against something by a crushing current. No, not right—the pressure was *in* me, not outside. Something inside me that used to go to Harvey now had nowhere to go. It built and built and I was afraid that I would fly apart.

Finally I drove Jordan over to some friends—people I've known only a few months—and begged them to watch him for a while. I must have looked deranged. They seemed surprised but said, "Of course, go ahead. Why don't you go to Napatree?" I drove through Westerly too fast, propelled by the yearning to let out of me the ugly sound I felt still building. But when I parked my car and ran, stumbling, up over the dunes to where I couldn't be seen, it wouldn't come. The gray waves were roaring in, ready to cover anything, but nothing came. I couldn't believe it. I just stood there feeling blank.

Disappointed, I headed slowly out toward the point. From time to time, I bent and picked up a translucent pebble. After a while, as I walked, I decided I should keep no more than three—a kind of exercise. So I kept searching and discarding, searching and discarding, for as long as it took to walk out to the point and halfway back, probably an hour—until I had the three most beautiful stones on that long stretch of beach. Then I walked up to where the waves end and stood there. The wind was not as cold as I had thought. I picked one of the stones out of my palm and forced myself to throw it far out into the ocean. "See?" I yelled at the wind, "I can do it. I can play your filthy game." And then I took the second one, "Here! Take it! I can stand it!" and threw it too, defiantly.

But then there was just one left. It was exquisitely hard to let go of that last one. I paced back and forth for a while, clutching for alternatives. Then I went back to the spot in the sand where I had started and simply stood there. The sky was gray, the sea was gray, the beach was gray. I pulled my arm up and did it. As my body came around on the follow-through, doubled over with loss, there appeared at my feet, instantaneously, three extraordinary yellow starfish.

Somewhere deep inside the pain, something shifted. Full of awe, I picked them up—fragile, perfect—and stood with my back to the ocean, absorbing what had happened. With them in front of me, in my hands, I slowly started the long walk back. On the way, I stopped and sat in the damp sand by some big old dock posts. I set the starfish down beside me and leaned sideways against the biggest post and felt the tear-restrainer loosen a little. The wood was cold and smooth against my cheek. It was sunk deep into the earth. It used to hold a pier. I hugged that old post, then, with both my arms. I hugged it and it held me up, and the real crying finally came.

———————————

Questions and Activities

1. Bring to mind the death of a loved one. What was your immediate reaction to the news of his or her death? What were your later thoughts, feelings, actions? How were these similar or different to those experienced by Ms. Blankenship after her husband's death?

2. The author of this personal account explained that her grief was magnified 3 months after her husband's death when she realized she had just used the last of his shaving cream. Was there some physical object that was particularly difficult for you to give up after a loved one's death? Why was it difficult for you? Was there a particular day that your grief once again intensified? Do you know what made that day more difficult?

3. The death depicted in this diary excerpt was the result of natural causes. Have you ever experienced the death of a loved one due to a suicide? Murder? Accident? Did your reactions vary with the type of death? Explain your answer.

4. Write a condolence letter or find a sympathy card that you would send to a bereaved friend. What attracted you to that particular card compared to others you saw? What message did it convey?

5. How would you have comforted Ms. Blankenship during the months after her husband's death? Would you have reacted to Ms. Blankenship differently if the death had been a suicide? A murder? An accident?

Glossary

Acute Grief: Grief that is felt during the period when somatic, intrapsychic, and behavioral reactions are most intense.

Anniversary Reaction: Exacerbation of grief precipitated by a special day related to the deceased (such as a birthday).

Anticipatory Grief: Grief experienced prior to the death of a loved one.

Bereavement: State of being that results from a significant loss.

Bereavement Overload: Extreme degree of grief triggered by multiple losses in a relatively short period of time.

Cathexis: Investment of psychic energy in an object.

Chronic Mourning: Grief that is unusually intense and extremely long-lasting (beyond 1 to 3 years).

Delayed Grief: Relatively extreme grief reaction long after the original loss that person is actually mourning.

Grief Work: Process by which individuals resolve their grief.

Hypercathexis: Investment of an extreme amount of psychic energy in an object.

Idealization: Distortion of reality regarding deceased; only the positive characteristics are remembered.

Identification: Manifestation by a survivior of symptoms, problems, or behaviors similar to those of the deceased.

Inhibited Grief: Prolonged absence of acknowledged grieving; however, physical symptoms are often manifest.

Intrapsychic: Pertaining to the emotions and mind.

Libido: Energy of love and pleasure.

Memorialization: Phenomenon where survivor pays homage to the deceased through a particular frequent ritual.

Mourning: Social prescription for way in which we are expected to display our grief.

Mummification: Phenomenon whereby the bereaved attempts to leave things just as they were when deceased was alive.

Object Loss: Loss of a loved one.

Preventability: Belief that factors contributing to the death might have been avoided.

Role Loss: Loss of one's position or status in society.

Somatic: Related to the body.

Thanatologist: Professional who specializes in the study of death, dying, and grief.

Suggested Readings

Dunne, E. J., McIntosh, J. L., & Dunne-Maxim, K. (Eds.) (1987). *Suicide and its aftermath: Understanding and counseling the survivors.* New York: Norton.

A compilation of 24 articles presented in the following sections: the social context of surviving suicide, the aftermath of suicide in families, implications for professionals, therapeutic approaches, and conclusions.

Rando, T. A. (Ed.) (1986). *Loss and anticipatory grief.* Lexington, MA: Heath.

This book provides specific information, techniques, and coping strategies that can help patients, families, and caregivers with the process of anticipatory grief.

Worden, J. W. (1982). *Grief counseling and grief therapy: A handbook for the mental health practitioner*. New York: Springer.

This volume describes the role of the mental health professional in helping clients cope with normal and abnormal grief reactions. It includes guidelines for conducting workshops and several sample vignettes for use in role playing.

Resources

The Grief Education Institute
2422 Downing Street
Denver, Colorado 80210
(303) 777-9234

Mothers Against Drunk Driving (MADD)
669 Airport Freeway
Suite 310
Hurst, Texas 76053
(817) 268-6233

Parents of Murdered Children, Inc.
100 E. 8th Street
Cincinnati, Ohio 45202
(513) 721-5683

References

Aiken, L. R. (1985). *Dying, death, and bereavement*. Rockleigh, NJ: Allyn & Bacon.

Andrews, G., Tennant, C., & Hewson, D. M. (1978). Life event stress, social support, coping style, and risk of psychological impairment. *Journal of Nervous Mental Disorders*, *166*, 307–316.

Barnes, M. J. (1978). The reactions of children and adolescents to the death of a parent or sibling. In O. J. Sahler (Ed.), *The child and death* (pp. 185–201). St. Louis: Mosby.

Ball, J. G. (1977). Widow's grief: The impact of age and mode of death. *Omega*, *7*(4), 307–333.

Battin, D., Gerber, I., Wiener, A., & Arkin, A. (1977). Clinical observations on bereaved individuals. In E. R. Prichard, J. Collard, B. A. Orcutt, A. H. Kutscher, I. Seeland, & N. Lefkowitz (Eds.), *Social work with the dying patient and the family* (pp. 80–96). New York: Columbia University Press.

Benoliel, J. Q. (1985). Loss and adaptation: Circumstances, contingencies, and consequences. *Death Studies*, *9*, 217–233.

Berman, L. C., & Bufferd, R. K. (1986). Family treatment to address loss in adoptive families. *Social Casework*, *67*(1), 3–11.

Bolton, I. (1986). Death of a child by suicide. In T. Rando (Ed.), *Parental loss of a child* (pp. 201–212). Champaign, IL: Research Press.

Bowlby, J. (1980). *Attachment and loss* (Vol. 3): *Loss, sadness, and depression.* New York: Basic Books.

Brasted, W. S., & Callahan, E. J. (1984). Review article: A behavioral analysis of the grief process. *Behavioral Therapy, 15*(5), 529–543.

Bugen, L. A. (1979) *Death and dying: Theory/research/practice.* Dubuque, IA: William C. Brown.

Buksbazen, C. (1976). Legacy of a suicide. *Suicide and Life-Threatening Behavior, 6*(2), 106–122.

Burgess, A.W. (1975). Family reactions to homicide. *American Journal of Orthopsychiatry, 45*(3), 391–398.

Calhoun, L. G., Abernathy, C. B., & Selby, J. W. (1986). The rules of bereavement: Are suicidal deaths different? *Journal of Community Psychology, 14*(2), 213–218.

Calhoun, L. G., Selby, J. W., & Abernathy, C. B. (1984). Suicidal death: Social reactions of bereaved survivors. *The Journal of Psychology, 116*(2), 255–261.

Cameron, P. (1987). Bereavement after loss of body function. In M. A. Morgan (Ed.), *Bereavement: Helping the survivors* (pp. 225–228). London, Ontario: King's College.

Charmaz, K. (1980). *The social reality of death: Death in contemporary America.* Reading, MA: Addison-Wesley.

Chesser, B. J. (1981). Coping with accidentally killing another person: A case study approach. *Family Relations, 30*(3), 463–473.

Chester, V. A., Jerardi, N. C., & Weger, J. M. (1980). Sudden death/lingering death. In B. A. Orcutt, E. R. Prichard, J. Collard, E. F. Cooper, A. H. Kutscher, & I. B. Seeland (Eds.), *Social work and thanatology.* New York: Arno Press.

Clark, D. B. (1981). A death in the family: Providing consultation to the police on the psychological aspects of suicide and accidental death. *Death Education, 5,* 143–155.

Clayton, P. (1975). The effects of living alone on bereavement symptoms. *American Journal of Psychiatry, 132*(2), 133–137.

Clayton, P. J., Desmarais, L., & Winokur, G. (1968). A study of normal bereavement. *American Journal of Psychiatry, 125,* 169–178.

Cook, J. A. (1983). A death in the family: Parental bereavement in the first year. *Suicide and Life-Threatening Behavior, 13*(1), 42–61.

Davis, B. H. (1987). Disability and grief. *Social Casework, 68*(6), 352–357.

Demi, A. S. (1984). Social adjustment of widows after a sudden death: Suicide and non-suicide survivors compared. *Death Studies, 8,* 91–109.

Demi, A. S., & Miles, M. S. (1987). Parameters of normal grief: A Delphi study. *Death Studies, 11*(6), 397–412.

Doyle, P. (1980). *Grief counseling and sudden death: A manual and guide.* Springfield, IL: Charles C Thomas.

Dunn, R. G., & Morrish-Vidners, D. (1987). The psychological and social experience of suicide survivors. *Omega, 18*(3), 175–215.

DuVaul, R., & Zisook, S. (1976). Unresolved grief. *Postgraduate Medicine, 59*(5), 267.

Eisenbruch, M. (1984a). Cross-cultural aspects of bereavement. I: A conceptual framework for comparative analysis. *Culture, Medicine, and Psychiatry, 3*(3), 283–309.

Eisenbruch, M. (1984b). Cross-cultural aspects of bereavement. II: Ethnic and cultural variations in the development of bereavement practices. *Culture, Medicine, and Psychiatry, 8*(4), 315–347.

Flesch, R. (1975). A guide for interviewing the bereaved. *Journal of Thanatology, 3*, 93–103.

Foeckler, M. M., Garrard, F. H., Williams, C. C., Thomas, A. M., & Jones, T. J. (1978). Vehicle drivers and fatal accidents. *Suicide and Life-Threatening Behavior, 8*(3), 174–182.

Frears, L. H., & Schneider, J. M. (1981). Exploring loss and grief within a wholistic framework. *The Personnel and Guidance Journal, 59*(6), 341–345.

Freese, A. (1977). *Living through grief and growing with it.* New York: Barnes & Noble Books.

Freud, S. (1917). Mourning and melancholia. In J. Strachey (Ed.), *The standard edition of the complete psychological works of Sigmund Freud* (Vol. 14, pp. 237–260). London: Hogarth Press, 1957.

Froiland, D. J., & Hozman, T. L. (1977). Children: Forgotten in divorce. *Personnel and Guidance Journal, 55*, 530–533.

Fulton, R. (1970). Death, grief, and social recuperation. *Omega, 1*, 23–28.

Gerber, I., Rusalem, R., Hannon, N., Battin, D., & Arkin, A. (1975). Anticipatory grief of aged widows and widowers. *Journal of Gerontology, 30*, 225–229.

Getzel, G. S., & Masters, R. (1984). Serving families who survive homicide victims. *Social Work, 65*(3), 138–144.

Ginn, P. D., Range, L. M., & Hailey, B. J. (1988). Community attitudes toward childhood suicide and attempted suicide. *Journal of Community Psychology, 16*(2), 144–151.

Glick, I., Weiss, R., & Parkes, C. (1974). *The first year of bereavement.* New York: Wiley.

Gorer, G. (1965). *Death, grief, and mourning.* London: Cresset Press.

Greenblatt, M. (1978). The grieving spouse. *American Journal of Psychiatry, 135*(1), 43–46.

Gut, E. (1974). Some aspects of adult mourning. *Omega, 5*(4), 323–342.

Hall, M. N. (1982). Law enforcement officers and death notification: A plea for relevant education. *Journal of Police Science and Administration, 10*(2), 189–193.

Hardt, D. V. (1978). An investigation of the stages of bereavement. *Omega, 9*(3), 279–285.

Hatton, C. L., & Valente, S. (1981). Bereavement group for parents who suffered a suicidal loss of a child. *Suicide and Life-Threatening Behavior, 11*(3), 141–150.

Hauser, M. J. (1987). In E. J. Dunne, J. L. McIntosh, & K. Dunne-Maxim (Eds.), *Suicide and its aftermath: Understanding and counseling the survivors* (pp. 57–70). New York: Norton.

Hay, J. (1985). An experience in listening. *The American Journal of Hospice Care, 2*(3), 45–46.

Heikkinen, C. A. (1979). Counseling for personal loss. *Personnel and Guidance Journal, 58*(1), 46–49.

Hurley, D. (1987). Children's views of family breakdown. In M. A. Morgan (Ed.), *Bereavement: Helping the survivors* (pp. 243–251). London, Ontario: King's College.

Jacobs, S. C., Kosten, T. R., Kasl, S. V., Ostfeld, A. M., Berkman, L., & Charpentier, P. (1987). Attachment theory and multiple dimensions of grief. *Omega 18*(1), 41–52.

Jewett, C. L. (1982). *Helping children cope with separation and loss.* Cambridge, MA: The Harvard Common Press.

Jones, W. H. (1979). Grief and involuntary career change: Its implications for counseling. *Vocational Guidance Quarterly, 27*, 196–201.

Kalish, R. A., & Reynolds, D. K. (1976). *Death and ethnicity: A psychocultural study.* Los Angeles: The Ethel Percy Andrus Gerontology Center.

Kastenbaum, R. (1969). Death and bereavement in later life. In A. H. Kutscher (Ed.), *Death and bereavement* (pp. 28–54). Springfield, IL: Charles C Thomas.

Kastenbaum, R. J. (1981). *Death, society and human experience* (2d ed.). St. Louis: Mosby.

Kavanaugh, R. E. (1972). *Facing death.* Baltimore, MD: Penguin Books.

Kleinman, A., Kaplan, B., & Weiss, R. (1984). Sociocultural influences. In M. Osterweis, F. Solomon, & M. Green (Eds.), *Bereavement: Reactions, consequences, and care* (pp. 199–212). Washington, DC: National Academy Press.

Krupnick, J. L. (1984). Bereavement during childhood and adolescence. In M. Osterweis, F. Solomon, & M. Green (Eds.), *Bereavement: Reactions, consequences, and care* (pp. 99–141). Washington, DC: National Academy Press.

Krupp, G. R., & Kligfield, B. (1962). The bereavement reaction: A cross-cultural evaluation. *Journal of Religious Health, 1*, 222–246.

Kübler-Ross, E. (1969). *On death and dying.* New York: Macmillan.

Lattanzi, M. E. (1982). Hospice bereavement services: Creating networks of support. *Family & Community Health, 5*(3), 54–63.

Lattanzi, M., & Hale, M. E. (1984). Giving grief words: Writing during bereavement. *Omega, 15*(1), 45–52.

Lindemann, E. (1944). Symptomatology and management of acute grief. *American Journal of Psychiatry, 101*, 141–148.

Lord, J. H. (1987). Survivor grief following a drunk-driving crash. *Death Studies*, *11*(6), 413–435.

Maddison, D., & Viola, A. (1968). The health of widows in the year following bereavement. *Journal of Psychosomatic Research*, *12*, 297.

Maddison, D., & Walker, W. (1967). Factors affecting the outcome of conjugal bereavement. *British Journal of Psychiatry*, *113*, 1057–1067.

Malinak, D. P., Hoyt, M. F., & Patterson, V. (1979). Adults' reactions to the death of a parent: A preliminary study. *American Journal of Psychiatry*, *136*(9), 1152–1156.

Marris, P. (1986). *Loss and change* (rev. ed.). New York: Anchor Books.

Miles, M. S., & Demi, A. S. (1984). Toward the development of a theory of bereavement guilt. *Omega*, *14*(4), 299–314.

Murray, R. (1987). Unemployment: Not only the loss of a job. In M. A. Morgan (Ed.), *Bereavement: Helping the survivors* (pp. 237–241). London, Ontario: King's College.

Newman, C., & Paris, C. (1987). Families in limbo: Picking up the pieces after a stroke. In M. A. Morgan (Ed.), *Bereavement: Helping the survivors* (pp. 211–223). London, Ontario: King's College.

Parkes, C. M. (1975). Determinants of outcome following bereavement. *Omega*, *6*(4), 303–323.

Parkes, C. M., & Brown, R. J. (1972). Health after bereavement: A controlled study of young Boston widows and widowers. *Psychosomatic Medicine*, *34*, 449–461.

Parkes, C. M., & Weiss, R. S. (1983). *Recovery from bereavement*. New York: Basic Books.

Parks, R. (1977). Parental reactions to the birth of a handicapped child. *Health and Social Work*, *2*, 51–66.

Peppers, L. G., & Knapp, R. S. (1980). *Motherhood and mourning: Perinatal death*. New York: Praeger.

Peretz, D. (1970). Development, object relationships, and loss. In B. Schoenberg, A. Carr, D. Peretz, & A. Kutscher (Eds.), *Loss and grief: Psychological management in medical practice* (pp. 3–19). New York: Columbia University Press.

Pine, V. R. (1976). Grief, bereavement, and mourning: The realities of loss. In V. R. Pine, A. H. Kutscher, D. Peretz, R. C. Slater, R. DeBellis, R. J. Volk, & D. J. Cherico (Eds.), *Acute grief and the funeral* (pp. 105–114). Springfield, IL: Charles C Thomas.

Rando, T. A. (1984). *Grief, dying and death: Clinical interventions for caregivers*. Champaign, IL: Research Press.

Raphael, B. (1980). A psychiatric model for bereavement counseling. In B. M. Schoenberg (Ed.), *Bereavement counseling: A multidisciplinary handbook* (pp. 147–172). Westport, CT: Greenwood Press.

Raphael, B. (1983). *The anatomy of bereavement*. New York: Basic Books.

Reilly, D. M. (1978). Death propensity, dying, and bereavement: A family systems perspective. *Family Therapy*, *5*(1), 34–55.

Rinear, E. E. (1975). Helping the survivors of expected death. *Nursing, 5*, 60–65.

Rubin, S. S. (1985). The resolution of bereavement: A clinical focus on the relationship to the deceased. *Psychotherapy, 22*(2), 231–235.

Rynearson, E. K. (1984). Bereavement after homicide: A descriptive study. *American Journal of Psychiatry, 14*(11), 1452–1454.

Sanders, C. M. (1979). A comparison of adult bereavement in the death of a spouse, child, and parent. *Omega, 10*(4), 303–322.

Sanders, C. M. (1980). Comparison of younger and older spouses in bereavement outcome. *Omega, 11*(3), 217–232.

Sanders, C. M. (1982). Effects of sudden vs. chronic illness death on bereavement outcome. *Omega, 13*(3), 227–241.

Schmidt, J. D. (1986). Murder of a child. In T. Rando (Ed.), *Parental loss of a child* (pp. 213–220). Champaign, IL: Research Press.

Schoenberg, B., & Carr, A. C. (1970). Loss of external organs: Limb amputation, mastectomy, and disfiguration. In B. Schoenberg, A. C. Carr, D. Peretz, & A. H. Kutscher (Eds.), *Loss and grief: Psychological management in medical practice.* New York: Columbia University Press.

Schuyler, D. (1973). Counseling suicide survivors: Issues and answers. *Omega, 4*(4), 313–321.

Schwab, J., Chalmers, J., Conroy, S., Farris, P., & Markush, R. (1975). Studies in grief: A preliminary report. In B. Schoenberg, I. Gerber, A. Wiener, A. Kutscher, D. Peretz, & A. Carr (Eds.), *Bereavement: Its psychosocial aspects* (pp. 78–87). New York: Columbia University Press.

Sheshkin, A., & Wallace, S. (1976). Differing bereavements: Suicide, natural, and accidental. *Omega, 7*(3), 229–242.

Simos, B. (1979). *A time to grieve: Loss as a universal experience.* New York: Family Service Association of America.

Solomon, M. I. (1983). The bereaved and the stigma of suicide. *Omega, 13*(4), 377–387.

Speece, M. W., & Brent, S. B. (1984). Children's understanding of death: A review of three components of death concept. *Child Development, 55*(5), 1671–1686.

Stephenson, J. S. (1985). *Death, grief, and mourning: Individual and social realities.* New York: Free Press.

Vachon, M., Lyall, W., Rogers, J., Freedman-Leftofsky, K., & Freeman, S. J. (1980). A controlled study of self-help intervention for widows. *American Journal of Psychiatry, 137*(11), 1380–1384.

Vachon, M., Rogers, J., Lyall, W., Lancee, W., Sheldon, A., & Freeman, S. (1982). Predictors and correlates of adaptation to conjugal bereavement. *American Journal of Psychiatry, 138*(8), 998–1002.

Wallerstein, J., & Kelly, J. (1976). The effects of parental divorce: Experiences of the child in later latency. *American Journal of Orthopsychiatry, 46*, 256–269.

Winkler, D. (1987). Psychosocial aspects of loss of a body function. In M. A. Morgan (Ed.), *Bereavement: Helping the survivors* (pp. 229–233). London, Ontario: King's College.

Wolfelt, A. (1983). *Helping children cope with grief.* Muncie, IN: Accelerated Development.

Worden, J. W. (1982). *Grief counseling and grief therapy: A handbook for the mental health practitioner.* New York: Springer.

Wright, L. S. (1976). Chronic grief: The anguish of being an exceptional parent. *Exceptional Child, 23,* 160–169.

3

THE BEREAVED FAMILY

Family Systems Theory   91

Developmental Stages of Families   93

Death as a Family Crisis   96

Variables Affecting the Family's Ability to Cope   96

Concurrent Stressors   97
Family Resources   100
Family's Perception of the Event   100

Adaptation of the Family Unit   101

Positive Outcomes   101
Negative Outcomes   102

Intervention with the Family System   106

Family Tasks Involved in Coping   106

Maintain Open Communication   107
Reassign Roles   107
Provide Support   109
Modify Relationships   109

Intergenerational Issues Related to Death   110

Family Rituals Related to Death   112

Prefuneral Rituals   113
Funerals and Memorial Services   113
Postfuneral Rituals   114

Summary   114

The experience of loss due to the death of a family member constitutes not only an individual crisis but a family crisis as well. A change in the composition of the family by even a single member has an impact on the dynamics of family interaction (Broderick & Smith, 1979). Additionally, even though individuals must cope with their own grief, they "must do it within the context of adjustment of all other people who are affected by the death" (Weinstein, 1979, p. 25).

Family Systems Theory

In the 1940s, Ludwig von Bertalanffy, a biologist, first proposed general systems theory to describe all living things. During the past several decades, theorists and practitioners have used the systems framework to understand the family. *Systems theory* includes several basic concepts: (1) First of all, a system, while consisting of interacting parts, is characterized by wholeness or unity. (2) Second, systems are governed by rules. (3) Third, systems can be described by some degree of openness. Following is a brief discussion of each of these concepts.

1. *A system, while consisting of interacting parts, is characterized by wholeness or unity.* In order to understand the whole, one must understand the parts, the interactions among the parts, and the relationship between the parts and the environment. Therefore, in order to understand the family as a system, one must look at individual members of the family, their relationships to each other, and their interactions with others outside the family. Families are composed of smaller units referred to as *subsystems.* It is useful to understand the subsystems of a family when attempting to understand the family as a functional unit.

Systems are entwined by *boundaries* which are abstract dividers between or among subsystems that define participation in them. Distinct boundaries can serve to define, protect, and enhance the integrity of individuals, subsystems, and families. Boundaries can change over time and with various situations. The extent of this change will be affected by characteristics of the boundaries (rigid, flexible, diffuse) in each family.

Theoretically, each individual can be thought of as a subsystem. Also, most families have marital subsystems, sibling subsystems, and parent–child subsystems. Other subsystems can be formed by generation, sex, function, or by a variety of other factors. In addition, each family has its own particular set of different subsystems. Often referred to as *alliances* or *coalitions,* these subsystems are defined by particularly close bonds between certain family members. Members of these subsystems are likely to feel closer to each other, do more activities together, be especially loyal and protective of each other, share opinions and see things the same way in the family, and support one another when disagreements within the family arise (Karpel & Strauss, 1983).

The death of a family member can have a unique impact on the members of subsystems of which that individual was a part. All family members may have lost the same person, but not the same relationship. Because subsystems within the family have been altered, the family as a whole will be out of balance and will need to reorganize.

2. *Systems are governed by rules.* Both overt and covert *rules* (shared norms and values that govern repetitive patterns of family functioning) help the system to maintain a steady state of dynamic equilibrium or balance, referred to as *homeostasis.* This homeostasis makes the system and the relationships of interacting persons within the system predictable. Schatz (1986) notes that the well-known family therapist Virginia Satir used a mobile to illustrate the concept of balance in a family system. When one element of the mobile is removed, the entire system is in a state of imbalance. In order for a system to change (that is, for a change in homeostasis to occur), rules must be modified so that a new balance can be achieved. A death results in disequilibrium in the family system and requires a readjustment among surviving family members. Thus, rules must oftentimes be changed following a death to allow the system to meet the needs of the individuals involved and the system as a whole (Goldenberg & Goldenberg, 1980).

In a family, rules govern the *roles* (expected behavior of family members), division of labor, power structure, and patterns of interaction. Some rules are overtly discussed and agreed upon. Other family rules are not openly discussed but are tacitly acknowledged and followed by family members. For example, it may be an unstated family rule that it is not okay to discuss the impending death of a family member or to show unrestrained emotion.

3. *A property of all systems is openness.* The terms "open system" and "closed system" refer to the extent to which a family is open or closed to new information and, thus, susceptible to change. An *open family system* is dynamic and open to events and feelings both within and outside of the family structure. Information is freely exchanged with others outside the system and between members within the system. In contrast, a *closed family system* tends to be rigid and insensitive. Family members are locked into strictly prescribed patterns with little tolerance for innovation or adaptive change.

Open and closed family systems react differently in response to a death. According to Bowen (1978), the open family is more likely to recognize the full meaning of the loss; thus, its members may suffer intense emotional responses. After going through a period of disorganization, the family reorganizes in new and effective ways to meet the needs of the individual family members. This result is due, in part, to the fact that family members not only react to the news of the death, but also respond to each other's needs by offering nurturance and support. Additionally, they are willing to accept help from others outside of their own system.

In an extremely closed system, the family is more likely to deny the loss, since acceptance necessitates change. Family members are locked into rigid ways of responding to each other, unable to respond appropriately to their current situation. Not only will the family have difficulty responding to the demands of the environment, but it may also be unable to respond to the needs of individual family members. Thus, they may be isolated in their grief. When families fail to respond openly to their loss, individual adaptation may be inhibited. The more closed a family system, the more likely that a death will be met in ways which are maladaptive for the family unit and consequently that it will have negative impacts on family members (Stephenson, 1985).

Developmental Stages of Families

As with individuals, families move through predictable developmental stages. While different theorists have proposed slightly different models of family development, Carter and McGoldrick (1980) have identified six stages in the family life cycle and the particular developmental tasks and changes associated with each stage (see Table 3.1).

Family roles change significantly upon entry to each new family stage. The resources, needs, and tasks of the family also vary in each stage of development. Healthy families proceed through each stage relatively smoothly, completing appropriate developmental tasks and modifying patterns of interaction accordingly. Unhealthy families have difficulty and are often unable to complete the developmental tasks associated with particular stages. Consequently, they may get "stuck" in a stage, performing tasks and maintaining patterns of interactions appropriate to that stage but inappropriate for later stages.

The timing of a death in the life cycle of the family is often an important variable in the adjustment of the family and of its individual members (Rolland, 1987). For example, a family that experiences the death of one of its adult members may expect an older adolescent to become a surrogate parent for younger siblings and a companion for the remaining parent, thus truncating the normal process of separation during this age stage. In many cases, this can be a threat to independence and also delay or pre-

Table 3.1
Stages of the Family Life Cycle

Family Life Cycle Stage	Emotional Process of Transition: Key Principles	Second-Order Changes in Family Status Required to Proceed Developmentally
1. Between Families: The Unattached Young Adult	Accepting parent-offspring separation	a. Differentiation of self in relation to family of origin b. Development of intimate peer relationships c. Establishment of self in work
2. The Joining of Families through Marriage: The Newly Married Couple	Commitment to new system	a. Formation of marital system b. Realignment of relationships with extended families and friends to include spouse
3. The Family with Young Children	Accepting new members into the system	a. Adjusting marital system to make space for child(ren) b. Taking on parenting roles c. Realignment of relationships with extended family to include parenting and grandparenting roles
4. The Family with Adolescents	Increasing flexibility of family boundaries to include children's independence	a. Shifting of parent-child relationships to permit adolescent to move in and out of system b. Refocus on mid-life marital and career issues c. Beginning shift toward concerns for older generation
5. Launching Children and Moving On	Accepting a multitude of exits from and entries into the family system	a. Renegotiation of marital system as a dyad b. Development of adult-to-adult relationships between grown children and their parents c. Realignment of relationships to include in-laws and grandchildren d. Dealing with disabilities and death of parents (grandparents)
6. The Family in Later Life	Accepting the shifting of generational roles	a. Maintaining own and/or couple functioning and interests in face of physiological decline; exploration of new familial and social role options b. Support for a more central role for middle generation

Table 3.1
(*continued*)

Family Life Cycle Stage	Emotional Process of Transition: Key Principles	Second-Order Changes in Family Status Required to Proceed Developmentally
		c. Making room in the system for the wisdom and experience of the elderly; supporting the older generation without overfunctioning for them
		d. Dealing with loss of spouse, siblings, and other peers, and preparation for own death. Life review and integration.

SOURCE: E. A. Carter & M. McGoldrick (Eds.) (1980), *The Family Life Cycle: A Framework for Family Therapy*, New York: Gardner Press, p. 17. Reprinted by permission.

vent the young person from leaving home to start his or her own adult life (Gordon, 1986).

In families that have difficulty accepting loss as a natural part of life, young adults may be unable to separate from their family of origin and venture out on their own as mature individuals. At the same time, family members may not be able to allow the young adults in the family to pull away as part of the normal emancipation process. As a result, the system becomes static and locked into a rigid pattern that is resistant to change. Persons within this type of system are unable to *individuate* (to move toward more autonomous functioning), and thus view themselves as extensions of their families rather than unique, separate individuals. At the extreme are pathologically *enmeshed families* which manifest "total togetherness." These families are composed of family members with little individual autonomy or differentiation (Sieburg, 1985). When a death actually occurs in enmeshed systems, it reconfirms the pain of separation and leads to further enmeshment.

Family psychopathology often centers around *family myths*, which serve the same function for families as defense mechanisms do for individuals. Family myths consist of beliefs accepted and adhered to by family members that defend against disturbances or changes in existing family relationships. For example, members of enmeshed families may all uphold the myth that "We are only safe if we all stick together and let no one else into our inner circle."

Death as a Family Crisis

Family stress theory provides a useful model for conceptualizing the family's response to a death. A classic model of family stress developed by Reuben Hill (1949) over 40 years ago serves as a basis for current theoretical work. In this model, a family crisis is viewed as arising from a stressor event interacting with both the family's current crisis-meeting resources and the family's definition or perception of the stressor. The *stressor event* is defined as a life event or occurrence that impacts upon the family unit and produces, or has the opportunity to produce, change in the family system. (This change may take place in various areas of family life, such as family goals, patterns of interaction, quality of relationships, roles, values, or boundaries.) These combined factors all influence the family's vulnerability and, in turn, determine to what degree the family will experience a crisis. A family crisis refers to disruption, disorganization, or incapacity in the family system. A death in a family (a stressor event) usually results in a family crisis because of the excessive demands placed on the family's resources and ability to cope.

While the early conceptions of family stress focused primarily on precrisis variables, McCubbin and Patterson (1983b) have elaborated on Hill's original model to take into account postcrisis variables that influence the family's ability to recover from a crisis (often referred to as the family's *regenerative power*). These additional postcrisis variables include (1) the concurrent life stressors and changes that make family adaptation more difficult to achieve, (2) the critical psychological and social resources the family seeks out and utilizes when managing crisis situations, and (3) the family's interpretation of the crisis experience. All of these factors contribute to the family's ability to cope and represent the processes the family engages in to achieve satisfactory crisis resolution.

The outcome to a family's crisis over time can vary considerably in terms of adaptiveness and can be viewed on a continuum from *maladaptation* to *bonadaptation*. At the negative extreme, maladaptation results in the curtailment of individual and family development. At the positive extreme, the outcomes of bonadaptation are the enhancement of development in individual family members and the enhancement of the family as a unit (McCubbin & Patterson, 1983b).

Variables Affecting the Family's Ability to Cope

As previously stated, a family's ability to cope with a family crisis such as death and recover from it will be determined by other stressors experienced concurrently, the resources of the family, and the family's perception of the event (see Figure 3.1).

Concurrent Stressors

The ability of the family to cope may be complicated by multiple stressors. Illness or death within the family does not preclude the possibility of other stressful situations occurring at approximately the same time.

Some stressors may be related to the illness or death itself, while others may be quite unrelated. Stressors have been categorized by family researchers as (1) situational (for example, war or unemployment), (2) normal developmental (for example, birth of first child or retirement), or (3) transitional (for example, divorce). Stressors encountered at the same time as the illness or death have a cumulative effect, and thus the family experiences "pile-up." *Pile-up* refers to the accumulation of normative and nonnormative stressors and intrafamily strains (McCubbin & Patterson, 1983a). As the pile-up of stressors continues, the resources of the family become increasingly taxed, and there is an increased risk that family coping will become dysfunctional (Crosby & Jose, 1983).

Stressors Related to Illness or Death. The family experiences a variety of stressors that are directly related to the illness or to the death itself. For example, providing care to a person who is seriously ill is physically and emotionally exhausting (Montgomery, Gonyea, & Hooyman, 1985; Pratt, Schmal, Wright, & Cleland, 1985). As the illness progresses and death approaches, the family is faced with multiple losses: expected loss of life, the loss of a healthy family member, and the loss of family life as it had been (Kupst et al., 1982). Each of these losses is stressful in and of itself and may trigger a grief reaction among individual members. Other frequent stressors include increased time commitments, disruption of family routines, lack of time for self and other family members, a sense of social isolation, and financial strain. Additional strains on the family such as interruption of career, housing adaptation, and postponement of planned family activities also precipitate stress (Kalnins, Churchill, & Terry, 1980).

Stressors Not Related to Illness or Death. Holmes and Rahe (1967) identified a number of stressful life events and ranked them in terms of their relative stress factors (see Table 3.2). Note that many of these factors occur with fair regularity and as such may well occur during the time that a family member is dying. Kalnins et al. (1980) interacted with 45 families

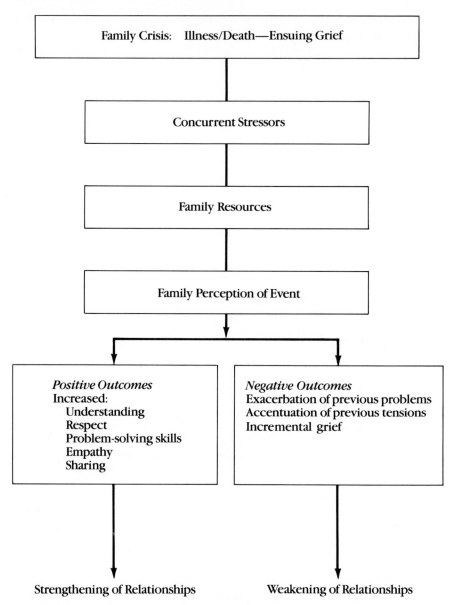

Figure 3.1 *Family Crisis Model: Death as an Example*

of leukemic children and found that they experienced a variety of concurrent stresses that had no direct relationship to the child's illness. These families experienced stressful events such as the death of another family member or friend, occupational changes, moving, and automobile accidents.

Normal developmental changes also constitute a source of stress. As individuals within the family develop and change over time, each must face new developmental issues and deal with new crises. The family system, too, changes over time and is faced with new challenges as noted earlier. The birth of a child, for example, is regarded by many to be a crisis in and of itself. Think of how much more difficult the situation becomes if the baby's parents are also caring for another child who is dying of cancer.

Table 3.2
The Social Readjustment Rating Scale

Rank	Life Event	Mean Value
1	Death of spouse	100
2	Divorce	73
3	Marital separation	65
4	Jail term	63
5	Death of close family member	63
6	Personal injury or illness	53
7	Marriage	50
8	Fired at work	47
9	Marital reconciliation	45
10	Retirement	45
11	Change in health of family member	44
12	Pregnancy	40
13	Sex difficulties	39
14	Gain of new family member	39
15	Business readjustment	39
16	Change in financial state	38
17	Death of a close friend	37
18	Change to different line of work	36
19	Change in number of arguments with spouse	35
20	Mortgage over $10,000	31
21	Foreclosure of mortgage or loan	30
22	Change in responsibilities at work	29
23	Son or daughter leaving home	29
24	Trouble with in-laws	29
25	Outstanding personal achievement	28
26	Wife begins or stops work	26
27	Beginning or end of school	26
28	Change in living conditions	25
29	Revision of personal habits	24

SOURCE: T. H. Holmes & R. Rahe (1967), The social readjustment rating scale, *Journal of Psychosomatic Research*, Vol. 11, p. 216. Copyright © 1967 Pergamon Journals, Ltd. Reprinted by permission.

Family Resources

Having resources available and being willing to use them can effectively mediate the effects of a family crisis. Resources can include (1) support and strengths within the family and (2) support and services from individuals and organizations outside the family system.

Three features seem to characterize families that are able to respond adequately to stressor events: involvement, integration, and adaptation. *Involvement* is the commitment that members make to the family and their participation in family life. *Integration* refers to the ability of family members to work together in order to assist in achieving both group and individual goals and in maintaining psychological equilibrium. *Adaptation* is the ability of the family and each of its members to change their responses to each other and to the outside world as situations demand (Glasser & Glasser, 1970).

McCubbin (1979) agrees that the internal resources of the family, such as integration and adaptability, are crucial to positive family functioning after a crisis but adds that families must also develop or strengthen their ability to seek community resources, external to the family itself. This need for external support was confirmed by Venters (1981) who studied families of children with cystic fibrosis. The life expectancy for individuals with cystic fibrosis is late teens or early twenties. In this study, Venters found that families who had a high level of functioning sought both practical help and emotional support from persons both inside and outside the family. Middle functioning families shared their burden extensively within the family structure and minimally outside. Finally, families determined to be low functioning had one or two persons within the families who were primarily responsible for the care of the sick child and did not request help or support from any external individual or group whatsoever.

Family adjustment to illness and death is also related to a variety of additional factors. These include interpersonal interaction styles, cultural expectations, characteristic modes of dealing with stress, a positive outlook on life, hope, and rules that allow emotional expression and role flexibility (Crosby & Jose, 1983; Koch, 1985; Nordlicht, 1982; Patterson & McCubbin, 1983).

Family's Perception of the Event

Crisis situations may be somewhat neutralized by the cognitive appraisal (Pearlin & Schooler, 1978) or the psychological evaluation (Lazarus, 1966) that is made of them. For example, factors such as religious beliefs affect the family's perception of the crisis (Pratt et al., 1985) and allow individual family members to regard the crisis as a test of their faith or a challenge by which their faith might become stronger. Stinnett, Knorr, DeFrain, and Rowe (1981) found that 56 percent of the "strong families" in their study indicated that a spiritual or religious belief allowed them to cope more effectively. Endowing an illness or death with a positive meaning may allow survivors to adjust more easily (Venters, 1981). In contrast, viewing a death as punishment for past deeds can have a negative influence on the resolution of grief.

At times, the family's perception of the crisis event even alters the feeling of being a family. Family members may perceive the death as "destroying our family" or "the loss of the person who gave life to our family." Bereaved mothers often talk about "not seeming to be a family anymore" after a child's death (Schatz, 1986). These perceptions are important and need to be addressed in any therapeutic intervention.

Adaptation of the Family Unit

The Chinese symbol for the word *crisis* is translated to mean "dangerous opportunity." Implicit in this translation is the understanding that the challenges that are precipitated by a death may result in either positive or negative changes for the family. According to Broderick and Smith (1979), it is unreasonable to expect that a family has a rule to deal with every possible situation. As a result, they may react to a novel or unanticipated situation in a wide variety of ways. Depending on the specific family, the response may be immobilization, break-up, or a marshaling of resources to create a new suitable response to the situation. Crises are not necessarily detrimental to the family. Often new and creative solutions are developed for reacting to situations, such that future crises may actually be dealt with in a more effective manner (Hansen & Johnson, 1979).

Positive Outcomes

Many families report closer bonds, better understanding and respect for each other's strengths, enhancement of mutual problem-solving skills, greater empathy, and increased sharing following the illness and/or death of a family member. DeFrain and Ernst (1978) studied the effect of Sudden Infant Death Syndrome on family survivors. They reported that in those cases where individuals turned to family members for support and that support was granted, family relationships were generally strengthened.

Klass (1986) explains that, for some families, a death creates a new bond as members draw together to deal with a shared crisis.

Mages and Mendelsohn (1979) have agreed, emphasizing that the experience of having cancer can affect individual development and family dynamics in positive ways , whether or not it ends in death:

> We have observed several instances in which patients whose personal affairs were in disarray used their experience with cancer to reorganize their lives by taking advantage of the new opportunities and sources of help that had become available. Less dramatic, but more frequent, is the quiet reassessment of values and goals that many patients go through, a reassessment that may lead to a keener appreciation of what is important in life and to more satisfying choices regarding the style and direction of their lives. The impact of illness leads some patients to become more constructively self-centered and more assertive in pursuing their personal goals. And for those couples and families who are able to master the stresses of cancer, the experience of surmounting crises together and perhaps communicating in ways in which they never have before may lead to a satisfying growth and deepening of relationships. We can hardly recommend cancer as a route to maturity, but, like other profound experiences, it can have the effect of clarifying the distinction between the trivial and the essential. (p. 278)

In his study of parents representing 100 families with a child who had cystic fibrosis, Venters (1981) found that approximately one-half of the families regarded their crisis as growth-producing. Many sought new solutions to dealing with problems and reducing stress.

Negative Outcomes

One cannot assume that all families will experience a positive outcome to the crisis of death. The phrase "dangerous opportunity" implies that there is a risk involved—a risk that the family may not possess the coping strategies to deal with the stress and conflict that arise after the death of one of its members. Several researchers have found that the death of a family member may produce a variety of negative outcomes.

Incremental Grief. Oftentimes, the crisis of illness or death does not draw family members closer together but rather causes significant discord. A model of incremental grief will be discussed which explains how one loss often triggers another loss. The resultant grief is magnified with each added loss. In order to simplify the discussion of this model, we shall examine it in terms of the survivors being a husband and wife. It should be remembered, however, that the model does apply to other surviving relationships (parent–child, sibling–sibling, and friend–friend, among others) and to grief precipitated by losses other than death.

As described in Chapter 2, there are many common manifestations of grief; however, each person's grief experience is ultimately unique. Each individual feels the loss in a very personal way, due to the specific relationship that was severed and due to variations in coping strategies. One spouse may be very depressed, guilty, and preoccupied with the death for many, many months after the loss of a child. The other spouse may be deeply saddened by the loss and very angry at the medical profession and other family members for a few months after the death. At a given moment in time, even while in the acute stage of grief, one spouse may feel moderately happy while the other is in anguish. This variability of grief-related experiences and time taken for resolution describes the *dissynchrony* or *asymmetry* of grief (Cook, 1984; Davies, Spinetta, Martinson, McClowry, & Kulenkamp, 1986; Owen, Fulton, & Markusen, 1982; Purisman & Maoz, 1977; Rando, 1985).

Both during an illness and following the death, family members often use *discrepant coping styles* (Christ, 1980; Cook, 1983; McGrory, 1978). Some survivors may vent their emotions openly while others inhibit their feelings. Some individuals wish to communicate openly and talk frequently about their grief while others regard their experiences as private and are reticent.

Due to the dissynchrony of grief and discrepant coping styles following the primary loss of death, there is often *secondary loss*—a loss which is a consequence of a death, the primary loss (Rando, 1984). In order to understand the impact of grief on surviving relationships, we will define the secondary loss in this context as a change in the predeath relationship regarded as stressful by the survivors. (Rando uses a broader definition of the term to refer to any loss, either physical or symbolic, that develops as a consequence of the death of a loved one).

The resultant strain on the relationship is often related to stresses that predated the death. The crisis precipitated by death often exacerbates already existing interpersonal problems or accentuates tensions already present. For example, a husband and wife may have never openly shared their emotions with one another (Geyman, 1983; Kerner, Harvey, & Lewiston, 1979). The death of their child simply made the ongoing silence in that area all the more noticeable, as well as painful, when one spouse desperately wanted to share feelings. In some instances, the stress caused by the death creates new problems for the survivors. For example, after the death of a child, one spouse may physically withdraw from a mate who chooses to deal with his or her grief privately. The rejected spouse may then seek extramarital relationships, even though that had never been a pattern prior to the child's death. Or, as another example, a parent who had never used alcohol or drugs previously may use them excessively after the death.

If the stress on a surviving relationship is significant, survivors often grieve not only the primary loss of the death but also grieve over the significant change in the predeath relationship with another survivor (secondary loss). This grief is termed *secondary grief* (Oltjenbruns, 1987) and emanates from the stressful change in a relationship with another survivor, not from the death itself.

Secondary grief is often characterized by one spouse being angry at the other for not understanding what he or she is experiencing or for not offering support when it is needed. A husband or wife who assumes that all people should grieve the same way may condemn the other, who is grieving differently. One parent may erroneously conclude that the other parent did not love the deceased child because he or she is not grieving openly and, as a result, inappropriately berate their mate for what is perceived to be a lack of attachment to the child who died. There is often a lack of understanding when an expectation of providing mutual support cannot be fulfilled. Grief is such a personally painful and draining experience that bereaved parents sometimes simply cannot reach out to help each other, even when they want to. As illustrated by these characteristics, secondary grief adds to the burden of family members who have experienced the death of a loved one (primary loss) and a significant change in a relationship with another survivor (secondary loss) (see Figure 3.2).

The importance of understanding the secondary grief phenomenon relates to modes of intervention. As discussed in Chapter 2, individuals need an opportunity to do their own grief work and be given support for venting emotions and sharing thoughts or beliefs. To deal more effectively with secondary grief, counselors, social workers, and others who help families must take a systems perspective, for this grief evolves not only from the individual's personal primary loss but also from the ultimate effect which that loss has had on the relationship with another survivor. In some instances, the secondary grief may permanently alter the relationship, or even terminate it, if appropriate systems-oriented intervention is not provided. For example, Kaplan, Grobstein, and Smith (1976) studied 40 families after the death of a child with leukemia. Serious marital problems were reported by the majority of the families. In addition, many families reported difficulties in parent–child communication. Eighty percent of the families who noted having problems believed that these had been precip-

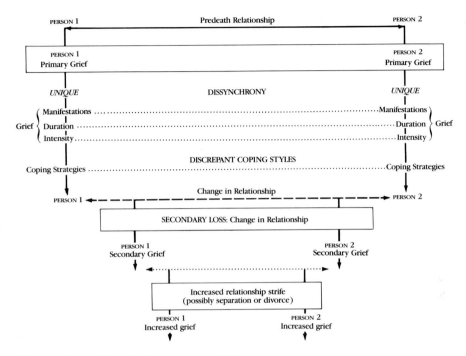

Figure 3.2 *A Model of Incremental Grief*

itated by the illness and subsequent death. Fish (1986) found 70 percent of bereaved parents in his study reported significant marital stress related to the loss. Only 24 percent felt that their shared loss had brought them closer together.

Although consistent data are not available regarding the number of divorces due to the death of a child, many bereaved couples are in serious marital difficulty within months after the death of a child, and divorce for these couples is a possibility if professional help is not obtained. It may well be that the secondary grief phenomenon is the more direct cause of the marital discord, rather than the primary loss—the death of a child. The individual who grieves the following losses—the primary loss (such as the death of a child), the resultant secondary loss (for example, change in relationship between husband and wife which causes increased stress), and a tertiary loss (ultimately, perhaps divorce)—experiences a shifting in the focus of the grief and also the added grief of multiple losses. This phenomenon is termed *incremental grief* (Oltjenbruns, 1987). Incremental grief is defined as the additive factor of grief due to multiple related losses. The grief resulting from a primary loss may trigger a secondary loss. The grief resulting from the secondary loss may then precipitate yet another loss.

Intervention with the Family System

The optimal time for intervention is during the early, acute stage of a crisis. It is during this time that the family is attempting to reorganize and new patterns of interaction are being established. When a terminal illness precedes a death, intervention should begin prior to the actual death, following the confirmation of the diagnosis. Shneidman (1971) has used the term *postvention* to refer to assistance offered to survivors *following* a death. It is at this time in the dying continuum that intervention most often occurs.

Herz (1980) has noted that families often do not seek help from family therapists for problems related to a recent or past death, but rather request help for other identifiable concerns. For example, parents may seek professional help because of a parent–child conflict or marital difficulties, without seeing the connection to a previous death in the family. In other cases, the death will not be mentioned because it is a taboo subject for family members. In these situations, the family's "presenting problem" may camouflage the underlying issue of impact of the death on the family system.

Grebstein (1986) points out that intervention with families often involves a strong educational component. If families are prepared for the issues they must face, they are more likely to avoid maladaptive coping and poor outcomes. The single most important task for the family therapist is to help the family talk openly about the death, its impact on them, and their emotional reactions to it. In this regard, therapists should be sensitive to the uniqueness of each family's reaction. Each family is different, and the therapeutic interventions required may vary considerably; however, intervention with a family system should focus on the following family tasks.

Family Tasks Involved in Coping

Each individual in the family performs certain death-related or grief-related tasks. Each communicates with the dying person, grieves for that person both before and after death, and relinquishes attachment to the person who has died. Other tasks are relevant to the family system as a whole. Family-oriented tasks include maintaining open communication, reassigning roles, acting as a support for other family members, and modifying relationships with external systems.

Maintain Open Communication

In Chapter 1, we stressed that shared communication is crucial if dying persons are to avoid a sense of isolation, abandonment, or an overwhelming sense of fear regarding their impending deaths. Both the dying individual and the family as a whole typically have a need for closure with one another. This can only occur if there is open communication. Engaging in a conspiracy of silence negates the opportunity for both the dying person and family members to plan for the future, deal with anxieties, and enjoy each other's company (Krant & Johnston, 1978).

Open communication not only increases the opportunity to interact positively with the dying individual, it also serves as a resource to the family as it strives to regain equilibrium (Kaplan, Smith, Grobstein, & Fischman, 1973).

> Families with open internal communication systems are more prone to resist the societal taboos surrounding the area of death, and are thus more likely to discuss and make realistic plans for the death of their members. . . . The degree to which it is permissible to express feelings of sadness and loss, as well as the less acceptable reactions of anger, guilt, and relief, seems to play a large role in determining the success of the readjustment period. (Vollman, 1971, p. 104)

If family members do not openly share their thoughts and feelings, the family may be at risk for experiencing negative outcomes. Lack of open communication increases the possibility of guilt, blame, and conflict (Derdeyn & Waters, 1981; Vess, Moreland, & Schwebel, 1985b).

Reassign Roles

After the death of one of its members, the family must reassign the roles which that person had performed. These roles consist of tasks that may be either instrumental or expressive in nature (Arndt & Gruber, 1977; Goldberg, 1973). *Instrumental tasks* include such activities as serving as primary breadwinner for the family or preparing meals. *Expressive tasks* facilitate the development of a favorable social–emotional climate within the family. They include such activities as promoting affectionate interactions or minimizing conflict.

The number of roles to be reassigned and the centrality of these roles to overall family functioning affect the intensity of the family crisis (Goldberg, 1973). "The specific roles depend on the family's stage in the family life cycle, which, in turn, will determine the roles that require reallocation" (Vess, Moreland, & Schwebel, 1985a, p. 2). If the family member who is ill or who has died is a parent/spouse, role reassignment may be all the more difficult than if it were a young child. In this situation, surviving family members are at risk for increased stress and disorganization, because a parent/spouse is likely to have fulfilled a combination of the following roles: financial provider, socializer and caretaker of children, and housekeeper, among others (Nye et al., 1976). The surviving parent, then, may attempt to assume too many additional roles, thereby experiencing *role strain*. In other instances, children may attempt to assume roles for which they have inadequate preparation and/or skill. If this is the case, not only do the children suffer, but the roles are likely to be performed inadequately.

Stress due to role reallocation may also be experienced while the dying person is still alive. For example, if family members are involved in providing care to the patient or if they must travel long distances to the hospital, they may experience what seem to be impossible demands on their time. These increased demands result from trying to perform their ongoing old roles, new roles related to the illness, and also some of the patient's former roles that have been reallocated to them.

The opportunity for a positive outcome to the process of role reallocation can be enhanced by a number of factors. Two of these will be briefly discussed here: (1) open communication among family members and (2) achievement (as compared to ascription) of roles.

Vess et al. (1985a) studied cancer patients and their families and found that open communication provided an opportunity to negotiate the reallocation of roles, which in turn diminished role strain and role conflict. Without good communication, roles are oftentimes simply reallocated by default, with little attention paid to how they might most effectively be fulfilled (Silverman & Englander, 1975).

In discussing assignment of roles, Aldous (1978) differentiates between the ascription of roles and the achievement of roles. She defines *ascribed roles* as those assigned by virtue of some characteristic over which a person has no control, such as gender or sex. For example, a daughter who is expected to perform housekeeping chores after her mother dies, simply because she is a girl, has an ascribed role. *Achieved roles* are acquired by the efforts and skill of the individual. A son or daughter who becomes involved with caring for a younger sibling because he or she has the skills and desire to do so has undertaken an achieved role. The method of assigning roles affects both the performance of the roles and the family environment. "Families who used achieved roles performed their reallocated roles at a higher level than did families who adopted ascribed roles. Specifically, these families were less likely to use a role overload pattern" (Vess et al., 1985a, p. 14).

Provide Support to Other Family Members

The outcome of a family crisis such as illness or death of a family member is affected by the presence or absence of family support. Support is needed both during the caregiving process (Pratt et al., 1985) and after the death (Crosby & Jose, 1983). Stinnett et al. (1981) studied the coping strategies of 66 families who had been identified as "strong families" by persons outside the family unit. When asked who was most helpful in dealing with a crisis, the most common response was family members. A major conclusion of the study was "the primary family unit itself became a major resource in coping with crisis . . . the strong family has a great deal to contribute to the strength of the individual" (p. 163).

It is important to note, however, that some family systems do not provide support to one another. Families that do not have good communication skills, respect, or empathy for each other may serve as a liability rather than a resource.

Modify Relationships with Social Networks

A fourth task that must be performed by surviving family members is to establish or modify relationships with other social networks (Arndt & Gruber, 1977; Goldberg, 1973). Individuals and families often do not have all of the resources that are necessary to deal with a severe crisis and may need to seek social support. *Social support* is defined as "individuals, groups, or institutions that provide assistance of varying degrees and forms to help another individual combat stresses that tax his or her personal resources" (Schilling, Gilchrist, & Schinke, 1985, p. 47). Social support can also be provided to the family system as a whole.

Unger and Powell (1980) explain that social networks may be either formal or informal in nature. *Informal support networks* refer to family members, friends, and neighbors. *Formal support networks* refer to organizations such as organized peer support groups or professionals such as doctors or counselors. Both formal and informal support networks can provide instrumental and/or emotional support or provide information regarding other networks.

More and more formal networks are being created to help dying individuals and their families. These include hospices and peer support groups such as CanSurmount and Make Today Count (for cancer victims and their families), Outstretched Hands and Widow-to-Widow (for widowed individuals), Parents Without Partners (for single parents who may have been widowed), Compassionate Friends (for parents whose children have died), and Heartbeat (for survivors of a suicide), just to name a few. Although many formal networks do exist, one cannot assume that they are necessarily used by all who may need them. Some family units do not search outward in their time of need and can "bankrupt themselves in time of tragedy" (Vollman, Ganzert, Picher, & Williams, 1971, p. 103).

Intergenerational Issues Related to Death

Some families who seek help may have loss-related problems that are not immediately apparent. At times, the loss may have occurred in previous generations. In order to adequately assess each family and identify the sources of difficulty, it is often helpful to do a *genogram*. A genogram is a structured family history in which the therapist diagrams information about the family, their relationships, and important family events (McGoldrick & Gerson, 1985). Through this process, the family's experience with death can be determined. The genogram, which typically covers the past three generations, is based on Bowen's (1976) theory that the effects of major losses in a family can be transmitted to subsequent generations if they are not worked through by the family when they occur. According to Bowen (1976), the death of a family member creates an "emotional shock wave" that is "a network of underground 'after shocks' of serious life events that can occur anywhere in the extended family system in the months or years following serious emotional events in a family" (p. 339). A death in a family system has the potential of disrupting the effective equilibrium of the system, which can result in a chronically dysfunctional family. When intervening in such a system, a balance must be maintained between encouraging expression of unresolved grief associated with a death and promoting healthy family interactions so that the family can continue to develop in the future.

Figure 3.3 illustrates the genogram done on the family of a 19-year-old college student who began to show anorectic behavior after leaving home for college. Karen, the student, had an older sister who was attending another college in the same geographical area. All members of Karen's family described themselves as open and loving and felt that they were closer than most families. The genogram provides insight into repetition of family patterns and the impact of critical events in the family's history.

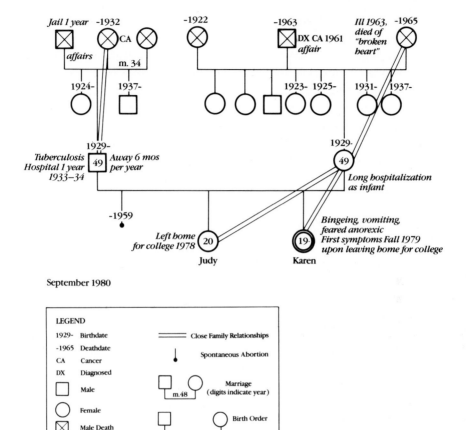

Figure 3.3   *The S. Family: An Example of a Genogram*

Source: Reproduced from *Genograms in Family Assessment* by Monica McGoldrick and Randy Gerson, by permission of W.W. Norton & Company, Inc. Copyright © by Monica McGoldrick and Randy Gerson.

The therapist concluded that Karen's difficulties leaving home were related to her special position in the family, due to the deaths of her maternal grandparents shortly after her birth. The special closeness of the family was explained by the parents' early childhood experiences with loss (death of Karen's paternal grandmother when her father was 3 years old) and separation (Karen's mother's long hospitalization as an infant and her father's hospitalization as a young child) (McGoldrick & Gerson, 1985).

Confused and fearful attitudes related to death can interfere with the normal processes of separation and individuation that are a natural part of progressing through the family life cycle. Worden (1982) has emphasized that one important reason for using a family systems approach is that unresolved grief may not only serve as a key factor in family pathology, but it may also contribute to pathological relationships across generations. Postponed mourning related to a death in one's family of origin at an earlier time can impede effective coping with emotional loss and separation within one's current family. Sometimes years later, remaining conflicts over loss and abandonment can be projected by adults onto their present-day families. Consequently, normal developmental change can become fearful, anxiety-laden matters (Pattison, 1977).

The genogram, in addition to discovering important clinical information from the past, can also have therapeutic benefits as families are given permission to discuss their previous losses (Grebstein, 1986). The assessment of a family should also include current level of functioning, family strengths and vulnerabilities, resources, and sources of support.

Family Rituals Related to Death

Most societies have rituals (such as funerals or memorial services) that serve as a public acknowledgment that a death has occurred. A *ritual* is a specific behavior or activity that gives symbolic expression to certain feelings or thoughts of groups and of individuals (van der Hart, 1983). They can be repeated or one-time acts. The acknowledgment of death on a formal level can promote acceptance on a more personal level. Rituals can provide powerful therapeutic experiences for families and symbolize transition, healing, and continuity. For a ritual to have optimal value, it must have meaning for its participants. A trend has emerged for funerals and memorial services to be more individualized and fit the needs of the bereaved family.

Families may also participate in private rituals that have special significance (for example, having a special meal in honor of the deceased and leaving an empty place at the head of the table on that particular occasion). In bereavement situations, sometimes the most meaningful rituals are silent, spontaneous, symbolic statements that represent unique feelings related to the deceased (sealed letters tucked underneath the casket pillow, a farewell salute, or a single rose placed on the casket are examples) (Conley, 1987). Family therapists often prescribe rituals to aid families in resolving their grief. These rituals need to fit the preferences of the particular family and be designed to (1) help the family accept the reality of the loss, (2) express feelings related to the loss, and (3) accomplish the tasks of grief work (Rando, 1985).

Prefuneral Rituals

Although we often regard the funeral or memorial service as the primary death-related ritual, there are a number of activities that take place prior to the funeral that serve as important leave-taking behaviors. These include submitting public notices of the death, viewing the body, selecting a casket and grave marker, and having a prefuneral prayer service (Bolton & Camp, 1987). Each of these activities helps the family to personally acknowledge that the death has occurred. The public notice of the death and prefuneral prayer service provide an opportunity to reach out for support.

Funerals and Memorial Services

As a ritual, funerals and memorial services fulfill a number of important functions both for the family and for the larger society (Charmaz, 1980; Friedman, 1980; Fulton, 1987). Specifically, they

1. Give recognition that a life has been lived

Photo 3.1 *Funerals provide an important opportunity for family members and friends to pay their respects to the deceased and to provide mutual support.*

2. Confirm the dignity and worth of human beings

3. Provide public recognition that the death has occurred

4. Allow the bereaved to publicly express and share the loss

5. Facilitate the expression of grief

6. Provide an immediate supportive network for the bereaved

7. Serve as a rite of passage from one status to another for both the deceased and the bereaved

8. Provide an opportunity to reestablish contact with distant relatives and promote group cohesion

Although funerals do serve many important functions, controversy exists surrounding the funeral industry. Many people question the high cost of funeral services in American society and emphasize the vulnerability of family members as they make "consumer" decisions during such an emotionally disruptive time. Some advocate making these decisions in advance of a death to reduce the stress of decision making during the stage of acute grief.

Postfuneral Rituals

Acknowledging gifts and cards, sorting and/or disposing of the deceased's personal effects, visiting the grave site, writing letters to inform others of the death, and removing a wedding ring are all types of postfuneral rituals. Although there is no definitive proof as to the impact of postfuneral activities on bereavement outcome, Bolton and Camp (1987) have recently done exploratory work in this area. While they were unable to draw any firm conclusions, these researchers did obtain results which suggest that postfuneral symbolic acts can facilitate grief work.

Summary

The death of a family member constitutes a family crisis as well as an individual crisis. Family systems react to death in ways that reflect their various characteristics (such as level of openness or existence of particular rules). The timing of the death in the family life cycle also affects the adjustment of the system. Crisis theory provides insight into the family's ability to adapt to the death of one of its members. Concurrent stressors on the family, resources of the family, and family perception of the death all have an impact on recovery patterns. Many families report a positive outcome in that members felt closer to one another as they struggled to deal with a shared crisis. In other situations, however, family members indicate that the death precipitated a number of negative outcomes due to the dissynchrony of individuals' grief experiences or discrepant coping styles. As a result, many survivors may experience a significant level of stress in their relationships.

Intervention with family members prior to the death can facilitate long-term adjustment. The process of adjusting involves many important tasks. The family reassigns roles that had been performed by the deceased. Family members strive to provide support to one another both before and after the death and seek help from other social networks. Participation in a funeral service or other ritual allows survivors to acknowledge that a death has occurred and provides a therapeutic experience that contributes to the resolution of grief.

 Personal Account

Pam Landon's son and daughter-in-law were killed in a fire in their apartment building. Her essay entitled "The Longest Day" recounts activities and feelings of that tragic day as well as the impact that the deaths had on the family system that survived.

The Longest Day

Pam Landon

> The call. The query. The downy cop.
> The wait till those remaining
> close in to shield each other's pain.
> The helpless disbelief, then certainty
> in the charred halls, and the small space
> beside the window; a last safety sought.
> Time stretched, collapsed and meaningless.
> The act of courage, manhood proved.
> An absolution in the sunny grove.

What we did not know then and do now know is that longest day in 1983, on which our son Kevin died at age 24, is a day that has no end.

No death of a family member or intimate other ends, even to the next generation, while memory lives. I still experience my mother's forever-

---

Pam Landon is Chair of the Department of Social Work at Colorado State University. Her personal account was written in 1987 as a contribution to this book.

painful story of dreaming nightly for years of vainly trying to touch a beloved sister-in-law who died on the day of my birth. My parents died 30 years ago. Often to this day, when I have a marvelously ridiculous encounter or experience a special moment, I think, "I've got to tell Mother about that." Six months after my parents' death, my Aunt Peg wrote me and said what I've found to be true. She said, "Time does not heal; what times does is allow the good memories to come true."

The death of one's child, or one's sibling, at a young age multiplies this ongoing reality because, I think, it is time-warped and not in the natural progression of expectation. You expect to bury your parents and even your spouse, but not your child or your childhood companion. It is shocking. It is not to be believed. It is not expected. You are not prepared, unless, perhaps in wartime or after a long illness. You are not ready. It is not fair. It should have been one of us, not him. It is out of season, and it remains raw and shocking and, most of all, present. Good memories do start to surface, and, after some time elapses, it is not always in the forefront of consciousness. But it is ever present and never loses the raw waves of pain. At least, that is so for his father and me to this present time.

If you live in our area, you may remember the story, which was well covered by the press. It is not uncommon, particularly in major cities. An old house, made over into apartments for the non-Yuppie young and others with either marginal incomes or preference for living "downtown," goes up in flames. It goes up in flames as a result of dried-out wallpaper and inadequate fire systems. It goes up in flames as a result of a drunken party and a small fire started in a wastebasket and human error. You may have seen pictures of the bodies of our son and his wife carried out on stretchers on the 5 o'clock news. We did. We are grateful that they were overcome by smoke and never felt the burning. The smell of the burned-out apartment remains forever in the senses; in the heart, the sorrowful pride for his courage shown in protecting his wife with his body till his death.

It is meaningful to have this opportunity, offered by good colleagues, to think about what this kind of loss meant to our family then, and what it means now, individually and collectively. It was also good to talk with each member about their reactions and thoughts and feelings then and now in a quiet and reflective way, instead of in the passing comments that we seem to have developed over time. Some issues seem to have become clearer to me regarding both our own individual and collective experiences, and how these may relate to other families. This is one reason for the writing. It may repay in part the many kinds of help that others gave to us.

What help do I remember?

The importance of information given. I will never forget Joe, the fire investigator who gave several hours of his time to tell us just what had and had not happened, or the neighbors who told us all they knew of his last hours; I also will never forget, at the opposite end, the official of the well-known disaster program, who when I called at 6:00 in the morning told me I would have to wait until the office opened at 8:30 to find out whether our child was living or dead.

The difference that caring makes: the caring of each of us for each other; of the tears in the eyes of the young policeman who came to the door to tell me what I already knew; of the colleague who became a friend, who came over while I was still in the shower and just "hung out" until my family could get home; of the people who worked with our son and invited us to a restaurant to buy us coffee and tell us what he had meant in their lives; of all the people who came, even out of sickbeds, to the memorial service; of all those who wrote, sent cards, gave contributions. For 2 or 3 weeks, the afternoon mail was a blood transfusion. I used to not go to funerals, not write because I didn't know what to say, not "hang out" because I might be excess baggage. No more. I know what it means. And I will err on the side of presence over absence.

The centrality of sharing: again each of us with each other; the shared experience of the two families which continues, in attenuated form, today; the young son of that family who carefully went through all the burned belongings so we would not have to; the unpressuring and continuing, to the present, offer of Compassionate Friends, the self-help group for parents who have lost children, for the knowledge of whose availability we were grateful, although we did not participate; the others who also lost children and told us how it has been for them; and those who continue to care, knowing there is no set time period for grieving. I wrote to my sister the next April:

> I think the shock and the kind of support you initially get hold you together for a while, and then at the time the world expects you to start getting it together is when you internally fall apart. At least this seemed so for me. Just when I think I'm "on top of it," the waves wash over.

The sharing helps. People experience their humanity in conjunction with other people. Communicating with those who have stood where we stand is for most a major experience in being heard and being understood.

However, if we define our own experience as being the same as that of another, we do individuality of person and family an injustice. Therefore, I'll talk about us as a family: what each person felt individually then and now, how each saw the family then and now, and our speculations as to the why of these feelings and perceptions. I'll offer as thoughts and speculations some reactions I believe may be universal to such an experience and some concepts about how families work that make the universal experience of the death of son and sibling idiosyncratically each family's own.

Our family nucleus is my husband, myself, our oldest son, who was 31 at the time of the death, and a daughter who was 22. Both sets of grandparents had long since died. I was the youngest of a large and very extended family. My husband was the only child of a family no longer in existence. He had two daughters by a previous marriage, one of whom had died 2 years earlier.

At the time of the death, our oldest son had recently remarried and, shortly before the longest day, had returned with his new wife, and we had held the first total family reunion in several years. That reunion was a wonderful and comforting happenstance. I wonder if it was happenstance. I also wonder if the wonderful weekend his father and I had spent with Kevin and his wife in the high country a few weeks before, where much had been talked out and a closer relationship had been established, was also happenstance, or preparation.

Our daughter had come West from Connecticut where she was living with my aunt and going to college. She was driving back East in the very early morning and heard of the fire on the radio and woke me with her phone call. She had heard of a fire in a downtown location and that two people had died. She, not knowing, was sure it was her brother and his wife. I, not knowing, was also sure. His older brother remembers his first reaction as one of "horror, numbness, and inevitability." This reaction I believe must be universal, except where one has a warning, such as after a long illness. Each of us remembers the initial reaction of horror but not of disbelief; in fact, as his father put it, there was a sense of "some way of forcing his own disaster." This may well have been an idiosyncratic factor of our particular family. This son had been an individual with a number of handicapping conditions—physical, intellectual, and emotional—and individually and as a family we had experienced a number of crises centered on him as he grew up. The prescience of disaster may well have been an outcome of this background.

Thus, the nature of the child who is gone is one of the factors that makes each experience different. The fact that our son had overcome multiple difficulties and had succeeded in living independently, completing school, working, and starting his own family and that this had taken a long time and a lot of concentration had different meanings for family members. For his sister, it came as no particular surprise because she had "always considered him her equal and had resented the fact that he got the most attention." For his father, the reaction was not only one of disbelief but also one of anger at the death that cut him off from enjoying his troubled son's coming of age and realizing his potential, anger that this son "was permitted to die as contrasted to someone else. I would much rather it had been me." For his older brother, who had understood and accepted an ongoing responsibility in necessary areas as part of his own future, this death came in sadness but also as a lifting of a burden. "I wish I still had that burden." For me, the loss was heightened by the years of intensive investment, fears, frustrations, and successes.

The nature of immediate and ongoing sorrow was experienced very differently. As his sister said, "What could you expect, we always have to deal with things each in our own way." For his father then and now, "The loss is horrendous. I was devastated. The pain is as sharp as it ever was, seeing a picture, hearing a song, being in a place that has him in it.'' His sister still waits for him to call with a question for her to answer. "Although our lives were very different, he was the person who shared my childhood and knew me in a way no one ever will. There is a forever void.'' For his brother, ''I can't really talk about the then. Too much remembered pain. The now is remote, pops up at bizarre moments on a quiet evening. Not sure of where or when it will end, but it had to be.'' For me, the sorrow was all-consuming then, a part of daily living now.

Possibly because of his centrality, guilt did not and does not appear to be a central issue for our particular family. His sister said: "Mostly it was scary. Not much guilt. We fought the last time we were together, but that was normal.'' His brother expresses more. "I felt guilt for not being there as often as I could have been, not being as much as I should have been.'' I do not see that as reality. His father does not speak of guilt. And mine are small ones—the fact that the day before he died, I had thought of stopping in to see them and did not because I was running late, and I would call them that evening and I did not. Small regrets, not big guilts. I think the feeling is sadness and ambivalence, not guilt.

All of us were impacted almost immediately by a sense of instantaneous change in the family. Systems theory would say, of course! As his father put it, "His disability tended to pull the family together in our concern for him; everyone shared in the knowledge and the responsibility.'' His sister said that he had been the "central one—the child still sort of at home, which left us free to do our own thing. He was the force that connected us all and he was gone.'' Initially, everyone perceived a closeness never experienced before. His father said, "No one really believed a sibling could die.'' His brother said, "His death forced his sister and me to grow up. . . . Death is a hefty dose of reality, and his death gave all of us a sense of mortality for each of us.'' His sister talked about that a lot. We all felt the need to communicate a lot more frequently. Both his siblings and I dreamed a lot about him for months. I still do; I don't know whether they do. I worried much more if I had not heard from everybody in a month. I was afraid to be alone, afraid something else would happen. In another part of me, I, like his brother, experienced some relief. We did not have to worry any more. He was all right. We were the ones that were hurting. We found comfort in different people at the time: his sister with an old and valued family friend, my husband with his new daughter-in-law. We are gentler and kinder with each other, and permanently both closer and freer.

Over time, roles have changed. His sister feels more important and more focused on as the only one not married. Has she taken his place as the central force? For his father, the death "clarified relationships with the other children and gave a better understanding of the family unit. Prior to that my understanding of family was intellectual, not emotional, because I never had a family.'' Our daughter corroborates this and says that he has grown more paternal, and we have become more important to him. For his brother, it has permitted completion of his emancipation and given him permission to concentrate on his own new family, himself and his career, and the birth of his own child. He feels a bit guilty about the relief. So do I.

Over time we have moved from the need for "circling the wagons." His sister said that we have fractured a bit, so that we can deal with his death and our lives each in our own way. "What do you expect, it's the way we always do." His father sees the family as less of a unit than when he was alive and as having permission to make changes and develop in a more normal manner. He predicts that it will pull back more closely in another 10 years when we all have more time and that this is the time to catch up with individual lives on a different level. I sense this, too, and am struggling to adjust to the sense that I am really older. Adjust, yes; accept, I doubt it, anymore than I can truly accept his death. It is as unacceptable as death out of its time is unacceptable. His father, after his initial anger at "being cheated out of seeing him develop and use some of the things I'd been able to give him," is more sanguine than I, for he asks, "Who am I to fight the Higher Power? Apparently it was in His scheme of things that he should die rather than I at this time." His sister talks of his death as almost something animate. "I hate it. I don't understand it. It leaves me with a huge question to which the only answer I have is that fate meant it to be for whatever reason." His brother does not believe there was any reason. I wait to learn it as I have other things over time. I think another universal variable affecting our experience is the nature of our individual spiritual belief systems.

A final factor, in addition to the stage of familial development when the death occurs, that influences and individualizes the experience could be entitled the family rules or messages, or "The Way We See Things." The centrality of this really came home to me in our discussions, along with its intergenerational nature, which I had never seen before. This theme came through from everybody. My husband said: "We had encouraged their disengagement and underwritten their right and necessity of finding their own lives." His sister said: "You taught us to do our thing and lead our own lives." His brother said: "You not only told us to do our thing; you showed us. Mom, you traveled two thousand miles from your family to do your own thing, and you showed us that this was okay." I quietly remember that my husband was the first of his family to leave northern New York, my father the first to come East, and my mother the only child to leave Waterbury for New York City.

There may be a number of other essential elements that make such experiences both the same and different for families. I am left to wonder if our particular family is an essentially disengaged or enmeshed family, or a good bit of both, which I suppose most families are. You who read this are inevitably much better evaluators of that than we who live it. We are not and will never be the same since the death. I think we've grown; whoever said growth occurs without pain? I look at pictures of our family together and separate, laughing, formal, climbing trees, acting as "the littlest angel," and now in graduation garb and holding the next generation. I feel as I do so often the presence of the child who has gone ahead. Perhaps this may have some use. As I look at the picture of the sunlit grove with the two intertwined birches, where our family said our last good-bye to him, I think of the poem the young brother in the other family tucked in my pocket that late afternoon, which perhaps is the right ending for now.

> The Lord walketh
> by my side
> Therefore I am
> Not Alone.
> My Loved Ones lost
> Walketh with the Lord.
> Therefore I am
> Not alone.
> As I walk
> I question not.
> I only live and
> Learn a lot.
> Thanks be to
> My Lord God of Wisdom.

This was the finest of gifts to give. He believed. I also may. Someday.

Questions and Activities

1. "The Longest Day" describes various family members' reactions to the death of an individual who was killed—a son, a brother. Reactions varied from person to person. Have you seen (or would you expect to see) such variation of grief reactions in your own family? Would your family be apt to have a "dissynchrony of reactions" or utilize "discrepant coping styles"? Would you expect a death of a family member to draw individuals in your family closer together or force them apart? What was the outcome in the Landon family after Kevin's death?

2. If a member of your family has died, bring that memory to mind. (If you have not had such a loss, imagine yourself in that situation.) What was most painful as you came to terms with the death? Were there any positive outcomes? What was most helpful to your family as you dealt with your loss? What was least helpful?

3. Imagine that someone in your family has died. What roles would need

to be reassigned? How would the reassignment most likely take place? Who would be most apt to take on those new roles?

Glossary

Achieved Roles: Roles acquired by the efforts and skill of the individual.

Alliance: When two persons join together because of common interests, such as within a family system.

Ascribed Roles: Roles assigned on the basis of some characteristic over which the person has no control (for example, gender or age).

Bonadaptation: The outcome of a family crisis that results in enhancement of development in individual members and the enhancement of the family as a unit.

Boundaries: Abstract dividers experienced between or among systems and subsystems that determine participation in them. Distinct boundaries can serve to define, protect, and enhance the integrity of individuals, subsystems, and families. Boundaries can change over time and with situations. The extent of this change will be affected by characteristics of the boundaries (rigid, flexible, diffuse) in each family.

Closed Family Systems: Families that are self-contained and organized to preserve the status quo and resist change.

Coalition: When two people in a triad join to counteract the power of the third person in an effort to keep the system in balance. For example, if one parent is overpowering, the other parent may form a coalition with a child to balance that power.

Crisis: An event or problematic situation confronting an individual or family that results in disruption of normal living patterns and is characterized by high levels of tension. A crisis produces temporary disequilibrium in the family system, resulting in varying degrees of disorganization and incapacity.

Discrepant Coping Styles: Differences in the ways that family members cope with a loss.

Dissynchrony (or Asymmetry) of Grief: Differences between individuals in their grief experience related to a particular loss and the time needed to resolve the loss.

Enmeshed Families: Families in which family members have little individual autonomy or differentiation due to diffuse boundaries between individuals and between subsystems.

Expressive Tasks: Activities that have emotional and social functions and facilitate positive development and interaction among family members.

Family Adaptation: Ability of the family and each of its members to change their response to each other and to the outside world as situations demand.

Family Integration: Ability of family members to work together in order to assist in achieving both group and individual goals and in maintaining family equilibrium.

Family Involvement: Commitment that members make to the family and their participation in family life.

Family Myths: Beliefs that are accepted and adhered to by family members that defend against disturbances or changes in existing family relationships.

Formal Support Networks: Support networks consisting of organizations and professionals that provide needed services to individuals and families.

Genogram: A structured family history typically covering three generations, in which the therapist diagrams information about the family, their relationships, and important family events.

Homeostasis: A steady state of dynamic equilibrium or balance.

Incremental Grief: The additive factor of grief due to multiple related losses.

Individuate: To move toward more autonomous functioning as a part of normal individual development.

Informal Support Networks: Support networks composed of family members, friends, and neighbors that offer assistance in times of stress.

Instrumental Tasks: Activities that contribute to the effective day-to-day functioning of the family.

Maladaptation: The outcome of a family crisis that results in curtailment of individual and family development.

Open Family Systems: Families that are open to new information and exchange from the internal and external environment and are, thus, more susceptible to change.

Pile-up: The accumulation of normative and nonnormative stressors and intrafamily strains.

Postvention: Assistance offered to survivors following a death.

Regenerative Power: The family's ability to recover from a crisis.

Ritual: A specific behavior or activity that gives symbolic expression to certain feelings or thoughts of groups and of individuals.

Roles: Expected behavior of family members.

Role Strain: Strain that occurs when a family member assumes too many roles.

Rules: Shared norms and values that govern repetitious patterns of family functioning.

Secondary Grief: Grief associated with a secondary loss (such as change in a predeath relationship with another survivor).

Secondary Loss: A loss (such as change in a predeath relationship with another survivor) that is the consequence of a death (primary loss).

Social Support: Individuals, groups, or institutions that provide assistance of varying degrees and forms to help individuals and families cope with stressful situations.

Stressor Event: A life event or occurrence that impacts upon the family unit and produces, or has the opportunity to produce, change in the family system.

Subsystems: Basic structural units of the family system. These smaller units can be determined by variables such as relationship, generation, sex, age, or function.

Systems Theory: A framework for studying a group of related elements that interact as a whole entity.

Suggested Readings

Guest, J. (1976). *Ordinary people.* New York: Ballantine.

> This novel explores the complexities of family dynamics after the accidental drowning of the oldest son.

Nichols, M. (1984). *Family therapy: Concepts and methods.* New York: Gardner Press.

> This book provides a comprehensive introduction to the field of family therapy. The author examines and compares the concepts and methods associated with the major approaches to the field and uses case studies to illustrate their application.

Sherman, R., & Fredman, N. (1986). *Handbook of structured techniques in marriage and family therapy.* New York: Brunner/Mazel.

> The authors describe a wide variety of structured family therapy techniques.

Each technique is preceded by a brief introduction providing a rationale and theoretical basis for its use. Guidelines are given for selecting and evaluating the effectiveness of techniques.

Resources

National Funeral Directors Association
11121 West Oklahoma Avenue
P.O. Box 27641
Milwaukee, Wisconsin 53227
(414) 541-2500

References

Aldous, J. (1978). *Family careers: Developmental change in families.* New York: Wiley.

Arndt, H., & Gruber, M. (1977). Helping families cope with acute and anticipatory grief. In E. R. Prichard, J. Collard, B. A. Orcutt, A. H. Kutscher, I. Seeland, & N. Lefkowitz (Eds.), *Social work with the dying patient and the family* (pp. 38–48). New York: Columbia University Press.

Bolton, C., & Camp, D. (1987). Funeral rituals and the facilitation of grief work. *Omega, 17*(4), 343–352.

Bowen, M. (1976). Family reaction to death. In P. J. Guerin, Jr. (Ed.), *Family therapy: Theory and practice* (pp. 335–348). New York: Gardner Press.

Bowen, M. (1978). *Family therapy in clinical practice.* New York: Aronson.

Broderick, C., & Smith, J. (1979). The general systems approach to the family. In W. R. Burr, R. Hill, F. I. Nye, & I. L. Reiss (Eds.), *Contemporary theories about the family* (Vol. 2) (pp. 112–129). New York: Free Press.

Carter, E. A., & McGoldrick, M. (1980). *The family life cycle: A framework for family therapy.* New York: Gardner Press.

Charmaz, K. (1980). *The social reality of death: Death in contemporary America.* Menlo Park, CA: Addison-Wesley.

Christ, G. (1980). Dis-synchrony of coping among children with cancer, their families, and the treating staff. In A. E. Christ & K. Flomenhaft (Eds.), *Psychosocial family interventions in chronic pediatric illness* (pp. 85–96). New York: Plenum Press.

Conley, B. H. (1987). Funeral directors as first responders. In E. J. Dunne, J.L. McIntosh, & K. Dunne-Maxim (Eds.), *Suicide and its aftermath: Understanding and counseling the survivors* (pp. 171–181). New York: Norton.

Cook, J. A. (1983). A death in the family: Parental bereavement in the first year. *Suicide and Life-Threatening Behavior, 13*(1), 42–61.

Cook, J. A. (1984). Influences of gender on the problems of parents of fatally-ill children. *Journal of Psychosocial Oncology, 2,* 71–91.

Crosby, J. F., & Jose, N. L. (1983). Death: Family adjustment to loss. In C. R. Figey & H. I. McCubbin (Eds.), *Stress and the family: Coping with catastrophe* (Vol. 2) (pp. 76–89). New York: Brunner/Mazel.

Davies, B., Spinetta, J., Martinson, I., McClowry, S., Kulenkamp, E. (1986). Manifestations of levels of functioning in grieving families. *Journal of Family Issues, 7*(3), 297–314.

DeFrain, J. D., & Ernst, L. (1978). The psychological effects of Sudden Infant Death Syndrome on surviving family members. *The Journal of Family Practice, 6*(5), 985–989.

Derdeyn, A. P., & Waters, D. B. (1981). Unshared loss and marital conflict. *Journal of Marital and Family Therapy, 7,* 481–487.

Fish, W. C. (1986). Differences of grief intensity in bereaved parents. In T. A. Rando (Ed.), *Parental loss of a child* (pp. 415–429). Champaign, IL: Research Press.

Friedman, E. H. (1980). Systems and ceremonies: A family view of rites of passage. In E. A. Carter & M. McGoldrick (Eds.), *The family life cycle: A framework for family therapy* (pp. 429–460). New York: Gardner Press.

Fulton, R. (1987). Death, grief and the funeral. In M. A. Morgan (Ed.), *Bereavement: Helping the survivors* (pp. 123–126). London, Ontario: King's College.

Geyman, J. P. (1983). Problems in family practice: Dying and death of a family member. *The Journal of Family Practice, 17*(1), 125–134.

Glasser, P. H., & Glasser, L. N. (Eds.). (1970). *Families in crisis.* New York: Harper & Row.

Goldberg, S. B. (1973). Family tasks and reactions in the crisis of death. *Social Casework, 54,* 398–405.

Goldenberg, I., & Goldenberg, H. (1980). *Family therapy: An overview.* Monterey, CA: Brooks/Cole.

Gordon, A. K. (1986). The tattered cloak of immortality. In C. A. Corr & J. N. McNeil (Eds.), *Adolescence and death* (pp. 16–31). New York: Springer.

Grebstein, L. C. (1986). Family therapy after a child's death. In T. A. Rando (Ed.), *Parental loss of a child* (pp. 429–449). Champaign, IL: Research Press.

Hansen, D. A., & Johnson, V. A. (1979). Rethinking family stress theory: Definitional aspects. In W. R. Burr, R. Hill, F. I. Nye, & I. L. Reiss (Eds.), *Contemporary theories about the family* (Vol. 1) (pp. 582–603). New York: Free Press.

Herz, F. (1980). The impact of death and serious illness on the family life cycle. In E. A. Carter & M. McGoldrick (Eds.), *The family life cycle: A framework for family therapy* (pp. 223–240). New York: Gardner Press.

Hill, R. (1949). *Families under stress.* New York: Harper & Row.

Holmes, T. H., & Rahe, R. (1967). Social readjustment rating scale. *Journal of Psychosomatic Research, (11),* 213–218.

Kalnins, I., Churchill, M. P., & Terry, G. (1980). Concurrent stresses in families with a leukemic child. *Journal of Pediatric Psychology, 5*(1), 81–92.

Kaplan, D., Grobstein, R., & Smith, A. (1976). Predicting the impact of severe illness in families. *Health and Social Work, 1*(3), 71–82.

Kaplan, D., Smith, A., Grobstein, R., & Fischman, S. E. (1973). Family mediation of stress. *Social Work, 18*, 60–69.

Karpel, M. A., & Strauss, E. S. (1983). *Family evaluation.* New York: Gardner Press.

Kerner, J., Harvey, B., Lewiston, N. (1979). The impact of grief: A retrospective study of family function following loss of a child with cystic fibrosis. *Journal of Chronic Disabilities, 32*, 221–225.

Klass, D. (1986). Marriage and divorce among bereaved parents in a self-help group. *Omega, 17*(3), 237–249.

Koch, A. (1985). "If only it could be me": The families of pediatric cancer patients. *Family Relations, 34*(1), 63–70.

Krant, M. J., & Johnston, L. (1978). Family members' perceptions of communication in late stage cancer. *International Journal of Psychiatry in Medicine, 8*(2), 203–216.

Kupst, M. J., Tylke, L., Thomas, L., Mudd, M., Richardson, L., & Schulman, J. L. (1982). Strategies of intervention with families of pediatric leukemia patients: A longitudinal perspective. *Social Work in Health Care, 8*(2), 31–47.

Lazarus, R. (1966). *Psychological stress and coping process.* New York: McGraw-Hill.

Mages, N. L., & Mendelsohn, G. A. (1979). Effects of cancer on patients' lives: A personological approach. In G. C. Stone, F. Cohen, N. E. Alder, & Associates (Eds.), *Health Psychology—A handbook* (pp. 255–284). San Francisco: Jossey-Bass.

McCubbin, H. (1979). Integrating coping behavior in family stress theory. *Journal of Marriage and the Family, 41*(2), 237–244.

McCubbin, H., & Patterson, J. (1983a). The family stress process: The double ABCX model of adjustment and adaptation. In H. McCubbin, M. Sussman, & J. Patterson (Eds.), *Social stress and the family: Advances and developments in family stress theory and research* (pp. 7–37). New York: Haworth.

McCubbin, H. I., & Patterson, J. M. (1983b). Family transitions: Adaptation to stress. In H. I. McCubbin & C. R. Figley (Eds.), *Stress and the family: Coping with normative transitions* (Vol. 1) (pp. 5–25). New York: Brunner/Mazel.

McGoldrick, M., & Gerson, R. (1985). *Genograms in family assessment.* New York: Norton.

McGrory, A. (1978). *A well model approach to care of the dying client.* New York: McGraw-Hill.

Montgomery, R., Gonyea, J., & Hooyman, N. (1985). Caregiving and the experience of subjective and objective burden. *Family Relations, 34*(1), 19–26.

Nordlicht, S. (1982). The family of the cancer patient. *New York State Journal of Medicine, 82*, 1845–1846.

Nye, F., Bahr, H., Bahr, S., Carlson, J., Gecas, V., McLaughlin, S., & Slocum, W. (1976). *Role structure and analysis of the family.* Beverly Hills, CA: Sage.

Oltjenbruns, K. (1987). *Impact of loss on surviving relationships: The "incremental grief phenomenon."* Unpublished manuscript, Colorado State University, Fort Collins, Colorado.

Owen, G., Fulton, R., & Markusen, E. (1982). Death at a distance: A study of family survivors. *Omega 13*(3), 191–225.

Patterson, J. M., & McCubbin, H. I. (1983). Chronic illness: Family stress and coping. In C. R. Figley & H. I. McCubbin (Eds.), *Stress and the family. Coping with catastrophe* (Vol. 2) (pp. 21–36). New York: Brunner/Mazel.

Pattison, E. M. (1977). The family matrix of dying and death. In E. M. Pattison (Ed.), *The experience of dying* (pp. 28–42). Englewood Cliffs, NJ: Prentice-Hall.

Pearlin, I., & Schooler, C. (1978). The structure of coping. *Journal of School Health and Behavior, 19*(1), 2–21.

Pratt, C., Schmal, V., Wright, S., & Cleland, M. (1985). Burden and coping strategies of caregivers to Alzheimer's patients. *Family Relations, 34*(1), 27–33.

Purisman, R., & Maoz, B. (1977). Adjustment and war bereavement. *British Journal of Medical Psychology, 50,* 1–9.

Rando, T. A. (1984). *Grief, dying, and death: Clinical interventions for caregivers.* Champaign, IL: Research Press.

Rando, T. A. (1985). Creating therapeutic rituals in the psychotherapy of the bereaved. *Psychotherapy, 22*(2), 236–240.

Rolland, J. S. (1987). Chronic illness and the life cycle: A conceptual framework. *Family Process, 26*(20), 203–221.

Schatz, B. D. (1986). Grief of mothers. In T. A. Rando (Ed.), *Parental loss of a child* (pp. 303–314). Champaign, IL: Research Press.

Schilling, R. F., Gilchrist, L., & Schinke, S. P. (1985). Coping and social support in families of developmentally disabled children. *Family Relations, 33*(1), 47–54.

Shneidman, E. S. (1971). Prevention, intervention, and postvention of suicide. *Annals of Internal Medicine, 75,* 453–458.

Sieburg, E. (1985). *Family communication: An integrated systems approach.* New York: Gardner Press.

Silverman, P., & Englander, S. (1975). The widow's view of her dependent children. *Omega, 6*(1), 3–19.

Stephenson, J. S. (1985). *Death, grief, and mourning: Individual and social realities.* New York: Free Press.

Stinnett, N., Knorr, B., DeFrain, J., & Rowe, G. (1981). How strong families cope with crisis. *Family Perspective, 15*(4), 159–166.

Unger, D. G., & Powell, D. R. (1980). Supporting families under stress: The role of social supports. *Family Relations, 29* (4), 566–574.

van der Hart, O. (1983). *Rituals in psychotherapy: Transition and continuity.* New York: Irvington.

Venters, M. (1981). Familial coping with chronic and severe childhood illness: The case of cystic fibrosis. *Social Science & Medicine, 15,* 289–297.

Vess, J. S., Moreland, J. R., & Schwebel, A. I. (1985a). An empirical assessment of the effects of cancer on family role functioning. *Journal of Psychosocial Oncology, 3*(1), 1–17.

the younger children in her study (ages 3 to 5) believed that dead people were capable of some activity, although they regarded dead people as "less alive" than living people. For example, one child in Nagy's study described a dead person as being able to eat and drink but not being able to move.

Some children believe that the person who is dead is in a state similar to sleep and can be awakened or is "broken" and can be fixed by an adult. Recall that preoperational thinkers are animistic in their thought patterns and often attribute life to inanimate objects. The belief that individuals are able to function, at least in an altered state, is possibly a variation of the child's normal animistic thought.

Finality. This component refers to the permanence of the state of death (that dead people do not return to life). Koocher (1974) studied 75 children between the ages of 6 and 15 years. Based on performance of particular reasoning tasks, he divided them into three groups: preoperational, concrete, and formal operational thinkers. He found that eight children in his sample responded to the question "How do you make dead things come back to life?" by identifying specific strategies to accomplish that task. One child, for example, explained, "Help them, give them hot food, and keep them healthy so it won't happen again" (p. 408). All of the children who answered the question as if you could bring dead persons back to life were preoperational thinkers between ages 6.0 and 7.1 years.

Children's cartoons and fairy tales often reinforce the preoperational child's misconceptions regarding the finality of death. Although they may be seriously maimed, mangled, and pulverized, many cartoon characters miraculously survive what would certainly be fatal if experienced by a "real" human. Snow White, although seemingly dead, was revived by Prince Charming's kiss.

Universality. Universality is the understanding that all human beings will someday die. White, Elsom, and Prawat (1978) used a sample of 170 children from kindergarten through fourth grade to study children's conceptions of death. After hearing a story about a character named Mrs. Wilson who dies at the end, each child was asked questions such as "Do you think that everybody will die someday?" (p. 308). Approximately 62 percent of the preoperational children ages 2 to 7 answered the question incorrectly by indicating that some people will not die.

Causality. Causality refers to those factors that can precipitate death (such as cancer, heart attack, or car accident). This component was a central focus of Koocher's (1974) interactions with 75 children, ages 6 to 15 years. When asked "What makes things die?"(p. 406), the subsample of preoperational thinkers in the study typically gave very specific responses that seemed to be very closely related to their own experiences and, therefore, Koocher concluded, reflected a strong sense of egocentrism, which is common in the preoperational period. Responses included: "They eat poison and stuff; pills, you'd better wait till your mom gives them to you." "Yes, you can die if you swallow a dirty bug" (p. 407).

Personification.   This is the belief that death is a concrete entity, such as a person or object. Nagy (1948), who studied Hungarian children, did not divide her sample into Piagetian stages, but rather divided her groups by ages. Children in her "Stage Two" group (ages 5 through 8) typically regarded death as a skeleton man or a monster and thought that persons might be able to escape death if they could run fast enough. The personification of death is one component that seems to be culture-bound. Replication studies of Nagy's work performed in this country have not found personification of death among American children (Childers & Wimmer, 1971; Gartley & Bernasconi, 1967; Melear, 1973). The cultural milieu has an effect on formation of the concept of death. Art and literature that were a part of the Hungarian cultural experience often depicted death as personified; current American art and literature do not.

Young Children's Understanding of the Concept of Illness

Children's understanding of illness also develops gradually. Bibace and Walsh (1979) reported that preoperational thinkers' explanations regarding the nature of sickness can be categorized as either phenomenism or contagion. A "phenomenistic" response is one that defines illness in terms of a single specific symptom, sensation, or object that the child has associated with the illness. One child in Bibace and Walsh's preoperational group explained, "A heart attack is from the sun" (p. 290).

Preoperational children also explained illness in terms of "contagion." When asked how an illness is caused, the children reflected close proximity as the causal link. A child who was asked how people catch colds responded, "Other kids." When probed further and queried, "How do other kids give you a cold," the child answered, "You catch it, that's all" (p. 290). These categories of responses, phenomenism and contagion, reflect normal characteristics of preoperational thought. Bibace and Walsh (1979) explain:

> The child is swayed by the immediacy of some aspects of perceptual experience. The primary characteristics of this stage include: concreteness or preoc-

cupation with external perceptual events; irreversibility, or the inability to con-
strue processes in reverse; egocentrism, or viewing the world from one's own
perspective, centering or focusing on a single aspect or part of experience to the
exclusion of the whole; and transductive reasoning, or thinking that proceeds
from one particular to another rather than from particular to general or vice
versa. (p. 290)

Redpath and Rogers (1984) asked 30 preschoolers a number of questions related to sickness, hospitals, medical personnel, and operations.
They found that these preoperational children usually described illness in
terms of restriction of activities rather than a change in their bodies. When
asked how a person gets sick, they answered, "cause you do" or confused
a cause with a symptom such as throwing up. They seemed unsure as to
why children would go to a hospital and once again confused cause and
effect by indicating "people got sick or hurt in a hospital."

Young children do not understand that health and illness are related
concepts. Natapoff (1982) reminds us that preoperational children are
unable to transform states for they are unable to reverse their thought processes. Therefore, young children do not perceive illness as related to
either a previous or future state of health. Furthermore, these children do
not understand the global aspects of health but rather focus on specific,
concrete components such as eating or drinking certain foods (such as
carrots, peas, and milk) that they felt were related to health.

Psychosocial Development

Toddlerhood: Autonomy versus Shame and Doubt

Erikson (1963) explains that infants strive to develop a sense of trust rather
than mistrust. Infants need to feel that they are safe in their physical and
social environment. Later as they become toddlers, they struggle to
become independent and to gain a sense of control over their environment. This is reflected in the crisis of autonomy versus shame and doubt.
Autonomy implies independence, while *shame* denotes a sense of being
bad or worthless, and *doubt* describes a belief that one is incapable of
mastering skills or making appropriate choices. A child who is encouraged
to learn basic self-care skills (to feed or dress himself, for example) in a
positive and supportive environment is likely to develop a sense of autonomy. On the other hand, a child who is repeatedly told in a stern voice
"Hurry up!", "You're making a mess!" or "You can't do anything right!" is
likely to develop a sense of shame and doubt. The same holds true for a
child who is rarely allowed to complete a task for himself or herself, for

there is an implication, even if it is not verbalized, that the child is incapable of doing it correctly.

In order to master a sense of autonomy, children must feel that they have a sense of control over their world. Control allows a sense of security, providing comfort in a world that might otherwise seem overwhelming and even frightening. A strong desire for control is frequently reflected in the toddler's use of language. "No!" and "Me do it!" are often repeated words and are certainly indicative of the child's desire, and even insistence, that he or she intends to do something in his or her own way and own time. Freedom of choice—what to eat, what to wear, what to play—can also lead to a sense of control. One hospital lab technician would allow her young patients some control over the procedure of drawing blood by playfully telling them, "You pick it (referring to the finger) and I'll stick it."

Security is derived from knowing what to expect from one's environment. A routine that helps structure the day is helpful to the young child by allowing a sense of control through knowing what to expect next. Rituals also promote a sense of control. In general terms, a *childhood ritual* is a stereotyped behavior performed to order one's environment. In some cases, rituals of childhood must be followed precisely or the child becomes frightened, hurt, or angry. One of the authors, as a young child, was convinced that a terrible fate would befall individual family members if she did not say, each and every night, "Good night; sleep well; sweet dreams; see you in the morning; don't let the bed bugs bite." This ritual was a time-consuming one in that it needed to be repeated for each individual in the family—mother, father, older brother, two younger sisters, and younger brother. (It was obviously worth the effort—each of these persons is alive and well today!) Security objects can also offer much comfort to many young children. Certain blankets, dolls, and items of clothing have all been endowed by individual children with the power to dry tears, quiet sobs, and soothe them to sleep.

Circumstances that are often related to the dying process may put toddlers "at risk" for developing a negative resolution to the crisis of autonomy versus shame and doubt and for developing a sense that they have no control over their environment. Toddlers who are dying may simply have limited physical capacities as compared to healthy children. These limitations, such as diminished stamina, weakness in certain parts of their bodies, and limited range of motion, can have an impact on the ease with which toddlers can master skills that allow them to feel autonomous.

Another factor that puts dying toddlers at risk in this stage is the tendency of many parents and medical personnel to show their concern for these children by being overprotective in many situations. Overprotection can deprive these toddlers of opportunities to explore their environment in whatever way they can and to do things for themselves. This, in turn, contributes to the potential development of feelings of self-doubt rather than confidence.

Another factor that may have an effect on the outcome of this developmental crisis is related to time. Individuals giving care to a dying toddler may feel very pressed for time. They are likely to have numerous other commitments and responsibilities needing their attention. Often they are overwhelmed by the sheer magnitude of the task of caring for a dying child. These caregivers, then, may be physically and emotionally exhausted. As a result, they look for shortcuts in the care of their sick children. Shortcuts include the caregivers' performing tasks or making choices rather than allowing the toddlers themselves to do so. For example, adults who are striving to save time often take responsibility for feeding the children rather than allowing them to feed themselves.

It is important that persons giving care to dying toddlers create an environment that allows for the development of a sense of autonomy rather than shame and doubt. Examples of strategies for developing such an environment are included here:

1. Provide opportunities to practice and master those skills that are age appropriate. For example, allow dying toddlers to walk unaided or feed themselves, as best they can, even if it takes longer.
2. Allow freedom of choice. This can be done by providing them with a variety of acceptable options. For example, allow dying children to select the toys they would like to take to the hospital or the pajamas that they would like to wear to bed.
3. Help the toddlers succeed at the tasks they do undertake. For example, if they wish to feed themselves, ensure that eating utensils are adapted, if necessary, so that they can be manipulated by the toddlers.
4. Try to maintain as many familiar routines as possible within the hospital environment.
5. If a routine has to be changed, explain the reasons why and what might be expected (for example, "You won't get to watch Sesame Street today because the nurse is going to give you a shot to make you sleep.").

Preschool Years: Initiative versus Guilt

Preschoolers are extremely curious creatures. They ask what seem to adults to be a never-ending series of "Why?" questions. They vigorously explore their environment and seek answers through experimentation.

These characteristics and activities set the stage for the psychosocial crisis of the preschooler as described by Erikson (1963) as *initiative versus guilt*. The positive resolution, initiative, involves defining a task and using one's personal resources to accomplish it. This challenge takes place at the time when the child is beginning to develop a conscience. Caregivers must help children develop an understanding of right and wrong without creating an unduly heavy burden of guilt for the shortcomings they often experience as they curiously explore the world around them.

Dying preschoolers, because of their severe illnesses, may be at increased risk for developing a sense of guilt rather than a feeling of initiative. Recall that preschoolers are very involved in many imaginative and creative processes. Additionally, they do not fully understand the world around them because of lack of experience and immature intellectual capacities. As a result of these factors, they cannot always separate fantasy from reality. Preschoolers, then, often feel guilty for events that are imagined or that are distorted variations of reality. Dying children may erroneously conclude that they are being punished for some wrongdoing such as fighting with siblings or not putting toys away. As a result, they may feel very guilty.

In order to develop a sense of initiative, children need to explore their environment, to become involved in a variety of creative experiences, and to have their curiosity satisfied. These tasks may be difficult due to the physical limitations and also environmental restrictions resulting from preschoolers' illnesses. There are a number of strategies that facilitate dying preschoolers' development of a sense of initiative rather than guilt. Examples are:

1. Listen to and observe carefully what these children are communicating regarding their feelings about their illnesses. Many will communicate in direct conversation; others will communicate indirectly through puppets or dolls, paintings, or telling stories about "other" children.

2. Reassure dying preschoolers that they did not cause their illnesses, that they are not being punished, and that all that can be done to help them is being done. This should be done in concrete terminology with as many specific examples as possible.

3. Provide an environment that is open to the children's sense of curiosity (for example, answer questions that they have about their own illnesses or other subjects in terminology they can understand; encourage them to tour the medical facilities to which they are about to be admitted).

Additional Needs of Dying Children

Several needs of dying young children have been discussed as they relate to cognitive and psychosocial development. Additional needs—trust, minimal separation, normalization—will now be examined and strategies for helping meet those needs will be suggested.

Trust

Many, if not most, terminally ill children seem to know that they are dying (Wass, 1984; Zeligs, 1974). This insight develops even if they are not directly told the truth about the expected outcome of their illness. Children may gain an understanding that they are seriously ill through a variety of cues in their environment. They may be hospitalized with little explanation as to what is wrong with them and no reference to when they will get better. Lack of such information, in this situation, may be quite different from other experiences with illness and may suggest to children that something is seriously wrong or else there would be comforting messages to the contrary. Due to others' tears, withdrawal patterns, hushed voices, or overheard comments, children may suspect that death is approaching. In addition, children may know they are dying by being sensitive to their own symptoms and changes in body functions (Bluebond-Langer, 1978).

Children may share that they are aware of the seriousness of their situation in a variety of ways. For example, Elisabeth Kübler-Ross describes a picture drawn by a young boy who had not been told directly of his impending death. In the drawing, he holds up a stop sign in an attempt to halt the forward movement of a big tank (death) that is approaching. Other children may indicate their awareness by statements such as "I am not going to get old" or "Christmas is going to come without me." Some children directly ask, "Am I going to die?"

Regardless of how children indicate awareness of their approaching death or ask for confirmation of their suspicions, others should give honest answers. Providing accurate information creates an environment of trust. Information about the illness, treatments, new environments, and other changes should be shared in language that the child can understand. Honesty is an important factor because dishonesty can seriously undermine the foundation of trust in a relationship between the child and parents or medical personnel. One of the authors still clearly recalls an incident that occurred many years ago during hospitalization for a tonsillectomy. The operation took place a couple of weeks prior to Easter; while the anesthesiologist put the ether mask on, he said, "Count to ten backwards and you will see the Easter bunny." She can still recall the anger at waking up without seeing the Easter bunny but rather experiencing a very sore throat. More importantly, she can remember the distrust that was a direct outcome of that lie.

Malice is not the motivation for withholding information from dying children or providing misinformation. Rather, there is the hope that these children will somehow be spared further distress. Unfortunately, this is usually not the case. As trust is undermined, children become increasingly fearful and feel a sense of isolation (Mrgudic, 1985; Wheeler & Lange, 1985). Additionally, there is the risk that a child will be told of the illness by someone outside of the family or medical staff—someone who assumed the child already knew about his or her serious illness. Chesler, Paris, and Barbarin (1986) share the following anecdote:

> Gradually she knew something was wrong even though we didn't tell her much. A teacher at school one day told the class our daughter had cancer—and she was sitting right there. That was the first she had heard of it. (p. 512)

There is evidence that children's fears magnify behaviors such as refusing treatment, agitated crying, and hostile outbursts, particularly in situations which they regard to be highly stressful (Broome, 1986). Since a great deal of a dying child's existence is stressful—ongoing medical exams, various treatment regimens, interactions with strangers—it is crucial that we find ways in which to minimize their fears. One of our best tools is honest communication, which builds a foundation of trust.

Minimal Separation

One of the primary fears of young children is that of separation (Rait & Holland, 1986). Although fear of separation is exhibited in many situations, it is heightened in the hospital setting (Earnshaw-Smith, 1981). Bowlby (1980) described the behavior of hospitalized children and determined that they pass through three stages related to the separation from their primary caregiver. Those stages include the following:

1. *Protest* marks the initial stage and is characterized by an urgent effort to recover his lost caregiver. The child "will often cry loudly, shake his cot, throw himself about, and look eagerly towards any sight or sound which might prove to be his missing mother" (p. 9).
2. *Despair* characterizes the second stage as the child's hope for his caregiver's return diminishes. "Ultimately the restless noisy demands cease: he becomes apathetic and withdrawn, a despair broken only

perhaps by an intermittent and monotonous wail. He is in a state of unutterable misery" (p. 9).

3. *Detachment* is the final stage and is characterized by an absence of attachment behavior (such as physically withdrawing, refusing to be held or cuddled) when the child is reunited with the caregiver.

As society becomes increasingly aware of the need to minimize a dying child's separation from loved ones, particularly parents, we have seen the introduction of a variety of innovations. For example, parents are allowed to "room-in" with their children. In some instances, parents actually share the same room; in others, parents stay in another room in the hospital set aside for that purpose. Communities sometimes provide temporary, low-cost housing for out-of-town families seeking medical care. An example of these types of facilities are the Ronald McDonald houses in a number of cities across the country, supported by the McDonald Corporation and local fund-raising drives.

Opportunities for parents and/or siblings to remain close provide benefit both to the terminally ill children and to their families. Children's separation anxiety and parents' ensuing guilt may both be minimized. Additionally, staying in living quarters that are in close proximity to the child reduces travel time and conserves physical energy.

In an increasing number of instances, children die either at home or in a hospice facility rather than in a hospital. Although there are many reasons for this occurrence, one of the primary reasons is to minimize the separation of dying children from their families.

Normalization

There are many changes in the lives of dying children that cannot be avoided and that often cause stress. It is helpful, therefore, to strive for normalization in other facets of life (Mrgudic, 1985). *Normalization* involves a consistency in interactions, activities, and routines that provides a sense of predictability, security, and comfort.

Children find comfort in continuing activities that they had enjoyed previously. These may include playing with siblings, going to preschool, and listening to bedtime stories. Involvement in these activities provides a sense of security and also underscores the need to focus on the fact that a dying child is also a living child.

Some hospitals try to normalize some of the activities related to meal times, since sharing food in a comfortable atmosphere is a focus of many family interactions. For example, one child-life program encourages all

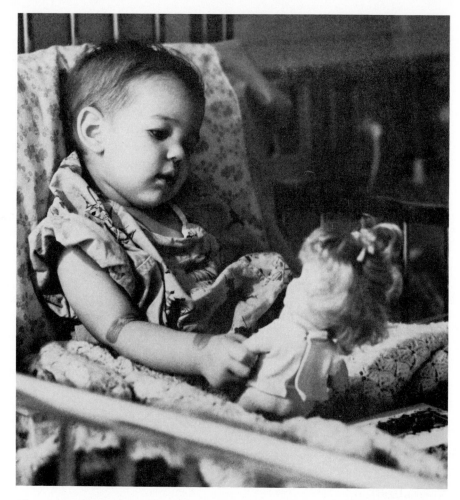

Photo 4.1 *Toys from home provide the hospitalized child with much comfort.*

family members to eat together in the playroom. Staff members often put sheets on the tables to serve as tablecloths and create various centerpieces to add color. Sometimes they even engage children in a cooking activity, such as preparing a dessert, so that they can share a "normal activity" together.

Because parents normally discipline their children, they should continue to provide appropriate guidelines and limits for those who are dying. Consistency in expectations and beliefs regarding right and wrong allows a child more easily to predict a parent's reaction and, as a result, engenders a sense of trust and control (Maccoby, 1980). Suddenly allowing a child to misbehave (simply because he or she is very ill) can endanger the safety of the child or others, damage property, and cause conflict and much more. Children who repeatedly disobey even after clear guidelines are given may be trying to communicate some symbolic message to others (Bigner, 1985). Parents and other caregivers should attempt to determine a child's motivation for misbehaving in order to more effectively deal with the underlying concerns. For example, a young boy who would repeatedly misbehave in the hospital playroom by throwing toys or being aggressive to other children finally told a staff member, "I want somebody to pay attention to me!—My parents never do!"

Parents of Dying Children

Stressors on Parents

Parents of dying children experience many psychological and physical stresses during the period of illness. Demands related to providing care to the sick child and demands related to a job often claim the majority of each day. Parents have less time to spend with their other children, who then may become hurt or angry and, as a result, add to the stress already being experienced. Diminished time to spend with one's spouse often weakens a familiar support system which, in turn, exacerbates feelings of distress. Activities that once provided pleasure and relaxation are forgone in order to deal with the additional time constraints, such as traveling to and from the hospital and/or providing care.

Physical exhaustion is common as parents struggle to perform multiple roles, including parent of sick child, parent of healthy child(ren), spouse, worker, and housekeeper, among others. Although it is difficult, if not impossible, to surrender certain roles, parents do welcome short-term respite from particular tasks. It can be particularly helpful for others to make specific offers of assistance (to cook a meal, clean house, babysit other children, or shop for groceries). Many parents note that they do prefer suggestions of specific ways to help in contrast to a more open-ended offer "to do anything I can—just let me know." This phraseology puts the burden on the parents to determine what needs to be done in relation to the other person's available resources, and, as a result, such offers of help often go unheeded.

Costs of medical treatments not covered by insurance add a great deal of stress to many families. Parents may have to work during a period when they want to spend increasing amounts of time with the child who is dying.

They feel torn between their commitments and experience feelings of guilt coupled with intense frustration. Medical bills may escalate to a point where families feel their impact for years to come.

Parents' Grief after Death of a Child

Death of one's own child is a catastrophic loss that contradicts the natural order of life (Sanders, 1979). Additionally, the child's death breaks one of the strongest bonds—that of parent and child. Parents may question their fundamental adequacy as adults, because they are so strongly socialized to protect their offspring. For years after the death, many parents still experience the pain of their loss and strive to deal with an "empty space" that results from the death (McClowry, Davies, May, Kulenkamp, & Martinson, 1987).

Valeriote and Fine (1987) explain that "when a child dies, the surviving family is at risk of system disorganization and dysfunction; a structural void is created which requires homeostatic adjustments. How the family makes this homeostatic adjustment is determined by: (1) the structure prior to the child's death (i.e., the role of the dead child . . .); (2) the family's ability to mourn; (3) the permeability of the boundary around the family. . ." (p. 214). Long-term effective coping is related to level of family support, quality of the parents' marital relationship, good coping of other family members, lack of additional concurrent stresses, and open communication among family members (Kupst & Schulman, 1988).

Bereaved parents often experience intense feelings of guilt (Edelstein, 1984; Friedman, 1974). Miles and Demi (1984) discuss a model describing five types of guilt observed in their clinical patients:

1. *Death causation guilt* involves the belief that the child's death was somehow caused by the parent. Causality may be linked, in the parent's mind, to either acts of *omission* such as failure to notice early symptoms of the illness or acts of *commission*, such as giving the child permission to cross the street by himself or herself. These acts may or may not have actually contributed to the death.

2. *Cultural role guilt* is the sense that the parent has failed in his or her prescribed role. The role of parent is based on expectations that he or she will love and protect the child at all times. When a child dies, there are feelings of guilt that the child was not protected. Parents might feel guilty when they recall a past incident when they became angry at their son or daughter.

3. *Moral guilt* is the feeling that the child's death was punishment or retribution for some transgression of the parent. Moral guilt may be

tied to experiences such as poor church attendance or dishonesty in business transactions.

4. *Survivor guilt* is the sense that death of one's child is a violation of the natural order of life. Parents are expected to die before their children; when this is not the case, they experience guilt.

5. *Recovery guilt* often occurs as parents begin to resolve their grief and once more begin to enjoy life. They feel guilty that, by not continuing to grieve, they are violating a societal standard and failing to care for their deceased child.

Miles and Demi (1984) performed a pilot study with 28 parents to determine the adequacy of their model. Of the parents studied, 57 percent identified guilt as their most distressing feeling following the death of their children. Fifty-four percent of the sample reported experiencing death causation guilt and/or cultural role guilt. An unexpected finding was six parents (21 percent) reporting a type of guilt related to their belief that they were not grieving appropriately. One parent, for example, said "I couldn't live up to society's expectations of me as a bereaved parent" (p. 304).

Rando (1983) investigated a variety of factors related to the outcome of grief in parents whose children had died from cancer. Her sample was comprised of 54 parents (27 married couples) whose children had died from 2 months to 3 years previously. Each parent was given a subsequent adjustment score that was analyzed in relationship to a variety of factors, including length of illness, length of time since death, parents' anticipatory grief, parental participation during child's hospitalizations, parental evaluation of the child's treatment, and previous loss experience. Factors that were related to a more positive level of subsequent adjustment included a moderately long length of illness (6 to 18 months), the experience of anticipatory grief, a moderate level of participation in the child's care, and few previous losses.

Both mothers and fathers experience acute grief after the death of a child. Cook (1983) found that both sexes were overwhelmed by the intensity of their feelings. Parents do, however, report somewhat different facets of grief. The fathers in Cook's study explained the loss as "something missing." One father remarked, "There's only three of us. It seems like the biggest problem is having the feeling that the family isn't complete any more. It seems like a void. There isn't enough activity" (p. 48). In contrast, mothers explained the loss in more personal terms and frequently linked the loss to a sense of loneliness, which was rarely described by fathers. Cook interpreted these differences in reaction to the type of interaction each parent had previously with the child. Mothers typically described a closer relationship with the child, one that was central to the mother's existence. During their daily routine, they were constantly reminded that the child was no longer a part of their lives. Tasks such as setting one less place at the table for dinner elicited painful memories and evoked a continuing sense of loss.

The men in Cook's (1983) study shared more often than did the women the feeling that they were responsible for managing or controlling other family members' grief. They felt responsible for "lifting the family's spirits" (p. 51), particularly their wives'. Closely related was the feeling the men had that they should grieve in private. Keeping their grief private often acted as a barrier to open communication with their wives.

Oftentimes men exhibit their grief through angry outbursts and irritability, frantic activity, and additional investment in work. These behaviors are sometimes used as avoidance techniques in order to protect the bereaved father from thinking about the loss. There is a point at which, however, even these men who may have inhibited their grief at the outset must face it.

Schatz (1986) explains the extreme difficulty that socialization into the traditional male role creates after the death of a child:

1. A man is socialized to be strong and to control his emotions, *yet* successful grief work depends on venting one's emotions.
2. A man is taught to protect his family and possessions; *however,* he was unable to protect his child from death.
3. A man is expected to be the problem solver—the person who can fix what is broken—*but* death cannot be avoided; it cannot be fixed.
4. A man is socialized to be the family provider, *but* his grief impairs his on-the-job functioning.
5. A man is taught to be self-sufficient, *yet* he needs others to support him during his grief.
6. A man is taught that if he works hard and acts responsibly he can control his own destiny; *however,* his life and that of his family seem to be out of control due to the death.

As our socialization practices change, men are likely to look at their roles differently. They need to understand that they have a right to grieve. Although they can be supportive to their families, they need to feel comfortable accepting support from others as well. Sometimes social support is not as readily available for men as it is for women, since many people think that men are not grieving and, therefore, do not offer the needed support.

Children as Grievers

Some people may question whether young children grieve as the result of experiencing a significant loss. It is certain that young children do grieve, although they may grieve in a somewhat different manner as compared to adults. This section identifies many of the common manifestations of children's grief as well as factors that may intensify the grief response. An expanded discussion of children's bereavement after the death of a parent or the death of a sibling is included in Chapter 5.

Elizur and Kaffman (1983) identified a variety of clinical bereavement symptoms in a sample of 25 Israeli children (ages 2 to 10 years at the time of death) whose fathers died in the October War of 1973. These symptoms included "regressive overdependent behavior, manifold fears, separation anxiety, night sleep disorders, discipline problems, restlessness, learning difficulties, eating disorders, enuresis (bedwetting), aggressive or inhibited behavior, and social withdrawal" (p. 668). Other common manifestations of children's grief include sadness, despair, lowered school grades, depression, death fantasies, somatic complaints, guilt due to magical thinking, fear of abandonment, rejection, temper tantrums, acting out behavior, explosive emotions, and feelings of helplessness (Davies, 1987; Greenberg, 1975; McCown, 1988; Roberts, 1981; Vipperman & Rager, 1980; Wolfelt, 1983).

Similar to grief reactions among adults, those of children are highly variable. Elizur and Kaffman (1983) found that bereavement symptoms were more intense in children who had a history of poor impulse control, a tendency to handle frustration with outbursts of rage, a pattern of withdrawal in other relationships, and higher levels of adjustment difficulties. They also discovered increased pathology in situations where there had been a great deal of family conflict or periods of long-term separation from the father prior to the death. Mothers' mourning patterns were related to their children's in that "where mothers exhibited over-restraint, withholding of emotional expression, and inability to share with the child expressions of grief and memories of the deceased, the children showed signs of considerable emotional distress during the first months" (p. 673). The latter finding confirms our understanding that involvement in a conspiracy of silence minimizes the opportunity to share feelings, magnifies fears, creates misunderstandings and confusion, and contributes to a sense of loneliness (Hardgrove & Warrick, 1974).

Although many adults would like to spare children from the knowledge that a loved one has died and from the subsequent grief, this is simply not possible, nor should it be attempted. Children need the opportunity to say good-bye, to share their feelings, to vent their emotions. Children need the same opportunities to accomplish their grief work as do adults. Adults, then, should be prepared to provide support to children who have experienced a loss. In those instances where the parents do not communicate openly with their children, it can be helpful to involve them in family counseling so that the therapist can model supportive ways to talk to children about death and grief (Warmbrod, 1986). Children may interpret a lack of acknowledgment of either the death or their feelings of grief as insensitivity, meanness, or lack of caring (Furman, 1978).

Many adults question whether children should be permitted to attend a funeral. It is often helpful to give the children themselves the choice as to whether they would like to attend. When the choice is their own, children are less likely to feel angry at someone else for having made a "wrong" decision. Prior to making a decision, children need information regarding the physical, social, and emotional environment in which the funeral will take place (Berlinsky & Biller, 1982). If children do choose to attend the funeral, they should be allowed the option of not participating in certain aspects of the ritual that might cause them discomfort (such as viewing an open casket). Advantages of attending the funeral include the opportunity to confirm the fact that the death has occurred, to observe that others share their grief, and to feel the support that is offered.

Giving children the choice to attend the funeral is not always possible or reasonable. Based on their usual parenting styles, some parents are simply not likely to provide the option. In other instances, someone else in the family may have such strong feelings against the child's going that it is not wise to give the choice. If the child does not attend the funeral, it is often helpful to encourage participation in some other ritual in order to formally say good-bye.

Although children's experience of bereavement is painful and ongoing, grief does not seem to be as all-consuming as it is for adults. Children can be very sad one minute, but playful and happy the next. Because young children have comparatively short attention spans and are quite easily distracted, adults frequently perceive that children have resolved their grief much sooner than actually is the case (Brenner, 1984; Salladay & Royal, 1981). This misconception that children's grief work is completed may cause premature withdrawal of support. As with adults, grief frequently lasts for an extended period of time, and concern and comfort are needed throughout. Another issue to consider is the fact that engaging in play may be the child's way of coming to terms with the loss. Play activities can provide a much needed catharsis of emotions or allow mastery of a particular concept. In other instances, a child's play may serve a function similar to an adult's preoccupation with work.

Death of a loved one has a different impact on children than on adults. Differential outcomes are related to a variety of factors, including cognitive understanding of the death and qualitatively different relationships between the deceased and adult survivors as compared to child survivors. In order to better understand the death from the child's perspective, we must provide opportunities for children to share their thoughts and feelings. Without this insight, we may not give the appropriate support. Pohlman (1984) stresses that adults should "listen carefully to their questions and comments, listening for emotional needs; not only the word content" (p. 124).

Children need accurate information about the death itself and the events that follow (the funeral service, burial, cremation). If children have misconceptions about these events, it is crucial that accurate information be given in concrete and specific terminology. For example, it is helpful to reassure children that the person who has died is not hungry or cold in the casket, does not wish to "get out" of the casket, and so forth (Furman, 1978). If we are honest with young children, they will still not fully understand the meaning of death, but they will learn that it is acceptable to discuss the death. Opportunities to talk can provide a great deal of comfort. Additionally, accurate information can help to alleviate young children's fears, build a sense of trust in others, and serve as the foundation for deeper understanding later on in the child's life, as maturation progresses (Berg, 1978).

Because young children think in concrete terms, rather than in the abstract, and because they tend to understand things in the literal sense, adults must be careful about how they explain circumstances surrounding a death. For example, if children are told that the deceased is "sleeping," they may assume that he or she will reawaken and come back to life. This is particularly likely for children under age 6, because they do not understand the permanence of death. Adults who tell children that the deceased has "gone on a long trip" may expect to hear responses such as "When is grandpa coming back? Will he bring me a present?"

We need not wait until the death of a loved one to teach children about death and grief. The ongoing rhythms of life and death in nature can serve as an impetus for discussion. The loss of a pet frequently triggers a grief response. Children who are allowed to grieve openly and to talk about their feelings can learn much from the experience.

Following the death of a loved one, young children often fear that others close to them will also die or that they themselves will also die (Havener & Phillips, 1975; Joseph, 1974). Children need to be reassured that death is the result of a very serious illness or accident and that others are not likely to die. Many children carry a heavy burden of guilt following the death of another. Because they have a difficult time separating fantasy from reality, children may assume they caused the death to occur. One 3½-year-old child was in anguish over his older brother's death. The child had told his sibling to "Go away! Get out of here!" when the older brother was teasing him. The next day, the older boy was killed when he fell off the roof of the family's garage. Fortunately, a neighbor finally asked the child why he repeatedly cried, "I am so bad! I wished that he would go away, but I didn't really mean it" during the weeks that followed. His response indicated that he thought he had killed his brother because he had been mad earlier. If the neighbor had not asked the boy to explain how he felt about his brother's death and why he felt he was "so bad," the child might not have been reassured that he was in no way responsible.

As the years pass after the death of a loved one and as children grow and mature in their thinking and emotional processes, they can be faced, once again, with resolving grief-related issues. For example, a 4-year-old girl whose father died in a car accident may not totally resolve her grief in the months or years immediately following the death. As she grows older and her concept of death matures, she will gain deeper understanding of the permanence of death and what it means never again to interact with her father. As she becomes capable of thinking in the abstract, she may philosophically question the meaning of the death. As she becomes an adolescent and searches for her own identity, she grieves her loss anew and wonders how she herself would have been different had her father lived. When she grows into young adulthood status and gives birth to her first child, she mourns another aspect of her much earlier loss—the fact that her own child will never know her father, the baby's grandfather.

Therapeutic Interventions for Dying and Grieving Children

Child-life Programs

In an effort to be as helpful as possible in meeting the needs of sick children (of all ages) and their families, many hospitals currently hire staff members called *child-life specialists*. These individuals play a very important role in preparing the child and family for what is to come. They serve as an emotional support in times of stress, and act as an advocate for the entire family. The training of this professional includes an academic background in child growth and development, family systems, facilitation of play activities, and communication skills. An understanding of a child's developmental level provides insights into the age-related needs, capabilities, and interests. This information is crucial if the child-life worker is to be successful in planning interventions that are appropriate for sick children of various ages. The child-life specialist understands that the crisis precipitated by the illness affects the entire family and that care must be taken to meet not only each individual's needs, but also those of the larger family system.

Preparation. Hospitalization itself, as well as various medical procedures, become all the more frightening if a child does not know what to expect or is confused about the illness itself (Golden, 1983). The following case studies shared by Petrillo and Sanger (1980) illustrate the confusion experienced by many children and illustrate the important need for preparation and clear, honest communication.

> Jenny developed precocious puberty and an insatiable appetite at age four because of a brain tumor. She attributed these symptoms to a little man in her stomach who ate her food and caused her trouble. (p. 70)

> At age five, Audrey required a nephrectomy for treatment of Wilm's tumor. After a five-year remission, she was readmitted with metastatic disease. Her nurse asked the reason for the large surgical scar on her abdomen. She explained, parts of my body get rotten. (p. 71)

The child-life worker prepares the child and other family members using a variety of strategies. A tour of the hospital a week or so before admission allows the child to become more familiar with the physical surroundings. Tours often include the check-in area, the operating area, and rooms on the pediatric floor (such as a patient's room and the playroom). Of the 62 pediatric hospitals studied by Peterson and Ridley-Johnson (1980), 74 percent reported using some sort of prehospitalization preparation techniques with children. Many offered the program to all children entering the hospital while others only utilized it with those undergoing surgery or other special procedures.

Children also gain comfort by being prepared for various medical procedures that they will encounter. A child-life worker should explain very carefully to the children what they will experience. Explanations become more clear to a child when there is opportunity for active involvement. For example, children who simply hear the terms "stethoscope" or "blood pressure cuff" may have very little comprehension of what they are or how they are used. Children, however, who are allowed to see and manipulate these devices have a much clearer understanding. Children can learn a great deal about an upcoming operation if they are shown a simplified model or picture of the human body. Location of the incision can be identified and an explanation given about the operation itself. Children can be shown how their bodies will change after the surgery. A demonstration of certain procedures can be performed on a doll (such as the application of a real cast). For example, one hospital uses a doll named Charlie to demonstrate how an IV is inserted in the wrist, with an explanation regarding the rationale for the procedure and how it will feel. Children often stick the doll with a real needle under the supervision of a staff member. The staff member can ask such questions as "Why does the nurse put the needle in your arm?" "What does Charlie have wrong with him?" or "Can you explain how the IV can help Charlie?" Many children often return to the playroom after they have had an IV and ask to play with Charlie again. The children experience a cathartic effect by repeatedly sticking the needle into the doll and once again process the experience and rationale behind it with a staff member. Books, films, and puppet shows can also be useful in helping to prepare children for upcoming events.

Thompson and Stanford (1981) make an important point when they stress that children do not acquire appropriate preparation merely through the availability of various props. Rather, the real value comes through the sensitive interaction with a trained individual who can give accurate information and emotional support as the props are being utilized.

Emotional Support.   By conversing with children and by watching their play, health-care professionals can learn a great deal about their emotional reactions to illness and hospitalization. Although they are not the only staff members providing emotional support, child-life specialists do play an important role. Because they are trained in child development, they may have insights that other personnel do not. Therefore, during interdisciplinary staffings, they can share important information about emotional concerns and helpful intervention strategies. By the very nature of their professional assignments within the hospital, child-life workers often have more time to spend with children and family members who are struggling with the emotional impact of an illness.

Child-life specialists and other staff members must be prepared to give emotional support for a variety of concerns such as those illustrated by the following anecdotes:

> When the nurse started an IV on Danny in preparation for chemotherapy, he screamed over and over again "I'm sorry; I said I'm sorry." As a way of explaining that the procedure was not a form of punishment he was introduced to needle

play in which the puppet who had a similar view of treatment was reassured. (Petrillo & Sanger, 1980, p. 69)

Will, age seven, developed visual disturbances and was hospitalized for diagnostic studies. His parents were so overwhelmed with the realistic possibility of a brain tumor that they could not discuss the illness with him. Will told his nurse that he had figured out he was admitted to have his eyes removed. (Petrillo & Sanger, 1980, p. 72)

Advocacy. Although medical staff are concerned about the well-being of their patients, it can still be useful to have someone acting as an advocate in their behalf. Policies, procedures, and the physical environment itself

Photo 4.2 *Hospitalized children can form important relationships with caring professionals.*

should be evaluated on an ongoing basis to ensure compatibility with the primary goal of meeting needs of patients and families. For many years, hospitals limited the number of hours that parents could spend with their sick child. Through the recent advocacy work of child-life specialists and others sensitive to emotional and social needs of young children, those restrictions have been greatly relaxed or even lifted. The policy of limiting visiting hours was found to be detrimental to children who feared separation from parents or who felt they were sick because of something they had done wrong and were being punished by their parents. Recall that separation anxiety and unfounded guilt are common during childhood. It was very beneficial to children and their parents to have persons within the health-related professions serve as advocates—individuals who understand the developmental needs of children and patterns of family interaction.

Child-life specialists have also had a positive impact by explaining the need for normality in children's lives. Play is an important part of a child's normal existence; as a result, many hospitals have playrooms or take games to a child's bedside. Staff members also encourage children to bring some of their own toys to the hospital and decorate their rooms. Until fairly recently, these procedures were not recommended.

Play Therapy

Play is an important part of young children's lives. It provides an opportunity to master skills, express ideas and feelings, deal with thoughts and emotions, and better understand one's environment. As is true for any child, play can become a valuable therapeutic modality for children who are dying or children who are grieving (Klein, 1979; Wheeler & Lange, 1985).

It is often difficult for children, especially younger ones, to articulate their concerns. Toys and other play materials can be regarded as a vocabulary through which children can communicate. The medium of play permits children to confront difficult situations on their own terms using a process over which they feel they have some control.

Pohlman (1984) recounts the activities of a group of 3-year-olds in her preschool classroom prior to the death of a peer due to cancer. The children engaged in a great deal of hospital play as they acted out the role of parent, nurse, or doctor. In many of these episodes, the preschoolers covered a doll's eyes to parallel real life. Their sick classmate had lost an eye to the cancer and was in the process of being fitted with a new prosthetic eye. The child who was sick engaged in similar types of play activities.

Art Therapy

Children who are dealing with either their own deaths or that of another can communicate through various art activities as well (Schmitt & Guzzino, 1985). Through their art, children often express their needs, fears, questions, and concerns (Lonetto, 1980; Lowenfeld & Brittain, 1975). Through observation, it becomes evident that children have many concerns regarding death and related emotions. Their art allows them to communicate with others symbolically. The art work can also serve as the focus of a discussion, as children explain what is meant by the use of a particular color or inclusion of a particular figure. The creative process itself may have a cathartic effect simply by allowing the children an opportunity to vent particular feelings (for example, admitting fear by sketching a small figure falling into a big, black hole). A child who was given clay to play with at preschool one day created a body with a grossly enlarged head. Shortly thereafter, he began to tear the head apart, saying "My mommy's head is going to explode!" He had overheard a conversation between his father and his aunt regarding the pressure being exerted by his mother's brain tumor. After the episode with the clay, this child admitted to being extremely upset by the belief that his mother was going to "explode" and brains would "spill out all over." This child had not voiced his fear earlier; it seemed he first needed to communicate it symbolically through the creation of a clay model. Once he had communicated the emotion, his father and teacher were able to provide information regarding his mother's medical situation to help reassure him.

There are a number of books currently available that include examples of children's art work as it relates to concerns of illness, death, and grief. The book entitled *There Is a Rainbow Behind Every Dark Cloud* (The Center for Attitudinal Healing, 1978) includes a compilation of pictures drawn by cancer patients between the ages of 8 and 19 years of age. Figure 4.1 illustrates one child's perceptions of how it feels to have to go to the hospital. Figure 4.2 is another child's response to the same request: "Draw a picture of yourself in the hospital." These two drawings are indicative of various concerns and would be good tools to elicit further conversation about such topics as medical procedures, loneliness, being in a strange environment, or feeling overwhelmed by all that goes on in a hospital. The sequel, *Straight from the Siblings: Another Look at the Rainbow* (The Cen-

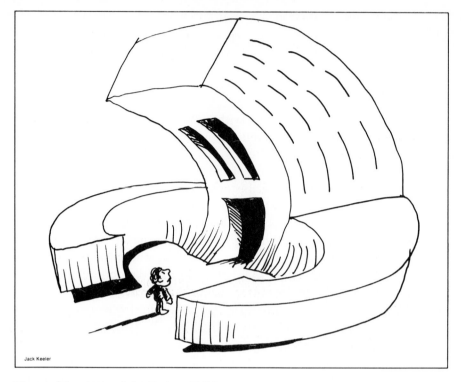

Jack Keeler

Figure 4.1 *Artwork by Dying Child*

Source: The Center for Attitudinal Healing (1978), *There Is a Rainbow behind Every Cloud,* Millbrae, CA: Celestial Arts, p. 21. Reprinted by permission.

ter for Attitudinal Healing, 1982) includes pictures portraying the siblings' perspectives of living with a sick brother or sister.

Linn (1982) used art work as a primary therapeutic modality in working with children whose siblings had died from a variety of causes. Her book *Children Are Not Paper Dolls* includes much of their art work. The drawing in Figure 4.3, with its accompanying caption, expresses a child's concerns about her brother's death and misgivings about sleeping in the room in which he died.

Bibliotherapy

Today there are many books written for children that provide insight regarding death and related emotional issues. (Selected examples are listed at the end of this chapter.) These books allow children to better understand that death is a natural part of life and that it is normal to feel sad or angry or any of a variety of other emotions. Children who have been unable or unwilling to articulate their own thoughts or feelings may feel more comfortable doing so after reading a story that somewhat parallels their own circumstances.

A number of authors have summarized and critiqued books that can be read to children of various ages (Bernstein, 1977; Fassler, 1978; Mills, Reister, Robinson, & Vermilye, 1976; Wass, 1984; Wass & Shaak, 1976). These book reviews can be useful for parents, teachers, and counselors who wish to become familiar with the available literature.

Summary

As children mature, they refine physical and cognitive capabilities and struggle to master varying psychosocial tasks. According to Erikson, for

Figure 4.2   *Artwork by Dying Child*

Source: The Center for Attitudinal Healing (1978), *There Is a Rainbow behind Every Cloud,* Millbrae, CA: Celestial Arts, p. 22. Reprinted by permission.

Figure 4.3   *Artwork by Grieving Child*

Source: E. L. Linn [Levy] (1982), *Children Are Not Paper Dolls,* The Publishers Mark, P.O. Box 6939, Incline Village, NV 89450. (Originally published by Harvest Printing, Greeley, CO.) Reprinted by permission.

example, a toddler attempts to develop autonomy rather than shame or doubt, while a preschooler faces a new crisis of initiative versus guilt. Illness puts children "at risk" for developing a negative resolution to these crises, and special care must be taken to ensure a positive outcome. Strategies should involve support for normal developmental needs as well as concern for issues specific to having a particular illness. Young children who are in Piaget's preoperational stage do not have a true understanding of the concept of death or illness. As a result, adults must be very careful to explain related issues in a way that is appropriate to their level of understanding.

Children who are dying need to feel they can trust the people around them. Caregivers and family members can enhance trust by giving appropriate information about what is transpiring, showing their concern, and allowing the child to communicate feelings. Additional needs of dying children are normalization and minimal separation from loved ones. Normalization of activities and routines can provide a sense of comfort and continuity. Life-threatening illnesses trigger many concurrent stressors. Ongoing contact with loved ones can provide additional strength to face them.

The death of a child typically triggers an intense grief reaction in the parents. Guilt is often a central theme to that grief reaction. Although there is some evidence that mothers and fathers grieve somewhat differently, both do experience acute grief. Their grief is often magnified by the wide variety of stressors that are concurrent with the period of bereavement.

Children who experience the death of a loved one also grieve. Although their grief experience is somewhat different from an adult's, there are many similarities. There are many therapeutic interventions that are helpful when giving support to dying or grieving children. These interventions include the involvement of child-life specialists in hospitals to prepare children for their experiences and to serve as an advocate. Play therapy, art therapy, and bibliotherapy are also powerful tools for helping these children.

℘ Personal Account

A young woman entered the hospital with the expectation that she would be treated for a serious infection and released within a few weeks. From the time her mother went into the hospital, 3-year-old Ariane began asking her father a variety of challenging questions. When her mother dies unexpectedly, Ariane vents her grief in child-like fashion, shows her support for her father as he grieves, and explores the meaning of death from a 3-year-old's perspective.

Conversations With Ariane

Nicholas Putnam

Nearly two years have passed since it happened. The pain in me has eased, and Ariane's questions come less often. The questions are easier to answer now. "Did Mommy like this place?" she asks. The memories and mystery of her passing, however, remain for us both.

My daughter and I lost Nina on January 23, 1978. She was not yet 30 and my daughter was not yet 4. She took with her an unborn child and left us behind in shock and grief. Such tragedies occur often enough, and usually they happen to someone else. When they happen to you, they are true emotional disasters. Adults and school-age children, if they are lucky, go through a period of grief which is both painful and healing. The well of sadness inside me occasionally seems almost dry and then at unexpected moments can fill suddenly and overflow. But what of our little girl? What of Ariane who at three lost the primary source of love, nurturance, identification, and companionship in her life? How can she deal with such a devastating rupture? In fact, she has survived. In small doses she has processed the information, felt the pain, and constructed a new reality for herself. It was an enormous task.

During the month after Nina's death I kept a diary of Ariane's remarks. I am still not sure why I did this. Maybe it was because Nina paid such close attention to all of the little things in Ariane's life. She delighted in Ariane's growth and personality. Perhaps I felt that by writing down Ariane's words I could take some of the sting out of them; I could help myself see these questions as a part of a process, something I could look back on, something "objective." I remember thinking at the time that a record like this could be of some help to others experiencing a similar tragedy. Then again, perhaps I made this diary because it was something I had already begun to do while my wife was still in the hospital. There are many things I did that I continue to do, possibly without reason, but which give me the sense that Nina is still a presence in my life.

It all began in my ninth and final year of training at UCLA. In July, the student years were to have ended, and Nina, Ariane, and I, and the baby she carried, were going to begin the productive middle years of our lives. On November 17, Nina went to the dentist to have a routine oral prophylaxis, to have her teeth cleaned. About three weeks later she began feeling poorly, with vague symptoms including occasional low-grade temperature and fatigue. On Christmas Eve she went to the emergency room at UCLA where an alert intern put together the facts of her recent trip to the dentist and the finding of a heart murmur, a murmur she had never had before. She was admitted to the hospital, and on Christmas Day it was confirmed that she had subacute bacterial endocarditis, an infection of one of the valves of the heart. Apparently the bacteria had traveled from her mouth during the oral prophylaxis and lodged on one of the heart valves, slowly growing there and causing her vague symptoms.

Ariane and I drove to the emergency room as soon as we learned that Nina was to be admitted to the hospital. We had been at a Christmas Eve luncheon, and Ariane knew that her mommy was not feeling well and was seeing a doctor. During the first visit, dressed in her Christmas dress of velvet, lace, and ribbon, she said very little. She appeared relieved when we left the emergency room. The next day was Christmas, and, before being hospitalized, Nina had prepared for Christmas with stockings, tree, and a huge gingerbread house. She had gone about town finding just the things that Ariane wanted. Santa Claus got all the credit, however, and Ariane was eager to get to the hospital as soon as possible to show Nina some of her gifts. That Christmas Day in the hospital, Ariane watched very closely the activities of nurses and doctors. She saw her mother wince and cry for a second as her intravenous medication was begun. Again she saw her mother's tears as she was told that the treatment for this disorder would require four to six weeks of hospitalization, but we all cheered up when we heard that the chances for complete recovery were good, provided she had the proper rest and treatment.

When I first met Nina, ten years ago, she had a little sign in her room from the movie, *Auntie Mame:* "Life is a banquet, and most poor beggars are starving to death." Life was meant to be a celebration. If she had to be in the hospital, we would all make the best of it—with visits, and wheelchair trips around the UCLA campus, card games, dominoes, and puzzles. Ariane was even allowed to try out her new roller skates in the hospital corridors. At least we knew why Nina had felt so tired during the last few weeks. At least now she would get better and go on with the business of life. Ariane began to take an interest in the activities of the doctors and nurses and asked for some IV tubing to start "treatment" on Betty. She and Betty, her doll, were inseparable.

The day after Christmas, Ariane asked an aunt, "Will Mommy die in the hospital?"

Adherence to a routine of daily living is important for children at this age, and so we tried as best we could to continue the routine of life at home. Still Ariane was able to visit Nina three or four times a week. On December 30, she asked me, "Do you know what Betty's thinking? Betty thinks very silly things. . . . Betty thinks doctors put you in the hospital and never let you come home."

"Gee, Betty's silly," I said.

"Betty thinks the doctors stick needles in your arms and your eyes and in your mouth and blood comes out."

"Betty doesn't know very much about what really happens in hospitals, does she?" I asked.

"No, she doesn't."

With her grandmother living in our home and frequent visits with her mother and days spent with friends, Ariane appeared to be adjusting to the new situation surprisingly well. She had a hard time conceptualizing a four-week period, but never asked directly when Nina was coming home.

On January 5, she told me, "Daddy, I'm having a hard time sleeping."

"Why?"

"I'm thinking too much."

"What about?"

"About Mommy."

"What about Mommy?"

"About all the nice things she did for me."

"Yes," I said.

"Daddy, how did she get to the hospital? Did she drive there?"

"She had to go there because she was sick. Some germs got into her heart, and the doctors have to give her medicine that will make her all better. She's going to come home in a little while, and she's going to be doing all those nice things again.

"I want she to come home now!"

"She will."

"Mommy is never coming home!" she challenged me.

"Yes, she is."

"No, she isn't."

Clearly, it was hard for her to imagine an end to the separation, and it was hard to separate Ariane and Nina after they had spent a day together in the hospital. But I found consolation in my knowledge that the treatment was going very well, that the complications, for Nina and for the unborn child, were going to be minimal and well within our ability to cope. At the suggestion of Ariane's nursery-school teacher we made a calendar. Nina was to come home in about two-and-a-half weeks and each night we would cross off a day. I moved the day of homecoming back a couple of days so that any last-minute delays would not be disappointing to Ariane.

"I will cross off all the days so she will come home now," Ariane decided one morning.

At last we came to the final week in the hospital. Now we were dealing with numbers that Ariane could understand, six days, four days, three days, only two days left until Mommy comes home. She was to be home on Sunday afternoon, January 22.

Friday morning, the 20th, at 4:45 A.M., the phone rings. The doctor tells me that Nina has had a seizure in the middle of the night and that her condition is serious. He wants me to come to the hospital immediately. At first I am confused as to how this could have happened, but suddenly terrible possibilities flood my mind: a major cerebral artery has burst open, an unexpected result of the endocarditis, which was virtually cured. I reel out of bed and begin to wail in anguish. Ariane is awakened. She says, "What's wrong? Don't cry, Daddy, everything's going to be okay."

The next four days form a painful blur in my memory. Nina is moved to the neurosurgical intensive-care unit (ICU). My mental stage changes from hopeful anticipation of her homecoming to anguish and despair at her rapid deterioration. Close friends gather from around the country and surround me. Ariane visits the hospital only once. She takes a quick look into the neurosurgical ICU to see her mother for the last time. Undoubtedly, she notes that some of her worst fears are confirmed. Mommy does have tubes coming from her mouth and head, and her eyes are taped shut. After staring for about twenty seconds from the doorway, she turns her head and asks to leave. She sees me distraught all of the time and in tears much of the time. There is a great influx of adults into her life as friends gather at the house and the hospital.

My mother had taken over her care since my wife had entered the hospital. At first Ariane directed some of her frustrations at her grandmother, whom she called Gigi. However, she also began to form a bond with her and made attempts to understand her new situation. On January 21, she and Gigi ate dinner alone. She played a game she often played with her mother: "Let's pretend we're two people at a restaurant."

"Do you have a daughter, lady?" asks Ariane.

"No, but I have a granddaughter."

"Yes, and her name is Jenny." Ariane continues with her fantasy.

"No, her name is Ariane," replies my mother.

"Does Ariane have a Mommy?"

"Yes, she does, but she's very sick and she's at the hospital."

Nina's chances for recovery dwindled over that long weekend. In a state of shock, I tried to prepare Ariane for what might happen. I told her that Mommy was very sick and that she could die. I told her that if Mommy died she would not be coming home ever again. I told her that we were hoping and praying that this would not happen. I felt that she might not possibly have any idea what I meant. She looked back at me with her big brown eyes, with only the faintest trace of tension showing about her mouth, and said, "Why do you tell me things I already know, Daddy?"

On Monday, January 23rd, at 1:00 P.M., my wife died. A neurologist whom I had known for several years was called to tell me that although her heart was beating, there was no evidence of any life in the brain. Shortly thereafter her heart began to fail and stop, and shortly after that the brief life of the unborn child was stilled. For about 30 minutes I couldn't stand up, and I could barely breathe.

"Jolly" West, the chairman of my department, somehow appeared at my side during this time and explained my body's reaction to me in a way that was rather clinical but quite reassuring at the same time. A state of shock had set in, and I felt completely numb. I felt nothing as I drove myself home. I remember stopping for gas. When I arrived home Ariane was playing with some neighbors. I told her I had something very important to tell her, and I picked her up and carried her down to a bench overlooking the ocean. I told her that something awful had happened. I told her the worst thing that could ever happen had happened. I began to cry. I told her that Mommy died and that she had gone to heaven. She looked at me for a moment and then she covered her ears, one at a time. She kept looking at me and saying, "Why do you tell me things I know already? Why do you tell me these things, Daddy?" Once again I told her that Mommy had gone to heaven and that we would not be seeing her, but that we would always love her, and that maybe her spirit would always be near us.

"Can we see her spirit, Daddy?"

"No, but we might feel it." I began to sob again.

"Daddy, you're dumb. You're telling me things I already know."

"But I have to tell you these things."

"I'm not going to listen to you. You're dumb."

Friends arrived from all over the country for the services. I became increasingly occupied with the arrangements and with the help and support of friends these normally distressing obligations became increasingly meaningful. At the services, which Ariane attended, our friends and I stood up and talked about the Nina we had known and loved. Ariane ran about the chapel but was not oblivious to the proceedings. She perked up when her name was mentioned and she ran up to me and to Nina's father to kiss us. She involved herself with many of the people who had come to visit and appeared quite cheerful. She knew the services related to her mother, but it soon became clear that death was a complete mystery to her. At the cemetery, a beautiful spot between mountains and sea, she ran about the grounds picking wildflowers and talking to friends. Finally, she settled down on the grass next to the coffin. She said, "This is my bedroom. I'm going to be next to Mommy, and I don't want anyone to disturb me." Then she stood up and began working the handle of the coffin back and forth and said, "Do you see what I'm doing? I'm pumping water into their eyes . . . for tears."

Although she appeared more serious than before, most could not detect a major change in her mood. A three-year-old, however, has very little idea of the permanence of death. Her confusion soon became evident. She began to ask, "Where is she?" "I want she here!" "Can I see her?" She looked over my shoulder as I showed some pictures of a recent family gathering to some friends. In these pictures Nina appeared beautiful as ever; radiant. Ariane pointed to her and said, "There's Mommy." But then she added, "Can I see her?"

I replied, "You can see her in the picture."

"No, I can't, she wasn't there. I didn't see her there."

After a week it was time for friends from out of town to leave. She became petulant when they said good-bye. At one point she threw a gift that a friend had given her across the room as he tried to say good-bye to her. Then she hugged him and said, "I don't want anybody to leave this house."

A week later we went out to the desert for a few days. There she developed an earache and woke up from sleep crying and demanding, "I want my Mommy. I want my Mommy!" This was too much for me to bear and I was unable to hold back my own tears. When she noticed my crying, she stopped hers and kissed me. I do know she sensed my suffering.

Despite these episodes during illnesses, her general behavior changed very little. If anything, she appeared more grown up than ever before. There certainly was no regression in her development. She continued going to nursery school and playing with her friends. In the midst of my suffering, I wondered at her ability to go on with life. She saw my crying spells and was comforting, and would say, "You're sad about Mommy." In her own way, however, she tried to grasp what had happened.

I have written down her comments whenever I have had the opportunity to do so. I have not done this because I feel that such comments are in any way typical of three-year-olds dealing with the death of their mother. Children's personalities are as varied as wildflowers. All of us, in our own ways, however, try to make sense of the world around us, and this was true of Ariane during these miserable days.

Ariane's comments about her mother were painful for me to hear, and they may be painful for others to read. But they do provide an opportunity to see how a three-year-old tries to come to terms with the loss of the most important person in her life.

For example, on February 9th she said, "I wish that nobody had taked away Mommy. . . . Only God did. . . . I wish I was magic and could fly up to the sky. I'm going to do magic and bring Mommy here."

Later that same day she ran into a friend in the supermarket. For a while the other little girl followed her around asking, "Did your Mommy die?" Ariane ignored her. Later we heard that that little girl subsequently became quite upset. In fact, many of Ariane's friends whose parents were divorced or separated appeared to take Nina's death with more visible stress than Ariane herself.

The following day she asked, "Does Great-grandma know Mommy's in heaven?"

"Yes."

"You fighted with Mommy, didn't you, and she went to the hospital?"

"When did I fight with her?"

"A long time ago," she said.

"Do you think she died because I fought with her a long time ago?" I asked.

"I don't like arguments, and Mommy shouldn't have goed to the hospital."

"People argue with other people at times, but that doesn't make anyone die. We all get mad at each other sometimes, but getting mad at somebody doesn't make them get sick and die, Ariane. Besides, I wasn't mad at

Mommy before she died. Mommy died because she got very, very sick. She got an infection in her blood.''

"I don't want to talk about it anymore." And later that day, singing: "Dear God, please make my Mommy come again . . . and everything will be all right . . . and I can just say the magic words and she will come home.''

In my anguish I tried to reassure her (and possibly myself) by telling Ariane that Mommy knew how we felt and perhaps her spirit was in the room with us. Ariane would reply, "I can't wait to go to heaven so she can hold me again.''

On February 15th, singing: "Sometimes when I cry Mommy comes right away . . . sometimes when I'm happy, let's not talk about sad, let's be happy every day." And later that day, "I want to sing a song about Mommy: I love my Mommy, Nina. When I was two and had long hair Mommy was here and she took me to the haircutter and they cutted my hair and she did ni-ice things for me and then she went to the hospital and now the end.''

We talked about possibly selling Nina's car during dinner one night. Ariane got up abruptly from the table and became quite upset: "You guys don't like my Mommy's car. . . . You're going to sell it. I don't want it selled." I answered her, "I know it makes you mad when we talk about selling the Pinto.''

"I'm not mad at Mommy; I'm only mad at God. I want to see her, hug her, and kiss her and give her my picture." The Pinto sits in my driveway to this day.

On my birthday, February 18th, she asked, "God took Mommy to heaven, didn't He?''

"Well," I tried to respond helpfully and yet honestly, "I guess so, she got sick, and I guess it was time for her to die, and God had something to do with it.''

"Well then, God can do magic and bring her back.''

"God can't do that, nobody can," I groped and hesitated. "You see, God can take her to heaven but nobody comes back from heaven.''

"Why not?''

"You'll understand when you grow up." And then I realized immediately that I didn't understand myself, so I added, "I don't know why; Daddy doesn't understand these things. I don't know if anybody understands God or why things happen in life." I continued to grope, "It's terrible that this happened, and we don't always understand God." Somehow I found myself increasingly inclined to use the concepts of heaven and God in dealing with Ariane's questions. This was difficult for me to do, as I had never had a strong belief in an afterlife. However, I was finding some comfort myself in the idea that there is something more to our existence than the short time we spend living on this planet.

In a restaurant one evening she searched through her grandmother's purse. She found a picture of Nina and held on to it, staring at it for quite some time. She said, "I'm going to hold on to this picture and look at it all day and all night and all the time. I'm going to give Mommy my picture." Ariane is an attractive child and, as often happens, a lady in the restaurant waved and winked at her. Ariane responded angrily, shaking her fist at the lady and sticking her tongue out. I scolded her, and she began to cry. It was time to leave, anyway, and I picked her up and carried her out to the car. She kept imploring, "I want my Mommy, I want to see her!" Her tears led to my tears. When she saw me crying, her tears suddenly changed to feigned tears of laughter. She said, "You see, we don't have to be sad all the time." The truth was that we couldn't both be sad at the same time. It was too frightening. When she was feeling okay, she could watch me cry and be comforting. When she needed to cry, it was important for her to feel that I could remain strong. Remarkably, she confined her questions and the open expression about the loss of her mother to a few brief moments each day. For most of the time life went on quite the same as usual.

She began to make an increasing commitment to her relationship with my mother. She gave my mother her own middle name. One night, laughingly, she told me, "Isn't it funny, you have a Mommy and your Daddy died, and I have a Daddy and my Mommy died. It's all together." However, she always included her mother when she talked about her family, saying, "I love a lot of people. I love Betty, Gigi, Mommy, and Daddy," adding several friends and neighbors as well. On our first return to the cemetery late in February, Ariane brought her Big Wheel and rode about on the grounds. She seemed happy to know that this was a special place where we thought about Mommy. She picked wildflowers and placed them in a vase over the plot. I told her that these would be nice flowers for Mommy. She asked, "Can Mommy see the flowers?" I told her that it makes us happy, and perhaps it makes Mommy happy, too, when we put flowers on her grave.

Ariane's experience with grief seemed to be quite different from mine. She dealt with this terrible loss in small increments, a few moments each day, although I imagine that she thought about and still thinks about it a good deal more. On February 23rd, she said:

"I don't like that doggy, Daddy."

"Why?"

"He's going to get a gun and kill us, Daddy, and we will go to heaven."

"Oh no," I laughingly reassured her.

"I don't want to go to heaven, and I don't want you to go to heaven or Gigi to go."

"Yes, we all want to live for a long time."

"Yes, I want you and Gigi to stay here so then you can take care of me."

Typically, for a child of three, she was concerned about the possibility of abandonment. A year later she would raise the possibility of something happening to me and then enumerate a number of possible solutions such as, "I could go live with Eric's family." I felt a sense of panic as I contemplated the possibility of her being left completely alone, should something happen to me.

Now, nearly two years later, I realize that I will never "get over" Nina's death: I believe I will eventually get used to it. There seemed to be a life-force in Ariane which helped her through the loss. She was able to live with something she didn't really understand. She made new attachments. She told her grandmother, "I'm lucky to have you." Was she repeating something I had said to her? Or was she beginning to sense the importance of her new relationship with her grandmother? Possibly it was a little of both.

I see Ariane's loss, and my own, and sometimes I see Nina's loss as well. During the month after her death I bought Ariane her first two-wheel bicycle. Watching her pedal the pink Schwinn about and seeing her delight at being able to ride it, brought to mind all of Nina's hopes for her. I felt so down at Nina's not being there that I was almost unable to complete the transaction with the salesman. And yet, I have gotten some comfort from the fact that Ariane has good feelings about her mother despite the loss. Many times she has looked at something in the house and said, "Mommy make that? I only like to look at that . . . reminds me of Mommy!" She asks me, "Did Mommy learn to swim when she was five?" "Did Mommy like to rollerskate?" She appears to have the capacity to identify with the mother she no longer has.

I cannot help my daughter understand something that I don't understand myself. I can't explain it in such a way that everything, or anything, seems logical or fair. As I grieved, and as I still do, I watch Ariane cope. Her confusion was enormous. Although exceedingly cheerful and full of life, one night at dinner, she abruptly turned to me and said:

"Hit me, Daddy!"

"But why should I hit you?"

"Because that's what happened to Mommy. She got hitted."

"I never saw Mommy get hit! No, Ariane, Mommy didn't get hitted. She got very sick, and she died."

"You're wrong, Daddy. You're telling me a lie. She didn't die, she got hitted, and went to heaven."

She looked for answers; from television she must have learned the association between violence (hitting) and death. She looked for psychological explanations for the loss. She wondered, did we get mad at her? Did she get mad at us and go away? But nothing seemed to fit or make sense. Her mother's death remained an enormous mystery. It was no less a mystery to me. And yet, not understanding, Ariane went on living, activated by some vital force within her. She took pleasure in little things and looked forward to the future, noting that she was "almost four, and when I grow up I can be a girl doctor." The presence of that life within her gave me strength and hope.

About a month after Nina died, Ariane asked me, "Daddy, do you miss Mommy?"

"Yes, I miss her very much."

"Do you miss me when I go away to school?"

"Yes I do."

And then realizing that in the past all people we have missed have returned, I added, "Missing Mommy is different, honey, because she can never come back. We can never see her, but we might feel that we're close to her sometimes."

"You're wrong, Daddy, I can see her." And then very softly she went on, "Every night after I'm asleep I see her . . . in a warm . . . cave."

I had no reply for this.

Still more softly, she said, "I stay with her all night until it's morning and I get up."

"That sounds very nice to me," I said. "That must feel very nice."

I learned to trust her capacity to find a pathway through these woods. I could see that she never turned around or slipped back. I could see that she continued to move forward, only occasionally looking back. I could see that she found resting places, warm spots, glimpses into the future, springs of hope.

We made the journey together, and each of us traveled alone. At times the woods were wet with rain, and yet there were periods of sunshine, song, and laughter. Through it all, we kept talking to each other. And we knew we were changed forever.

Questions and Activities

1. Was it "normal" for Ariane to throw a gift across the room and then tell a friend, "I don't want anyone to leave this house"? Explain your answer. What is the primary issue being dealt with here? Give other examples of the same issue from other parts of this personal account.

2. Summarize various components of the concept of death. Illustrate each of these components by giving examples from "Conversations With Ariane" and from your own personal experience. Do you agree with the approach that the author took in explaining to Ariane about her mother's death? Would you have said or done anything differently?

3. If you were the parent of a 5-year-old terminally ill child and were directly asked "Am I going to die?", how would you respond? Explain your answer.

4. As a young child were you ever protected by your family from some "crisis" situation (such as death, divorce, alcoholism, abusive behavior)? If so, how did they protect you? How did you feel when you were not allowed to communicate openly with others or not allowed to participate in various activities? What do you wish had been done differently?

Glossary

Accommodation: Process by which present schemes are modified or new schemes are created.

Animism: Belief that inanimate objects are alive.

Assimilation: Process by which new stimuli are incorporated into existing schemes.

Autonomy: Positive outcome of Erikson's second psychosocial crisis; relates to independence.

Bibliotherapy: Use of books as a therapeutic modality.

Causality: Factors that precipitate death.

Centration: Act of focusing on a single prominent characteristic of an object to the exclusion of others.

Childhood Ritual: A stereotyped behavior performed to order one's environment.

Child-life Specialist: Professional who serves as an advocate for children and their families in a medical facility.

Concreteness: Inability to deal with abstractions.

Deductive Reasoning: Ability to think from a general rule to a specific case.

Doubt: Negative outcome of Erikson's second psychosocial crisis; relates to a belief that one's self is incapable.

Dual Monologue: Conversation in which both speakers are talking about distinctly different topics.

Egocentrism: Inability to process information from another's viewpoint.

Finality: Death as a permanent state.

Guilt: Negative outcome of Erikson's third psychosocial crisis; relates to a distorted belief that one is responsible for certain outcomes, such as someone's death. Apart from the negative resolution of an Eriksonian crisis, guilt is a common manifestation of the grief response.

Inductive Reasoning: Ability to think from specific examples to a general rule.

Initiative: Positive outcome of Erikson's third psychosocial crisis; relates to a sense of curiosity and creativity.

Irreversibility: Inability to understand that something may change and then return to its original state. Inability to mentally reverse the transformation.

Nonfunctionality: Cessation of all physical processes.

Normalization: Consistency in interactions, activities, and routines that provides a sense of predictability, security, and comfort.

Personification: Belief that death is a concrete entity, such as a person or object.

Operations: Ability to mentally manipulate internal representations of objects.

Preoperational Stage: Second of Piaget's cognitive stages.

Schemes: Organized patterns of behavior and perception that one constructs to interpret some aspect of one's experience. Children's schemes are action oriented.

Sensorimotor Stage: First of Piaget's cognitive stages.

Shame: Negative outcome of Erikson's second psychosocial crisis; relates to a sense of being bad or worthless.

Transductive Reasoning: Thought based on reasoning from one specific instance to another specific instance.

Universality: Understanding that all humans will someday die.

Suggested Readings

Arnold, J. H., & Gemma, P. B. (1983). *A child dies: A portrait of family grief.* Rockville, MD: Aspen Pub.

   Focusing on the death of a child and its multiple ramifications, this book specifically addresses the death of an infant, a younger child, and an older child. The authors emphasize that, while there are common components in the grief experience, there are also distinct differences in the ways in which parents deal wih these deaths.

Corr, C. A., & Corr, D. M. (Eds.). (1985). *Hospice approaches to pediatric care.* New York: Springer.

   This edited volume provides valuable information on needs of dying children, their families, and their caregivers in a hospice context.

Schaefer, C. E., & O'Connor, K. J. (1983). *Handbook of play therapy.* New York: Wiley.

In addition to reviewing major theoretical approaches to play therapy, the authors discuss specific techniques and activities for practitioners.

Children's Fiction Books on Death and Grief

Angell, J. (1977). *Ronnie and Rosey.* Scarsdale, NY: Bradbury.

Thirteen-year-old Ronnie's father dies. Both Ronnie and her mother have difficulty filling the void caused by his loss.

Bond, N. (1984). *A Place to Come Back to.* New York: Athenum.

Charlotte's friend Oliver faces the traumatic death of his great uncle, who is also his guardian. Charlotte finds it difficult to meet Oliver's needs as he comes to terms with the death.

Branfield, J. (1982). *The Fox in Winter.* New York: Atheneum.

A teenage girl befriends a proud old man after the death of his wife. She is able to share in many of his memories.

Bunting, E. (1980). *The Empty Window.* New York: F. Warne.

C. G. and his brother, Sweeney, capture a parrot for their friend Joe Rizzio, who has only a short time to live. The difficult part, though, is giving the gift to Joe, face-to-face. This story explores the confusing emotions surrounding the death of a friend.

Bunting, E. (1982). *The Happy Funeral.* New York: Harper & Row.

When Laura's grandfather dies, the young Chinese-American girl is unhappy and confused. She does not understand her mother's words, "When someone is very old and has lived a good life, he is happy to go." But Laura helps her family prepare for the funeral. As the ceremony draws to a close, Laura is still unhappy, but her sorrow is mixed with the loving memories of her grandfather.

Carrick, C. (1976). *The Accident.* New York: Seabury Press.

Christopher's dog is hit by a truck and killed. He deals with his feelings of guilt and depression.

Clifton, L. (1983). *Everett Anderson's Goodbye.* New York: Holt, Rinehart and Winston.

This is a touching portrait of a little boy who is trying to come to grips with his father's death. We see him struggle through many stages, from denial and anger to depression and, finally, acceptance.

DePaola, T. (1973). *Nana Upstairs and Nana Downstairs.* New York: Putnam.

Tommy loved visiting with his grandmother and great-grandmother on Sunday afternoons. But one day, when Tommy ran upstairs to see Nana, her bedroom was empty. This is a heartwarming story of that special relationship between the very young and the very old and the moment when the two must part.

Fassler, J. (1971). *My Grandpa Died Today.* New York: Behavioral Publications.

When his grandfather dies, David must struggle to understand and accept his death. In doing so, David learns a little bit more about life.

Haddad, C. (1984). *The Last Ride.* New York: Dodd, Mead.

Doug prohibits one friend from going home with a drunk driver. Others, however, are killed in a fatal crash. He feels responsible.

Harris, A. (1965). *Why Did He Die?* Minneapolis: Lerner Publications.

When his friend's grandfather dies, Scott's mother discusses death with him.

Hermes, P. (1982). *You Shouldn't Have to Say Goodbye.* San Diego: Harcourt Brace Jovanovich.

Thirteen-year-old Sarah must come to terms with the fact that her mother is dying of cancer.

Hickman, M. (1984). *Last Week My Brother Anthony Died.* Nashville: Abingdon.

A small girl describes her feelings of grief after the death of her 4-week-old baby brother.

Hoopes, L. (1981). *Nana.* New York: Harper & Row.

It is the little girl's first morning without Nana. The girl watches and listens to the mornings, calling to the chickadee, the way Nana taught her. Lyn Hoopes's gentle words share with young children a spiritual sense of life, helping them to better understand the loss of a loved one.

Madler, T. (1980). *Why Did Grandma Die?* Milwaukee: Raintree Children's Books.

This book presents major concepts related to death. Dying is a part of life. Death is not temporary, as many young children tend to believe. Also introduced are some common funeral customs and exposure to common feelings of grief.

Peavy, L. (1981). *Allison's Grandfather.* New York: Scribner's.

Erica knew that Allison's grandfather was dying, but she didn't really feel like asking about dying. Not out loud. Instead, she thought about Allison's grandfather last summer on his ranch.

Simon, N. (1979). *We Remember Philip.* Chicago: A. Whitman.

Sam and his classmates try to find a way to comfort their teacher. His teacher's son was killed in a mountain-climbing accident.

Simon, N. (1986). *The Saddest Time.* Chicago: A. Whitman.

Various vignettes discuss death related to a variety of different contexts including illness and accidents.

Tobias, T. (1978). *Petey.* New York: Putnam.

Playing with Petey was a fun part of Emily's day. When she came home from school, the little gerbil was always there in his cage waiting for her. Now Petey was going to die. This is the story of Emily's love for a friend. Her loss teaches her that life brings both change and continuity.

Resources

Candlelighters Childhood Cancer Foundation, Inc.
1901 Pennsylvania Avenue, N.W., Suite 1001
Washington, D.C. 20006 (202) 659-5136

The Compassionate Friends, Inc.,
National Headquarters
P.O. Box 3696
Oak Brook, Illinois 60522
(312) 990-0010

Make-A-Wish Foundation
2600 North Central, #936
Phoenix, Arizona 85004
(602) 240-6600

Ronald McDonald House
Children's Oncology Services, Inc.
500 North Michigan Avenue
Chicago, Illinois 60611
(312) 575-7048

References

Berg, C. (1978). Helping children accept death and dying through group counseling. *Personnel and Guidance Journal, 2*, 169–172.

Berlinsky, E., & Biller, H. B. (1982). *Parental death and psychological development.* Lexington, MA: Lexington Books.

Bernstein, J. E. (1977). *Books to help children cope with separation or loss.* New York: Bowker.

Bibace, R., & Walsh, M. E. (1979). Developmental stages in children's conceptions of illness. In G. C. Stone, F. Cohen, & N. Adler (Eds.), *Health psychology: A handbook* (pp. 285–301). San Francisco: Jossey-Bass.

Bigner, J. J. (1985). *Parent–child relations: An introduction to parenting* (2d ed.). New York: Macmillan.

Bluebond-Langer, M. (1978). *The private worlds of dying children.* Princeton, NJ: Princeton University Press.

Bowlby, J. (1980). *Attachment and loss* (Vol. 3): *Loss, sadness, and depression.* New York: Basic Books.

Brenner, A. (1984). *Helping children cope with stress.* Toronto: Lexington Books.

Broome, M. E. (1986). The relationship between children's fears and behavior during a painful event. *Children's Health Care, 14*(3), 142–145.

Center for Attitudinal Healing, The. (1978). *There is a rainbow behind every dark cloud.* Millbrae, CA: Celestial Arts.

Center for Attitudinal Healing, The. (1982). *Straight from the siblings: Another look at the rainbow.* Millbrae, CA: Celestial Arts.

Chesler, M. A., Paris, J., & Barbarin, O. A. (1986). "Telling" the child with cancer:

Parental choices to share information with ill children. *Journal of Pediatric Psychology, 2*(4), 497–516.

Childers, P., & Wimmer, M. (1971). The concept of death in early childhood. *Child Development, 42*(4), 1299–1301.

Cook, J. A. (1983). A death in the family: Parental bereavement in the first year. *Suicide and Life-Threatening Behavior, 13*(1), 42–61.

Davies, B. (1987). After a sibling dies. In M. A. Morgan (Ed.), *Bereavement: Helping the survivors* (pp. 55–65). London, Ontario: King's College.

Earnshaw-Smith, E. (1981). Dealing with dying patients and their relatives. *British Medical Journal, 282,* 1779.

Edelstein, L. (1984). *Maternal bereavement: Coping with the unexpected death of a child.* New York: Praeger.

Elizur, E., & Kaffman, M. (1983). Factors influencing the severity of childhood bereavement reactions. *American Journal of Orthopsychiatry, 53*(4), 669–676.

Erikson, E. (1963). *Childhood and society* (2d ed.). New York: Norton.

Fassler, J. (1978). *Helping children cope.* New York: Free Press.

Flavell, J. J. (1985). *Cognitive development* (2d ed.). Englewood Cliffs, NJ: Prentice-Hall.

Freiburg, K. L. (1979). *Human development: A life-span approach.* North Scituate, MA: Duxbury Press.

Friedman, S. B. (1974). Psychological aspects of sudden unexpected death in infants and children. *Pediatric Clinics of North America, 21,* 103–111.

Furman, E. (1978). Helping children cope with death. *Young Children, 33*(4), 25–32.

Gartley, W., & Bernasconi, M. (1967). The concept of death in children. *The Journal of Genetic Psychology, 110,* 71–85.

Golden, D. B. (1983). Play therapy for hospitalized children. In C. E. Schaefer & K. J. O'Connor (Eds.), *Handbook of play therapy.* (pp. 213–233). New York: Wiley.

Greenberg, L. I. (1975). Therapeutic grief work with children. *Social Casework, 56,* 396–403.

Haley, J. (1985). Dealing with children's pain: Learning from personal experience. *The American Journal of Hospice Care, 2*(3), 34–40.

Hardgrove, C., & Warrick, L. H. (1974). How shall we tell the children? *American Journal of Nursing, 74*(3), 448–450.

Havener, R. M., & Phillips, W. (1975). The grieving child. *The School Counselor, 22*(5), 347–351.

Joseph, S. M. (1974). *Children in fear.* New York: Random House.

Klein, D. (1979). Rx for pediatric patients: Play while you wait. *Young Children, 34*(2), 13–19.

Koocher, G. P. (1974). Talking with children about death. *American Journal of Orthopsychiatry, 44*(3), 405–411.

Kupst, M. J., & Schulman, J. L. (1988). Long-term coping with pediatric leukemia: A six year follow-up study. *Journal of Pediatric Psychology, 13*(1), 7–22.

Linn, E. L. [Levy, E. L.] (1982). *Children are not paper dolls.* Incline Village, NV: The Publishers Mark. (Originally published by Harvest Printing, Greeley, CO).

Lonetto, R. (1980). *Children's conceptions of death.* New York: Springer.

Lowenfeld, V., & Brittain, W. L. (1975). *Creative and mental growth.* New York: Macmillan.

Maccoby, E. E. (1980). *Social development: Psychological growth and the parent–child relationship.* New York: Harcourt Brace Jovanovich.

McClowry, S. G., Davies, E. B., May, K. A., Kulenkamp, E. J., & Martinson, I. M. (1987). The empty space phenomenon: The process of grief in the bereaved family. *Death Studies, 11*(5), 361–374.

McCown, D. E. (1988). When children face death in a family. *Journal of Pediatric Health Care, 2*(1), 14–19.

Melear, J. (1973). Children's conceptions of death. *Journal of Genetic Psychology, 123*(2), 359–360.

Miles, M. S., & Demi, A. S. (1984). Toward the development of a theory of bereavement guilt in bereaved parents. *Omega, 14*(4), 299–314.

Mills, G., Reister, R., Robinson, A., & Vermilye, G. (1976). *Discussing death: A guide to death education.* Homewood, IL: ETC Publications.

Mrgudic, K. (1985). Jeremiah's story: Living well with terminal illness—A child's experience with death. *The American Journal of Hospice Care, 2*(6), 17–21.

Nagy, M. (1948). The child's theories concerning death. *Journal of Genetic Psychology, 73*, 3–27.

Natapoff, J. N. (1982). A developmental analysis of children's ideas of health. *Health Education Quarterly, 9*(2), 34–45.

Peterson, L., & Ridley-Johnson, R. (1980). Pediatric hospital response to survey on prehospital preparation for children. *Journal of Pediatric Psychology, 5*(1), 1–7.

Petrillo, M., & Sanger, S. (1980). *Emotional care of hospitalized children: An environmental approach* (2d ed.). Philadelphia: Lippincott.

Piaget, J. (1963). *The origins of intelligence in children.* New York: International Universities Press.

Piaget, J. (1968). *Six psychological studies* (A. Tenzer, Trans.). New York: Vintage Books.

Pohlman, J. C. (1984). Illness and death of a peer in a group of three-year-olds. *Death Education, 8*(2), 123–136.

Rait, D.S., & Holland, J. (1986). Pediatric cancer: Psychosocial issues and approaches. *Mediguide to Oncology, 6*(3), 1–5.

Rando, T. A. (1983). An investigation of grief and adaptation in parents whose children have died from cancer. *Journal of Pediatric Psychology, 8*(1), 3–20.

Redpath, C. C., & Rogers, C. S. (1984). Healthy young children's concepts of hospitals, medical personnel, operations, and illness. *Journal of Pediatric Psychology, 9*(1), 29–39.

Roberts, C. L. (1981, February). Helping children cope with death. *Educational Leadership*, pp. 409–410.

Salladay, S. A., & Royal, M. E. (1981). Children and death: Guidelines for grief work. *Child Psychiatry and Human Development, 11*(4), 203–212.

Sanders, C. (1979). A comparison of adult bereavement in the death of a spouse, child, and parent. *Omega, 10*(4), 303–320.

Schatz, W. H. (1986). Grief of fathers. In T. Rando (Ed.), *Parental loss of a child* (pp. 293–302). Champaign, IL: Research Press.

Schmitt, B. B., & Guzzino, M. H. (1985). Expressive therapy with children in crisis: A new avenue of communication. In C. Corr & D. Corr (Eds.), *Hospice approaches to pediatric care.* New York: Springer.

Schuster, C. S., & Ashburn, S. S. (1986). *The process of human development: A holistic life-span approach* (2d ed.). Boston: Little, Brown.

Speece, M. W., & Brent, S. B. (1984). Children's understanding of death: A review of three components of a death concept. *Child Development, 55*, 1671–1686.

Thompson, R. H., & Stanford, G. (1981). *Child life in hospitals: Theory and practice.* Springfield, IL: Charles C Thomas.

Valeriote, S., & Fine, M. (1987). Bereavement following the death of a child: Implications for family therapy. *Contemporary Family Therapy, 9*(3), 202–217.

Vipperman, J. F., & Rager, P. M. (1980, March/April). Childhood coping: How nurses can help. *Pediatric Nursing*, pp. 11–18.

Warmbrod, M. E. (1986). Counseling bereaved children: Stages in the process. *Social Casework, 67*(6), 351–358.

Wass, H. (1984). Parents, teachers, and health professionals as helpers. In A. Wass & C. Corr (Eds.), *Helping children cope with death: Guidelines and resources* (2d ed.) (pp. 75–130). New York: Hemisphere.

Wass, H., & Shaak, J. (1976). Helping children understand death through literature. *Childhood Education, 53*(2), 80–85.

Wheeler, P. R., & Lange, N. F. (1985). Improving care for hospitalized terminally ill children. In C. Corr & D. Corr (Eds.), *Hospice approaches to pediatric care* (pp. 43–60). New York: Springer.

White, E., Elsom, B., & Prawat, B. (1978). Children's conceptions of death. *Child Development, 49*, 307–311.

Wolfelt, A. (1983). *Helping children cope with grief.* Muncie, IN: Accelerated Development.

Zeligs, R. (1974). *Children's experience with death.* Springfield, IL: Charles C Thomas.

5

School-age Years

Physical Development 185

Cognitive Development 185

Characteristics of Concrete
  Operational Thought 185
School-age Child's Concept of
  Death 188
School-age Child's Concept of
  Illness 189

Psychosocial Development
189

The Culture of Childhood 189
Erikson's Crisis: Industry versus
  Inferiority 191

**Additional Needs of Dying
School-Age Children** 192

Pain Management 193
Continued School Attendance
  194
Continued Peer Interaction
  195

Children as Survivors 196

Death of a Parent 196
Death of a Sibling 200

Summary 204

When comparing the school-age child (ages 6 to 11) to the preschool child (ages 3 to 6), we see notable differences in the physical, cognitive, and psychosocial realms of development. School-agers refine many physical skills, such as running and skipping, and are able to do increasingly difficult tasks requiring fine motor coordination. They spend greater amounts of time in peer interaction, both in school and in their neighborhoods. School-agers are more flexible in their thinking and have a more realistic understanding of death.

Physical Development

Given opportunities to practice them, most school-age children learn new physical skills rapidly. They spend seemingly countless hours engaged in such physical activities as playing ball, riding bicycles, and climbing playground equipment. Their level of success in mastery of such skills often influences their level of acceptance in particular peer groups.

As children enter the school-age years, they become increasingly concerned about their physical appearance and capabilities. Shortcomings or differences become a source of embarrassment and discomfort and affect the development of self-concept (VanderZanden, 1985).

Cognitive Development

According to Piaget's theory of cognitive development, school-age children between the ages of approximately 7 and 11 are commonly capable of thinking at the *concrete operational level*. Operations allow us to mentally manipulate objects and determine relationships among them (Piaget & Inhelder, 1969). For example, categorizing children by sex and age involves the operation of classification. Determining who has been sick the shortest time and who has been sick the longest involves the operation of seriation. Children in the concrete operational stage are "bound by immediate physical reality and cannot transcend the here and now, consequently, during this period, children still have difficulty dealing with remote, future, or hypothetical matters" (VanderZanden, 1985, p. 294).

Characteristics of Concrete Operational Thought

Although still somewhat limited in its scope, concrete operational thinking is marked by major advances over preoperational thinking. Concrete

185

operational thought is characterized by diminished egocentrism, decreased animism, and lessened confusion between reality and fantasy. Concrete operational thinkers are able to decenter their focus of attention, attend to transformations, and master concepts related to conservation. These cognitive capabilities do not all develop at the same time; rather, they develop gradually and become refined over time.

Diminished Egocentrism.   Younger preoperational thinkers often tend to perceive the world from only one viewpoint—their own. Concrete operational children much more clearly and consistently understand that others may think differently from the way that they do. Older children, then, care about what their peers think about them. As a result, they put much time and energy into trying to be similar to others and avoiding becoming outcasts. Children whose bodies have changed due to the ravages of illness often are painfully aware of others' reactions toward them.

Decentration.   Whereas preoperational thinkers focus their attention on one dimension at a time, concrete operational children decenter their attention and consider multiple factors simultaneously. For example, the concrete operational child understands that a friend can be happy and worried at the same time—happy that the leukemia has currently gone into remission but worried that the illness will recur.

Transformations.   Concrete operational thinkers are able to perceive intermediate steps that lead up to a particular outcome. Younger children perceive only the final state. An older child recalled his sister's illness gradually limiting her attendance at school. She shifted from full days to half days to two mornings a week. A younger child could only describe the final outcome and could not explain the gradual change.

Reversibility.   Preoperational children's thinking is marked by an inability to regain an initial state. Concrete operational thinkers can reverse thought processes. For example, the older child may understand that his father is currently very sick and confined to bed but remembers that he was much healthier at one time and used to participate in many physical activities. Therefore, he is capable of understanding that his father can possibly regain his health.

Conservation.   Concrete operational thinkers are able to understand that certain characteristics of an object do not change (volume, mass, weight), even if other dimensions are transformed. For example, a concrete operational thinker would understand that $\frac{1}{2}$ ounce of medicine is the same whether it is taken from two spoonfuls or one. A preoperational child who has focused on the number of spoonfuls would regard the two as having contained more medicine, even though it still totals to $\frac{1}{2}$ ounce.

Related Phenomena. Although thought has become more logical, school-age children still hold some magical beliefs. Most of us can remember a time when we took great pains to ensure the physical welfare of our mothers—by not stepping on a crack! On our birthdays, we guaranteed our wishes' coming true by refusing to tell our siblings what we had hoped for as we blew out the birthday candles. As twilight fell, we searched for the first star and wished upon it "Star light, star bright, first star I see tonight. I wish I may, I wish I might. . . ." Because belief in magic is such a normal part of both the preschool years and the school-age years, it is quite common to hear sick children ask the powerful adults in their lives (parents, doctors, nurses) to "fix me" or "make me better," fully believing that they have the power to do so, particularly if the child wishes hard enough that it be accomplished. When adults do not have the power to heal them or make them totally comfortable, some children misinterpret the lack of power as deliberate unwillingness or a desire to punish them due to some perceived wrongdoing. Recall, once again, that many sick children feel guilty, thinking they caused their own illnesses by being bad.

Increased cognitive abilities do facilitate the mastery of language that allows the child to engage in telling jokes and riddles. Many have a death-related theme and, in some instances, may be told as an invitation for further discussion of death or grief. One classic joke is the following:

> How do you make a dead man float?
>> Well, you take a dead man, two scoops of ice cream. . . .

Rosenbloom (1976, pp. 49–50) has provided examples of school-age riddles concerning death, illness, and medical procedures:

> How can you tell if a mummy has a cold?
>> He starts coffin.

> What is the famous last word in surgery?
>> Ouch.

> What would you call a small wound?
>> A short cut.

School-age jokes concerning suicide also exist. Rosenbloom's (1984) collection of jokes includes the following:

> A man wanted to commit suicide. To make sure he did the job, he got a bottle of poison, a rope, a gun, some gasoline and matches. Pouring the gasoline all

over his clothing, he climbed a tree and crawled out on a branch overhanging a lake. He hung himself from the limb, drank the poison, set his clothing on fire, and then shot himself. Alas! He missed his head, the bullet hit the rope, he fell into the water, and the water put the flames out. He swallowed so much water that the poison became harmless. Then he had to swim as hard as he could in order to save his life. (p. 323)

There was a young feller named Clyde,
Who fell down a sewer and died.
    Now, he had a brother
    Who fell down another,
Would you call that double sewer-side? (p. 356)

School-age Child's Concept of Death

This section will examine the school-age child's understanding of the various components of the concept of death that were reviewed in Chapter 4. Recall that preschool children do not fully understand the elements of nonfunctionality or universality. In their extensive review of studies examining children's understanding of the concept of death, Speece and Brent (1984) have concluded that the majority of children at the concrete operational stage have acquired the death-related concepts of nonfunctionality, finality, and universality.

Nonfunctionality.   In contrast to the young children in her study (ages 3 to 5) who believed dead people could act and perceive, Nagy (1948) found that the older children (5 to 9) understood that dead persons do not feel, breathe, eat, and so forth.

Finality.   Koocher (1974) asked the children in his study "How do you make dead things come back to life?" Whereas 40 percent (8 out of 20) of the preoperational children felt that this feat was possible, the older children recognized that death is permanent. One representative answer was "By thinking about them; then they can live in our mind, but you can't really make them come alive again" (p. 408).

Universality.   White, Elsom, and Prawat (1978) questioned children in their study: "Do you think that everybody will die someday?" (p. 308). Sixty-two percent of the concrete operational thinkers answered this question correctly, compared to 38 percent of the preoperational thinkers.

Causality.   When asked by Koocher (1974) "What makes things die?" preoperational thinkers typically gave answers that were closely tied to their own experience and, therefore, reflected a sense of egocentrism characteristic of that period. The children in the concrete operational stage, however, identified specific weapons or illnesses. One 7-year-old responded, "Knife, arrows, guns, lots of stuff. Do you want me to tell you all of them? (Interviewer: As many as you want.) Hatchets and animals, and fire and explosions too" (p. 407). Although these answers are less egocentric than those given by preschoolers, they are still very concrete in nature as compared to adolescents' responses, which reflect deterioration of life processes or destruction of vital organs.

School-age Child's Concept of Illness

Bibace and Walsh (1979) studied children's perceptions given by illness. As noted in Chapter 4, the most common explanations of preoperational children were categorized as "contagion explanations" (71 percent). Concrete operational thinkers, however, gave markedly different proportions of types of responses. Only 17 percent gave contagion explanations, while 75 percent gave responses that were categorized as "contamination explanations." In these explanations, children were able to articulate the causal link between the source of the illness (for example, germs) and the illness itself. In contrast to the preoperational child, the concrete operational thinker no longer focuses on a single symptom but rather attempts to integrate multiple symptoms. Concrete, visible bodily processes are discussed. Additionally, "the egocentricity of the earlier stage is less apparent, as the child describes illness as a more general phenomenon ('People get measles,' rather than 'I got measles'; 'Colds come from cold air,' rather than 'A cold is from the wind and I went to the doctor')" (p. 293).

Bibace and Walsh (1979) also noted that concrete operational thinkers' newfound capability of reversing thought processes was apparent in many of their responses. Many children explained that a person who was sick might once again become well.

Psychosocial Development

The Culture of Childhood

The culture of childhood embodies many factors. Berger (1983, p. 334) explains, "While playing together, children in middle childhood transmit and develop their own subculture ... complete with language, dress codes, and rules of behavior that adults often do not notice." From age 5 or 6 onward, involvement in school is a focal point of most children's daily activities. They spend many hours a day learning those skills and subjects that our society deems to be valuable. Additionally, children engage in many extracurricular activities (clubs and sports, among others) which provide increased opportunities to develop competencies that provide a sense of pride as well as pleasure.

School-age children expand their social environment well beyond their family boundaries. They have many opportunities to interact with other children as they play in their neighborhoods and as they attend school. Peer groups become an important social force during this life stage and serve many different functions. They provide opportunities to develop a variety of interpersonal skills as children communicate with one another, learn to cooperate, assert themselves, and interact in many different ways. Children derive a sense of belongingness from membership in a peer group, which, in turn, promotes a sense of security and self-confidence. That sense of belonging, however, typically carries with it a definite price. Children must adhere rigidly to a set of group norms, behaviors, and standards for physical appearance. Individual differences often lead to a child's being ostracized. Children typically rank members of a group in hierarchical fashion along a variety of dimensions, such as physical attractiveness or athletic capability. Children then use rankings of particular characteristics to make judgments regarding who is to be regarded as popular and who is to be rejected. A number of researchers have found a relationship between popularity and social desirability (Langlois & Stephan, 1977; Lerner & Lerner, 1977). A child who has experienced many physical changes as the result of a life-threatening illness is at risk for being regarded as "ugly" or "strange" and, therefore, for being rejected from the peer group. Kleck, Richardson, and Ronald (1974) have noted that rejection is all the more difficult for children to deal with if they are unable to change the personal trait causing the isolation.

Compared to preschoolers, school-age children have much greater mastery over the use of language. They are able to share information, communicate ideas, and express their desires. Words themselves are imbued with a great deal of power. For example, name-calling can have a dramatic effect on a child's mood. Many childhood fights begin with taunts such as "Crybaby" or "Fatso." Some children fight words with words and retort, "Sticks and stones may break my bones, but names will never hurt me." Other children seem to be emotionally devastated by having been labeled in a negative fashion. A child who has undergone chemotherapy and has lost his hair is at great risk of being publicly taunted with "Baldy" unless children are told the relevant circumstances.

Erikson's Crisis: Industry versus Inferiority

The crisis of school-age children, as explained by Erikson (1963), is that of *industry versus inferiority*. During this period, children focus much of their energy on learning new skills, making things, and being productive. If allowed to do these activities successfully and in a way which allows them feelings of pride and competency, school-age children will develop a sense of industry. Peers become increasingly important during the school-age years, and children desire to be accepted by their peers and regarded as an equal, if not a superior, match to others. If they consistently fail, school-agers develop a sense of inferiority rather than industry.

Dying children may be in danger of developing a negative outcome to their crisis situation and a feeling that they are inferior to those around them. Dying school-age children are very capable of making the determination that they are different from their healthy peers. In addition, medical procedures and/or progress of their disease often bring about changes in their physical appearance. These children typically do not have the same energy levels as their peers and therefore cannot participate in the same variety of activities or perform at the same level of expertise.

Photo 5.1 *School-age children need the opportunity to become involved in developmentally appropriate activities.*

Oftentimes, dying school-age children are restricted from going to school for part, if not all, of the course of their illness. This separation from the school environment removes them from a typical pattern of interaction with their peers and also makes it more difficult to learn and master skills that are essential to developing a sense of industry.

Strategies that can be helpful in counteracting a sense of inferiority in dying school-age children include the following. Each is based on the premise that the child is desirous of these activities.

1. Allow children to normalize their physical appearance to as great a degree as possible. For example, allow them to select a fashionable wig or hat if hair loss has occurred.

2. As energy allows, encourage peer interaction and involvement in normal recreational activities. For example, these school-agers may wish to play a variety of video games with one another.

3. Facilitate the children's involvement in school activities. Examples include allowing them to attend school on a very flexible schedule, sending tutors to the medical facility, and having peers take homework assignments to them.

4. Encourage dying children to develop new interests and skills that they can be proud of and that can be shared with others. For example, encourage them to show new magic tricks, photo albums, or stamp collections to family and friends.

Additional Needs of Dying School-age Children

Children need to be allowed to be children. Even dying children want to engage in play activities, attend school, and interact with peers. Focusing exclusively on a child's illness or on the child's normal developmental needs can cause despair (Katz, Kellerman, Williams, & Siegal, 1975; Van Eys, 1977). We need to acknowledge both the reality of the disease and the need, within limitations prescribed by the disease, to pursue normal activities and interests. Although Levenson and Cooper (1984) made the following statement regarding chronically ill children, it can be generalized to dying children as well:

> As a group, distinctive needs have been identified. To avoid or negate these differences denies many of the realities that shape the child's existence. Conversely, too much focus on differences can be disturbing to the child and exacerbate feelings of alienation and lowered self-esteem. Assurance that they are "like everyone else" can appear as not credible and inaccurate to children daily confronted with their limitations. (p. 448)

With this in mind, important needs of the school-age child are pain man-agement, continued school attendance, and continued interaction with peers.

Pain Management

Although the control of pain was discussed in Chapter 1 as a common need of the dying, this topic will be examined once again as it relates spe-cifically to children. Haley (1985) identifies two different types of pain. *Disease-related pain* relates to the progression of the disease itself. For example, pain caused by intestinal blockage, growth of a tumor, bone frac-tures, or distention of tissue would be disease-related. *Procedural pain* is caused by medical procedures themselves. Insertion of needles in order to start an IV or draw blood, bone marrow tests (for example, to determine suitability of a bone marrow transplant after diagnosis of leukemia), and surgery (such as to remove a malignant brain tumor) are causes of proce-dure-related pain.

Because children cannot communicate their feelings or thoughts as clearly and as directly as adults, it is crucial that caregivers derive insight from their nonverbal cues and also provide opportunities for children to express themselves. Infants depend on an adult's ability to differentiate among qualitatively different cries—a "hurt" cry versus a "hungry" cry. Toddlers communicate nonverbally through actions such as clenching teeth, opening eyes very wide, rubbing an area, losing interest in play, or kicking or hitting the caregiver who intends to carry out a procedure pain-ful to them.

Preschool children have language capacity that allows them at least some ability to explain how they feel. Even so, it may be very difficult for the child to accurately describe the pain or localize it. While experiencing pain in his chest, a child may explain that his stomach hurts. Preschool children, who live in the here and now, often do not derive comfort from hearing that the pain will end. The hurt is now and seems as if it will last forever. Preschoolers fear intrusive procedures (Rait & Holland, 1986) and imagine devastating outcomes, such as all their blood running out of the hole in the finger where some blood was drawn.

School-age children are able to better understand the cause of the pain and also that it may be time-limited. This age group worries, however, that the pain may limit their involvement in activities with their peers. There may be some sex-related differences related to the reaction to pain. In one particular study, school-age boys said they "felt brave," while girls felt "nervous or afraid" (Haley, 1985). These differences would seem to reflect differences in childhood socialization practices.

In addition to developmental level, Haley (1985) also stresses that parental attitudes and cultural background influence the child's unique pain experience. Children can learn constructive pain management techniques from parents who portray a calm attitude. Their fears can be magnified, on the other hand, by a parent who is overly concerned and highly anxious.

The child's cultural background also influences the perception or expression of pain. For example, some ethnic groups are taught to deny pain and are hesitant to request pain relief. Others feel it very appropriate to express pain by moaning, talking, or gesturing. Still others are taught to control pain through visual imagery or other mental exercises.

Knowledge that children's pain experiences vary somewhat depending on developmental stage, parental attitude, and cultural background can be helpful as one interacts with children in pain. It is important, for example, to explain upcoming procedures in language they can understand. Opportunity to talk, draw pictures, or engage in dramatic play—in conjunction with support from a sensitive adult—can help children ask questions, express their fears, and integrate the experience of pain into the rest of their experiences, allowing them to retain a sense of control. Precautions should be taken to minimize procedural-related pain and teach children effective strategies for minimizing all types of pain (using self-distraction or relaxation techniques, for example). Heightened confidence in one's ability to cope diminishes fear of an anticipated painful event and also increases ability to withstand actual pain (Ross & Ross, 1985).

Continued School Attendance

Because school attendance is such a focal point in their lives, most dying children prefer to return to school, if at all possible. Participation in school activities can promote a sense of normality within certain limiting parameters. In addition to continuing their academic development, these children are able to maintain a sense of control and are allowed to continue relationships with teachers and peers (Cairns, Klopovich, Hearne, & Lansky, 1982; Ross, 1984).

Levenson and Cooper (1984) identify four major areas of concern regarding the teachers' roles in meeting the needs of children with cancer:

1. *Communication:* Teachers and parents need to share information.
2. *Organization:* Teachers should plan appropriate strategies to pro-

mote the child's academic progress prior to and during the reentry period.

3. *Identification of emotional problems:* School staff should be alert to emotional concerns and behavioral changes in order to work cooperatively with parents in facilitating the child's readjustment to school.

4. *Identification of physical problems:* Teachers need to recognize fatigue or other physical changes resulting from the illness or the therapy so that they may appropriately adapt teaching styles, assignments, and instructional equipment.

Each child should have an individualized education plan (IEP) that considers the following: (1) long-term goals and short-term objectives, (2) specialized services needed by the child to function successfully, and (3) modification of standards of competency (Deasy-Spinetta & Tarr, 1985).

Continued Peer Interaction

Children who are seriously ill continue to derive comfort from continued peer interaction. Sick children's psychological adjustment and self-acceptance are influenced by the perceptions and reactions of their peers (Potter & Roberts, 1984). Teaching the dying child how to communicate with peers about the illness can facilitate a positive psychological outcome. Weitzman (1984) suggests that parents or teachers discuss with the sick child the variety of possible reactions of peers and even role play appropriate types of interactions with them. Healthy peers may also have many questions or even anxieties related to their friend's illness. Parents, teachers, and school counselors, among others, can be very helpful by answering questions openly and honestly and by sharing information on an appropriate developmental level.

Sachs (1980) described a situation in which an 8-year-old's classmates visited him whenever they were able. This child had osteogenic sarcoma (a type of bone cancer). His leg had been amputated, and he had lost his hair due to chemotherapy treatments. The school counselor became aware that the child's peers were curious about a number of issues and had queried, "'We saw him fall and cut his foot—did that have anything to do with his leg being amputated?' 'Do you get cancer because you fell?' 'Are tumors and amputations contagious?' 'When you remove part of the body does it stop cancer?'" (Sachs, 1980, p. 330). The school counselor and nurse were able to provide much useful information by using visual aids to describe normal and abnormal cell growth, the use of chemotherapy and its side effects, the reason for the amputation, and related matters. Additionally, they showed an artificial limb and demonstrated how it worked.

Although sharing this type of factual information is crucial to classmates' understanding of a dying child's experience, the discussion should also allow an opportunity to share feelings. Classmates need to feel comfortable talking about their reactions and gain solace. Anxieties about such factors as physical differences, mood changes, or uncertain outcomes of the disease may affect continuing peer relationships. Children need support and guidance as they strive to overcome their concerns.

Children as Survivors

Death of a Parent

Although there are many resources available to those who wish to study the effect of parental death upon children, this section shall review only a limited number. Berlinsky and Biller (1982) did a thorough review of the related literature by examining over 200 studies. These authors suggested an organizational model for understanding factors influencing adjustment subsequent to a parent's death. Berlinsky and Biller note that these factors include the type of death (sudden or prolonged illness, suicide, homicide, war); parent's age, sex, and relationship with the child; the child's preparation for and involvement in the mourning process; and the child's age, sex, personality, and cognitive level. Additionally, family characteristics such as family structure, patterns of adjustment, cultural background, and religiosity must be examined for fuller understanding of the effect of parental death upon a child's behavior.

Upon completion of their literature review, Berlinsky and Biller drew a number of conclusions, including the following:

1. Because mothers and fathers typically play different roles and fulfill different needs, loss of a mother would be expected to have a somewhat different outcome than that of a father. Unfortunately, many studies ignore that probability and regard children of deceased parents as a homogeneous group.

2. There are a variety of common reactions to the death. Children typically experience some guilt, believing that something they did do or failed to do led to the death. The children also often regret the nature of their relationship with the deceased parent (wishing they had been closer or kinder, for example). Many children are angry at the deceased parent for having deserted them, particularly because children typically believe that the parent's primary purpose is to take care of them.

3. Children are likely to experience adverse effects if they are not given accurate information about the parent's death. Peers can often repeat exaggerated versions of the death based on conversations with adults. For example, one young child was in anguish thinking her mother had been decapitated in an auto accident. The daughter had seen a great deal of blood on her mother's dress after the accident, and children at school had told her "your mom's head was cut off." Although fatally injured due to severe head wounds, this woman had not been decapitated. Once the daughter was clearly given this truthful information, she was able to successfully continue her grief work.

4. Children should be informed about customs dealing with death, and expectations should be discussed. (Will there be a casket? if so, will it be open?)

5. Younger children seem to be more adversely affected by the death of a parent than are older children. It is hypothesized that these findings may be related to the younger child's inability to clearly understand the meaning of death, to their greater need for parental supervision, or to the lack of accumulated benefits of being from an intact family. These hypotheses need to be carefully tested before more definitive statements can be made.

6. The family situation is likely to change after the death of a parent; this occurrence, in turn, affects the child's subsequent adjustment. Family circumstances that may be altered include emotional and physical availability of the surviving parent, employment status of the remaining parent, functional roles played by each family member, and entry into the family of a parent substitute (a new spouse or a paid caregiver).

7. The child's relationship with the surviving parent is typically modified. Many children worry about the parent's welfare, fearful that he or she, too, may die and leave the child alone. Children may struggle against any separation from the parent, thinking that their presence will ensure the parent's safety. Some children take on extra responsibilities, hoping to spare the parent from additional stress. In some instances, children emotionally withdraw from the parent in order to protect themselves from another potential loss.

8. In some situations, there may be a positive outcome to the death of a parent. For example, the death of an abusive or an uninterested parent may have a positive influence on a child's self-concept and emotional adjustment. Even if the death is regarded by the child as a loss, he or she may ultimately become more resourceful as a result of the loss.

In conclusion, Berlinsky and Biller (1982) recommended that researchers proceed by doing more carefully designed and controlled studies regarding children's adjustment to parental death. Because factors such as sex of parent, child's age at the time of the death, and suddenness of death have an influence on the outcome, these variables should be taken into consideration when determining the research design.

Ikeman and her colleagues (1987) have studied a variety of issues related to childhood bereavement. They have found that the relationship between the surviving parent and the child becomes strained for a number of reasons. Since the surviving parent is dealing with his or her own grief and is also often responsible for roles that had once been performed by the dying/deceased parent, the surviving mother or father may have decreased awareness of the child's needs. Additionally, the surviving parent may be so emotionally drained that there is little energy or attention left to give the child. As a result, the child may experience a double loss— one parent is dying or has died, the other has withdrawn. The child then often becomes angry at the surviving parent whom he or she holds responsible for all of the negative changes in the family's life.

In their study, Kaffman and Elizur (1979) controlled for the sex of the parent who died (the father) and the type of death (killed suddenly in war). They then compared the adjustment of young children between the ages of 2 and 6 to that of older children between the ages of 6 and 10. The 24 children studied were living on a kibbutz, a type of commune, in Israel. None of the children had been identified as having any unusual problems prior to the death of their fathers in the October 1973 war. Each child's behavior was reported by mothers and teachers over a period of 1 to 6 months after the death. All of the families were middle class. The survivors did not have to fear financial stress after the death because food, clothing, and lodging were provided by the kibbutz. The similarity of circumstances of the children in this study provided controls not present in most other studies related to parental death.

Children in this study exhibited a variety of grief reactions similar to those noted earlier. Kaffman and Elizur (1979) found that almost all the children in their sample

> expressed their distress through noticeable behavioral changes and marked increase in the amount and severity of psychological symptoms. The reactive behavioral symptoms included a wide range of problems such as increased aggressiveness, tantrums, augmented dependency, separation anxiety, diverse fears, sleep problems, restlessness, changes in scholastic performance, discipline problems, wandering, daydreaming, eating problems, enuresis, thumbsucking, tics, excessive sibling rivalry, etc. (p. 220)

Overt sadness, crying, preoccupation with the deceased father, imitation of and identification with the father, searching for a "substitute" father, and striving to remember the father were also common responses. Many children were able to directly relate their feelings of sadness with their father's death. One 6-year-old boy said, "Mommy, I loved Dad and now my heart hurts so much that it goes to my stomach and I can't eat."

The researchers discovered a number of differences between responses of the younger children (2 to 6) and the older children (6 to 10). The remembering activities of younger children typically centered around "shared experiences," such as recalling times shared with their father, looking at photograph albums, listening to tape recordings of his voice, or holding his personal effects. The older children processed the death at a somewhat different level. In addition to the shared experiences, they frequently asked to go to the cemetery or expressed their longing in a new context (one unrelated to past shared experiences). One $6\frac{1}{2}$-year-old boy made up new words to a popular song: "If I could travel to faraway places, if I could come back home, and see my father, not only my mother, if all our wishes could come true . . ."

Thirteen out of the 24 children talked about their fathers as if they were still alive. Ten of those 13 were preschoolers. They repeatedly made statements about their father's expected return, and many thought that their fathers were alive in their photographs. A $4\frac{1}{2}$-year-old girl asked her father's photograph, "Daddy dear, why don't you answer me? . . . Where is the war?"

Younger children also differed from the older children in a variety of other symptoms, which the researchers categorized as "behavioral symptoms" in contrast to "grief reactions." Younger children showed a greater increase in problems related to separation from their mothers, excessive demands on adults for assistance, nighttime fears, and rejection of strangers than did the older children. The older children, however, showed a greater increase in quietness.

The literature related to the effect of parental death on the adjustment of surviving children clearly indicates the need for sensitive support and understanding. The intervention strategies discussed in Chapter 4 also apply in these situations.

It is difficult to conclude with any degree of certainty the long-term effects of parental death on individual children. Many variables influence the outcome, including sex of parent, quality of interaction with family members, age of child, and addition of surrogate parents. One drawback to much of the research that has examined the long-term influence of parental death on children's later adjustment is the use of subjects who have sought psychological intervention, rather than a random sample of survivors (Berlinsky & Biller, 1982). A clinical sample can give biased

results since these individuals (by nature of their selection) have identifiable adjustment difficulties.

Death of a Sibling

Predeath.   Siblings have unique needs after the death of a brother or sister. They also have special needs throughout the course of a life-threatening illness. When one child becomes seriously ill, parents have a diminished amount of time to spend with other children in the family. Healthy
children may become hurt, angry, or jealous when parents are unable to
give them the same attention they received earlier (Kinrade, 1985). Martin
(1985) explains that home care for the terminally ill child may have multiple benefits for the siblings. The family has more time to spend together
because the parents spend less time away from home visiting the sick
child. Furthermore, siblings may derive satisfaction from contributing to
the care of their dying brother or sister. After the death, the children may
once again feel deprived of the parents' attention, as the parents struggle
to do their own grief work.

Koch-Hattem (1986) interviewed 33 siblings of children with cancer
(the cancer was currently in remission but the children were still receiving
chemotherapy). Twenty-seven of the 33 siblings were older than the
patient, while six were younger than their sick brother or sister. A significant number of siblings reported feeling bothered, sad, and scared more
frequently after the onset of the illness than they had prior to that time.
They also said that the patient seemed to be angry at them more often
following the diagnosis than prior to it.

The siblings reported that they dealt with their own varied feelings in
different ways. They vented their feelings by becoming angry or crying.
They sought comfort from others. A frequent reaction was one of caring—
many focused their attentions on the child who was sick. A few indicated
that they wished they could change places with the patient. One child
shared, "Why couldn't it be me instead of him? Cause he's so little and so
young that I probably could take shots better than he could" (p. 114).
Twenty-two of the 33 siblings expressed fears that their siblings would
experience a relapse or death. One 11-year-old sibling said of her 3-year-
old sister, "I listen to her sleep, and I worry about her. I'm afraid her tumor
will come back" (p. 114).

Koch-Hattem (1986) also asked the siblings in her study what would
help them through the course of a brother's or sister's illness. Many noted
they would like to learn more about the patient's disease and its treatment.
The researcher suggests that parents keep communication lines open with

healthy siblings. For example, if parents hear a child get up to go check on his or her sibling, they might take the opportunity to talk to the child about how the whole family worries at times. Children whose parents allow them to share their own needs and fears make better adjustments than children who are not given this same opportunity (Cole, 1986). Parents should also reassure siblings that others in the family are not likely to become seriously ill and answer any questions that arise.

Postdeath.   Research done with siblings of deceased children indicates that these children often display a variety of behavior problems shortly after the death (Binger et al., 1969; Kaplan, Grobstein, & Smith, 1976; Spinetta, Swarner, & Sheposh, 1981).

Using the standardized Child Behavior Checklist, McCown and Pratt (1985) found that children grieving the death of a sibling displayed significantly more behavior problems in comparison to standardized norms. Problem behaviors included hyperactivity, arguing, excessive talking, running away, nightmares, clinging to adults, and withdrawal. Of the three groups studied (ages 4 to 5, 6 to 11, and 12 to 16), the group comprised of 6- to 11-year-olds showed the greatest disturbance. The authors (McCown & Pratt, 1985) conclude:

> Several explanations are possible. First, the 6- to 11-year-olds fall within the psychosocial stage described by Erikson as Industry versus Inferiority. The loss of a sibling at this phase may lead to a sense of self-vulnerability and inferiority. A second potential explanation for problems may be related to the 6- to 11-year-olds' death conceptualization. It is between the ages 6 and 11 (about age 9 or 10) that the critical conceptualization of death as universal and personal takes place in the child's understanding. School age children 6 to 11 make a transition from preoperational to concrete operational modes of thinking. They find death bewildering and seek a cause and explanation. For the child in this age group who is making the transition to concrete thought, the event and cause of sibling death may evoke confusion. The increased behavior problems may be a reflection of that confusion and concern. (p. 333)

In addition to behavior disturbances, guilt is one of the most frequent reactions to a sibling's death. It is related to hostile thoughts common to sibling rivalry and the belief that such thoughts were responsible for the death (Cain, Fast, & Erickson, 1964; Weston & Irwin, 1963). Because surviving children often think that they caused the death, these children sometimes conclude that they should not derive pleasure from life anymore. Some feel they should have died with, or instead of, the sibling. Not only do children feel guilty about the death, they often increase their burden of guilt by assuming they have caused other family members' reactions (such as parental withdrawal or a sibling's behavior problems). After working with 58 children, ages $2\frac{1}{2}$ to 14, who had experienced the death of a sibling, Cain et al. (1964) found that the "guilt was variously handled by each child in accord with his unique personality structure, with reactions including depressive withdrawal, accident-prone behavior, punishment-seeking, constant provocative testing . . . and many forms of acting out" (p. 743). A conspiracy of silence surrounding the death may alter family communication patterns. Krell and Rabkin (1979) describe this as a "conspiracy of guilt." The conspiracy of guilt is often present even though neither parent nor sibling could have done anything to prevent the death. For example, a parent may think, "If only I had checked the brakes on Joni's bike, she would have stopped in time" when, in fact, this may not have been the case.

It is crucial that children's guilt feelings be explored and alleviated. This is true whether the child in no way contributed to the death or was, in fact, instrumental in causing it. Unfortunately, in those cases where a sibling did contribute to the death, it is common for the parents inappropriately to reassure the child that he or she did not cause the death (even when the surviving child knows he or she had), label the death an accident, and/or prevent an open discussion with the child. Cain et al. (1964) found that in such cases parents engaged in these avoidance activities for the following reasons:

1. Parents felt that talking about the incident would only upset the surviving child more.
2. Parents were frightened of magnifying their own intense grief.
3. Parents were fearful of rage that they had suppressed in order to protect the surviving child.
4. Parents wanted to avoid open assessment of blame so that they might not have to succumb to their own self-accusations and resultant feelings of guilt.

It is helpful for open communication to take place so that each family member might deal with the guilt stemming from feelings that he or she had contributed to the death. Unfortunately, this often does not occur. Rosen (1985) interacted with 159 persons between the ages of 15 and 74 who had experienced the death of a sibling prior to the age of 20. Sixty-two percent of the sample reported that they had never discussed the death of the sibling with another family member. Twelve percent said they occasionally mentioned the deceased sibling, while 26 percent participated in extended family discussions.

"The death of a child leaves a legacy that influences all future transactions among the surviving family members. . . . the survivors—both parents and the remaining child or children—must adapt to a new reality" (Krell & Rabkin, 1979, p. 471). As noted in Chapter 3, family members change roles or perform new tasks in order to regain a sense of equilibrium. For example, some parents place an added emotional burden on a surviving child by expecting him or her to perform the same functions or achieve the same goals as the sibling who died (Cain & Cain, 1964; Poznanski, 1972; Zeligs, 1974). This phenomenon is known as the *replacement child* syndrome. Identity issues become complicated by the parent's expectation that the surviving child, to some extent, become the deceased child so that he or she, too, might continue to live. The surviving child may interpret the parents' desire as indicating that they wished that *he* or *she* had died instead. This interpretation magnifies already existing grief reactions such as anger, sadness, or guilt. In other situations, parents choose to have another baby to replace the child who has died and, in extreme instances, even give the new baby the deceased child's name.

Following the death of one child, parents may overprotect others in the family by increasing vigilance over their activities and discouraging free exploration of their environment. "Every foray into new experiences is considered by the parents to be fraught with danger, and constant warnings immobilize the child and prevent the incorporation of a suitable range of experiences essential to adequate and flexible coping responses" (Krell & Rabkin, 1979, p. 475). As described in Chapter 4, there are many strategies helpful to resolving children's grief. School teachers and counselors play an important role in facilitating children's coping. Appropriate support is predicated on their understanding the normal grief process and resulting behavior problems. Binger (1973) reported that many surviving siblings exhibit poor school performance or school phobias. These, too, require sensitivity and understanding. School-age children dread being regarded as different out of fear of feeling inferior. Teachers, therefore, should be sure that their discussions about or interactions with the children do not cause them to be ostracized by classmates.

Because peer interaction is such an important part of the culture of childhood, peer support groups comprised of others who have experienced severe illness or the death of a sibling provide an important therapeutic environment (Koch-Hattem, 1986). One of the more unique support groups of this type gathers at a camp called Camp Amanda for a weekend. The purpose of this camp is twofold: (1) to allow children to run and play and laugh and make noise again, and (2) to meet other boys and girls their own ages who have also had a death in the family. By meeting others like themselves, the children discover that they all share similar feelings, that those feelings are normal, and that they are okay for having them (Zimmerman, 1985). At a program similar to Camp Amanda—the

Bannock Bereavement Retreat—children who have experienced the death of a loved one meet with hospice personnel to discuss illness and death (Moyer, 1988).

Summary

Hallmarks of school-age development include refined physical skills, a shift from preoperational thinking to concrete operational thinking, and increased peer interaction. Additionally, school-agers strive to develop a sense of industry that allows them to be proud of their productivity. If children become seriously ill at this stage, they are at risk of being deprived of opportunities to enhance their physical capacity, rejected by their peers because they are different, and developing a sense of inferiority rather than industry.

Dying children can better retain a sense of control if pain is well managed. Continued school attendance and continued peer interaction also help children maintain a sense of control.

School-age children must cope with a variety of thoughts and feelings as they deal with the death of a parent. These may include guilt, misconceptions about the cause of death, desire to protect the surviving parent, and much more. The death of a sibling also precipitates a wide variety of reactions both before and after the death. Children often experience many fears related to the illness, have a desire to learn much more about the disease, and sometimes act out their feelings in an inappropriate fashion. An added burden may be parents' expectations that the surviving child, in essence, replace the deceased.

Personal Account

The following article explains how a teacher helped her fourth-grade students cope with the sudden death of a classmate. In a classroom context, the teacher gave her students permission to grieve and used the tragedy as an opportunity for learning and growth.

From *Journal of School Health*, Vol. 52, No. 2, February 1982, pp. 104–107. Copyright © 1982, American School Health Association, Kent, OH 44240.

The Death of a Classmate: A Teacher's Experience Dealing with Tragedy in the Classroom

Beth J. Evans

This past year, one of my fourth grade students died unexpectedly on a Sunday afternoon.

The following morning two of her friends, immediately upon entering the classroom, asked to speak to me and told me that Jill would not be in class for a while. One friend stated that "Jill had passed on" while the other youngster remarked that "Jill had passed out."

Crises do not respect age, and as much as we would like to, we cannot "protect" our students by not acknowledging and dealing with the traumatic events that confront them. We, as teachers, must be as willing and ready to offer the necessary emotional support as we are willing to teach our students academic subjects.

On Monday, my first reaction—a reaction common to all—was one of denial. I explained to the girls that the expression "passed out" is a temporary condition whereas "passed on" means to die. As I defined these phrases I also was trying to deny the possibility that Jill had died. Because the girls were so distraught, I assured them I would attempt to get the facts by calling the home and report back to them immediately.

My telephone call to Jill's home confirmed that Jill had died suddenly of what appeared to be a malfunctioning of the heart. I knew it was important and necessary to work quickly, for the children had sensed that something was wrong and rumors had already begun to circulate. I had to acknowledge the reality, tell the truth and establish a support system that would meet the emotional needs of the students. G. Kliman in *Psychological Emergencies of Childhood* states that the sooner a child is informed of a tragedy; the more opportunity there is to react with the adult and peer support; and the more organized and supportive the adult structured environment, the better.[1] In addition, not to do this would involve a loss of the children's self-esteem, for I would be giving these fourth-graders the message that it is not important for them to know and to respond as necessary.

After privately talking to the two girls, I gathered the children to discuss Jill's death. I was aware some children had already confronted death on an intimate level—the death of a parent, and for one student the death of both parents. Thus, a discussion of the death of a classmate could be a painful, but important experience. H. Moller notes that school personnel, such as teachers or guidance counselors should provide opportunities for bereaved children to talk about death in order to help children work through their grief.[2]

I informed the students that Jill, a bright, active and well-liked classmate had died and shared with them the few known facts. I shared my shock, sorrow, confusion and anger, and encouraged them to do so also. Emotions ran high; some cried, some demanded to know how this could happen to an eight year old, and others were angry at the unfairness of losing a friend, classmate and neighbor. During the discussion, the classmates related their personal experiences ranging from the death of a grandparent, a neighbor's cat, to the death of a pet dog. The latter youngster was still angry because she was not informed of her pet's death until she returned home from camp at the end of the summer.

I acknowledged that we were entitled to all our feelings—anger, guilt, sadness, the unfairness, the loneliness and the scariness. I emphasized that sharing our feelings would make it easier, but not less painful, for each of us to deal with the tragedy and face the next few days.

Confronting death leaves us with a variety of responses such as feelings of helplessness, confusion and fear. A. Kliman in *Crisis: Psychological First Aid for Recovery and Growth* points out that our psychological defenses at these times can be either adaptive or maladaptive. This holds true for children as well, for they are socially, intellectually, and emotionally immature, and have a harder time distinguishing between reality and fantasy.[3] Therefore, in addition to sharing the truth with them, I wanted the children to participate in the mourning process, providing opportunities to find the most adaptive ways for these youngsters to move from a helpless position to one of coping and mastery of the crisis.

The initial involvement was to collect money and send flowers. It was a true, caring gesture as they collected more than the suggested amount taken from both their snack money and from their piggy banks.

Writing condolence cards to Jill's parents was a very valuable experience, for it was a way to express their grief. The letters were a personal way of expressing sorrow, for most of them related thoughts about that child and his or her relationship with Jill. Before sending the cards, the children read and shared them with the class.

Since school is a place where learning takes place, I tried to maintain an atmosphere in which it was *safe* to ask, know and gather facts even on a topic such as death. I incorporated the different aspects of this tragedy into many different curriculum areas.

Jill's death was discussed during our daily current events session. The children brought in the reports of Jill's death that appeared in the local newspaper, as well as her obituary. They discussed these articles with one another including their reactions on how it felt to read about the death of their classmate and friend.

In addition to writing cards, the children read the cards other classes sent to us. Vocabulary words such as obituary, coffin, autopsy, funeral, cremation, wake and in memoriam were taught.

One of the most valuable experiences in the mourning process was utilizing the class newspaper. The children dedicated the next issue in Jill's memory. They wrote both factual articles and their own personal memories. All the children had the option to include at least one thought about their classmate. The newspaper served an additional purpose. It was published on what would have been Jill's ninth birthday and gave us another opportunity to share our feelings. These fourth graders eagerly shared their copy of the newspaper with schoolmates, friends and family.

The school nurse-teacher explained the importance of the heart and how it works. These lessons in science and health also emphasized that it is the norm for almost all children to reach adulthood, thus reassuring these students that their lives were not in danger. It was necessary to frequently remind them that they were healthy children who most likely would grow up to lead normal, active lives and that sudden death of children rarely happens.

This also led to a discussion on the average life span in the U.S., thus involving math. Some students chose to research what the average life span is, while others reported their findings with graphs and charts.

Our science unit on "Living Things" enabled us to discuss the life cycle of a leaf and plant as well as that of the human being. The children made charts illustrating different stages of human and plant growth. They also observed and logged the stages of development of plants that were in the classroom. This was valuable to the children for M. Rudolph in *Should the Children Know?* emphasizes that children who have experiences with living things including dying plants will become familiar with the life cycle and will gradually understand human health.[4]

Many children expressed the desire to attend either the wake or the funeral. First, we discussed some of the funeral rituals of different religious groups, such as a wake, the sitting of "shiva," and open and closed coffins.

When children know what to expect at a wake or funeral, they are better able to handle a difficult emotional experience. Attending the wake or funeral would help to confirm that which was hard for the children to believe—that Jill was dead. Also G. Kliman notes that children between the ages of three and ten tend to invent elaborate resurrection fantasies. Therefore, it is less frightening for children to participate in such procedures as a funeral and "see" for themselves rather than deal with their fantasies and perceptions of what is happening.[1]

It is the policy of the school board that parental permission is required for children to leave the school building during the school day. I contacted all the parents and encouraged them to allow their children to attend the funeral. We, as educators, have a responsibility to help parents understand that we neither protect nor help children by not allowing them to participate in rituals such as funerals. Since not all parents agreed to let their children attend the funeral, I, and those classmates accompanied by a parent, represented these children.

After returning from the funeral the children shared what had happened as well as their feelings. The children were open and interested in knowing specific details and many of their questions—such as what did the coffin look like, were her eyes opened, did she look the same as when she was alive—were answered. This was appropriate behavior, for Gordon and Klass observe in *They Need to Know* that children from ages seven to eleven are at a developmental stage where they may be more fascinated with the physical aspects of disposal than with the emotional aspects of the funeral.[5]

Furthermore, the children's interest in knowing the truth was not morbid, but rather realistic, healthy and left less to their imagination. What is not known is usually more frightening than that which is known. By talking about that which is scary, we can help children deal with it.[3]

Following Jill's death, I scratched our normal schedule and allowed time to discuss this tragic event whenever the need arose. But, I was also careful not to dwell on this topic for too long.

For the first week following the announcement of Jill's death there were many requests to see the school nurse-teacher. A. Kliman alerts us that children who are the friends and classmates of the deceased child are "indirect victims" and are subject to "the guilt of the survivor," which manifests itself in new physical and psychosomatic illnesses and in accidents, both at home and at school.[3] This was evident in my classroom. The children had complaints of hearts that hurt (the cause of Jill's death) as well as stomach aches, headaches and frequent minor accidents resulting in limping legs and sprained fingers. The school nurse-teacher, after examining the children and aware of their vulnerabilities as "indirect victims," was supportive and reassured the children that they were not seriously ill and helped them "talk out" the reasons for their illnesses.

Jackson explains that the feelings of grief for children are more likely to be worked out through their behavior. He states that this can include angry, boisterous and noisy behavior.[6] During this period I observed that the children's feelings and emotions spilled into their behavior both inside and outside the classroom. Bickering, unwarranted outbursts and needless arguments took place in the cafeteria and on the playground. Their disruptive behavior gradually subsided as their angry feelings were "talked out," and channeled into more positive behavior. At this time some children found it difficult to concentrate and were inattentive, others were "models" of good behavior.

Fourth graders are chronologically completing the stage of magical thinking when they believe what they think, wish or say can make something happen. Under stress it is easy for all of us, especially children, to regress to this stage. G. Kliman states that "children feel the emotion of guilt even more intensely if they happen to be young enough to imagine they are magically responsible for the person's death."[1]

Before Jill's death one child wished that I would move Jill's seat—she did not want to sit next to her. Another student was worried—he had pushed Jill on the lunch line. These are just two instances where it was necessary to remind them that their thoughts or actions did not cause Jill's death, thus helping to relieve them of guilt feeling.

At the children's request, Jill's desk remained in the room for the next few weeks, making the loss of their classmate very real and concrete. The desk became a link which enabled the classmates to reflect on her absence, their sadness and loneliness and provided the healing time to help them accept and recover from their loss.

It is important for teachers as well as parents to realize that when an important person dies it is not helpful to immediately discard all evidence of that person's life. To do so gives a message to others, including children, that the deceased person was not important, and/or we didn't care about that person. It leaves children confused for they are then unable to express their grief, which involves talking, sharing and remembering with family and friends, thereby making mourning that much harder. Grollman emphasizes this point by urging us not to attempt to eradicate the memory of the loved one. Children want some tangible reminders of the deceased and pictures are helpful for remembering, as are other mementos.[7]

Her work, especially her autobiography and self-portrait, done at the beginning of the school year remained on display. The children would frequently read and look at these and then discuss with me or a few of their classmates her wishes, hopes and facts of her life gleaned from the autobiography. These fourth graders were truly mourning in an age-appropriate way.

The children will not forget Jill. At appropriate times she will be remembered, such as when the class photos arrive, for the children are now able to share and express their feelings.

Mourning involved discussing a scary subject and realizing that our classmate was no longer with us, except in our memories. But it is more important that the children are now able to continue growing, strengthened and prepared both emotionally and academically to face life.

Summary

Educators have a responsibility to help children deal with crises, such as death, by doing the following:

(1) acknowledge the reality as soon as possible,

(2) provide an environment where children feel comfortable discussing their feelings,

(3) provide learning opportunities with curriculum so children may understand what has transpired.

It is my hope that the means I used to incorporate the subject of death into the curriculum can be adapted by other educators. Additional resource material can be found in *They Need to Know*[6] and *Discussing Death.*[8]

References

1. Kliman GW: *Psychological Experiences of Childhood.* New York, Grune & Stratton, 1968, p 136.

2. Moller H: "Death: Handling the Subject and Affected Students in the Schools" in Grollman EA (ed): *Explaining Death to Children.* Boston, Beacon Press, 1967, p 163.

3. Kliman AS: *Crisis: Psychological First Aid for Recovery and Growth.* New York, Holt, Rinehart and Winston, 1978, pp 5–7.

4. Rudolph M: *Should the Children Know?* New York, Schocken Books, 1978, pp 45–46.

5. Gordon AK, Klass D: *They Need to Know.* Englewood Cliffs, Prentice-Hall, 1979, p 55.

6. Jackson EW: *Telling a Child About Death.* New York, Channel Press, 1965, pp 68–70.

7. Grollman EA: *Talking About Death* (rev. ed). Boston, Beacon Press, 1976, p 59.

8. Mills GC: *Discussing Death.* Homewood, Ill, ETC Publications, 1976.

Questions and Activities

1. In the article "The Death of a Classmate," the teacher used a variety of techniques to help her young students cope with the sudden death of a classmate. Identify the specific intervention strategies used.

2. Could the teacher have done anything else to help her students cope with this sudden loss? Was it appropriate to bring up the subject of Jill's death during the months after the death?

3. The teacher contacted the parents of all of her students to obtain permission for them to attend Jill's funeral. If you were the teacher making that contact, what would you say? What suggestions would you give to the parents to help them deal with the situation at home?

4. If Jill had died of a long-term illness rather than dying suddenly, should the teacher have interacted differently with her students? What could she have done prior to the death to help both Jill and her classmates?

5. Do you remember any conversations you had as a child with classmates or teachers about the subject of death? What were they like? Were they helpful? Realistic?

Glossary

Concrete Operational Stage: Third of Piaget's cognitive stages, associated with school-age children.

Conservation: Understanding that certain characteristics of an object do not change in spite of modifications in its appearance.

Disease-Related Pain: Pain caused by the progression of the illness itself.

Industry: Positive resolution of Erikson's school-age crisis. Industry is associated with feelings of pride and competency resulting from successfully learning new skills, making things, and being productive.

Inferiority: Negative resolution of Erikson's school-age crisis. Involves feelings of being inferior to those around oneself.

Procedural Pain: Pain caused by medical treatments.

Replacement Child Syndrome: Expectation that a surviving child will perform the same functions or achieve the same goals as the sibling who died.

Transformations: Ability to perceive intermediate steps that lead to a particular outcome.

Suggested Readings

Gordon, A. K., & Klass, D. (1979). *They need to know: How to teach children about death.* Englewood Cliffs, NJ: Prentice-Hall.

This book emphasizes the importance of children learning about death and dying and suggests ways for parents and teachers to introduce children to this sensitive subject. The authors include a special section on coping with death in the school setting and provide examples of appropriate curricula and death education for grades K–12.

Mills, G. C., Reisler, R., Jr., Robinson, A. E., & Vermilye, G. (1976). *Discussing death: A guide to death education.* Homewood, IL: ETC Publications.

A curriculum guide on death education with sections organized by age level (5 to 6 years, 7 to 9 years, 10 to 12 years, and 13 to 18 years). It includes very practical information for teachers. Each death-related concept is followed by a description of learning opportunities and objectives, details of suggested activities, instructional notes to teachers, and a list of resources.

Thomas, J. L. (Ed.). (1984). *Death and dying in the classroom: Readings for reference.* Phoenix, AZ: Oryx Press.

This volume contains a variety of readings of interest to teachers. Very practical and applied in focus, the articles address topics related to dealing with death-related situations and issues in the classroom.

Resources

Children's Oncology Camps of America
c/o The Children's Memorial Hospital
2300 Children's Plaza
Chicago, Illinois 60614
(312) 880-4564

Sky High Hope Camp
Oncology Department
Denver Children's Hospital
(303) 861-8888

References

Berger, K. S. (1983). *The developing person through the lifespan.* New York: Wadsworth.

Berlinsky, E. B., & Biller, H. B. (1982). *Parental death and psychological development.* Lexington, MA: Lexington Books.

Bibace, R., & Walsh, M. E. (1979). Developmental stages in children's conceptions of illness. In G. C. Stone, F. Cohen, & N. Adler (Eds.), *Health psychology: A handbook* (pp. 285–310). San Francisco: Jossey-Bass.

Binger, C. M. (1973). Childhood leukemia—Emotional impact on siblings. In E. J. Anthony & C. Koupernik (Eds.), *The child in his family: The impact of disease and death* (pp. 195–209). New York: Wiley.

Binger, C., Ablin, A., Feuerstein, R., Kushner, J., Loger, S., & Mikkelson, C. (1969). Childhood leukemia: Emotional impact on patient and family. *New England Journal of Medicine, 280,* 414–418.

Cain, A., & Cain, B. (1964). On replacing a child. *Journal of the American Academy of Child Psychiatry, 3,* 443–455.

Cain, A., Fast, I., & Erickson, M. (1964). Children's disturbed reactions to the death of a sibling. *American Journal of Orthopsychiatry, 34,* 741–745.

Cairns, N., Klopovich, P., Hearne, E., & Lansky, S. (1982). School attendance of children with cancer. *The Journal of School Health, 52,* 152–155.

Cole, E. (1986). Anticipatory grief of parents and siblings of children with chronic terminal illness. *Advances in Thanatology, 5*(4), 23–26.

Deasy-Spinetta, P., & Tarr, D. (1985). Public law 94–142 and the student with cancer: An overview of the legal, organizational, and practical aspects. *Journal of Psychosocial Oncology, 3*(2), 97–105.

Erikson, E. (1963). *Childhood and society* (2d ed.). New York: Norton.

Haley, J. (1985). Dealing with children's pain: Learning from personal experience. *The American Journal of Hospice Care, 2*(3), 34–40.

Ikeman, B., Block, R., Avery, J., Niedra, R., Sulman, J., Trentowsky, S., & Yorke, E. (1987). Grief work with children: Access, clinical issues, community advocacy.

In M. A. Morgan (Ed.), *Bereavement: Helping the survivors* (pp. 105–119). London, Ontario: King's College.

Kaffman, M., & Elizur, E. (1979). Children's bereavement reactions following death of the father. *International Journal of Family Therapy, 1*(3), 203–229.

Kaplan, D., Grobstein, R., & Smith, A. (1976). Predicting the impact of severe illness in families. *Health and Social Work, 1*, 71–82.

Katz, E., Kellerman, E., Williams, K., & Siegel, S. (1975). School intervention with pediatric cancer patients. *Journal of Pediatric Psychology, 2*(2), 72–76.

Kinrade, L. C. (1985). Preventive group intervention with siblings of oncology patients. *Children's Health Care, 14*(2), 110–113.

Kleck, R., Richardson, S., & Ronald, L. (1974). Physical appearance cues and interpersonal attraction in children. *Child Development, 45*, 305–310.

Koch-Hattem, A. (1986). Siblings' experience of pediatric cancer: Interviews with children. *Health and Social Work, 11*(2), 107–117.

Koocher, G. P. (1974). Talking with children about death. *American Journal of Orthopsychiatry, 44*(3), 405–411.

Krell, R., & Rabkin, L. (1979). The effects of death on the surviving child: A family perspective. *Family Process, 18*, 471–477.

Langlois, J., & Stephan, C. (1977). The effects of physical attractiveness and ethnicity on children's behavioral attributions and peer preference. *Child Development, 48*, 1694–1698.

Lerner, R., & Lerner, J. (1977). Effects of age, sex, and physical attractiveness on child-peer relations, academic performance, and elementary school adjustment. *Developmental Psychology, 13*, 585–590.

Levenson, P., & Cooper, M. (1984). School health education for the chronically impaired individual. *Journal of School Health, 54*(11), 446–448.

Martin, B. (1985). Home care for terminally ill children and their families. In C. A. Corr & D. M. Corr (Eds.), *Hospice approaches to pediatric care* (pp. 65–86). New York: Springer.

McCown, D., & Pratt, D. (1985). Impact of sibling death on children's behavior. *Death Studies, 9*, 323–335.

Moyer, J. A. (1988). Bannock bereavement retreat: A camping experience for surviving children. *The American Journal of Hospice Care, 5*(2), 26–29.

Nagy, M. (1948). The child's theories concerning death. *Journal of Genetic Psychology, 73*, 3–27.

Piaget, J., & Inhelder, B. (1969). *The psychology of the child*. New York: Basic Books.

Potter, P., & Roberts, M. (1984). Children's perception of chronic illness: The roles of disease symptoms, cognitive development, and information. *Journal of Pediatric Psychology, 9*(1), 13–25.

Poznanski, E. (1972). The "replacement child"—A saga of unresolved parental grief. *Journal of Pediatrics, 81*, 1190–1193.

Rait, D. S., & Holland, J. (1986). Pediatric cancer: Psycho-social issues and approaches. *Mediguide to Oncology, 6*(3), 1–5.

Rosen, H. (1985). Prohibition against mourning in childhood sibling loss. *Omega, 15*(4), 307–316.

Rosenbloom, J. (1976). *Biggest riddle book in the world.* New York: Sterling.

Rosenbloom, J. (1984). *Laughs, hoots, and giggles: Riddles, jokes, knock-knocks, and put-downs.* New York: Sterling.

Ross, D. M., & Ross, S. A. (1985). Pain instruction with third- and fourth-grade children: A pilot study. *Journal of Pediatric Psychology, 10*(1), 55–63.

Ross, J. (1984). Resolving nonmedical obstacles to successful school reentry for children with cancer. *Journal of School Health, 54,* 84–86.

Sachs, M. (1980). Helping the child with cancer go back to school. *The Journal of School Health, 50*(6), 328–331.

Speece, M. W., & Brent, S. B. (1984). Children's understanding of death: A review of three components of a death concept. *Child Development, 55,* 1671–1686.

Spinetta, J., Swarner, J., & Sheposh, J. (1981). Effective parental coping following the death of a child from cancer. *Journal of Pediatric Psychology, 6*(3), 251–263.

Van Eys, J. (1977). The outlook for the child with cancer. *The Journal of School Health, 47*(3), 165–169.

VanderZanden, J. W. (1985). *Human Development* (3d ed.). New York: Knopf.

Weitzman, M. (1984). School and peer relations. *Pediatric Clinics of North America, 31*(1), 59–69.

Weston, D., & Irwin, R. (1963). Preschool child's response to death of infant sibling. *American Journal of Diseases of Children, 106,* 564–567.

White, E., Elsom, B., & Prawat, B. (1978). Children's conceptions of death. *Child Development, 49,* 307–311.

Zeligs, R. (1974). *Children's experience with death.* Springfield, IL: Charles C Thomas.

Zimmerman, J. (1985). Amanda the panda. In C. A. Corr & D. M. Corr (Eds.), *Hospice approaches to pediatric care* (pp. 179–194). New York: Springer.

6

ADOLESCENCE

Death-related Experiences of Adolescents 216

Adolescents' Understanding of Death 218

Formal operational Thought 218
Adolescent Egocentrism 223

Needs of the Adolescent with a Life-threatening Illness 224

Privacy 225
Positive Body Image 226
Expression of Individuality 228
Independence and Control 232
Peer Interaction 236

Helping Adolescents Cope with Life-threatening Illnesses 239

The Grieving Adolescent 241

Adolescent Manifestations of Grief 241
Coping with Loss during Adolescence 243

Adolescent Suicide 247

Causes of Suicide 247
Suicide Prevention, Intervention, and Postvention 249

Summary 252

Adolescence is a transitional life stage bridging childhood and adulthood and culminating in the achievement of adult status. The transitional nature of adolescence can be seen in almost every aspect of the individual's life. Not only are most developmental processes going through dramatic and rapid change, but these changes are occurring at different rates. Because of the combined effects and special nature of these changes, adolescents confront unique issues during this critical period of life (Lerner & Hultsch, 1983). Due to the degree of change during this age span, many developmentalists have divided adolescence into two stages: early adolescence (12 to 16 years of age) and later adolescence (17 to middle 20s) (Schiamberg, 1985).

Death-related Experiences of Adolescents

Much has been written about the isolation of today's young people from death and death-related events. While death and dying may appear to have little to do with the life of a young person, closer examination shows that this is not the case. Recent data suggest that adolescents have more experience with death than is generally recognized. In a survey of over 1000 high school juniors and seniors, 90 percent of the students had lost someone they cared about through death. A high percentage of these losses were among friends; about 40 percent of the sample had experienced the death of a friend their own age (Ewalt & Perkins, 1979). This figure is not surprising considering the increase in adolescent suicide over the past several years. Ewalt and Perkins (1979) also found that approximately 20 percent of high school students in their study had actually witnessed a death.

As one considers the experiences of adolescents in contemporary society, it is clear that death is not a stranger to them and that their experience with it is by no means negligible. In addition, adolescents are exposed to information almost daily regarding global conflict, the threat of nuclear war, and the possibility of total annihilation during their lifetimes. They are also aware that they may be required to participate in activities related to military conflict. At the same time, adolescents of today have felt the impact of the tragic deaths of some of their popular idols (rock stars, actors) and have witnessed the reality of political assassinations.

Despite adolescents' increased exposure to death, Kalish (1985) has described adolescence itself as the healthiest period of the entire lifespan: "The vulnerability of infancy and childhood has been replaced by a much more robust quality, and the accrued health problems and stresses of the adult years have not yet begun" (p. 239). Consequently, the death

216

rate of adolescents is the lowest of any age group. When death does occur, it is usually the result of accidents, suicides, or homicides. Many adolescents thus die under tragic circumstances, either suddenly or after a brief period in intensive care.

Of the life-threatening illnesses adolescents may experience, cancer is the most common. In fact, cancer is the fourth most common cause of death among adolescents in the United States (United States Bureau of the Census, 1983). Although adolescents can be diagnosed as having any of a variety of cancers (among them Hodgkin's disease and brain tumors), leukemia is the most common type of cancer during this age stage. Some types of cancer are particularly associated with the adolescent years (for example, certain tumors of the bone such as Ewing's sarcoma and osteogenic sarcoma) and are found less frequently in other age groups. Figure 6.1 shows the relative incidence of major malignancies during adolescence. Cancer in adolescents is usually treated aggressively with some combination of chemotherapy, radiation therapy, and surgery.

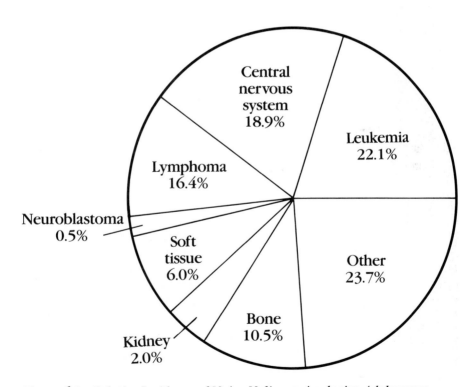

Figure 6.1 *Relative Incidence of Major Malignancies during Adolescence*

Source: A. J. Altman & A. D. Schwartz (1978), *Major Malignancies of Infancy, Childhood, and Adolescence,* Philadelphia: W. B. Saunders Co., p. 3. Reprinted by permission.

Cancer was once almost always fatal, but advances in medical science have resulted in longer remissions (disease-free states) and more apparent "cures" of cancer patients. Survival rates as well as courses of treatment do vary, however, for different types of cancer. It is legitimate in many cases to view adolescent cancer as a chronic disease with an uncertain outcome, as medical treatment may continue for many years. Because young people with cancer are living longer and fewer are dying of the disease, more and more adolescents are alive who have or have had a malignancy (Blumberg, Lewis, & Susman, 1984).

Adolescents' Understanding of Death

Significant changes occur in cognitive abilities during adolescence. These cognitive changes have far-reaching effects on the way adolescents view life and death and on the types of questions and concerns they have about the dying process.

Formal Operational Thought

Cognition undergoes both quantitative and qualitative change during adolescence. Not only do adolescents acquire more information, but the way they process this information is distinctively different than younger age groups. Piaget (1972) has proposed the stage of *formal operations* as the last stage in his structural approach to cognitive development, following the earlier sensorimotor, preoperational, and concrete operational stages. According to Piaget, the formal operational stage begins at approximately 11 or 12 years of age and continues to develop gradually over a period of several years.

The entire reasoning process is altered upon entering the formal operations stage of cognitive development. Perhaps the most striking characteristic of formal operational thought is its flexibility. Upon reaching this stage, the adolescent is no longer tied to the observable. He or she can reason logically with abstractions that may have no basis in reality. In fact, formal operators seem to enjoy thinking about hypothetical situations. In addition, their approach to problem solving becomes increasingly systematic; possible solutions to a problem are generated and then evaluated. This hypothetical-deductive style of reasoning includes considering hypothetical "if/then" propositions and carrying them to a logical conclusion. With the expanded thought capacities of the adolescent, the way the world is organized is no longer seen as the only way it can be. The ability to think abstractly, hypothetically, and counterfactually allows the adolescent to consider possibilities for change. Anything and everything can become the focus of this type of thinking (Lerner & Hultsch, 1983). Shaffer (1985) captures the essence of formal operational thought in the following statement:

> In sum, formal-operational thinking is rational, systematic, and abstract. The formal operator can now "think about thinking" and operate on *ideas* as well as tangible objects and events. Piaget believes that these new cognitive abilities are almost certain to have a dramatic impact on the adolescent's feelings, goals, and behaviors, for teenagers are suddenly able to reflect on weighty abstractions such as morality and justice, as well as more personal concerns such as their present and future roles in life, their beliefs and values, and the way things "are" as opposed to the way things "ought to be." Consequently, the adolescent approaching intellectual maturity is apt to become a bit of a philosopher, and his or her preoccupation with thinking and its products is the hallmark of the formal-operational period. (p. 355)

Neimark (1979) in reviewing research in this area found that some adolescents and adults never reach the formal operations stage. Therefore, a certain percentage of adolescents, especially younger ones, may still be rather concrete in their thinking. Possible explanations for this include a limited intellectual capacity or a lack of environmental demands that require performance at the formal operational level of intellectual functioning. Shaffer (1985) has concluded that the failure of individuals to use formal operational thought is due primarily to lack of experience with formal operations rather than inability to reason at that level.

Cognitive changes reflecting formal operational thinking affect the adolescent's ability to comprehend death and related concepts. Adolescents' maturing ability to use abstract reasoning and to understand symbolism allows them to more fully grasp the meanings of life, death, and time. Abstract concepts such as "eternity," "the purpose of life," and "acceptance of death" can now be considered. Adolescents can consider the interrelationships of several variables (for example, length of life, quality of life, and effects of medical intervention) rather than focusing on each variable in isolation. Because they can deal cognitively with hypothetical situations, they are able to consider various possibilities when presented with a question such as "What would you do if you knew you were going to die next month?"

Accompanying the development of logical thought is the drive to explore the world of ideas, ideologies, and theories. The newly developed cognitive abilities prompt the adolescent to ponder the meaning of life and death. As Hankoff (1975) has pointed out, it is natural for adolescents to consider the limits of life and the meaning of death as they explore the reaches of their own minds.

In comparing questions about death and dying among junior high, high school, and college students, Cook and Oltjenbruns (1982) obtained results that show the strong influence of cognitive development on the individual's specific concerns about death. These investigators concluded that 11-year-olds are seeking different information and asking qualitatively different questions than are older adolescents (see Table 6.1). Junior high school students asked questions that focused on concrete events and physical appearance (such as "What do people look like when they die?"). Their questions tended to be fact oriented ("How much does a funeral cost?") and frequently required only a yes–no response ("Is death a bad thing to watch?" "Do some people die happy?" "Do the muscles and stuff still move after the person is dead?"). Most of the questions of the junior high school students indicated that they viewed death as a single event rather than a process. Because of their age, the majority of the junior high school students were still in Piaget's concrete operational stage.

In contrast, the questions of high school juniors showed that they had made a shift to abstract thinking. They appeared more interested in understanding the dynamics of grief, dying, and death than in just obtaining facts and figures. Rather than asking questions that typically started with "what" or "how many," as was true of the junior high school students, the questions of the high school juniors often began with "why" or "how." Many of their questions indicated that they had begun to question their own values and personal philosophies related to life and death. For example, one student asked, "Why treat someone who will die anyway?" Another questioned, "How do people prepare for the end?" The high school juniors no longer viewed death as an event, but rather as a process.

An analysis of the questions asked by college juniors indicated even further cognitive change. While similar to the high school juniors in many respects, college students demonstrated an increased understanding of the complexity of death-related events. Showing the ability to manipulate more than two categories of variables simultaneously (characteristic of formal operational thinkers), the college students asked questions such as "Does research show that most people fear death, and does this feeling relate to age?" College students also asked questions that challenged widely held ideas about the dying process and questions that showed an unwillingness to simply accept the view of authorities ("Do you think Kübler-Ross's model of the five stages of dying has been used to dehumanize the dying by putting a label on them?"). Other questions showed what Piaget has described as the ability to think in relativistic terms, rather than being bound to absolutes. This characteristic of formal operational thought was illustrated in the following questions: "How does the type of death affect family interactions?" "When parents are faced with the death of a child, is their reaction different than that of a child faced with the death of a parent?" This research shows that the cognitive maturation process continues during the adolescence period and influences the ability to comprehend complex concepts, determines the types of questions and concerns adolescents may have about death, and modifies their own experience of the death of a loved one.

Table 6.1
Developmental Changes in Questions about Death

Junior High Students ($N = 41$)
Questions illustrated concrete thinking, a concern with appearance, and the idea that death is an event, not a process. Many questions required a yes-no or a simple factual response.
Do some people die happy?
How many shots do you give a dying person each day?
How much does a funeral cost?
What do people look like when they die?
What do you do with a body right after a person dies?
How many people die?
Does everyone have to die when they get old?
Is death a bad thing to watch?
Do the muscles and stuff still move after the person is dead?
Why does people's hair fall out with chemotherapy?

High School Juniors ($N = 47$)
Questions illustrated a shift to abstract thinking, a desire to understand the dynamics of the death and dying process, and an examination of personal values and philosophies.
Will people automatically act differently toward a terminally ill person?
Do the dying have long periods of depression?
How do people prepare for the end?
Why would someone want to be cremated?
Why would someone want to view a body?
What is a dying person's reaction to death?
What is the best way to share grief?
Why treat someone who will die anyway?
Do dying people seem to treasure life more than other people?

Table 6.1
(*continued*)

College Juniors ($N = 62$)

Questions illustrated understanding of interrelated variables and abstract con-
cepts, unwillingness to simply accept all that authorities teach, and relativistic
thinking.

Do you believe that people ever reach the "last stage" (so-called) of acceptance?
　Or do you think resignation or acknowledgment would be a better term?
Do you think that Kübler-Ross's model of the five stages of dying has been used
　to dehumanize the dying by putting a label on them?
What are some different points of view on life after death and ways to cope with
　one's own death?
How does the type of death affect family interactions?
Does research show that most people fear death and does this feeling relate to
　age?
How many people find cremation harder to cope with than what they had previ-
　ously presumed?
When parents are faced with the death of a child, is their reaction different than
　that of a child faced with the death of a parent?
How do you go about donating your body to science?

SOURCE:　A. S. Cook & K. Oltjenbruns (1982), A cognitive-developmental approach to death
education for adolescents, *Family Perspective,* Vol. 16, p. 12. Reprinted by permission.

　　Contemporary concerns related to death and dying often involve important ethical issues. Closely related to changes in cognitive development
are changes in the manner in which one judges behavior and thinks about
moral dilemmas, usually referred to as *moral reasoning* (DePalma &
Foley, 1975; Piaget, 1932). A key developmental task of adolescence as
identified by Havighurst (1972) is the acquisition of a set of values and an
ethical system as a guide to behavior—in other words, developing one's
own personal ideology. The development of a personal ideology is closely
related to adolescents' attempts to define themselves and to express who
they are as individuals. Each adolescent struggles with developing a
coherent value system that includes attitudes toward life and death. Peers,
parents, school, and religion are all important influences as the adolescent
develops his or her standards for living. Successful completion of this
developmental task is made possible by, among other factors, the adolescent's ability to conceptualize on an abstract level. The adolescent cancer
patients studied by Orr, Hoffmans, & Bennetts (1984) stated emphatically
that they did not want to be given false promises or aggressive therapy if
death was inevitable. Honesty was a standard they wanted their health care

providers and their parents to uphold. While they considered it vital to maintain hope and consider the possibilities of a cure, they did not believe in deception, and they readily articulated this belief.

Adolescent Egocentrism

Egocentrism is expressed in different ways at each stage of cognitive development. During adolescence, individuals become preoccupied with their own thought processes, leading to limitations on their newly developed cognitive abilities. Elkind (1967) has labeled this phenomenon *adolescent egocentrism*. Because adolescents are preoccupied with their own thinking and their thoughts of themselves, combined with a self-consciousness about their physical and sexual changes, they create an *imaginary audience* and believe that they are continually under observation by others. Manaster (1977) describes the concept of imaginary audience as follows:

> The adolescent is said to be anticipating the reactions of the persons around him as if they saw him with his eyes, seeing his strengths, weaknesses, and concerns as he does for himself. And he thinks they are as intensely interested in the minutiae of his appearance and behavior as he is. This tremendous pressure of always being on stage in front of an "imaginary audience" accounts in part for adolescent self-consciousness, overreaction to self-perceived successes and failures, and a need for privacy and seclusion. . . . (p. 47)

Physical changes associated with disease can be especially problematic for younger adolescents, due to this developmental phenomenon.

According to Elkind (1970), adolescent egocentrism declines at about the age of 15 or 16 as older adolescents begin to realize that their feelings are not that different from the feelings of others and that they are not really standing in the middle of center stage all the time. At this point, a more realistic self-concept emerges. Correspondingly, formal operations are becoming better established at this time as well.

While failing to separate their concerns from those of others, adolescents overdifferentiate their own feelings and see them as new and different, believing that perhaps they have never been experienced so intensely by anyone else. Therefore, they regard themselves as special and unique. This leads to a second aspect of adolescent egocentrism—*the personal fable*. The personal fable is the belief the adolescent holds that he or she is a one-of-a-kind individual (Elkind, 1970). This exaggerated sense of uniqueness, which often persists into late adolescence, can lead to the feeling that one is immune from the bad things that happen to others. The rules that govern other people's lives somehow do not apply to them. As a result, adolescents typically believe that death only happens to others and that it could not possibly happen to them or their family. This belief contributes to adolescents' propensity to participate in a variety of death-defying and dangerous activities and display daredevil behavior.

While part of the normal adolescent reaction, the view that one is indestructible can also contribute to denial in response to the diagnosis of a terminal illness. Blumberg et al. (1984) point out that this denial in adolescent cancer patients can be very adaptive. In fact, they have suggested that caregivers encourage adolescents to use some minimal degree of denial as a valid way of adapting to their disease by encouraging adolescents to continue their normal activities. Denial can be maladaptive, however, if it interferes with adequate medical intervention or results in participation in certain activities against medical advice (Moore, Holton, & Martin, 1969).

Zeltzer (1980) has noted that adolescents have a resiliency that comes from their views of themselves as immortal. Viewing death as something in the distant future enables adolescents with cancer to cope better with setbacks in the course of their illness. Examining the effectiveness of experimental drugs after the failure of conventional treatment, Susman, Pizzo, and Poplack (1981) found that their adolescent patients displayed an inordinate degree of hope in the remission-inducing potential of the chemotherapy. The majority of adolescents thought they would survive even though the odds were against them.

Needs of the Adolescent with a Life-threatening Illness

All of the developmental processes of adolescence have implications for the individual's ability to cope with death, dying, and grief. Adolescents with life-threatening illnesses have special needs and concerns. These needs relate to the developmental issues associated with the period of adolescence and include the following: (1) the need for privacy, (2) the need for a positive body image, (3) the need to express individuality, (4) the need for independence and control, and (5) the need for peer interaction. These needs must be considered in order to provide optimal care for the adolescent patient. In this section, important changes in the areas of physical, cognitive, and psychosocial development will be discussed and related to the needs of adolescents with life-threatening illnesses.

In working with adolescent patients, the emphasis is less on rehabilitation (returning the person to his or her previous level of functioning) and more on fostering development so that it will continue as closely as possible to that of their agemates (Blumberg et al., 1984). Adolescents with life-threatening illnesses are very much like healthy adolescents. They all confront the normal stresses and challenges of this stage of life. In addition, adolescents with health problems must face the added stresses associated with their particular disease process and its implications for their psychosocial functioning. Additional change precipitated by illness may be particularly anxiety provoking during a life stage already filled with multiple and rapid changes.

Privacy

Adolescence begins biologically when endocrine glands release hormones into the blood stream, which in turn initiate physical and sexual changes. The 1- to 2-year period that follows is referred to as puberty. Puberty usually begins in females around the age of 12, and in males at approximately age 14. During this period, individuals experience a growth spurt and add several inches to their height. Increases in weight and changes in body shape also occur during this time. Wide individual differences do exist, however, as to when the growth spurt begins and the extent to which it occurs (Gander & Gardiner, 1981). Another important aspect of puberty is the development of primary and secondary sex characteristics that signal the beginning of sexual maturation. Changes that occur at this time include the development of breasts in females and facial hair in males.

Because new hormones are being produced, adolescents not only begin to look different but they feel different as well. The physical and hormonal changes associated with puberty produce changes in the person's emotional functioning that result in sexual drives and other feelings not previously experienced (Lerner & Hultsch, 1983). The physiological changes of puberty have symbolic value as well. The altered appearance of the adolescent serves as a signal to society that a new person is emerging within the adolescent. "What the adolescent experiences internally, family members are able to view externally, the two views giving consensual validation to each other of the life cycle change which is occurring" (Hankoff, 1975, p. 374).

Adolescents are acutely aware of the development of secondary sex characteristics. Their egocentrism causes them to feel that others are also focusing on changes in their body. Late maturers and early maturers may be especially sensitive during early adolescence. This sensitivity needs to be acknowledged and respected by health care professionals. Privacy can be assured by performing physical examinations behind a closed curtain or a closed door and by entering their rooms only after knocking. Mitchell (1980) found male adolescents' self-consciousness concerning a physical examination conducted by a female more related to "what the other guys would think" than to the actual experience. These findings have implications for the way opposite-sex nursing and medical staff prepare adolescents for potentially embarrassing medical procedures such as urinary catheterization, sponge baths, and pelvic examinations.

The need for privacy extends into other areas as well. The right to private conversations with friends, siblings, or medical staff is important to the adolescent. If conversations held in confidence are not kept confidential, then the adolescent's trust will be jeopardized. Because of the many issues that they are facing, adolescents may also want some private time away from parents and medical staff. Quiet time for reflecting and contemplating one's life experience becomes increasingly important with age.

Positive Body Image

Although they are normal, the physical changes that occur in the body of the adolescent can be a source of anxiety and concern. Physical appearance is very important at this stage, and adolescents may worry, for example, that they are too tall, that their noses are crooked, or that their teeth are too big. Adolescents typically spend considerable time each day grooming, evaluating their physical appearance in the mirror, and trying to become accustomed to their changing bodies. As Manaster (1977) points out: "For adults, the question 'How do I look today?' can generally be answered 'Like I looked yesterday.' For adolescents, it is a real question, which they can answer by frequently inspecting and modifying the way they look, and incorporating this information into their changing body concept" (p. 272). The concern of adolescents over their body image is magnified by our society's emphasis on physical appearance. Body image is the result of several factors, including ideas about how adolescents think they look, how they think others view them, their fantasies about how they would like to look, and whether they mature earlier or later than their peers. An adolescent with a positive body image is more likely to develop a positive self-image (Gander & Gardiner, 1981).

In addition to adapting to the normal changes in appearance, adolescents with life-threatening diseases must cope with changes resulting from the disease process. An adolescent with cystic fibrosis or end-stage renal failure will enter puberty later than his or her peers because of growth failure. Consequently, they sometimes look years younger than their chronological age and may be treated more like children than adolescents. This can cause anger and frustration. Such maturational discrepancies can also lead to feelings of "being different" and to social isolation (Blum, 1984).

Often the side effects of treatment pose an even greater threat to body image than the disease process itself. These changes may include stunted growth, obesity, severe weight loss, radiation dermatitis, or changes in appearance resulting from amputation and other types of surgery (Kellerman & Katz, 1977). In a recent study of adolescents with cancer, the young patients emphasized their need to be informed of side effects in advance. They also felt it would have been useful to talk to someone their own age who had already gone through the treatment in order to be better prepared. As one adolescent expressed it: "Kids can explain it better." In discussing the specific effects of chemotherapy, the adolescents did not emphasize nausea and vomiting (athough these were common side effects) as much as changes in physical appearance and abilities. Hair loss, cushingoid facies (that is, "moon face"), and the inability to participate in favorite physical activities were mentioned as especially difficult by the adolescents who had undergone chemotherapy. Some of the changes caused embarrassment and threatened the young person's self-esteem. No matter how well they felt, the adolescents were constantly reminded of their illness by the visible side effects of the treatment (Orr et al., 1984). In fact, they may often perceive these changes to be more problematic than the actual disease (Susman, Pizzo, & Poplack, 1981; Wasserman, Thompson, Wilimas, & Fairclough, 1987).

As we have seen, adolescents have a strong need to develop and maintain a positive body image. Caregivers should recognize the importance of this need and provide support and encouragement to the young person attempting to deal with unpleasant physical changes. For example, *alopecia* (hair loss) resulting from chemotherapy can be particularly difficult for adolescents with cancer to accept. It may affect their perceived sexual attractiveness as well as their peer relations. Zeltzer, LeBaron, and Zeltzer (1984) reported that adolescent amputees thought that hair loss was even more difficult to cope with than loss of a limb. For these adolescents, walking on crutches or using a prosthesis was seen as a physical accomplishment by peers and required less explanation than did baldness. Many patients fear that their hair will not grow back, and consequently need reassurance that it indeed will. They may want to wear a wig, scarf, or hat to enhance their appearance and to make them feel more comfortable until they regain their hair.

It should be remembered that adolescents are very particular about what they wear, and they usually have definite preferences. It is very important that they have the opportunity to choose clothes that help them feel good about themselves. Clothes can be selected to minimize the changes in physical appearance caused by weight gain or loss (Blumberg et al., 1984). If the adolescent has been hospitalized for an extended period of time, he or she may want to find out about current styles in clothing from peers or from magazines in order to select new clothes that are regarded as fashionable.

Just as the normal adolescent spends much time grooming, adolescents with life-threatening illnesses may also appear preoccupied with their daily grooming routine. It is important to them not to look different from their peers. While perhaps appearing excessive to parents, the extra time and energy required for daily hair washings and application of cosmetics may be crucial for the sick adolescent to feel comfortable around others.

Expression of Individuality

Erikson (1959), in positing his series of developmental psychosocial crises, proposed *identity versus role confusion* (*identity diffusion*) as the critical developmental issue to be resolved during adolescence. The adaptive challenge of self-definition and commitment to a role is the major developmental task of this life stage. The many changes that occur during adolescence raise the question of "Who am I?" Perceptions about themselves formulated in concrete terms must be reinterpreted in the broader abstractions of formal operational thought. This period of personal definition and reorganization facilitates the adoption of a role in society and commitment to an ideology. Discovering attitudes, ideals, and roles that one will carry into adult life contributes to a stable and consistent sense of self. On the other hand, being unsure of who one is and where one is going leads to a prolonged sense of identity diffusion. Adolescents with a life-threatening illness may have particular difficulty resolving identity issues. Their uncertain and often limited future can interfere with positive identity development.

Experimentation is often seen in the adolescent's search for his or her own identity. Anyone who has lived with an adolescent is familiar with the mood swings, extremism, and strong displays of emotion typical of this age group. Adolescents try out new behaviors and ways of relating in order to assess the reaction of others and to engage in reality testing. Experimentation is a primary characteristic of adolescent behavior, and everything is a ready target including clothes, hairstyles, attitudes, friendships, and roles. Much of the perceived inconsistency in any particular adolescent relates to this type of experimentation, as he or she conceives of various potentialities for being and behaving. Also contributing to the apparent inconsistency and lack of maturity in the personality of adolescents is the fact that they are facing a myriad of new situations in which they simply do not know how to act. Dating, work roles, their transitional status, and so forth all put adolescents in a situation in which they are unsure of what is expected of them and how well they will perform. They therefore appear awkward and inconsistent as they try out different roles and ways of fulfilling them to find out what comfortably fits and what they will carry with them into adulthood (Manaster, 1977).

In an attempt to find oneself, the adolescent may try out one role one day (with its corresponding set of behaviors and attitudes) and another role the next, temporarily investing himself or herself in a variety of roles. The experimentation of this period is sanctioned by the laxness of society in enforcing adult rules on adolescents and the difference in responsibility assigned to adolescents as compared to adults (Manaster, 1977). Erikson (1959) uses the term *psychosocial moratorium* to describe the relatively hands-off posture of society toward adolescents. Adolescents are allowed some time to engage in the process of finding themselves and their place in society. The time allotted for this process varies not only in families and by social group, but across cultures as well. Growing up in a family with open communication and few restrictions on the individual members can provide a facilitative context for the successful resolution of this search (Lerner & Hultsch, 1983).

The development of "self" emerges out of interaction with others and also out of internal dialogue with one's thoughts and feelings. Identity can be thought of as the "me" in each person. Erikson (1959) viewed identity as including self-esteem, or our feelings about ourselves. A strong and stable identity gives an individual a consistent psychological basis for dealing with the demands of reality.

During this period, adolescents also have a strong interest in the identity of others. For example, knowing some personal information about health care professionals, rather than just the fact that they are doctors or nurses, seems to be important. In one study of adolescents with cancer, the investigators found that this type of sharing was necessary for the development of trust on the part of the young patient. The researchers suggest that appropriate self-disclosure may help health care professionals establish rapport with their adolescent patients and encourage cooperation (Orr et al., 1984).

Adolescents with a life-threatening illness are at risk of a negative resolution of the major psychosocial crisis of this life stage, *identity versus role confusion* (*identity diffusion*). They may develop a distorted image of themselves as a result of the disease process and its treatment (due to ongoing and dramatic change in physical appearance, for example). Adolescent patients may also have a diffused sense of self due to being in the "patient role" or the "dying role" for a prolonged period and not having the opportunity to experiment with various roles in a normal setting.

The development of identity requires opportunities for self-expression. Self-expression, so valued by the adolescent, is difficult to achieve when parents continue to provide for one's basic needs, when weakness and pain restrict activities, and when the individual is uncertain of his or her skills and abilities (Eisenberg, Sutkin, & Jansen, 1984). Caregivers in a medical setting need to give special attention to the need of adolescents to express their individuality. Flexible hospital policies and regulations that allow adolescents to wear their own clothes and personalize their rooms (perhaps put their favorite posters on the wall) can be particularly significant and can give the message to young patients that they are unique individuals with special interests, abilities, and traits regardless of their physical condition. Providing recreational activities that encourage self-expression (for example, painting or woodworking) can also provide for the expression of a variety of personal feelings that adolescents may not be able to express verbally.

Photo 6.1 *Adolescents with life-threatening illnesses have a need to express their individuality. Room decorations, clothing, and their own artistic work can be important statements about how they view themselves.*

Continuity versus discontinuity in the adolescent's life is also a key identity issue. Adolescents with serious diseases need help continuing normal, everyday activities as much as possible. Adolescents need opportunities to be themselves and to show others who they are (S. J. Berman, 1980). One way of maintaining continuity is by keeping one's identity as a student. Maintaining the role of student, in whatever capacity is feasible, helps an adolescent maintain a sense of normality at a time when he or she may be feeling very different from peers.

Adolescent cancer patients, while feeling that it is important to return to school, understandably have some concerns about it (Office of Cancer Communications, 1980). Some of their concerns can be alleviated if caregivers plan for their eventual return. Hospitals, schools, and tutors as well as teachers of the homebound can help the adolescent keep up with classwork and thus make the transition back to full-time or part-time student easier. It is also important for parents to maintain contact with the school and inform staff of their adolescent's needs in anticipation of his or her reenrollment. Adolescents returning after hospitalization may have some difficulty handling the demands of school because of frequent absenteeism. They may also not feel well enough or have sufficient energy to complete their work or to spend a full day at school. Regardless, there seems to be general agreement that adolescent cancer patients should return to school as soon as possible to begin reestablishing a normal life-style (Blumberg et al., 1984).

A return to school usually means a return to peers and peer activities. These activities can have special meaning during the teen years. Adolescents may request that their schedule for chemotherapy treatments be changed to enable them to attend a school dance or a sports event. Flexibility on the part of the medical staff is important as long as it does not jeopardize the patient's medical condition.

Part of the adolescent's identity relates to his or her plans for the future and the roles he or she wishes to assume upon reaching adulthood. As adolescents mature, they often think of their future in terms of education, career, family, and life-style. Planning for career and life goals is difficult when a life-threatening illness occurs. If they know they will not have the opportunity to live as an adult, adolescents with illnesses diagnosed as terminal often feel cheated and angry because of their illness. When the dying trajectory is uncertain, a lack of clarity about future possibilities and limitations can leave the adolescent unable to make definite plans (Rando, 1984). In some cases, they may even be reluctant to explore options for fear of having their expectations inappropriately raised. These adolescents also have some special concerns about their future that involve much more than their survival. For example: "Will anyone want to marry me if I have had cancer? Will I be able to have children?"

In spite of existing uncertainty about their future (which may vary considerably for different individuals), adolescents should be encouraged to make realistic plans. Nannis et al. (1982) suggest that a perception of some control of the future is positively correlated with optimism and participation in activities of daily living. The adolescent may need some adult assistance and guidance in charting his or her future. For example, if treatment interrupts the adolescent's education, then plans regarding college or employment may have to be altered or delayed. For young people with a certain death trajectory, their "future" may be limited to only a few months. These adolescents will need help coping with the fact that they will not have the opportunity to complete some important life goals, such as finishing high school or obtaining a college degree.

Not all of the adolescent's thoughts about the future will be reality-based. Fantasizing about the future is a part of normal adolescent development and should not be considered aberrant in adolescents with life-threatening illnesses. While some of their fantasies may seem quite unrealistic (for example, becoming a rock star), they may be important in helping the adolescent maintain positive emotional adjustment (Nannis et al., 1982).

Independence and Control

Havighurst (1972) identifies achieving emotional independence from parents and other adults and establishing new and more mature relations with agemates of both sexes as important developmental tasks of adolescence. These tasks operate in a complementary fashion to help adolescents become emancipated from their parents in preparation for leaving home at the beginning of their adult years. The end goal is to maintain affection for each other and develop interdependence while at the same time breaking the dependency bond remaining from childhood.

Ansbacher and Ansbacher (1956) in their book on Alfred Adler quote his views regarding the centrality of the independence issue for the adolescent:

> For almost every child, adolescence means one thing above all else: he must prove he is no longer a child. . . . Very many of the expressions of adolescence are the outcome of the desire to show independence, equality with adults, and manhood or womanhood. The direction of these expressions will depend on the meaning which the child has attributed to being "grown-up." (p. 439)

Ambivalence marks both parental and adolescent attitudes toward the developmental task of achieving emotional independence. This ambivalence centers around the needs to relinquish childhood ties while developing appropriate independence behaviors. Adolescents want to have more control over their lives, yet they are unsure of giving up the parental protection that diminishes with their increasing autonomy. For parents, the development of independence on the part of their adolescent means a corresponding loss of power and influence for themselves. Parents are not sure that their "child" can make it without them, and the adolescent may be unsure as well because he or she is not yet ready to deal with the world in a mature, adult-like manner.

Parenting style affects how well and how smoothly the adolescent masters the task of independence. Parents with extremely authoritarian or permissive parenting styles often encounter difficulties with their adolescent and may impede their child's progress toward becoming a mature, autonomous adult. In contrast, a democratic approach to parenting facilitates a positive self-concept and independence (Baumrind, 1983; Gander & Gardiner, 1981). Depending on the dynamics involved, the quest for independence may become a power struggle between adolescents and their parents. The more control the parents maintain, the more likely adolescents will battle with them to show their own control. Rebellion and rejection of parental values sometimes accompany this process.

Relationships between terminally ill adolescents and their parents may be especially difficult. Adolescents, particularly younger ones, may vacillate between the desire to be independent from parents and the need to depend on parents for support and protection. The tendency to temporarily regress and become dependent is especially pronounced during high stress periods such as those following diagnosis, relapse, or treatment (such as chemotherapy) (Zeltzer, LeBaron, & Zeltzer, 1984). For example, when adolescents are ill from treatment they may revert to a dependent, child-like state. As soon as the symptoms and side effects subside, they are likely to rebuff parental attention. This dependence–independence cycle can be very confusing for parents. As one parent commented: "When she zigs I zag and we just can't seem to get our zigs and zags synchronized" (Farrell, 1981). Parents may try to show their concern by overprotecting their adolescent at a time when, if the adolescent were healthy, they would be learning to let go (Kellerman & Katz, 1977). In fact, the parents' own sense of loss of control may intensify their concern and caretaking of their adolescent. This attempt on the part of parents to combat their own feelings of helplessness may be viewed negatively by the adolescent. S. J. Berman (1980) uses a quote from an 18-year-old patient to illustrate the embarrassment felt in response to the parent's inappropriate attempts to help her:

> My mother thinks I'm two years old again. She hovers over me. When the doctor comes in to talk to me, she talks for me as if I cannot talk. It really bothers me, even though it probably makes her feel better to do these things. (p. 2)

Moore et al. (1969) cite dependence versus independence as one of the central challenges for adults in dealing with adolescents who have cancer. Diagnosis of particular diseases and the treatments that follow can threaten the adolescent's sense of control and independence. Adolescents tend to perceive more self-control over their illness and their symptoms when their disease is one, such as diabetes, that can be controlled through diet regimens and self-administered medications. In contrast, less control is perceived with diseases such as cancer and renal dysfunction in which treatments and medications are administered in medical settings by medical personnel (Kellerman, Zeltzer, Ellenberg, Dash, & Rigler, 1980). A diagnosis of cancer, for example, can lead to an emotional crisis with concomitant feelings of anxiety, depression, and helplessness. While loss of control is an issue for all cancer patients, it has a heightened impact on adolescents because of the developmental tasks they are facing. At a time when they are gaining increasing personal autonomy and mastery over their environment, adolescent cancer patients may find themselves having to cope with a variety of intrusive medical procedures in a hospital setting that encourages passivity and dependency (S. J. Berman, 1980). As the adolescent's discomfort level rises at the same time independence is threatened, characteristic behaviors of individuals may become exaggerated. For example, a 16-year-old who has always been direct and outspoken may appear belligerent at times. Another adolescent who has always been rather daring may take more defiant risks (Plumb & Holland, 1974).

In some cases, power struggles can develop between parent and adolescent that can jeopardize the patient's physical well-being. S. J. Berman (1980) describes a case of a 16-year-old female who refused food as a way of both asserting her independence and testing her mother's concern. This behavior was in response to her mother's focused attention on her food intake and her attempts to "baby" her daughter as she stood over her 12 to 14 hours a day. The adolescent was using the only thing she felt was hers—her body—as a means of maintaining control. Once it started, the power struggle escalated to a point that neither individual could easily break away from it. This situation was resolved by giving the adolescent more legitimate control so that she did not have to use her physical control in a maladaptive way.

These power struggles can also extend to the doctor–patient relationship. Lack of involvement in decisions about their treatment and in communications about the nature and progression of their illness can result in lack of cooperation and, in some cases, actually sabotage the medical staff's treatment plan. Frustrated adolescents, fearing that they are being forced to regress to an earlier developmental stage, may also rebel by refusing treatment, breaking hospital rules, and participating in forbidden activities (Blumberg et al., 1984). This noncompliance and uncooperativeness may be the only way they have of exerting some control over their lives.

To increase compliance, the adolescent's sense of control should be fostered to enhance his or her feelings of self-worth and psychological well-being and to avoid the treatment program itself from becoming the target of control (Zeltzer, 1980). Participating in treatment decisions and being informed of their progress and options is a major issue for adolescents. In interviews with parents of cancer patients in this situation, Farrell (1981) found that parents were concerned about their adolescent's degree of involvement in discussions with the health care professionals. While wanting to protect their children from the implications of their diagnosis, all the parents in the study recognized the need of the child to be involved in ongoing decision making with the treatment team. Open and honest communication enhances interaction between the adolescent and significant others, and it should be present from the time of diagnosis and continue throughout the treatment process.

Despite potential problems that may arise between adolescents and their parents, some adolescent patients feel that they can rely on their parents more than anyone else. As one adolescent expressed it: "Your parents are your best friends, they'll never desert you" (Office of Cancer Communications, 1980). Adolescents with life-threatening illnesses can feel guilty for being dependent on others and for the extra burden their illness puts on their family. Adolescent patients may be concerned about the cost of their medical treatment, the time the parents have lost from work, and family plans that are spoiled (missed vacations, among other things) due to their illness. Getting a driver's license is a common goal among adolescents, well or ill. Adolescents with life-threatening illnesses often want to increase their level of responsibility in the family by driving themselves to the hospital or clinic for their treatment (Blumberg et al., 1984). By doing so, they feel they are easing the burden of their illness on their parents as well as demonstrating their competence.

The research of Seligman (1975) and others has clearly shown that the perception of control reduces anxiety and contributes to greater stress tolerance. Their findings suggest that perceiving control, even if one does not necessarily use it or even in fact have it, is an important factor in successfully dealing with adverse situations. Maximizing the participation of terminally ill adolescents in their daily lives can have positive effects both from a therapeutic and a developmental perspective. Because control has many facets, adding to and supporting the adolescent's sense of autonomy and involvement in certain areas of his or her life can mitigate the effects of lack of control in other areas (Nannis et al., 1982).

Choices and input should be provided whenever possible for the adolescent patient (for example, letting the adolescent help plan his or her diet or giving choices related to physical care and recreation). Doing things, even small ones, by themselves or with minimal assistance can help adolescents experience some autonomy even during a period when they may be highly dependent on health care professionals. Some physical distance from parents and other caregivers can also be healthy for the adolescent. During a ''well'' period, adolescents often want to return to school. On their own territory, adolescents may feel safer acting out and asserting themselves. Finally, encouraging and giving opportunities to adolescents to assist other patients can reassure them that they have something to offer, rather than always being the recipient of care and support.

Peer Interaction

One of the most notable social changes during adolescence is the increased importance of peer groups. The peer group serves several important functions for the adolescent, and these functions appear to be interrelated. One of the most important functions is the granting of status at a time when the adolescent is striving for self-definition. Status is earned through the adolescent's own efforts, and interaction with the social environment facilitates identity development. Peer relationships provide latitude for adolescents to test themselves and try out a variety of roles, since peers are more tolerant of extremes in behavior. In this context, the adolescents can extend the boundaries of their sense of self and expand the range of their behaviors. The extent to which this is allowed is based on reactions and approval from peers. Toward the end of adolescence, the peer group loses some of its potency as a socialization agent. The more confident individuals feel about themselves and their own judgment, the less influence others will have on them.

A second function of the peer group is to facilitate the adolescent's quest for independence from parents and to give focus and support to the adolescent as he or she resists adult standards and control. While emotional bonds to parents are still maintained, the relationship eventually matures as adolescents move toward exercising greater personal autonomy. Identification with a peer group and adherence to its norms aids the adolescent in the transition from emotional dependence on parents to interdependence in a variety of relationships. Agemates offer support, security, and a feeling of "belonging" for the adolescent while he or she is negotiating this transition.

Maintaining positive relationships and frequent interaction with peers is critically important to adolescents with life-threatening illnesses. One of the favorite activities of individuals in this age group is to "hang out" with each other, away from adult scrutiny (Farrell & Hutter, 1980). The disease and its treatment can unfortunately limit opportunities for peer contact and, thus, interfere with the accomplishment of peer-related developmental tasks. When adolescents are separated from their friends, they are also separated from valuable emotional support.

Adolescents with life-threatening diseases are afraid of being regarded as different from their classmates and of being rejected by them. They are also unsure how to respond to others' questions and how to handle teasing. Some of these individuals impose isolation on themselves and withdraw from peers rather than risk rejection. Physical limitations (such as an amputation that interferes with participation in athletics, dancing, or other social activities) can contribute even more to this sense of being different. The individual's perception of his or her social status may be distorted, thus contributing to feelings of inadequacy and incompetence (Blumberg et al., 1984).

Adolescents with cancer report that they are bothered more by stares of and avoidance by peers than they are by direct questioning. Healthy adolescents, however, may often hesitate to mention the subject of their friend's disease. In a project sponsored by the National Cancer Institute, adolescent cancer patients recommended telling friends the truth about their cancer, its treatment, and its side effects. One patient told of the strengthening of a friendship by this type of sharing: "And I prepared one of my better friends. I told her I'm going to come home and probably I'm going to be bald, I'm probably going to look like I'm sicker than a dog. And she said okay, just as long as you're you" (Office of Cancer Communications, 1980). Other cancer patients may lose some of their friends because the situation is more than their peers can handle.

Interestingly, peers of adolescents with cancer generally report positive feelings toward the person and say they admire the way he or she manages the disease. One study found that some adolescents felt uncomfortable with their ill friend and worried about saying the wrong thing. Most felt that they acted no differently toward the person because he or she had a life-threatening disease; one-third said they had talked with the person about their illness. Only 14 percent, however, had visited their friend when he or she was absent from school (Hodges, Graham-Pole, & Fong, 1984).

Lack of peer interaction can lead to feelings of isolation and rejection by the dying adolescent. Peer interaction can be facilitated in a number of ways. One is by encouraging the visitation of friends both at the hospital and at home, and helping them feel comfortable when they do visit. Visitors provide a vital link to the events external to the hospital situation (Denholm, 1985). This function is described by Kline & Schowalter (1974), who state: "Rarely have I heard an adolescent patient dominate conversations with hospital stories or complaints or illness . . . discussions with visitors cover all kinds of outside happenings to bring the patient up-to-date" (p. 47). Peers can also promote recovery and provide an opportunity for ventilation of feelings.

Inflexible policies, an institutional atmosphere, and lack of privacy and space can discourage visits from healthy adolescent peers. Geographical distance and transportation can also make it difficult for younger adolescents to visit their hospitalized friends. Installing a phone by the adolescent's bed or providing equipment for tape-recorded correspondence can help the person maintain contact with friends on a regular basis.

Hospitalized adolescents can also have positive interactions with other adolescents in their same situation. Allowing adolescents to have adolescent roommates and establishing teen wards in hospitals can provide ongoing peer interaction. Sometimes deep friendships are formed among adolescent patients. It is not unusual for a hospitalized adolescent to experience the death of another young patient on the ward. After leaving the hospital, adolescents who had been hospitalized together often continue to maintain contact and inquire about each other's condition.

Opportunities for group activities in a hospital setting can be enhanced by the availability of a recreation room containing age-appropriate equipment (a stereo, video games, a pool table, a Ping-Pong table). Bringing albums and videos from home and sharing them with other hospitalized peers can help the adolescent feel more connected to "the real world."

There are times, however, when adolescents will not want companionship. Farrell and Hutter (1980) have observed that any adolescent with cancer will have some "bummer" days, which are usually precipitated by bad news and exhaustion. Adolescents may want to shut the world out and be left alone on these days. Time away from the intrusion of hospital routines can be especially therapeutic at this time. Special areas on the hospital grounds such as outdoor lounges can be designed with this purpose in mind.

Helping Adolescents Cope with Life-threatening Illnesses

Adolescents with life-threatening illnesses appear to cope remarkably well (Zeltzer, Kellerman, Ellenberg, Dash, & Rigler, 1980). Research has shown that, in general, chronically ill and terminally ill adolescents seem to have a higher tolerance for stress than do their healthy peers. These findings suggest that adolescents with life-threatening diseases learn to live with their health problems and to cope effectively (Bedell, Giordan, Amour, Tavormina, & Boll, 1977). In fact, Kellerman et al. (1980) found a negative correlation between anxiety and time since diagnosis, indicating that, with time, increased coping skills are developed and adjustment occurs. Overall, adolescents who face potentially fatal health conditions appear to be psychologically healthy and well adjusted and to have generally hopeful, positive outlooks (Zeltzer et al., 1980).

Adolescents with life-threatening illnesses appear to be more concerned with day-to-day inconveniences and immediate sources of distress than worries about death (Zeltzer et al., 1984). When asked about their futures, Zeltzer et al. (1980) found that 95 percent of the adolescents in their sample reported that they expected their condition to improve, even though 30 percent were in relapse at the time of the study.

Adolescents use a variety of coping techniques to help them deal with their illnesses. In addition to the use of denial, discussed in a previous section, prevalent coping mechanisms of adolescents include overcompensation, intellectualization, and anger. Adolescents in their attempts to deny their illness and appear "normal" may try to overcompensate by outperforming their peers and proving their abilities. Intellectualization, used more by older adolescents than younger ones, can reduce anxiety by repressing emotions while focusing on intellectual aspects of the illness. Activities such as researching the illness and asking detailed questions about the treatment process can reduce their uncertainty as well. Anger regarding the illness and its effects may be channeled in many different directions. Often it is displayed in the form of "acting-out" behavior and rebellion against authority figures (Moore et al., 1969).

Adolescents also acquire more mature coping strategies, such as altruism (helping others) and humor, which help them maintain a positive attitude (Pattison, 1977). Zeltzer et al. (1984) reported that adolescents feel that the major factors helping them cope with cancer are maintaining a sense of humor, thinking pleasant thoughts, hearing of other patients who are doing well, and having someone to talk to when they are afraid.

In addition to individual coping skills, peer support can also be valuable, and the effectiveness of support groups in helping adolescents cope with life-threatening disease has been demonstrated in several studies. Orr et al. (1984) recommend using closed groups (membership does not change) instead of open groups (new members can be added at any time) for adolescents. It takes time to develop trust and rapport, and the addition of new members alters group dynamics and affects the quality of interaction. In their 18-month experience with a series of open groups for seriously ill, hospitalized adolescents, Blum and Chang (1981) found that group members had a sense of constantly "beginning over again." Orr et al. (1984) found in their observations of a 3-month closed group for adolescents with cancer that particularly difficult topics and areas of vulnerability were typically not discussed until after the fourth session, when the psychological comfort level within the group had increased.

Printed materials can also have therapeutic value. In order to help adolescents cope with cancer, the National Cancer Institute (1982a, 1982b) has developed materials designed for an adolescent audience which address concerns of individuals in this age group who have cancer. These materials can be an important aid for teachers, serving as a catalyst for meaningful classroom discussion. Through this avenue, adolescents can have their questions answered and also develop more understanding of the needs of their peers who have cancer.

For the adolescents who recover from cancer, several beneficial aspects of the experience can be identified. These adolescents often experience feelings of mastery and self-confidence in relation to having conquered the disease. Other outcomes mentioned by adolescents include greater sensitivity and ability to help friends with their problems, increased introspection, the development of coping skills, and a tendency to place less emphasis on physical appearance (Orr et al., 1984).

Few studies have been done on long-term survivors of adolescent cancer. Wasserman et al. (1987) have emphasized the need for such studies because by the year 2000, based on present cure rates, 1 in 1000 people between the ages of 20 and 29 will have survived cancer during their younger years. In their study of individuals who had completed treatment for Hodgkin's disease and had been considered cured for at least 5 years, Wasserman et al. (1987) found high levels of adjustment. Many of the former patients were young adults at the time of the study and were leading essentially normal lives and adjusting to the demands of school, work, and personal relationships. The individuals felt that because of their experience with cancer they had an increased appreciation of being alive and an improved outlook on life.

The Grieving Adolescent

Adolescent Manifestations of Grief

The impact of a loss and the subsequent experience of grief during adolescence will depend on the type and quality of the relationship and the degree of ego maturity attained by the adolescent before the loss. Many adolescents experience the death of a parent, sibling, or friend during their teenage years; however, the first encounter that most adolescents have with death is the death of a grandparent. In some cases, relationships between adolescents and their grandparents are quite close. These relationships, not having the turmoil of parent–child interactions, may represent safety and security for the adolescent. In other situations, the relationship may be more distant, and the adolescent will be less likely to experience intense grief at the time of the grandparent's death. However, the death may still serve to remind the young person of the frailty of life and of the fact that death is the ultimate destiny of humans. The grandparent's death may also have a profound impact on the adolescent's parent, which in turn will have consequences for the adolescent.

The manifestations of grief in adolescence are similar to those of adulthood. LaGrand (1981) found depression to be a common response among older adolescents to loss of a loved one. Other prevalent manifestations of grief included feelings of emptiness, crying, headaches, insomnia, digestive upsets, and exhaustion. Balk (1983) also obtained similar findings in his study of 33 adolescents who had experienced the death of a sibling. Balk noted the similarity of these reactions with those of bereaved adults, but he also emphasized the enduring quality of some of the adolescent grief reactions. At the time of the study (4 to 84 months after the death, with an average of 23.6 months), the most persistent grief responses were confusion and depression, and at least one-third of the sample also continued to feel guilt and loneliness. All but two of the adolescents said that their sibling's absence was more poignantly felt on occasions such as holidays, the sibling's birthday, or the date of the sibling's death; about half of the teenagers thought they had seen or heard the deceased sibling. In some cases, school performance also continued to be affected. While the performance of most of the adolescents returned to normal (half reported poor study habits and a decline in grades immediately after the death),

Photo 6.2   *Many adolescents experience the death of someone close to them during their teenage years.*

approximately 25 percent continued to have academic difficulties at the time they were interviewed. Balk concluded that for many of these adolescents their previous loss was still a source of current pain, and he reported that tears, shaking, shortness of breath, and periods of heavy sobbing were not uncommon during the interviews he conducted.

According to Raphael (1983), adolescent mourning is likely to extend over a considerable period of time, as the loss is slowly resolved. Active grieving may occur intermittently when circumstances are favorable for the expression of grief. It may also be delayed until the surviving parent is able to respond to the adolescent's needs or a sensitive teacher provides the opportunity for the adolescent to share memories and feelings pertaining to the deceased.

The grief process may also be extended because of the adolescent's tendency to idealize the deceased. In the instance of death of a parent, this idealization combined with the normal ambivalence in adolescent–parent relationships can produce a great deal of guilt and self-blame. Surviving adolescents may ask themselves: Why did I not appreciate my father when he was still alive? Why was it so important for me to prove that I didn't need him anymore? An adolescent may fear that the deceased parent did not know how much he or she was loved because of the adolescent's recent rebelliousness and increased attachment to a peer group (Raphael, 1983).

Grief may also be complicated when the significance of a relationship is not acknowledged. During adolescence, boyfriend–girlfriend relationships are common. While these relationships may not ultimately be permanent ones, they can involve intense feelings of attachment and perhaps sexual intimacy. No matter how strong the bond between the pair, primary bonds are viewed by society as being with the family of origin, and therefore the adolescent's grief for a boyfriend or girlfriend may be ignored or not understood. This is even more likely in early adolescence, when couple relationships receive less sanction. One young adolescent expressed his pain and lack of support following the death of his girlfriend this way:

> Jenny was my girl. She was special and private, and she was mine. When she died, they wouldn't even let me go to the funeral. I loved her and she loved me . . . and *them* . . . *they* knew nothing, nothing, about what it was like for us. *They* were too old to know. They treated me as though she was theirs and as though I didn't care.
>
> Steve, age 16 (Raphael, 1983, p. 139)

The emotional intensity of adolescence adds to the feelings of loss after a death. Recognizing the significance and strength of love relationships during youth and providing opportunities for mourning are critical for the successful resolution of grief in these circumstances.

It is normal for grief sometimes to temporarily reemerge after a loss. The pain of an earlier loss can be reawakened during adolescence by developmental events and markers (such as high school graduation or leaving home to attend college) that would have held special significance for the deceased. The absence of the loved one is keenly felt, and happiness surrounding the occasion is mixed with feelings of sadness associated with the loss (Johnson & Rosenblatt, 1981).

Coping with Loss during Adolescence

While resembling adults' reactions, adolescents' ways of coping with a significant loss have some unique components. Following the death of a loved one, adolescents may have a particularly intense display of emotions or, to avoid being perceived as childish, adolescents may present a stoic, unemotional demeanor to hide their inner feelings. In their proud attempts to demonstrate independence and control, they may refuse to allow themselves the support of others (Eddy & Alles, 1983). They may also be hesitant to show their grief for fear that they may be considered different or abnormal. Because of the adolescent sensitivity to the views of others and the possible lack of knowledge about the normality of grief, emotional responses may be either suppressed or repressed (Raphael, 1983). The difficulties in expressing grief during adolescence are captured in the following statement by a 14-year-old male:

> When my mother died I thought my heart would break. Yet I couldn't cry. It was locked inside. It was private and tender and sensitive like the way I loved her. They said to me, "You're cool man, real cool, the way you've taken it," but I wasn't cool at all. I was hot—hot and raging. All my anger, all my sadness was building up inside me. But I just didn't know any way to let it out. (Raphael, 1983, p. 176)

The expression of grief can be even more difficult if the bereaved adolescent feels that the topic of death is taboo in his or her family. Wass (1979), in her study of 144 high school seniors, found that 39 percent said that death was never discussed in their families, and another 25 percent indicated that the subject was only talked about briefly and only when necessary. The topic can be especially difficult to approach if the death involved a close family member. Sometimes adolescents feel they must protect their parents from additional sadness and emotional pain; therefore, they may avoid mentioning their own concerns and feelings.

It has been argued that adolescents are especially vulnerable to the impact of a crisis and, as a result, their mental health may be at risk. Indeed, bereavement outcomes are often quite complex following a significant loss during adolescence (Cho, Freeman, & Patterson, 1982). For instance, the crisis of a death may actually strengthen the adolescent's immediate coping abilities, but it can also leave him or her vulnerable as new developmental and family issues are faced. Aubrey (1977), in reviewing cases seen at a university counseling center, has noted that a high incidence of students seeking counseling have experienced a significant earlier loss. While this information was elicited in clinical interviews, few students initially cited adjustment to the loss as their presenting problem. The loss-related issues that surface during counseling can be quite varied. For example, a young woman may have deep-seated fears of womanhood and sexual activity because of associations formed years earlier when her mother died of breast cancer. Another example would be a young man who has unrecognized hostility toward his stepfather for trying to take his deceased father's place and anger toward his mother for remarrying rather than "remaining loyal."

Aubrey (1977) has emphasized the need to accept the adolescent's own way of coping with a loss, and she views art, music, and drama as having a critical role in helping adolescents deal with their feelings. According to Aubrey: "When sad or depressed, many adolescents almost automatically put on a record or tune in their favorite radio station. Deference to parental feelings about such 'escapism' may make some adolescents refrain from activities that could be highly cathartic" (p. 137). Given the freedom to use their own coping devices, many adolescents will do so instinctively. Parents and clinicians need to be more flexible and creative in helping young people deal with death and encourage them to use their preferred resources and types of support.

If adolescents are given support from adults and peers, they are often able to cope effectively with the death of a loved one. Adolescents tend to take a more active role in funerals and memorial services as they get older, which can often help to facilitate a positive resolution of grief. In addition, young people often remember deceased persons and mourn their death through socially constructive acts. For example, following the death of a teacher students may volunteer to help raise money for research in order to help conquer the disease that caused the death. After a classmate commits suicide, friends may offer to participate in a suicide prevention program.

On the other hand, when denial of death is reinforced by family and friends and when opportunities for grieving are not provided, adolescents may vent their feelings through destructive acts. Unable to express their grief in socially acceptable ways, adolescents may "act out their tears" through delinquent behaviors (Shoor & Speed, 1976). Rosenblatt and his colleagues (Rosenblatt, Jackson, & Walsh, 1972) go so far as to suggest that a great deal of antisocial behavior in our society is the result of anger associated with repressed grief.

Acting-out may also occur in the form of sexual behavior. The need to be comforted and consoled, if not met by family members, may be sought in sexually oriented relationships outside of the family. While not helping to resolve the individual's grief, these relationships may temporarily take away some of the emotional pain, provide physical comfort, and allow for the discharge of tension. In some circumstances, the individual may become extremely promiscuous, unconsciously desiring in some way to replace the lost person through a pregnancy (Raphael, 1983). In studying adolescent pregnancy, Coddington (1979) has noted the high frequency of loss in the background of adolescents who become pregnant.

The acting-out of grief by the bereaved adolescent can be just a temporary phase or it can become a more permanent pattern. Factors affecting the duration of this behavior include the family's ability to perceive and respond to the adolescent's needs (allowing for the resolution of grief) and the availability of other forms of intervention (Raphael, 1983).

In some circumstances, suicide can be an outcome of loss. Balk (1983) found in the 33 adolescents he studied that thoughts of suicide were reported after the death of a sibling and were associated with feelings of depression and family arguments. Twelve adolescents thought of suicide in the few weeks after their sibling died, and nine had considered it several months or years after the death. These adolescents saw suicide as a means of being reunited with their siblings and as a way of escaping their troubles.

Cain (1978) has noted the additional risk to adolescents when parental death is due to suicide. In such situations, the young person's sense of self can be negatively affected. The legacy of parental suicide can result in the lowering of self-esteem as the survivor views himself or herself as "not worth hanging around for." This perceived parental rejection may pose a serious threat to identity development. Identification with a parent may also assume a pathological, destructive quality when the parent commits suicide. Under extreme circumstances, the process of overidentification with the deceased can lead to suicide attempts by the griever. The strength of this identification can clearly be seen when the adolescent chooses the anniversary of the parent's death, the same method, and/or the same location to attempt his or her own suicide.

The dynamics of the family can also affect the adolescent's grief outcomes. If family members are unable to grieve, they may vent their anger within the family in inappropriate ways. The adolescent may become the family scapegoat, functioning both as a target of unexpressed family emotion and also as the vehicle by which the family's pain is acted out through the adolescent's misbehaviors. The adolescent may also experience strong familial pressures to assume the role of the deceased parent. If such a role is assumed, it can have negative implications for identity development and can result in a premature and perhaps inappropriate definition of who the adolescent is and can be. Assuming the role of the deceased may also interfere with the adolescent's normal strivings for individuation and separation from his or her family. The individual may feel tremendous internal struggles as family expectations conflict with developmental imperatives.

Despite the difficult issues that may be confronted, most adolescents cope successfully with the pain of loss and continue to lead well-adjusted lives. In addition, the grief experience almost always has a maturing effect.

A serious life crisis at this age teaches adolescents many hard lessons and provides an initiation into the realities of life.

Adolescent Suicide

While adolescent suicide is not a new phenomenon, its occurrence has increased at an alarming rate. As a result, the topic has received considerable attention recently from the media, from school personnel, and from mental health professionals. Between 1960 and 1980, adolescent suicide increased 237 percent, currently making suicide the third leading cause of death in this age group (Maris, 1985). While youth suicide rates have increased, the suicide rates for individuals over age 30 have decreased. Proportionately, approximately 11 percent of all deaths among 15- to 24-year-olds in our society are caused by self-inflicted means (A. L. Berman, 1986). Of additional concern is the fact that 1 out of every 1000 adolescents attempts suicide, and many more at least consider it (Walker & Mehr, 1983). These figures are even more alarming when one considers the fact that many suicide attempts are not reported and many suicides are recorded as accidents. Therefore, the available statistics may actually underestimate the extent of this problem.

Causes of Suicide

Suicide is a complex behavior with multiple determinants. No easy answers are found when families ask "Why?" with regard to the self-destructive acts of their loved ones. When left, suicide notes like the following one offer few reasons for the self-inflicted death (A.L. Berman, 1985, p.151).

Dear Mom, Dad, and everyone else,

I'm sorry for what I've done, but I loved you all and I always will, for eternity. Please, please, please don't blame it on yourselves. It was all my fault and not yours or anyone else's. If I didn't do this now, I would have done it later anyway. We all die some day, I just died sooner.

Love,
John

Suicide is an act of desperation by a person who believes that his or her only remaining option is self-destruction. This inability to consider alternative ways of dealing with a present crisis is referred to as *tunnel vision*

(Hatton, Valente, & Rink, 1977). Tunnel vision reduces one's field of perception so that only one single alternative appears viable.

The inability to see available choices and options is affected by emotional depression, which is prevalent among many suicidal adolescents. Depression often involves feelings of helplessness and hopelessness. Consequently, suicidal individuals often feel that nothing that they can do will make a difference. Suicidal thoughts occur when individuals are unable to mobilize their resources, view themselves as powerless, anticipate that their situation will not improve, and can see no other way to escape their emotional pain (Fairchild, 1986). While viewing suicide as their only option, individuals considering suicide have very ambivalent feelings. Most suicidal persons do not really want to die, but they do not want to continue living in their current state of despair.

As an indication of this ambivalence, individuals contemplating suicide often communicate their need for help. Approximately three out of four people who eventually kill themselves have given some clues to friends, family, or other significant people in their life. These clues can be verbal ("If things don't get better, you'll be reading about me in the paper") or behavioral (giving away valued possessions). Because of the popular myth that people who talk about suicide don't actually commit it, these clues are often ignored (Kastenbaum, 1986).

More subtle clues also may not be attended to because they go unrecognized or undetected. Hart and Keidel (1979) have suggested a number of signs to watch for among teenagers that may indicate significant problems and possibly high suicide potential. These signs include the following: (1) subtle signs of self-destructive behavior, such as carelessness or accident-prone behavior, (2) exaggerated or extended apathy, inactivity, or boredom, (3) academic decline, (4) involvement in substance abuse (drugs, alcohol), (5) tearfulness, depressed feelings, or an unusually long grief period following a loss, (6) decrease in verbal activity and withdrawal from peers and previously enjoyed activities, (7) recent hostile behavior or an increase in interpersonal conflict, (8) a decrease in ability to tolerate frustration, (9) truancy from school and running away from home, and (10) physiological and behavioral indicators such as loss of appetite, excessive eating, or sleep disturbance. All of these behaviors may be indicative of depression. While depression is often associated with suicide, it is less easily identified in adolescents than in adults because of the natural mood swings experienced by those in the adolescent age group. It should be remembered that depression may manifest itself in a variety of ways in teenagers (Martin & Dixon, 1986).

Research findings suggest that adolescents of today view suicide as a more acceptable alternative than adolescents of the past. In their study,

Perkes and Schlidt (1979) found that 60 percent of adolescents in their sample felt that every person should have the freedom to die. Boldt (1982) concluded that youth of today are more accepting of suicide than their parents' generation. High school seniors in his study, when compared with adults, viewed suicide in terms that were less judgmental of the individual and less stigmatizing. They were also less inclined to think of suicide in religious or moral terms, and they placed greater emphasis on the individual's right to die. These more accepting attitudes of contemporary youth may influence suicidal behavior by showing more tolerance and less fear of it. Unfortunately, these attitudes are prevalent at a time when young people are confronted with the unique stresses and strains of modern life.

Suicide Prevention, Intervention, and Postvention

Prevention refers to actions taken to avoid a stressful or harmful situation, while *intervention* includes therapeutic efforts to reduce the intensity and negative effects of a crisis or difficult situation. *Postvention* involves dealing with the aftermath of a traumatic event and minimizing the impact (Shneidman, 1981; Valente & Saunders, 1987). Attempts to reduce the incidence of adolescent suicide require attention to all of these areas.

In order to prevent suicides, Maris (1985) suggests that we give young people in general an optimism for the world they live in and its future: "Any suicide is a waste. Young suicides are particularly tragic, since many have really never lived. To help people live, we have to restore a sense of hope about the goodness, purpose, pleasure, and viability of life itself" (p. 108).

In addition, specific programs that increase the self-esteem, decision-making abilities, and coping skills of adolescents have an important role in suicide prevention. Individuals with poor self-concepts and few problem-solving skills are at risk for mental health problems. Impulsivity and few alternative strategies for coping can turn suicidal thoughts into suicidal behaviors (A. L. Berman, 1986). Fairchild (1986) suggests that many skills can be taught through *developmental counseling* in the schools. Developmental counseling attempts to prevent potential crises from occurring by initiating contact with students before they have a need to contact a counselor. Counselors work with students in small groups to help them become more aware of themselves, how they interact with their environment, and how to effectively cope with the various tasks involved in growing up. At times, counselors may come into the classroom and use group discussions, formal presentations, and structured activities to assist students in addressing personal issues. Students are not the only focus for school personnel using this approach. Outreach programs that target their efforts at improving family communication and enhancing parenting skills can also have preventative value.

In addition to programs aimed at general affective needs of students, schools and communities have developed programs specifically aimed at preventing adolescent suicides. A primary objective of these programs is to educate teachers, parents, and adolescents themselves about the warning signs of suicide (Peck, Farberow, & Litman, 1985). Early identification allows the opportunity for prevention. Schools, especially, have been identified as having a critical role in suicide prevention since they interact with most of the youth in our society (Ross, 1985). Teachers often play an important role by detecting up distress signals from suicidal children and adolescents. As teachers become better informed, many more suicidal tragedies might be avoided. Appropriate referrals by teachers need to occur before the crisis of suicide is imminent.

Peers can also be taught to identify suicidal signs and make appropriate referrals. When surveying high school students, Nelson (1988) found that 34 percent indicated prior experience with suicidal peers. Teenagers often share their concerns with each other rather than approaching an adult, which supports the need for programs that teach students how to respond effectively in these situations. To encourage peer participation in suicide prevention, many pilot youth suicide prevention programs have been initiated in which adolescents themselves take an active role (A. L. Berman, 1986). For example, in Vancouver, British Columbia, and San Mateo, California, community suicide prevention centers have collaborated with school personnel in training students as peer counselors. Training, supervising, and supporting the adolescents who choose to participate are critical elements in the success of these programs (Valente & Saunders, 1987).

Well-trained specialists are needed for intervention once an adolescent has been identified as suicidal. Most school systems today have a staff of mental health professionals who can provide counseling and consultation. Appropriate and timely intervention often involves helping the suicidal adolescent to see viable alternatives to his or her situation and to develop coping skills and resources. It is important to recognize, however, that individuals who have attempted suicide are likely to try again. Four out of five people who kill themselves have made previous attempts (Martin & Dixon, 1986). Fairchild (1986) emphasizes that frequent counseling contacts with suicidal students are necessary. Even though the immediate threat of suicide may seem to have passed, the following 2 or 3 months are considered critical. It is during this period that some students attempt suicide after apparent improvement (Morgan, 1981). Many times the adolescent's issues are inseparable from family issues, and intervention at the family level is needed (Walker & Mehr, 1983). Depending on the circumstances, the adolescent and family may be referred by school personnel to family therapists, child psychologists, or social workers.

Suicide is of much concern on college campuses as well. In a study of college students, Carson and Johnson (1985) found that 20 percent of their sample (drawn from social science classes) had seriously considered committing suicide. While those who had considered suicide had not actually experienced more stressful life events than other students, they reported more stress symptoms and appeared to have fewer resources to help them deal with their emotions and problems. The investigators suggest that services such as counseling centers, crisis hotlines, and suicide prevention offices be provided on campus for students to receive information and assistance in dealing with suicide issues and that efforts be made to inform all students about the availability of these services. By educating students about alternatives to suicide, teaching them better coping skills, and expanding their available resources, hopefully the likelihood of suicide on college campuses can be reduced.

Unfortunately, many suicide programs in schools tend to deemphasize bereavement and fail to have a postvention component to address the aftereffects of a suicide on a school population. Although no research exists that indicates the frequency with which adolescent suicide is related to bereavement, the literature suggests that the experience of loss, especially when accompanied by depression and feelings of alienation, can lead to suicidal thoughts (Richman, 1986). Classmates, friends, and school staff need a forum for sharing their grief. Special events, student assemblies, and individual consultations can all provide mechanisms for meeting the needs of individual survivors. In situations in which peer counselors were involved with the victim, they may have feelings of failure and guilt because they were not able to prevent the suicide. Special attention needs to be given to these adolescents as well as to teachers or counselors who may have similar feelings.

Young people, especially adolescents, are also highly vulnerable to the influence of others. When a suicide occurs in a school, subsequent suicide attempts or completions by others may follow. The first suicide possibly serves as a model and gives permission to others considering suicide. A. L. Berman (1986) suggests that it is important to address the phenomenon of "contagion" through our interventions and preventative programming efforts. Because of widespread belief in the *contagion theory*, some adults have been reluctant to discuss suicide because they fear that talking about it will encourage suicidal behavior in young people. Ross (1985), however, has been unable to find strong empirical evidence to substantiate this view. Ross insists that the "rule of silence" following a suicide should be considered dangerous because it deters important discussions that could help prevent many suicides and that could also help many adolescents deal with grief.

We will continue to see innovative programs develop as schools and communities grapple with the problems associated with adolescent suicide. Already several state legislatures (California, New Jersey, Louisiana, Florida) have mandated suicide prevention programs in their high schools (Valente & Saunders, 1987). We hope we will begin to see a corresponding decrease in the frequency with which young people take their lives as the effectiveness of these programs improve.

Summary

Adolescents are not strangers to death. Many have faced the death of a close friend or family member. A number must deal with their own impending death.

Piaget believes adolescents are capable of formal operational thinking, which allows much more flexibility in thought as well as attention to abstract ideas than at earlier stages of thinking. As a result, individuals in this stage are able to much more fully understand the concept of death and related spiritual and ethical issues.

Adolescents with life-threatening illnesses face the same developmental tasks as healthy adolescents, but they have special needs associated with their particular illness. For example, ill adolescents struggle to maintain a positive body image. This task is a particular challenge, given the normal, rather dramatic, physical maturational changes of adolescence. The need for privacy is closely related to these physical changes, as well as adolescents' sense of egocentrism. In addition, adolescents struggle to resolve the crisis of identity versus role confusion. As a result, adolescents strive to express their individuality, seek independence and control, and develop more mature relationships with parents and peers.

The grieving adolescent manifests a wide variety of emotions and behaviors. If given support, adolescents often participate in socially constructive acts that demonstrate caring for the deceased and successfully come to terms with their grief. However, if adolescents are not allowed to deal with their grief openly, it may surface in maladaptive or antisocial behaviors.

The incidence of adolescent suicide has increased at an alarming rate. Suicide is a complex behavior with multiple determinants; however, it often involves tunnel vision (the inability to see available alternatives) and it is often associated with depression. Young people considering suicide may give a variety of clues that can be interpreted as cries for help. In an effort to reduce the number of adolescents who take their lives each year, mental health professionals and school personnel are currently implementing programs that emphasize prevention, intervention, and postvention.

 Personal Account

In May 1974, a year after being diagnosed with leukemia, Carol Trautmann graduated from high school at 17. She died the following April. In this article, "The Absence of the Dead," her mother describes the events of that period, her interactions with Carol, and the special nature of their mother–daughter bond.

The Absence of the Dead

Mary Winfrey Trautmann

It is a spring like no other, erratic and wild, blustering with tumult. In May, wind and rain swirl; a heavy branch breaks from the top of the silk oak tree and shatters across the front yard. "That came close, didn't it?" I say to my husband as we pick up fragments of bark and splintered wood. I think back to January, the very start of 1973, the days sheeted with rain, the long, unusually wet winter for California, the sudden lurch into spring.

Carol has been watching us from the house. She comes outside to help. Her bedroom lies under the silk oak's restless branches and she is thoroughly alarmed. "Keep calm, Carol," Paul advises. "One tree limb doesn't make a cyclone."

The rain persists and then a great many flowers and fruit trees bloom all at once—the two-toned ornamental peach, purple jacaranda, the neighbor's white magnolia, a host of red and orange hibiscus and oleander, until the bright rioting colors seem to be running a race. High flowering and gusts of wind, of course, bring the fine pollen which causes Carol to sneeze and cough. She has been coughing a long time, I reflect uneasily, taking solace in the fact that a local doctor has prescribed an asthma drug for her, a fluid that she drinks daily. Still, the cough continues.

Carol does not want to see another doctor. She knows she is allergic to a large number of epidermals; this is nothing to become excited about. She is planning a beach trip with her club friends, accumulating stewpans and long-stemmed spoons. It is her responsibility, she explains with mild self-satisfaction, to bring down enough cooked food for everyone on the first night and sufficient supplies to last through the succeeding two days and nights.

On the first night of Easter vacation she carries a simmering casserole for twenty girls to the beach, positioning the dish beside her in the car and watching over it with a wary eye. When she returns in a few days, I am truly alarmed. She has lost weight, is still coughing. Her light skin has paled to alabaster, the brown eyes are puzzled, secretive. I decide to take her to an allergist at once.

Years ago when she was barely seven, Carol underwent a battery of tests, some 250 separate injections and was found to be allergic to almost everything in the world except newsprint and tissues and ink. For a couple of years she submitted to regular shots of antigens, then quit quite precipitously. "I'm sure I'm going to outgrow this junk." And her prediction seemed true enough. Now, though, this particularly windy spring, I tell myself it is absolutely necessary to reevaluate the allergy picture. She may be compelled to renew the shots whether she likes the idea or not. Adolescence, I remind myself, quoting from the universal lexicon that all mothers seem to read, adolescence is a time of serious stress.

Just before the trip to the allergist, Paul asks me whether Carol is "on anything," as he obliquely puts it. She had stood outside his shop door talking one afternoon, turned and stumbled. I tell Paul not to worry; the doctor will have an explanation.

On the way to the allergist's office, Carol, who insists upon driving, swerves unexpectedly, narrowly misses a collision with another car. While we wait to hear the results of her laboratory tests, Carol becomes dizzy and vomits into a basin. I suspect pneumonia, anemia, bronchitis. But no one will tell me anything; no one feels equal to telling me or my daughter the truth. I cannot discover just what it is the laboratory tests have revealed. Rather, I am met by evasions and apologies: "This isn't my field. . . . Why don't you see so-and-so?"

Our family physician, clearly shocked by some news bulletin we do not possess, insists that Carol enter the hospital immediately. Here we find a man who does speak out the truth—coldly and harshly as if he takes a perverse gratification in announcing disaster.

"No good white cells left to speak of. Very little chance. . . . Maybe she will be admitted to the City of Hope, I'll try. . . . If they are studying her particular kind of leukemia, they may accept her as a patient." It is Sunday when he utters those words. May 13. Mother's Day.

The days waver by. When Paul visits the City of Hope on his lunch hour or at night, just before treatment, accompanied by Julie, Carol's fourteen-year-old sister, he acts cheerful; he can often behave as if the leukemia were basically a chimera, a bad nightmare that will somehow vanish at an undisclosed moment. He jokes, teases Julie, says to Carol, "Hey, Car-oleeo, what's the latest hot scoop on the news, what's Nixon been up to?'' Toying with the mechanisms in the room, he lightly touches the controls that raise and lower the bed and states, "I'll bet you don't even know who designed these contraptions," and we hear again the story of Howard Hughes and the evolution of the modern hospital bed. Carol begins to glow, a camaraderie is established. Then a nurse enters to start an IV and she grabs my fingers.

By now we realize that her veins are small and difficult to locate. We are compelled to concentrate on a matter none of us has ever considered before—the size and availability of veins. "But I think of them all the time, I honestly do," a young nurse confides to me. She is constantly studying the blood vessels in other people's forearms, she says, glancing at my wrists. My eyes follow hers; the pulsating cords I see traveling down my arms would obviously be easy to pierce. Compared to mine, Carol's veins are like slim blue threads.

It is only the start, the first series of treatments, and Carol cannot resist playing practical jokes now and again. One night after Paul arrives and the IV stand is wheeled in, she fakes a cry of pain, holds the back of her hand to her mouth in an attitude of despair, creates a flurry, so that the nurses gather around the bed like a host of fidgety bees. Nothing whatsoever has happened. The next day I see her stun a group of awestruck friends by placing her hands on her throat in a pose worthy of Bette Davis and declaiming huskily, "I've only got two more weeks." She settles back to watch everyone's reactions, wide-eyed, a small observant sphinx. It is absurd, pure teenage soap opera—excruciating, lethal.

Before the series concludes, the hematology team interrogates Carol during a "grand round" of Wing Five. "Yes," she admits under their scrutiny and questions, "yes, I have noticed lesions on my back and hips, too. Loss of weight, yes." Paul and I listen, discover more details, learn of new symptoms. She has been aware of the red dots on her skin for several weeks; conscious, also, of a too-rapid heartbeat. "And have you had any problems with vision, Carol?" one of the men asks. Again the answer is yes.

There are intimations and warnings which Carol has been disregarding. At sixteen she cannot take such cryptic signals seriously. She surrounds herself with joy and friendliness, walks in an aura of sunlight. It is easy to laugh: a fresh joke, a hoary pun, her dog worrying a rag, the pomposity of a hospital, can cause a rivulet of laughter to escape from her, a sound, one of the nurses whispers to me, that the whole staff delights in hearing. They do not mind her practical jokes, they all love Carol.

It is less easy to laugh when the nausea comes at night, following chemotherapy, with a remorselessness she will never discuss. In the morning we see the untouched food, the listlessness, the dawdling over breakfast for hours before she at last requests a milk shake or limeade from the small kitchen around the corner.

Carol shrugs at the festive-looking trays that are brought over regularly from the main cafeteria. "Bring me a big dill pickle from the German deli-catessen, will you please, Mother?" she pleads, or else asks, "Have the birds left any apricots on the tree at the top of the hill?" I carry paper bags filled with oranges and apricots and store them in the kitchen cubicle on Wing Five. I place enormous pickles immersed in pickle juice in plastic envelopes beside Carol's tray.

Admittedly, there is not enough for me to do here, yet I cannot leave the hospital for long; I am pulled into its smooth-flowing rhythms as snugly as a leaf riding into an eddy. A furious suspense grips me. I have no more strength than the leaf. Nothing in my life has prepared me for this intol-erable suspense, no event, conditioning, or previous crisis—not child-birth, not the death of either of my parents.

I invent things to do, begin reading the history of the City of Hope. I spend an hour surveying abalone jewelry and embroidered cotton blouses in the gift shop, move across the hall to the racks of stationery and candy. It is simple enough to select brightly colored jelly beans for Carol, but what do *I* want? The choice becomes fateful, overwhelming me. I cannot make up my mind. My brain seems composed of alien dry cogs that barely turn and so I decide nothing, simply buy more jelly beans.

I conceal the bewilderment that encompasses me in ever-increasing rip-ples by being as functionally useful as possible. I change the water in the flower containers in Carol's room, tug the portable telephone about, and take down messages. I am present; on the spot, at the moment the IV is begun and Carol wants to clutch me. The books I read, the letters I write, even the diary entries, are a façade concealing my actual preoccupation, the vigil that absorbs me. While Carol sleeps or watches television and the hot summer days undulate past, I observe every changing nuance of her face and body.

A student nurse, earnest and purposeful, takes me aside and says, "I don't honestly know what your relationship with your daughter is, but anyhow, perhaps when Carol sees you coming here every day she realizes you are neglecting other responsibilities and this fact," the student nurse contin-ues firmly, "may well add to her own feelings of depression—the with-drawal she is struggling with." She gestures toward the untouched school-books that Carol has left in view. "What is here, what is she taking in school? Chemistry, history, advanced foods. . . . Well, why not call her counselor, find a tutor, someone to renew her interest in studying? . . . Now when I was sixteen . . . at that age, I could never have spoken to my mother about my feelings about myself. Perhaps she needs to be alone more, perhaps she just needs to cry."

"Do you remember the boy across the hall in room 531?" Carol asks sud-denly, as if a total random thought has entered her mind.

Something in her voice subdues me and I wait, not wanting to intrude with my immediate recollections.

"Mother, I think he died last night. Oh, yes, I do; I think I saw it happen." She is answering the puzzlement on my face, the unspoken denials. "Birdie tried to cover it up. But everything moved so fast, she was too late. It was right before dinner."

"But Carol, I was here, too," I blurt out.

"Yes. You were watching television. Your back was to the door. But I was looking and I could see him on the bed and an oxygen tent went in with a lot of people and then a stretcher and then, Mom, you know what? Birdie came in my room and asked if she could eat a peach, and shut the door. *She shut the door!*"

I continue to say nothing.

"Yesterday he talked to me," she says softly. "And he was just fine, walking around, barely even using his walker, and laughing. Do you remember how he used to eat so much?"

I nod my head, picturing the young man, a Mexican with some sort of back injury, leaning on the modified walker, talking Spanish to the orderly; I visualized the plates heaped with tostadas and rice, the flirtation tentatively begun with Carol.

"He had leukemia," she says. "And he liked me." She grows silent as if thinking about what the two of them held in common or had briefly shared—the strange unpredictable illness, the random conversations, room 531, Wing Five.

Moments afterward I encounter Dr. Graham at the nursing station. She informs me that the boy in room 531 did indeed die during the supper hour on the preceding night. A death on the Wing cannot be kept secret, the patients feel it, she admits reluctantly. "It's as if they have a sixth sense and can tell when someone dies."

She waits a moment and then says, "I am surprised Carol will not discuss this matter with me. But she won't, she doesn't say anything to the nurses either. She is keeping it to herself, suppressing the whole thing, Mrs. Trautmann." I feel that in some obscure way I am undergoing a reprimand.

"It is better for her to ask questions," the doctor says. "She should bring her suspicions out in the open. It is better to talk about death." Turning away abruptly she adds, "Teenagers are always the worst, they do not want to accept anything."

St. Patrick's Day, 1975. Carol's breakfast tray arrives with a slice of green-and-white frosted cake and a tiny Erin Go Bragh flag stuck in a pot of flourishing shamrocks.

There is no talk of death today. Dr. Kellon, Carol says, is searching for a bone-marrow donor; a transplant is still a possibility. Her platelet count is up, the hemoglobin at the twelve mark. She's having lots of visitors.

During some slack time after lunch I ramble through the extensive grounds that surround the City of Hope, losing my way more than once among the terraces and buildings. Repeatedly, it seems almost by prearrangement, I end up scrutinizing the façade of the weathered structure known as Hillquit, where tuberculosis patients were formerly housed during the early days of the medical-research center.

Hillquit is flanked by a row of large tattered eucalyptus trees. It is only when I examine them closely, walking near to the dusty branches and peering past the flaking bark at the grey trunks that I see certain of these trees wear metal plaques. The plaques are chained around the tree trunks like necklaces or charm bracelets and are engraved with names and dates. They are, in fact, memorials.

The wind has blown a considerable scattering of leaves, bark slivers, and pods upon the grass. The impression of their fragrance and shivering silver-green movement goes with me when I re-enter the corridors of Wing Five and almost without reflecting upon the matter, I describe the trees to Carol. Her response is instantaneous. "Oh, mother, can I have a tree, promise me, can I?"

I am unprepared for this reaction and my face shows it.

She repeats her request. "Promise me, mother, promise me, please."

I promise her a tree.

Carol's telephone call startles me early the next morning. She is in profound distress, her voice scarcely audible. Her friend Gayle died in February, two weeks ago, Dr. Kellon has just told her. Died of bleeding in the brain, the onrush of too many white cells, Carol laments brokenly. She cries, I cry, hard driving tears.

I find some words. "But no one ever really dies. They just change, take on a different form." She welcomes my words, whispers that Dr. Kellon will be starting a new treatment tonight. However, when I reach the hospital, the nurse is already in the room adjusting the paraphernalia to begin a series of cytoxin and cytosine injections, the c. and c., as she calls this treatment, which is to be administered around the clock at ten and two and six. Carol, having misunderstood her doctor's directive, is washing her hair in the shower. She emerges explosively.

"I want to wash it while I can," she shouts through the dribbles of water. "It's going to fall out, you know!" She blows her nose fiercely and demands that the injection be postponed.

I sit in silence while my daughter weeps for Gayle and for her own yellow hair soon to be sacrificed.

The nurse motions me into the hall. "I've seen good results from this treatment," she says. "As for the side effects, I've been advising Carol that not everyone loses hair with c. and c. Some do, some don't. It's not certain.

"Carol is terribly upset just now," I venture.

"Oh, of course. We all understand. She *should* feel anger. She *should* cry. She's a young girl and she's doing badly and she knows it." The memory of Gayle absorbs us both, even though we do not refer to her by name.

Gayle, I think wistfully, the absent friend, the contestant who has just abandoned the race.

The air throngs with death. The actress Susan Hayward dies. Aristotle
Onassis dies. The Brazilian father who was flown to the City of Hope from
Rio de Janeiro last month dies. The widow, ringed by her family in the TV
lounge, gesticulates, all black eyes and nervous motion. The young son,
she vows, is now to become head of the family.

Easter Sunday, 1975. Carol comes to the house with her friend, Les.
"Mother, I'm having chills," she says. "I just want to take a nice hot bath."
She sluices hot water over herself and stands close to the electric wall
heater in the bathroom.

"But Carol," I protest, "I don't really believe this is the right thing to
do for the hematoma." She is doctoring herself again, I think desperately.
The thermometer reads 104 degrees. Chills and fever. I reach for the
telephone.

Carol's friend Rick drives her to the City of Hope in the enormous
camper that he has borrowed for the holiday trip to the Colorado River. A
cluster of good friends goes along, sits beside her, stays near at hand during
the admissions procedure, never a rapid process, and this afternoon, endless. They huddle together in the outpatient waiting room while a doctor
is found who can examine her, someone else who can X-ray her. The hospital is understaffed. It is Easter, an inappropriate day for an emergency.

Carol clutches my hand, voiceless, looking angry, worried, resigned,
annoyed. A nightmare is being played out before me in slow motion. No
one can locate the hospital aides. The elevator jams on its way to the lab,
stalls with Carol on a gurney and me beside her. She is X-rayed incorrectly;
the procedure has to be repeated. Walking in a nightmare, I tell my daughter's good friends, anxiously assembled, that she is to remain in the hospital. She will be treated for an infection. Some pain is as yet unaccounted
for but the X-rays have turned out satisfactorily. Everyone is relieved and
departs. Carol is wheeled to Wing Five, this time to a room near the nursing
station. She grits her teeth. "So here I am, down where all the basket cases
are cared for."

Carol drifts into an entrancement as if a charm had been pronounced, a
spell cast. She slips out of this bemusement only when visitors, her father,
her sisters, come to talk and linger. Then she rallies, the brooding eyes
kindle. When people leave, she glides under the entrancement again.

Someone makes a mistake. Carol is transported on a tall white gurney
down cluttered halls and up to another floor for an abdominal examination. The order is cancelled. We reverse our path, proceed through the
same halls past clinics and staring eyes. We meet Dr. Graham. Her eyes lock
with mine and for an instant I see the taunting question in their depths:
"You realize what this is at last, finally, don't you, Mrs. Trautmann?"

I place a couple of chairs together, sleep next to her bed; for two nights I keep this post. When morning arrives I begin my diary writing again. She notices and smiles. I start to sketch her profile upon white paper, attempting to reproduce the contour of the nose, the unruly hair, the smudged eyes, her hand which, as it grasps the cup, stays steady, stays poised.

"It is no longer a policy of the City of Hope to plant trees as personal memorials. . . . Those eucalyptus trees were established many, many years ago."

After an interval of polite fencing, my telephone call is transferred to the Los Angeles office of the administrative director whose brisk voice assures me, "Everything that *can* be done *will* be done." However, when I repeat my wish to plant a tree on the grounds, he objects with vigor. "It just isn't practical. It simply doesn't work out. We gave up the practice, oh, decades ago. We had to. The plaques hanging on the trunks get ruined; they become illegible. High winds out of the San Bernardino mountains sometimes wreck the trees. People come back later, can't find their tree, and complain."

I wait until he has run down.

"I promised her a tree." Silence. When he speaks again his tone has altered slightly.

"I'm going to refer you to the superintendent of grounds, Mrs. Trautmann. You can discuss the matter further with him. What kind of tree did you say you wanted to plant?"

"A lemon tree."

Monday morning, after the usual delays and re-routing at the switchboard, the voice of the superintendent of grounds, Mr. Cameron, finally reaches my ears. "I don't know exactly where we'll put that lemon tree yet, but your daughter's going to have one. But no plaque around the trunk," he cautions. "The plaques get torn off anyway. They're not worth it."

At the nursery in Whittier I am promised one Eureka lemon tree in a fifteen-gallon can, about seven feet high, already bearing lemons and yellow winter leaves that will turn dark green in time. Delivery will take two weeks, enough time certainly for the selection of an appropriate site.

The actual tree-planting ceremony takes place on a warm day in June. A circle of people gathers; poetry is read; Dr. Ed Bloomfield speaks to us about hope—the word, the hospital, and "the hope that before this tree reaches its full stature a cure will be found for the illness that took Carol from us." Paul and I are the first to shovel dirt around the tree's roots. Others pick up the spade and throw on more soil. The tree is planted.

The last time I visited Carol's tree I observed that it now stands on the circumference of a children's playground and is part of a border of greenery that shelters behind a strong metal fence.

Leukemic children and infants suffering from catastrophic illness are no longer sequestered on a roof top. They play in a large circle of sand edged by a concrete sidewalk; and they can choose from among a fine selection of playground equipment that includes a jungle gym made of logs, a sheet metal slide, and a large rubber tire swing. The circle of sand and the collar of cement both sweep past the lemon tree. A few toy plastic cars and digging spoons are scattered near its slender trunk.

The branches shiver softly, laden with their yellow and dark-green leaves; several small green globes, the rind just beginning to turn golden, swing freely in the depths of Carol's tree. It is still the only lemon tree on the grounds, more than doubled in height and daily growing taller.

Questions and Activities

1. What coping techniques did Carol and her family use to deal with her illness?

2. Identify specific characteristics and behaviors that Carol exhibited that are typical of adolescents. What other characteristics and behaviors appear to be unique to Carol's own personality and the Trautmanns' family dynamics?

3. Cite interactions that Carol and her family had with the hospital staff. In what ways were these interactions helpful? Did any of the situations create psychological stress, rather than alleviating it? Did the staff show an understanding of normal adolescent development? Give examples.

4. While hospitalized, Carol experienced the deaths of two peers who were also ill. As a caregiver, what would you have told Carol about the deaths in both of these situations? When and how would you have shared the news with her?

5. Think about the communication patterns in the Trautmann family. What words would you use to describe the quality of the communication? Describe the family dynamics (rules, roles, subsystems, and so forth) that influenced the level and type of communication surrounding Carol's illness and impending death.

6. In what ways was planting the lemon tree on the hospital grounds therapeutic for her mother? What did it symbolize for her?

Glossary

Adolescent Egocentrism: Preoccupation of adolescents with their own thought processes and their thoughts of themselves.

Alopecia: Hair loss (for example, from chemotherapy).

Contagion Theory: Belief that talking about suicide will encourage suicidal behavior.

Developmental Counseling: Attempts to prevent potential crises by helping students become more aware of themselves, how they interact with their environment, and how to effectively cope with the various tasks involved in growing up.

Formal Operational Stage: Refers to Piaget's fourth stage of cognitive development, beginning in adolescence and continuing through adulthood.

Identity: Positive resolution of Erikson's psychosocial crisis associated with adolescence; it implies self-definition and commitment to a role.

Imaginary Audience: Belief held by adolescents that they are continually under observation by others.

Intervention: Therapeutic efforts to reduce the intensity and negative effects of a crisis or difficult situation.

Moral Reasoning: Process of judging behavior and thinking about moral dilemmas.

Personal Fable: Feeling, common among adolescents, that one is immune to the bad things that happen to others.

Prevention: Actions taken to avoid a stressful or harmful situation.

Postvention: Dealing with the aftermath of a traumatic event and minimizing the impact.

Psychosocial Moratorium: Relatively "hands-off" posture of society toward adolescents to allow them time to engage in the process of finding themselves and their place in society.

Role Confusion (Identity Diffusion): Negative outcome of Erikson's adolescent crisis; individuals having this outcome are unsure of who they are and where they are going.

Tunnel Vision: Inability to consider alternative ways of dealing with a crisis.

Suggested Readings

Blum, R. (Ed.). (1984). *Chronic illness and disabilities in childhood and adolescence.* Orlando, FL: Grune & Stratton.

This book discusses the major physical, social, psychological, educational, and rehabilitative needs of children and youth with chronic illnesses and disabilities. Written from a multidisciplinary perspective, the text covers such diverse topics as social and political issues; ethical concerns; and special educational, nutritional, and sexual considerations. Specific illnesses covered include sickle cell anemia, cancer, cystic fibrosis, and chronic kidney disease.

Corr, C. A. , & McNeil, J. N. (Eds.). (1986). *Adolescence and death.* New York: Springer.

This collection of articles examines a broad array of issues related to death, dying, and grief during the adolescent years. Topics covered include death themes in adolescent music, the influence of the nuclear threat on adolescent development, guidelines for helping dying and grieving adolescents, needs of suicidal adolescents and suicide survivors, and counseling adolescents in a variety of death-related situations.

Krementz, J. (1981). *How it feels when a parent dies.* New York: Knopf.

This book contains deeply moving accounts by 18 children and adolescents who have experienced the death of a parent. Ranging in age from 7 to 17, these young survivors speak openly about their loss and share a variety of feelings.

Mack, J. E., & Hickler, H. (1981). *Vivienne: The life and suicide of an adolescent girl.* Boston: Little, Brown.

This is the story of a young girl who committed suicide at age 14. Insights into her life and death are gained through her diary entries, poems, school compositions, and letters. Vivienne's family, a teacher at her school, and a psychiatrist collaborated on this book.

Resources

American Association of Suicidology
2459 South Ash Street
Denver, Colorado 80222
(303) 692-0985

Leukemia Society of America
733 Third Avenue; 14th Floor
New York, New York 10017
(212) 573-8484

Cancer Information Service
National Cancer Institute
Building 31, Room 10A24
Bethesda, Maryland 20892
(800) 422-6237

References

Ansbacher, H. L., & Ansbacher, R. R. (Eds). (1956). *The individual psychology of Alfred Adler: A systematic presentation in selections from his writings.* New York: Basic Books.

Aubrey, R. R. (1977). Adolescents and death. In E. R. Prichard, J. Collard, B. A. Drevitt, A. H. Kutscher, I. Seeland, & N. Lefkowitz (Eds.), *Social work with the dying patient and family* (pp. 131–145). New York: Columbia University Press.

Balk, D. (1983). Adolescents' grief reactions and self-concept perceptions following sibling death: A study of 33 teenagers. *Journal of Youth and Adolescence, 12*(2), 137–161.

Baumrind, D. (1983). Authoritarian vs. authoritative parental control. In J. J. Conger (Ed.), *Contemporary issues in adolescent development.* New York: Harper & Row.

Bedell, J. R., Giordan, B., Amour, J. L., Tavormina, J., & Boll, T. (1977). Life stress and the psychological and medical adjustment of chronically ill children. *Journal of Psychosomatic Research, 21*(3), 237–242.

Berman, A. L. (1986). Helping suicidal adolescents: Needs and responses. In C. A. Corr & J. N. McNeil (Eds.), *Adolescence and death* (pp. 151–166). New York: Springer.

Berman, S. J. (1980, September). *Adolescent coping with cancer: The issue of control.* Paper presented at the Annual Meeting of the American Psychological Association, Montreal, Canada.

Blum, R. W. (1984). The dying adolescent. In R. W. Blum (Ed.), *Chronic illness and disabilities in childhood and adolescence* (pp. 159–176). Orlando, FL: Grune & Stratton.

Blum, R. W., & Chang, P. (1981). A group for adolescents facing chronic and terminal illness. *Journal of Current Adolescent Medicine, 3,* 7–12.

Blumberg, B. D., Lewis, M. J., & Susman, E. J. (1984). Adolescence: A time of transition. In M. G. Eisenberg, L. C. Sutkin, & M. A. Jansen (Eds.), *Chronic illness and disability through the life span: Effects on self and family* (pp. 133–149). New York: Springer.

Boldt, M. (1982). Normative evaluations of suicide and death: A cross-generational study. *Omega, 13*(2), 145–157.

Cain, A. C. (1978). The impact of parent suicide on children. In O. Sahler (Ed.), *The child and death* (pp. 202–210). St. Louis: Mosby.

Carson, N. D., & Johnson, R. E. (1985). Suicidal thoughts and problem-solving preparation among college students. *Journal of College Student Personnel, 26*(6), 484–487.

Cho, S. A., Freeman, E. M., & Patterson, S. L. (1982). Adolescents' experience with death: Practice implications. *Social Casework, 63,* 88–94.

Coddington, R. D. (1979). Life events associated with adolescent pregnancies. *Journal of Clinical Psychology, 40,* 180–185.

Cook, A. S., & Oltjenbruns, K. A. (1982). A cognitive developmental approach to death education for adolescents. *Family Perspective, 16,* 9–14.

Denholm, C. L. (1985). Hospitalization and the adolescent patient: A review and some critical questions. *Children's Health Care, 13*(3), 109–116.

DePalma, D. J., & Foley, J. M. (Eds.). (1975). *Moral development: Current theory and research.* New York: Wiley.

Eddy, J. M., & Alles, W. F. (1983). *Death Education.* St. Louis: Mosby.

Eisenberg, M. G., Sutkin, L. C., & Jansen, M. A. (1984). *Chronic illness and disability through the life span: Effects on self and family.* New York: Springer.

Elkind, D. (1967). Egocentrism in adolescence. *Child Development, 38,* 1025–1034.

Elkind, D. (1970). *Children and adolescents: Interpretive essays on Jean Piaget.* New York: Oxford University Press.

Erikson, E. H. (1959). Identity and the life cycle. *Psychological Issues, 1,* 50–100.

Ewalt, P. L., & Perkins, L. (1979). The real experience of death among adolescents: An empirical study. *Social Casework, 60,* 547–551.

Fairchild, T. N. (1986). Suicide intervention. In T. N. Fairchild (Ed.), *Crisis intervention strategies for school-based helpers* (pp. 321–369). Springfield, IL: Charles C Thomas.

Farrell, F. A. (1981). *Interviews with five sets of parents of adolescents with cancer.* Unpublished manuscript, University of Arizona, Tucson, Arizona.

Farrell, F., & Hutter, J. J. (1980). Living until death: Adolescents with cancer. *Health and Social Work, 5,* 35–38.

Gander, M. J., & Gardiner, H. W. (1981). *Child and adolescent development.* Boston: Little, Brown.

Hankoff, L. D. (1975). Adolescence and the crisis of dying. *Adolescence, 10*(39), 373–389.

Hart, N. A., & Keidel, G. C. (1979). The suicidal adolescent. *American Journal of Nursing, 79*(1), 80–84.

Hatton, C. L., Valente, S. M., & Rink, A. (1977). *Suicide: Assessment and intervention.* New York: Appleton-Century-Crofts.

Havighurst, R. J. (1972). *Developmental tasks and education* (3d ed.). New York: David McCay.

Hodges, M. H., Graham-Pole, J., & Fong, M. L. (1984). Attitudes, knowledge, and behaviors of school peers of adolescent cancer patients. *Journal of Psychosocial Oncology, 2*(2), 37–46.

Johnson, P., & Rosenblatt, P. (1981). Grief following childhood loss of a parent. *American Journal of Psychotherapy, 35,* 419–425.

Kalish, R. A. (1985). *Death, grief, and caring relationships* (2d ed.). Belmont, CA: Brooks/Cole.

Kastenbaum, R. J. (1986). *Death, society, and human experience* (3d ed.). Columbus, OH: Charles E. Merrill.

Kellerman J., & Katz, E. B. (1977). The adolescent with cancer: Theoretical, clinical, and research issues. *Journal of Pediatric Psychology, 2*(3), 127–131.

Kellerman, J., Zeltzer, L., Ellenberg, L., Dash, J., & Rigler, D. (1980). Psychological effects of illness in adolescence. I. Anxiety, self-esteem, and perception of control. *The Journal of Pediatrics, 97*(1), 126–131.

Kline, J., & Schowalter, J. E. (1974). How to care for the "between-ager." *Nursing, 4*(11), 42–51.

LaGrand, L. E. (1981). Loss reactions of college students: A descriptive analysis. *Death Education, 5*, 235–248.

Lerner, R. M., & Hultsch, K. F. (1983). *Human development: A life-span perspective.* New York: McGraw-Hill.

Manaster, G. J. (1977). *Adolescent development and the life tasks.* Boston: Allyn & Bacon.

Maris, R. (1985). The adolescent suicide problem. *Suicide and Life-Threatening Behavior, 15*(2), 91–109.

Martin, N. K., & Dixon, P. N. (1986). Adolescent suicide: Myths, recognition, and evaluation. *The School Counselor, 33*(4), 265–271.

Mitchell, J. R. (1980). Male adolescents' concern about a physical examination conducted by a female. *Nursing Research, 29*, 165–169.

Moore, C., Holton, C. P., & Martin, G. W. (1969). Psychological problems in the management of adolescents with malignancy. *Clinical Pediatrics, 8*(8), 464–473.

Morgan, L. B. (1981). The counselor's role in suicide prevention. *The Personnel and Guidance Journal, 59*, 284–286.

Nannis, E. D., Susman, E. J., Strope, B. E., Woodruff, P. J., Hersh, S. P., Levine, A. S., & Pizzo, P. A. (1982). Correlates of control in pediatric cancer patients and their families. *Journal of Pediatric Psychology, 7*(1), 75–84.

National Cancer Institute. (1982a). *Help yourself: Tips for teenagers with cancer.* Washington, DC: Adria Laboratories in cooperation with the National Cancer Institute.

National Cancer Institute. (1982b). *Help yourself: Tips for teenagers with cancer: Four audio plays.* Washington, DC: National Cancer Institute.

Neimark, E. D. (1979). Current status of formal operations research. *Human Development, 22*, 60–67.

Nelson, F. (1988). A research note on knowledge of youth suicide among high school students. *Journal of Community Psychology, 16*(2), 241–243.

Office of Cancer Communications, National Cancer Institute. (1980). *Pretest report: Statements on issues of concern to adolescents with cancer.* Unpublished report.

Orr, D. P., Hoffmans, M. A., & Bennetts, G. (1984). Adolescents with cancer report their psychological needs. *Journal of Psychosocial Oncology, 2*(2), 47–59.

Pattison, E. M. (1977). *The experience of dying.* Englewood Cliffs, NJ: Prentice-Hall.

Peck, M. L., Farberow, N. L., & Litman, R. E. (Eds.). (1985). *Youth suicide.* New York: Springer.

Perkes, A. C., & Schlidt, R. (1979). Death-related activities of adolescent males and females. *Death Education, 2*, 359–368.

Piaget, J. (1932). *The moral judgment of the child.* New York: Free Press.

Piaget, J. (1972). Intellectual evolution from adolescence to adulthood. *Human Development, 15*, 1–12.

Plumb, M. M., & Holland, J. (1974). Cancer in adolescents: The symptom is the thing. In B. Schoenberg, A. C. Carr, A. H. Kutscher, D. Peretz, & I. K. Goldberg (Eds.), *Anticipatory grief* (pp. 193–209). New York: Columbia University Press.

Rando, T. A. (1984). *Grief, dying, and death: Clinical interventions for caregivers.* Champaign, IL: Research Press.

Raphael, B. (1983). *The anatomy of bereavement.* New York: Basic Books.

Richman, J. (1986). *Family therapy for suicidal people.* New York: Springer.

Rosenblatt, P. C., Jackson, D. A., & Walsh, R. P. (1972). Coping with anger and aggression in mourning. *Omega, 3*(4), 271–284.

Ross, C. P. (1985). Teaching children the facts of life and death: Suicide prevention in the schools. In M. L. Peck, N. L. Farberow, & R. E. Litman (Eds.), *Youth suicide* (pp. 147–169). New York: Springer.

Seligman, M. E. P. (1975). *Helplessness: On depression, development and death.* San Francisco: W. H. Freeman.

Schiamberg, L. B. (1985). *Human Development* (2d ed.). New York: Macmillan.

Shaffer, D. R. (1985). *Developmental psychology: Theory, research, and applications.* Monterey, CA: Brooks/Cole.

Shneidman, E. (1981). Postvention. *Suicide and Life-Threatening Behavior, 11*(4), 349–360.

Shoor, M., & Speed, M. H. (1976). Death, delinquency, and the mourning process. In R. Fulton (Ed.), *Death and identity.* Bowie, MD: Charles Press.

Susman, E. J., Pizzo, P. A., & Poplack, D. G. (1981). Adolescent cancer: Getting through the aftermath. In P. Ahmed (Ed.), *Living and dying with childhood cancer* (pp. 99–117). New York: Elsevier.

United States Bureau of the Census. (1983). *Statistical abstracts of the United States* (103d ed.). Washington, DC: U. S. Government Printing Office.

Valente, S. M., & Saunders, J. M. (1987). High school suicide prevention programs. *Pediatric Nursing, 13*(2), 108–112, 137.

Walker, B. A., & Mehr, M. (1983). Adolescent suicide—a family crisis: A model for effective intervention by family therapists. *Adolescence, 18,* 285–292.

Wass, H. (1979). *Dying: Facing the facts.* Washington, DC: Hemisphere.

Wasserman, A. L., Thompson, E. I., Wilimas, J. A., & Fairclough, D. L. (1987). The psychological status of survivors of childhood/adolescent Hodgkin's disease. *American Journal of Diseases of Children, 141*(6), 626–631.

Zeltzer, L. K. (1980). The adolescent with cancer. In J. Kellerman (Ed.), *Psychological aspects of childhood cancer.* Springfield, IL: Charles C Thomas.

Zeltzer, L., Kellerman, J., Ellenberg, L., Dash, J., & Rigler, D. (1980). Psychologic effects of illness in adolescence. II. Impact of illness in adolescents—crucial issues and coping styles. *The Journal of Pediatrics, 97*(1), 132–138.

Zeltzer, L., LeBaron, S., & Zeltzer, P. (1984). The adolescent with cancer. In R. W. Blum (Ed.), *Chronic illness and disabilities in childhood and adolescence* (pp. 375–395). Orlando, FL: Grune & Stratton.

7

Young Adulthood

Major Causes of Death during Young Adulthood   269

Needs of Young Adults with Life-threatening Illnesses   270

Developing Intimate
   Relationships   270
Expressing Their Sexuality   272
Receiving Realistic Support of
   Goals and Future Plans   275

Acquired Immune Deficiency Syndrome (AIDS)   279

Grief of AIDS Victims   281
Grief of AIDS Survivors   283
Ethical Issues Related to AIDS
   284

The Grief of Young Parents
285

Miscarriage   286
Stillbirth and Death of a
   Newborn   287
Sudden Infant Death Syndrome
   289
Abortion   290

Death and War   291

Personal Consequences of
   Combat   292
Healing the Emotional Wounds
   296

Writing during Bereavement
300

Summary   302

The period of young adulthood extends throughout one's twenties and thirties. Whereas adolescence involves the crystallization of identity, early adulthood involves the exploration of "still-uncharted depths of that identity" (Schiamberg, 1985). The maximum unfolding of our capabilities and opportunities occurs during the early years of adult life. It is the first time in our lives that we as individuals can be truly autonomous, making our own decisions and living with the consequences. This life stage is one of decision making. Choices about relationships, work, and life-style made at this time help shape and define the remainder of adult life.

For the majority of individuals, young adulthood marks the beginning of many life events and roles—the commitment to a career, the beginning of a marriage, and the initiation into parenthood. Hopes, aspirations, and goals are now beginning to be translated into experience. The high energy level of young adults allows them to live their lives to the fullest. Peak physical strength is achieved in the twenties (Stevens-Long, 1988), and young adults use their physical strength and stamina as they pursue vigorous, active life-styles. The physical zest of this stage is the antithesis of illness and death.

When a terminal illness does occur, young adults react to the knowledge of their impending death with frustration and disappointment. They feel angry and cheated out of their lives. They are on the threshold of fulfilling their dreams and aspirations, only to have their lives cruelly interrupted (Pattison, 1977). More than at any other time in adult life, the young adult has both more to lose and less to reflect back on. The losses are even more acute because the person will not live to see the promise of relationships fulfilled or experience the future of significant others (such as children) (Rando, 1984). Pattison (1977) has remarked on the tenacity with which young adults hold onto life. They are actively pursuing their life goals, and their intensity for life makes them impatient with illness and angry at the threat of death. As Pattison has expressed it, death during young adulthood is "dying with the harness on."

Major Causes of Death during Young Adulthood

For individuals in their twenties and early thirties, accidents continue to be the leading cause of death, followed by suicide. Young adults are physically active and are often involved in leisure and recreational activities that can be potentially dangerous. Activities such as motorcycle racing and sky diving, for example, may be viewed as even more exciting because of the element of risk involved (Pattison, 1977). Diseases are less common causes of death until age 35, when cancer becomes the leading cause,

269

closely followed by heart disease (United States Bureau of the Census, 1987).

Needs of Young Adults with Life-threatening Illnesses

Young adults have their own developmental concerns, and these concerns must be considered by caregivers attempting to meet the needs of terminally ill individuals in this age group. Three specific needs of dying young adults will be considered in depth. These needs are: (1) the need to develop intimate relationships, (2) the need to express their sexuality, and (3) the need for realistic support of their goals and future plans.

Developing Intimate Relationships

Erikson (1959) has identified *intimacy versus isolation* as the major psychosocial issue to be resolved during the young adult years. Intimacy involves the ability to experience an open, supportive, and close relationship with another person, without fear of losing oneself in the process. The establishment of intimacy with a significant other implies the capacity for mutual empathy, the ability to help meet each other's needs, the acceptance of each other's limitations, and the commitment to care deeply for each other. An intimate relationship may be sexual or nonsexual, and it can range from a marital relationship to a deep friendship or a sibling relationship. Both individuals in an intimate relationship bring their own personal strengths and resources as well as their limitations to the relationship, and both partners are affected by the nature of their interpersonal interaction. Prior to adulthood, individuals' identities are too fragile and their egos are too immature to attain the mutuality involved in truly intimate relationships.

Intimacy is the basis for mature love relationships, and the ability to develop intimate relationships is related to the positive resolution of psychosocial crises of earlier developmental periods. For example, trust is a prerequisite for the development of intimacy, and a sense of identity is also important. It is difficult to share and give of ourselves if we do not know who we are as distinct individuals. Failure to develop intimate relationships can lead to preoccupation with oneself and superficial relationships with others. Erikson (1959) has used the term "isolation" to describe this outcome.

Cozby (1972) has emphasized the importance of self-disclosure in the development of intimacy, trust, and understanding with others. The process of self-disclosure is based on reciprocity, and it is critical for the formation and strengthening of close relationships. Little by little, this reciprocal exchange of personal information takes place as the individuals involved feel safe enough to risk self-disclosure (Derlega & Chaikin, 1975). Individuals move slowly in revealing themselves until they feel confident that their disclosures will be respected and accepted by the other person. The process is disrupted when one member does not reciprocate. As intimacy is increased, communication is facilitated and feelings are expressed more openly and honestly. Through this process, some of our deepest emotions are shared.

Having a close relationship with a significant other has been shown to help adults cope with stressful periods. According to Lowenthal and Weiss (1976), "intimacy is a sine qua non of hope" for many individuals (p. 13). For dying young adults, intimacy with a significant other can be an important avenue for ventilating fears and concerns related to dying and assuaging their feelings of emotional isolation. It can also help them feel valued as unique persons when the emphasis in the relationship is on who they are in the here and now, rather than on who they possibly could have become.

Different levels of intimacy will be attained with different individuals, depending on the nature of the relationship. Trust and self-disclosure are often overlooked as important aspects of the professional–patient relationship. Compliance with medical procedures and opportunity to share fears and concerns are intricately tied to quality of relationships between patients and professional caregivers. Professionals who desire to communicate on a less superficial level with their patients have to be willing to share something of themselves as individuals separate from their roles. The dying individual will need to communicate with the caregiver as a person as well as a professional.

Concerns related to intimacy can also extend to family members and friends. If not married, young adults may have to depend on their parents for caregiving and non-family members may be minimally involved. Depending on the age of the young adult's parents, their physical capacity for caregiving may be diminished and siblings may be called upon to assume some of the caregiving responsibilites. Because many young adults live some distance away from their parents, having a terminal illness may necessitate relocating to the city in which their parents live. This relocation can result in separation from important social support systems. When geographical distance is not a factor, friends often want to be actively involved in caregiving and should be allowed to do so.

Following a diagnosis of a serious illness, intimate relationships of the young adult can be threatened. In some situations, intimate companions may pull away because of their own fear and confusion. For example, they may equate cancer with death and feel they will not be able to cope with the consequences. On the other hand, young adults with life-threatening illnesses may themselves pull away from relationships because they feel they have no future and therefore nothing to offer those close to them. Furthermore, parents and siblings may try to protect the dying young adult from pursuing mature relationships with others for fear he or she will be hurt. Taking emotional risks is part of living, and young adults with life-threatening illnesses have every right to engage in the risks associated with establishing new relationships (Gideon & Taylor, 1981). Mutuality in adult relationships involves giving as well as receiving, and the "giving" component may have special significance for dying young adults as they become the recipients of increased care and attention from family members and health care professionals.

It is important for professional caregivers to be aware of the quality and availability of intimate relationships in the patient's life and to be supportive of these relationships. Including the significant other in discussions of the illness and its implications can help allay fears and reduce confusion. It may also aid the patient and his or her significant other in making difficult decisions regarding their future together. An open and honest exploration of the issues involved assists young adults in determining what they can offer each other. The relationship may be redefined as the dying individual's condition changes. Sometimes original plans will be changed (for example, marriage plans may be canceled), but the relationship may still remain as a support and provide intimate companionship for the dying individual.

If the dying individual is hospitalized, the physical setting can have implications for the fulfillment of intimacy needs. Facilities should be designed to facilitate ongoing relationships rather than inadvertently foster isolation and loneliness. Allowing for privacy and visitation of both family and non-family members can be crucial to sustain emotional support for young adults.

Expressing Their Sexuality

Sexuality is a natural expression of intimacy in couple relationships, and individuals with life-threatening illnesses share the need to be affectionate and to express themselves sexually. Human sexuality is life affirming and can enable one to feel more like a living individual than a dying individual. Unfortunately, the sexual needs of the dying are often ignored; dying individuals are treated as though they are asexual beings.

Adults are sexual beings regardless of their age, physical status, or stage in life. Expressing our sexuality contributes to our sense of worth and communicates some of our deepest emotions. Recognizing this, Gideon and Taylor (1981) have proposed a sexual bill of rights for dying persons. They believe that the dying have a right to be sexual in the broadest sense of the term. In their view, sexuality and intercourse are not necessarily the same. Sexuality encompasses a wide range of feelings, attitudes, and behaviors; one's sexuality can be expressed in many ways. If individuals are aware of this, then loss of ability to express themselves sexually through intercourse will be less damaging to the person's sexual identity and self-esteem.

Feeling attractive and positive about ourselves physically is an important aspect of our sexual identity. Though a positive sexual identity can be facilitated by feeling desirable, many dying individuals fear they will be criticized if they purchase new clothes so close to their anticipated death or spend money to enhance their physical appearance. Our physical appearance is the most visible aspect of our sexuality, and dying individuals should be given opportunities to engage in activities that promote acceptance of their changing bodies. Gideon and Taylor (1981) also insist that it is the individual's right to maintain control over his or her own body. Some individuals will refuse disfiguring surgeries (despite the recommendations of their physicians) in order to preserve their physical integrity and maintain a positive body image. For example, a breast cancer patient may opt for less radical surgery even though she is told that her risks of recurrence will be greater.

Leviton (1978) has stated that the intimacy and sexual needs of the terminally ill need to be legitimized. Willingness on the part of caregivers to openly discuss these needs can help in having these needs met. The dying and their partners also need access to counseling and information that will help in accommodating the physical changes occurring in their bodies. Because of taboos in our society surrounding sex and sexuality, both patients and caregivers find it difficult to bring up the subject. Spouses may also fail to bring up sexual issues because they sense the professional's discomfort with the topic. Unfortunately, this situation can have devastating consequences for a couple. For example, one young woman, Mary, came home from the hospital after a series of cancer treatments with only a few months to live. Her husband, Tom, took a leave of absence from his job to care for her, with the assistance of a local hospice, during her remaining time. Mary wanted to be physically intimate with her husband in order to reaffirm their relationship and to have the comfort and reassurance of being held and loved. Sexual issues were not discussed with her physician, and Tom incorrectly assumed that intercourse would be too physically taxing and painful for Mary and that it might worsen her condition, and thus, hasten her death. Tom even started sleeping on a cot rather than in their bed so that Mary would be more comfortable. Mary did not share her feelings and assumed that Tom should know that she wanted him to be physically close, as she always had. When Tom failed to respond in familiar ways, she interpreted his withdrawal as rejection. As the months passed, Mary felt more and more distanced from Tom because of these misunderstandings regarding her needs for sexual intimacy. To avoid this situation, couples need to be aware of each other's fears and concerns. This awareness can be encouraged by sensitive professionals with training in sexuality and medicine. Open communication between partners should be encouraged to facilitate the mutual meeting of their needs.

Changes in body function affecting sexuality often occur as a result of the patient's disease and related medical treatment. These changes can surprise, frighten, and sometimes demoralize couples and result in a drastic reduction in sexual activity, although such reduction is unnecessary. When medical personnel openly discuss anticipated changes and effects on sexuality, couples can be helped to understand what is happening and adjust or adapt their sexual practices accordingly. For example, radiation therapy to the vaginal area may leave it drier and less elastic, requiring the use of lubricants for pleasurable intercourse. Drug therapy may also affect sexual functioning. For instance, major tranquilizers such as Thorazine can reduce sexual interest and inhibit ejaculation. If not prepared for these side effects, the individual may attribute these changes to his or her own inadequacies and thus experience a great deal of anxiety. Many times couples need specific suggestions about sexual practices. For example, one couple felt awkward until they learned that the husband's colostomy bag could be placed in such a way as to permit holding and cuddling each other comfortably. For other couples, new positions for intercourse or different ways of releasing sexual tension will need to be explored (Gideon & Taylor, 1981).

Some diseases and their treatments can result in impotence (for example, estrogen treatment given to males for prostate cancer), while others result in sterility but not necessarily impotence (such as removal of the testes). Impotence and frigidity can also be caused by general ill health. Fatigue and chronic pain often accompany terminal illnesses and can result in a general lack of interest in intercourse. In fact, patients with chronic pain often report a decrease in the frequency and quality of their sexual activity. Lack of confidence in one's ability to perform can lead to a poor self-image, which can further contribute to impaired sexual functioning (Gideon & Taylor, 1981).

Institutional settings, such as hospitals, can sometimes interfere with a partner's ability to share physical displays of affection. Privacy is essential for a couple to show their love and support in an intimate way, and hospitals provide few opportunities for private moments. Having a loved one sleep quietly next to them can provide tremendous comfort to some dying individuals. To accommodate these intimacy needs, hospital rules and regulations must be relaxed and hospital staff must maintain nonjudgmental and accepting attitudes.

Receiving Realistic Support of Goals and Future Plans

Young adulthood is a time of dreams and aspirations, and individuals in this age group often feel shortchanged when faced with a life-threatening illness. They need help in evaluating their futures and deciding on appropriate goals for the time they have remaining. Future plans for the young adult often involve marriage, children, and career goals. The particular disease, the prognosis and associated dying trajectory, the individual's personality and coping style, and available social supports all contribute to the definition of what is "realistic" and "appropriate." Young adults need to talk about the future and the implications for themselves and their loved ones.

Marriage. The decision of whether or not to marry should be determined by the individuals involved. Couples may decide they want to go through a formal ceremony to publicly show their commitment to each other despite a very negative prognosis for the terminally ill partner. The realities of the illness should be made clear to each individual, but whatever the couple's decision, it should be supported by friends and family. Sometimes the pair will not want to plan a future together as a married couple. The individual with the disease may be concerned about the possibility of a recurrence and the burden it would place on the spouse if they were married. The healthy individual may feel he or she does not have the personal strength to cope with the uncertainty of the disease process and the probability of widowhood at an early age. In these situations, couples can benefit from timely therapeutic intervention. Marriage therapists can work with the two individuals, both together and separately, to help clarify each person's feelings and facilitate understanding of the partner's fears and concerns. The outcome of therapy will vary for each couple; some will recommit to the relationship and resume their plans for marriage, while others will decide that marriage is not the best option for them. Whatever the outcome, the integrity of the relationship can often be preserved and any negative consequences for the two individuals can be avoided. Guilt, martyrdom, and fear of hurting the other person are inappropriate motivations for marriage. Individuals with life-threatening illnesses, if they do marry, deserve a relationship based on love and trust rather than sympathy.

If the dying individual is already married, he or she may want to discuss the spouse's future. The survivor's happiness and satisfaction in a future marital relationship may be very important to the dying person. The dying partner may feel a strong desire to discuss remarriage and be supportive of the spouse. Common reactions of the spouse often include statements such as "That's in the future—we have a long time together yet" or "That's silly, you know I could never be married to anyone but you." For some individuals, the mention of their remarriage suggests betrayal, and assistance may be needed to redefine what future relationships will mean after the death of their spouse. A vow never to remarry can cause emotional problems years later when they meet someone with whom they want to share their life. An honest sharing of feelings is appropriate whenever the subject is mentioned. The future is important to the dying young adult, and it should not be a taboo subject in which communication is closed by "pat" responses. Although the discussion may be painful because it involves acknowledging the reality of one individual's eventual death, each person can benefit from this type of sharing with his or her marital partner. Both will have unique concerns about the future, and partners should listen to each other rather than assuming that they know the other's agenda of issues.

Children.   Some married couples want to have a child together even after receiving a terminal diagnosis for one of the partners. Gideon and Taylor (1981) have asserted that dying persons have the right to bear or father children within the confines of full understanding between the two parents.

Sometimes couples will view children as an important and lasting manifestation of their love for each other. While knowing that their time is limited, they may wish to have children as a way of having a part of themselves survive death. Other motivations for having children at this time can include demonstrating one's masculinity or femininity, wanting the opportunity to experience the parental role, enhancing one's feelings of competence or achievement, exerting some control over one's life, providing an avenue for the expression of nurturance, and tapping into the universal life–death cycle through the creation of another human being.

A woman's decision regarding whether or not to have a baby usually involves medical considerations. Being pregnant can preclude many types of medical treatments for women with life-threatening diseases because of the potential danger to the fetus. Also, the hormonal and other bodily changes that occur during pregnancy can exacerbate the illness and associated symptoms.

Sterility is a possible side effect of some medical treatments. Wasserman, Thompson, Wilimas, and Fairclough (1987) have suggested that male patients be encouraged to bank their sperm prior to receiving cancer treatment because reproductive capacity can be negatively affected by both chemotherapy and radiation treatments, although this is not inevitable. New developments in the field of infertility (such as artificial insemination and *in vitro* fertilization) create an increasing number of options for men and women who survive cancer and want to be parents. If the treated partner is not sterile, a couple may wonder about the effects of the cancer therapy on the children they might have. Such concerns are not easily answered because the long-term effects of cancer therapy are not fully known.

Decisions regarding childbearing should be made only after an in-depth exploration of the implications. Discussion of issues regarding single parenting, the probability of a future marriage with another partner, and medical issues for both the unborn child and the terminally ill adult are necessary for responsible decision making. Concerns regarding children also involve financial matters. Dying individuals with young children will want to know that their children's needs will be met. Many young adults have limited savings and assets and have devoted little time to planning for financial security. Having a clear picture of how their family will be supported and cared for following their death can be reassuring and can help give them more peace of mind. After receiving full and complete information and weighing their options, some couples decide to go ahead and have children despite their limited time together as a family.

Career. Work and education are other issues that are paramount in the lives of young adults. Our occupations and vocations help define a significant aspect of our "self" and contribute to our feelings of competence. According to Stevens-Long (1988), "an occupation provides an important social and personal anchor, a stronghold of identity. It is impossible to really understand adult life without a thorough understanding of the role of work during the life cycle" (p. 152).

Young adults with a life-threatening illness may choose to continue in their work or student roles for as long as possible. For some individuals, finishing a university degree or a work project will be very important. In a school environment, college and university advisors can be helpful in clarifying what goals are realistic, given the person's diagnosis. They can also serve as advocates and help the student avoid some obstacles by providing accurate information and effectively communicating with other offices on campus when appropriate. In a work environment, employers can be supportive of work-related goals by maintaining a "place" at the work setting for the individual (office or desk) and providing extra assistance (clerical help, modified equipment, and so forth) as it is needed. Work policies that allow part-time employment, flexible hours, and "at-home" work can be critical for terminally ill employees who wish to be productive as long as they are physically able. Even though friends and family members may feel the individual should "slow down and enjoy the last remaining months," the wishes of the dying individual should be respected. When dying individuals are no longer able to work, they may find it reassuring to review their work accomplishments and the contributions they have made in this sphere of their lives.

Young adults who survive a life-threatening illness may also have work-related concerns. In a study of long-term survivors of Hodgkin's disease, Wasserman and her colleagues (1987) found that this group identified job discrimination as a major problem. In order to avoid potential prejudice, some of the individuals in the study said that they do not mention that they have had cancer on their job applications. They felt this action was justified because they were considered cured of cancer and their previous health problems would not adversely affect their present work performance. Some subjects still had strong feelings about career opportunities that were closed to them because of their experience with cancer. For example, young adults who were excluded from military service felt that this had a negative impact on their lives (for example, by depriving them of the opportunity to use the GI bill to help further their education).

Employers are often concerned about the effect that hiring a former cancer patient will have on their insurance program. The young adults in the Wasserman et al. (1987) study frequently mentioned the problems they had obtaining health and life insurance. While almost two-thirds of the sample had some form of health insurance coverage, it was usually through a group plan associated with their own jobs or through coverage provided through their spouse's or parents' place of employment. Even among the individuals who were covered by a group insurance plan, some still encountered difficulties. One person's group policy excluded all cancer-related problems. Another man was unable to accept a better position because he would have lost his group coverage. Without the group option, however, health insurance for these former cancer patients was either expensive or unobtainable. In addition, less than one-third of the sample had life insurance policies, and some of these policies contained a cancer exclusion clause.

Acquired Immune Deficiency Syndrome (AIDS)

Today, many young adults face the threat of death by a disease called Acquired Immune Deficiency Syndrome (AIDS) which, prior to 1981, was essentially unknown both to the public-at-large and to the medical community. Once the syndrome was better understood, however, cases could be traced back to as early as 1972. Since that time, it has spread across the United States and at least 90 other countries at an alarming rate. AIDS is a disorder in which a severe deficiency develops in a person's immune system. The individual is then extremely vulnerable to disease conditions that a healthy immune system would normally fight effectively. Today, AIDS has reached epidemic proportions and carries with it the psychological impact of a modern-day "black plague" (Batchelor, 1984). In its May 9, 1988, "AIDS Weekly Surveillance Report," the Centers for Disease Control reported that 34,526 people in the United States have died of AIDS since June 1981 (Public Health Service Centers for Disease Control, 1988). Of this number, 566 were children under the age of 13 at the time of their diagnosis. Table 7.1 provides information regarding the cumulative number of AIDS cases diagnosed as well as deaths, by transmission categories.

In the initial stages of the epidemic, the majority of AIDS victims in this country fell into one of four high risk groups: (1) homosexual men, (2) intravenous drug users, (3) hemophiliacs receiving clotting factor infusions, and (4) infants of mothers who either had AIDS or who fall into one of the high risk groups (Siegal & Siegal, 1983). Currently, however, AIDS is found in every segment of our population and appears likely to spread well beyond the groups where it was initially found to be most prevalent. As seen in Table 7.2, individuals of any age may acquire AIDS.

Currently, there are many more questions regarding AIDS than there are answers. Most leading scientific and medical researchers believe that it is caused by a virus (variously called HTLV–III, LAV, and HIV) that is spread by intimate sexual contact or exchange of infected blood. It is not transmitted by casual interaction such as hugging, kissing, crying, coughing, sneezing, and so forth.

In an unprecedented public education effort, the U.S. Surgeon General's Office, in conjunction with the Centers for Disease Control, mailed an eight-page brochure entitled "Understanding AIDS" to more than 100 million homes in the United States during the spring of 1988. The focus of the brochure was how a person contracts AIDS and what precautions to take to avoid the disease. Although millions of dollars are being spent on AIDS research, there is currently no known cure or preventive vaccine available. The diagnosis of AIDS is typically preceded by the following symptoms: severe weight loss, night sweats, swollen lymph glands, and a general malaise. Tests will show antibodies to the AIDS virus in the blood. The pre-AIDS condition is referred to as *AIDS-related complex* (ARC).

Individuals suffering from AIDS have no capacity to fight a wide variety of infections that a healthy immune system could combat effectively; therefore, this group is highly susceptible to illness. A conclusive diagnosis of AIDS is reached by the presence of very serious (and otherwise rare) diseases such as Kaposi's sarcoma (an atypical form of cancer) or Pneumocystis carinii pneumonia. Homosexuals are more likely to present Kaposi's sarcoma as the initial manifestation, while individuals with a history of intravenous drug usage more often experience other opportunistic infections (Enlow, 1984; Lopez & Getzel, 1987).

Table 7.1

Cumulative Number of AIDS Diagnoses and Deaths, by Transmission Categories (June 1981–May 9, 1988)

Transmission Categories	Cumulative Cases and Deaths			
Adults/Adolescents	*Number*	*(% All Cases)*	*Deaths*	*(% All Cases)*
Homosexual/Bisexual Male	38371	(63.3)	21236	(62.5)
Intravenous (IV) Drug Abuser	11256	(18.6)	6311	(18.6)
Homosexual Male and IV Drug Abuser	4489	(7.4)	2663	(7.8)
Hemophilia/Coagulation Disorder	597	(1.0)	353	(1.0)
Heterosexual Cases	2489	(4.1)	1341	(3.9)
Transfusion, Blood/Components	1492	(2.5)	1004	(3.0)
Undetermined	1929	(3.2)	1052	(3.1)
SUBTOTAL	60623	(100.0)	33960	(100.0)
Children				
Hemophilia/Coagulation Disorder	55	(5.7)	33	(5.8)
Parent with/at risk of AIDS	747	(76.8)	432	(76.3)
Transfusion, Blood/Components	133	(13.7)	80	(14.1)
Undetermined	38	(3.9)	21	(3.7)
SUBTOTAL	973	(100.0)	566	(100.0)
TOTAL	61596		34526	

SOURCE: Public Health Service Centers for Disease Control (1988), *AIDS Weekly Surveillance Report,* May. Washington, DC: United States Government Printing Office.

Table 7.2
Cumulative Number of AIDS Diagnoses, by Age at
Diagnosis (June 1981–May 1988)

Age Group	Cumulative Cases	
	Number	*(% All Cases)*
Under 5	819	(1)
5–12	154	(0)
13–19	260	(0)
20–29	12743	(21)
30–39	28556	(46)
40–49	12792	(21)
Over 49	6272	(10)
TOTAL	61596	(100)

SOURCE: Public Health Service Centers for Disease Control (1988), *AIDS Weekly Surveillance Report,* May. Washington, DC: United States Government Printing Office.

Grief of AIDS Victims

Until a cure is found, the diagnosis of AIDS is equivalent to a death sentence. As a result, individuals with AIDS have needs and concerns similar to those discussed in Chapter 1 as common to the dying process. Because their death is certain, they also grieve in anticipation of the impending death.

Due to the nature of the illness, however, there are some rather unique circumstances that complicate the grief process and make coming to terms with death more difficult. Because many people in our society are exhibiting extreme fear of AIDS due to its many unknown factors, its victims are often ostracized to the extent that they are being treated as modern-day lepers. Social supports are withdrawn, and discussions of large-scale quarantine are common. In some settings, AIDS victims have been fired from their jobs. More recently, the courts have ruled in favor of AIDS victims' rights to continue their employment. Michael Collen, an AIDS victim, shared that "AIDS patients suffer in two basic ways: We suffer from a life-threatening illness, and we suffer from the stigma attached from being diagnosed with AIDS" (Siegal & Siegal, 1983, p. 183).

Patrick Haney was diagnosed with AIDS in 1984. Prior to his death in 1988, he summarized a few of the struggles he and others faced as AIDS victims. Of great concern is the fact that the shame and stigma associated

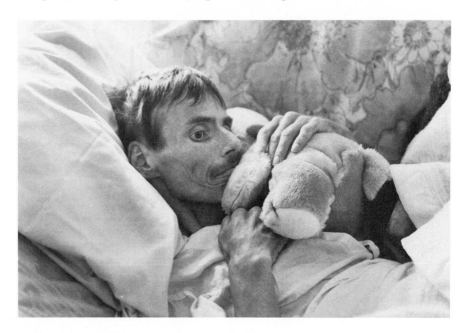

Photo 7.1   *AIDS patients often face rejection, stigmatization, and isolation.*

with the disease cause persons with AIDS to hide their initial symptoms or deny their diagnosis. As a result, they often do not get appropriate medical care and may continue practicing unsafe sexual activities and put others at risk of contracting the virus. Additionally, if persons with AIDS refuse to share with others about their illness, due to the shame and blame involved, they deny others the opportunity to be supportive. This even further isolates the individual with AIDS. Isolation is a major problem. While isolation and alienation result from the withdrawal of social support, medical treatment often involves physical isolation which, in turn, magnifies the sense of social isolation (Price, Omizo, & Hammett, 1986).

The fact that AIDS is most often transmitted as a result of one's own lifestyle choice (such as sexual contact or drug usage) may lead to self-condemnation and severe guilt. (A notable exception, however, is having received a transfusion of blood that was already infected with the AIDS virus.) A normal grief reaction commonly involves such feelings, but they are exacerbated by this particular illness. Other common grief reactions include fear, shock, panic, and denial. The diagnosis of AIDS may heighten those responses unless victims are provided with accurate information and sensitive psychological support (Kennedy, 1987; Wolcott, Fawzy, Landsverk, & McCombs, 1986). Group counseling sessions have become an important therapeutic mode for AIDS victims, since other patients can share their fears and provide factual information, social support, and physical comfort (Morin, Charles, & Malyon, 1984). This type of support can be crucial, as many AIDS patients report a diminished interaction with their former network of friends. A study by Donlou, Wolcott, Gottlieb, and Landsverk (1985) suggested the following factors as likely reasons for the change in interactions: diminished energy of the AIDS victim, avoidance by friends for fear of being stigmatized, and friends' withdrawal due to fear of disease.

Grief of AIDS Survivors

Those who grieve the death of an AIDS victim not only experience the common somatic, behavioral, and intrapsychic symptoms of grief, but they must also face societal stigma, rejection, and a sense of isolation (Altman, 1986; Geis, Fuller, & Rush, 1986). In the early 1980s, AIDS was thought to be primarily a disease of homosexuals (and even called the "gay plague"). This fact caused those who suffered from this syndrome to be shunned by a social structure which condemned that population's life-style.

Families who have never admitted to others outside the family that a son or brother is gay may be particularly unwilling to do so when AIDS is diagnosed. Through their denial, they often sacrifice the support that at least some friends or family members would like to give. Lovers of AIDS victims also may be shunned by families who do not accept their homosexual lifestyle. As a result, a lover may not even be recognized as one who legitimately should be allowed to participate actively in the care of the AIDS victim and later in the funeral (Shearer & McKusick, 1986) or be understood by others to be grieving the death of a significant other (Doka, 1987).

Survivors of homosexual AIDS victims—lovers, family members, and friends—are also frequently ostracized by the larger society and even members of the medical community (Fuller, Geis, & Rush, 1988). Because we do not know the precise mechanisms by which AIDS spreads, many fear that it may be caused by casual contact, even though medical evidence indicates otherwise. Nonetheless, AIDS survivors (regardless of how the victim contracted the illness—blood transfusion, drug usage, sexual activity) are frequently socially isolated for fear that the bereaved survivor may also carry the virus and spread it to others (Carl, 1986).

Added to the stress of rejection, stigmatization, and isolation, survivors must also deal with their own fears about the illness. Whether or not they, in fact, do carry the virus, they must deal with that possibility. "AIDS tests" actually test for the presence of antibodies to the virus, not the AIDS virus itself, and therefore do not yield conclusive results for a period of months immediately after transmission of the virus may have occurred. Further, a positive result on an AIDS test does not necessarily mean the individual will develop the symptoms of AIDS. Mental health professionals have found extreme stress in a group they label the *worried well*—individuals who do not have AIDS at present but fear they will develop it—and the *walking wounded*—individuals who may have an early form of the syndrome (Forstein, 1984). Geis et al. (1986) found in talking to homosexual lovers of AIDS victims that they frequently respond with a sense of fatalism ("If my number is up, it's up") or an obsession ("I think about it all the time, I'm sure I'm going to get it") (pp. 51–52). Even those who do not test positive on the antibody test may report feeling that their own lives are in jeopardy, and may suffer from depression and health-related anxiety (Galea, Lewis, & Baker, 1988).

Given the rapid spread of AIDS through all segments of our population, it is evident that we must search for answers to the medical questions related to this disease. It is also imperative that we deal with the issues that currently prevent victims and survivors alike from getting the human support that we give to others who are dying or grieving.

Ethical Issues Related to AIDS

In addition to unique grief-related issues, AIDS gives rise to a variety of ethical issues. These concerns, in turn, may have an effect on the grief process. E. Nichols (1986), writing for the Institute of Medicine—National Academy of Sciences, identifies what she perceives to be a few of the ethical issues related to the AIDS syndrome:

1. Who should pay for patient care, given skyrocketing medical costs?
2. Should insurance companies be permitted to screen for HTLV–III antibodies (evidence that the individual has been exposed to the AIDS virus) although the individual will *not necessarily develop AIDS?*
3. Who is liable in cases where an individual has had a blood transfusion and been infected?
4. What are the rights of AIDS victims in the school system, workplace, and so forth?
5. Is mandatory screening for AIDS a health necessity or is it an invasion of privacy?

Another important issue is related to the fact that screening tests for the AIDS virus are not 100 percent accurate; some persons are erroneously told they carry the AIDS virus (the test may give false positive results). How ethical is it to give a test that is not 100 percent accurate? If the test is deemed necessary, who is responsible for the negative impact on the individuals receiving false positive results? What is entailed in that responsibility?

These ethical questions underscore the fact that AIDS affects all of us, not simply those who adhere to a particular life-style. In the not too distant future, it is quite likely that each of us will somehow be directly and personally touched by this modern epidemic.

The Grief of Young Parents

Young parents sometimes experience a miscarriage or the death of an infant. The U.S. National Center for Health Statistics reported that in 1985, 1.06 percent of live births ended in death prior to the infants' becoming one year of age, with over half of these deaths occurring within the first 28 days after birth. Additionally, it is estimated that 15 to 20 percent of all pregnancies end in miscarriage (Borg & Lasker, 1981).

There is a growing body of evidence that indicates parents actively grieve after the death of a very young infant, even though the baby lived only a short time. One of the earliest studies was done by Kennell, Slyter, and Klaus (1970), who interviewed 20 women whose children had died between 1 hour and 12 days after birth. Each interview was evaluated for the presence of six signs of mourning: sadness, loss of appetite, inability to sleep, increased irritability, preoccupation with the lost infant, and inability to return to normal activities (p. 345). All of the women reported a sense of sadness and preoccupation with thoughts of the baby. The majority also reported irritability, insomnia, and loss of appetite.

A mourning score was given to each woman on the basis of the number of signs present and the duration of the symptoms. In comparing the nine mothers in the "high mourning" group compared to the "low mourning" group, the researchers found high mourning was significantly associated with previous loss of a baby and positive feelings about the pregnancy. The researchers did not find a relationship between the mourning score and the length of the baby's life. Lack of relationship between the grief score and the baby's life was confirmed by Peppers and Knapp (1980), who studied 65 women who experienced the death of a child between the twenty-eighth week of pregnancy and the fourth week of life. In addition to the six signs of mourning used by Kennell et al., Peppers and Knapp (1980) also noted feelings of anger, guilt, time confusion, and depression. These two researchers theorize that the grief experienced was due to the mother's becoming very attached to the baby early in the prenatal period.

Wolff, Nielson, and Schiller (1970) interviewed 50 women whose children died at birth or shortly thereafter and followed their progress over a span of 3 years. Forty-eight exhibited what were thought to be normal grief reactions. Klaus and Kennell (1976) draw a close parallel between the *perinatal bereavement syndrome* (grief related to miscarriage, stillbirth, or death of a newborn) and the symptoms of grief described in Lindemann's (1944) classic study, which was discussed in Chapter 2.

Miscarriage

Miscarriage, sometimes referred to as a spontaneous abortion, is the unwillful termination of a pregnancy prior to the point of viability. Miscarriages may be due to a variety of factors, including improper implantation of the fertilized ovum or abnormality of the embryo. In almost all instances, there is nothing whatsoever that can be done to prevent the miscarriage; it is a biological process over which the woman has no control. She did not cause it; she cannot prevent it.

Because miscarriage involves the loss of an unborn child, many have doubted whether a significant loss has truly occurred (Reinharz, 1988) and therefore, have not understood that grief is a likely consequence. As a result, couples who have experienced a miscarriage often get little or no support (Leff, 1987; Lietar, 1986). Recent research, however, has provided evidence that most women grieve after a miscarriage. Although there is anecdotal evidence and strong reason to believe that men also grieve in these situations, empirical evidence that shows their response to this type of loss is lacking. We hope this void in the research will soon be filled. Lietar (1986) notes that "the amount of grief over a miscarriage will not be determined by the time between conception and aborting, but by the meaning that the pregnancy held for the couple and a number of other factors such as the desire for parenthood, religious training, cultural mores, and the positive value placed on the pregnancy by the couple's social and environmental milieu" (p. 124).

Miscarriage involves two different losses: the loss of a baby who will never be born and also the loss of a dream for what the child would have become. In an interview reported by Borg and Lasker (1981), a woman who had experienced a miscarriage stated: "By the end of three months of my pregnancy the baby was already going through college in my mind.

During that period I had such an active fantasy life; I fell in love with that baby. When I saw the fetus the fantasy became a person and it was more than the death of a fantasy; it was a real baby I lost" (p. 34). It has only been within the past few years that we have recognized the intensity of feeling after a miscarriage. One example of a recent medical response to this insight is that many hospitals now make arrangements for women who have had a miscarriage (or experience a stillbirth) to have the opportunity to move off of the maternity ward. However, this choice as to whether the woman moves from the obstetrical unit to another location should be given to the parents. J. A. Nichols (1986) reports that approximately 50 percent of the women she studied preferred being moved so that they did not have to watch other parents interact with their new babies. Many other mothers, however, perceived that moving them to another area negated their loss by implying they had simply been hospitalized for a medical procedure.

A strong sense of guilt is often evidenced in parents after a miscarriage. Many erroneously feel that they somehow contributed to the termination of the pregnancy through such factors as too much or too little exercise, improper nutrition, continuation or discontinuation of work, or other reasons. Seibel and Graves (1980) reported that one-quarter of the women in their study felt that they had done something to cause the miscarriage. Parents should be given accurate information regarding pregnancy and miscarriage, emphasizing the unlikelihood that they were responsible (Shaw, 1983). Together with the sense of guilt, many couples are burdened by the thought that they have failed at what they regard as one of life's normal processes—procreation. They may then assume that their femininity or masculinity is in question (Gilson, 1976).

Stillbirth and Death of a Newborn

If fetal death occurs after the twenty-eighth week of prenatal development, the term *stillbirth* is used rather than the term *miscarriage. Newborn death* is one that takes place within a few hours or days after birth. Collectively, these are termed *perinatal deaths.* Society often tends to negate all of these losses as being unimportant. After all, the parent did not really know the child—or so others assume. As a result, many discount the parents' grief (Hutchins, 1986). Another reason why family and friends may discount the grief of the parents is the fact that *they* themselves have not had an opportunity to interact with the baby and therefore do not share the parents' anguish (Palmer & Noble, 1986).

Another factor that complicates grief following a perinatal death is its

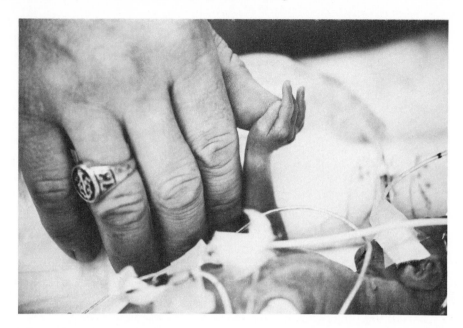

Photo 7.2   *Parents bond very early with their infants and, as a result, often grieve intensely after the death of a newborn.*

lack of focus. The families have experienced a significant loss, yet they have few shared memories that may ultimately sustain families experiencing the death of an older child. Medical personnel and mental health practitioners are now recommending that parents be given an opportunity to share what they can with the child in order to facilitate their ensuing grief. Hutchins (1986) explained that families need to say "hello" before they can say "good-bye."

Strategies for helping the brief existence of the baby seem more real include the following:

1. Name the child so that he or she is regarded as a person.
2. After giving information as to what the baby will look like and feel like, allow parents to hold their child. Time alone with the baby should be provided, if it is desired.
3. Provide a concrete memento of the child's existence—a picture, a lock of hair, a footprint.
4. Share details about the baby—length, weight, hair color.
5. Provide information from the autopsy.
6. Encourage participation in rituals (funeral or memorial service) which validate that a loss has occurred.

Although each of these strategies have been found to be helpful to many families, parents should be given the choice as to what they prefer. Forced participation may cause psychological harm (Kellner, Best, Chesborough, Donnelly, & Green, 1981).

Leff (1987), who is herself a practicing physician, notes that professional caregivers can be of help to parents experiencing a pregnancy loss in the following ways: (1) not abandoning the failed mother-to-be; (2) providing areas within hospitals where women may deliver fetuses; (3) acknowledging the mourning process, with its individual variations; (4) treating the dead fetus with respect; and (5) encouraging the study of the unique needs of the failed father-to-be, the burdens placed on the marital relationship, and the most effective treatment approaches toward alleviating unwarranted and, at times, paralyzing guilt (p. 113).

One factor that contributes to the uniqueness of a perinatal death is that it is in such contrast to the joy surrounding an expected birth. The anticipation of one of life's most profoundly happy events is shattered with little or no warning. Individuals who were involved in the positive anticipation withdraw due to misunderstanding or discomfort. Persons who have not yet heard of the death write or call to ask for news—expecting that it is good—only to find the baby has died.

Sudden Infant Death Syndrome

Estimates vary, but approximately 10,000 infants die each year from Sudden Infant Death Syndrome (SIDS) in the United States alone. It is the primary cause of death of infants between the ages of 1 week and 1 year. Infants, who seemingly are in good health, die suddenly and unexpectedly with little or no struggle. Typically, the infant has been put down to sleep; when the caregiver later checks on the baby, he or she has died.

Recent efforts to find the cause of SIDS have resulted in numerous theories; however, no clear-cut answer has been discovered. In 1975, Beckwith catalogued 73 different theories related to the etiology of SIDS. Since that time, many more have been explored but no totally conclusive answers found. Some of the more recent ones include focus on the following variables as either causes or correlates: cardiac imbalance, infection, electrolyte imbalance, allergies, DPT immunizations, abnormal maternal placenta, and morphologic abnormalities (Swoiskin, 1986).

Markusen, Owen, Fulton, and Bendiksen (1978) argue that grief due to SIDS is extremely difficult to resolve. DeFrain and Ernst (1978) collected questionnaire data from 32 parents whose infants died from SIDS. All of these parents rated SIDS as the most severe crisis they had ever experienced and reported that it took approximately 16 months to regain the level of personal happiness experienced prior to their infant's death. They noted that it took a somewhat shorter time to return to a fairly smooth level of family functioning. Many factors contribute to the intensity of the parents' bereavement. Because the death is sudden and unexpected, the parents are unable to psychologically prepare for the loss (Lowman, 1979; May & Breme, 1982). Because the cause of the death is unknown, many parents assume they were responsible and experience intense feelings of guilt. For example, parents often question whether their baby choked to death or suffocated and whether they could have somehow prevented the death (Pomeroy, 1969; Smialek, 1978). An autopsy often alleviates some of the guilt experienced by parents or blame placed on other caretakers. Although the autopsy does not identify the specific cause of death, it does prove the baby did *not* choke or suffocate (Aadalen, 1980; Bergman, Pomeroy, & Beckwith, 1969). Sharing the autopsy report can serve as a valuable counseling tool (Kotch & Cohen, 1985).

Parents need support as they mourn the death of their infants. Unfortunately, in some circumstances, persons wrongly blame the parents for the death or even accuse them of child abuse (Chng, 1982). Others negate the loss with the recommendation that the couple try to have another baby as soon as possible (Bergman, 1974).

Fortunately, the National SIDS Foundation (NSIDSF) is involved in attempts to provide support to families dealing with the tragedy of their infants' death. The primary goals of the foundation include the following (Williamson, 1986):

1. Providing services to families and other caregivers
2. Educating professionals and community members to better understand the sensitive issues related to SIDS
3. Promoting major research efforts related to causation and, ultimately, prevention

Abortion

In contrast to a miscarriage (that is, a spontaneous abortion), *abortion* is the deliberate termination of a pregnancy. The U.S. Center for Health Statistics reported that there were over 1.5 million abortions in the United States during 1985.

In their extensive review of the literature, Doane and Quigley (1981) estimated that 5 percent of women experience adverse psychological and emotional effects after an abortion. Fogel (1981) estimates that number to be somewhat higher—10 percent. Women who do experience grief explain that it is characterized by sorrow, anger, guilt, or yearning for the lost child (Joy, 1985).

A number of factors may exacerbate the feelings of grief following an abortion (Harris, 1986; Peppers, 1987; Worden, 1982):

1. The belief that abortion is morally wrong and regret that the decision was made may trigger a grief response.

2. Prior emotional disturbance may cause the woman to be more vulnerable to stress.

3. Ambivalence about having the abortion often triggers questions later on about the appropriateness of the decision.

4. Pressure to have an abortion against one's own wishes may elicit feelings of exploitation, anger, and grief.

5. Later timing of the abortion (such as second trimester) contributes to the likelihood of stronger bonding to the baby. The pain experienced by the woman during this time frame is also typically more intense.

6. Abortions performed for medical reasons due to fetal malformation increase feelings of guilt. The parents feel responsible for having created an "imperfect" child and also may feel guilt for choosing to terminate the pregnancy rather than care for the child.

7. Lack of support from family and friends may exacerbate negative emotions. Although it is legal in this country, abortion is often regarded as taboo. Additionally, women may be ashamed or embarrassed and not tell others about the abortion.

8. Women may perceive that they are being punished by those who disagree with their decision.

Death and War

In order to pursue victory, countries call upon their strongest in times of war. It is not surprising, therefore, that military troops are largely composed of young adults. In fact, many nations routinely prepare their young men, and sometimes their young women, to participate in the defense of their homelands. Young adults, however, are likely to have had limited experience with death and loss prior to their military service.

War always involves death and killing. Participation in combat requires taking the lives of other human beings and fighting for your own survival.

In war, conventional rules and moral sanctions regarding killing do not apply. Taking someone else's life is often not only necessary but also considered heroic. The same action under other circumstances would be considered murder.

Hendin and Haas (1984) charge that society has been slow to recognize the personal price that combat soldiers pay in service to their country. According to these authors: "Only since World War II have we begun to realize that killing, sustained exposure to the possibility of sudden death, and witnessing the violent deaths of friends have lasting traumatic consequences for a high percentage of combat soldiers" (p. 6). They also point out the tendency of American civilians to view postwar difficulties as weaknesses because of their idealized hero image of soldiers.

Personal Consequences of Combat

The most recent war in America's history was the Vietnam conflict. This war began as a civil war in the late 1950s and did not officially end until 1975. In 1965, the first U.S. troops were sent to participate in the Vietnam war and the last U.S. ground forces did not depart until 1973. The heaviest U.S. military involvement was between 1965 and 1969. Many of the readers of this text have siblings, friends, or parents who were directly involved in this war. Some of them may have been killed or wounded. In fact, during the duration of this war, almost 60,000 American soldiers were killed and over 330,000 were wounded (Parson, 1986).

Recently, much has been written about the adjustment of veterans of the Vietnam war. It is estimated that as many as 50 percent of the 800,000 combat veterans who were involved in the Vietnam conflict still suffer from unresolved war experiences (Shehan, 1987). More than two decades after the peak years of the Vietnam war, those who participated in it reported significantly more emotional and interpersonal problems than their peers who did not (Card, 1987; Hogancamp & Figley, 1983). Without question, any war can have a powerful impact; however, the Vietnam war had some unique aspects that have complicated the adjustment process of veterans.

This war was different from other American wars in several respects. First of all, the soldiers who fought in Vietnam were the youngest in our history. The average age of soldiers was 19.2 years as compared to 26 years for those in World War II (Brende & Parson, 1985).

Second, soldiers typically entered Vietnam alone or with strangers, in contrast to previous American wars in which soldiers went to their assignments in groups that had trained together. Soldiers often left the Vietnam war alone as well or were transferred as individuals. In previous wars, group members would often remain together for the duration of their mission.

Third, the possibility of death was more of a constant and pervasive threat. Because it was a guerilla war, ambushes were common and combat techniques such as booby-trapping were frequently employed. Also, because it was a civil war, the enemy was often indistinguishable from the ally (Shehan, 1987).

Fourth, combat in Vietnam involved the killing of women, children, and the elderly to a degree unparalleled in earlier wars. In many situations, the soldiers were attempting to save their own lives (for example, a soldier shooting a Vietcong woman who was attempting to throw a grenade at him or his squadron); at other times, civilians were killed inadvertently or in retaliation for deaths caused by their countrymen. Hendin and Haas (1984) believe that the deaths of these nonmilitary individuals have played a significant role in the stress disorders of Vietnam veterans. They committed acts that, under normal situations, would be inconceivable to them. When they returned home to a "normal life," they continued to be plagued by these (and other) images of the war.

Fifth, the Vietnam war was unpopular in the United States. Soldiers on the front line did not feel that they had the united support of the civilians they were representing. Toward the end of the conflict in Vietnam, antiwar protests were common in the United States. Many of the soldiers themselves questioned why they were there. While many had joined the armed forces, others had been drafted (often unwillingly) into military service. The political divisiveness over the war and the lack of support for returning soldiers have contributed to widespread problems among Vietnam veterans (Keane & Fairbanks, 1983). Their homecoming experiences often were characterized by ambivalent and sometimes hostile responses from civilians as compared to heroes' welcomes and parades for veterans of earlier military actions.

Finally, the Vietnam war differed from previous American wars in that the final objective was not achieved: The United States failed to keep Communism out of South Vietnam. Although the American troops were not defeated militarily, soldiers did not feel the glory of "winning" a war. In fact, many felt that they had made great sacrifices for nothing.

The young adults who returned from Vietnam had experienced a variety of significant losses. All had lost their innocence and youth. While many had been boys when they left the United States, they were men when they returned. Most had lost peers on the battlefield and with them important friendships and attachments that grew out of surviving together in a combat zone. Still others were injured and lost body parts and/or functions, a permanent and visible reminder of their time in Vietnam (Parson, 1986). For many, a vision and a set of ideals had also been lost. The world now seemed less predictable, less safe, and less sane.

Post-traumatic Stress Disorder. For many Vietnam veterans, the emotional scars are still healing. The aftereffects exhibited by a significant number of veterans constitute a syndrome identified as *post-traumatic stress disorder* (PTSD). PTSD is defined as a delayed but persistent condition characterized by nightmares, loss of control over behavior, emotional numbing, withdrawal, and hyperalertness with anxiety and depression (American Psychiatric Association, 1987). This disorder results from a *traumatic stress*, defined as a situation or event which is generally outside the range of normal human experience, and which, as such, would evoke significant symptoms of distress in almost anyone. In addition to war, other traumatic stress situations may also produce symptoms of PTSD. These include other deliberate human-caused disasters (for example, bombings, death camps), natural disasters (floods, earthquakes), accidental disasters (plane crashes and auto accidents), and violent personal assaults (rapes). Pearce and her colleagues (1985) found that the first category—deliberate disasters, such as war—produced the most severe PTSD symptoms.

When PTSD symptoms have been analyzed for Vietnam veterans, four major components have been evident: (1) depression, (2) residual guilt or grief, (3) reexperiencing the trauma, and (4) detachment and anger (Silver & Iacono, 1984). Also, the specific patterns of symptoms are somewhat unique for war veterans. Table 7.3 summarizes the symptoms associated with each of these categories. An examination of these symptoms shows that the adjustment problems of Vietnam veterans have affected every sphere of their lives. Of special interest are the grief-related components of PTSD. Veterans often feel guilt, shame, and remorse about what they did in Vietnam. They also grieve over the losses that they themselves experienced as a result of the war. In addition, they frequently report feeling *survivor guilt*, which is guilt over having survived when many others have died. Large numbers of veterans felt guilty leaving Vietnam, concluding that they were abandoning their friends who stayed behind. They later felt additional guilt that they had "made it" when they learned that one of their friends had not. In extreme situations, survivor guilt can induce feelings of needing to "pay one's dues" for surviving. This attitude can be manifest in ways that can have very destructive and negative consequences (such as starting fights, engaging in behaviors that elicit rejection from family members and friends, or getting involved in a high frequency of

Table 7.3
Symptoms of Post-traumatic Stress Disorder

Symptoms

Factor I Depression
  Trouble concentrating
  Low interest in job or other activities
  Feeling worthless or unsure about self
  Difficulty keeping a job
  Depression
  Suicidal feelings or attempts
  Problems with memory

Factor II Residual Guilt or Grief
  Guilt about what I did in Vietnam
  Guilt for surviving Vietnam
  Grief or sorrow

Factor III Reexperiencing the Trauma
  Nightmares
  Violent dreams or fantasies
  Flashbacks to Vietnam
  Reacting when surprised by using military training

Factor IV Detachment and Anger
  Feeling angry or irritable
  Losing temper easily
  Difficulty in relations with others
  Mistrust of others or government
  Jumpiness or hyperalertness
  Feeling emotionally distant from family and others
  Anxiety
  Difficulty feeling emotions
  Painful moods and emotions
  Feeling separated from others, from country or society
  Fear of loss of control
  Depression
  Having arguments with others

SOURCE: From S. M. Silver & C. U. Iacono (1984), Factor-analytic support for DSM-III's post-traumatic stress disorder, *Journal of Clinical Psychology,* Vol. 40, No. 1, p. 8. Reprinted by permission.

accidents). These individuals feel that they do not deserve to be alive and enjoying life.

Which individuals are more likely to develop PTSD? Do predisposing factors place certain individuals at greater risk? Foy and Card (1987) found that combat exposure was related to PTSD symptomatology although premilitary adjustment was not. An earlier study also found that childhood and preservice experiences did not play a major role in the development of post-traumatic stress disorders (Solkoff, Gray, & Keill, 1986). These investigators did find that veterans diagnosed with PTSD, as compared to veterans who were not, more frequently sustained injuries in the war and had more death-related experiences. They were involved more personally in killing, and they were in combat for a longer period of time. More of their friends were killed, and they reported feeling more guilt over surviving. The group of veterans who had symptoms of PTSD also tended to have fewer contacts with other veterans after they were discharged.

Healing the Emotional Wounds

Until recently, there have been few therapeutic programs designed specifically for Vietnam combat veterans. Figley and Salison (1980) have emphasized the value for veterans of contact with their peers of the Vietnam era: "Those who share the injuries are major sources of reassurance, strength, encouragement, guidance, and counsel" (p. 139). This type of contact can occur on an informal basis or through support programs operated primarily by Vietnam veterans, such as the Veterans Administration's Operation Outreach.

Most veterans with symptoms of PTSD can also benefit from individual therapy. According to Tick (1985), combat veterans often need therapeutic grief intervention because they are in a state of *psychic numbness*. Lifton (1970) has described this condition as occurring when one is "intellectually aware of death and suffering but emotionally desensitized to them" (p. 222). This state helps keep strong emotional feelings at a distance. In combat situations, psychic numbing may be necessary for survival and effective functioning. Outside of a combat situation and over an extended period of time, it can lead to alienation from one's own feelings. One veteran described his emotional numbness this way: "I couldn't feel anything. I didn't want to feel anything. Feeling is too painful. I think I killed myself inside to help me forget" (Parson, 1986, p. 15). For Vietnam veterans who experience psychic numbness for a prolonged period, the grieving process is often incomplete, distorted, chronic, or frozen. Unless intervention occurs, the person will likely experience depression and despair (Tick, 1985).

This alienation from feelings can create a powerful obstacle in interpersonal relationships as well. Wives and girlfriends often feel that they, too, are victims of the war. In support groups, veterans' wives often describe their husbands as emotionally distant and unable to express and share their feelings. They also report that their spouses have a "leave-me-alone" attitude and appear aloof. In addition, some men returned from Vietnam with drug and alcohol problems and others became verbally or physically abusive, thus adding to stress on the spouse (Shehan, 1987). Some of these problems were exacerbated by the new policy begun in the Vietnam war of flying combatants home quickly after their tour of duty was finished. Soldiers were often back home with their families within 36 hours from the time they were processed out of Vietnam. As one veteran said: "One day I was out in the bush, killing . . . , seeing buddies get killed, covered in mud, trying to sleep at night with the threat of ambush by the VC and two days later I was trying to talk to my family at the dinner table. I couldn't tell them what I had been through. They couldn't have understood it" (Brende & Parson, 1985, p. 73). This type of situation was especially difficult because many of these men had fantasized about coming home, and they were not prepared for the adjustments that they and their families would face upon their return.

Most intervention strategies designed for use with veterans' war-related problems have focused almost exclusively on the individual veteran and have, unfortunately, given little attention to relationships with family members (Hogancamp & Figley, 1983). Shehan (1987), however, has addressed the importance of intervention with spouses and has offered several suggestions for assisting wives of men returning from combat. According to Shehan, support groups for spouses can provide an atmosphere in which wives can openly express their concerns. Many blame themselves for their husband's emotional distance and feel tremendous guilt as a result. These groups can also educate wives about symptoms of PTSD and reinforce the idea that their husband's behavior is related to this disorder. Mutual support and empathy can also be experienced as these women share their common concerns.

Family therapy approaches can also be used to improve communication among family members. Increased communication can aid the husband in successfully working through the trauma of the war and also increase the wife's satisfaction with the marital relationship. Although spouse support has been shown to be a significant factor in the adjustment of returning veterans (Solkoff et al., 1986), many spouses are unsure of how to be supportive. For example, some are uncertain about whether to ask questions about Vietnam and confused about when they should accept their husband's silence. Many veterans may be hesitant to discuss their combat experiences for fear of rejection, and they will react strongly to responses that are interpreted as judgmental or condemning. Shehan (1987) suggests that wives be trained to provide empathic responses. She also considers it important for veterans' wives to be desensitized to the disturbing details of the Vietnam combat experience, so that the shock and trauma will be minimized when their husbands share their own experiences. Reading personal accounts of the war written by other veterans may be helpful in this regard.

To aid in their healing, Vietnam veterans need the recognition from American civilians that they failed to receive when the war was over. Recent films such as *Platoon* and *Heavy Metal Jacket* have facilitated a better understanding of what Vietnam veterans actually experienced on a day-to-day basis during their term of duty and the issues that they continue to confront today. These films have also stimulated discussion between veterans and nonveterans. Resolution of grief among Vietnam war veterans continues to be facilitated by the Vietnam Memorial—our country's tribute to those who died in Vietnam. This monument was dedicated in November

Photo 7.3 a & b   *Those who returned from the Vietnam War experienced a variety of losses, but only in the past several years have those losses been acknowledged.*

1982, nearly a decade after the longest and costliest war ever fought by the United States was over. The following passage written by a Vietnam veteran, Jim O'Meara, illustrates the poignancy of this symbolic structure for those who survive:

> There isn't anything else like it. It's a black, polished granite cliff, formed into a shallow "V," that has the names of the missing and dead from the Vietnam War inscribed on it in white letters. 57,939 of them. It's technically a "Memorial," but that doesn't begin to cover what it means. "Monument" isn't right either. Most of the Veterans who went there for the dedication called it, simply, "The Wall."
>
> At first, I was skeptical. For me, Vietnam was thirteen years ago, buried somewhere back in my mind. I hadn't heard much about the memorial, and I was leery of bringing up old feelings, of waking up at night, sweating, with the smell of dry, red central highlands dust mixed with hot canvas in my nostrils and the heat of helicopter blades in my ears, or dealing with the deep, bitter emotions, the feeling of betrayal at the reception I'd received when I got back. Like most of the other Vietnam veterans, I never spoke about it.
>
> I heard the rumor that the State of Wyoming was paying for air fare to fly some guys to Washington, D. C. for the dedication. No, I told myself, don't get involved. But it wouldn't go away. I told my wife about it.
>
> "You're going, of course," she said.
>
> "Can we afford it?" I asked.
>
> "Does that make any difference? You were there, you should go."
>
> On Friday, I went to see the Wall. I went alone, when not so many people would be there. I thought it might be a heavy time for me. From the subway station, it's about a mile down a grassy mall, past the Washington Monument and along a pond, to where the memorial was supposed to be. I'd heard about it, but I wasn't sure what it would actually look like. As I got closer, I saw some guys sitting around in small groups or walking alone, wearing old fatigue uniforms or parts of them. I didn't know what to expect. Lots of anxiety.
>
> I walked over a small rise, and saw it. It looked small and black. I felt a little disappointment, it wasn't tall and grand. It was even below ground level. I was looking into the shallow V. From where I was, you couldn't tell its size. I started walking toward the apex.
>
> As I walked closer, down the long slope toward the bottom of the apex, the polished black granite arms tapered off on either side. I was about ten feet from the Wall when the impact of the thing hit me. From ten feet higher than my head, stretching out of sight on either side, were the names of 57,939 people. The dead and the missing from Vietnam. I was slammed with the enormity of it all, the weight of those people who were not here, who had died because they had been asked, or sent, to do a job their nation wanted done. Emotions washed across me, and my eyes filled with tears. I moved away and sat alone on the grass.
>
> Time passed, an hour or so I guess, and I picked up a brochure that said how to find the year and the month you were looking for. I went back to the Wall and found the names I had come to see. I said to myself the things I had to say. I read a little further and found some names I hadn't expected to find. I thought they'd made it home. I sat on the grass, then, for a very long time.

Later, I watched a couple, obviously tourists, start at one end and walk toward the apex, chatting and looking around. About three-quarters of the way down, I saw it hit them, too. They suddenly knew what it was and what it meant. In the last analysis, this is what Vietnam was all about, 57,939 people listed on the Wall and millions of veterans who, in their minds somewhere, sat on the grass abandoned and alone, betrayed by the nation they'd fought for.

If the Wall could do that, I thought, it's doing all that could be asked of it.

Writing during Bereavement

Writing during bereavement can be therapeutic for many individuals. According to Lattanzi and Hale (1984):

> Writing can be a helpful and healing experience for grieving persons. It has not been fully explored or understood as a coping response in relation to the grief process. Just as people are changed by the experience of grief, the experience of expressing their grief can also change them. Shakespeare wisely advised us to "give grief words." It is generally acknowledged that the expression of grief can soften the impact and contribute to the management of the experience. (p. 45)

These authors point out that throughout time, people have described some of their deepest thoughts and feelings through their writings. An examination of some of the best-known literature throughout the centuries will reveal an abundance of books, plays, and poetry that convey themes of grief and loss. While Lattanzi and Hale (1984) emphasize that writing as a coping technique will not be therapeutic for all persons or in all situations, they feel that in many instances it can facilitate positive outcomes. "By tapping one's creative energy, writing can be not only a way for the bereaved to address their despair, but also a means of instilling hope through exploring the meaning of the experience" (p. 52).

Individuals may choose to put their grief into words for varying reasons. Writing, especially for professional writers and journalists who have experienced a profound loss, may be a natural way to express their pain. It can also be a way to immortalize the deceased or the writer's relationship with the deceased. Grieving individuals may also feel a sense of responsibility to share their experience with a larger audience in an attempt to educate or enlighten others.

Many personal accounts of bereavement have been published in books and magazines. The authors of these works often express the hope that others will find comfort or in some way benefit from their literary contribution. Through this process, the death is seen as having some positive consequences. Others do, in fact, seem to derive meaning from these works. Many individuals who are grieving often request written materials to help them better understand the grief process. Reading an account of another person's bereavement can sometimes reassure them that their grief is normal and that they, too, can cope.

In addition to published materials, individuals often find therapeutic expression in more personal forms of writing, such as diaries and journals. At times, writing is a vehicle for stating that which cannot comfortably be said aloud. If writings are shared with significant others, they can often be an avenue for increased communication and emotional support. The process of writing can also provide valuable insights and perspectives. As time passes, a review of earlier writings can help the bereaved recognize the personal changes they have experienced and the healing that has occurred.

Summary

Intimacy versus isolation is the psychosocial crisis of young adulthood. Dying persons of this age span strive to become emotionally close to others—a task that is especially difficult because limited time raises questions as to whether one should marry, have children, and so forth. Investment of time in career or additional education are other important issues as these young adults seek fulfillment of aspirations. Survivors may feel guilty about developing new relationships or may face economic pressures associated with raising children alone.

Although the modern-day AIDS epidemic affects people of all ages, the highest death rate has taken place among young adults. Due to the stigma and fears of this particular disease, special problems exist for both the AIDS victims and their survivors.

Young adulthood marks the beginning of parenting for many individuals. The termination of a pregnancy through miscarriage or the death of a newborn precipitates a grief reaction, even though many in our society do not recognize the intensity of the loss.

In times of war, many young adults and their families face multiple traumas. While all wars involve death and destruction, each particular war has its own special issues that may leave invisible emotional scars. Post-traumatic stress and survivor guilt still haunt the lives of many Vietnam war veterans. These individuals and their families need recognition and support for the losses they incurred while serving their country.

Writing during bereavement can be meaningful for many grievers. Individuals may find therapeutic expression in personal forms of writing, such as journals and diaries. Many persons share their writings with others through published accounts of their experiences with loss.

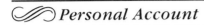 ## Personal Account

"Story of a First-Born" documents the brief life of the author's first-born son Michael. The article gives a day-by-day account in which modern hospital policies and practices control much of what happens in the life of Michael and his parents.

Story of a First-Born*

Wende Kernan Bowie

In the last two decades, popular informative literature and the burgeoning availability of natural childbirth training classes have almost erased the image of fear and pain that most of our mothers associated with childbirth, creating in its place a much more fearless, hopeful outlook on the process of birth and fetal development. The practice of obstetrics, pre-natal and neonatal care has improved, brushing away much of the mystery and uncertainty of the past. The voluminous literature written for expectant parents is overwhelmingly optimistic; there are statistics and more statistics to show the decreasing incidence of birth defects and fetal or neonatal deaths.

But despite the impression an expectant mother gets, mishaps to mother and infant during pregnancy and birth continue to occur. The percentages are decreasing, but the actual number is still quite large. In 1974 in the United States, it is estimated that 660 mothers died as a result of complications of pregnancy, childbirth and the puerperium. It is estimated that each year over 200,000 infants have defects that are evident at birth or during the first few years of life. Almost 20 percent of the newborns or more than 600,000 infants per year require care for some form of illness during the newborn period.[1]

What happens to the mother and infant when there is trouble? What normal emotional changes can she expect to have if her child is either ill at

From *Omega: Journal of Death and Dying*, Vol. 8, No. 1, pp.1–17. Copyright © 1977. Baywood Publishing Co., Inc. Reprinted by permission.

*All the names mentioned in this article are fictitious, except for my own, my husband's and my son's.

[1]Statistics are estimates given by the National Foundation March of Dimes.

birth or needs intensive care for a few days after its birth? How can she best deal with the situation if she must leave her infant in the hospital? What resources are available to her both inside the hospital and at home? What role can her husband take, and what is the status of the pediatrician should the infant be hospitalized in an intensive care unit? These and many other questions can and should be answered within the popular literature, not to frighten, but to inform and prepare expectant parents, so that they do not become mere victims, but active, knowledgeable participants in the process of curing and nurturing their seriously or not so seriously ill infant.

Michael

My husband and I shared our culture's optimism toward childbirth as we approached the coming of our first child last spring. My pregnancy had been a happy one. I was healthy, and I worked until two weeks before Michael was born. My husband and I began Lamaze training, and toward the end of March, I went into labor and was admitted to our community's excellent teaching hospital, where our child was to be delivered. The story of how we two—prospective parents totally unprepared for anything to go wrong—dealt with what happened follows.

Monday March 24th

As my husband left my women's hospital room that bright afternoon, I said to him, "Lee, we have a son! We have a son!" I was happy; I was exhausted; and I couldn't possibly sleep; I wanted to call just one more person to tell them our child was finally born! I wanted to tell the world.

That was the last happy moment I was to have for a long time, and as I write this now, I look back on it as Camelot. My newborn baby weighed in at a healthy 7 lbs. 2 oz., and I felt joyful and awed when they placed him in my arms and wheeled us in our triumphant journey out of the delivery room.

That evening an intern came to my room to tell me that there was trouble with my child; he had been born with a high percentage of red blood cells; they had drained some blood from his body and had replaced it with plasma to thin it out so that his heart would not have to work so hard to pump thick blood. The intern informed me that without this exchange transfusion, Michael would have died within hours of a cerebral hemorrhage, but that he thought they had probably transfused him in time. I was also told that Michael was still "downstairs" under observation in a special nursery, but that he would be brought up to the regular nursery on my floor by midnight or so.

I was dismayed. I called Lee who came right over. We talked the whole thing over with the intern again. "Was there any brain damage?" we asked. Luckily, the answer was no. Midnight did not seem very far away, and I needed some sleep before then, so Lee went back to a friend's house, and I lay back, trying unsuccessfully to rest.

But my episiotomy started to hurt. I was exhausted. I felt like a victim, and I didn't really know how my baby was. Midnight came and went and I fabricated reasons why the nurses had not brought Michael to my room. Perhaps they were planning to bring him to me for the 4 a.m. feeding. I tried to protect myself during those early morning hours from realizing that something was seriously wrong.

Tuesday March 25th

I slept only an hour or two all night. I was very worried and upset by this time, almost to the point of panic. I had waited all night for the nurses to bring Michael to my room; no one had told me why he was not with me. A group of doctors came to see me. I could hear them reviewing my case outside my room in low voices. It made me angry. I thought they were concealing facts from me. "Why didn't someone tell me about my baby?", I thought.

Finally, the doctors stood at the foot of my bed. One of them told me that my blood pressure was too high. I said, "Of course my blood pressure is too high, I'm worried about my baby!" Honestly, I was thinking, what happens to me is so very unimportant; of course I have high blood pressure! I've not slept a wink for waiting all night and worrying and hoping. The doctor replied curtly that he certainly knew more about my condition than I did and asked me to bare my knee so that he could check my reflexes. My reflexes were fine. The doctor turned on his heel and without another word to me, left the room, followed by the others. I was once again left alone with my thoughts, which were becoming progressively more ominous. There was not a word about Michael.

If it hadn't been for Lee, I couldn't have dealt adequately with this day. Later, after he arrived, we were told Michael was to be kept "downstairs" "a while longer." They suspected there was something wrong with his heart. The news was getting worse and worse. We were both horribly anxious. No one had any definite answers. Had my head been clear at the time, I would have realized that there was one set of doctors dealing with my physical self and another set of doctors dealing with Michael's physical self. None of them were very aware or sensitive in dealing with the emotional stress on me which was, due to the separation between me and my infant, becoming progressively more serious.

Where in heavens name *was* "downstairs" anyway?

At about this point in our thoughts, a student nurse came into the room with some pills for me. When I asked what they were, she replied that they were valium and phenobarbital and that they would "really knock me out." I didn't want to take them, because I wanted to have a clear head to understand what the doctors had to say about Michael. I wanted to see him! The only way to find out what these pills were for was to call the doctor, so Lee did. It took Lee two insistent requests to get past the nurse at his office. The nurse did not know why I had to take the pills; she simply said that I must take them. Finally the doctor came on the line and the following conversation ensued: "Mr. Bowie, I prescribed those pills for your wife, do you know what will happen if she doesn't take them?" In kind, Lee responded, "No, but I think it would be nice if somebody told us." And finally, the doctor said, "There's a good chance she may have convulsions." Of course that settled it. I took the tranquilizers, but it certainly took a lot of panache on Lee's part to find out why they were necessary. Of course I was not allowed to walk, as I was not trusted to keep my balance under such heavy medication.

So, drugged, and in a wheelchair, I was taken to see my baby for the very first time. I was not prepared for this by anything I had read, heard, or learned during my pregnancy, and I had acquired a considerable amount of knowledge about birth, babies and hospitals through Lamaze training, a baby care course, and much reading of the literature. Most of all, I did not know what I was going to do about nursing my baby if he was to be kept "downstairs." I wanted to nurse him. I had decided long before to breast feed my baby. At this point, though, I was embarrassed to insist and afraid to ask about it.

The observation nursery was part of the newborn intensive care unit at this hospital. It was a room, neon-lit, with one whole wall of observation windows. It contained a lot of equipment—isolettes, bilirubin lights, scales, examining tables, another scrub sink, oxygen outlets, heart and respiration monitors and, last but not least, babies. Visitors had to wear a sterile gown from neck to mid-calf, which tied in the back. We had to scrub with yellow soap from fingertip to elbow and to remove all rings, watches and jewelry every time we entered the nursery. Eventually I stopped wearing my wedding and engagement rings altogether as I had to remove them to a safe place so often, I was afraid I'd lose them.

Most of the newborn babies spent twelve hours at this nursery being observed for irregularities and then were transferred up to the healthy nursery on the maternity floor. Michael had been here for twenty-four hours. He was pointed out to us. He was being given oxygen in a hood, but it was possible to disconnect the hose from the hood, pick him up, and hold him with the tube pointed directly under his nose. So I sat there in my wheelchair holding my baby for the very first time and holding the oxygen tube to his nose; my husband and the nurse watched Michael and me. Later I was given a bottle of formula to feed him. It took some juggling, but Lee held the oxygen tube and I held Michael and fed him. I wondered if I would be able to nurse Michael when my milk came in, and I did not dare ask why Michael was getting oxygen. I felt privileged just to be allowed to hold him. He was adorable.

When we were finished feeding him, there was nothing left to do there, so Lee took me back to my room. It was then that the flood of maternal feelings overcame me. The sense of separation from Michael was unbearable. I felt a strong need to be near him. It was agony, and I was very frightened that this separation would interfere with my future relationship with this baby for whom I was responsible.

Wednesday March 26th

Michael, we discovered, was a puzzle to all his doctors. He breathed too fast, and the eight specialists who were trying to diagnose his problem were stymied. First they thought it was his heart; but the pediatric cardiologist we spoke to told us it probably was not; then they thought it was his kidneys; but after tests, they discovered it was not. Michael was an enigma. I was, I must admit, a bit proud of having given birth to an enigma. To me he was a lovable enigma.

Thursday March 27th

Michael, they said, had early signs of a bacterial infection. He would need, they said, to stay in the hospital for at least ten more days. I was not relieved to hear this. How could I stand being separated from him for that long! It seemed like the last straw—I collapsed into tears. He was *my* baby! I wanted him near me!

When I saw him next he had an intravenous needle in his head! They had shaved his hair in an ugly strip in order to find the veins. They had placed a plastic bag over his penis to collect a 24-hour urine sample for diagnostic studies. He was in an isolette, his legs were tied down and his hands also, so he wouldn't push away his tubes and his oxygen mask. I was afraid, so afraid to touch him.

Friday March 28th

At eight in the morning the intern came into my room and told me without ceremony that he thought it was time I went home—that the hospital was no place for me. "It's up to my private obstetrician to tell me when to go home," I replied. After all, I had been on phenobarbital continuously; they had finally stopped giving it to me Thursday night. My blood pressure was still not down to normal. I did not feel reassured at all about my physical condition. And most of all, I did not want to leave my baby there. But I never had a chance to say this last; I sensed that the intern did not want to hear about it, did not consider it a part of his job to discuss this difficult issue with me. The intern, who looked and acted, incidentally, at least ten years my junior, told me that well, "we" are "watching over you" when your doctor isn't here, and that "we" think it is time you left here.

Check-out time at the hospital was 2 p.m. My obstetrician usually came to see me about that time. I told the intern that I was not going anywhere until I got the okay from my obstetrician. My husband was teaching that day, and he could not drive me home until evening. In most cases patients in a hospital are happy to be told to leave, but my case was very different, because leaving the hospital meant leaving my baby. I wished I had been given some advance warning; I knew that I needed time to prepare myself for the wrenching sadness, fear and disappointment of going home with no baby to put into the cheerful nursery Lee and I had prepared.

Somehow I got through that day. I just had to grit my teeth and get through it. I walked down to the nursery one last time to see Michael and wondered what it would be like to be so far away from him. I wondered what it would be like to be at home, alone, recovering from the birth, with no baby to nurse, with my milk coming in. Lee came and helped me pack. We left in the evening.

Saturday March 29th

I tried to resume my normal life, but I was still very tired. I had not asked them at the hospital whether I could breast-feed. I took it for granted that I would not be allowed to. They did say that I could express milk and freeze it in two ounce quantities, and that they would then feed it to my baby. But they would not begin doing this until I could produce the 8 ounces per day which was Michael's diet. I was desperately worried that I would not be able to produce that amount, and without Lee's constant encouragement and support I would never have been able to do it. I used a hand pump and my breasts were very sore. It was all I could do to express milk every four hours. I was exhausted from the birth too.

I hoped that Michael would improve and would by some miracle stop breathing too fast. Michael's pediatrician told us that sometimes babies have difficulty at first, but with proper treatment, the rapid breathing diminishes. No one finds out why it happened, but the baby develops normally from then on. My constant thought during all of this uncertainty about Michael's future was that if he should come home I should keep my milk flowing so that I would be able to breast-feed him. It, the breast-feeding, was very important to me; I thought that without it I would be unable to develop a good mother–infant relationship.

I was miserable at home. It was my first baby and I had looked forward to the responsibility of caring for him eagerly, though not without the usual trepidations. My fears about my ability to really love and nurture my baby were greatly magnified because we were apart and because the nursery provided for all Michael's needs. They asked no help from me. I feared that this alienation from my baby would continue into our future relationship. There was one thing that I alone could give Michael: my breast milk. And to this end Lee and I worked to stimulate my breasts to produce.

Sunday March 30th

Lee and I went in to see Michael. Dr. Cousins, Michael's pediatrician, was there and several other doctors. Michael was tired. I watched as Dr. Cousins examined him. It was agony to see other people touch Michael. He still seemed a part of myself, but separated, kept in a hospital nursery, where I had "visiting" privileges—I had not even changed his diapers yet, and I had fed him only three or four times. He was almost a week old. I was afraid that if he ever came home he would seem like someone else's child.

I felt very strange with these new feelings—I had never thought before I gave birth that I would experience such intense and disparate emotions. The strength of my love for Michael was almost overwhelming at times, especially when Dr. Cousins examined him that day. I had to leave the room because when Dr. Cousins picked him up and let his head fall back, it came home to me as at no other time that Michael was indeed a very sick baby. I wanted to deny that knowledge as long as I could. I wanted to hold Michael and love him and touch him and care for him and these were all new feelings for me. I was embarrassed to admit them to the nursing staff or the team of doctors because my emotional life was so unfamiliar to me. In this medical context, I wondered what use I could be and where I could fit in.

The medical staff looked at Michael from one perspective—that of diagnosing him. They still didn't know what was wrong. I looked at Michael from another—I was his mother and I wanted desperately to be near him. I hated to see other people touch him.

I finally got the courage to express some of these feelings to Dr. Cousins, and he said that they were the most natural ones in the world. He immediately got the consent of the specialists to allow me to breast-feed Michael in a day or so, as soon as he was off the antibiotics. This was just wonderful! But if I had not had the courage to ask, would anyone have offered to let me breast-feed? If I had not had Dr. Cousins to intercede for me, would I have been deprived of even this?

At this point in the attempts to diagnose Michael's troubles, the doctors thought he had a weak heart. They thought that he either had some viral infection of the muscle or that he had a congenital heart defect. But they didn't know the answers. Dr. Cousins told us that allowing the breast-feeding was extremely unorthodox; in fact, it had probably never been done before. But it was the happiest moment of my life when I was told that I could breast-feed my baby. I wondered if I would have to do it in public the very first time.

Monday March 31st

Finally, seven full days after Michael was born, my milk really came in. Perhaps psychologically it had something to do with my knowledge that I could breast-feed the next day, and I had better be ready so that it would be easy for him! If in fact he had a weak heart, I did not want to exhaust him with the breast-feeding. It takes more energy for a baby to nurse. I could not go to the hospital every three hours and nurse Michael, I was too tired, it was too far to drive, it would adversely affect my milk supply. I therefore had to pump part of the milk and let Michael nurse for only some of the feedings. The milk which was pumped was then frozen and carried into the hospital. The nurses would feed Michael my breast milk by bottle.

We rented a breast pump, electric, from La Leche League for $ .25 a day so that I could express milk. In spite of my determination to provide my baby with milk, I could not have done so without that pump. Nor could I have done so without my husband's constant encouragement.

Tuesday April 1st

My first experience breast-feeding Michael did not go too well, but it makes me laugh to think of it. He was accustomed to the taste of formula which was much sweeter or at least quite different in taste from breast milk. With the help of a nurse from the maternity floor who was asked to come especially for the occasion, I placed my little baby on a pillow before me as I sat on a rocking chair and positioned him at my breast. He closed his tiny mouth on my rather large nipple, then promptly wrinkled his nose, pulled his head away and clamped his rebellious mouth shut tightly. My God, I thought, he is rejecting me, my soul, my breast and my whole being. I was crushed; I was dismayed that this tiny being so soon was ready to push me away. Nothing, no trick we tried could persuade him. Luckily we had a bottle of breast milk nearby for just such an emergency, but it was the same, Michael rejected both the nipple and the bottle. So we decided that he needed a few trials with breast milk to get him used to it.

Wednesday April 2nd

I decided to go in twice a day to breast-feed him. It was a complicated procedure. Each time, he had to be removed from his oxygen-giving iso-lette. Then he had to be weighed, both before and after meals, to determine how much fluid he was getting. It was an unreliable measure, but it made the medical staff happy.

After the first dismal trial Michael caught on fast. For me, it was wonderful. Lee always came with me. (I was feeling strange anyway, nursing my baby for the first few times, and to be on stage in the observation nursery compounded my awkwardness and embarrassment.) But I remembered those moments as the happiest that the three of us were to have together.

And Lee, well, he watched with pleasure, encouraged and provided support—these were warm and loving times.

Thursday April 3rd

After we had breast-fed Michael about four times and things began to settle down to a sort of routine, our pattern was disturbed by the sudden appearance one morning, just as I was about to start feeding Michael, of two pediatric cardiologists, a man and a woman who requested they be allowed to, in their words, "watch Michael's behavior at the breast."

Nursing was the one privacy I had been allowed. Yet how could I refuse them this intrusion? They really had me over a barrel; they had control of my son, after all, and I did not dare say no.

My first thoughts were, will Michael and I perform according to their expectations? Will we pass the test? What will they be looking for? Will they be judging my performance also? Will my milk let down with two perfect strangers watching?

In short, this is what happened: Michael, asleep, and I, wide-awake, adrenalin pumping, settled into the armchair; one cardiologist stood to my left, the other to my right. There I was, my breasts full of milk, bare and ready, but Michael slept on. I tried my best to rouse him; he would half open his eyes, only to close them again and slumber on. He would not wake up. Then the female cardiologist broke in, "Now, when you feed this baby, I want to see no fooling around; he must get right down to the business of eating and waste no time outside of his isolette. He must be breathing room air no longer than necessary." Michael remained asleep. Finally, when it became clear that he just wasn't interested in his breakfast that day, the cardiologist asked, "Have you ever breast-fed a baby before?" I felt defensive and surprised at the question. "No," I responded truthfully, "this is my first baby." She walked out of the room briskly, leaving me, breasts still bare, sitting in an armchair. As she left she threw over her shoulder, "Well, we shall just have to get someone down here who knows what they're doing."

I sat there for a minute, trying unsuccessfully to regain my dignity and composure, but it was difficult, as I was still half naked, and frightened that every second out of the isolette would bring about Michael's demise. I finally just gave Michael to Lee, stood up, buttoned my blouse and stalked, shaking, out of the nursery, to compose myself in the waiting room, which I supposed was my proper place now that my competency as a mother had been called into question.

Looking back on the incident objectively, I suppose that the cardiologist, puzzled by Michael's symptoms herself, felt uncomfortable in not having any ready answers about his condition, and therefore, felt more at ease accusing *me* of incompetence than herself. At the same time I wondered whether perhaps the woman was unused to dealing with the vagaries of mother love and breast-feeding when perhaps she had taken refuge in the sterility and cut-and-dried security of the medical world. Perhaps she was threatened by the whole scene, never having chosen to have the experience herself.

I was furious. I wanted to scream questions after her: Don't mothers and fathers have any rights when their own child is critically ill? Is nothing sacred? Does the medical staff have to examine, observe and dissect everything? Can I feed my baby only if I measure up to your medical standards of competency? Do I have to go to nursing school to be competent enough to understand what is happening to my child?

Friday April 4th

Michael's condition had not improved; it was his second week of life. He still breathed too fast, and his heart sounds were not good. The cardiologists had decided to perform a more invasive test on him to determine whether there were any structural abnormalities in his heart; the procedure was called cardiac catheterization. They explained it to us briefly; the catheterization required written permission from us, and we had been standing by for two days to give it. A resident from the neonate unit had called us at midnight Thursday night to inform us that they were ready and to get our permission by phone. Apparently he didn't know that a telephoned permission was not legally binding unless it was also telegrammed and witnessed by a third party listening in. Anyway, at midnight Thursday night we all thought that everything was set for Michael to be catheterized the next day.

We waited all day for word from the hospital, expecting any minute word that the test had been completed and perhaps the first results. Late in the afternoon Lee was on the telephone when his call was interrupted on an emergency. Of course he thought that something terrible had happened to Michael and he suffered much unnecessary emotional stress on account of it. The cardiologists had Michael in the laboratory, but had refused to proceed without a telegrammed consent from us, thus, the emergency. Compared to what was to come, this was a very minor mix-up. However, consent duly given properly, the test proceeded. Lee and I waited some more by the phone. Luckily we had some friends with us whom we knew very well.

Finally, three hours after we had telegrammed our consent, Dr. Brown, the cardiologist, called and gave us the horrible and shocking story. Something had gone wrong with the procedure—through a technician's error, an anesthetic called Lidacaine had been injected into Michael's heart instead of dye. His heart had stopped for fifteen minutes. The cardiologists had been able to monitor the circulation and therefore knew exactly how much external cardiac massage to deliver. Dr. Brown said that he thought they had prevented any brain damage, but they couldn't guarantee it. My immediate reaction was to think and say—Oh, Michael, you can have no arms, no legs, but if you have no brain, you're lost!

But Michael was still alive; he needed a respirator to help him breath; he was on heavy doses of phenobarbital to control convulsions which are a side-effect of Lidacaine; he was on high oxygen and he was placed in the intensive care unit; but, brain-damaged or not, he lived.

With Dr. Brown's immediate admission of error, Lee and I knew we had found someone we could trust. After that we turned often to Dr. Brown because we respected him for his honesty. He also turned out to be our most reliable source of information regarding the details of Michael's care. Without him we would have known very little about the plans the staff had for Michael.

Saturday April 5th

The first time we saw Michael after the damaging mishap was heartbreaking. Thursday I had been breast-feeding this adorable little baby of ours, and Saturday he looked near death. He was very pale in comparison to his pinkness of two days before; his head was tipped upwards and there was a tube (endotracheal) stuffed down his throat which delivered oxygen to his lungs and expanded them for him. His hands and feet were tied down to prevent his dislodging his endotracheal tube and his intravenous tube; he was in a drugged stupor from the heavy doses of phenobarbital being given to prevent possible convulsions from the Lidacaine. Michael needed heroic support measures to sustain his life until the effects of the Lidacaine wore off.

I looked at him just once and the tears rolled down my face. I turned away. I could not bear the sight. There was nothing I could do for him.

It was at this time that I first realized that Michael might very well die, and I look back on this day as a turning point in my mind. I began to lose hope. I ceased to be able to see Michael as my adorable brand new first baby. I could not see beyond the tubes which sustained him. Michael became figuratively the property of the intensive care nursery. Even Dr. Cousins, our trusted pediatrician, told us that he was now merely a figurehead, and had no real control over what happened to our son. He was no longer even the physician of record, once Michael had been placed in intensive care.

I knew then that Michael, Lee and I were in for a long haul. I was living literally from moment to moment. I knew that I could not continue for long this way, thinking constantly that good news might break, thinking constantly that Michael would be home with us soon. Michael was in intensive care now. I tried to think now in terms of weeks rather than days. I continued daily entries in my journal because I had a strong intuitive feeling that these days were precious. The journal also helped me to keep a record of events as they happened. My story continues, in narrative form, based on those journal entries.

Coping

In order to deal with our feelings of anxiety over our son's condition and our mutual feelings of impotence and frustration at being unable to help our son grow in any way—at being unable to have any control whatsoever over the details of his care—at being superficial adjuncts to the process of treating him, we took different tracks which turned out to be mutually beneficial and mutually adaptive.

Lee, an academic by profession, turned to knowledge. Through his reading, intensive study and constant questioning of the medical staff, he kept us both very well informed of every detail of Michael's condition, from blood gas reports to cardiac anatomy and eventually to neuroanatomy. I, on the other hand, and in response to entirely different personal needs, continued milk expression, and tried in other ways to maintain a contact and a relationship with our child. Although it only takes a few seconds to read my brief account of what we did during this time in order to deal with the horrendous strain in our lives, it was a full time job for two intelligent people to stay on top of the situation. It took virtually all of my resources to deal especially with the medical and nursing staff. For one thing, we had to be available at odd times during the day in order to speak to the medical staff about Michael; we could only speak to them when *they* had the time; never did the staff consider that we might not be available to speak to them; and never did they make it easy for us to talk to them, except when they needed permission to perform a medical procedure.

I tried, then, after the cardiac catheterization fiasco, to reconcile myself to the fact that Michael was going to be in that intensive care unit for quite a while longer. I visited him daily. I called to see how he was doing usually twice a day. Michael was being fed intravenously, as the endotracheal tube which helped him breathe made it impossible to feed him by mouth. Later, the order was given to feed him by stomach tube. I continued to express milk into sterile 2 ounce bags, which would then be kept frozen, and thawed to be fed to him by stomach tube. At this point, much to my sadness, there was really nothing I could do except express milk, so I clung to this; I felt useless and cheated and continually anxious and preoccupied. If only someone had told me what to do, even feed my baby by stomach tube, I would have been overjoyed to have a useful and necessary task.

The doctors were still uncertain as to what was wrong with him. His rapid breathing had not diminished; it was therefore decided to keep him on the respirator in a more permanent way. The endotracheal tube was a temporary breathing tube which reached his lungs through his mouth. It was decided to perform a tracheostomy which is a surgical procedure necessitating a slit in his trachea into which would be introduced a plastic tube which would more or less permanently be in his trachea. Permanently, that is, until he did not need it any more. To this tube would be attached hoses delivering oxygen in measured amounts. I was told that it is extremely rare for a baby to have a tracheostomy repair any sooner than six months after it was performed originally, so I knew that Michael would be in the hospital for at least that long. In the back of my mind I also knew that the diagnosis of a possible weakness of the heart muscle due to infection or other cause was by no means certain. Each day I hoped that Michael would improve, and each day I called the hospital before visiting only to discover that basically Michael's condition remained unchanged. Except for minor variations in the respirator settings or small changes in the amount of breast milk he was allowed, Michael's care remained the same. The nurses changed shifts every eight or twelve hours and I got to know some of them a little. They were responsible for carrying out the orders regarding Michael's basic care. I took each day as it came, as much as possible. I lived from one visit to the next, as if the visits were the only real events in my life.

The fact that Lee and I wanted detailed information on Michael's care was a surprise to the nurses. One of them even tried to hide Michael's chart from Lee, saying, when he asked for it, that it was "where it belonged" (in a drawer, out of sight). We were told that "Most parents were not in the least interested in blood gas reports, respiratory rate, or the number of times the baby vomited during the night." But Lee insisted on having access to the chart. He was not like "most parents" in this respect. Both of us resented deeply being stereotyped in this way. We both found ourselves feeling defensive about wanting medical information.

Dr. Brown was a rare exception to what I have said previously about the people we encountered in the medical world. He was an extremely reliable source of information. We usually spent an hour with him once a week, during which time we asked all the questions we had stored up in our minds. He answered all of the ones he could in great detail, and he was quick to admit if he was not able to answer them. Always during these weekly sessions we wanted to ask what were Michael's chances for survival, and if he survived, would he be disabled in any way? These were the questions that Dr. Brown could not answer. He still maintained that Michael probably had a viral infection of the heart muscle, and to this end X-rays were taken every few days to see if his heart size had decreased, indicating that the infection had subsided. Always during our meetings, Dr. Brown gave us the latest results, and always they were the same, no change in heart size. Lee and I always hoped for good news. We were constantly on tenterhooks. Dr. Brown never let us give up hope, nor did we want to.

Nonetheless, Lee and I had good reason to doubt the competency of even so great an institution as this intensive care unit—the error during the cardiac catheterization—the sloppy administration of the consent forms for that test—and the occasional misinformation we were given by the resident on duty in the unit. Because this was our son, and because the doctors did not seem to be able to give us any firm answers, Lee and I on more than one occasion had cause to question the actions taken by the intensive care unit staff regarding Michael.

Cause to Question

One incident was particularly frightening. Michael's condition when he was five weeks old warranted frequent blood tests. His blood gas levels indicated how well or how poorly his heart was functioning. The tests caused the red blood count to decrease faster than his body could replace it. At some point we knew that he would require a transfusion. In addition to this impending transfusion, Michael was due for yet another attempt at breathing without the help of the respirator.

This was the situation one Friday in early May when Lee and I had one of our talks with Dr. Brown. Dr. Brown told us that Michael was to have a transfusion that afternoon, and he was careful and considerate to warn us that the extra blood in his system would exacerbate his symptoms—fluid retention and rapid breathing. As we drove home that day we were not particularly worried, and we were glad that the oxygen-carrying ability of his blood was to be improved. Around eight that night we called to see how Michael was tolerating the transfusion. We were told that no transfusion had occurred. This puzzled us, as Dr. Brown had seemed so sure that Michael was to be transfused that day.

The following morning, when I went to visit him, I was greeted at the door by a nurse, all smiles, telling me that Michael had again been taken off the respirator and was trying to breath on his own. I hid my alarm, but I was very concerned that they had taken Michael off the respirator when a transfusion was imminent. Both actions at once would most certainly put his heart in jeopardy. I felt that the doctors were not giving Michael every chance to succeed off the respirator. I was both angry and alarmed. I had no illusions this time of hope for Michael's success. I went home, and Lee and I tried to get hold of Dr. Brown, but of course, it being Saturday, he was unavailable. There was nothing to do but watch helplessly the following sequence of events—Sunday, Michael needed frequent suctioning to remove fluid from his lungs; he was breathing rapidly and with difficulty; he was tired and could hardly eat. Sunday night he was given a slow transfusion. Monday he was even more tired and his breathing was more labored. So we were not surprised when by Tuesday Michael was put back on the respirator; his congestive symptoms had been aggravated by the transfusion. We finally got in touch with Dr. Brown who was as surprised as we were that Michael had been taken off the respirator. We had called the resident on duty and asked him why this had been done. His reply was that it seemed like a good thing to do at the time! He sounded so cavalier about it—I wish someone had consulted us first!

Apparently the administrative set-up could not prevent this sort of thing happening because Dr. Brown, a pediatric cardiology fellow, acted in an advisory capacity on Michael's case; the final decisions were made by the intensive care unit staff. The resident on duty often made decisions such as the one to take Michael off the respirator; however, the resident was still only a doctor in training. Lee and I could not understand why, if the consensus was that Michael was a heart patient, the ICU did not take the advice of the cardiologists more seriously. We made an appointment with the Director of the unit and questioned him about this. He replied that in the future he would try to increase communication between the cardiologists and the intensive care unit staff. His answer hardly placated us, but under the circumstances we could not have accomplished more. Michael's pediatrician was right; he had advised us prior to this meeting that doctors do not like to be questioned on medical matters by laymen and that we had better restrict our comments to a criticism of the administration of the ICU rather than a criticism of the medical decisions made by the staff. This was a very difficult interview to conduct, but I thought that Lee had done so with great tact and delicacy.

The upshot of this interview with the Director was that our complaint got back to the resident in charge of the unit who then had a discussion with Dr. Brown, and asked him not to talk to us any more about Michael's care because it was confusing us! It seemed then that given the facts we were still stereotyped into "confused" parents. Implied was the comment that the less we knew about the better. I hope that it is clear what we were up against in our search for straight answers and information. I hope that it is also clear how, when faced with hard lay questions regarding medical decisions, the medical profession closed in its ranks. Dr. Cousins, Michael's pediatrician, too, had received a call from someone in the unit who begged him to head off our queries. The staff just didn't know what to do about us, he was told. To our relief and satisfaction, Dr. Cousins stood up for us, replying that the fault was not by any means with us, but lay with the administration of the unit. He said, "There's nothing wrong with them! Any problems that you have are of your own making!" Had not Dr. Cousins supported us, who knows just how awful it might have been!

Perhaps in an attempt to deal with their own anxieties in relating to a mother and a critically ill infant, or perhaps in a misguided attempt to help, it was not unusual for hospital personnel to tell us their own tales of sadness and despair. If I could pick one of the sequence of events as a crowning blow, a last straw, it would be the following. Tuesday night after the mix-up in the transfusion I went in to see Michael. The excerpt from my journal speaks for itself.

He's back on the respirator as of 4:30 p.m. at two breaths per minute, 40% oxygen—he looks O.K. colorwise, but his legs lie limp. He's awake and lookin' all around with his big blue eyes. An older nurse is taking care of him. She is giving him his first feeding by bottle, as he's been too tired to suck all day. He's been throwing up too and they've had to suction his lungs much more frequently.

Damn it—I could have told them this would happen on Sunday!

Nurse tells me that cardiac babies make up with their eyes what they can't do with their arms and legs. That they're smart and never miss a trick with their eyes; whereas other babies spend so much time moving around and sucking their thumbs that they miss alot that is going on around them. Then she told me of her little niece who had an operation for patent ductus and lived to the age of three years.

I tried to be nice and said well, at least if Michael dies I will have done everything I could to make his stay here happy.

This only egged her on.

Meanwhile, she's feeding Michael the bottle while he's lying on his side in bed— not in her arms—she's clucking and cooing over him and doing all the mothering herself—and I want to wring her neck as I stand by watching and feeling as if *my* brand of mothering isn't good enough, and it really is the only thing I have to offer him that until this moment gives me pleasure too. And she is taking it all away.

I did not return to the hospital for five days after this. My milk supply reached dangerously low levels, because I felt superfluous and I was discouraged. I wished this horrible suspense of not knowing whether Michael would live or die would end. I became so desperately unhappy that I truly believed that I wanted him to die. I wished desperately that he would live, and I also wished that he would die. The two desires lived constantly in my mind side by side. I felt shattered. I was deeply angry. I wanted to hit people. More and more during the month of June, my thoughts turned to death. I began thinking about euthanasia and wondered if it was a possibility in Michael's case. I had heard that there are some babies two years old who never have been off a respirator. I could not stand it that long. But, I realized that if this came to pass, I would have to stand it as I had done so far. I was in continual misery. I gave up milk expression and tried to appreciate Michael as much as I could. He was still fun to hold, even though he still only weighed seven pounds.

Toward the end of June we found out that Michael was going to die. The doctors had discovered that he had massive arterio-veinous malformations in the midbrain. An operation would leave him a vegetable for a few years, but the malformations would eventually reform, and he would die. The neurosurgeons advised against operating. He had never had a chance from the second month of his in utero development on. We were told that Michael had at most six months to live.

The sudden spectre of my baby's certain death frightened, shocked and awed me. I did not feel relief. I wanted to stay away from Michael—to begin to forget (I thought) right away. I did not want to see him again. But I woke up one morning after about two days with the sudden realization that the fact he was to die didn't really change anything. He had not died yet! I knew that I would forever regret it if I did not make the utmost of the precious time we had left together. So I continued to go and visit him every day.

On one of those days, I was called into the Director's office. The resident in charge was there also. The Director told me in a long speech that the unit had done everything possible for my baby. No further therapeutic procedures would help him recover. I was told that in cases like this there are considered two parallel factors—the patient and the parents. I was terrified—frozen in fear—during the interview. It seemed so vague as to what exactly was expected of me, and this frightened me more. I did not want to watch Michael fade, sicken, suffer and die. I was very frightened of this too. We were moving out of state in one month, and I told the Director that if Michael were still alive, I could not leave him here, but would have to take him to another ICU in the town in which we were to live. I did not want Michael to suffer in a prolonged, futile struggle when all he could ever hope to have would be more of the same. This was all I could convey to the two doctors. I told them that my husband's feelings were much the same. In the end any decisions that might or might not be made were left up to the intensive care unit and to the natural course of Michael's illness. It seemed unfair that the only time that anyone in the hospital was interested in my thoughts and feelings about Michael's care was in regards to his death.

I urged Lee to come with me to see Michael for the same reasons that I went to see him, and toward the end, Lee did come. We took pictures and I fed Michael his beets. His dietary restrictions were lifted, and for a few days he drank lots of formula and we all spoiled him as much as we could. One of the nurses brought him a baseball cap that said Junior League on it. He looked adorable and he just loved his meals.

At home we always waited for the phone to ring with the final news. I hoped it would not happen that way, but that we would get some warning. I began to think of burial and where it should be.

One day we called the hospital to inquire about Michael, and the resident in charge told us that he had just given Michael some morphine, as he was extremely uncomfortable, struggling for air. Lee and I let an hour go by before we went to the hospital to give the morphine a chance to take effect. Michael was white. He lay limp on his pillow with his eyes opening and closing slowly. Lee said that he was cold to the touch. I took one look and covered my eyes—he was so obviously dying. No one spoke to us and no one looked up when we entered the nursery. All we could hear were the machines bubbling and sighing—and Michael lay white on his bed. I didn't think he'd last the night. It was very quiet.

We left the hospital. We didn't know what to do with ourselves, not wanting to go home for the inevitable phone call. Finally we went home and the resident called to tell us that Michael had died ten minutes after we left. We were shaking inside.

Questions and Activities

1. Identify and discuss specific needs of Michael's parents. Be sure to address unique needs of both the mother and the father. How did the hospital interfere with the fulfillment of those needs? What was done or could have been done in terms of staff support, hospital facilities, rules, and so forth to be more helpful to Michael's parents and reduce their stress and uncertainty?

2. Were Michael's mother and father viewed by the medical staff as part of the caregiving team? In what ways could they have more actively participated in Michael's care, given his critical condition?

3. What type of death trajectory is illustrated in this case study? What reactions are associated with this type of trajectory and how were they manifested by Michael's parents?

4. Have certain psychological costs been paid as medicine has become more sophisticated? Give several examples from Michael's case. Is this a necessary consequence of modern medicine?

Glossary

Abortion: Deliberate termination of a pregnancy.

AIDS–related Complex (ARC): Pre-AIDS condition.

Intimacy: The positive outcome of Erikson's young adulthood crisis. Intimacy involves the ability to experience an open, supportive, and close relationship with another person, without fear of losing oneself in the process.

Isolation: The negative outcome of Erikson's young adulthood crisis. Isolation is the inability to develop intimate relationships which leads to preoccupation with oneself and superficial relationships with others.

Miscarriage: Unwillful termination of a pregnancy prior to the point of viability.

Newborn Death: Death that takes place within a few hours or days after birth.

Perinatal Bereavement Syndrome: Grief related to miscarriage, stillbirth, or death of a newborn.

Perinatal Death: Refers to a miscarriage, stillbirth, or a newborn death.

Post-traumatic Stress Disorder: A delayed but persistent condition resulting from a traumatic stress.

Psychic Numbness: Intellectual awareness of death and suffering, concurrent with emotional desensitization that may be necessary for survival and effective functioning, as in a combat situation.

Stillbirth: Fetal death occurring after the twenty-eighth week of prenatal development.

Sudden Infant Death Syndrome (SIDS): The primary cause of death of infants between the ages of one week and one year. Athough many theories exist, the cause of SIDS is not known.

Survivor Guilt: Guilt over having survived when others have died.

Traumatic Stress: A situation or event which is generally outside the range of normal human experience, and which, as such, would evoke significant symptoms of distress in almost anyone.

Worried Well: Individuals who do not have AIDS at present but who fear they will develop it.

Walking Wounded: Individuals who have an early form of the AIDS syndrome.

Suggested Readings

Brende, J. O., & Parson, E. R. (1985). *Vietnam veterans: The road to recovery.* New York: Plenum Press.

This book provides a brief overview of the Vietnam war, discusses the long-term effects on those who participated in it, and examines the major issues related to recovery. Interspersed throughout the book are quotes from Vietnam veterans. Of special interest is a chapter on the adjustment of women and ethnic minorities involved in the war.

Gong, V., & Rudnick, N. (Eds.) (1986). *AIDS: Facts and issues.* New Brunswick, NJ: Rutgers University Press.

This edited volume is a compilation of 25 articles written by professionals from a number of different fields—health care, education, social welfare, and law. The book focuses on various topics including facts and fallacies, medical perspectives, high-risk factors, social responses, research in cure and prevention, and coping strategies. A glossary of AIDS-related terms is also included.

Progoff, I. (1975). *At a journal workshop.* New York: Dialogue House Library.

A practical guidebook for using a journal as a means of personal growth. It contains a variety of thought-provoking exercises and techniques.

Resources

HOPING (Helping Other Parents in Normal Grieving)
1215 East Michigan Avenue
Lansing, Michigan 48909
(517) 483-2344

National Sudden Infant Death Syndrome Clearinghouse
8201 Greensboro Drive, Suite 600
McLean, Virginia 22102
(703) 821-8955

AIDS Action Council
2033 M Street, N. W., Suite 801
Washington, D.C. 20036
(202) 293-2886

Veteran's Administration
810 Vermont Avenue, N. W.
Washington, D.C. 20420
(800) 332-6742

References

Aadalen, S. (1980). Coping with sudden infant death syndrome: Intervention strategies and a case study. *Family Relations, 29*, 584–590.

Altman, D. (1986). *AIDS in the mind of America.* Garden City, NY: Anchor Press/ Doubleday.

American Psychiatric Association. (1987). *Diagnostic and statistical manual for mental disorders* (3d ed.—Revised). Washington, DC: Author.

Batchelor, W. F. (1984). AIDS: A public health and medical emergency. *American Psychologist, 39*(11), 1283–1284.

Bergman, A. (1974). Psychological aspects of sudden unexpected death in infants and children. *Pediatric Clinics of North America, 21*(1), 115–121.

Bergman, A. B., Pomeroy, M. A., & Beckwith, J. B. (1969). The psychiatric toll of the sudden infant death syndrome. *General Practice, 40*(6) 99–105.

Borg, S., & Lasker, J. (1981). *When pregnancy fails: Families coping with miscarriage, stillbirth, and infant death.* Boston: Beacon Press.

Brende, J. O., & Parson, E. R. (1985). *Vietnam veterans: The road to recovery.* New York: Plenum Press.

Card, J. J. (1987). Epidemiology of PTSD in a national cohort of Vietnam veterans. *Journal of Clinical Psychology, 43*(1), 6–17.

Carl, D. (1986). Acquired immune deficiency syndrome: A preliminary examination of the effects on gay couples and coupling. *Journal of Marital and Family Therapy, 12*(3), 241–247.

Chng, C. L. (1982). Sudden infant death syndrome: An inexplicable tragedy for the family. *Family Perspective, 16*(3), 123–128.

Cozby, P. C. (1972). Self-disclosure, reciprocity, and liking. *Sociometry, 35*, 151–160.

DeFrain, J. D., & Ernst, L. (1978). The psychological effects of sudden infant death syndrome on surviving family members. *The Journal of Family Practice, 6*(5), 985–989.

Derlega, V. J., & Chaikin, A. L. (1975). *Sharing intimacy.* Englewood Cliffs, NJ: Prentice-Hall.

Doane, B. K., & Quigley, B. Q. (1981). Psychiatric aspects of therapeutic abortion. *Canadian Medical Association Journal, 125,* 427–432.

Doka, K. J. (1987). Silent sorrow: Grief and the loss of significant others. *Death Studies, 11*(6), 455–469.

Donlou, J., Wolcott, D., Gottlieb, M., & Landsverk, J. (1985). Psychosocial aspects of AIDS and AIDS-related complex: A pilot study. *Journal of Psychosocial Oncology, 3*(2), 39–55.

Enlow, R. W. (1984). Epidemiology and immunology of Acquired Immune Deficiency Syndrome. In S. Nichols & D. Ostrow (Eds.), *Psychiatric implications of Acquired Immune Deficiency Syndrome* (pp. 1–16). Washington, DC: American Psychiatric Press.

Erikson, E. H. (1959). Identity and the life cycle: Selected papers. *Psychological Issues,* Monograph No. 1.

Figley, C., & Salison, S. (1980). Treating Vietnam veterans as survivors. *Evaluation and change: Services for survivors* [Special issue]. 135–141.

Fogel, C. I. (1981). Abortion. In C. I. Fogel & N. F. Woods (Eds.), *Health care of women: A nursing perspective* (pp. 524–538). St Louis, MO: C.V. Mosby.

Forstein, M. (1984). AIDS in the "Worried Well." In S. Nichols & D. Ostrow (Eds.), *Psychiatric implications of Acquired Immune Deficiency Syndrome* (pp. 49–60). Washington, DC: American Psychiatric Press.

Foy, D. W., & Card, J. J. (1987). Combat-related post-traumatic stress disorder etiology: Replicated findings in a national sample of Vietnam-era men. *Journal of Clinical Psychology, 43*(1), 28–31.

Fuller, R. L., Geis, S. B., & Rush, J. (1988). Lovers of AIDS victims: A minority group experience. *Death Studies, 12*(1), 1–7.

Galea, R. P., Lewis, B. F., & Baker, L. A. (1988). Voluntary testing for HIV antibodies. *Journal of the National Association of Social Workers, 33*(3), 265–268.

Geis, S. B., Fuller, R. L., & Rush, J. (1986). Lovers of AIDS victims. *Death Studies, 10*(1), 43–53.

Gideon, M. D., & Taylor, P. B. (1981). A sexual bill of rights for dying persons. *Death Education, 4,* 303–314.

Gilson, G. (1976). Care of the family who has lost a newborn. *Postgraduate Medicine, 60,* 67–70.

Haney, P. (1988). Providing empowerment to the person with AIDS. *Journal of the National Association of Social Workers, 33*(3), 251–254.

Harris, B. G. (1986). Induced abortion. In T. Rando (Ed.), *Parental loss of a child* (pp. 241–256). Champaign, IL: Research Press.

Hendin, H., & Haas, A. P. (1984). *Wounds of war: The psychological aftermath of combat in Vietnam.* New York: Basic Books.

Hogancamp, V., & Figley, C. (1983). War: Bringing the battle home. In C. Figley & H. McCubbin (Eds.), *Stress and the family: Coping with catastrophe* (Vol. 2) (pp. 148–165). New York: Brunner/Mazel.

Hutchins, S. H. (1986). Stillbirth. In T. Rando (Ed.), *Parental loss of a child* (pp. 129–144). Champaign, IL: Research Press.

Joy, S. S. (1985). Abortion: An issue to grieve. *Journal of Counseling and Development, 63*(6), 375–376.

Keane, T. M., & Fairbanks, J. A. (1983). Survey analysis of combat-related stress disorders in Vietnam veterans. *American Journal of Psychiatry, 140,* 348–350.

Kellner, K., Best, E., Chesborough, S., Donnelly, W., & Green, M. (1981). Perinatal mortality counseling program for families who experience a stillbirth. *Death Education, 5,* 29–35.

Kennedy, M. (1987). AIDS: Coping with the fear. *Nursing, 17*(4), 45–46.

Kennell, J., Slyter, H., & Klaus, M. (1970). The mourning response of parents to the death of a newborn infant. *New England Journal of Medicine, 283,* 344–349.

Klaus, M. H., & Kennell, J. H. (1976). *Maternal–infant bonding.* St. Louis, MO: C. V. Mosby.

Kotch, J., & Cohen, S. (1985). SIDS counselor's report of own and parents' reactions to reviewing the autopsy report. *Omega, 16*(2), 129–139.

Lattanzi, M., & Hale, M. E. (1984). Giving grief words: Writing during bereavement. *Omega, 15*(1), 45–52.

Leff, P. (1987). Here I am, Ma: The emotional impact of pregnancy loss on parents and health-care professionals. *Family Systems Medicine, 5*(1), 105–114.

Leviton, D. (1978). The intimacy/sexual needs of the terminally ill and widowed. *Death Education, 2,* 261–280.

Lietar, E. F. (1986). Miscarriage. In T. Rando (Ed.), *Parental loss of a child* (pp. 121–128). Champaign, IL: Research Press.

Lifton, R. J. (1970). *History and human survival.* New York: Random House.

Lindemann, E. (1944). Symptomatology and management of acute grief. *Journal of Psychiatry, 101,* 141–149.

Lopez, D., & Getzel, G. (1987). Strategies for volunteers caring for persons with AIDS. *Social Casework, 68*(1), 47–53.

Lowenthal, M., & Weiss, L. (1976). Intimacy and crisis in adulthood. *Counseling Psychologist, 6*(1), 10–15.

Lowman, J. (1979). Grief intervention and sudden infant death syndrome. *American Journal of Community Psychology, 7*(6), 665–677.

Markusen, E., Owen, G., Fulton, R., & Bendiksen, R. (1978). SIDS: The survivor as victim. *Omega, 8*(4), 277–283.

May, H. J., & Breme, E. J. (1982). SIDS family adjustment scale: A method of assessing family adjustment to sudden infant death syndrome. *Omega, 13*(1), 59–74.

Morin, S. F., Charles, K. A., & Malyon, A. K. (1984). The psychological impact of AIDS on gay men. *American Psychologist, 39*(11), 1288–1293.

Nichols, E. (1986). *Mobilizing against AIDS: The unfinished story.* Cambridge, MA: Harvard University Press.

Nichols, J. A. (1986). Newborn death. In T. Rando (Ed.), *Parental loss of a child* (pp. 145–158). Champaign, IL: Research Press.

Palmer, C. E., & Noble, D. (1986). Premature death: Dilemmas of infant mortality. *Social Casework, 67*(6), 332–339.

Parson, E. R. (1986). Life after death: Vietnam veteran's struggle for meaning and recovery. *Death Studies, 10,* 11–26.

Pattison, E. M. (1977). *The experience of dying.* Englewood Cliffs, NJ: Prentice-Hall.

Pearce, K. A., Schauer, A. H., Garfield, N. J., Ohlde, C. O., & Patterson, T. W. (1985). A study of post-traumatic stress disorder in Vietnam veterans. *Journal of Clinical Psychology, 41*(1), 9–14.

Peppers, L. (1987). Grief and elective abortion: Breaking the emotional bond. *Omega, 18*(1), 1–12.

Peppers, L., & Knapp, R. J. (1980). Maternal reactions to involuntary fetal/infant death. *Psychiatry, 43,* 155–159.

Pomeroy, M. R. (1969). Sudden death syndrome. *American Journal of Nursing, 69*(9), 1886–1890.

Price, R. E., Omizo, M. M., & Hammett, V. L. (1986). Counseling clients with AIDS. *Journal of Counseling and Development, 65*(2), 96–97.

Public Health Service Centers for Disease Control. (1988). *AIDS Weekly Surveillance Report* (May). Washington, DC: U.S. Government Printing Office.

Public Health Service Centers for Disease Control. (1988). *Understanding AIDS.* (HHS Publication No. [CDC] HHS-88-8404). Washington, DC: U.S. Government Printing Office.

Rando, T. A. (1984). *Grief, dying, and death: Clinical interventions for caregivers.* Champaign, IL: Research Press.

Reinharz, S. (1988). What's missing in miscarriage? *Journal of Community Psychology, 16*(1), 84–103.

Schiamberg, L. B. (1985). *Human development* (2d ed.). New York: Macmillan.

Seibel, M., & Graves, W. (1980). The psychological implications of spontaneous abortion. *Reproductive Medicine, 24,* 161–165.

Shaw, C. T. (1983). Grief over fetal loss. *Family Practice Recertification, 5,* 129–145.

Shearer, P., & McKusick, L. (1986). In L. McKusick (Ed.), *What to do about AIDS: Physicians and mental health professionals discuss the issues.* Berkeley, CA: University of California Press.

Shehan, C. L. (1987). Spouse support and Vietnam veterans' adjustment to post-traumatic stress disorder. *Family Relations, 36,* 55–60.

Siegal, F. P., & Siegal, M. (1983). *AIDS: The medical mystery.* New York: Grove Press.

Silver, S. M., & Iacono, C. U. (1984). Factor-analytic support for DSM–III's post-traumatic stress disorder for Vietnam veterans. *Journal of Clinical Psychology*, *40*(1), 5–14.

Smialek, Z. (1978). Observations on immediate reactions of families to sudden infant death. *Pediatrics*, *62*(2), 160–165.

Solkoff, N., Gray, P., & Keill, S. (1986). Which Vietnam veterans develop posttraumatic stress disorders? *Journal of Clinical Psychology*, *42*(5), 687–698.

Stevens-Long, J. (1988). *Adult life* (3d ed.). Palo Alto, CA: Mayfield.

Swoiskin, S. (1986). Sudden infant death: Nursing care for the survivors. *Journal of Pediatric Nursing*, *1*(1), 33–39.

Tick, E. (1985). Vietnam grief: Psychotherapeutic and psychohistorical implications. In E. M. Stern (Ed.), *Psychotherapy and the grieving patient* (pp. 101–115). New York: Haworth Press.

United States Bureau of the Census (1987). *Statistical abstract of the United States: 1988* (108 ed.). Washington, DC: U.S. Government Printing Office.

Wasserman, A. L., Thompson, E. I., Wilimas, J. A., & Fairclough, D. L. (1987). The psychological status of survivors of childhood/adolescent Hodgkin's disease. *American Journal of Diseases of Children*, *141*(6), 626–631.

Williamson, P. (1986). National Sudden Infant Death Syndrome Foundation. In T. Rando (Ed.), *Parental loss of a child* (pp. 509–512). Champaign, IL: Research Press.

Wolcott, D. L., Fawzy, F. I., Landsverk, J., & McCombs, M. (1986). AIDS patients' needs for psychosocial services and their use of community service organizations. *Journal of Psychosocial Oncology*, *4*(1), 135–146.

Wolff, J. R., Nielson, P. E., & Schiller, P. (1970). The emotional reaction to a stillbirth. *American Journal of Obstetrics and Gynecology*, *108*(1), 73–77.

Worden, J. W. (1982). *Grief counseling and grief therapy: A handbook for the mental health practitioner*. New York: Springer.

8

Middle Adulthood

Major Causes of Death during Middle Adulthood 328

Needs of the Dying at Midlife 330

Reevaluating One's Life 330
Continuing Roles 331
Putting Affairs in Order 332

Coping with a Life-threatening Illness: Considerations of the Specific Disease Process 332

Heart Disease 333

Cancer 337
Amyotrophic Lateral Sclerosis 346

Losses during Midlife 354

Loss of a Spouse 354
Loss of a Former Spouse: Grief after Divorce 360
Loss of a Parent 362

Summary 365

The years of middle adulthood include the forties, fifties, and the beginning of the sixties. These middle years of life are often referred to as the "prime of life." It is a time of achievement. At this point, individuals have accumulated a broad range of personal, social, and work skills; they are usually at their peak in terms of vocational development. By midlife, the quest for the adolescent dream has been replaced by the protection of gains (Schiamberg, 1985). Competencies, skills, relationships, and lifestyles that have been developed are maintained and nurtured.

As with previous life stages, new challenges are encountered and new perspectives are also gained during the middle years. In midlife "the impetuous drive of youth mellows to the steady pull of maturity. A growing sense of the surety and familiarity of oneself, one's marriage, one's spouse leads toward a possible appreciation of the more subtle and muted rewards of life" (Pattison, 1977, p. 25). Butler and Lewis (1982) attribute this increased appreciation of life to the restructuring and reformulation of concepts of time, self, and death that occur during middle age.

Some individuals experience a midlife crisis when confronted with the fact that life is not filled with unlimited time. Stephenson (1985) has described the midlife crisis as a form of anticipatory grief—grief over loss of youth, opportunities, endless life. This crisis is often prompted by developmental events that signal that persons are getting older (for example, the event of the last child leaving home, changes in physical appearance associated with aging, such as graying hair, or menopause marking the end of childbearing ability in women). By mourning these losses, the individual can better accept his or her own aging process and the transition to another life stage. Coming to terms with the midlife transition allows individuals to more fully value and appreciate their lives.

Major Causes of Death during Middle Adulthood

By the end of young adulthood, death due to disease increases significantly. For middle-aged males, heart disease is the leading cause of death, followed by cancer. The order is reversed for females, whose primary cause of death in the middle years is cancer. The most common types of cancer are also different for males and females. Breast cancer is responsible for most malignancies in women, while lung and prostate cancer are the most prevalent types of cancer found among the male population. Lung cancer, however, is the leading cause of cancer deaths in both groups (American Cancer Society, 1987). Figure 8.1 shows the current percentages of cancer deaths by site for both sexes.

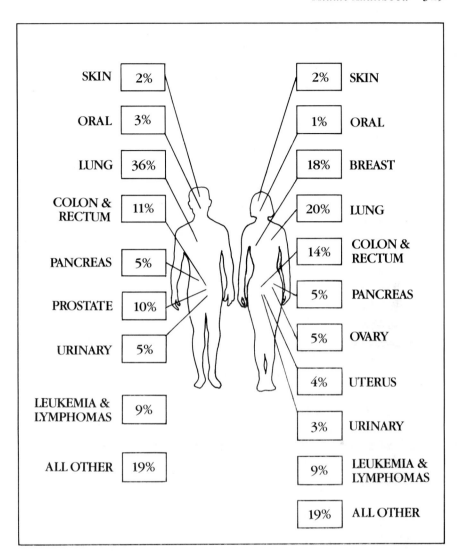

Figure 8.1   *Cancer Deaths by Site and Sex (United States: 1987 Estimates)*

Source: *Cancer Facts and Figures—1987,* New York: American Cancer Society, p. 12. Reprinted by permission.

Needs of the Dying at Midlife

The needs of the dying at midlife relate to responsibility for others and increased self-reflection. These needs include (1) the need for reevaluation of one's life, (2) the need for continuation of roles, and (3) the need to put affairs in order.

Reevaluating One's Life

Middle age is a period of reevaluation. While reevaluation can occur during any life stage, this process has a special quality during middle adulthood. According to Schiamberg (1985), the primary concern of the middle-aged person can be viewed as that of the proverbial man who wondered aloud if his glass was half empty or half full. Individuals at midlife are faced with limited future choices while also being acutely aware of the influence of past decisions and events on their lives. Midlife is, therefore, a period of questioning. Questions such as "What is the meaning of my life?" and "Should I continue in the same direction?" are commonly asked by individuals at this time. This type of life evaluation has been referred to as *stock-taking* (Butler & Lewis, 1982). Individuals take stock of their lives with full awareness that what they find is and will continue to be their life unless they make some changes soon. This questioning is a normal and natural part of midlife, as individuals become increasingly conscious of their own mortality and the fact that their time is running out. For the first time, these individuals realize that they have more time stretching out behind them than in front of them.

Stock-taking occurs in terms of one's relationships, career, achievements, values, and other commitments made earlier in life. The outcomes of this reevaluation take several directions. Following the assessment of previous choices, individuals may recommit themselves to the path previously chosen, or their assessment may result in major life changes. The decision to pursue new directions or relationships at this stage are reflected in midlife career changes and the high rate of divorce during the middle years. Regardless of the outcome, the individual must come to grips with his or her actual achievements in relation to the hopes and aspirations of young adulthood.

For the individual facing death in the middle years, this reevaluation will be accelerated and compressed into the remaining time the individual has left. The individual may appear quiet and introspective to others while engaging in this process. One outcome of this stock-taking is the need to mourn losses: goals never attained, aspirations never reached, and deeds never done. Another aspect of this mourning stems from the meaning one attributes to one's life. Positive conclusions drawn about one's life after the midlife evaluation imply that the individual has much to lose. Impending death will raise issues and remind the individual of all he or she will be leaving behind.

Continuing Roles

Roles are important to the middle-aged individual. Much of an individual's identity is derived from his or her adult roles. In the early years of adulthood, self-perceptions help determine what roles are chosen. As an individual moves through adulthood, the enactment of these roles affects one's sense of self. Thus, as the individual assumes more roles, his or her identity becomes more complex and differentiated.

Through one's roles, individuals are able to make lasting and significant contributions. Erikson (1968) has identified the central issue of midlife as *generativity versus stagnation*. Generativity is reflected in a deep concern for the next generation and a desire to contribute to the future. Generativity is achieved through the channeling of one's energy and creativity in a direction that will produce lasting and worthwhile results—a legacy for the future. Failure to develop a generative life-style in midlife will result in self-indulgence and stagnation (Erikson, 1968).

Individuals facing death at midlife may ask themselves: Have I made a significant contribution to the next generation? Have I been a productive and creative member of society? It is important for the dying individual to be supported in maintaining his or her adult roles whenever possible. Too often, the dying person is seen only as "ill" and "dying" and is not given opportunities to function as a father, a spouse, a mentor, a friend, and so forth. Giving advice to a younger colleague, helping to complete plans for reorganization of their company, and providing emotional support to family members are examples of important goals of the middle-aged person coping with a life-threatening illness. By continuing to participate in life and ongoing relationships, individuals will be more likely to positively resolve the generativity versus stagnation conflict and to feel they are leaving behind a legacy after their death. They will also face death with a strong sense of personal identity and a better understanding of the purpose of their lives.

Putting Affairs in Order

Middle age is the life stage in which individuals have the greatest responsibilities. Leadership positions in work settings and community organizations are typically held by those in their middle years. It may also be a time of heightened psychological pressures and financial demands as support is provided for other family members. Adolescent children may still be in college or establishing themselves as young adults. In addition, the parents of middle-aged individuals are aging and may begin to need more assistance and attention from their adult children than ever before.

For the terminally ill individual at midlife, responsibilities and obligations to others are of the utmost importance. Dying at this time is a disruption of ongoing relationships and involvement with others. Faced with impending death, the middle-aged person will be less concerned about death per se and more concerned about his or her responsibilities and obligations to loved ones that may go unmet after death. Therapeutic intervention will often involve helping the person plan for those who will be left behind: spouse, children, aging parents, and employees, among others. The person usually wants to carry out his or her duties to whatever degree possible through making appropriate arrangements and plans prior to death (Pattison, 1977; Rando, 1984).

Coping with a Life-threatening Illness: Considerations of the Specific Disease Process

The psychological issues related to coping with a life-threatening illness are directly related to the specific realities of the patient's disease (Mages & Mendelsohn, 1979). Each disease has its own particular course, symptoms, treatment options, and stages. The issues associated with each of these factors can present unique adjustment difficulties. Gould (1980) has emphasized that cancer patients have been the focus of the majority of studies on adaptation to terminal illness. He maintains that while the findings obtained from this research may hold true for cancer patients, they may have limited applicability to other terminal illnesses. In the following sections, we will illustrate this point by describing three very different diseases: (1) heart disease, (2) cancer, and (2) amyotrophic lateral sclerosis. Heart disease and cancer are leading causes of death in the United States, while amyotrophic lateral sclerosis is a low-incidence disease.

Heart Disease

> He awoke at 7 a.m. with pain in his chest. The sort of pain that might cause panic if one were not a doctor, as he was, and did not know, as he knew, that it was heartburn.
>
> He went into the kitchen to get some Coke, whose secret syrups often relieve heartburn. The refrigerator door seemed heavy, and he noted that he was having trouble unscrewing the bottle cap. Finally, he wrenched it off, cursing the defective cap. He poured some liquid, took a sip. The pain did not go away. Another sip; still no relief.
>
> Now he grew more attentive. He stood motionless, observing symptoms. His breath was coming hard. He felt faint. He was sweating, though the August morning was still cool. He put his fingers to his pulse. It was rapid and weak. A powerful burning sensation was beginning to spread through his chest, radiating upward into his throat. Into his arm? No. But the pain was getting worse. Now it was crushing—*"crushing,"* just as it is always described. And worse even than the pain was the sensation of losing all power, a terrifying seepage of strength. He could feel the entire degenerative process accelerating. He was growing fainter, faster. The pulse was growing weaker, faster. He was sweating much more profusely now—a heavy, clammy sweat. He felt that the life juices were draining from his body. He felt that he was about to die. (Lear, 1980, p. 11)

Cardiovascular diseases are responsible for nearly one-half of all deaths in the United States. Of the cardiovascular diseases, myocardial infarction (commonly called heart attack) is the most prevalent (see Figure 8.2). In fact, heart attacks are the leading cause of death among Americans. In 1984, it was estimated that each year as many as 1,500,000 individuals in the United States will have a heart attack and about 540,000 of them will not survive (American Heart Association, 1987).

Because of the nature of myocardial infarction, it can usually be viewed as having an uncertain outcome with an uncertain time of death. The tra-

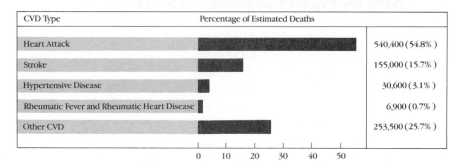

Figure 8.2 *Estimated Deaths Due to Cardiovascular Diseases by Major Type of Disorder (United States: 1984 Estimates)*

Source: American Heart Association, copyright © *1987 HEART FACTS*. Reproduced with permission.

jectory can change, however, if the cardiovascular system becomes severely damaged or diseased. Medical interventions, such as surgery and heart transplants, can also alter the death trajectory. The issues that the person with heart disease faces are significantly different than those with other life-threatening illnesses. All, however, must deal with the possibility (and in some cases, the certainty) of death. (A glossary of terminology related to heart disease and stroke can be found at the end of this chapter.)

Survival after a Heart Attack.   Death from a heart attack is typically sudden, with little warning. Approximately 60 to 70 percent of heart attacks occur outside hospitals (Daniel, 1986). Most heart attack victims who do not survive die within 2 hours after their first symptoms appear. Despite efforts to educate the public about this fact, many individuals experiencing a heart attack delay seeking help. The initial tendency seems to be to explain the chest pain in some other way (such as attributing it to severe indigestion). Eventually, when the pain does not subside or becomes overwhelming, the person having the heart attack is taken to a hospital. Efforts in the hospital are focused on survival because there is nearly a 50 percent mortality rate during the 30 days following a heart attack (Daniel, 1986).

Once admitted to a hospital, heart attack patients are usually placed in a coronary care unit (CCU) where they are continuously monitored by sophisticated equipment. Although this array of machinery can be frightening to some patients, Hackett and Cassem (1979) report that most find it reassuring. At times in the CCU environment, individuals are close to other critically ill persons and may observe the cardiac arrest of another patient. While this event often causes alarm and raises fears among other patients on the unit, they often comment that they are reassured by the speed with which the medical team responds and the amount of time spent resuscitating the person. When patients survive this experience, they typically have difficulty recalling anything about the event. Some say that they vaguely remember "being thumped on the chest and hearing voices." Survivors sometimes report that they have recurrent nightmares afterwards and have states of chronic anxiety. Often they feel different from other people because of this experience (Hackett & Cassem, 1979).

Recovery following a Heart Attack.   Survivors of heart attacks are usually encouraged by their physicians to participate in cardiac rehabilitation programs, as these programs have been shown to produce very positive results (Block, Boyer, & Imes, 1984). The essential component of these programs is exercise training or physical conditioning, which begins within 4 to 8 weeks after the patient's discharge from the hospital and con-

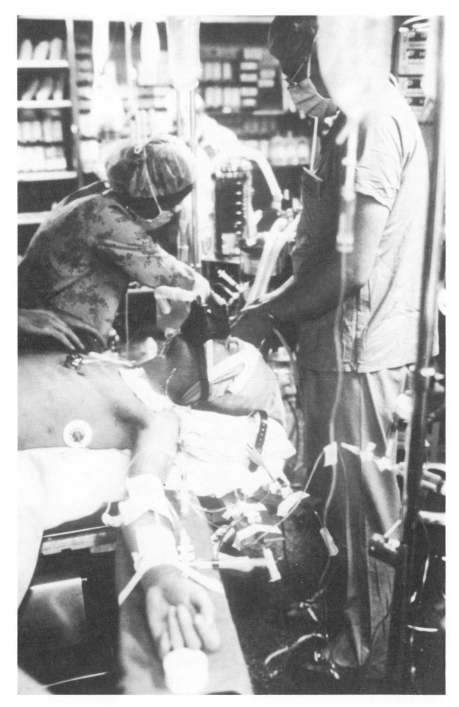

Photo 8.1 *Sophisticated modern equipment helps save many lives each year.*

tinues on a weekly basis for the next 3 months. These programs often have a counseling and education component as well. Oldenburg, Perkins, and Andrews (1985) have emphasized that counseling and education should begin as soon as possible and should not be delayed until the outpatient cardiac rehabilitation program begins. These investigators found that psychological and educational interventions with patients in the days following the heart attack had positive short-term and long-term effects on psychological, physical, and life-style functioning.

The specific type of intervention used will vary with the psychological characteristics of the patient. Approaches that may be effective with one group of cardiac patients may be contraindicated for another. For example, one group of patients may experience disabling anxiety and depression about their disease that prevents them from actively participating in their treatment. Fears of future cardiovascular damage and pessimism about the future pose barriers to recovery that can lead to chronic cardiac invalidism. These patients often become highly dependent, and they are typically noncompliant in rehabilitation programs. They are at high risk for having a second heart attack. A time of particular risk for this type of patient is the transfer from the CCU with its constant medical surveillance to a regular medical unit in the hospital. Loss of the continuous monitoring often results in increased anxiety and panic in these patients, which can precipitate another heart attack.

In contrast, another group of patients refuse to acknowledge that they have had a heart attack and deny that it will have much impact on their lives. Because of their maladaptive denial, they are excessively independent. Because they see little need for participation in a rehabilitation program, they run a greater risk of complications and recurrence. Other groups of patients are able to acknowledge their illness yet manage their feelings about it, thus leading to more positive health outcomes (Sulman & Verhaeghe, 1985).

Rehabilitation of a cardiac patient always involves addressing family issues. The crisis of a heart attack is a major threat to the stability of a family system. In hospital settings much attention is given to the patient because of his or her critical condition, and the important role of families is often ignored. The family's attitudes and patterns have an extremely potent influence on the heart attack patient's behavior, and they are important factors affecting that individual's resumption of normal activities.

The family's involvement is vital throughout the recovery process. According to Sulman and Verhaeghe (1985):

> As the patient improves the family needs specific information about levels of activity, the purpose and effects of medication, recommended changes in diet

and smoking habits, methods of reducing stress and resumption of sexual inter-course. This information can reduce the impact of new anxieties as the family shifts its focus from survival of the patient to long-range adaptation. (p. 15)

The response of family members can either aid the patient during the rehabilitation process or interfere with it. Some family members may attempt to overprotect the heart attack patient and encourage increased dependency. Others may deny that there is a problem and refuse to make the adjustments that are necessary for the well-being of the family member with heart disease.

Caregivers also need to recognize that family members will also have a variety of feelings that are related to the heart attack. Family members may feel anxious and sad about the future of their family, the uncertainty of the health and longevity of a loved one, and changes in daily living patterns. At the time of hospital discharge, spouses may feel ill-prepared to cope with heart disease in their family and manifest a variety of fears. Worries and concerns about financial issues also often surface after the first crucial weeks in the hospital are over, and special needs may arise in circum-stances in which a procedure such as coronary artery bypass surgery is rec-ommended. In addition, personality changes in a person after a heart attack (such as increased cautiousness and fearfulness) can result in strain between family members and increased stress and tension in the family.

Despite the problems associated with heart disease, many individuals and families cope well with it and continue to live normal lives. Dhooper (1983) found that nearly half of the families in her study felt that they had emerged from the crisis of a heart attack stronger and at a better level of functioning than they had been before the event. Many families adopt healthier patterns of living and begin focusing more on prevention.

Cancer

Cancer is actually a group of diseases rather than a single disease. Over 250 different kinds of cancer have been identified (DeVita, 1980). All of them have at least one factor in common—uncontrolled growth of malig-nant cells. (A glossary of cancer terminology can be found at the end of this chapter.)

Experiencing any form of cancer is also not a single stressful event, but rather a continuing condition with a series of threats of varying intensity and duration. Therefore, what it means to have cancer and the issues asso-ciated with the disease change over time. Mages and Mendelsohn (1979) have delineated several stages of the disease and the particular psychological issues and adaptive tasks associated with each stage (summarized in Table 8.1). Their discussion examines the following progression in the course of the illness: discovery and diagnosis, primary treatment, remission with return to normal activity, recurrence and spread of the disease, and terminal illness. Fortunately, a significant number of cancer patients will not reach the last two stages in this sequence. Because the majority of information on adaptation to cancer has focused on the acute stages of the disease (initial diagnosis, treatment, and terminal stages), little is known about the long-term adaptations of those who have survived cancer. As we

Table 8.1
Issues and Tasks Related to Coping with Cancer

  I. ISSUE: Discovery of cancer.
      ADAPTIVE TASK: To seek appropriate treatment.

 II. ISSUE: Primary treatment.
      ADAPTIVE TASK: To recognize and cope with the situation and one's emotional reactions and to integrate the experience of illness with the rest of one's life.

III. ISSUE: Damage to one's body from the cancer and/or treatment.
      ADAPTIVE TASK: To mourn the loss, replace or compensate for lost parts or functions, and maximize other potentials in order to maintain a sense of self-esteem and intactness.

 IV. ISSUE: Returning to normal activities and maintaining continuity in life roles.
      ADAPTIVE TASK: To understand and communicate one's changed attitudes, needs, and limitations in a way that permits functioning within one's social and physical environment with a minimum of constriction of one's life.

  V. ISSUE: Possibility of recurrence and progression of the disease.
      ADAPTIVE TASK: To learn to cope with this uncertainty and to continue appropriate medical follow-up.

 VI. ISSUE: Persistent or recurrent disease.
      ADAPTIVE TASK: To exercise freedom of choice when possible and accept one's dependence on others when necessary, while continuing appropriate treatment.

VII. ISSUE: Terminal illness.
      ADAPTIVE TASK: To prepare for the final separation from family and friends, to put one's affairs in order, to use medical and personal resources to minimize pain, and to retain as much self-sufficiency and personal dignity as possible.

examine unique adjustments associated with each stage of the disease, Mages and Mendelsohn's work will be discussed in more detail.

I. ISSUE: Discovery of cancer.
ADAPTIVE TASK: To seek appropriate treatment.

The symptoms of cancer are usually discovered by the individual, although sometimes cancer is detected by a physician during a routine physical examination. By the time the symptoms appear, the cancer has been growing for some time. The initial symptoms may be painless and innocuous and therefore easy to ignore. A medical diagnosis is sometimes delayed until after the symptoms have worsened and significant others have urged the individual to see a physician. The period between discovery of symptoms and the decision to consult a physician can be one of great apprehension.

In Stolar's (1982) study of 80 women who had undergone a mastectomy for treatment of breast cancer, she found that 86 percent of her sample had discovered the lump in their breast themselves, and three-quarters of the women had talked with others (usually their spouse) about discovery of the lump before consulting a physician. Among the sample, 45 percent had a mastectomy less than 2 weeks after discovering the lump. Some of the women delayed surgery due to inadequate or inappropriate medical care. Most of the delays, however, were due to the following: the woman ignoring or denying her condition; not wanting to change immediate work, vacation, or personal plans; or believing the lump was not malignant due to having had several benign lumps previously. Needless to say, delays in receiving medical treatment can be extremely dangerous, even though many lumps are benign. More than 80 percent of the women had received a routine medical checkup during the year prior to their diagnosis, indicating a high level of health awareness among the sample. The fears associated with cancer, however, can often result in avoidance behaviors, to the detriment of the individual's physical well-being.

II. ISSUE: Primary treatment.
ADAPTIVE TASK: To recognize and cope with the situation and one's emotional reactions and to integrate the experience of illness with the rest of one's life.

At the turn of the century, virtually no cancer treatment was available. By the time the National Cancer Institute was formed in 1937, only 20 percent of patients with cancer were considered curable. Surgery and radiotherapy improved significantly in the late 1950s, which resulted in an increase of 33 percent in the cure rate. By 1980, approximately 41 percent of all cancer patients in the United States could be cured, and that figure has risen to 50 percent with currently available treatments. It must be remembered, however, that survival rates may vary tremendously, depending on the particular type of cancer involved (DeVita, 1980; Roberts, 1984).

Successful treatment of cancer involves destruction or removal of all cancerous tissues to prevent progression and recurrence of the disease. Unless the disease is treated, the cancerous cells will continue to reproduce. In addition to the effects at the primary site, the cancer may spread to adjacent tissues or other parts of the body through *metastasis*. Metastasis is a process whereby cancer cells break away from the primary site and travel to distant secondary sites through the bloodstream, lymph system, or body tracts.

Specific treatments vary with the type of cancer and its location in the body. Common therapeutic interventions include surgery, radiation therapy, and chemotherapy. One type of treatment may be very successful in treating one type of cancer and ineffective in treating another. Often a combination of treatment strategies is used, with each having a particular purpose in the treatment regimen.

The primary treatments for cancer can be as frightening as the cancer itself, and the period of treatment is typically one of distress. As Mages and Mendelsohn (1979) have noted:

> Unlike many illnesses in which one comes to the doctor feeling sick and then feels better after treatment, the reverse is often true with cancer. For many patients, the primary treatment has the characteristics of a traumatic experience: There is a sudden catastrophic event, assault on one's body, and disruption of normal life, all of which lead to a sense of being overwhelmed. (p. 262)

Surgery.   The greatest percentage of cancer cures have been due to modern surgery. Many types of cancer require surgical removal of the malignant mass together with adjacent tissue.

Gallo (1977) views the preoperative period as the time to begin receiving professional support. The majority of breast cancer patients in her study reported the preoperative period to be one of the most difficult for them. Their concerns about survival seemed to be particularly strong during this time.

Surgery often results in some degree of physical disfigurement. Following surgery, the introduction of reconstructive and rehabilitative techniques (a prosthesis, for example) can be important components in the adjustment process. The impact of radical surgery on the person's life will be lessened and recovery time reduced as improvements continue in this area.

Radiation Therapy. Radiation therapy, used on more than half of cancer patients in the United States, uses ionizing radiation to destroy cells. While affecting both normal and cancerous tissue, radiation damages cancer cells more because of their rapid growth. Not all forms of cancer respond to this modality of therapy; in fact, some are relatively resistant to radiation. In instances in which cures are not achieved, radiation can at least slow the growth of many types of malignancy.

Radiation therapy is usually administered during frequent, intensive treatments, sometimes as often as several times a week over a period of several months. It frequently causes uncomfortable side effects, such as fatigue and general weakness. Other specific side effects are confined to the area of the body being treated (for example, hair loss when the head is irradiated or nausea and vomiting when the gastrointestinal tract is involved). The radiation dose is determined by the stage of the disease and the patient's ability to withstand the side effects, always weighing potential risks against possible benefits (Barstow, 1982).

As Barstow (1982) points out, cancer patients often have a sense of dread regarding radiation therapy. The patient is usually referred to a specialist for radiation therapy by his or her primary physician. According to Barstow (1982):

> During the therapy itself the patient often feels isolated and abandoned. He or she is undergoing a different, often frightening type of treatment, under supervision of a new physician, in a new place that may be a long distance from home. The patient may find communication with the new physician difficult and may feel separated from family and friends who usually provide support. (p. 36)

Additional strains may stem from the amount of traveling often required to obtain treatments, the extended disruption of one's normal routine, the constant reminder of the disease, and financial concerns.

Chemotherapy. Chemotherapy refers to the use of drugs to treat cancer. A typical treatment regimen might involve 6 weeks of intensive chemotherapy, with a brief respite before another series is started. While designed to attack the rapidly dividing cancer cells, chemotherapeutic agents are toxic and have an effect on the entire system. A patient's drug program is closely monitored, with much attention paid to the patient's response to treatment. Chemotherapy can bring a number of unfavorable and uncomfortable side effects, including the following: loss of hair, insomnia, nausea, difficulty in eating and digestion, bleeding sores around

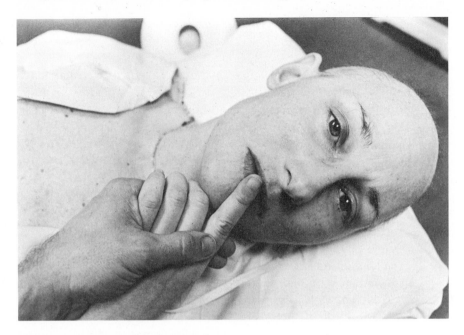

Photo 8.2   *The primary treatments for cancer and associated side effects can be as frightening for patients as the cancer itself.*

the mouth, ulceration and bleeding in the gastrointestinal tract, and other toxic effects. Not all patients, however, will experience all of these side effects or experience them with the same degree of severity.

III. ISSUE: Damage to one's body from the cancer and/or treatment.

ADAPTIVE TASK: To mourn the loss, replace or compensate for lost parts or functions, and maximize other potentials in order to maintain a sense of self-esteem and intactness.

Mages and Mendelsohn (1979) report that readily visible disfigurement from the disease or its treatment can lead to a devastating loss of self-esteem and to reclusive behavior. Injury or disfigurement of private parts of the body, while having less impact on one's public life, may impair sexual functioning and interfere with intimate relationships. Some of the physical changes are temporary (hair loss as a result of chemotherapy, for example), while others are permanent and require long-term adjustment.

The impact of loss of a body part or function depends on a person's self-concept. The more secure individuals are in their relationships with others and in their sense of worth, the more capable they will be of adjusting to the loss and maintaining a positive self-image (Gallo, 1977). However, adjustment to physical disfigurement is always a challenge in a society that places a premium on physical appearance and offers constant reminders of the cultural ideal of physical attractiveness.

Attitudes of significant others toward the body change will also affect the individual's attitude. For example, if a husband is repulsed by his wife's scars from breast surgery, it will greatly affect her adjustment. Gallo (1977) recommends actively involving the spouse when working with breast cancer patients. Support from loved ones and reassurance of one's desirability are especially important. One former mastectomy patient expressed it this way:

> I feel strongly that the husband who probably has many questions, fears, etc. is rather left out of the picture and as a result cannot intelligently give his wife the support and encouragement she needs. I think very few husbands are prepared for what a mastectomy operation looks like—I know I was scared to show my husband mine. I watched him like a hawk to see what reaction he would have . . . he didn't let me down. (Stolar, 1982, p. 32)

Anderson and Jochimsen (1985) have pointed out that difficulty with sexual functioning is highest for cancer patients with the disease located at a sexual body site. Two groups that are particularly at risk are women with breast cancer or gynecological cancer (that is, cancer of cervix, endometrium, or ovary). Breast cancer patients, in particular, may feel that they have been mutilated. They often fear losing their "wholeness" and "femininity" as a result of losing a breast (Stolar, 1982). Partners may refrain from close physical contact for fear they may hurt their spouse at the surgery site or possibly remind her of changes in her body. When changes in sexual behaviors occur, it is important to understand their origins in order to offer appropriate intervention (Anderson & Jochimsen, 1985).

IV. ISSUE: Returning to normal activities and maintaining continuity in life roles.

ADAPTIVE TASK: To understand and communicate one's changed attitudes, needs, and limitations in a way that permits functioning within one's social and physical environment with a minimum of constriction of one's life.

If rehabilitation efforts are to be successful in helping the individual achieve a new level of adjustment, then the specific problems that patients face during this stage need to be known. In an attempt to obtain pertinent information in this area, Heinrich, Schag, and Ganz (1984) developed The Cancer Inventory of Problem Situations. After administering it to 84 cancer patients, the investigators concluded that cancer has a significant impact on psychosocial and physical functioning. Moderate to severe problems were found in personal care, activity management, involvement with the health care system, work, and interpersonal interactions. The path to recovery involves dealing with each of these problems effectively.

Some of the issues that cancer patients face are less tangible. Mages and Mendelsohn (1979) have reported that cancer patients say they have been changed by the experience of cancer. They have developed new attitudes toward time, mortality, and their priorities in life, in addition to having changed their perspectives toward work and their personal relationships. Individuals find they are often treated differently by family, friends, and coworkers as a result of their illness. Adjustment involves maintaining a sense of identity and role continuity while integrating the experience with their disease into their philosophy of life. Programs such as CanSurmount and Reach for Recovery can provide valuable support in this process, as individuals interact with others who have had cancer and have successfully recovered.

V. ISSUE: *Possibility of recurrence and progression of the disease.*

ADAPTIVE TASK: *To learn to cope with this uncertainty and to continue appropriate medical follow-up.*

In many cases, primary treatment results in eradication of the disease. Usually, however, it is years before the cancer patient can be assured that a recurrence will be unlikely. "Cured" is a difficult concept in cancer care. Some tumors may recur after long periods of remission, and a small percentage of patients develop secondary malignancies as a consequence of radiation and chemotherapy. While it is difficult to say with accuracy when an individual has been "cured," 5-year survival with no recurrence of the disease represents a cure for most types of cancer (Roberts, 1984).

Roberts (1984) points out that fears of recurrence are based on reality—physicians can provide no guarantee that all cancer cells have been eradicated as a result of treatment. Cancer patients, therefore, are left with varying degrees of uncertainty. The fear of recurrence tends to be strongest immediately after the primary treatment and gradually diminishes over time. For some individuals, the fear will persist for years or it may be reactivated at follow-up visits, by new symptoms that may be unrelated to the cancer, and by events or environmental cues that remind them of their vulnerability and their experience with cancer. At times, this fear can be paralyzing and it can profoundly affect the person's life decisions (Mages & Mendelsohn, 1979). In this regard, Roberts (1984) has made the following observation:

> Although the possibility of recurrence is always present, in some patients fear becomes excessive and debilitating. Some individuals feel extremely vulnerable, as if a sword is hanging over them, ready to drop at any time. These excessive fears are known as the *Damocles syndrome*. Fear of recurrence can lead to a debilitating preoccupation with the disease. Every cough, every ache is thought to signal that the cancer has returned. Some former cancer patients repeatedly seek medical reassurance. Others go to the opposite extreme, avoiding physicians entirely and neglecting essential health monitoring and maintenance programs. (p. 98)

Roberts (1984) suggests that physicians provide solid information about the chances of recurrence and development of secondary malignancies. In addition, it is recommended that recovering cancer patients be prepared for the fears that they are likely to experience so that they will recognize that the fears are normal.

VI. ISSUE: Persistent or recurrent disease.

ADAPTIVE TASK: To exercise freedom of choice when possible and accept one's dependence on others when necessary, while continuing appropriate treatment.

If primary treatment fails or the disease reappears, the issues the individual faces are markedly changed. The person is no longer considered a cancer "survivor." Consequently, he or she will likely experience new physical symptoms, continued treatment, pain, progressive deterioration, and eventually death. While hope may continue for an extended remission or for remaining periods of comfortable and productive life, the patient's experience will be very different than that of the disease-free survivor.

The failure of individuals to control their disease by their own efforts and those of their physicians can be extremely disturbing. Individuals at this point must cope with feelings of powerlessness. They must struggle to maintain a sense of self-sufficiency and control over their lives. As they experience the impact of cancer on their bodies as well as on their careers and personal relationships, feelings of helplessness are often accentuated. To avoid succumbing to fear, despair, and passivity, these individuals will need a great deal of support and encouragement.

VII. ISSUE: Terminal illness.

ADAPTIVE TASK: To prepare for the final separation from family and friends, to put one's affairs in order, to use medical and personal resources to minimize pain, and to retain as much self-sufficiency and personal dignity as possible.

At this point, the individual must face and come to terms with impending death. The quality of the individual's remaining life will be greatly influenced by the daily management of pain and other symptoms, the supportiveness of the psychosocial environment, and the opportunities for open and honest communication. As was indicated in Chapter 1, the dying have a variety of needs that must be addressed by health care professionals. Only when these needs are met can the dying be expected to meet the adaptive demands associated with this stage of their illness.

Amyotrophic Lateral Sclerosis

A type of *motor neuron disease* with a course very different from cancer is amyotrophic lateral sclerosis (ALS). ALS is a disabling, terminal, and rapidly progressing neurological disorder that most commonly affects adults between the ages of 35 and 60. It also affects twice as many men as women. The motor neurons of the spinal cord, brainstem, and cortex of an ALS victim gradually degenerate. As a result, voluntary muscles atrophy; however, the sequence will vary for different individuals. For example, one person may be virtually immobile at some point in the disease process while speech and breathing capabilities remain intact. Another ALS patient may have loss of speech while most other motor functions are nearly normal. Typically, eye muscles, bowel and bladder sphincters, and involuntary muscles (such as the heart) are unaffected. In the natural course of the disease, death usually occurs as the result of respiratory failure when thoracic and upper airway muscles fail. While usually rapid, the rate of progression shows considerable individual variation. The duration of the disease also varies, but averages 3 years. While 50 percent of ALS patients do not live more than 3 years, 20 percent are alive 5 years after their diagnosis and 10 percent live for 10 years or longer (Camerino & Wilner, 1986; Leach & Kelemen, 1986; Sinaki, 1980).

According to Gould (1980), patients dying of this disease undergo a significantly different psychological process than do patients dying of cancer. Cancer patients rarely experience the physical and functional impairment of ALS patients; when they do, it does not involve such an extended period of time. Also, much less is known about this disease than is known about more prevalent diseases such as cancer. In most countries the incidence of ALS is less than 2 cases per 100,000 population, and it is responsible for only about 1 out of every 1000 deaths (Juergens & Kurland, 1980). ALS remains the cruel enigma it has been since it was first recognized 100 years ago. Currently, little is known about its cause and no effective cure exists. For ALS patients, the terminal phase of this disease can be viewed as spanning the entire duration of the illness.

Diagnosis. While the cancer patient may be asymptomatic and experience little difficulty at the time of diagnosis, the ALS patient initially consults medical specialists because of the presence of disturbing symptoms (limb weakness, awkwardness of gait, and slurred speech, among others). Because the illness seems "real" from the start, a definitive diagnosis for the ALS patient may actually be a source of relief (Gould, 1980). While most people have some familiarity with cancer, ALS is largely unknown among the general public. Therefore, the ALS patient usually has little or no personal knowledge of the disease or the disease's symptoms or prognosis. Some patients may have heard of "Lou Gehrig's Disease" (referred to by this name because of the famous baseball player who had ALS), and physicians may use this limited knowledge to convey information to them about the illness. In a study of ALS patients, Horne and Fagan (1983) found that in most cases patients were told that they had ALS but were given few details about the course of the disease. The participants in the study felt that information is crucial at all stages of the illness. They expressed a desire to know what to expect and to understand what is happening from a medical perspective. Few patients or families had been given information regarding resources, and they had to discover support services such as the Les Turner ALS Foundation on their own.

ALS is not a disease that is simple to diagnose in its early stages. No specific laboratory test for the disease exists, and diagnosis is usually based on clinical symptoms and the patient's medical history. In most cases, diagnosis is made by a neurologist after the disease is well established. Patients often first go to their family physicians, who often attribute the ALS symptoms to other causes. As the disease progresses, the patient is usually referred to a neurologist. Even when the neurologist suspects ALS, he or she may be hesitant to give a definitive diagnosis because ALS has such a grave prognosis and some of its symptoms are very similar to those of other neurological diseases. The patient may be subjected to unnecessary treatment until a correct diagnosis is obtained (Mulder, 1980).

Symptoms. Gould (1980) describes the general symptoms and progressions of ALS as follows: "This illness robs the person of various physical abilities while preserving their personality and intellect. They are the 'same person,' but trapped in a body that allows progressively diminishing levels of physical competence, autonomy, independence of action, and social interaction." The course of ALS is one of progressive muscular weakness and loss of physical ability. Little physical pain is experienced by ALS patients, unlike cancer patients, who often face intense pain in the terminal stages of their illness. (Pain can result from muscle spasms or complications such as immobilized joints, but with good physical care it

Photo 8.3 *Because individuals with ALS retain their cognitive clarity, they may also maintain a sense of social and intellectual competence that can compensate for declining physical abilities.*

is not normally part of the disease.) Because analgesics are not needed for the control of pain, ALS patients usually maintain their cognitive clarity until the time of death.

According to Moos and Tsu (1977), the type and location of symptoms are a major component in defining the exact nature of the tasks that patients and their families must face and their requirements for adaptation. Different organs and functions have psychosocial significance that may have little relationship to biological factors related to survival. The onset of ALS has two primary forms. In one form of ALS, *progressive muscular atrophy* (wasting away), the initial symptoms are weakness and *fasciculations* (small, local, involuntary contractions of muscle fibers) in one or both hands. In its other form, *progressive bulbar palsy* (loss of the ability to control movement), the initial symptoms are difficulty in breathing, speaking, and swallowing. Regardless of the initial symptoms, ALS patients eventually experience all of these symptoms as the disease progresses. Camerino and Wilner (1986) found that ALS patients with initial bulbar symptoms and their caregivers experienced greater psychosocial stress than did patients whose initial symptoms involved weakness in the extremities. The researchers concluded that the impaired ability to communicate was a major factor in the higher psychosocial stress experienced by those with bulbar palsy. The inability to verbalize their needs and emotions combined with the relatively short course and rapid progression of the illness can result in emotional and social isolation on the part of the patient. While this study examined differences in ALS groups based on initial symptoms, the data showed that beginning symptomatology of the illness had an enduring effect on stress even after the full range of symptoms typically associated with ALS appeared. Camerino and Wilner (1986) emphasize that special effort should be made to improve the communication and social interaction ability of all ALS patients, especially those who experience early difficulty in this area.

Treatment.   The treatment options and experience of the ALS patient are in marked contrast to the individual with cancer, who often feels ambivalent about his or her treatment. While cancer treatment may be necessary in an attempt to save lives, it often causes severe discomfort and psychological stress in cancer patients. In ALS, treatment is either unavailable or discouraged because of its lack of effectiveness. In almost all cases, experimental drugs and procedures used with this disease (usually administered at ALS research centers) are benign, with few side effects and limited invasiveness. This treatment, while offering little hope of survival, can have very beneficial effects. The patient's distress may be lessened by the clinical interest shown and the general hospital care. Also, patients may derive satisfaction from the idea that they may be helping future victims of the disease (Gould, 1980).

Unfortunately, because no cure exists for ALS, many physicians consider it to be "untreatable." Gould (1980) reports that in many of his interviews with ALS patients, they report that their physicians basically instructed them to "go home and wait to die" after giving them their diagnosis without offering minimal hospital treatment or referring them for other services. Patients perceived this "there's nothing more that I can do" attitude as emotional abandonment. While physicians currently may not be able to provide a cure or abate symptoms associated with this disease, they can have a crucial role in providing emotional support and referring ALS patients to other professionals (such as occupational therapists, speech therapists, family therapists, or nutritionists) who can assist them.

The goals of treatment in ALS are to help patients cope with their disabilities and to help them be independent as long as possible. These goals can be met through a variety of community and professional services, specialized equipment, and modification of the physical environment (Sinaki, 1980). Maintaining autonomy for a person who has ALS is an ongoing concern, as new issues and challenges are constantly presented (Cassel, 1980). A variety of interventions can be crucial in assisting the ALS patient in maintaining his or her autonomy and continuing family and work roles.

A physical therapy program can keep muscle strength at the maximal level during the changing stages of the illness, prevent complications secondary to the disuse of muscles and immobilization, and maintain the patient at his or her optimal functional level for as long as possible. Moxley (1980) reported that a regular, individualized exercise program which is carefully monitored can have beneficial effects for ALS patients. Patients who survive longer than the average prognosis of 3 years show a remarkable capacity to compensate for loss of motor skill, which enables them to continue their regular daily activities for years in some cases.

Great progress has been made in the development of technologies to assist patients with ALS. Elaborate devices exist for assisting communication, eating, and other functions. Occupational therapists can help patients learn to use and apply various devices for independence in self-care.

As weakness progresses from one group of muscles to another, requirements for devices to assist the patient change and new problems arise in coping with the activities of daily living. Communication deficits present special challenges. Because the retention of mental alertness is common among patients in advanced stages of ALS, even the most severely paralyzed person has the potential to continue meaningful relationships if a method of communication can be developed. If not, the person will become increasingly isolated from family and friends and experience much frustration. Different communication aids will be appropriate at different stages of the illness. Usefulness of any apparatus will be determined by the specific disabilities of the individual and the extra time and effort required to master a complex device. Problems of increasing paralysis may limit the useful life of any device and make it impractical in terms of the time, effort, and cost involved.

Some communication devices are not specifically designed for ALS patients and therefore may not meet their specific needs (voice amplifiers that increase volume but not intelligibility, for example); others require manipulation that is difficult or impossible for an ALS patient. More appropriate devices, especially for advanced stages of the disease, include those that can be triggered by eye blinking, as this ability is always preserved in ALS.

Adaptation. A diagnosis of ALS has traditionally been equated with hopelessness. Mulder (1980) points out, however, that some patients with ALS live productive lives long after their diagnosis, continuing to work and fulfill their family roles and responsibilities. In fact, some have made significant contributions in spite of advanced ALS. Mulder feels that the ability of the ALS patient to cope with his or her disease has been largely overlooked in the medical literature. Gould (1980) agrees that little is known about the psychological aspects of ALS and attributes this to (1) the small population available for study and (2) the transient care of the patient, as ALS patients typically do not stay in active treatment for long.

Gould (1980) has described ALS patients as having a reputation for "heroic stoicism." As a group, they appear to adjust unusually well to their illness, showing resourcefulness, strong motivation, and positive attitudes. He has encountered many patients diagnosed with ALS in their prime of life, unable either to speak or write, who still manage (despite the great effort required) to communicate with the outside world.

Patients often experience considerable discouragement and dysphoria. They may feel angry or depressed because of their increasing physical limitations. Once they adjust to one change in their physical ability, another usually follows shortly thereafter. Emotionally, ALS patients experience recurring grief with each subsequent loss. At times, they may be embarrassed about their physical appearance and lack of physical abilities, have a lowered sense of self-worth as they become increasingly dependent on others, and feel guilty about the burden placed on family members. The fear of abandonment by significant others may also be present as their condition deteriorates (Leach & Kelemen, 1986).

As a defense mechanism, Gould (1980) has observed that ALS patients tend to maintain a strategy of *partial denial* throughout their illness. In this partial denial, reality is not denied as much as it is redefined. Through this process, hope is maintained—hope for more time or hope for maintaining the capacity to communicate. This is viewed by Gould as a highly adaptive and healthy response.

Denial is also seen as a defense against the threatened loss of significant relationships, which explains why patients tend to use denial in their interactions with certain individuals more than others. For example, individuals with ALS may share deeper concerns and speak more candidly about their diagnosis and prognosis with medical consultants than with family members. Also, expressions of doubt and discouragement may be verbalized to aides rather than to physicians because patients fear such comments may be viewed by their doctors as criticism and lack of confidence in their professional services. Gould (1980) feels that mental health professionals may be persons with whom patients can share deeper concerns. Family therapists can be very instrumental in establishing communication in families that have not had the opportunity to discuss their feelings about the illness and the anticipated death with each other.

Until the final stages of the illness, most individuals with ALS are treated as outpatients, continuing to live and function within their families and communities. ALS affects not only the patient, but has serious emotional, social, and financial consequences for family members. With ongoing changes in the patient's ability level, their lives require repeated adjustments. The duration and progression of ALS can severely tax the resources of the patient and family.

Extensive modification of family roles and responsibilities is often required. However, ALS patients may be able to maintain many of their normal roles longer than patients with other diseases. Because ALS patients retain their cognitive clarity, they may also be able to maintain a sense of social and intellectual competence that can compensate for the loss of strength and kinetic control. For example, a mother with ALS may be too weak to walk or prepare meals but will continue to occupy her role by planning family meals, directing the preparation of dinner, or eating with the family from her bed or chair. In contrast, by the time the mother with cancer becomes bedridden, she is often too sick to maintain household responsibilities.

As patients become increasingly disabled, family members must assume more and more responsibility for their care. No matter how much sophisticated equipment one has, personal care of the ALS patient in the later stages of the illness requires a tremendous amount of time and energy. As the disease progresses, some patients need constant attention, which, in some cases, necessitates hiring others to assist family members. At times, the demands on the caregivers can be overwhelming, and families may need additional relief. Short periods of hospital-based treatments can give overly stressed families a period of rest and recuperation during these times.

Support can be provided to families through offering information, experience, and empathy. Families need education regarding what to expect as the illness progresses. Intervention with family members involves instructing and assisting family members in techniques used in the patient's health care. A recent study (Norris, Holden, Kandal, & Stanley, 1986) reported that, under favorable conditions, effective home care can be provided for severely paralyzed ALS patients. The investigators found that motivated family members and friends could be trained in 2 to 4 weeks in the necessary physical care techniques, including tracheostomy and gastrostomy care, respirator adjustments, and deep tracheal suctioning. With appropriate intervention, family members can feel more comfortable in their caregiving role and the patient can benefit as well. Norris et al. (1986) found that home care, in contrast to hospital care, was associated with improved patient morale.

Family members need support in preserving the maximum degree of autonomy for the patient. Outside perspectives and consultation can help balance unrealistic expectations and premature invalidism (Sebring & Moglia, 1987). Family members may also need help to explore their feelings of responsibility and powerlessness and to set realistic limits for their caregiving (for example, a daughter may feel that she should drop out of college for 2 years to help her mother care for her father). Angry feelings concerning the patient's illness may need to be expressed and legitimized. If not dealt with openly, the anger may be directed toward a scapegoated family member who is healthy and "can take it." Conflicts precipitated by the illness and those that are lingering from before the illness was diagnosed can be addressed and, in some cases, resolution can be achieved before the death occurs. It is unrealistic to assume, however, that a history of conflictual relationships can be altered during a brief period in which the family is under additional stress.

Adaptation of the individual and family can be hampered throughout the duration of the disease by factors related to its low incidence in the general population. First of all, information and resources are likely to be limited. Medical centers specializing in this disease are likely to be quite distant from the patient's home, possibly in another state. Lack of experience with the disease among health care professionals may delay diagnosis and prevent the patient from receiving appropriate therapeutic interventions. Unless family members are given information from a reliable source, they may not know what to anticipate during the course of the disease. Also, ALS symptoms such as slurred speech may be mistaken by lay persons unfamiliar with the disease as indications of intoxication.

Second, support to the patient and family may be less than in the case of other diseases. Friends may withdraw from the patient and family because they are not sure what to expect when they visit and are unsure about ways to assist persons with physical disabilities and communication difficulties. Their discomfort and lack of knowledge may keep them from providing welcome support. Social interaction is increasingly valued as social activities outside the home become more and more restricted due to the patient's condition. Formal support groups are less available to those with ALS because only one or two individuals in an entire city may have the disease. Likewise, support groups for families are also difficult to find. When available, ongoing groups designed to provide support and information to ALS patients and their families have been shown to enhance coping. Although participation in such a group usually involves associating with other patients at more advanced stages of the illness and possibly experiencing the death of a group member, these factors do not deter participants from ongoing involvement (Kitto, Garry, & Roelofs, 1986). Because such groups are not available in most areas, families may choose to participate in activities sponsored by organizations that focus on other but related, more prevalent, diseases (for example, the Muscular Dystrophy Association).

Losses during Midlife

Loss of a Spouse

Loss of a spouse at midlife involves a variety of adjustments. Emotional responses, role loss, social adjustments, and financial issues must all be faced (see Figure 8.3). Unfortunately, a disproportionate amount of research has been done on widows, and few studies have focused on the unique concerns of widowers (Clark, Siviski, & Weiner, 1986).

Emotional Adjustment. Loss of a spouse involves loss of a primary relationship. Depending on the length of the marriage, many couples at midlife have shared their youths, had children together, and supported each other during many life transitions and family crises. They have been friends, companions, and sexual partners. Loss of this "significant other" at midlife can have a profound emotional impact. Loss of a husband or wife is, in fact, ranked on life event scales as one of the most stressful of all potential life changes (Holmes & Rahe, 1967).

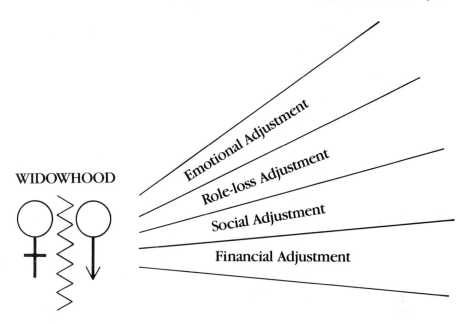

Figure 8.3 *Major Aspects of Adjustment to Widowhood*

The grief response of widows and widowers often involves a feeling of being abandoned or deserted. Widowers, in particular, often say that they feel they have lost "a part of themselves" (Glick, Weiss, & Parkes, 1974). The remaining spouse often has concerns about being left as a single parent. The thought of raising children alone can be frightening for some.

Anger and guilt may also be strong components of the grief experienced in conjugal bereavement. Anger is often present if the bereaved feels that the deceased's death was induced or hastened by failure to seek medical care, lack of compliance with the physician's advice, or continuation of self-destructive habits. Failure to prepare for the family's financial well-being in the event of death can also be a source of anger. Maddison and Raphael (1975) have reported that the widows in their study felt that others were sometimes shocked by their expressions of anger toward the deceased. These investigators indicate that the outcome of bereavement tends to be more negative when the bereaved feel they do not have a supportive environment in which to share the full range of emotions they are experiencing. Friends were considered supportive if, in addition to accepting the widow's feelings, they also allowed the bereaved to discuss her past life, her relationship with her husband, and events surrounding his death. An excessive focus by friends on the present and future while ignoring the past was seen by some recently widowed individuals as unhelpful.

Role Loss and Related Adjustments.   Widowhood is a very disorganizing experience. In addition to a personal loss, the individual often faces a major role loss as well. Reorganization of social roles is required whenever roles are removed or added, or when the relative importance of existing roles is altered. The degree of role change experienced following the death of a spouse varies widely in different societies. In modern Western societies such as the United States, the degree of role change necessitated by death of a spouse is significant (Lopata, 1972). The widowed individual often has to expand his or her role and assume family roles left by the deceased. In the context of the nuclear family, much interdependence exists among family members. With only two adults in most households, loss of one of them results in a major role loss. In many American families, a clear division of labor still exists. Husbands, for example, have traditionally assumed the role of primary wage earner while wives have taken primary responsibility for household tasks and child rearing. If gender roles were well defined in their marriage, the widowed individual will find that he or she will be assuming many unfamiliar tasks. In marriages in which roles have been jointly shared rather than assigned by gender, the transition may be smoother. However, all individuals widowed at midlife may experience role overload as they assume the sole responsibility for parenting teenage children and the financial and emotional demands associated with the parenting role.

Not only are additional roles often assumed after widowhood, but a major role is lost as well. Unless remarriage occurs, the individual is no longer a "wife" or a "husband." The loss of this role can be particularly devastating if the person has derived much of his or her life satisfaction from it. Many women, in particular, find themselves in this situation when they have devoted their adult lives to the role of wife and mother. As children grow up and leave home during the parents' middle years, the marital relationship becomes even more important. Lopata (1973) found that widows who assigned the highest priority in their lives to a wife role, rather than a parent role or an occupational role, had the most difficulty adjusting to widowhood. For a woman who has invested most of her "self" in being a wife, the death of her husband can result in a major identity crisis. Accustomed to deriving her status and identity from her husband, she must now redefine who she is in the absence of that relationship. This identity struggle can be very difficult and confusing. Women who previously have had stable images of themselves and their role in life often have these images shattered by the experience of widowhood.

For other individuals, the loss of the spouse role is not as traumatic. For some, the marital role is viewed as one among a complex of many satisfying roles in which they are involved. More and more women today are engaging in multiple roles and expanding their views of themselves as they enter nontraditional arenas. If these current trends continue, the transition to widowhood may be made somewhat easier, reducing the degree of change precipitated by the loss and increasing the continuity available to the individual.

Social Adjustment. Loneliness is frequently identified as a major problem of widows and widowers. In fact, it is often seen as their single greatest concern (Carey, 1979; Clark et al., 1986). Upon the death of a spouse, individuals lose a companion as well as a significant source of emotional support. In addition, other relationships are altered as well.

Osterweis, Solomon, and Green (1984) have referred to widowhood as a time of "social marginality" for many. A factor contributing to isolation is the couple orientation among the middle class in our society. This couple orientation often makes those who do not have a partner feel like a "fifth wheel" in social situations. Lynn Caine (1974) relates the social awkwardness of not having a marital partner in the following passage from her book *Widow*:

> I met my friends for lunch. Someone suggested going to the theatre with our husbands that evening. It was awful—I felt so alone. My husband's name came up because he would have enjoyed this play. They got embarrassed. Imagine— I had to comfort them. When we left there was some discussion about picking me up. I wanted to drive myself even though I had never gone out alone at night. Then they got into this kind of nonsense. I'll never agree to that again, and I'm not sure they want me anymore either.

Having an "available" male or female in social groups composed of primarily middle-aged couples can be very threatening during middle age when divorce rates are high. Individuals may fear that their spouses may become attracted to the unattached person in the group. Also, the presence of a widow or widower in the group reminds others of their own vulnerability and that of their spouse. Our avoidance of death in American society sometimes extends to those who have been widowed as well. These factors operate to prevent, in many cases, the widowed from remaining integrated in their former social networks.

The impact of widowhood on a woman's friendship patterns is largely determined by the number of the widow's friends who have been widowed previously. Being the first widow in one's social group is especially difficult and is more likely to be the case for younger women. If many of her friends have been widowed, a newly bereaved individual will typically find more support and understanding for her situation (Troll, Miller, & Atchley, 1979). Widowers are less likely than widows to have close, intimate friendships that could serve as a buffer against loneliness and isolation. Also, widowers are less likely to have friends who have been widowed because of the lower frequency of widowhood among males. When together as a couple, husbands often depend on their wives to maintain kinship and social ties. The widower's social contacts are therefore sharply reduced upon his wife's death (Lopata, 1980).

The younger the widow or widower, the greater the chances of remarriage. However, widowers are likely to remarry sooner than widows. For example, 50 percent of the widowers but only 18 percent of widows questioned in one survey had remarried by the first year of bereavement (Glick et al., 1974). It may be difficult for both middle-aged males and females to meet single persons, and dating can seem very awkward after many years of marriage. Sometimes adolescent or adult children may object strongly to their parent being replaced, and therefore provide little support for the surviving parent's attempts to seek adult companionship.

The tendency to idealize the deceased can also interfere with developing new relationships. Lopata (1979) used the term *husband sanctification* to refer to the tendency of bereaved widows to overly idealize their deceased husbands. (This concept can also apply to males who have been widowed.) The women in Lopata's study described their late husbands as unusually good fathers, husbands, and men in general. Some even said that the deceased had no faults. When this idealization is exaggerated, few living males will be able to compete with the perfection attributed to the widow's former husband.

Financial Adjustment.   A major aspect of adjustment that is often overlooked relates to financial issues. Dealing with financial issues at a time of great emotional pain can be overwhelming to both widows and widowers. Widows especially may have had little experience with financial matters, and the stresses in this area usually increase after losing a spouse. First of all, huge medical expenses may remain after a long, extended illness. Understanding and taking action related to insurance benefits, burial policies, and other financial and legal concerns can be frustrating and require a great deal of time and energy. The less experience one has had in this area, the more stressful it will probably be. Acquiring financial knowledge can be an important way to help women prepare for widowhood. Gaining experience in financial decision making can lower the anxieties associated with these tasks.

Financial issues pertinent to widowhood are too often ignored by middle-aged couples. Nuckols (1973) found that 71 percent of the husbands of the large sample of nonelderly widows he studied had not made out a will. Discussing these topics can be threatening because it forces them to think of the possibility of separation through death—a thought that is anxiety-provoking for many individuals. Adults at midlife usually expect that they will have many years left to live and, therefore, feel no rush to put their affairs in order. As a result, middle-aged widows often find themselves with inadequate resources, which usually necessitate a change in life-style.

Because financial status is usually lowered after death of a husband, in many cases middle-aged widows are forced to seek employment (if not already employed). Unfortunately, they are often ill-equipped to enter the labor market. Many widows of today invested themselves in the roles of wife and mother to the exclusion of a career role. In one study of 300 urban widows, Lopata (1973) found that 26 percent had never worked and 40 percent did not work during marriage, but almost half had to seek jobs after their husbands died. After 30 years or more with little or no work experience outside the home, most widows have difficulty finding suitable employment and many must settle for unskilled, low-paying positions. The financial plight of widows may be much improved in the future as increasing numbers of women obtain higher levels of education, enter professional fields, and combine occupational roles with family roles. However, women still tend to earn less than men even when they have equivalent positions or levels of training.

Interventions and Outcomes. Programs designed to support widows and help them resolve their grief have been shown to be very beneficial. Barrett (1978) found that women who participated in a therapeutic group for 7 weeks showed significantly more improvement than those widows who did not participate in an intervention program. The type of group seemed to make little difference. Women with the group experience reported higher self-esteem, greater optimism regarding their future, and a greater ability to express their grief. Other researchers have concluded that groups are beneficial for providing support, reassurance, education, and information to the bereaved (Kirschling & Akers, 1986).

Therapeutic groups can be especially helpful for widows and widowers considered to be at risk for a poor recovery. A group of Canadian researchers found that recovery after loss of a spouse was related to availability of social support, situational variables, and personality. Vachon and her colleagues (1982) found that the widows who were the most distressed 2 years after the death of their husbands had (1) fewer social supports, (2) greater health problems, (3) greater financial stress, and (4) lower emotional stability and higher anxiety. The widows in this study ranged in age from 27 to 69, with a mean age of 54 years.

The marital tie itself also appears to be an important predictor of recovery after bereavement. Parkes and Weiss (1983) have associated poor recoveries with conflictual marriages in which the survivor had very ambivalent feelings, rather than mostly loving or nonloving feelings. The bereaved spouses in this category showed less emotion immediately after the death but displayed more problems than other widows when they were interviewed approximately 1 year later. Strong feelings of anger and guilt were also linked to poor long-term outcomes.

Of those who do make a successful adjustment, some of the outcomes may be unexpected. Silverman (1982) has observed that conjugal loss can initiate a process that can lead to "dramatic growth or quiet reorientation." In Golan's (1975) view, personal growth occurs when the widows and widowers give up their self-image as being a "partnerless half" and begin to recognize and develop their individuality. Barrett (1978) found that individuals who had attended groups for widows were less predisposed to remarry than their counterparts in a control group. Perhaps these women felt more confident, as a result of the group intervention, of their ability to make it on their own without a husband.

Loss of a Former Spouse: Grief after Divorce

Several authors have compared the loss of spouse through divorce to loss due to death (Kitson, Lopata, Holmes, & Meyering, 1980; Raphael, 1983). The losses (emotional, social, financial) experienced appear to be similar in both experiences. In divorce, however, the adjustment process may be complicated by feelings of failure and rejection. Also, since the former spouse is still alive, resolution may be difficult because of the possibility (real in some instances and imagined in others) of being reunited. For some individuals, the element of choice may be a critical variable in adjustment. If both partners decide that a divorce is in their best interests, the grief associated with the ending of the spousal relationship may be minimized. However, if disagreement exists, guilt may be a predominant emotion experienced by the initiator of the divorce, while anger is keenly felt by the partner resisting the divorce. The circumstances surrounding any particular divorce must always be considered when examining the effects on the individuals involved. As high divorce rates continue, mental health professionals need to be cognizant of the grief associated with divorce and separation. Three main tasks of divorced individuals are (1) to resolve feelings related to the loss, (2) to redefine their relationship to their former spouse, and (3) to adjust to a life in which the divorced partner is no longer a significant part.

What happens if death of a former spouse occurs before grief associated with the divorce has been resolved? Unfortunately, little is known about the impact of death after divorce. Doka (1986) has noted that most grief studies have tended to focus on survivors who have had identifiable and recognized role relationships to the deceased, such as the spouse and children. Other significant relationships are often ignored. He points out that lack of a socially recognized and sanctioned relationship may in fact disenfranchise the bereaved. In other words, the person's grief may not be recognized or supported by others even though he or she is experiencing a typical grief reaction. Other groups, in addition to divorced couples, that may experience *disenfranchised grief* are cohabitating couples, homosexuals, and individuals involved in extramarital relationships. The very nature of these relationships may intensify or complicate grief while traditional sources of support are either limited or lacking.

Ex-spouses have had a significant relationship together, oftentimes for many years. This relationship combined with the divorce is likely to engender strong, but perhaps ambivalent, feelings. In some situations, one partner may still be in love with his or her former spouse; in others, the adults have established new relationships yet remain friends. While some couples are emotionally distant following their divorce and rarely interact, contact continues on some level for many individuals, especially those who have had children together. However, individuals outside of the relationship assume the bond to have been effectively ended with the divorce.

Raphael (1983) has stated that ambivalent relationships, concurrent crises, and previous losses can negatively influence the course of grief. These conditions are often found in situations in which divorce precedes death. In an exploratory study, Doka (1986) interviewed adults who had experienced a divorce which was then followed by the death of their former spouse. Most of the individuals reported experiencing a major sense of loss at the time of the divorce, despite the existence of long histories of marital conflict. Time appeared to be a necessary but not sufficient factor in resolving the divorce-related loss. In most cases, resolution can occur within a few years after the marriage is terminated. Some individuals, however, may not have resolved the loss even years later.

After the death of a former marital partner, the degree of loss experienced by the surviving ex-spouse was varied. Half of the individuals in Doka's (1986) study described the impact of the death as minimal and felt emotionally uninvolved. One woman said that she felt as if a distant relative or remote friend had died. For the remainder of the sample, strong affective responses were evident. This reaction was especially strong when the loss associated with the divorce had not been fully resolved prior to the death. One respondent described her reactions "as normal and poignant as any widow." Feelings of guilt and regret were prevalent among several of the survivors. As one woman expressed it: "I felt devastated—I never really stopped loving him. I felt guilty—guilty about the divorce, the death. Maybe he would still be alive if I hadn't thrown him out" (p. 444). The ambiguity of the ex-spouse's role made it especially difficult if he or she visited the former spouse at the hospital or attended the funeral. While these actions were often prompted by feelings of concern or obligation, these experiences were often ones of discomfort and confusion. The ex-spouse often felt uncomfortable and out of place. One woman described her visit to her former husband in the hospital in the following way: "I visited but I saw him and his new wife and his new friends and I felt very ill at ease. I didn't know what to say or how to act. They didn't either" (p. 446).

Difficulties at the funeral included questions of seating (should the ex-spouse sit beside *their* children in the section reserved for his family?) and emotional reactions to the eulogy (for example, a minister focused on the present marriage of 4 years duration without mentioning the previous marriage of 25 years). Some ex-spouses anticipated difficulties associated with the funeral and chose not to attend. By doing so, they were denied the therapeutic benefit of rituals related to death and public mourning.

Social support was also often lacking. Respondents reported that their friends did not know what to say or how to respond to their needs during bereavement. If the survivor had also remarried, it was sometimes difficult to share that grief with the new spouse. As one woman stated: "Whenever I mention Stan (the late ex-spouse) my John stiffens" (Doka, 1986, p. 446). Relationships with former in-laws may be tense and nonsupportive. In some instances, in-laws blamed the death on the ex-spouse (in-laws assumed that a heart attack was caused by the stress of the divorce, for example).

In addition to minimal social support, grieving ex-spouses may feel a lack of support in other spheres of their lives as well. Because the deceased is not considered "a family member," the ex-spouse may not be given time off from work or other special considerations, even though intense grief might be felt. Also, persons who would like to seek comfort from the church may refrain from doing so because of the absence of religious sanction of the divorce.

Loss of a Parent

Losing one's parents during one's own midlife is viewed as a normal event. In fact, it is the most common type of bereavement during the middle adult years. As individuals age, their parents age also and death is inevitable. Regardless of the normalcy of this process, the death of a parent during our adult years can affect us deeply (Myers, 1986). Moss and Moss (1983) have noted that, despite the frequency of this type of death, only a few researchers have explored the impact of parental death at midlife. Most research on the effect of parental death has focused on young children or adolescents as survivors.

The death of an older parent brings the adult child face-to-face with death and his or her own finiteness:

> The loss of parent represents the removal of a buffer against death. As long as the parent was alive the child could feel protected, since the parent by the rational order of things was expected to die first. Without this buffer, there is a strong reminder that the child is now the older generation and cannot easily deny his or her mortality. (Moss & Moss, 1983, p. 72)

Osterweis, Solomon, and Green (1984), describing this type of death, refer to it as giving the adult children a "developmental push" into their next stage of maturity, in which they feel the weight of responsibility as the oldest generation in the family. As a result, they may feel that they must assume responsibility for additional family members, take over operation of a family business, and/or begin to view themselves as the patriarch or matriarch of the extended family. This developmental transition can lead the surviving adult child to a renewed commitment to care for others, the establishment of a stronger sense of identity, and a deeper understanding of life and its cycles.

The parent for whom the adult is grieving is, in part, the parent from one's childhood years. Therefore, the loss of a parent may have many meanings for surviving adult offspring. It may mean the loss of that "perfect," unconditional love experienced during childhood, a loss of security and support, or a giving-up of the "child" within themselves since their parent is no longer present. Accepting the death means acknowledging that one's family of origin is irreplaceably lost (Moss & Moss, 1983). One study found that death of a mother was more difficult than death of a father, possibly because of the mother's earlier status as the nurturing caregiver (Horowitz et al., 1984). Rather than reflecting differences in parental relationships, the findings may simply be suggesting that death of a second parent is more difficult than the death of the first, because women typically outlive men. When the mother dies, adult children may mourn the loss of having "parents" in addition to mourning that specific loss (Osterweis, Solomon, & Green, 1984).

Parent–child relationships change over time. As children become adults, marry, and begin their own families, their family commitments and ties are shared with their spouse, their own children, their parents, and their in-laws. The elderly parent is often seen as being in a "post-parental" stage, as their "children" are mature adults themselves (Troll et al., 1979). When comparing adult responses to the death of a child, a spouse, and an older parent, Sanders (1980) found that death of a child produced the most difficult and prolonged grief. Death of an elderly parent was often anticipated because of the individual's age and/or physical condition and resulted in less severe grief reactions in general than did death of a spouse or child. As Moss and Moss (1983) have observed, adult children are some-what braced for the death of their aged parents. Also, loss of a parent at this stage in life is generally less disruptive in terms of their everyday lives and requires fewer adjustments. Survivors are usually able to meet the heavy demands of their families and jobs despite their recent loss (Sanders, 1980).

While loss of an older parent may not be as devastating as other types of loss, it has its own unique adjustments and associated issues. The parent-child relationship is one of a kind. As one adult son reflected upon the death of his mother: "This was my mother; the word 'mother' brings on a flow of feeling and past experiences and years of living together, loving together, and hating, too. . . . It was not an impersonal fact of someone having cancer and dying, but it was a basic relationship that can never be repeated, a piece of eternity, never to be the same anymore" (Moustakas, 1961, p. 19).

Some adult children may react with ambivalence to the death of an aged parent. A sense of relief may be experienced if the death occurs after a long, extended illness, and the surviving adult may feel guilty for wishing the death to occur because of the strains of caregiving. In other situations, the adult child, while grieving for the loss, may feel good about the circumstances under which the death took place (for instance, a quick death with little pain). However, few children regard their parents as having died "the right way and at the right time" (Moss & Moss, 1983).

The nature and intensity of the grief response will certainly be influenced by the history of the particular parent–child relationship. In unhealthy family systems, death of a parent may indicate an end to destructive family ties, an opportunity to be free of parent expectations, or a chance to be truly independent as an adult (Moss & Moss, 1983). In these situations, grieving can be complicated by the mixed reactions the death will bring and the symbolic significance of the death. Oftentimes, old parent–child relationship difficulties are not simply resolved by the death of the parent. This prior relationship can have an enduring influence on the individual's identity, feelings of self-worth, and patterns of relating to others, which are not easily altered. Therapeutic intervention may be needed for the individual to be able to redefine himself or herself in the absence of a strong parental figure and overcome negative familial influences.

Few close relationships are free of conflict. Even in healthy families, an adult child may harbor unresolved feelings regarding an earlier event involving his or her parent. Following a parental death, these events are part of the memory of the deceased. As the adult child matures and faces the ongoing challenges of adulthood, he or she may begin to view the situation from the parent's perspective and substitute forgiveness and understanding for blame. In some cases, this reinterpretation of a significant aspect of the parent–child relationship can be important in the resolution of grief.

Summary

Middle-aged persons typically take stock of their lives and then face the decision to recommit themselves to choices made earlier or make changes. Many individuals at midlife desire to be remembered as someone who made contributions to others in their family or to the larger society. Dying persons at this age are often less concerned about death per se and more concerned about responsibilities and obligations to others that they fear may go unmet after they die.

Differences in dying trajectories and disease symptoms, treatments, and incidence have a tremendous impact upon both the dying individual and loved ones. Heart disease, cancer, and ALS serve as examples of these differences and their effects. Common physical changes, psychological reactions, and coping mechanisms are discussed.

The loss of a spouse during middle age precipitates a variety of emotional responses. Additionally, survivors must cope with loss of a crucial role and social support and often must face changes in financial status. Currently, there are many support groups for widowed individuals that can help survivors deal with their multiple losses. Loss of a former spouse may also cause grief, even if the couple had been divorced for some time prior to the death. This is particularly true if the grief triggered by the divorce itself had not yet been resolved.

Loss of one's parents during one's own midlife is the most common type of bereavement during these years. It involves many aspects—facing one's own mortality, accepting that one's own family of origin is irreplaceably lost, and feeling the burden of responsibility for the younger generations.

⟨⟩ *Personal Account*

Cecil Neth, a seasoned journalist dying of ALS, writes about coming to terms with death. With his characteristic humor and insight, he discusses the hard facts related to the disease and his concern for the impact it will have on members of his family.

The Courage to Face Death

Cecil Neth

I believe I was, until a few months ago, fairly typical. Thoughts of dying were always thoughts of dying on my own terms.

Death would drift by when the right factors converged. Enough insurance. A secure home. All the children out of school and doing well. It would arrive on my schedule and I, an aging sage, would depart with just the proper measure of patriarchal dignity.

Things are not working out that way.

Last Nov. 5, late in the afternoon, Dr. Burk Jubelt, an associate professor of neurology at the Northwestern University Medical School, told me, as gently as anyone could, that I was dying, ready or not.

I have amyotrophic lateral sclerosis, or ALS, an inexorably terminal neurological disorder.

It is commonly known as Lou Gehrig's disease. Gehrig, an all-star New York Yankees first baseman, gave the disease his name by dying of it twice—once in fact in 1941 and by inference the following year in *Pride of the Yankees,* with an assist from Gary Cooper. ALS was a mystery then, with no known cause and no treatment. It is the same mystery now, more than a century after its identification in France as a singular and specific ailment.

The available knowledge is worth a paragraph.

ALS is a disorder of the anterior horn cells in the spinal cord. The horn cells control muscle movement. ALS wastes the skeletal muscles. Voluntary movements from the neck down are lost. So, often, is the ability to speak and swallow. The heart and other internal organs work. Patients remain in control of eye muscles and bladder and bowel functions. They can hear. The mind is active, retaining what one researcher termed "totally preserved cognitive clarity and psychic energy." The sexual appetite persists—a bit of cosmic mischief amid the ruins.

From Cecil Neth, The Courage to Face Death, *Chicago Sun-Times,* June 29, 1986, pp. 1, 64–65. Reprinted by permission.

Everything else is a statistic or statistical extrapolation. ALS generally strikes individuals past 40. The annual incidence is a fraction more than one person in each 100,000.

Each patient has a statistical probability of living from three to five years after diagnosis, but that is deceptive. It is impossible to know how long the disease was active before diagnosis. Many patients last less than a year after getting the word. A very few live more than a decade.

And that's that, except for the fact that virtually no one dies of the paralysis that is the final stage of ALS. The weakened body becomes susceptible to common ailments, such as pneumonia—and, I am beginning to suspect, the mute and wearying frustration of contending with an agile mind in a motionless body.

Sportswriter John Lardner once described a noted shortstop as being not so much big as he was small. That's me: Moderately short. More light than heavy. No room for muscles that ripple. So I was surprised when some did.

I was shaving and noticed a rhythmic movement of muscles in my shoulders and upper chest. I took inventory and found a few ripples on my calves and thighs.

The rippling—twitching, actually—is termed fasciculation. It appears in some patients and not in others, but for me it was the first overt symptom of ALS.

Diagnosis, even for the extensively skilled neurologists, is primarily visual. They also tug at the limbs and digits to gauge muscle strength. They employ electromyography—devilish tests with the impact of cold-morning jump-starts—to measure the disease's progress. But diagnosis is mostly by eyeball.

That means that doctors unfamiliar with the disease can easily miss the boat, and do. It means that individuals like me can discover a fasciculation and say, "Oops, too many martinis."

That was my response. I retreated to beer for a week, then reverted. The next symptom was difficulty opening my balcony door with the left hand. I decided I needed more exercise.

Even when my left foot began to drag occasionally and when leg and toe cramps in the night became common, I attributed the difficulties to blips in my lifestyle. I thought only marginally about seeing a doctor.

ALS is, after all, a nearly painless disease without, in most instances, an abrupt deterioration. It strikes mostly older folks like me who don't see anything terribly unusual about a stubborn body part.

And there is no immediate danger from self-deception. ALS is as untreatable in the beginning as at the end. The danger in not attending to symptoms is that they are insidious. They pile up, the muscle loss continues, and injury becomes a constant possibility. My own enlightenment began last summer.

When I returned to the *Sun-Times* in 1984 after a teaching hiatus in Colorado, Jane stayed behind with the family. She had a job she liked. The kids were in school. Our home has a nice view of the Rockies. I became a commuter husband.

That permitted me to ignore the muscular changes when alone at home in Chicago and to shrug them off amid all the activity when at home in Colorado.

Jane did urge me to see a doctor. I agreed, but procrastinated. I had passed three physicals in the past year, all with perfect numbers. I eventually visited a Chicago internist—who, I learned later, had correctly diagnosed ALS. But I blew off the neurological appointment he had needed for confirmation.

About that time I began to stumble and fall. I could give my body orders, but it didn't always obey.

I fell from a dining chair while reaching for a magazine. I had a cheap folding chaise lounge for watching television. I tumbled several times while getting up from it. I slipped going down the stairs to the street, but didn't fall. I fell once while crossing Lincoln Avenue near my apartment.

Jane arrived in Chicago last July with our 11-year-old son, Alex. She was concerned with the degree of physical change. I said I would see a doctor again after our trip east.

I fell twice in Maine, once painfully. I discovered I could no longer tie a decent fisherman's knot. The cramps, similar to good, old-fashioned charley horses, regularly woke me up.

Back in Chicago, with Jane and Alex safely in Colorado, I saw Dr. Raymond Curry of the general medicine department of the Northwestern University clinic on East Superior. He arranged a neurological examination that somehow was gummed up. While awaiting another exam, I fell down again.

The date was Oct. 2. I hit the sidewalk adjacent to Welles Park on North Lincoln. I fractured my left cheekbone in three places, spent seven hours in the Passavant emergency room, underwent surgery and connected with Dr. Jubelt, who four weeks after I left the hospital told me why I was no longer nimble.

I couldn't tell Jane with a phone call. I decided to wait until I returned to Colorado for the Thanksgiving holiday.

I needed the time to sort out my own reactions. I needed to discover whether I could be as objective as I wanted to be. I have spent a career in pursuit of objectivity and have found it elusive. But I felt that without a good grip on it, there would be a temptation to lie down and give up.

I drew a mental line in the dirt between self-interest and self-pity and practiced stepping back and forth. I believe I won.

I flew to Colorado and told Jane just before Thanksgiving. I told her I thought that if we kept a sense of the absurd, we could manage. She said that if I could do it, so could she. We are still working at it.

I told the five older children during their Christmas vacation from school. I asked them to keep a sense of humor, but not to giggle when I fell down. I haven't probed, but they seem on the surface to be doing splendidly.

Yet it hasn't been easy for Jane, or the kids, or for me.

For one thing, there is going to be a bottom line. It can't be talked or daydreamed away.

For another, I need so much care that my family has no chance to escape the inevitable.

Because I chose a profession that requires only two fingers and a word processor, I am still able to work a full day five days a week for the *Sun-Times*.

Because I have what everyone should have, compassionate bosses, I work and am writing this from my Colorado home.

The last months in Chicago were flat-out miserable. Once at work, I was fine. Writing is inherently sedentary. It was the getting to and from work that pained.

My left arm and hand weakened first, then the left leg. The most important loss, except for the instability caused by a wobbly leg, was that of grasping strength.

Dressing for work—and getting undressed at night—became time-consuming labor. Shaving, bathing and brushing my teeth required more time and some new maneuvers.

Once dressed and on the street, there was another challenge, the No. 11 CTA bus. It required a sturdiness of limb that I no longer had and that a newly acquired cane couldn't replace.

Going south in the morning, I could usually persuade the driver not to start the bus until I was seated. Going north in the evening, no way.

I gave up on buses when one driver lurched away from Grand and Michigan, leaving me flat on my back in the aisle like an upended turtle. From then on, it was a cab twice a day between Lincoln and Lawrence and 401 N. Wabash. That smarts.

Meanwhile, of course, I had given up cooking.

Then, in early February, I went west to upend my family's routine.

Our home is typical Colorado subdivision. In the basement level there is a dandy family room, a dormitory bedroom and a nice bath. When I first arrived home, I worked downstairs. Now, because the stairs are too risky for me, I work on the main level. It is taking on some of the aspects of a nursing home.

I have a walker for short trips, and a wheelchair that has become a nearly constant companion. The dining table has been moved so that there is room at one end for me to wheel to meals. For relaxation, I have an electrically powered chair that lays me down, then lifts me to a standing position. There will soon be a wheelchair ramp to the back yard. I will need a speaker phone. The list goes on. But mechanical devices are only that.

My day begins when Jane helps me out of bed, helps me into clothes and buttons and zips them. The day ends when she undoes the morning's work and points me toward the bed.

She has to serve my food and cut what needs to be cut. She has to wrestle the wheelchair into and out of the car. In a restaurant, she has to open the men's room door and stand by for the call that means she can open it again to retrieve me. She worries each time that I will fall and that she will have to rush in, devil take the hindmost.

I feel alternately frustrated and guilty because I can't manage myself. I have gone bananas twice, crying and ranting with irrational anger. Once it was because of the difficulty of chasing pieces of salad across a plate.

Jane is always concerned that she is not doing enough, or that she is not doing what she does quickly enough. She worries when she has to leave me alone. But we talk, and we are learning. Disputes end amicably. Except for one.

We continue to differ on the matter of qualifications for a home helper when the time comes to hire one.

I want her to have nice legs.

I set out with a single purpose: To explain an obscure disease and its impact on a family. I hope I have done so.

I have held back a bit. Some experiences should remain locked in the attic. But I also have saved some tag ends for last. Bear with me.

This first concerns silence and whether I can deal with it if it comes.

Not everyone with ALS loses the ability to speak, although most do. Perhaps I will be among the fortunate. But what if I am not?

There are electronic devices now and others in development that permit a form of writing. One version, I am told, operates something like a ouija board.

But such machines are awfully expensive and may be forever out of reach of my wallet.

Moreover, machines, including the small marvel I am now using, are wearying.

There will be silent down time, perhaps a lot of it. That means being seriously alone with my thoughts, master of both question and answer, but communicator of neither.

That strikes me as the ultimate intrapersonal confrontation, a monkish exercise for which few of us are prepared.

There are the eyes, which should last. There will be visual stimulation.

But there will often be nothing new to look at. That "preserved cognitive clarity" to which the researcher alluded will demand words. What then?

My recent vision of hell has been one of being pointed toward television and left there. But I won't have to watch. There will be a more challenging alternative.

This is about Alex.

One approach to dealing with certain death dictates full family involvement. The family supposedly lessens the trauma by becoming its own candid support group.

OK. I told Jane candidly, and the five older kids candidly.

But for months after the rest of the family knew, I stubbornly and wrongly insisted that Alex, the youngest, not be told. I couldn't do it, so I wanted no one else to do it.

I told him the obvious—that I have a muscle disease. He didn't pursue it. I knew he worried about me, and there were moments when I wanted to tell him the truth because I wanted to say how much I loved him and to let him hear how deeply it cuts to know I won't see him grow up.

It hurt that he trusted me implicitly and that I was deceiving him. But I couldn't face that instant when he would be fully aware and we would be together, alone, with neither of us able to reach out far enough.

So my decision was taken mostly out of cowardice, although not wholly because of it.

At 12, Alex is nine years younger than the next oldest, Marcy. Young sons of older-than-average fathers sometimes have problems, and so do the fathers.

Alex and I haven't because we like the same things. We like reading, early morning birdwatching, fishing through the evening and baseball. Last summer was his sixth year in youth baseball. He is not fast but plays center field competently and hit .400 for the season.

Like his older siblings, he is just what is wanted when the order for a new child is written.

When I thought in the past of dying on my own terms, Alex set the limits. I needed to see him out of school and grown.

Hal is grown and out of school. Shelley, Caitlin, Cara and Marcy are grown and nearly out of school.

I know them and am happy and satisfied that they have remained friends with each other and that they are intelligent and compassionate adults.

Alex will be that kind of person, too, I am sure. Yet only a freak of nature could permit me to know. There won't be one. I understand what is happening to me and how quickly.

And of all things I confront, he is the toughest because he is so young.

His knowing makes it better for him. Still, I grieve selfishly because he has to know.

I would like ALS to have a high enough profile so that more people could know it's out there, crouching. Lou Gehrig's disease rings few bells now.

Why not quietly begin referring to ALS as David Niven's disease? Or Charlie Mingus's disease? More people still watch old Niven movies or listen to Mingus jazz than peruse old Gehrig stats.

Heavyweight champion Ezzard Charles was an ALS victim, and he whipped Joe Louis. Former Sen. Jacob Javits of New York died of ALS this spring. Monsieur Nortier in the *Count of Monte Cristo* had symptoms suspiciously like those of ALS. Nortier's disease has a nice sound, a touch of class.

I will accept suggestions—even place my own sibilant name in nomination.

Roll it on the tongue. Cecil's disease. Can't you just hear the giggling in the labs?

Questions and Activities

1. What issues does Cecil Neth seem to be facing as he discusses his impending death? What attitudes, behaviors, or coping mechanisms does he display that are characteristic of the middle years of life?

2. From the information provided in the article, what personal attributes does Cecil Neth have that help him cope with his disease in its predicted course?

3. Consider the impact of the particular disease on the dying process. In general, how does ALS differ from heart disease and breast cancer in terms of the following: diagnosis, initial and later symptoms, death trajectory, treatment issues, common fears and concerns of individuals with the disease, effects on family members, need for specialized services, and availability of support?

4. Denial is often demonstrated by individuals in the initial stages of many diseases. What function does it serve? In what ways may denial be functional? Dysfunctional?

Glossary

Atrophy: A process of wasting away; a decrease in size of an organ or tissue.

Conjugal: Pertaining to a marital relationship.

Damocles Syndrome: Excessive fear of recurrence that can lead to a debilitating preoccupation with a disease.

Disenfranchised Grief: Grief that is not socially sanctioned or recognized because the survivor did not have a recognized role relationship to the deceased (such as cohabitating couples or homosexual partners).

Fasciculations: Small, local, involuntary contractions of muscle fibers.

Generativity: A deep concern for the next generation and a desire to contribute to the future by channeling one's energy and creativity in a direction that will produce lasting and worthwhile results.

Husband Sanctification: The tendency of bereaved widows to overly idealize their deceased husbands.

Motor Neuron Disease: A disease of the motor neurons, characterized by degeneration of anterior horn cells of the spinal cord, the motor cranial nerve nuclei, and the pyramidal tracks.

Palsy: Temporary or permanent loss of sensation or loss of ability to move or to control movement.

Partial Denial: Reality is redefined in order to maintain hope in the face of a life-threatening illness, such as ALS.

Prosthesis: An artificial device to replace a missing part of the body.

Stagnation: Negative resolution of Erikson's middle adulthood stage. Results in focusing inward on oneself rather than contributing to others.

Stock-taking: The questioning and life evaluation that occurs at midlife as individuals become increasingly aware of their own mortality.

*Terminology for Heart Disease, Stroke, and Related Disorders**

Aneurysm: A ballooning-out of the wall of a vein, an artery, or the heart due to weakening of the wall by disease, traumatic injury, or an abnormality present at birth.

Angina Pectoris: A condition in which the heart muscle itself doesn't receive a sufficient blood supply, resulting in pain in the chest and often in the left arm and shoulder. This is the primary symptom of ischemic heart disease.

*Source: *1987 Heart Facts*, © 1987 American Heart Association, pp. 28–31. Reproduced with permission.

Arrhythmia (or Dysrhythmia): An abnormal rhythm of the heart.

Arteriosclerosis: Commonly called "hardening of the arteries," this term includes a variety of conditions that cause the artery walls to thicken and lose elasticity.

Atherosclerosis: A form of arteriosclerosis in which the inner layers of artery walls become thick and irregular due to deposits of a fatty substance. As the interior walls of arteries become lined with layers of these deposits, the arteries become narrowed, and the flow of blood through the arteries is reduced.

Blood Pressure: The force of pressure exerted by the heart in pumping blood; the pressure of blood in the arteries.

Cardiac Arrest: When the heart stops beating.

Cardiovascular: Pertaining to the heart and blood vessels.

Cerebrovascular Accident: Also called cerebral vascular accident, apoplexy, or stroke, this describes an impeded blood supply to some part of the brain.

Congestive Heart Failure: The inability of the heart to pump out all the blood that returns to it; this condition results in the backing-up of blood in the veins that lead to the heart and sometimes in the accumulation of fluid in various parts of the body.

Cyanosis: Blueness of skin caused by insufficient oxygen in the blood.

Defibrillator: An electronic device that helps to reestablish normal contraction rhythms in a heart that is malfunctioning.

Electrocardiogram (ECG or EKG): A graphic record of electrical impulses produced by the heart.

Heart–Lung Machine: An apparatus that oxygenates and pumps blood while a person's heart is opened for surgery.

Hypertension: An unstable or persistent elevation of blood pressure above the normal range. Same as high blood pressure.

Myocardial Infarction: The damaging or death of an area of the heart muscle (myocardium) resulting from a reduced blood supply to that area.

Occluded Artery: An artery in which the flow of blood has been impaired by a blockage.

Stroke (also called Apoplexy, Cerebrovascular Accident, or Cerebral Vascular Accident): An impeded blood supply to some part of the brain.

Vascular: Pertaining to the blood vessels.

Cancer Terminology*

Benign Tumor: An abnormal growth that is not cancerous and does not spread to other areas of the body.

Biopsy: The surgical removal of a small piece of tissue for microscopic examination to determine if cancer cells are present.

Blood Count: Examination of a blood specimen in which the number of white blood cells, red blood cells, and platelets are determined.

Bone Marrow: The soft, fatty substance filling the cavities of bones. Blood cells are manufactured in bone marrow. The bone marrow is sampled in leukemia, lymphoma, multiple myeloma, and other cancers affecting blood cells to determine the diagnosis and response to treatment.

Cancer: A general term for a large group of diseases, all characterized by uncontrolled growth and spread of abnormal cells. Cancer cells are abnormal and eventually form tumors that invade and destroy surrounding tissue.

Carcinoma: A form of cancer that develops in tissues covering or linking organs of the body, such as the skin, the uterus, the lung, or the breast.

Chemotherapy: Treatment of disease, such as cancer, by drugs.

Colostomy: A surgical procedure that creates an artificial opening in the abdominal wall for elimination of body wastes from the colon. It can be either temporary or permanent.

Cyst: An abnormal sac-like structure that contains liquid or semisolid material and may be benign or malignant. Lumps in the breast are often found to be harmless cysts and not cancer.

Diagnosis: The process of identifying a disease by its characteristic signs or symptoms and through laboratory findings.

Etiology: Study of the causes of disease.

Five-Year Survival: A term commonly used as the statistical basis for successful treatment. A patient with cancer is generally considered cured after 5 or more years without recurrence of disease.

Hodgkin's Disease: A form of cancer that affects the lymph system.

Hysterectomy: The surgical removal of the uterus. May be combined with removal of the ovaries (oophorectomy).

---

*Source: *Cancer Word Book* (1985), New York: American Cancer Society. Reprinted by permission.

376 Developmental Perspectives on Dying and Grieving

Leukemia: Cancer of the blood-forming tissues (bone marrow, lymph nodes, spleen). Leukemia is characterized by the overproduction of abnormal, immature white blood cells.

Melanoma: A type of skin cancer. While most skin cancers rarely spread to other areas of the body and are easily treated and cured, melanoma can be more aggressive if not detected early.

Metastasis: The spread of cancer cells to distant areas of the body by way of the lymph system or bloodstream. The term, metastases, refers to these new cancer sites.

Neoplasm: Any new abnormal growth. Neoplasms may be benign or malignant, but the term is generally used to describe a cancer.

Oncology: The science dealing with the physical, chemical, and biological properties and features of cancer, including causes and the disease.

Palliative Treatment: Therapy that relieves symptoms, such as pain, but does not alter the course of disease. Its primary purpose is to improve the quality of life.

Prognosis: A prediction of the course of disease; the future prospects for the patient.

Prosthesis: An artificial replacement for a missing part of the body, such as a breast or limb.

Relapse: The reappearance of cancer after a disease-free period.

Remission: Complete or partial disappearance of the signs and symptoms of disease in response to treatment. The period during which a disease is under control. A remission, however, is not necessarily a cure.

Sarcoma: A form of cancer that arises in the supportive tissues, such as bone, cartilage, fat, or muscle.

Suggested Readings

Caine, L. (1974). *Widow.* New York: William Morrow.

> Lynn Caine candidly shares her experience of being widowed, her emotional responses during the period of bereavement, and the societal response to her loss. Her book gives a moving account of the realities of this type of loss at midlife.

Lear, M. W. (1980). *Heartsounds.* New York: Simon & Schuster.

> Martha Lear tells the story of her physician husband's own encounter with heart disease. The book begins at the time of Hal Lear's first heart attack and takes us through their lives until the time of his death, 2 years later.

Lynch, D., & Richards, E. (1986). *Exploding into life.* New York: Many Voices Press.

This is the story of one woman's life with, and eventual death from, breast cancer. The story is told through the patient's diary and through photographs taken by an intimate friend.

Resources

American Heart Association
7320 Greenville Avenue
Dallas, Texas 75231
(214) 373-6300

American Cancer Society, Inc.
(CanSurmount, Reach to Recovery, I Can Cope)
3340 Peachtree Road, N.E.
Atlanta, Georgia 30326
(404) 320-3333 or (800) 227-2345

Les Turner ALS Foundation
3325 West Main Street
Skokie, Illinois 60076
(312) 679-3311

References

American Cancer Society. (1987). *Cancer facts & figures—1987.* New York: American Cancer Society.

American Heart Association. (1987). *1987 Heart facts.* Dallas, TX: American Heart Association.

Anderson, B. L., & Jochimsen, P. R. (1985). Sexual functioning among breast cancer, gynecologic cancer, and healthy women. *Journal of Consulting and Clinical Psychology, 53*(1), 25–32.

Barrett, C. J. (1978). Effectiveness of widows' groups in facilitating change. *Journal of Consulting and Clinical Psychology, 46,* 20–31.

Barstow, L. F. (1982). Working with cancer patients in radiation therapy. *Health and Social Work, 7*(1), 35–40.

Block, A. R., Boyer, S. L., & Imes, C. (1984). Personal impact of myocardial infarction: A model for coping with physical disability in middle age. In M. G. Eisenberg, L. C. Sutkin, & M. A. Jansen (Eds.), *Chronic illness and disability through the life span: Effects on self and family* (pp. 209–221). New York: Springer.

Butler, R. N., & Lewis, M. I. (1982). *Aging and mental health* (3d ed.). St Louis, MO: C. V. Mosby.

Caine, L. (1974). *Widow.* New York: William Morrow.

Camerino, V. J., & Wilner, P. J. (1986). Amyotrophic lateral sclerosis and Parkinson's disease: An analysis of physical and psychosocial stresses. *Advances in Thanatology, 5*(4), 1–7.

Carey, R. G. (1979). Weathering widowhood: Problems and adjustments of the widowed during the first year. *Omega, 10,* 163–174.

Cassel, C. (1980). Patient autonomy as therapy. In D. W. Mulder (Ed.), *The diagnosis and treatment of amyotrophic lateral sclerosis* (pp. 325–332). Boston, MA: Houghton Mifflin.

Clark, P. G., Siviski, R. W., & Weiner, R. (1986). Coping strategies of widowers in the first year. *Family Relations, 35*(3), 425–430.

Daniel, A. (1986). Coronary heart disease: An overview. In M. L. Pollock & D. H. Schmidt (Eds.), *Heart disease and rehabilitation* (2d ed.)(pp. 69–83). New York: Wiley.

DeVita, V. T. (1980). *Cancer treatment.* Washington, DC: U.S. Department of Health and Human Services.

Dhooper, S. S. (1983). Family coping with the crisis of heart attack. *Social Work in Health Care, 9*(1), 15–31.

Doka, K. J. (1986). Loss upon loss: The impact of death after divorce. *Death Studies, 10*(5), 441–449.

Erikson, E. H. (1968). Generativity and ego integrity. In B. L. Neugarten (Ed.), *Middle age and aging* (pp. 85–87). Chicago: University of Chicago Press.

Gallo, F. T. (1977). Counseling the breast cancer patient and her family. *Family Therapy, 4*(3), 247–253.

Glick, I. O., Weiss, R. S., & Parkes, C. M. (1974). *The first year of bereavement.* New York: Wiley.

Golan, N. (1975). Wife to widow to woman. *Social Work, 20,* 369–374.

Gould, B. S. (1980). Psychiatric aspects. In D. W. Mulder (Ed.), *The diagnosis and treatment of amyotrophic lateral sclerosis* (pp. 157–165). Boston: Houghton Mifflin.

Hackett, T. P., & Cassem, N. H. (1979). Psychological management of the myocardial infarction patient. In C. A. Garfield (Ed.), *Stress and survival: The emotional realities of life-threatening illness* (pp. 201–212). St. Louis, MO: C. V. Mosby.

Heinrich, R. L., Schag, C. C., & Ganz, P. A. (1984). Living with cancer: The cancer inventory of problem situations. *Journal of Clinical Psychology, 40*(4), 972–980.

Holmes, T. H., & Rahe, R. H. (1967). The social readjustment rating scale. *Journal of Psychosomatic Research, 11,* 213–218.

Horne, R., & Fagan, M. (1983). *Focus group summary.* Skokie, IL: Les Turner ALS Foundation, unpublished manuscript.

Horowitz, M. J., Weiss, D. S., Kaltreider, N., Krupnick, J., Marmar, C., Wilner, N., & DeWitt, K. (1984). Reactions to the death of a parent. *Journal of Nervous and Mental Disease, 172*(7), 383–392.

Juergens, S. M., & Kurland, L. T. (1980). Epidemiology. In D. W. Mulder (Ed.), *The diagnosis and treatment of amyotrophic lateral sclerosis* (pp. 35–46). Boston: Houghton Mifflin.

Kirschling, J. M., & Akers, S. (1986, September/October). Group experience for the recently widowed: A bereavement follow-up study. *The American Journal of Hospice Care*, pp. 24–27.

Kitson, G. C., Lopata, H., Holmes, W., & Meyering, S. (1980). Divorces and widows: Similarities and differences. *American Journal of Orthopsychiatry, 50*(2), 291–301.

Kitto, J., Garry, K., & Roelofs, G. (1986). A model for information and support to amyotrophic lateral sclerosis patient. *Muscle and Nerve, 9*(5), 102.

Leach, C. F., & Kelemen, T. (1986). Reflections on suffering prompted by ALS. *Loss, grief, and care: A Journal of Professional Practice, 1*(1), 57–67.

Lear, M. W. (1980). *Heartsounds*. New York: Simon & Schuster.

Lopata, H. Z. (1972). Role changes in widowhood: A world perspective. In D. O. Cowgill & L. D. Holmes (Eds.), *Aging and modernization* (pp. 275–303). New York: Appleton-Century-Crofts.

Lopata, H. Z. (1973). *Widowhood in an American city*. Cambridge, MA: Schenkman.

Lopata, H. Z. (1979). Widowhood and husband sanctification. In L. A. Bugen (Ed.), *Death and dying: Theory/research/practice* (pp. 205–211). Dubuque, IA: William C. Brown.

Lopata, H. Z. (1980). The widowed family member. In N. Datan & N. Lohmann (Eds.), *Transitions of aging* (pp. 93–118). New York: Academic Press.

Maddison, D., & Raphael, B. (1975). Conjugal bereavement and the social network. In B. Schoenberg, I. Gerber, A. Weiner, A. H. Kutscher, D. Peretz, & A. C. Carr (Eds.), *Bereavement: Its psychosocial aspects* (pp. 26–40). New York: Columbia University Press.

Mages, N. L., & Mendelsohn, G. A. (1979). Effects on patients' lives: A personological approach. In G. C. Stone, F. Cohen, N. E. Alder, & Associates (Eds.), *Health psychology—A handbook* (pp. 255–284). San Francisco: Jossey-Bass.

Moos, R. H., & Tsu, V. D. (1977). The crisis of physical illness: An overview. In R. H. Moos (Ed.), *Coping with physical illness* (pp. 3–21). New York: Plenum Press.

Moss, M. S., & Moss, S. Z. (1983). The impact of parental death on middle aged children. *Omega, 14*(1), 65–75.

Moustakas, C. E. (1961). *Loneliness*. Englewood Cliffs, NJ: Prentice-Hall.

Moxley, R. T. (1980). The role of exercise. In D. W. Mulder (Ed.), *The diagnosis and treatment of amyotrophic lateral sclerosis* (pp. 195–213). Boston: Houghton Mifflin.

Mulder, D. W. (1980). Introduction. In D. W. Mulder (Ed.), *The diagnosis and treatment of amyotrophic lateral sclerosis* (pp. 1–6). Boston: Houghton Mifflin.

Myers, E. (1986). *When parents die: A guide for adults*. New York: Viking.

Norris, F. H., Holden, D., Kandal, K., & Stanley, E. (1986). Home nursing care by families for severely paralyzed patients. *Muscle and Nerve, 9*(5), 104.

Nuckols, R. (1973). Widows study. *JSAS Catalog of Selected Documents in Psychology, 3*, 9.

Oldenburg, B., Perkins, R. J., & Andrews, G. (1985). Controlled trial of psychological intervention in myocardial infarction. *Journal of Consulting and Clinical Psychology, 53*(6), 852–859.

Osterweis, M., Solomon, F., & Green, M. (Eds.) (1984). *Bereavement: Reactions, consequences, and care.* Washington, DC: National Academy Press.

Parkes, C. M., & Weiss, R. S. (1983). *Recovery from bereavement.* New York: Basic Books.

Pattison, E. M. (1977). *Death throughout the life cycle.* In E. M. Pattison (Ed.), *The experience of dying* (pp. 18–27). Englewood Cliffs, NJ: Prentice-Hall.

Rando, T. A. (1984). *Grief, dying, and death: Clinical interventions for caregivers.* Champaign, IL: Research Press.

Raphael, B. (1983). *The anatomy of bereavement.* New York: Basic Books.

Roberts, L. (1984). *Cancer today: Origins, prevention, and treatment.* Washington, DC: National Academy Press.

Sanders, C. M. (1980). A comparison of adult bereavement in the death of a spouse, child, and parent. *Omega, 10*(4), 303–322.

Schiamberg, L. B. (1985). *Human development* (2d ed.). New York: Macmillan.

Sebring, D.L., & Moglia, P. (1987). Amyotrophic lateral sclerosis: Psychosocial interventions for patients and their families. *Health and Social Work,* 12(2), 113–120.

Silverman, P. R. (1982). Transitions and models of intervention. *Annals of the Academy of Political and Social Science, 464*, 174–187.

Sinaki, M. (1980). Rehabilitation. In D. W. Mulder (Ed.), *The diagnosis and treatment of amyotrophic lateral sclerosis* (pp. 169–194). Boston: Houghton Mifflin.

Stephenson, J. S. (1985). *Death, grief, and mourning: Individual and social realities.* New York: Free Press.

Stolar, G. E. (1982). Coping with mastectomy: Issues for social work. *Health and Social Work,* 7(1), 26–34.

Sulman, J., & Verhaeghe, G. (1985). Myocardial infarction patients in the acute care hospital: A conceptual framework for social work intervention. *Social Work in Health Care, 11*(1), 1–20.

Troll, L., Miller, S., & Atchley, R. C. (1979). *Families in later life.* Belmont, CA: Wadsworth.

Vachon, M. L. S., Sheldon, A. R., Lancee, W. J., Lyall, W. A. L., Rogers, S., & Freeman, S. J. J. (1982). Correlates of enduring distress patterns following bereavement: Social network, life situation, and personality. *Psychological Medicine, 12*, 783–788.

9

Late Adulthood

Developmental Themes of Late Adulthood 382

Major Causes of Death among the Elderly 383

Needs of the Dying Elderly 384

Maintaining a Sense of Self 385
Participating in Decisions Regarding Their Lives 386
Being Reassured That Their Lives Still Have Value 388
Receiving Appropriate and Adequate Health Care Services 389

Quality of Life Issues 391

Suicide and the Elderly 394

The Elderly as Grievers 400

Disability and Loss 400
Widowhood: Loss of a Spouse 401
Loss of an Adult Child 406
Grandparents as Grievers 408
Loss of a Pet 410

Summary 413

Death is often associated with the later years of life. In 1987, more than 70 percent of the deaths in the United States occurred among individuals who had passed their sixty-fifth birthday (Fulton, 1987). The average life expectancy of Americans in 1985 was 74.7 years, with women on the average living approximately 8 years longer than men (American Association of Retired Persons, 1987).

Despite the high frequency of deaths occurring during the later years of life, most older individuals lead healthy, active lives. As individuals age, however, a greater likelihood exists that they will experience deteriorating health and disabling conditions. Many gerontologists (professionals who study the process of aging, or *gerontology*) have found it useful to distinguish between the "young-old" (55 to 74 age group) and the "old-old" (those 75 years of age and older), due to the large differences between these two age groups (Kart, 1985). Unfortunately, much of the research on the elderly has failed to differentiate findings based on this classification.

Developmental Themes of Late Adulthood

The prevalence of death in the later years is related to a number of developmental themes of late adulthood. Erikson (1950) has postulated *"ego integrity* versus despair" (the last of his eight stages) as the critical developmental issue for the aged. Resolving this issue positively involves acceptance of one's personal experiences. According to Erikson, the achievement of inner balance and harmony is directly linked to coming to terms with one's past and the successful resolution of earlier developmental tasks. When ego integrity predominates, it is often accompanied by the wisdom that has often been associated with the later years of life (Erikson & Erikson, 1981). Resolution of this issue in terms of despair occurs when the elderly view their lives as poorly spent and feel that it is too late to compensate for unfortunate choices made earlier in life. For these individuals, death will often come too soon.

Robert Butler (1963) has proposed that reminiscence in the elderly is part of a normal, healthy process brought about by the approach of death. He used the term *life review* to describe this process of surveying and reflecting upon one's past. During reminiscence, past experiences are spontaneously brought to consciousness for review and possible reinterpretation and reintegration. Reconsideration of the past often results in revised or expanded meanings and the resolution of old conflicts. Such reorganization of past experience may give new and significant meanings to one's life, thus helping to prepare for death.

Consistent with Butler's observation are empirical findings related to

382

shifts in intrapsychic personality dimensions as individuals age. Neugarten (1977) has reported an increase in introspection and self-reflection during the second half of life. Referred to as *interiority*, this tendency appears to be even more pronounced in late adulthood.

While other age groups may also reminisce and engage in introspection, Butler and Lewis (1982) point out that the intensity of these mental activities is most striking in the later years of life. During this period, a reassessment of life occurs as the elderly realize that their personal myth of invulnerability and immortality can no longer be maintained. As individuals advance in age, they begin to accept that they too will die.

Studies have shown the elderly to be significantly less fearful of death than younger individuals (Bengston, Cuellar, & Ragan, 1977; Kalish & Johnson, 1972; Kalish & Reynolds, 1976). Kalish (1985a) has offered three possible explanations for the diminished fear of death found among older persons. First of all, older persons may accept death more easily because they have been able to live a full lifespan. Second, the elderly may be socialized to accept their own deaths through repeated experiences with the deaths of others. The third possible explanation is that the elderly may perceive the costs of giving up life to be lower because they view their lives as having less value than the lives of younger persons.

Major Causes of Death among the Elderly

Death in old age can be the result of a number of different disease processes. The most common cause of death among individuals age 65 and over is heart disease. Cancer is the second most frequent cause of death among the elderly until the age of 85, when it assumes third position and is replaced by cerebrovascular disease (stroke). Other diseases that are responsible for a significant number of deaths in advanced old age (85 and older) are pneumonia, influenza, and atherosclerosis (the build-up of fatty deposits in the walls of arteries, which interferes with circulation) (United States Bureau of the Census, 1987).

The changes in the body that are associated with aging tend to be gradual. As one ages, systems of the body become less efficient and less well integrated. Much variability exists, however, among individuals in the rate of physical aging. The changes that occur in the body over time are cumulative. As individuals age, the progressive effects of years of poor dietary habits and sedentary life-styles can take their toll and affect the normal aging process. Also, a lifetime of exposure to cigarette smoking or polluted air can sometimes produce the first signs of health impairment in old age when systems begin to wear down. It is difficult at times to distinguish between changes associated with "normal aging" and physiological changes resulting from particular dietary and life-style practices prevalent in our culture.

Many elderly individuals function well physically in the absence of demands on their physiological systems. However, the aged body is vulnerable and becomes more so with time. It can no longer deal as effectively with physiological stress. As the effectiveness of the immune system decreases, the individual becomes more susceptible to disease, both degenerative diseases associated with aging and infectious diseases (Perlmutter & Hall, 1985).

The deterioration of the cardiovascular system in particular is associated with age. As cells age, the overall efficiency of the system is reduced. Eventually, the system wears out because cells of the heart, arteries, veins, and capillaries cannot divide and reproduce. Rates of coronary artery disease are also very high in the United States and other highly industrialized nations. With this disease, the amount of blood supplied to the heart is deficient because of blood vessel constriction. In the case of atherosclerosis, arteries are occluded (obstructed), which forces the heart to work harder to force blood through them. Strokes can occur when blood flow is restricted to the brain, usually resulting in either disability or death.

Due to advanced health-related technology, many older individuals tend to survive longer with major health problems. When in the past they would have died, modern medical interventions often prolong their lives for many years. Nursing homes and other long-term care institutions have been developed as an option of care for older individuals in these circumstances. While only 5 percent of the elderly are residents of long-term care institutions at any one time, a significant number of deaths occur there. Over 85 to 90 percent of persons who enter nursing homes do not leave them alive (Butler & Lewis, 1982). In the twentieth century, long-term care institutions are increasingly a place of final residence for a substantial number of elderly.

Needs of the Dying Elderly

The dying elderly, like other age groups, have unique needs that are linked to their particular developmental stage. Four specific needs of elderly people with life-threatening illnesses are as follows: (1) maintaining a sense of self, (2) participating in decisions regarding their lives, (3) being reassured that their lives still have value, and (4) receiving appropriate and adequate health care services.

Maintaining a Sense of Self

According to Tobin (1985), one of the primary developmental tasks of late adulthood is the maintenance and enhancement of the individual's sense of self. A stable sense of self can be critical for successfully facing the later years of life and the changes it brings (Lowenthal & Chiriboga, 1973). Preserving their identities as unique individuals is essential in order for the elderly to end their lives with a sense of integrity.

Ego integrity can be facilitated through the life review process, as the elderly reminisce about the roles they played, the relationships they had, and their own particular life circumstances. To reexamine their lives through their memories can reaffirm their identity in old age and validate who they are and have been in life. Reminiscing can also strengthen emotional bonds between individuals and promote family cohesiveness as significant aspects of family history are shared. With additional information about elderly persons from these individuals' stories of their past, professional caregivers also have the opportunity to relate to older persons as individuals rather than as "patients," "nursing home residents," or "senior citizens."

In order to aid the elderly in maintaining their sense of self, Verwoerdt (1985) has suggested adjusting the environment to the person rather than adjusting the person to the environment. For example, when individuals are placed in institutional settings a dramatic change in their behavior can oftentimes be observed. Removed from familiar surroundings and faces and placed in a strange environment, the elderly may feel that they have been separated from most of what has made their lives meaningful. Thus, they may become disoriented and withdrawn. Institutions such as nursing homes can recognize each person's individuality and uniqueness by taking individual differences into account. Ways of doing this include allowing the nursing home residents to furnish their rooms with their personal furniture, decorating their rooms with important photographs and mementos, and encouraging contact with people and events outside the nursing home. Additionally, directors of activity programs should inquire about each person's interests and past activities and incorporate them into the program instead of simply offering a standard slate of recreational events. Residents are often capable of using some of their skills and abilities in the nursing home setting. By emphasizing the remaining abilities of the elderly rather than their disabilities, their feelings of self-esteem and worth are enhanced.

Matthews (1976) has also suggested that the self-identity of the dying elderly can be maintained when they give others tangible items that are a reflection of themselves (for example, planning or participating in the distribution of important personal items to relatives or friends). Many individuals see their personally valued possessions as extensions of themselves. Giving a treasured keepsake to a loved one who will value it can be a reminder of one's enduring significance to others.

Participating in Decisions Regarding Their Lives

Dowd (1980), using the perspective of social exchange theory, has stated that the problems of the aged in twentieth-century industrial societies are primarily due to the decreasing power of the elderly. He argues that, due to practices such as retirement, the elderly are more likely to be economically and socially dependent than other adults. As a consequence, they gradually lose power as their opportunities to offer and exchange services decrease. Thus, they are placed in a position in which compliance with the wishes of others may be their only remaining option.

Older individuals have a right to maintain as much control over their lives as possible. Unfortunately, this right is often disregarded as the individual ages. When the deteriorating physical condition of older persons necessitates a change in their living situation, they are often excluded from discussions about plans for their future. Well-meaning family members and physicians may want to spare the elderly from the difficult choices to be made, when in fact they may be making the situation more painful and frightening by excluding them.

Older individuals value their independence and express concern over being dependent on their children (Troll, 1971). Many times families of the elderly are not fully aware of housing options or community support services that could allow their aged parent to retain some degree of independence while obtaining needed care. Out of concern for their parent's safety, adult children often insist that the elderly move in with them. If this situation is not feasible or fails to work, a nursing home placement is often considered.

Commenting on nursing home environments, Solomon (1982) suggests that moving into a nursing home can lead to learned helplessness. Life in this setting can threaten the elderly's remaining feelings of mastery and control as they are socialized into the nursing home routine. In this environment, many of the decisions and responsibilities of the older person (including what to eat and when to sleep) are taken away, and patients are labeled as sick and helpless regardless of their actual condition. Even the best-run institutions seem to limit the residents' option to exercise choices.

Schulz (1976) demonstrated that loss of control over aspects of their own lives contributes to feelings of depression, physical decline, and premature death in the institutionalized aged. Maizler, Solomon, and Almquist (1983) have used the term *psychogenic mortality* to refer to a syndrome in which a patient's psychological condition triggers physical reactions that lead ultimately to death. Stenback (1975) has referred to this state as "giving-up withdrawal," which he describes as the somewhat conscious decision made by a person after appraising his or her life situation and concluding that it is not worth living. Verwoerdt (1976) has added that with "giving-up" there is "a sense of complete loss of control and intactness of self. In such a state of hopelessness and helplessness, the entire homeostatic machinery may collapse" (p. 28).

Butler and Lewis (1982) have observed that much of the authoritarianism in institutions is designed to meet the needs of providers rather than the consumers of services. Patients in nursing homes and hospitals often are not aware that they have rights as well. These rights, mandated by the federal government, include (1) the right to obtain complete and current information from their physician regarding their diagnosis, treatment, and prognosis, in terms that they can understand; (2) the right to give informed consent before any procedure or treatment is begun and to be given information on alternatives; (3) the right to refuse treatment to the extent permitted by law; and (4) the right to refuse to participate in experimental research. Long-term care residents maintain their rights as citizens and can legally voice grievances and recommend changes in policies and services. Yet even if residents are aware of their rights, they may remain silent for fear of retaliation.

Intervention programs, however, do seem to be effective. When nursing home residents are allowed to take responsibility for some aspects of their lives, positive results are obtained. In studies that have introduced choices (such as having several entrees available for a meal instead of one) and responsibilities (planning social events for the facility, for example), the investigators have consistently found residents to be happier and more active as a result of the intervention (Banziger & Roush, 1983; Rodin & Langer, 1977).

Retaining a sense of control in our lives appears to be critical for positive mental health (Seligman, 1975). The elderly need avenues for the expression of their competence and remaining independence. They also need opportunities to participate in the decisions that will affect them. The extent to which they are capable of utilizing these opportunities will vary widely, depending on their current mental and physical condition.

Being Reassured That Their Lives Still Have Value

Social gerontologists have used the term *ageism* to refer to discrimination against the elderly solely on the basis of their age (Butler, 1975). In our youth-oriented society, this negative bias exists against older individuals in virtually every area of their lives. The old are viewed in stereotypical ways that do not fit the majority of individuals in the over-65 age group. Conceptions of the elderly as unproductive, dependent, and incompetent result in low social value being attached to the elderly segment of our population. These attitudes can also influence attitudes of older persons toward themselves. In addition to loss of their work role, sensory impairment, and decline of other functions, ageism can be a potent force in the lives of the elderly.

Sense of worth and value can be even more of an issue for the elderly who are terminally ill. They may fear that their social death will precede their physical death. This fear may be validated as they observe hospital or nursing home staff avoiding them and visits from family decrease. For many people, aging is associated with death, and contact with the elderly evokes fears and anxieties about both of these processes in themselves. Baltz and Turner (1977) found that effective versus ineffective nursing home aides could be differentiated on the basis of their attitudes toward illness and death. Those with negative attitudes toward illness and death were more likely to have difficulty relating to the residents and have a higher turnover rate. Baltz and Turner recommended that these attitudes be considered when employing aides, as a means of improving the quality of life in nursing homes. The fears and feelings of family members may also interfere with positive interaction with their elderly relatives. York and Calsyn (1977) have emphasized the importance of providing support and guidance to families of institutionalized elderly. Although these researchers found that most of the families in their study visited institutionalized relatives, these visits were not enjoyable in many instances, and family members reported feelings of guilt and frustration. As more opportunities for satisfactory patterns of interaction are established in institutional settings, family visits will be associated with concern and pleasure rather than obligation and guilt.

Gustafson (1972) has pointed out that messages of value can also be conveyed by actions that give the elderly a "living" rather than a "dying" status. Providing the individual with new glasses, dental work, physical therapy, and other aids and services can serve as important symbols of their social value. These acts also imply that the elderly have "a future," however short it might be.

The elderly need to feel that their lives are valued and that they are still important to other people. Conveying to the elderly a sense of their continued value and significance as human beings can greatly influence the remaining quality of their lives. If they feel more connected to life than to death, they will maintain their will to live. Professional caregivers should recognize this need as a major psychosocial issue in their treatment of the dying elderly.

Receiving Appropriate and Adequate Health Care Services

The elderly, in addition to other age groups, are entitled to receive quality health care and appropriate services. *Geriatrics* is the field of medicine that focuses on care of the elderly. Few physicians have been attracted to this area because, unfortunately, it is not seen as having the status or professional challenge of other specialties. Of even more concern is the evidence of age bias among the medical profession.

Gruber (1977) has used the terms "defeatism, negativism, and professional apathy" to describe the attitudes of physicians toward caring for the elderly. In a recent study, a random sample of private-practice physicians representing seven specialties were asked to record the amount of time they spent with each patient over several typical office days. When the results were examined by age of the patients, the investigators found that the physicians spent considerably less time with individuals in the over-65 age group than with patients in the other age groups. This finding held true for office, hospital, and nursing home visits (Kane, Solomon, Beck, Keeler, & Kane, 1981). These results are the opposite of what one would expect, because individuals over the age of 65 are the heaviest consumers of medical services in this country (Davidson & Marmor, 1980).

Miller and his associates (1976) found that only 38 percent of the medical profession said that they would put forth equal effort on the young and old. According to Sudnow (1967), older individuals in hospital wards and emergency rooms are less likely than younger people to receive a thorough medical examination should they be admitted in critical condition. Simpson (1976) made similar observations in Great Britain. These findings are alarming because of their important implications for the quality of medical care provided to the elderly. Lack of knowledge about the aging process among physicians can also lead to misdiagnoses and inadequate treatment plans in some cases. Early symptoms may be simply dismissed and attributed to "just aches and pains that go along with being old." Delay in treating many life-threatening diseases can be fatal. A national survey in 1976 revealed that only 15 of 96 medical schools in the

United States offered separate courses on aging as part of their curricula; however, 3 years later this figure had increased substantially, to 61. The current high level of interest in aging in this country may well stimulate changes in the training and subsequently the attitudes of physicians toward providing medical treatment for the aged (Kane et al., 1981).

Despite these predicted shifts in attitudes and training priorities, older individuals as a group may continue to be at risk of receiving less than adequate health care due to economic factors. Medicare, a national health insurance program designed for the elderly, was created by Congress in 1965 as part of the amendments to the Social Security law. Financed through the Social Security tax, the passage of Medicare was seen as a major breakthrough toward providing adequate health care for older Americans. It was designed to provide coverage related to episodes of acute illness. A separate program, Medicaid, provides health care for the indigent of all ages. While the Medicare program is limited in scope, its budget has continued to grow, due in large part to the increased number of aged individuals in our society. Recent measures to curb this growth have resulted in a system referred to as the *prospective-payment system* (PPS). Under this system, hospitals are paid a predetermined amount for a patient's treatment. This amount is determined by the *diagnostically related group* (DRG) in which the particular treatment is classified. If the patient's bill is less than the DRG amount, the hospital keeps the balance; if it is more, the hospital must absorb the difference (Scott, 1984). This system can potentially have a negative effect on the elderly if they are discharged from hospitals prematurely or when complicated cases are avoided by physicians for economic reasons.

In addition, Wattenberg and McGann (1984) have concluded that Medicare fails to provide many needed services. Due to these gaps in coverage (including hearing aids, dental care, preventative services, and long-term nursing home care, among other services), many older persons purchase supplemental private insurance policies. Unfortunately, many people tend to purchase policies that duplicate Medicare coverage rather than supplementing it. Oftentimes, elderly individuals do not realize the limitations of their coverage until they are in a critical health crisis. Despite the existence of Medicare, Medicaid, and private insurance options, the elderly pay 29 percent of their health bills themselves, and annual medical bills for this age group have increased over 500 percent since the mid-1960s (Fisher, 1980). As health care costs continue to soar in this country and the income of the elderly remains fixed, individuals in this age group are in jeopardy of receiving inadequate and insufficient health care services.

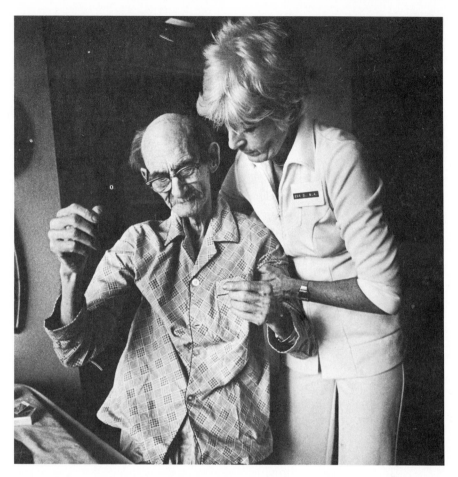

Photo 9.1 *As health care costs continue to soar, adequate and sufficient health care services for the elderly are in jeopardy.*

Quality of Life Issues

Discussions of "death with dignity" are particularly relevant to the elderly. Because of advancements in health care, nutrition, and sanitation, individuals are living longer than ever before. But, as Smith (1985) has pointed out, these added years do not guarantee quality of life for older people. The elderly are more likely today than in the past to have chronic illnesses or conditions (for example, the aftereffects of a major stroke) that leave them severely incapacitated. In the past, they would have been much more likely to die a swift, sudden death. Today, modern technology allows them to survive for what may be a period of many years. For some of these individuals, the circumstances of their existence can be considered a "living death" (Smith, 1985).

Marshall (1980) has suggested that there are circumstances under which dying is "legitimized." He proposed that death can legitimately be preferred to life when a person (1) is unable to be active, (2) is unable to be useful, (3) becomes a burden on others because of physical or social dependency, (4) loses mental abilities, or (5) has progressively deteriorating physical health and associated physical discomfort. Our own personal system of values would influence each of us in our view of the legitimacy of preferring death under any of the above circumstances. Kalish (1985b) notes that societal values have a strong influence as well. Americans value autonomy, independence, competence, activity, involvement, health, and growth. When these are not present, we interpret our quality of life as greatly diminished. Other societies with different values would not agree with the preceding criteria for having a worthwhile life. Other cultures, however, might consider death to be preferable to bringing shame to one's family, being captured in battle, or being possessed by evil spirits.

As more and more older individuals survive into their advanced years with major disabling conditions, new issues are raised in the euthanasia controversy. *Euthanasia,* often referred to as "mercy killing," literally means a quiet and peaceful death. One of the most controversial aspects of the debate surrounding it relates to passive euthanasia versus active euthanasia.

Passive euthanasia means failing to take an action that will sustain life; in other words, allowing a person to die without providing medical intervention (Smith, 1985). Opponents of passive euthanasia argue that there is danger of abuse. Diminished effort may be put toward preserving the lives of less valued members of society, and older persons may indeed be vulnerable to this type of misuse. Their lives and, therefore, the meaning of their deaths may be devalued. Religious and moral arguments are also used against passive euthanasia. Public acceptance of passive euthanasia, however, has continued to grow over the past several decades. With the current emphasis on death with dignity and the rights of the terminally ill, the right to die under certain circumstances has gained considerable support. More and more individuals have started to raise questions such as the following: Is artificially supported life really "life"? and What constitutes "quality-of-life" and who defines it? These important ethical issues will continue to be in the forefront of discussions for years to come as our society grapples with these difficult life and death dilemmas.

Active euthanasia involves a conscious action taken to cause or hasten death (Smith, 1985). One example that has received much public attention recently is the case of Roswell Gilbert, a 75-year-old Florida retiree. Gilbert shot his wife, Emily, to death in 1985 to relieve her from "further suffering and degradation." His wife of 51 years had been diagnosed as having Alzheimer's disease and painful osteoporosis. Gilbert said that he never loved his wife as much as the day he shot her. Gilbert was charged with first-degree murder and given a life sentence. As a result of much media coverage, this case and others have stimulated discussion about active euthanasia among the general public.

Ward (1980), in a study of attitudes toward active euthanasia, found that the aged were less accepting of this practice than were younger age groups. Of the older individuals in the study, those who were least satisfied with their lives were the most accepting of euthanasia. Ward suggested that some older individuals may be less supportive of euthanasia because of their lower status in society and concerns about the possibilities for *gerontocide* (the killing of older members of a society). Many may fear that euthanasia may become more prevalent because of economic factors such as the cost of nursing home care or because of the burdens that frail elderly may place on their families and society.

In contrast to the point of view of many experts, Rachels (1975) has argued that there is no moral difference between active and passive euthanasia. He points out that the process of "being allowed to die" can be relatively slow and difficult, whereas being given a lethal injection can be quick and painless. While the outcome of both is the same—death of the patient—Carson (1979) believes that outcome must be weighed against other factors such as condition of the patient, the intentions of those attending the patient, and most important, the wishes of the patient.

The condition of many older dying individuals may be such that they are unable to communicate whether they want to continue to live or be allowed to die. Unless they have prepared a living will or similar document, it is up to physicians and families to determine the best course of action (or inaction). While previous statements made by the person (for example, "I don't want to live hooked up to machines") may offer some guidance, in many cases the wishes of the person will have to be assumed. Facing the real situation can be very different than thinking in hypothetical terms.

With regard to the dilemmas of physicians in such situations, Carson (1979) has said:

> Upon entering their profession, physicians assume a dual obligation: to prolong life and to ease suffering. When these obligations conflict, as they com-

monly do near the end of a patient's life, physicians must often choose between extending a life while increasing suffering and assuaging suffering at the risk of hastening death by, for example, increasing pain medications to near lethal levels. (p. 365)

The decisions related to preserving life become more difficult as the definition of "living" becomes more complex.

Suicide and the Elderly

White elderly males are more likely to commit suicide than any other age group. Their self-inflicted deaths reach a peak between the ages of 80 and 84 (Zarit, 1980). Suicide attempts by people younger than 35 fail more often than they succeed, but after the age of 50 suicide attempts are likely to be successful. Once the person passes age 65, the attempt rarely fails (Butler & Lewis, 1982). Older individuals considering suicide are less likely than younger people to ask for help; therefore the possibilities for intervention may be fewer. At the Suicide Prevention Center in Los Angeles, only 2.6 percent of the calls they receive are from individuals over the age of 60. This figure is extremely low in view of the fact that the elderly, while comprising only 11.8 percent of the population, account for 18.8 percent of all the suicides in this country (Farberow & Moriwaki, 1975; National Center for Health Statistics, 1986). While suicide threats are relatively uncommon in this age group, they should be taken very seriously when they do occur. Some individuals may deliberately cause their deaths by indirect means such as starving themselves, refusing to take prescribed medication, or delaying medical or surgical treatment. Health care providers should give serious consideration to behaviors that might indicate self-destructive tendencies (Butler & Lewis, 1982).

Approximately 75 percent of all people who take their own lives visit a physician shortly before their suicide (Miller, 1979). Blazer (1982), however, reports that physicians are poor in predicting the imminent suicide of patients they are treating. One of the main factors associated with the risk of suicide among the elderly is depression. The individual may experience hopelessness and despair with the onset of a physical illness or after the death of a spouse. Some individuals express a sense of worthlessness as they grow older and fail to see purpose and meaning in their lives. Suicide usually does not occur during a deep depression but rather when the depression begins to lift. Two alternative explanations for this situation have been proposed. Either the older person has the energy available to commit suicide as the depression starts to subside or the decision itself to commit suicide provides what they perceive to be a solution or a way out of their emotional pain, which temporarily lifts their spirits (Butler & Lewis, 1982; Stenback, 1980).

Figure 9.1 shows that the suicide rate of elderly white males between the ages of 65 and 74 is twice that of aged black males, almost 5 times that of aged white females, and more than 17 times that of aged black females. Between the ages of 65 to 74, male suicides outnumber female suicides 5 to 1. This ratio continues to increase with age so that by age 85 it is 11 to 1. The reasons for this gender difference in suicide rates among the elderly

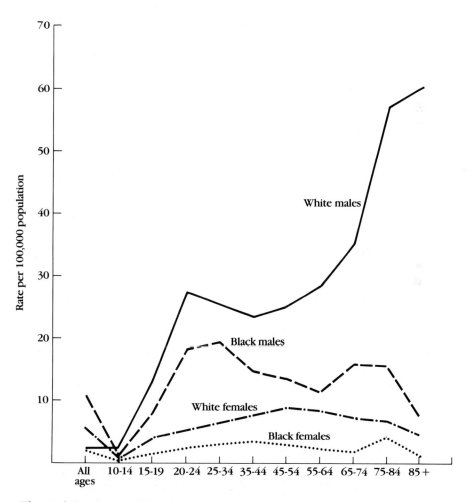

Figure 9.1   *Suicide Rates, by Sex, Race, and Age Group, 1985*

Source: United States Bureau of the Census, *Statistical Abstract of the United States: 1988* (108th edition), Washington, DC: United States Government Printing Office, 1987, Table 124.

is not clear, but researchers who study suicide have several hypotheses. It is thought that retirement may have a major role in the suicide of elderly males. Among today's older generation, retirement is a major life transition that occurs far more frequently for males than for females. Retirement not only means leaving the work force when one may still be competent and capable of working, it also involves a change of routine and lack of economic contribution to society. Following retirement, the elderly often feel unproductive and devalued. For many, it can symbolize a lowering of social status and income and the start of a decline in physical and mental health. In addition, men may have difficulty adjusting to a domestic role involving work in the home, a role with which women are familiar. Older white females and ethnic minority males and females may not be affected as much by these losses because they have had to adjust to dependency and lower status all of their lives. In contrast, white males in general are accustomed to having more power and influence and, thus, have the greatest adaptation to make after retirement (Miller, 1979; Stenback, 1980).

Retirement may also reduce the social support available to males. Miller (1978) found social isolation to be related to suicide among the elderly. In his study of 301 white male suicide victims in Arizona, he found that almost three times as many elderly who committed suicide as compared to elderly who died of natural causes had no confidant at all. In addition, he determined that the suicide group had significantly fewer visits from friends and family than did the control group. Friendships are often linked to a person's other life roles. For example, friendships often develop among coworkers. Consequently, when a man retires he also may suffer a loss of personal relationships and meaningful social contact. Having someone to confide in and express your feelings to can be critical at this stage of life, when individuals are experiencing numerous types of losses. Lack of this type of support can lead to despair and depression.

While we have some understanding of the factors leading to suicide among the elderly, McIntosh (1985) has pointed out that suicide prevention among the high-risk older population has been neglected. Because the elderly tend not to utilize formal suicide prevention services, alternative strategies need to be developed for this age group.

When discussing the prevention of suicide among the elderly, it is imperative to ask the following question: Do individuals have a right to determine the time and circumstances of their death? This question has been the focus of much debate between proponents and opponents of "rational suicide." *Rational suicide*, according to its advocates, has the following characteristics: (1) the mental processes leading to the individual's decision to commit suicide are unimpaired by psychological illness or severe emotional distress, and (2) the motivation for the decision would be understandable to the majority of the members of the person's community or social group (Siegel & Tuckel, 1984).

The libertarians' argument is a good example of a right-to-suicide position, since it has been widely accepted by advocates of rational suicide. Libertarians argue that suicide is not a crime and that everyone should have the right to end their lives. In their view, suicide must be considered an offense against God, society, or ourselves in order for it to be considered a crime. According to the libertarians, it is not an offense against God because our God-given reason offers us suicide as an alternative. With regard to society, they argue that little harm is done and, at worst, the individual is no longer a resource to society. This argument is even stronger in the case of the elderly who often have fewer major responsibilities than in earlier stages of adult life. The libertarian view also emphasizes that suicide is not an offense against oneself but may, in fact, be strongly in one's self-interest. The individual, they argue, is the best judge of what is in his or her best interest and that decision should be strictly left up to the individual (Moody, 1984).

On the other side of the debate is the sanctity-of-life argument that maintains that suicide should never be permitted under any circumstances. Human life is seen as sacred and it is to be protected at all costs. Proponents of this view believe that there are no legitimate grounds for killing oneself or others. According to this view, the choice of life is not a decision that belongs to human beings (Moody, 1984).

A second position that argues against rational suicide is the view of suicide as indicative of mental illness or emotional disturbance. Questioning the validity of the concept of rational suicide, Siegel and Tuckel (1984) point out that one of the inherent problems of the rational suicide position is the exclusive focus on thought processes when the urge to commit suicide "usually originates in the realm of feelings and emotions and not in the domain of evaluative reasoning in which the individual can objectively assess his or her situation" (p. 267). Closely linked with the philosophy of suicide prevention programs, this view is common in the mental health field. Suicide prevention is based on the premise that life is a good thing and that it is better to live than to die. Arguments in favor of suicide prevention, however, are often less applicable to the aged than to other age groups, according to Moody (1984). Consider his arguments, which follow, related to deliberate choice, future outlook, obligations to others, and disruption of the natural life cycle.

Deliberate choice: The state of mind leading to suicide may only be temporary; people often change their minds about living when their suicide attempt is interrupted and help is offered. The elderly person, however, may have selected this alternative after years of thought about the matter. This decision may reflect the fundamental values of that individual. For example, an elderly man who had been widowed for many years stated in his suicide note that he wished to depart from this world with his physical and intellectual powers intact and before he became a burden to anyone. He was choosing to end his life before he reached a stage of debilitation and dependence.

Future outlook: No matter how bad present circumstances are, a possibility exists that one's life will improve in the future. While the future is unpredictable in earlier life stages, the elderly face a limited life expectancy with the likelihood of diminished abilities and irreplaceable losses.

Obligation to others: The person attempting suicide usually has family and friends who will be affected by the death. The elderly have fewer interpersonal obligations as a result of retirement, children leaving home and moving away, and death of friends and relatives.

Disruption of the life cycle: Suicide is a premature termination that deprives the individual of a full life. Upon reaching advanced old age, individuals have lived out their natural lifespan. When an elderly person dies, we do not feel that the death is premature or unfair. Death in old age is thought of as the normal time of death.

Following his discussion of these issues, Moody (1984) raises the question: "What objection can there possibly be to an old person, who has lived a full lifespan, whose external obligations are fulfilled, who faces the prospect of infirmity and decline, and who rationally and deliberately chooses suicide as the form of death?" (p. 71).

While these traditional arguments against suicide may not be as easily applied to the elderly population, there are other arguments that have special relevance for this age group. First of all, it may be said that the high suicide rate among older individuals may be a result of living in a society that devalues its older people, is unresponsive to their needs, and strips away much of the meaning from their lives by encouraging their disengagement from major life roles (through retirement, in particular). If this is the case, then prevention efforts need to be much broader in scope and involve changing societal attitudes, policies, and practices that decrease the quality of life for older Americans. While many elderly will still have physical limitations and health concerns to cope with, these by themselves do not usually prompt individuals to end their lives. For example, suicide rates among terminal cancer patients are no higher than they are among the general population (Siegel & Tuckel, 1984).

Second, the low rate at which suicidal elderly seek psychological help may be affected by the bias of mental health workers against the elderly, rather than indicating that these older individuals do not desire any services. In discussing the prevalence of ageism in the mental health field, Butler and Lewis (1982) have stated that professionals are often pessimistic about the possibility of change among older individuals. They are also less likely to use psychotherapy as a method of treatment, and they are more likely to prescribe medication. They also may equate aging with inevitable decline and fail to recognize that late adulthood can be a very satisfying and rewarding period of one's life. Furthermore, they may consider it futile to invest effort in a person with a limited life expectancy. All of these factors contribute to fewer and oftentimes poorer quality of services for older adults.

Unless changes in society's attitudes toward the elderly are made, suicide rates among the elderly are unlikely to decrease. In fact, many researchers fear that they may increase. Although unlikely to occur, extremely high suicide rates among the elderly of the future could have far-reaching implications. According to Siegel and Tuckel (1984): "If suicide were to become an accepted norm, this might intensify pressure on these individuals to end their lives so they would not be a burden to their families or society. The option to commit suicide might easily be converted into an obligation to take their own lives" (p. 268). Presently, suicide is not seen as an acceptable means of ending one's life. Only 39 percent of Americans believe that a person has the right to end his or her own life if that individual has an incurable disease (Johnson, Fitch, Alston, & McIntosh, 1980), and fewer support the choice to end one's life in other circumstances. Indications are, however, that suicide as an alternative is becoming more acceptable among younger age groups, which will affect their attitudes in their later years of life.

In summary, the current issues of suicide in later life are historically unprecedented. First of all, never before have so many individuals lived to experience advanced old age. As stated earlier in this chapter, modern medical technology has made it possible for older individuals with severe chronic diseases and disabilities to survive. Second, due to the rapid rate of social change that has occurred in our society, many of these individuals will have lost some of the traditional roles (such as head of the family or worker) that gave meaning to their lives and made life worth living (Moody, 1984). As these trends continue, new questions regarding the right to end one's life will emerge. Quality of life issues will become more complex, and many ethical questions will need to be addressed.

The Elderly as Grievers

Disability and Loss

Oftentimes, the elderly experience grief related to the accumulation of physical changes that occur with age. Physical changes are inevitable as individuals grow older, and these changes may be perceived as states of loss or threats of loss. Body image may be altered due to such common age-related changes as reduced muscle strength, sensory loss, and changes in appearance. While the extent of these losses and the reactions to them vary considerably, over time these losses accumulate and threaten one's identity, independence, and self-esteem. For some elderly persons, these changes involve disability, chronic health problems, and restricted mobility. These losses lead the elderly and their families to make many psychological adjustments and adaptations. By recognizing and mourning each loss, individuals and their families can begin to come to terms with aging and the approach of death, thereby helping to retain the integrity of the remaining life of the elderly.

In certain age-related diseases that are not a part of normal aging, symptoms such as memory loss, personality change, and diminished intellectual capacities are experienced by the older person. Prior to the actual death of these elderly persons, many families face an *ambiguous loss.* An ambiguous loss occurs when a person is still physically present but is perceived as being psychologically absent (Boss, in press). The grief of family members cannot be resolved because the final death and loss are yet to occur. An example of this type of loss can be seen in families of victims of Alzheimer's disease. In the early stages of the disease, individuals seem forgetful and have difficulty remembering recent events (for example, that they made a phone call or turned off the stove). As the disease progresses, they become more confused and their judgment becomes increasingly impaired. Slowly, their behaviors become more and more inappropriate and their personalities appear altered. In addition, language becomes limited; Alzheimer's patients may have difficulty communicating their thoughts. Before death occurs, individuals with Alzheimer's disease move into an almost infantile state and need assistance with eating, dressing, and personal hygiene (Belsky, 1984).

In Alzheimer's disease, as with other types of *dementia,* the person that loved ones once knew is dying a little at a time, and "only fragments of familiar behaviors and personality remain as sorrowful reminders to the family of what has been lost" (Kapust, 1982, p. 79). Watching these changes can be extremely painful, and family members often feel a sense of helplessness and outrage. Toynbee (1968) has commented that an assault by nature on human dignity occurs when the death of the human spirit precedes the death of its body. Kapust (1982) has described living with dementia as "an ongoing funeral" for the healthy spouse and other family members. She points out that although the family grieves for the losses, no formalized rituals exist to help them through this time. Lezak (1978) also supports this view: "The spouse cannot mourn decently. Although he lost his mate as surely and permanently as if by death, since the familiar body remains, society neither recognizes the spouse's grief, nor provides the support and comfort that surrounds those bereaved by death."

In summary, loss associated with aging prompts many reactions among family and friends that make interactions and extended care very difficult. The family's grief is often accompanied by feelings of helplessness. The family can do nothing to alter the situation, but they must cope with the changes that occur and observe the continued deterioration until death comes.

Widowhood: Loss of a Spouse

Loss of a spouse is a common occurrence during the later years of life. Because marital partners rarely die at the same time, either a husband or a wife eventually must face the loss of this primary relationship. The remaining spouse is typically a female (see Table 9.1). In fact, between

Table 9.1
Percentage of Widowed Individuals, Classified by Sex and Age Level

Age	Men	Women
35–44 years	0.4	2.0
45–54 years	1.2	7.0
55–64 years	3.7	17.4
65–74 years	9.3	38.9
over 75 years	22.7	67.7

SOURCE: United States Bureau of the Census (1987), *Statistical Abstract of the United States,* Washington, DC: United States Government Printing Office.

the ages of 65 and 74 only 9.3 percent of males are widowed, while over a third of the females are widowed (38.9 percent). After the age of 75, 67.7 percent of elderly women are widowed, as compared with 22.7 percent of older men in this age category (U.S. Bureau of the Census, 1987). Both the longer lifespan of women and the tendency to marry men older than themselves contribute to these differential rates. Due to their lower numbers, considerably less research has been done on widowers than on widows.

Adjustment of Widows and Widowers. Carey (1979) found that males were significantly better adjusted than females 13 to 16 months following the death of a spouse. Several possible explanations were given for this finding. First of all, women in American society have been encouraged to base much of their self-identity on their marital role. Traditionally, much of a wife's status has been derived from her husband's occupation and social standing in the community. Death of a husband raises significant questions about the wife's identity and future role. The death not only signifies object loss, but role loss as well. For males, there is more continuity in these areas. Second, Carey (1979) concluded that the financial difficulties and safety concerns of widows outweigh the unique adjustments experienced by widowers, such as learning to prepare meals and perform domestic chores. Finally, remarriage is easier for older males than for older females following death of a spouse due to both the higher ratio of females in their age group and the social sanctions against women marrying men younger than themselves. While remarriage for both sexes becomes increasingly less probable with age, widowers are more likely to remarry and to do so sooner after the spouse's death than are widows (Aiken, 1985).

Ball (1977) has attributed the difficulties associated with a widow's grief to the fact that "she is generally an older person in our youth-dominated society; she is single in a couple-oriented society; she is female in a male-dominated society; she is often poor in a very affluent society" (p. 307). Most of our information on the experience of widows is based on data from older women who have had traditional marriages and assumed traditional roles. As today's younger women age and are widowed, their adjustments may be quite different. Compared with elderly women of today, they will be better educated, more identified with a work role, and have higher earning potential. They will also have more experience with financial matters.

Berardo (1970), in contrast to Carey, found that men had more difficulty than women in adjusting to the death of a spouse. According to Lopata (1980), widowers are often socially isolated and lonely after the death of their wife. In addition to being a companion, the wife often assumes the role of maintaining contact with relatives and family friends and organizing social events. Upon her death, social contact for the husband may be sharply reduced. Widowers are also less likely than widows to have a close friend other than their spouse.

As previously stated, most widowed males do remarry. For those that do not, their own risk of dying is increased during the months following the death of their spouse (Jacobs & Ostfeld, 1977). A longitudinal study showed that the mortality rate drops to normal for widowers who remarry, but it remains elevated for those who do not (Helsing, Szklo, & Comstock, 1981). The mortality rate of widowers is also higher than that of widows (Lopata, 1980). The death of a spouse clearly has profound effects on the survivor, but the toll it takes on health seems to be greater for men.

Rather than debating which gender suffers the most and has the greatest adjustment, it is more productive to understand the unique adjustments of both males and females who have been widowed. Future research is likely to help us learn more about this major life transition.

Effects of Age on Adjustment. Following the death of a spouse, older widows and widowers appear to adjust better than younger ones (Ball, 1977; Carey, 1979). Younger individuals are more likely to feel cheated by losing a spouse so early in a marriage. They are also more likely to report more illnesses and more intense and prolonged grief reactions than older individuals (Ball, 1977; Maddison & Viola, 1968). Older women in particular are likely to anticipate the death of their spouse as he advances in age. She may engage in mental rehearsals of her own potential widowhood as she watches other friends and relatives lose loved ones. Thus, she has the opportunity to make plans in the event she should survive her spouse. For the young married person, loss of a spouse is usually totally unanticipated and few if any preparations have been made for this eventuality.

Sanders (1980) found that while younger widows may initially have more difficulty adjusting to loss of a spouse, this trend is reversed after 18 months. One explanation for this shift can be found in the research of Barrett and Schneweis (1980). These investigators found that, among the sample of older widows they studied, the needs of the recently widowed were the same as the needs of those widowed years previously. They concluded that time is given too much credit as a healer for the elderly widowed. Younger individuals who are widowed, however, have often begun their process of adjustment by the second year of bereavement. Based on their findings, Barrett and Schneweis urge service providers to the elderly to abandon the myth that only the recently widowed need assistance.

Moss and Moss (1984) have argued that the elderly widow(er) after many years of marriage continues to maintain a deep attachment to the deceased. They emphasize that this emotional tie persists through the grieving period and that it is potentially a significant and permanent theme in the elderly person's life. Rather than viewing this persistent tie to the deceased as pathological and nonadaptive, Moss and Moss see it as normal, having been formed out of many years of being together. It also has the potential for enhancing the widow(er)'s identity and sense of well-being. By remaining affected by the memory of the deceased, continuity is maintained by integrating the past with the present.

The memory of the deceased spouse appears to be a welcome one for the elderly, and it can serve as an emotional resource. Many times photographs of the deceased will be used to create a sense of presence. When widow(er)s enter a nursing home and are restricted to bringing only a few personal possessions, treasured pictures of the deceased spouse or the couple together are often included. The elderly often report feeling "the caring presence" of their spouse years after the death. When making decisions, they frequently continue to consider what the deceased would think or do in a similar situation (Moss & Moss, 1984). The deceased in a sense becomes an "internal referee" influencing the widow(er)'s behavior (Bowlby & Parkes, 1970).

Moss and Moss (1984) point out that our society supports this persistent tie among the elderly widowed. Family and friends continue to recognize the elderly widow(er)'s link to the deceased spouse, as indicated by such phrases as "Mr. Hill's widow." Women tend to keep their deceased husband's name (Mrs. John Smith), and therefore they have daily reminders of their identity as the wife of their spouse. The home of the elderly also serves to support the emotional bond between the couple. Elderly widows are more likely than younger widows to continue to live in the same home after the death of their husband (Lopata, 1973). The home and neighborhood can serve as a constant reminder of the love and caring involved in the marital relationship and evoke a sense of continued care and security.

When examining the grief process and the subsequent adjustment, age appears to be a particularly salient factor. Developmental stage of the griever, length of the relationship, and length of life remaining can significantly alter the way in which one copes with a loss.

Interventions for the Widowed.   In 1968, Berardo commented that widowhood had been a neglected aspect of the family life cycle for both sociological researchers and family therapists. By the 1980s, however, interest in this life transition has resulted in a considerable amount and diversity of research (Balkwell, 1981). During the past decade, many programs and services have been developed for widows and widowers, and we are increasingly gaining information regarding the effectiveness of these interventions.

Hiltz (1975) has reported that discussion groups can be used effectively as a therapeutic technique with the widowed, but they can also be useless or detrimental under certain circumstances. She emphasizes that a well-trained discussion leader is crucial. This individual must be able to work effectively with the emotional issues associated with widowhood and be sensitive to the dynamics of the group. Selection of participants also appears to be important. If group participants cannot relate well to each other, intervention will not be effective. Hiltz states that members of each group should be fairly homogeneous in terms of age and types of concerns expressed. It is also important for the participants to recognize that it will take several months before they experience significant changes in their coping abilities.

Self-help groups offer a relatively new approach to aid for the widowed, and they have recently gained wide acceptance in the United States. Self-help groups are "composed of members who share a common condition, situation, heritage, symptom or experience. They emphasize self-reliance and generally offer a face-to-face or phone-to-phone fellowship network, available and accessible without charge. They tend to be self-supporting rather than dependent on external funding" (Lieberman & Borman, 1979, p. 2). The self-help group emphasizes the power of its members to assist one another rather than depending on the help of professionals. Through this type of group, individuals can gain a sense of community and feel that they are helping themselves as well as others.

Lund, Dimond, and Juretich (1985) found that a sizeable number (44 percent of the 61 subjects in their sample) of older adults expressed interest in participating in a bereavement self-help group. They emphasized that interest in participating in a self-help group does not necessarily imply lack of social support in the elderly person's life. A significant number of their potential participants reported having strong support networks. These individuals were coping well but they were interested in additional psychosocial benefits from this type of intervention.

The Widow-to-Widow program is another innovative approach to supporting individuals who have been widowed. Developed by Phyllis Silverman (1967, 1972) at Harvard University in the late 1960s, the structure and content of the program are based on extensive research. Silverman found that few widows sought services until several years following the death of their spouse. Even then, grief was rarely identified as the presenting problem, although delayed grief reactions were sometimes identified in the course of therapy. Silverman conceptualized widowhood as a major life transition rather than a crisis. This transition was viewed as extending over a number of years and requiring major changes in self-concept, roles, and tasks. Her program was designed for the entire population of widowed individuals, rather than only serving individuals identified as high-risk or in definite need of intervention. In the Widow-to-Widow program, widows themselves become caregivers to the recently widowed. They provide emotional support, serve as a role model, and act as a bridge person in the transition from wife to widow. Because of her own experience, a widow has special empathy for other widows. She is therefore more likely to accept the new widow's distress over an extended period of time. In addition, her services are more likely to be accepted than professional services, as there will be less stigma attached.

Vachon and her associates (1980), in a 2-year investigation of post-bereavement adaptation, studied widows who were paired with other widows for emotional support and practical assistance. They found that women receiving this intervention followed the same course of adaptation as those that did not; however, the adaptation of the intervention group was accelerated.

The results of the studies on intervention with widows have been encouraging. As new programs are introduced and evaluated, more information will be available regarding appropriate models of service delivery, precautions to take when designing and implementing programs, and critical factors to consider for timely intervention.

Loss of an Adult Child

The death of a child is traumatic for parents, regardless of the age of the child. Death of a child, when compared to other types of loss, has been shown to produce the most intense grief and the widest range of reactions (Sanders, 1980). While numerous studies have examined grief related to the death of young children, relatively few researchers have focused on the death of adult children.

As more elderly live to advanced old age, it is increasingly probable that one of their children will die before they do. A survey of a national sample of elderly found that 1 out of every 10 older persons who have had children experienced the death of at least one of them when the parent was age 60 or older (Moss, Lesher, & Moss, 1986). While their children were typically middle-aged at the time of their deaths, some could have been elderly themselves.

When a child of any age dies, the death disrupts the anticipated order of the generational cycle. Moss et al. (1986) describe this sense of untimeliness as follows: "Parents who have experienced decades of the natural rhythm of life, of the orderliness of family development, report feeling that their world view has been violated, that life has become chaotic and unpredictable. There is a profound existential sense of insecurity which emerges when the rational order of things has gone awry" (p. 213). In the case of the death of adult children, aged parents question why their lives have been spared when their offspring are taken in the prime of their lives. This is particularly true of the frail elderly who have seemingly healthy adult children with a spouse and children of their own.

For some frail elderly, well-meaning relatives may withhold specific details surrounding the death or not inform them of their child's illness or death at all in an attempt to protect them from the pain of grief. Brubaker (1985) illustrates this in the following example:

> An elderly woman may be a resident of a long-term care facility when her daughter becomes ill with cancer. The family makes the decision not to tell the mother about her daughter's illness out of concern that this will upset her. Also, the family believes that it is likely that the mother will die before the daughter. When the daughter dies, the family again decides to "spare" the mother by hiding this information. The mother frequently questions family visitors and nursing home staff about why the daughter no longer visits. She is anxious about her daughter's well being and becomes concerned that she has offended the daughter in some way. Although she is not aware of the daughter's death, she does mourn for loss of a relationship with her daughter. (pp. 39–40)

Grief resolution among elderly parents may be especially difficult for the following reasons: (1) They may have fewer options for reinvesting in other relationships following the loss; (2) they have fewer diversions such as employment to provide temporary relief from their emotional pain; (3) health problems and transportation difficulties may prevent them from participating in grief groups; (4) they may have less support for their grief because of a dwindling support network and because society is more likely to view the deceased's spouse and children as the primary grievers; (5) the elderly parents may have little involvement in rituals that can help in the resolution of grief (planning the funeral or sorting through personal items belonging to the deceased, for example), as the spouse of the deceased will usually assume this responsibility; (6) the elderly are more likely to have medication prescribed for their emotional distress, which can interfere with grief work; and (7) they may have limited strength and endurance to help them cope with the intensity of the loss (Rando, 1986).

Death of an adult child may also result in additional crises for and compound the grief of the older adult. Moss et al. (1986) suggest that the risk of institutionalization of the elderly may increase with the death of an adult child. Adult children are often caregivers for their elderly parents, and their absence may leave the elderly with little or no assistance. Thus, death of an adult child may increase the need for formal services for the surviving parent.

The bond between elderly parents and their adult children is unique. The older parent who loses a child generally views the relationship from a lifelong developmental perspective, and the image of the child spans a long time frame—from childhood through adulthood—and is tied to the survivor's history as a parent (Moss et al., 1986).The death of an adult child can threaten the elderly's sense of continuity and generativity, which is important to successful aging. If the deceased adult child was seen as "the one to carry on the family name" or was the primary person responsible for operating the family business, the elderly parent may feel that the future of their family is at stake as well (Rando, 1986).

Many parents who have lost adult children report a greater closeness among surviving members of the immediate family, including their spouses, their other adult children, their grandchildren, and their deceased child's spouse (Shanfield, Benjamin, & Swain, 1984). With increased closeness, difficult issues and concerns can be more easily resolved. Other surviving parents, however, experience distancing from family members. In addition to the loss of a son or daughter and what that loss symbolizes, the elderly parent may also lose contact with grandchildren and in-laws, especially if remarriage of the adult child's spouse occurs. Watching someone take over their deceased child's role in the family can be especially difficult for older parents, and grandparents often fear that their grandchildren will forget the deceased parent (Rando, 1986).

Grandparents as Grievers

While individuals usually become grandparents for the first time during middle age, grandparenting is a role that continues into the later years of life. Approximately 70 percent of the elderly in the United States have grandchildren (Schiamberg, 1985). Children and adolescents today are more likely to have grandparents who are living, as more older Americans are surviving to reach advanced old age. For older family members, grandchildren can symbolize a type of immortality because part of the elderly (the family name, genes, and so forth) lives on through future generations. Many grandparents have a special relationship with one or more of their grandchildren. A strong bond can be created without the friction that is often present between parents and children (Perlmutter & Hall, 1985; Wilcoxon, 1986).

Much of the literature on the death of children centers on the grief of parents and siblings. The grief of grandparents has largely been ignored by researchers. The grief they experience in relation to their fatally ill grandchild is usually threefold, as they grieve for their beloved grandchild, for their own son or daughter, and for themselves. Additionally, Hamilton (1978) has observed that grandparents are often more alone in their grief than any other group, and they often expect themselves to cope well so that they can be more of a support to their adult children and serve as a role model. The grandparent–grandchild relationship is a significant one, and it deserves greater attention than it has received from mental health professionals.

Grandparents usually experience denial upon hearing about their terminally ill grandchild's diagnosis. They report that parents have often waited several days before calling them with the news. Gyulay (1975) describes parents of terminally ill children as being surrounded by concentric circles of disbelief, with the most immediate circle being that of their own parents, the child's grandparents. Grandparents tend to show more denial and tend to be less accepting of the diagnosis than parents. Distant relatives show this to an even greater extent because of the tendency for reality distortion to increase with remoteness from the immediate family (Hamilton, 1978).

Once the denial (which may occur over an extended period of time) subsides, grandparents often feel anger and resentment. The anger can take many forms. Sometimes, grandparents feel angry toward the child's parents for not taking better care of their grandchild. They may also feel anger toward God and ask that their lives be taken and that the life of the child be spared. As the illness progresses and the child's condition worsens, grandparents often become depressed.

Grandparents experience a range of emotions in addition to their grief. While they usually want to help as much as possible, they may be unable to offer much assistance because of poor health or other factors such as lack of transportation, limited financial resources, and reduced physical capacities. This situation may be met with feelings of guilt and frustration. When they do offer advice, financial aid, and services such as babysitting, their offers are sometimes not accepted by their adult children for a variety of reasons. Some adult children may want to protect their parents from additional stress or see them as having few resources to give. Others may want to provide all the care to the young child themselves and fail to recognize the needs of grandparents to share in the caregiving.

Additional guilt may be felt by the grandparents for failing to notice the early symptoms of the illness in their grandchild. They assume that, with their greater life experience and exposure to illness, they should have detected that something was wrong and done something about it. If allowed to provide care for the child, grandparents may be frightened by some of the child's unfamiliar symptoms and medical needs. While many older people have cared for the sick and dying in their lifetimes, the context was very different in most cases. Hospitals and modern medicine may threaten their feelings of competency as caregivers at a time when it is critical for them to show how deeply they care. As a result, they may feel an intense sense of failure as both parents and grandparents. In their futile efforts to show they care, they may overindulge the child and buy anything he or she wants in an attempt to find a role for themselves (Hamilton, 1978).

In some families, conflicts erupt between the elderly and their adult children. Old issues may resurface as a result of the stress family members are currently experiencing. The parent's management of the dying child may be questioned as well. Grandparents sometimes feel that the parent is letting the child do things that may be harmful. Adult children may find they need some distance from their elderly parents as they try to cope with the harsh reality they are confronting. It may be a particularly difficult situation when genetically transmitted diseases (such as Tay-Sachs disease) are involved. Members of the older generation may be unable to acknowledge the presence of a "bad seed" in their families or they may have extreme guilt over the "inheritance" that has been passed on to their grandchild (Bozeman, Orbach, & Sutherland, 1955; Hamilton, 1978).

Before grandparents can begin to resolve their feelings and accept the death of their grandchild, they have many questions that must be answered. Groups for grieving grandparents that include medical personnel can be helpful in answering these questions and providing support (Friedman, Chodoff, Mason, & Hamburg, 1963; Hamilton, 1978).

Loss of a Pet

While the death of a pet is often the first exposure to death for many children, it may also be the final cause for grieving for some older individuals (Kalish, 1985). Recent studies have substantiated the strength of the bond between humans and animals. Not only can pets contribute to one's quality of life, but they also appear to satisfy basic human needs for love and companionship. The majority of pet owners report receiving more companionship from their animals than from neighbors and friends. In fact, many say their pets are as important to them as family members and relatives (Sussman, 1985).

Levinson (1972), in his book *Pets and Human Development,* suggests

Photo 9.2 *Beloved pets can offer companionship and reduce isolation for the widowed elderly.*

that pets can help human beings from infancy to old age solve developmental issues by providing an avenue for the expression of affection, nurturance, and competence. For the elderly, these functions of pet ownership may be especially important. As an age group experiencing a variety of losses, the elderly often experience diminished self-esteem, threatened images of self-identity, and exclusion from meaningful social participation as an accompaniment to these losses. Pets can serve special needs in the lives of the elderly by relieving loneliness, giving a sense of usefulness and purpose, and contributing to a sense of continuity and structure. Elderly pet owners continue to feel loved and valued by their animals despite changes in their appearance, income level, and physical abilities. Pets can also have symbolic value for the elderly. For example, following the death of a spouse, a family pet may be associated with feelings surrounding earlier family relationships and therefore serve as a link with the past (Ryder, 1985).

Loss of a pet tends to elicit the normal range of responses associated with grief. However, when a pet dies, others tend not to acknowledge the significance of the loss. The human–pet bond is discounted by comments such as "It was only a dog. You can get another one." For the elderly, death of a pet may mean much more than simply the loss of a valued relationship. The event can also represent the end of a era, a social and emotional void, and the beginning of the unknown. When this loss occurs to elderly who have few remaining friends and family, their reasons for living may be challenged (Cowles, 1985; Quackenbush, 1985; Shirley & Mercier, 1983).

Loss of a companion animal by the elderly is often not due to the actual death of the pet. Rather, older individuals may be forced to give up their pets if they move into senior citizen housing programs or nursing homes. Even if the elderly continue to remain in their own homes, they may develop physical problems that are incompatible with pet ownership. Reduced and fixed income may also make it difficult to provide for a pet's needs, especially during times of illness. A single pet surgery can easily cost from $200 to $400, which is almost the total monthly income of many older individuals; some treatments can be considerably higher. When the elderly are no longer able to care for their pets, younger animals are sometimes placed with a relative or friend so that the previous pet owner still has some contact with them. When older, sick animals are involved, *euthanizing* (the act of causing death painlessly so as to end suffering) the pet may be the only alternative left to the elderly pet owner. Depending on the circumstances surrounding the loss, the grief experienced by the bereaved pet owner may involve a great deal of anger and guilt (Nieburg & Fischer, 1982).

Recognizing the needs of pet owners in anticipation of or following a loss, the Veterinary Teaching Hospital at Colorado State University has established a resource program, referred to as CHANGES, for individuals dealing with grief-related issues pertaining to their pets. In addition to offering counseling and support, the staff gives guidance on how to explain the death of a pet to children, assists owners in making decisions about euthanasia, and makes appropriate referrals for those individuals needing further assistance. Involving professionals from a variety of disciplines, this program also provides instruction and training for veterinary students on the human–animal bond, the experience of grief, and their role in the grief-related situations they will encounter in the practice of their profession.

Summary

Individuals in their later years attempt to come to terms with their past through the process of life review. If a person concludes that his or her life has been well spent, ego integrity is the predominant outcome, as compared to despair.

The dying elderly have unique needs that are linked to their developmental stage. Preserving their individual identity is essential to maintaining a sense of ego integrity. Elderly patients need to participate in decisions regarding their lives and thereby retain a sense of independence and control. In a youth-oriented society, family members and health care professionals need to reassure older persons that their lives still have value because the elderly sometimes fear that they will die a "social death" prior to their actual physical death. If the elderly are to receive quality health care, professionals working with the elderly need a better understanding of the aging process, and ageism among health care professionals must be recognized and eliminated. Currently, geriatrics as a specialty is attracting few physicians at a time when the elderly population is rapidly increasing. Although medical technology contributes to increased longevity for those in the late adult years, it does not guarantee continued quality of life. Our society faces many challenges as we deal with issues related to "death with dignity" regardless of a person's age.

Depression among elderly persons is a major contributor to the relatively high suicide rate in this age group (especially for white males). These individuals may experience hopelessness and despair with the onset of physical illness, following the death of a spouse, or as a result of age-related transitions such as retirement. Unfortunately, suicide prevention with this age group has been largely neglected.

Older adults must cope with many losses. As one ages, the deaths of family members and friends occur with increased frequency. Other losses are the result of age-related role shifts and physical changes. Loss of a spouse is a common occurrence during late adulthood. Widowed individuals face many adjustments. In the past decade, programs have been developed to serve the varied needs of these survivors. As more individuals live to advanced old age, the probability increases that they will experience the death of an adult child. While the adult child may also be elderly, to lose a child at any age is very difficult for a parent. During the later years of life, loss of a child is often associated with loss of a major source of support. Although not as common as other types of loss, older adults sometimes experience the death of a grandchild. This event can be a particularly difficult one because, like the death of a child, it is not the usual course of events. Additionally, many individuals in society ignore the needs of grieving grandparents and are unaware of their unique concerns. Finally, many older persons have pets who fulfill special needs in their lives and give them a sense of usefulness and purpose. When their animal companions die, they often experience grief, but the intensity of their feelings is often not acknowledged by others.

ᓚᕱᗢ *Personal Account – #10*

In the following article, Dr. Hilfiker discusses ethical dilemmas related to the care of elderly patients with debilitating diseases. Through the frank sharing of his thoughts and feelings, he provides insight into the emotional demands on physicians as they make life and death decisions in these situations. He also raises important ethical questions related to quality health care for the elderly and emphasizes the need for guidelines to assist physicians in their decision making.

Allowing the Debilitated to Die: Facing Our Ethical Choices

David Hilfiker, M.D.

The phone wakes me; it is 3 a.m.

"Hello, Dr. Hilfiker? This is Ginger at the nursing home. Mrs. Toivonen has a fever."

Despite my tiredness my mind is immediately clear. Elsa Toivonen, 83 years old. Confined to the nursing home ever since her stroke three years ago. Bedridden. Aphasic. In an instant I remember her as she was before the stroke: her dislike and distrust of doctors and hospitals, her staunch pride and independence despite her severe scoliosis, her wry grin every time I suggested hospitalization for some problem. I remember admitting her to the hospital after her stroke, one side completely paralyzed, globally

From *New England Journal of Medicine*, 1983, Vol. 308, pp. 716–719. Copyright © 1983 Massachusetts Medical Society. Reprinted by permission.

aphasic, incontinent, and reduced to helplessness. And I remember those first few hospital days in which I aggressively treated the pneumonia that developed as a complication, giving her intravenous antibiotics despite her apparent desire to die. "Depressed," I had thought. "She'll get over it. Besides, she may recover substantially in the next few weeks." She recovered from the pneumonia, but she remained paralyzed and aphasic. For the past three years she had lain curled in her nursing-home bed, a grim reminder of the "power" of modern medicine.

"David?" Ginger's voice brings me back to my tired body.

"Oh . . . yes. Any other symptoms?" I know already that I'm going to have to go in, but I try to postpone the decision for a few minutes.

"Well, it's hard to tell. She hasn't been eating much the last few days, and she's had a little cough. Her temp started during the evening."

"What's her temperature now?"

"One hundred three point five, rectally."

"Oh . . . all right," I say reluctantly. "I'll be right in."

Ginger is waiting for me in the dark hall of the nursing home, just outside Mrs. Toivonen's room, chart in hand. "She looks pretty sick, David."

She does, indeed! Wasted away to 69 lb., decubitus ulcers on her back and hip, peering at me from behind her blank face—I'm used to all that from my monthly rounds. But this morning there is no movement of her eyes, no resistance to my examination, nothing to indicate that she is really there. There is little more to the history of Mrs. Toivonen's fever than what I gathered over the phone, and her aphasia precludes much of an interview. My examination is brief, directed pointedly toward the usual causes of fever in the elderly. (I remember the *Journal* article* suggesting that nursing home patients received less thorough attention simply because they were debilitated. It's true, of course, and I can't defend it, but I know that if Joe Blow, 47-year old schoolteacher, were in the emergency room with a fever I would be spending an hour talking with him and examining him thoroughly.) I try to assuage my guilt with the thought that I can't exhaust myself now in the middle of the night if I'm going to be able to give decent care to all the other patients, beginning at eight in the morning.

Listening to Mrs. Toivonen's chest, I hear the expected rales, and I complete the rest of the examination without finding anything else.

"I think she's got pneumonia," I say to Ginger, and we both look down at Mrs. Toivonen's withered body. I wonder to myself what I'm going to do now.

I ask Ginger to call the technician out of bed for a chest x-ray, and I write orders for a urine culture. While waiting for the x-ray, Ginger and I sit at the nurses' station, writing our respective reports.

*Brown N.K., & Thompson D.J. (1979) Nontreatment of fever in extended-care facilities. *New England Journal of Medicine*, 300, 1246–50.

Ginger looks up. "Mabel Lundberg said she hoped there wouldn't be any heroics if Mrs. Toivonen got sick again."

"I know," I answer. "She talked with me. What does she mean by 'heroics'?" Mabel is the only friend Mrs. Toivonen has, her only visitor; she probably knows better than anyone what Mrs. Toivonen would really want. But the only relative, a distant niece living in another state, has called some months ago asking that "everything possible" be done for her aunt. "Everything possible," "heroics": it all depends on the words you choose.

Essentially alone, foggy from tiredness in the middle of the night, I will make decisions that will probably mean life or death for this poor old woman. I think back to medical school and university hospital, where $1,000 worth of laboratory and x-ray studies would have been done to make sure she really did have pneumonia: several views of the chest, urine cultures, blood cultures, throat cultures, sputum for stain and culture (obtained by inducing this 69-lb, 83-year-old lady to expectorate or by transtracheal aspiration), blood counts, Mantoux test, lung scans to rule out emboli—the list is only as limited as one's imagination. And each study is "reasonable" if we really mean to be thorough; I can almost hear the residents suggesting obscure possibilities to demonstrate their erudition. (And they are not wrong, either. Can any price be put on a human life? Is it not worth anything to discover a rare, potentially fatal, but curable illness?)

There in the middle of the night I consider "doing everything possible" for Mrs. Toivonen: transfer to the hospital, intravenous lines for hydration and antibiotics, thorough laboratory and x-ray evaluation, twice-daily rounds to be sure she is recovering, more toxic antibiotics, and even transfer to our regional hospital for evaluation and care by a specialist. None of it is unreasonable, and another night I might choose just such a course. But tonight my human sympathies lie with Mrs. Toivonen and what I perceive as her desire to die. Perhaps it's because Ginger is working, and I know how impatient she is with technologic heroics; perhaps it's because I've been feeling a little depressed myself in the past few days; perhaps, I think to myself, it's because I'm tired and lazy and don't want to bother. In any event I decide against the heroics.

But I can't just do nothing, either. My training and background are too strong. I do not allow myself to be consistent and just go home. Compromising (and ultimately making a decision that makes no medical or ethical sense at all), I write orders instructing the nursing staff to administer liquid penicillin, to encourage fluid intake, and to make an appointment with my office so I can reexamine Mrs. Toivonen in 36 hours. On my way out of the dark hospital, I talk with the x-ray technician and check the x-ray film: It is questionable at best. With her severe scoliosis Mrs. Toivonen is always difficult to x-ray, and the chronic changes in her lungs make early inflammation difficult to detect. I thank the technician for the x-ray, wondering to myself why I ordered it. Driving home, I wonder why practicing medicine is so often dissatisfying; as usual it takes me an hour to get back to sleep.

In my own practice and in the physician practices I see around me, the old, chronically ill, debilitated, or mentally impaired do not receive the same level of aggressive medical evaluation and treatment as do the young, acutely ill, and mentally normal. We do not discuss this reality or debate its ethics, but the fact remains that many patients are allowed to die by the withholding of "all available care." There seems to be, however, a general denial of this reality: A widespread misperception exists that all patients receive (or at the very least should receive) the maximal possible care for any given medical problem. In medical schools, in medical literature, even in conversation between physicians it is assumed that all patients (with the possible exception of the "terminally ill" who have requested no heroics) receive the maximal possible care. Because the reality is so grossly different from the perception, there is little discussion of this extraordinarily common, deeply profound ethical problem. Practicing physicians are left to fly by the seat of their pants.

I will not pretend in this brief space to advance a particular solution to this ethical dilemma; my purpose is rather to sketch its outlines and to stimulate discussion about a situation that seems to have been ignored.

Although some persons may be tempted to dismiss the problem with the simple assertion that all patients deserve maximal care, that assertion would only heighten the relevance of this discussion, since current practice is so different from what it describes. In our nursing home, for example, there is a middle-aged woman who has been comatose for five years as a result of an accident. Although there is no meaningful chance that she will ever improve, she is certainly not "brain dead" and is supported only by routine nursing care that consists of tube feedings, regular turnings, urinary catheters, and good hygiene; she is on no respirator or other machine. If her physician were somehow to discover on routine examination that she was in imminent danger of a myocardial infarction, few persons would, I think, recommend full-scale evaluation for possible coronary-artery bypass surgery. The decision not to offer her maximal care might be justified in any one of several ways, but most often the question would simply not arise. It would simply seem obvious to the practicing physician that this particular patient should not receive such heroic treatment.

I think few would quarrel with the decision to withhold such evaluation and treatment. But once we have allowed that some persons should not receive some treatments that might prolong their lives, we must then begin the thorny ethical process of drawing lines: which patients, which treatments? Once we have allowed that our comatose patient should not receive bypass surgery, we must decide what kinds of treatment we should be prepared to offer her: aneurysmectomy for a dissecting aortic aneurysm? appendectomy? hospitalization for pneumonia? intravenous infusions for fluid loss with diarrhea? oral antibiotics for a bladder infection? tube feedings? routine nursing care? Each person may draw the line differently, but once it is accepted that heroic treatment will not be offered, we must decide what we will then do.

Because of our expertise, we physicians ordinarily have the responsibility and the power to make such decisions. As good physicians we must of course try to include the patient and the family in such important deliberations, but our ability to phrase options, stress information, and present our own advice gives us tremendous power. This power becomes for all practical purposes absolute when we are dealing with incapacitated patients, especially if family members are far away or otherwise not closely involved.

One would expect, then, that we would have special training or at least some resources to which we might turn when such common problems arise. But our collective denial that we make such decisions has left us without resources. There has certainly been a great deal published about the termination of life-support measures for persons with brain death, but that problem is both simple and uncommon compared with the one we are discussing; the solutions there are primarily technical rather than ethical. There has also been much discussion about the care of the terminally ill (cancer) patient, but that situation is also much more clear-cut than the usual one of the debilitated elderly patient, because the cancer patient and his or her physician can know that the illness is terminal within a certain period of time. We physicians therefore reassure ourselves that we are not so much "withholding available treatment" as "allowing the person to die with dignity." (The professional ethicist may see little distinction between the terminally ill cancer patient and Mrs. Toivonen, but the certainty of the former's death within a very short time compared with the possibility of the latter's living for years creates an important distinction for the practicing physician.) Also, the relatively rapid course of terminal cancer allows the patient to know, while still completely lucid, that the illness is terminal; the patient can thus participate fully in the discussion of the matter before decisions are made. Although there has been much energy devoted to the ethics of treating the brain-dead and the terminally ill patient, the much more common situation of the elderly, debilitated patient who contracts an acute illness seems to have been left relatively unaddressed.

Ethicists have advanced two seemingly helpful suggestions. Some have suggested that the practicing physician sit down with his patients to discuss, in advance, what the patient might like done under certain circumstances. Others have suggested a "living will," that would direct the physician to a particular course of action if the patient became disabled. Although these are helpful ideas, they suffer from some serious problems.

First of all, few in our society want to think seriously about their aging and death. Apart from offhand comments ("I hope they don't let me linger on like that!''), most persons do not wish to confront the eventual loss of their powers. Few are likely to make out a living will or pay their physician for the privilege of discussing the possibility of their own incapacity.

Secondly, in our mobile society a patient who has discussed such issues with his personal physician will probably be attended by someone else when these issues arise.

Furthermore, persons' ideas about the quality of life change drastically as they age, especially in the last years of their lives. The 21-year-old who wants to be shot rather than suffer the imagined ignominy of a nursing home is only too grateful to accept the nursing-home bed and warm meals when he turns 85. A living will or a frank conversation with one's physician even at age 55 would rarely reflect what one's wishes would be at age 70.

Finally, and most important, it is simply too difficult to define all the varieties of illness, suffering, prognosis, and treatment with sufficient precision for the definitions to be of much help in the actual situation. A physician may know, for instance, that the patient does not want to be "kept alive" "unnecessarily" "if I'm a vegetable" and there is "no hope of improvement." The real-life situation is, unfortunately, much more complex. What constitutes keeping a person alive? Is it giving him a warm room and regular meals rather than allowing him to lie at home paralyzed and with no heat? Is it giving him an intravenous infusion? Routine antibiotics? And what quality of life constitutes "being a vegetable"? Furthermore, in real life there is rarely any certainty about prognosis. Improvement may be unlikely, but it is often possible. So, even in the best case, in which a self-aware person had talked with his physician or made out a recent living will, the complexities of the actual situation would probably render those efforts of little practical use to the physician. And because of his debilities or the seriousness of his acute illness, the patient himself is rarely fully available to the physician at the needed moment.

If the professional ethicists have not yet provided much help in this most difficult situation, the law has been positively confusing. As I understand it, many recent court decisions have suggested that the courts must authorize the withholding of treatment in any particular case. Although I would not argue with the attempt to relieve the physician of this responsibility, the facts are that these decisions usually need to be made quickly (within hours or days), repeatedly (options with respect to quality of life, prognosis, and treatment may vary from day to day), and with a considerable degree of medical expertise. In my opinion, it is ridiculous to believe that the courts could (even if we thought they should) decide such matters promptly. It will be interesting to see how the courts finally settle this issue, but I expect that physicians will get little help, regardless.

In fact, then, the primary-care physician faces this complex dilemma alone. Because we have ignored the frequency with which such situations arise and their tremendous ethical importance, we force the physician into making profound ethical choices unprepared. He or she may try to share the decision with the family (who may know how the patient would decide in such a situation), but most often the family has even less idea of what to do than the physician on whom they rely for guidance. (And even when someone in the family does have a definite idea of what should be done, the physician needs to judge the ethics of that decision anyway, because our society does not indiscriminately assign the right to refuse treatment to any relative who might think he knows what is best.) For better or for worse, the decision returns to the physician.

What does one do, then? We have developed no rational way to decide what treatment to give and what to withhold once it has been decided to withhold "heroics." Perhaps my own most frequent response (and I do not admit this easily) is not to make a conscious decision at all. Aware that Mrs. Toivonen has a fever, I may decide to see her at the end of office hours and then, in the rush of late-afternoon appointments, "forget" to drop by the nursing home until the next morning, by which time she will be either better or so much worse that "it won't help much to put her in the hospital, anyway," Or if I do examine her promptly, my examination will not be so thorough as it might be, and I will decide that the fever is "only a virus" when I really haven't excluded all the likely possibilities. Or, as I did this time, I will give some treatment that will probably help but that is not as aggressive as it could be.

The problem is simply too difficult for me as a single human being to face in a conscious way. How do I consciously decide to let this person die when everything in my being says that life has the ultimate value? How can I make a decision about the quality of this life? How can I know what the patient would want? Yet, on the other hand, how can I inflict the pain of aggressive treatment, and the suffering of further living, and spend the scarce resources of time and money on this person who is so obviously "trying" to die? And so, all too often, I don't make a conscious decision at all. I simply act, do something, make a decision without really considering the meaning of what I do, for the real meaning is too painful.

At other times I do my best to make a conscious, rational decision, but this is little better. Since I am operating in a vacuum and have no reliable criteria on which to base a decision, my choice is ultimately guided by my feelings, prejudices, and mood more than by my reason.

Physicians have been making these decisions routinely, of course, ever since we acquired the power actually to influence the course of disease. As far as I can determine, however, we have not yet admitted to ourselves the awesomeness of our situation. We have been forced into the role of God, yet we hardly seem to have recognized it. For my part, the underlying irrationality of my decisions has gnawed at me; the life-and-death importance of my actions has kept me awake at night; the guilt and depression of never really knowing whether I have acted properly have been overwhelming. I would suggest that it is time we publicly examined our role in these situations, offered each other some guidelines, and came to some consensus about our responsibility. There is clearly no way to avoid these awesome decisions; let us at least come to them better prepared and with a clearer understanding of what we do.

Questions and Activities

1. Who has the right to define "quality of life"? Individuals and their families? Physicians? The legal system? Ethicists?

2. What is *your* definition of quality of life? If you had been in Dr. Hilfiker's position, would you have responded differently to Mrs. Toivonen's situation? What issues must be considered in this type of situation?

3. If you agree that some persons should not receive particular treatments that will extend their lives, at what point do you draw the line? Which patients? Which treatments? Is there a difference between prolonging life and prolonging death?

4. Who should have priority in attaining access to limited resources such as renal dialysis or organ transplants? Should age of the patient be a factor in these decisions? If so, why?

5. Interview several elderly persons and inquire about their attitudes toward "quality of life" issues. Do they appear to have strong opinions about how they want to spend their final days? How are the issues different for them than they were for their parents a generation ago? How has the context of death changed?

6. From the information you are given about Mrs. Toivonen, identify a variety of losses that she had experienced. As a member of the nursing home staff, what could you do to enhance her quality of life given her current condition?

Glossary

Active Euthanasia: A conscious action taken to cause or hasten death, with the intent of being merciful to the individual.

Ageism: Discrimination against the elderly solely on the basis of their age.

Aphasia: Absence or impairment of the ability to communicate through speech, writing, or signs, due to dysfunction of brain centers.

Ambiguous Loss: A loss that is not clear such as when a person is physically present but is perceived as being psychologically absent (for example, victims of Alzheimer's disease).

Dementia: Progressive mental deterioration due to organic disease of the brain; typically, impairment of memory is one of the earliest signs.

Despair: The negative resolution of Erikson's late adulthood stage. The elderly view their lives as poorly spent and feel that it is too late to compensate for unfortunate choices made earlier in life.

Diagnostically Related Group (DRG): Diagnostic group in which a particular treatment is classified in order to determine the amount of a payment under a prospective-payment system.

Ego Integrity: The positive resolution of Erikson's late adulthood stage. It results in the positive acceptance of one's own life experiences.

Euthanasia: Literally, a quiet and peaceful death; often referred to as "mercy killing."

Euthanizing: The act of causing death painlessly so as to end suffering.

Geriatrics: The field of medicine that focuses on the care of the elderly.

Gerontocide: The killing of older members of a society.

Gerontology: The study of the psychological, sociological, and biological aspects of the aging process.

Interiority: The introspection and self-reflection observed among the elderly.

Life Review: The process of surveying and reflecting upon one's past through reminiscence.

Passive Euthanasia: Failing to take an action that will sustain life; allowing a person to die without providing medical intervention.

Prospective-payment System (PPS): A system by which a predetermined amount is paid by Medicare for a patient's medical treatment.

Psychogenic Mortality: A syndrome in which a person's psychological condition triggers physical effects that lead ultimately to death.

Rational Suicide: A much debated concept related to an individual's conscious and presumably rational decision to end his or her life.

Self-Help Groups: Intervention groups composed of members with similar experiences which emphasize mutual support.

Suggested Readings

Callahan, D. (1987). Terminating treatment: Age as a standard. *Hastings Center Report, 17*(5), 21–25.

The author discusses what he terms two competing fears related to elderly persons who are dying: abandonment and lack of care on the one hand, and excessive treatment and painful extension of their lives on the other. When faced with difficulty regarding the ability to make an accurate prognosis about the person's ability to live a satisfying life after a particular treatment, the author advocates the use of age as a guiding criterion.

Coleman, P. G. (1986). *Ageing and the reminiscence process: Social and clinical implications.* Chichester, England: Wiley.

Coleman reports on data he obtained over the course of 15 years on the function of reminiscence in old age. He uses case studies to illustrate the various forms that reminiscence takes, the circumstances in which it is elicited, and the differences among individuals in their use of memories from the past.

Jury, M., & Jury, D. (1978). *Gramp.* New York: Penguin Books.

Photographers Mark and Dan Jury document with sensitivity and compassion the slow death of their grandfather. Through the eyes of Frank Tugend's grandsons, the reader witnesses the strengthening of bonds as family members share in caregiving at home and allow a loved one to die with dignity.

Mace, N. L., & Rabins, P. V. (1981). *The 36-hour day.* Baltimore: The Johns Hopkins University Press.

The authors have written a very practical and detailed reference book to assist family members of patients with dementia. Medical problems, mood disturbance, memory loss, and daily care issues are discussed and useful suggestions are provided. Also addressed are the effects of caregiving on the caregiver.

Resources

Alzheimer's Disease and Related Disorders Association
70 East Lake Street
Chicago, Illinois 60601
(312) 853-3060

American Association of Retired Persons
1909 K Street, N.W.
Washington, D.C. 20049
(202)872-4700

CHANGES
Veterinary Teaching Hospital
Colorado State University
300 West Drake
Fort Collins, Colorado 80523
(303) 491-7101

Widow-to-Widow Program
Needham Community Council
51 Lincoln Street
Needham, Massachusetts 02192
(617)444-2415

References

Aiken, L. (1985). *Death, dying, and bereavement.* Boston, MA: Allyn and Bacon.

American Association of Retired Persons. (1987). *A profile of older Americans.* Washington, DC: AARP.

Balkwell, C. (1981). Transition to widowhood: A review of the literature. *Family Relations, 30,* 117–127.

Ball, J. F. (1977). Widow's grief: The impact of age and mode of death. *Omega, 7*(4), 307–333.

Baltz, T. M., & Turner, J. G. (1977). Development and analysis of a nursing home screening device. *The Gerontologist, 17,* 66–69.

Banziger, G., & Roush, S. (1983). Nursing homes for the birds: A control-relevant intervention with bird feeders. *The Gerontologist, 23,* 527–531.

Barrett, C. J., & Schneweis, K. M. (1980). Stages of widowhood. *Omega, 11*(2), 97–104.

Belsky, J. K. (1984). *The psychology of aging: Theory, research, and practice.* Monterey, CA: Brooks/Cole.

Bengston, V. L., Cuellar, J. B., & Ragan, P. K. (1977). Stratum contrasts and similarities in attitudes toward death. *Journal of Gerontology, 32,* 76–88.

Berardo, F. M. (1968). Widowhood status in the United States: Perspective on a neglected aspect of the family life cycle. *The Family Coordinator, 17,* 191–203.

Berardo, F. M. (1970). Survivorship and social isolation: The case of the aged widower. *The Family Coordinator, 19,* 11–25.

Blazer, D. (1982). *Depression in late life.* St. Louis, MO: C. V. Mosby.

Boss, P. (in press). *Family stress management.* Beverly Hills, CA: Sage Publications.

Bowlby, J., & Parkes, C. M. (1970). Separation and loss within the family. In E. J. Anthony & C. Koupernik (Eds.), *The child in his family* (pp. 197–216). New York: Wiley.

Bozeman, M. F., Orbach, C. E., & Sutherland, A. M. (1955). The psychological impact of cancer and its treatment. *Cancer, 8,* 1.

Brubaker, E. (1985). Older parents' reactions to the death of adult children: Implications for practice. *Journal of Gerontological Social Work, 9*(1), 35–48.

Butler, R. N. (1963). The life review: An interpretation of reminiscence in the aged. *Psychiatry, 26,* 65–76.

Butler, R. N. (1975). *Why survive? Being old in America.* New York: Harper & Row.

Butler, R., & Lewis, M. (1982). *Aging and mental health* (2d ed.). St. Louis, MO: C. V. Mosby.

Carey, R. G. (1979). Weathering widowhood: Problems and adjustment of the widowed during the first year. *Omega, 10*(2), 263–274.

Carson, R. A. (1979). Euthanasia or the right to die. In H. Wass (Ed.), *Dying: Facing the facts* (pp. 360–374). Washington, DC: Hemisphere.

Cowles, K. V. (1985). The death of a pet: Human responses to the breaking of a bond. *Marriage and Family Review, 8,* 135–148.

Davidson, S. M., & Marmor, T. R. (1980). *The cost of living longer.* Lexington, MA: D. C. Heath.

Dowd, J. (1980). *Stratification among the aged: An analysis of power and dependence.* Monterey, CA: Brooks/Cole.

Erikson, E. H. (1950). *Childhood and society.* New York: Norton.

Erikson, E. H., & Erikson, J. M. (1981). On generativity and identity: From a conversation with Erik and Joan Erikson. *Harvard Educational Review, 51,* 249–269.

Farberow, N. L., & Moriwaki, S. Y. (1975). Self-destructive crises in the older person. *The Gerontologist, 15,* 333–337.

Fisher, C. R. (1980). Differences by age groups in health care spending. *Health Care Financing Review, 1,* 65–90.

Friedman, S. B., Chodoff, P., Mason, J. W., & Hamburg, D. (1963). Behavioral observations on parents anticipating the death of a child. *Pediatrics, 32,* 610.

Fulton, R. (1987). The many faces of grief. *Death Studies, 11*(4), 243–256.

Gruber, H. W. (1977). Geriatrics—Physical attitudes and medical school training. *Journal of American Geriatrics Society, 25,* 494–499.

Gustafson, E. (1972). The career of the nursing home patient. *Journal of Health and Social Behavior, 13,* 226–235.

Gyulay, J. E. (1975). The forgotten grievers. *American Journal of Nursing, 75,* 1476–1479.

Hamilton, J. (1978). Grandparents as grievers. In O. J. Z. Sahler (Ed.), *The child and death* (pp. 219–225). St. Louis, MO: C. V. Mosby.

Helsing, K. J., Szklo, M., & Comstock, G. W. (1981). Factors associated with mortality after widowhood. *American Journal of Public Health, 71,* 802–809.

Hess, B. (1972). Friendship. In M. W. Riley, M. Johnson, & E. Foner (Eds.), *Aging and society: Vol. 3. A sociology of age stratification* (pp. 357–393). New York: Russell Sage Foundation.

Hiltz, S. R. (1975). Helping widows: Group discussions as a therapeutic technique. *The Family Coordinator, 25,* 331–336.

Jacobs, S., & Ostfeld, A. (1977). An epidemiological review of the mortality of bereavement. *Psychosomatic Medicine, 39,* 344–357.

Johnson, D., Fitch, S. D., Alston, J. P., & McIntosh, W. A. (1980). Acceptance of conditional suicide and euthanasia among adult Americans. *Suicide and Life Threatening Behavior, 10*(3), 157–166.

Kalish, R. A. (1985a). Death and dying in a social context (2d ed.). In R. H. Binstock & E. Shanas (Eds.), *Handbook of aging and the social sciences* (pp.149–170). New York: Van Nostrand.

Kalish, R. A. (1985b). *Death, grief, and caring relationships* (2d ed.). Monterey, CA: Brooks/Cole.

Kalish, R. A., & Johnson, A. I. (1972). Value similarities and differences in three generations of women. *Journal of Marriage and the Family, 34,* 49–54.

Kalish, R. A., & Reynolds, D. K. (1976). *Death and ethnicity: A psycho-cultural study.* Los Angeles: University of Southern California.

Kane, R. L., Solomon, D. H., Beck, J. C., Keeler, E., & Kane, R. A. (1981). *Geriatrics in the United States: Manpower projections and training considerations.* Lexington, MA: D. C. Heath.

Kapust, L. R. (1982). Living with dementia: The ongoing funeral. *Social Work in Health Care, 7*(4), 79–91.

Kart, C. S. (1985). *The realities of aging: An introduction to gerontology* (2d ed.). Boston: Allyn & Bacon.

Levinson, B. M. (1972). *Pets and human development.* Springfield, IL: Charles C Thomas.

Lezak, M. D. (1978). Living with characterologically altered brain injured patients. *Journal of Clinical Psychiatry, 39,* 592–597.

Lieberman, M., & Borman, L. (1979). *Self-help groups for coping with crisis.* San Francisco: Jossey-Bass.

Lopata, H. Z. (1973). *Widowhood in an American city.* Cambridge, MA: Schenckman.

Lopata, H. Z. (1980). The widowed family member. In N. Datan & N. Lohmann (Eds.), *Transitions of aging* (pp. 93–118). New York: Academic Press.

Lowenthal, M. F., & Chiriboga, D. (1973). Social stress and adaptation: Toward a life-course perspective. In C. Eisdorfer & M. P. Lawton (Eds.), *The psychology of adult development and aging* (pp. 281–310). Washington, DC: American Psychological Association.

Lund, D. A., Dimond, M., & Juretich, M. (1985). Bereavement support groups for the elderly: Characteristics of potential participants. *Death Studies, 9,* 309–321.

Maddison, D., & Viola, A. (1968). The health of widows in the year following bereavement. *Journal of Psychosomatic Research, 12,* 297–306.

Maizler, J. S., Solomon, J. R., & Almquist, E. (1983). Psychogenic mortality syndrome: Choosing to die by the institutionalized elderly. *Death Education, 6,* 353–364.

Marshall, V. W. (1980). *Last chapters: A sociology of aging and dying.* Monterey, CA: Brooks/Cole.

Matthews, S. (1976). Old women and identity maintenance: Outwitting the grim reaper. In L. Lofland (Ed.), *Toward a sociology of death and dying.* Beverly Hills, CA: Sage Publications.

McIntosh, J. L. (1985). Suicide among the elderly: Levels and trends. *American Journal of Orthopsychiatry, 56*(2), 288–293.

Miller, D. B., Lowenstein, R., & Winston, R. (1976). Physicians' attitudes toward the ill aged and nursing homes. *Journal of the American Geriatrics Society, 24,* 498–505.

Miller, M. (1978). Geriatric suicide: The Arizona study. *Gerontologist, 18,* 488–496.

Miller, M. (1979). *Suicide after sixty: The final alternative.* New York: Springer.

Moody, H. R. (1984). Can suicide on grounds of old age be ethically justified? In M. Tallmer, E. R. Prichard, A. H. Kutscher, R. DeBellis, M. S. Hale, & I. K. Goldberg (Eds.), *The life-threatened elderly* (pp. 64–92). New York: Columbia University Press.

Moss, M. S., Lesher, E. L., & Moss, S. Z. (1986). Impact of the death of an adult child on elderly parents: Some observations. *Omega, 17*(3), 209–218.

Moss, M. S., & Moss, S. Z. (1984). Some aspects of the elderly widow(er)'s persistent tie with the deceased spouse. *Omega, 15*(3), 195–206.

National Center for Health Statistics. (1986). Advance report on final mortality statistics, 1984. *Monthly Vital Statistics Report, 35*(6, Suppl. 2), 40–41.

Neugarten, B. L. (1977). Personality and aging. In J. E. Birren & K. W. Schaie (Eds.), *Handbook of the psychology of aging* (pp.626–649). New York: Van Nostrand.

Nieburg, H. A., & Fischer, A. (1982). *Pet loss.* New York: Harper & Row.

Perlmutter, M., & Hall, E. (1985). *Adult development and aging.* New York: Wiley.

Quackenbush, J. (1985). The death of a pet: How it can affect pet owners. *Veterinary Clinics of North America: Small Animal Practice, 15*(2), 395–402.

Rachels, J. (1975). Active and passive euthanasia. *New England Journal of Medicine, 292,* 78–80.

Rando, T. A. (1986). Death of the adult child. In T. A. Rando (Ed.), *Parental loss of a child* (pp. 221–238). Champaign, IL: Research Press.

Rodin, J., & Langer, E. J. (1977). Long-term effects of a control-relevant intervention with the institutionalized aged. *Journal of Personality and Social Psychology, 35,* 879–902.

Ryder, E. L. (1985). Pets and the elderly: A social work perspective. *Veterinary Clinics of North America: Small Animal Practice, 15*(2), 333–343.

Sanders, C. M. (1980). Comparison of younger and older spouses in bereavement outcome. *Omega, 11*(3), 217–232.

Schiamberg, L. B. (1985). *Human development* (2d ed.). New York: Macmillan.

Schulz, R. (1976). Effect of control and predictability on the physical and psychological well-being of the institutionalized aged. *Journal of Personality and Social Psychology, 33,* 563–573.

Scott, S. (1984). The Medicare prospective payment system. *American Journal of Occupational Therapy, 38*(5), 330–334.

Seligman, M. E. P. (1975). *Helplessness: On depression, development, and death.* San Francisco: W. H. Freeman.

Shanfield, S. B., Benjamin, A. H., & Swain, B. J. (1984). Parents' reactions to the death of an adult child from cancer. *American Journal of Psychiatry, 141*(9), 1092–1094.

Shirley, V., & Mercier, J. (1983). Bereavement of older persons: Death of a pet. *The Gerontologist, 23,* 276.

Siegel, K., & Tuckel, P. (1984). Rational suicide and the terminally ill cancer patient. *Omega, 15*(3), 263–269.

Silverman, P. R. (1967). Services to the widowed: First steps in a program of preventive intervention. *Community Mental Health Journal, 3,* 37–44.

Silverman, P. R. (1972). Widowhood and preventive intervention. *The Family Coordinator, 21,* 95–102.

Simpson, M. (1976). Brought in dead. *Omega, 7,* 243–248.

Smith, W. J. (1985). *Dying in the human life cycle: Psychological, biomedical, and social perspectives.* New York: Holt, Rinehart & Winston.

Solomon, K. (1982). Social antecedents of learned helplessness in the health care setting. *The Gerontologist, 22,* 282–287.

Stenback, A. (1975). Psychosomatic states. In J. G. Howells (Ed.), *Modern perspectives in the psychiatry of old age* (pp. 269–289). New York: Brunner/Mazel.

Stenback, A. (1980). Depression and suicidal behavior in old age. In J. E. Birren & R. B. Sloane (Eds.), *Handbook of mental health and aging* (pp.616–652). Englewood Cliffs, NJ: Prentice-Hall.

Sudnow, D. (1967). *Passing on: The social organization of dying.* Englewood Cliffs, NJ: Prentice-Hall.

Sussman, M. B. (1985). Pet/human bonding: Applications, conceptual and research issues. *Marriage and Family Review, 8,* 1–4.

Tobin, S. (1985). Psychodynamic treatment of the family and the institutionalized individual. In N. Miller & G. D. Cohen (Eds.), *Psychodynamic research perspectives on development, psychopathology, and treatment in later life.* New York: International Universities Press.

Toynbee, A. (1968). *Man's concern with death.* New York: McGraw-Hill.

Troll, L. E. (1971). The family of later life: A decade review. *Journal of Marriage and the Family, 33,* 263–290.

United States Bureau of the Census. (1987). *Statistical abstract of the United States: 1988* (108th ed.). Washington, DC: U. S. Government Printing Office.

Vachon, M. L. S., Sheldon, A. R., Lancee, W. J., Lyall, W. A. L., Rogers, J., & Freeman, S. J. J. (1980). A controlled study of self-help intervention for widows. *American Journal of Psychiatry, 137,* 1380–1384.

Verwoerdt, A. (1976). *Clinical geropsychiatry.* Baltimore: Williams & Wilkins.

Verwoerdt, A. (1985). Individual psychopathology in senile dementia. In N. Miller & G. D. Cohen (Eds.), *Psychodynamic research perspectives on development, psychopathology, and treatment in later life.* New York: International Universities Press.

Ward, R. A. (1980). Age and acceptance of euthanasia. *Journal of Gerontology, 35*(3), 421–431.

Wattenberg, S. H., & McGann, L. M. (1984). Medicare or "Medigap"? Dilemma for the elderly. *Health and Social Work, 9*(3), 229–237.

Wilcoxon, S. A. (1986). Grandparents and grandchildren: An often neglected relationship between significant others. *Journal of Counseling and Development, 65*(6), 289–290.

York, J. L., & Calsyn, R. J. (1977). Family involvement in nursing homes. *The Gerontologist, 17*, 500–505.

Zarit, S. H. (1980). *Aging and mental disorders: Psychological approaches to assessment and treatment.* New York: Free Press.

PART III

Implications for Caregivers

10

Needs of Professionals Who Work with the Dying and Grieving

Concerns of Professionals
434

Personal Grief Reactions   434
Work-related Stress   441

Coping Mechanisms   445

Individual Strategies   446
Agency and Institutional
  Support   449

**Professional Training
Programs**   452

Preparing Professionals to Cope
  with Death, Dying, and Grief
  452
Preparing Professionals for
  Multidisciplinary Work   454

**Caring for the Dying: An
Opportunity for Growth**   455

Summary   456

$\mathbf{T}$hroughout this text we have examined the needs of individuals and families touched by death and bereavement. Strategies for meeting these needs and various intervention techniques have also been presented. In this final chapter, the focus of our attention will be on professional caregivers—the individuals who play a critical role in meeting the needs of the dying and their families. In their efforts to help others, they often fail to address their own needs and concerns. What are the effects of working in situations that involve grief and loss on a regular basis? What coping mechanisms do psychologists, social workers, physicians, nurses, clergy, therapists, and other professionals use to maintain both the quality of patient care and their own emotional well-being? How can training programs and institutional support be improved to prepare future professionals for the death- and grief-related situations they will face and for avoiding the consequences of "burnout"? This chapter will explore answers to these questions and consider the unique emotional demands of working in professions in which loss is a common element.

Concerns of Professionals

Individuals planning to work in the physical and mental health care fields often have concerns about their ability to work effectively with the dying and their families. Others have questions about the occupational hazards of this work in terms of personal stress (Benoliel, 1988). Until recently, little has been written to help individuals address these concerns and to assist them in coping with the personal aspects of their professions.

Personal Grief Reactions

Grief is a common reaction of professionals to the suffering, loss, and death of patients. Working in a professional role does not protect individuals from the emotional impact of death-related experiences. While the grief reactions of professional caregivers are similar to those of the patient and family discussed in earlier chapters, they are usually of less intensity and shorter duration (Swanson & Swanson, 1977). While all situations involving death can have a potential effect on human service professionals, the situational context in which care is provided and the type of death both appear to have a strong influence on the reactions of caregivers.

Variables Affecting Grief Reactions.   Age of the patient is an important variable affecting the grief response of professionals. Grief reactions among health care workers are especially pronounced following the death of an infant or child as, for example, in the case of Sudden Infant Death Syndrome (SIDS). While SIDS usually strikes in the home, such a death can also occur in medical settings. After a particular SIDS death at the Minneapolis Children's Health Center, a follow-up study focused on the effects of the death on the hospital team involved in the infant's care. In nearly all of their reactions, the nursing staff mirrored the questions and concerns of families who have lost a child to SIDS. All expressed shock and disbelief upon discovering or learning about the death. Feelings of guilt were strongly related to the amount of responsibility each nurse had for the infant. The nurse who was the primary caregiver engaged in exhaustive self-questioning of her actions, similar to "the kind of haunted and tormented thinking that families go through" (Friedman, Franciosi, & Drake, 1979, p. 539). Staff members expressed apprehension about adequate staffing and began checking more frequently on sleeping children. Affect disturbance was more pronounced and of longer duration in the staff member who had spent the most time with the SIDS victim. She was initially fearful of handling other infants and reported frequent crying, appetite problems, and bad dreams associated with the death. All of the staff were eager to go over the autopsy findings with the staff pathologist, and they had questions about whether they could have predicted or prevented the death of the infant. The information and reassurance provided through the group's discussion of the autopsy report was important in helping the staff cope with their feelings associated with this crisis. Recovery from this incident was also related to support from other staff members and from the infant's physician. This case illustrates the need for timely intervention and the importance of allowing each professional involved with the patient an opportunity to express his or her feelings and receive support following this type of death (Friedman et al., 1979).

Part of the trauma associated with SIDS is due to its sudden and unexpected occurrence in an assumed "well" population. The age of the patient, however, also influences the grief reactions of staff members in medical care settings in which all patients are gravely or seriously ill. For example, the death of a child on an Intensive Care Unit (ICU) elicits a different response from staff members than does the death of an older person. When a dying child is on the unit, nurses make concerned comments more frequently and attend to the young patient with extra diligence as compared to older patients. When the child dies, the staff is more likely to feel guilty and question what else they could have done for the child. In contrast, the usual concern over the death of a geriatric patient relates more to issues of pain control and death with dignity. In addition, staff members are more likely to accept an injured elderly person's statement about being ready to die than a similar statement from a younger person. Death of an older person is often met with comments such as "He has had a good life" or "She has lived 84 years" (Swanson & Swanson, 1977).

While grief appears to be generally less intense in response to the death of an older patient, grief reactions are still prevalent for those working with this age group. Lerea and LiMauro (1982) asked nurses and nurses' aides from a general hospital and three geriatric centers if they had ever grieved in response to a patient's physical or emotional condition. In each setting, the majority of staff reported having experienced grief reactions. Mourning was reported by 98 percent of the nursing staff at the 500-bed general hospital. In general hospitals, positive results are more often anticipated as a result of medical intervention; therefore, the staff are often not prepared for the death or deterioration of a patient. The incidence of bereavement reported by staff at the geriatric centers was lower (63 percent), presumably because one expects more patient losses in this type of facility and can more readily accept death or disability in an older population. The most common psychological reactions for both groups included thinking and talking about the patient (92 percent) and feelings of helplessness (84 percent). Fatigue was the physical response most frequently recalled (55 percent). It should be noted, however, that the full range of grief reactions as typically reported by the bereaved were observed in this sample (see Table 10.1). More than 1 month following the grief-related incident, psychological and physical grief reactions were still present for 50 percent of the general hospital staff and 38 percent of the geriatric staff. No differences were found between the grief reactions of nurses and nurses' aides.

In addition to age, a number of other patient variables can also affect the intensity and type of grief reactions experienced by professional caregivers. For example, Lerea and LiMauro (1982) reported that cancer was the diagnosis that elicited grief reactions most often among the respondents in their sample. Also, Vachon and her associates (1978) found the stress level of oncology nurses to be twice as high as that of nurses involved in other medical units and only slightly lower than that of newly bereaved widows. In contrast, ICU nurses often react to patients treated for drug overdoses and self-inflicted injuries with feelings of irritation, anger, and resentment because these cases take time away from other patients. Degree of consciousness of the patient also seems to have an effect on the caregiver's grief response. ICU nurses show less grief following the death of someone who enters the unit in a comatose state because the person's

Table 10.1
Percentage of Health Care Workers Experiencing Physical and
Psychological Grief Reactions

Physical	%	Psychological	%
Fatigue	55	Thinking or talking about the patient	92
Headache	44	Feelings of helplessness	84
Sighing respiration	42	Crying or despondency	53
Insomnia	41	Disbelief or shock	51
Loss of appetite or overeating	40	Difficulty concentrating	51
Dry mouth	35	Anger toward others	50
Restless or lethargic	34	Anxiety	47
Numbness	31	Irritability	43
Nausea or acid stomach	31	Guilt	37
Excessive perspiration	30	Withdrawal or feelings of aloneness	37
Constipation or diarrhea	16	Difficulty remembering	29
Dizziness	15	Apathy	22
Shortness of breath	13	Indecisiveness	20
Sexual difficulties	11	Tardiness or absenteeism	15

SOURCE: From E. L. Learea & B. F. LiMauro (1982), Grief among healthcare workers: A comparative study, *Journal of Gerontology,* Vol. 37, No. 5, p. 606. Copyright © 1982 The Gerontological Society of America. Reprinted by permission.

nonalert state prevents much emotional involvement on the part of the staff. Swanson and Swanson (1977) point out that one of the most difficult patients for the ICU nurse to care for is the individual who enters the unit in an alert state and then deteriorates. The longer the patient is on the unit in an alert state and able to communicate, the stronger the staff response will be. When it is apparent that the individual is dying, the attending nurse will often show signs of mild depression. "The nurse appears sad, works with less speed and zeal, and appears less interested in her job" (p. 246). At this point, the nurse often tends to withdraw emotionally from the patient and to show greater interest and concern for the monitors and the "busy work" involved in caring for the patient. Often when a death appears imminent, the ICU nurse, in order to avoid involvement with the actual death, will work hard to keep the patient alive so that he or she will not die on that shift but on someone else's.

Vulnerabilities of Professional Caregivers. As professional caregivers increasingly attempt to respond to the psychosocial needs of the dying, stronger attachments to the patient will be made, leaving the caregiver even more vulnerable to experiencing grief. Fulton (1979) has noted that this can be accentuated in the absence of strong family support for the dying. This support may be lacking due to disrupted family systems, distance among family members created by social or geographic mobility, disengagement of family members from the dying individual, and the tendency of individuals today to die in institutions. These sociological trends are contributing to the development of a role for the caregiver as a *surrogate griever* (one who grieves in the place of family members).

In some medical and mental health specialties death is encountered infrequently, although no specialty is "death-free." Other caregivers who deal with the dying on a regular basis run the risk of *bereavement overload.* This term, introduced earlier in the text, refers to the situation in which a griever must deal with several deaths in close succession and does not have the time to cope with the first death before he or she is confronted with another. If this accumulated grief is not resolved, the caregiver can be vulnerable to the same range of pathological grief reactions as any other griever. In addition to multiple losses, several other factors can interfere with adequately processing and working through grief (Lazure, 1979). Those factors most relevant to the caregiver role include unresolved guilt concerning the care of the patient, social negation of the loss (the impact on the caregiver is not acknowledged by others), and the assumption that one has to be "strong" because of a given occupation or role.

In discussing health care professionals and the grief they experience, Shanfield (1981) refers to them as "survivors of complex and manifold losses" (p. 385). While grief among medical workers is usually associated with the debilitating illness or death of a patient, other types of loss are frequently encountered as a consequence of working with dying patients. For example, loss of the caregiver's idealized role expectations may precipitate a separate but related grief reaction (Shanfield, 1981). Medical and nursing schools have a strong curative orientation that emphasizes technical skills geared toward treating disease and saving lives. For many physicians and nurses, to lose a patient to death is to face defeat. In fact, our idealization of medical workers often involves an image of omnipotence that can save us from "the enemy"—death. To work with dying patients means to confront one's limitations as a professional caregiver and to encounter the universal truths of life and death as part of the human experience.

Grief reactions of professionals are complex and reflect multiple losses on a number of levels. According to Pattison (1977), understanding a dying person demands insight into our own issues surrounding death. Working with the dying may evoke intense personal feelings and arouse pervasive fears (Weisman, 1970). Thus, individuals who work with the dying continually confront their own mortality and that of their loved ones. Previous losses are reawakened, and future losses are anticipated.

Grief Following Suicide.   Although most mental health professionals do not have the opportunity to work with the terminally ill on a regular basis, they do frequently work with individuals who are depressed and suicidal. Regardless of the quality of care provided, a suicide may be attempted or completed while an individual is seeing a psychologist, social worker, marriage and family therapist, pastoral counselor, psychiatrist, or other type of psychotherapist. One recent study found that 38.2 percent of a random sample of American psychotherapists had experienced the suicide of a client (Lapp, 1986).

According to Millen and Roll (1985), one of the most potentially shattering emotional experiences a psychotherapist can have is the death of a client by suicide. This experience can precipitate both a personal and professional crisis. While the research in this area is sparse, the available literature does indicate that mental health professionals are vulnerable to grief reactions similar to those of friends and family members of the suicide victim (Sanders, 1984). The longer the therapist has been associated with the suicide victim and the more intense the professional–patient relationship, the stronger the grief reaction.

Upon learning of the suicide, psychotherapists commonly express disbelief. At times, this reaction may be demonstrated by requesting additional verification of the death (for example, asking to see the coroner's report). Anger is also a common component of the therapist's grief—anger toward the suicide victim for having "betrayed" the therapist, anger toward the family for not having been more watchful, and anger turned inward toward oneself for not having prevented the suicide from occurring (Sanders, 1984). The professional questions what he or she could have done differently ("Should the last session have been longer and more focused?", "Why didn't I call her that day?") and often experiences guilt. The consequences of these grief responses can be especially negative because one's feelings of professional competence are threatened. These feelings can be heightened if grieving families displace their own anger and guilt onto the professional and blame him or her for the death (Sanders, 1984).

Therapists who experience a suicide in their work need emotional support, time to reflect, and relief from high-stress tasks. Unfortunately mental health professionals, like families of suicide victims, commonly feel isolated in their grief. Outlets for discussing the suicide are limited for professionals because of ethical issues surrounding confidentiality. Their work context (whether private practice, crisis center, inpatient facility, or outpatient facility) can make a difference regarding the support available to therapists (Jones, 1987). A private practice setting can be the most isolating for therapists in grief, while available support is likely to be greater for therapists employed in community agencies, hospitals, or psychiatric facilities. A positive and nonjudgmental staff response can do much toward enhancing the therapist's ability to deal with a suicide. The opportunity for discussion in a supportive atmosphere can help therapists sort through feelings of inadequacy and failure. Although sharing the details of the incident with respected colleagues is often therapeutic, this type of interaction may be avoided because of feelings of shame and embarrassment.

Marshall (1980) has suggested that mental health facilities develop procedures to aid professional staff in the aftermath of suicide. The forum designed for this purpose should be separate from any administrative effort to determine negligence. Also, Dunne (1987) emphasizes that attempts to support the staff should not be confused with the *psychological autopsy*. Years ago Shneidman (1969) introduced the psychological autopsy procedure, recognizing that a process of examination could be useful following a suicide. The focus of this formal review is on establishing events that led to the suicide in order to identify causal factors. It is more appropriately held some weeks or months following the suicide, after the initial shock has subsided and feelings have been addressed, when staff members can benefit from a closer look at their role, if any, in the death.

Jones (1987) recommends the establishment of ongoing support groups for grieving therapists. Following the suicide of one of his patients, he organized such a group. Of the therapists who attended, their patients' suicides had occurred from a few days to 20 years prior to their involvement in the support group. Many participants commented that this was the first time they had been given an opportunity to "talk it out."

In addition to providing an opportunity to explore feelings related to the suicide, support groups can help therapists deal with related professional concerns. Jones (1987) has reported that the experience of a patient suicide can affect professional attitudes and practices in a variety of ways. Some therapists become more conservative in the management of other patients who are potentially suicidal, and, in some cases, this conservatism results in inappropriate hospitalization. Other therapists refuse referrals of patients who are identified as suicidal risks in order to avoid suffering another loss by suicide. Many question their worth as therapists or the value of therapy itself and, consequently, consider leaving their profession. Some positive outcomes for therapists who are able to work through these issues include paying greater attention to suicidal behaviors, attempts, and gestures. Goldstein and Buongiorno (1984) found that therapists who survived the suicide of clients engaged in more explicit questioning and exploration of their clients' suicidal thoughts and feelings than they had done previously.

The resolution of this type of bereavement, with all of its ramifications, can take many months or even longer. For resolution to be facilitated, therapists need to acknowledge their grief. They must also remind themselves that suicides will occur despite the best treatment. Upon resolution of this experience, the therapist often crosses a threshold in terms of professional maturation. Sanders (1984) describes the significance of the experience this way:

> The first patient suicide, at least, becomes an initiation rite, an undesired challenge, which not only humbles one but also becomes a transforming and maturing experience. The therapist not only faces a significant object loss with all the accompanying grief reactions of anger, guilt, and sadness, but also suffers a chink in his professional armor as well. Some of the magical expectations of therapeutic omnipotence must be relinquished. At the same time, however, a deeper sensitivity is realized, a keener compassion to patient suffering. (p. 30)

Summary. In summary, while research shows general patterns of grief responses for professionals in a variety of situations, it should be emphasized that these are generalizations. People react to death in unique ways based on their own coping styles, personalities, and experiences with loss.

Work-related Stress

Job stress can affect an individual's health, personality, and job performance (Kroes, Margolis, & Quinn, 1974). During the past several years, the topic of job-related stress has received a great deal of attention, and the term *burnout* has become a familiar word. Burnout is a syndrome of mental and physical exhaustion, low morale, cynicism, and despair that occurs frequently among individuals who do "people work" (Maslach, 1982). Edelwich (1980) has referred to burnout as involving a progressive loss of idealism, energy, and purpose. It can happen to anyone regardless of age, discipline, or degree of formal training.

What are the consequences of burnout? The research on burnout shows the consequences to be serious for clients/patients, agencies, professional staff members, and their families. Burnout can lead to deterioration in the quality of services. It has also been shown to be an important factor in job turnover and absenteeism. Furthermore, burnout has been shown to be correlated with several indices of personal stress, including illness, increased use of alcohol and drugs, and psychological problems. Professionals who describe themselves as "burned out" also report higher levels of marital and family conflict (Freudenberger, 1974; Maslach, 1976; Pines & Maslach, 1978).

Stress Due to Professional Roles.   Some stress experienced by health care workers may be inherent in their respective professional roles as they are currently defined. Physicians have the burden of ultimate responsibility for their patients. While physicians have the primary role in treatment decisions, nurses perform many of the diagnostic and treatment procedures. Therefore, nurses spend a relatively large amount of time with patients and may be the ones who have to face the anger and dissatisfaction of families with the patient's treatment regimen. Families may consider it unsafe to confront or criticize physicians, as they are in charge of the fate of their loved one. On intensive care units, the rotation of attending physicians with their varying treatment and ethical approaches can make the role of the nurse even more difficult (Marshall & Kasman, 1980; Schowalter, 1978).

Other professionals can also be affected by the status hierarchy in the health care field. Child-life workers and recreational therapists often see aspects of the patient that go undetected by nurses and physicians. These individuals may become frustrated as they attempt to share these insights if their input is not respected and they are not seen as having a legitimate role on the health care team (Schowalter, 1978).

Stress in Intensive Care Units.   Daley (1979) has suggested that burnout can be better understood if the nature of the specific stressors involved in the work environment is considered. For example, nurses and their coworkers in certain medical settings are more likely to be faced with multiple stressors and demands than those in other settings. Staff members working in intensive care units, emergency rooms, coronary care units, and oncology wards seem to be especially vulnerable to stress due to (1) the tremendous pressure under which they work, (2) the high level of performance that is expected on a regular basis, and (3) the unrealistic expectations that patients and families in these units often have (Jacobson, 1978; Vachon, 1979).

An examination of the work environment in an intensive care unit (ICU) illustrates the extraordinary stressors that many professional caregivers face on a regular basis. The ICU is different from other areas of the hospital. The physical environment contains a massive array of sensory stimuli. The flashing lights and beeping and buzzing monitors of the sophisticated ICU equipment are in constant motion. Gurgling suction pumps and whooshing respirators provide other background sounds. While habituation to these stimuli occurs with time, their ever-continuing presence can still contribute to stress. The human environment in the ICU includes desperately ill or injured human beings connected to the machinery. Many are between life and death. Working in the ICU involves seeing disfigurement and hearing sounds associated with discomfort and pain. These sights and sounds present a strong element of surrealism. Hay and Oken (1977) have pointed out that this environment

> directly challenges the definition of being human, one's most fundamental sense of ego integrity, for nurse as well as patient. Though consciously the nurse quickly learns to accept this surrealism, she is unremittingly exposed to these multiple threats to the stability of her body boundaries, her sense of self, and her feelings of humanity and reality. (p. 383)

The work load of the ICU staff is also unique. Vital signs must be monitored at 15-minute intervals (sometimes more often). Tracheas must be suctioned, intravenous infusions changed, respirators checked, EKG monitors interpreted, and so on, and so on, and every step must be charted. Every procedure is potentially life saving, and any error may be life threatening. Subtle changes in the patient's condition may be of critical significance. As part of the daily routine, the ICU nurse faces the ever-present possibility of confronting death. A patient's death is a significant loss. The intense and intimate contact promotes emotional attachment of ICU nurses to their patients, especially those that are conscious and verbal. Even if the patient lives, they do not leave the unit "well." The ICU successes are usually still seriously ill and are transferred to another unit in the hospital.

In summary, working on an intensive care unit requires great vigilance and stamina. An ICU patient's life can depend on the care received during this critical period in the illness or injury. The quality of care is a function of both the professional skills and the psychological state of the caregivers. If staff stress and anxiety are excessive, it can reduce efficiency and the ability to make decisions. The outcomes can be fatal for the patient and also greatly threaten the physical and emotional well-being of the caregiver.

Stress in Hospices. Increasingly, medical care is provided outside a hospital context, through programs such as hospices that provide alternative models of care. In home-based hospice programs, caregivers do not have the opportunity to maintain a familiar work environment. They are constantly having to adjust to new settings as they work with different families in their own homes. Furthermore, caregivers may experience a form of culture shock as they shift from working in an acute care environment to a palliative care setting such as a hospice in which their roles, responsibilities, and orientation are different. In contrast to traditional medical care settings, quality of life is of paramount importance, rather than prolongation of life. Caregivers are also expected to have greater skill in addressing psychosocial issues than is typically the case in acute care hospitals (Rando, 1984). These aspects of hospice care, combined with the hospice philosophy, can result in some unique stresses for staff members such as the following ones identified by Vachon (1979).

> Difficulty accepting the fact that the patients' physical and psychological problems cannot always be controlled;
>
> Frustration at being involved with a patient's family only after their emotional resources have been drained by the illness;
>
> Disappointment if expectations for patients to die a "good death"—however this may be defined—are not met;
>
> Frustration at having invested large amounts of energy in caring for people who then die, taking this investment with them;
>
> Anger at being subjected to higher-than-standard performance expectations in prototypal facilities exposed to considerable scrutiny and publicity;
>
> Difficulty deciding where to draw limits on involvement with patients and their families, particularly during off-duty hours; and
>
> Difficulty establishing a sense of realistic limitations on what the hospice service, which is expected to be all-encompassing, can actually provide.

Vachon (1976, 1978, 1979) was one of the first researchers to address the unique strains of working with the terminally ill and the implications for quality caregiving. More recently, a number of studies have examined additional sources of work stress for professionals and volunteers involved in hospice work (Paradis, 1987). In one study (Yancik, 1984) that examined three hospices funded by the National Cancer Institute, 93 professional staff members were asked, "What are the three most stressful events you experienced professionally as a hospice worker in the last three months?" The subjects described 242 situations, which were then categorized. Approximately half of the stressful situations related to issues of staff support. The most prevalent concerns in this category centered around conflicts with other staff members, administrative problems, and work and emotional overload. One staff member commented: "We have an ongoing problem of providing support to each other and ourselves. We have needs that are not always heard or responded to, but the expectation is to continue to offer 'good work to others'" (Yancik, 1984, p. 25).

The second category, which accounted for slightly more than 37 percent of the incidents, emphasized concern for patients and families as a source of stress. At times, feelings of sorrow or loss were especially strong with regard to a particular patient. In other circumstances, staff members felt frustrated in their attempts to support the patient and family. For example, family members were sometimes already exhausted from coping with the illness by the time the patient entered the hospice program (Yancik, 1984).

Management of the disease process was only a minor source of stress for most hospice staff workers. The specific situations mentioned in this category revealed feelings of helplessness and vulnerability associated with the limitations of medical intervention (Yancik, 1984).

Yancik (1984) found that the types and frequencies of stresses varied with each hospice facility. The differences were most pronounced in the area of staff support. This finding has important implications for hospice programs and shows that an organization can effectively intervene to reduce staff members' stress.

In another study of hospice nurses, investigators Moser and Krikorian (1982) examined satisfactions as well as stresses. Their results concerning stresses were similar to those obtained by Yancik (1984). When the nurses were asked what gave them satisfaction in their work, working conditions were cited in only about 30 percent of the responses, whereas the satisfaction derived from working with patients and families accounted for over half of the reported incidents. Although potentially a source of significant stress, direct interactions with patients and their families can also be the most meaningful and satisfying aspect of hospice work.

While hospice work involves a variety of potential sources of stress, Vachon (1986) found that hospice workers in fact have fewer manifestations and reports of stress than do health care workers in other settings, such as emergency centers or intensive care units. Reasons for this finding were attributed to the hospice emphasis on philosophy of care, team support, and team building.

Coping Mechanisms

Stress arises out of transactions between individuals and given milieus (Lazarus & Cohen, 1977). Pearlin and Schooler (1978) have emphasized that the meanings attached to potentially stressful events depend on the particular individual participating in the event. Individual differences in perceptions, interpretations, and coping capacities can make the difference between those who suffer deeply and are immobilized and those who are challenged and grow.

Individual Strategies

Professionals have a responsibility to care for themselves as well as for their patients. They must replenish themselves if they are to continue to be effective in giving of themselves to others. Unlimited giving without replenishment leads to burnout (Marshall & Kasman, 1980). Part of nurturing oneself includes learning to cope with the stresses and strains of one's work. In order to survive and grow as they work with the dying, caregivers need to assume some responsibility for reducing their own stress levels.

According to Pearlin and Schooler (1978), individuals cope in three basic ways: (1) by cognitively controlling the meaning of the experience, which neutralizes its stressful character, (2) by managing to accommodate the stressor after it has arisen, and (3) by modifying or eliminating stressful situations. In order to cope by any of these means, specific coping strategies must be employed.

Photo 10.1   *In order to avoid burnout, professional caregivers must learn to control their own stress levels.*

Perception of the Experience.   Stress lies to a great extent in our perceptions of life events, rather than in the events themselves. The ways in which we define our work and our professional roles will determine whether we view our work as frustrating or fulfilling. Sutterley (1982) has pointed out that a great deal of stress arises from belief systems that are unrealistic and problematic. Distress occurs when incongruency exists between our visions and ideals and the realities of our work situation.

Bugen (1980) views the internal resources of the caregiver to be an important dimension of managing stress. He defines *internal resources* as "those abilities, attitudes, values, beliefs or techniques that help people handle difficult moments or periods of time" (p. 246). In Bugen's discussion of internal resources of caregivers working with the terminally ill, he refers to the importance of giving up idealistic and perfectionistic goals. He points out that it is important for the caregiver to differentiate between the process and the outcome of caregiving. It is possible to invest in the process of helping a patient without expecting to cure that individual. While caregivers will not always be able to save lives, they will be able to make the process of dying easier and to help individuals achieve a higher quality of life during their remaining time.

Some of the professional caregivers' expectations for patients are related to their own needs. According to Lattanzi (1983), training programs for those who work with the terminally ill should not only encourage an increased awareness of the needs of others, but an increased knowledge of one's own self as well. She urges caregivers to examine their motivations for working with the dying and to gain insight into how their motivations can affect their interactions with patients and families. Insight into their own needs, vulnerabilities, and expectations can allow professional and volunteer caregivers to separate their own issues from those of their patients.

Management of Stress.   Some degree of work-related stress is unavoidable. It is only when it becomes excessive and unmanageable that it can have detrimental effects. Part of learning to cope with adult life includes acquiring healthy ways to handle the daily hassles that we encounter.

Learning to cope with a demanding occupation requires a recognition of one's stress level and a concerted effort to regulate it. Self-regulation of stress can involve a variety of approaches. Regular physical exercise can be effective in discharging tension as well as increasing physical stamina and fitness (deVries, 1975). A high level of physical wellness, developed through proper nutrition and exercise, can combat the potentially detrimental effects of stress on the body. For individuals who are experiencing excessive muscle tension, biofeedback and relaxation training can be useful in lowering physiological arousal levels. No technique will work, however, unless the individual incorporates the skills into his or her daily life (Sutterley, 1982).

Marshall and Kasman (1980) recommend a "decompression" routine after work to serve as a transition between work and private time. This routine needs to include an activity that is enjoyable and relaxing for the person (e.g., running, walking, listening to music). This type of activity can facilitate a shift from the role of "caregiver" with its accompanying pressures and concerns to the multiple roles involved in one's personal life. By releasing the mental and physical tensions accumulated during the day and achieving a state of relaxation, more quality time outside of work can be experienced and enjoyed.

Taking time off for rest and relaxation can also be important. Allowing time for oneself can be critical for maintaining vitality and a high level of caring at work on a long-term basis. Too often, caregivers have difficulty setting limits and feel guilty for thinking of themselves instead of their patients. However, failure to establish their own physical and mental health needs as a high priority can lead to burnout and the inability to provide quality care to others (Maslach, 1982).

The ability of a caregiver to adapt to the stresses of work is also related to the availability of an effective support system. Having an available source of emotional support has been shown to be an important moderator of stress (Cobb, 1976; LaGrand, 1980). A social network consists of a person's relationships with family, friends, neighbors, coworkers, and any other individuals or groups with whom the person interacts. *Support networks* can be formal (the relationship with a counselor in the client role, for example) or informal (a personal friend), and the type of support offered can take several distinct forms. Support systems can offer emotional support through empathic listening and genuine caring or material support in the form of tangible goods and service (such as covering a weekend shift for a coworker when he or she has had a particularly difficult week). In addition, support can be given by providing needed information and perspectives. For example, information about the anger experienced by many dying patients helps health care providers reinterpret uncomfortable interactions that they have had and helps them understand that these feelings are normal and not neccesarily the result of something they have done wrong.

Modification or Elimination of the Stressor.   The most drastic step in coping with work-related stress is changing jobs, work settings, or professions. Although this may sometimes be the best course of action, it can often be avoided by learning to monitor stress levels and intervening before they become excessive and lead to burnout. A variety of personal indicators that can be useful in monitoring stress levels are listed in Table 10.2. Pines, Aronson, and Kafry (1981) have identified four intervention strategies for preventing burnout: (1) being aware of the problem, (2) taking responsibility for doing something about it, (3) achieving some degree of cognitive clarity about the stressful situation, and (4) developing new tools for coping and improving the range and quality of old tools. They point out that individuals experiencing stress perceive that they have far less control over their work situations than they actually do. By working with one's supervisors and peers, it is often possible to alter some aspects of the work environment that contribute to stress and to implement programs and policies that will increase job satisfaction.

Monitoring personal reactions to stress is an ongoing process. Edelwich (1980) has emphasized that burnout can be cyclic and repeat itself many times in the same particular job situation. Having successfully intervened in the burnout cycle does not make one immune to work-related stress.

Agency and Institutional Support

Pattison (1977) has used the term *death saturation* to refer to the limits of personal tolerance for death-related work. He emphasizes that we can only work for so long with so much personal investment and intensity before we reach our limits. Our bodies get fatigued and need sleep in order to function well. Likewise, human spirits also get exhausted. It is important for individuals to recognize their personal saturation points and give themselves opportunities for reprieve and reconstitution. Organizations can also avoid death saturation and burnout among their caregivers by reducing stressful working conditions, giving group support, and providing ongoing educational opportunities.

Reducing Stressful Working Conditions.   Many hospices have experimented with a variety of work patterns aimed at reducing staff stress. Hospice of Marin County in California found that a 4-day work week with an occasional night or weekend on duty improved staff attitude and level of efficiency (Lamers, 1978). Hospice of New Haven has used part-time staff and a "day-away" system to provide needed relief and to prevent staff exhaustion (Lack, 1978). Careful monitoring of caseloads and the demands of each individual case can also be beneficial. Time off after deaths that are particularly difficult (such as death of a child) can be critical for the patient's primary care nurse and volunteers.

Vachon (1979) has suggested job rotation as another solution. Occa-

Table 10.2
Indicators of Burnout

Health Indicators	Excessive Behavior Indicators	Emotional Adjustment Indicators	Relationship Indicators	Attitude Indicators
Fatigue and chronic exhaustion	Increased consumption of caffeine, tobacco, alcohol, over-the-counter medications, psychoactive prescription drugs, illicit drugs	Emotional distancing	Isolation from or overbonding with other staff	Grandiosity
Frequent and prolonged colds		Paranoia	Responding to clients in mechanical manner	Boredom
Headaches		Depression: loss of meaning, loss of hope	Increased isolation from clients	Cynicism
Sleep disturbances: insomnia, nightmares, excessive sleeping		Decreased emotional control	Increased expressions of anger and/or mistrust	Sick humor—aimed particularly at clients
Ulcers	High-risk-taking behavior: auto/cycle accidents, falls, "high-risk" hobbies, general proneness to accidents and injuries, gambling, extreme mood and behavioral changes	Martyrdom	Increased interpersonal conflicts with other staff	Distrust of management, supervisors, peers
Gastrointestinal disorders		Fear of "going crazy"		Air of righteousness
Sudden losses or gains in weight		Increased amount of time daydreaming/ fantasizing	Increased problems in marital and other interpersonal relationships away from work, including relationships with one's children	Hypercritical attitude toward institution and/or peers
Flare-ups of preexisting medical disorders: diabetes, high blood pressure, asthma, etc.	Increased propensity for violent and aggressive behavior	Constant feelings of being "trapped"		Expressions of hopelessness, powerlessness, meaninglessness
Injuries from high-risk behavior	Over- and undereating	Nervous ticks	Social isolation: overinvolvement with clients, using clients to meet personal and social needs	
Muscular pain, particularly in lower back and neck	Hyperactivity	Undefined fears		**Value Indicators**
Increased premenstrual tension		Inability to concentrate		Sudden and often dramatic changes in values and beliefs
Missed menstrual cycles		Intellectualization		
		Increased anger		
		Increased tension		

SOURCE: From J. F. X. Carroll & W. L. White (1982), Theory building: Integrating individual and environmental factors within an ecological framework. In W. S. Paine (Ed.), *Job Stress and Burnout: Research, Theory, and Intervention,* Beverly Hills, CA: Sage Publications, p. 44. Reprinted by permission.

sionally assigning nurses to other units in the hospital gives them a chance to see more patients who are responding well to treatment. In hospice situations, volunteers can also benefit from job rotation by participating in varying responsibilities. In addition to working directly with patients and families, hospices usually also need volunteers to work in the administrative office, answer telephones, give community presentations, publish newsletters, and participate in a variety of training and educational programs. Alternating their time among these various roles can help individuals revitalize between cases.

The physical setting can also affect stress levels and needs to be carefully planned. In discussing the physical design of intensive care units, Hay and Oken (1977) have proposed a circular pattern in which patients occupy "spokes of a wheel" separated by dividers. Glass enclosures can reduce the sensory bombardment of the ICU and be a barrier to contagion while still allowing patients to be in view of a central "hub" nursing station.

A physical setting that allows for some staff privacy will help reduce the stress of working in a unit in which the behavior of caregivers is so open to scrutiny. Staff members need some privacy to work out possible disagreements among themselves and to openly express their emotions away from patients and family members. It has frequently been observed that caregivers often use humor to reduce the emotional impact of their work. Joking, laughing, even singing can sometimes be observed in critical care settings. It usually occurs in small groups and is usually brief. While appropriate humor can be therapeutic for caregivers and reduce tension, relatives of critically ill patients may have difficulty understanding this response (Hay & Oken, 1977; Swanson & Swanson, 1977).

Giving Group Support. Structured group support can be critical in coping with work-related stresses. Providing a forum for open discussion has been shown to be effective on oncology wards as well as in other settings (Newlin & Welisch, 1978). While emotional support is often available from family members and friends, they may have difficulty relating to the caregiver's specific concerns. Sometimes, significant others simply get tired of hearing about their loved one's "death work."

Organized support groups composed of coworkers who meet regularly can serve several different purposes. First of all, they provide an outlet for the expression of feelings. Feelings are not only heard by others but validated by them as well. Staff members discover that they are not alone in experiencing the stress and grief associated with terminal patient care. In addition, individuals can learn useful coping strategies from other group participants. Younger, less experienced group members can model themselves on professionals who have been able to cope with their job demands, achieve job satisfaction, and manage their stress effectively. An added benefit of this type of support is the group cohesion that it promotes. This cohesion extends beyond the actual group meeting and can lead to better working relationships and less staff conflict.

Providing Ongoing Educational Opportunities.   Organizations, institutions, and agencies can also support their staff members by providing relevant educational and training opportunities. There is constant need for individuals working with the critically and terminally ill to be aware of new information and to upgrade their skills (Bugen, 1980). Not only are continued education and training necessary for quality patient care, but these factors have been shown to be stress reducers as well (Gronseth, Martinson, Kersey, & Nesbit, 1981). Regular in-service sessions can guard against stagnation, enhance job satisfaction, and increase caregivers' feelings of competence in dealing with patient issues. Through an organized educational program, staff members can work together to question past approaches and consider new avenues in view of recent research developments (Lattanzi, 1983).

Professional Training Programs

Preparing Professionals to Cope with Death, Dying, and Grief

Death education is a relatively new concept in professional training programs. Even though significant advances have been made in the last 2 decades, evidence suggests that present efforts in death education are still not sufficient to meet the needs of professionals working with dying and grieving individuals.

As late as 1980, over half of 800 Canadian physicians, residents, and medical students sampled said that they did not feel their skills were adequate to meet the psychosocial needs of their terminally ill patients (Perez, Gosselin, & Gagnon, 1980). In 1975, only 7 out of 107 American schools surveyed had a full-term course in the area of death and dying. Forty-four schools reported having a "mini-course," and an additional 42 had a "lecture or two" on the subject. Of the medical school deans who reported having some type of death education content in their curriculum, 73 percent had introduced it during the 5 years prior to the study (Dickinson, 1976). A similar survey conducted in 1980 showed that the number of full-term death education courses had increased only slightly, from 7 to 16. These courses were commonly taught using a team approach, with instructors representing a variety of disciplines. While physicians, psychiatrists, and theologians most typically served as faculty, also included in high numbers were psychologists, sociologists, nurses, philosophers, social workers, and attorneys (Dickinson, 1981).

Increased attention has been given to death education in professional schools during the 1980s. Dickinson, Sumner, and Durand (1987) found that 96 percent of medical schools, 95 percent of nursing schools, and 68 percent of pharmacy schools now offer some death education in their curricula. A multidisciplinary approach to teaching the subject matter is used in the majority of medical schools. Pharmacy schools use a team approach about half of the time, and nursing programs rarely use multiple instructors in their thantology offerings. Also, it must be noted that less than 25 percent of these professional schools offer a complete course on death, dying, and grief.

Medical school faculty sometimes argue that there is not enough time in the curriculum to include more instruction in death education. Offering another perspective, Olin (1972) has observed that medical students spend time learning about many rare diseases that they will probably never encounter. He then raises the point that dying may be thought of as a serious clinical condition that occurs frequently and therefore has a valid and important place in medical education.

Professionals who are called upon to offer emotional support to dying and grieving individuals also receive little preparation for this role. In their survey of theology schools, Kalish and Dunn (1976) found that the majority did not offer courses on death, dying, and bereavement. Even though the topic was included in some courses on pastoral counseling, it received little in-depth coverage. Family therapists are also often ill-prepared to work with families with loss-related issues. In a related study, a random sample of members of the American Association for Marriage and Family Therapy was questioned about their training and experience in death, dying, and grief. While 97 percent felt that training in this area was important for a therapist, only 24 percent were satisfied with the amount of death education they received in their professional training programs. The majority of therapists in the sample had counseled dying persons and had worked with grieving families. These therapists expressed the need for additional training to increase their expertise in working with grief and loss issues (Stephenson, 1981).

Professional training programs in the mental and physical health care fields can play an important role in preparing individuals to cope with the unique demands of working with the dying and their families. This preparation includes both the acquisition of a range of professional skills, a base of knowledge, and an examination of one's own feelings and attitudes.

Kastenbaum (1977) has suggested that the most successful death education efforts seem to be those that integrate intellectual content with the opportunity to explore feelings and attitudes. Although formal training on how to help dying individuals and grieving families has increased, little training is designed to help professionals deal with their own personal feelings of loss, grief, and self-doubt (Neimeyer, Behnke, & Reiss, 1983). Nurses trained in sophisticated techniques of medical care are sometimes no better equipped than aides in coping with their own emotional responses to illness and death. Maslach (1976) has charged that many educational institutions actually teach health care providers to disassociate their feelings and emotions from intellectual concerns by encouraging fragmented and dehumanized perceptions of patients.

After reviewing the clinical literature, Shady (1976) and Schulz and Aderman (1976) have concluded that caregivers must deal with their own feelings about death in order to effectively and comfortably deal with a person facing death. According to Bugen (1980), all professionals have significant emotional needs that they must cope with to ensure successful intervention with dying and grieving individuals. Unless these needs are acknowledged, the helping relationship may be jeopardized. Emotions, particularly anxiety, can affect professional perceptions, diagnoses, and even treatment of patients. Death anxiety can lead to avoidance of dying persons by professionals (Neimeyer et al., 1983) as well as inability to engage in direct, honest communication (Kastenbaum, 1977). Death anxiety can even cause the professional to project his or her feelings onto the patient. After listening to an acute leukemia patient speak in a death and dying seminar, psychology graduate students who reported high levels of anxiety during the presentation tended to view the individual as more denying, more angry, less accepting, and less hopeful than did students with low anxiety levels. While the same person was observed by all the students simultaneously, perceptions varied as a result of the observer's own emotional responses (Bugen, 1980).

Preparing Professionals for Multidisciplinary Work

In this chapter, we have discussed personal reactions of professionals and their need for support from peers as they face the stresses of working with the dying. However, individuals working together on multidisciplinary teams often have difficulty providing support to each other. The *multidisciplinary* approach involves more than a variety of professionals (physicians, nurses, clergy, psychologists, social workers, child-life specialists, and occupational therapists, among others) providing care. It includes the belief that a team approach with professionals from several disciplines working together can provide integrated optimum care for patients. The process of working together implies cooperation, communication, and common goals.

In reality, professionals in each discipline have little experience in working on multidisciplinary teams. Most individuals become part of a team after having been socialized into their respective professions during their many years of training. Professional socialization refers not only to the cognitive aspects of education in which skills and knowledge are acquired but also to the acquisition of attitudes, feelings, and values (Cartwright, 1979). Each member of the team speaks a different jargon, has a unique orientation, and possesses a distinct set of professional skills. When these differences are great they can interfere with clear communication and group cohesion.

Professional training programs can be instrumental in preparing students to assume professional roles in which they interact effectively with other professionals. Mutual respect and understanding are critical for professionals to function as a team. These can perhaps be developed through increased interaction during the critical socialization period. The inclusion of courses in professional training programs (psychology graduate programs, medical schools, nursing schools, pastoral counseling curricula) that involve faculty and students from several disciplines can have positive outcomes if accompanied by faculty commitment to interdisciplinary exchange and cooperation.

If professionals can get beyond the battleground of disciplinary turf issues, they can learn to nurture each other and provide collegial support. If not, they not only fail themselves and their colleagues, but also their patients. The more they are able to work through their own personal and professional issues, the better quality of care they will be able to provide for dying individuals and their families. With this goal comes the rewards and satisfactions of defining one's work in terms of integrity, meaning, and value.

Caring for the Dying: An Opportunity for Growth

Despite the grief and stress experienced by professionals, many of them spend their lives working with the dying and find innumerable rewards and satisfactions. It has often been said that we have much to learn from the dying. In the process of providing our services, we can enlarge our personal capacities as we learn to cope with our own concerns and anxieties. Pines and her colleagues (1981) have emphasized that a crisis can be a trigger for personal growth. When one's psychological equilibrium is disrupted, the adaptational process that follows can lead to a new reality within the person, involving new insights and perceptions. If this change is positive, it can be considered "growth" (Price & Murphy, 1984).

As professionals work with the dying and their families, they often find that their coping skills are increased, their support systems are strengthened and expanded, and their priorities are reordered. Working with the dying can teach us much about life and living. Elisabeth Kübler-Ross, who has worked with many terminally ill individuals, has often spoken about the enriching aspects of this experience. In her book *Death: The Final Stage of Growth* (1975), she says: "Facing death means facing the ultimate question of the meaning of life. If we really want to live we must have the courage to recognize that life is ultimately very short, and that everything we do counts" (p. 126).

Summary

Psychologists, family therapists, social workers, clergy, physicians, nurses, and other professionals experience many stresses as a result of ongoing interactions with the dying and the bereaved. Grief is a common reaction, although its intensity depends on a number of factors, including patient variables and other losses experienced by the caregiver. Job-related stresses should be closely examined in order to determine possible solutions for avoiding or diminishing the risk of staff burnout. Both individual staff members and supervisors need to be aware of warning signals and develop appropriate coping mechanisms as well as methods of prevention.

During the last decade, more and more professions have realized the importance of training their students in theory and application of knowledge related to death, dying, and grief. Many professional curricula now include at least some focus on these topics. Others are in the process of developing courses in these areas. Evidence suggests, however, that present efforts in death education are still not sufficient.

Many disciplines have developed over time in order to treat various needs of individuals and families. In our complex world, a team of professionals from various backgrounds is often called for in order to give clients optimal holistic care. In order to help different professions to work together effectively, a multidisciplinary perspective must be introduced and demonstrated in professional training programs.

Despite the stresses experienced, helping professionals find many rewards in working with the dying and the grieving. Personal skills and insights are developed that can enrich all facets of their lives.

$\mathcal{D}$ *Personal Account*

Four therapists describe the mourning process each experienced following the death of a patient by suicide. All of the suicides occurred in 1976, when the therapists were in clinical training at the same medical facility. To facilitate the resolution of the grief associated with the suicides, the therapists met as a group for over a year. In addition to describing their own experiences in this article, the authors give suggestions for ways training programs can help therapists when this type of crisis occurs.

The Working Through of Patients' Suicides by Four Therapists

Susan Kolodny, D.M.H, Renee L. Binder, M.D., Abbot A. Bronstein, Ph.D., and Robert L. Friend, M.D.

During the Spring of 1976 each of the four authors, then trainees in the Department of Psychiatry, Mount Zion Hospital and Medical Center, San Francisco, had a patient commit suicide. For each this was the first patient suicide, a powerful personal experience for which we had little preparation. Though we had studied suicidal behaviors, we had heard little about therapists' reactions to patients' suicide and found the literature on the subject to be sparse.

One month after the fourth suicide, we started meeting to discuss our cases and our reactions. Important differences among us were apparent, but more striking were the similarities. The realization of shared responses helped us to master the experience and suggested that a description of the cases and our reactions might be of value to others.

Review of the Literature

Theoretical discussions about suicide and suicidal behaviors have been a part of psychology and sociology for many decades. Yet, despite this wealth of material and the frequency with which suicides occur among patients in treatment (Litman, 1965), including the fact that in one university training center 16 percent of all residents in psychiatry had had a

This paper was presented at the Department of Psychiatry Grand Rounds, University of California Medical Center, San Francisco, May 17, 1977. The authors would like to express their appreciation to Drs. Edward Weinshel and David H. Rosen for their helpful comments and suggestions on a previous draft of this paper.

From *Suicide and Life-Threatening Behavior,* 1979, Vol. 9, No. 1, pp. 33–46. Reprinted by permission of Guilford Publications.

patient commit suicide (Rosen, 1974), only a few articles in the literature directly approach the problem of therapists' reactions to patients' suicides.

Most writers attempt to explore the suicide process in the hope of sensitizing clinicians to the important transference and countertransference cues during therapy (Havens, 1965; Bloom, 1967; Wheat, 1960). In contrast, Litman (1965), in a study based on interviews with more than 200 psychiatrists and psychologists, focused on how psychotherapists actually reacted to a recent patient suicide and cited a number of reactions reported by the therapists. These included feelings of disbelief and shaken self-confidence; partial identifications with patients, resulting in dreams and accident proneness by the therapists after the suicides; feelings of guilt and anger at supervisors, relatives of the patients, or the dead patients themselves.

The findings presented here are in some ways similar to those of Litman (1965) and Bloom (1967). The authors, however, go on to consider the process whereby therapists attempt to understand and master the experience following a patient's suicide and the implications that process has for training.

Cases and Reactions

We shall first describe the four patients, the therapy, and the therapists' individual reactions to the suicides up to the time that the therapists began meeting together as a group.

Mr. P

The Case. I was in my first year of clinical training when I saw Mr. P, a bright, articulate 23 year-old college student. He had come to the Crisis Clinic in the midst of his second acute psychotic decompensation. He suffered from what he recognized were hallucinations and delusions. Antipsychotic medications were administered and, when he refused hospitalization, I agreed to work with him in closely supervised outpatient crisis intervention therapy, stressing that if his condition worsened, he would be hospitalized. I met with Mr. P five times over two-and-a-half weeks. He failed to show for the sixth appointment or for an interview which he and I had arranged at a halfway house.

Mr. P initially continued to decompensate, but then his manifest psychotic symptoms seemed to clear. Though he was depressed and spoke of previous suicide attempts, he appeared hopeful, denied present suicidal intent, and seemed to form a good preliminary alliance with me. He showed insight into the meaning of his symptoms and spoke openly of his sexual identity confusion and its relationship to his psychotic episodes. All of this made me feel cautiously hopeful that Mr. P could be followed as an outpatient.

I liked Mr. P and I worried about him but was reluctant to risk his apparent trust by an involuntary hospitalization. I alternated, as he did, between feeling hopeful and despairing. He had some intact ego functions, but his lengthy psychiatric history did not suggest a good prognosis. I worried because he had no support system, but his apparent willingness to move into the halfway house made me feel that he would have a supportive environment that would help him through the present crisis.

When Mr. P failed to appear for his sixth appointment, I phoned his dorm. It was Monday; he had not been seen since Saturday. Tuesday, his car was found by the Golden Gate Bridge, where it was presumed to have been left several days before. Wednesday, I received a flurry of long-distance calls from his worried family. Thursday, the patient's uncle came to San Francisco, searched the patient's room, and found suicide notes for each member of his family. Mr. P's body was never found.

Therapist's Reactions. Upon hearing from a psychiatric technician that Mr. P's car had been found at the bridge, I felt a wave of panic, but did not for a moment doubt that he had killed himself. I was concerned about whether I would be able to function with patients and in conferences until the weekend. When I heard a second technician remark that he had figured the patient was suicidal, I walked off too angry to speak. A third technician called after me, telling me not to be upset. I wondered how people could say such useless things to one another at such a time. I felt alarmingly alone.

I then began questioning and doubting my therapeutic decisions. Should I have hospitalized him against his will? Would things ultimately have turned out differently if I had? Should I have picked up clues? Hadn't I in fact picked up clues and chosen to ignore them? I recalled having ominous feelings after my last session with him. Why hadn't I taken these more seriously as warnings? I wondered, too, if a more experienced therapist would have done differently. Had my supervisors—I had spoken to more than one of them about Mr. P—supported my decisions because of some inadvertent distortion I had made in telling them of the case?

I wondered if something I had said or done was responsible. Had my mentioning a possible referral for long-term therapy been experienced as a rejection? Had my identifying with him and with some of his intellectual interests fooled me into having too much faith in his apparent capacity to function?

I was alarmed at finding myself called upon to be supportive of others at such a time and surprised to find I could do so. I was able to be helpful on the telephone with Mr. P's family both before and after the suicide notes were found. I spoke at length with Mr. P's uncle almost immediately after he discovered the notes and found myself able to be helpful to him and to give him the solace he so clearly sought.

During that week in which the bad news had come in increments—the missing patient, the found car, the suicide notes—and for days after, I turned to a close friend for comforting. I discussed Mr. P with supervisors in an attempt to learn whatever I could and to see if I had done something wrong. I sought reassurances that I had made no dreadful error. I found relief in talking to those staff members who made themselves available to listen and felt impatient with those whose first response was to say, "Oh let me tell you about my patient who killed himself." I felt relieved that I and the supervisor with whom I had spoken the most about Mr. P were able not only to analyze the sessions, but also to talk candidly about our mutual sadness.

After a few weeks I received a visit from Mr. P's family. As a result of that meeting, I understood the patient better and felt I had possibly helped his family somewhat in their efforts to gain some sense of closure. A few weeks later I presented the case in a conference. The empathy and interest of my colleagues helped me to come to terms with the loss. I felt weathered by the experience, initiated. I thought about the meaning of the title "Doctor," its responsibilities, and the assumptions people make about those who hold it. I was sobered by being myself grieved and yet being in a position to have to comfort others.

For months after Mr. P's disappearance, I would think of him whenever I crossed the bridge and imagine him dead and floating in the water. At times I would think of him and start to cry. Sometimes it seemed as if he had no alternative at all.

I became worried that other patients would kill themselves. I hospitalized patients more frequently than before and had fantasies of requiring outpatients to sign oaths that they would not kill themselves. I did not feel I could tolerate ever having to have such an experience again. By the time the group of therapists began meeting, however, three months after Mr. P's death, I felt I had some distance from the experience. But the sadness remained for a long time.

Ms. C

The Case. I was in my second year of clinical training when I began treating Ms. C, then 24 years old and recently discharged following hospitalization for her second acute psychotic decompensation. I saw Ms. C as an outpatient twice weekly for one year and then three times weekly for six months in supervised, psychodynamically oriented psychotherapy. Ms. C then terminated treatment abruptly after 18 months—four months prior to her suicide.

Ms. C was a bright, charming, and vivacious, single, white college graduate. She had been diagnosed as a schizophrenic with depressive features during her first hospitalization at age 21. I, however, saw her as manic-depressive, circular type, and treated her with lithium carbonate. I felt hopeful that with what I considered to be the correct diagnosis and the appropriate treatment the patient would do well.

I found Ms. C attractive and appealing and felt the patient worked hard and well in therapy. Often I felt flattered by Ms. C, who would acknowledge the benefits of both psychotherapy and lithium therapy. I found myself harboring rescue fantasies with respect to the patient. At one point, for example, I met with Ms. C and her parents and when the parents overtly demeaned the patient, I found myself identifying with Ms. C and defending her against her parents, as well as telling them that she would get better.

At times during treatment I found myself worrying about Ms. C. I sometimes felt angry at the patient, who would come in three times a week and in a hopeless and helpless fashion, complain about her parents and her life. I felt that I had constantly to instill hope in the patient and that the patient expected me to perform miracles.

Seventeen months into treatment, Ms. C was found wandering on the Golden Gate Bridge, having left a note which said "I can't imagine being a sad, fat, 40 year-old supported by her parents." Though she denied suicidal intent, she was rehospitalized. Therapy then resumed for one month, after which I took a one-month vacation. The day I was to have my first post vacation appointment with Ms. C, the patient was rehospitalized for another acute manic attack. I contacted Ms. C and was informed that she had found a new therapist on her own and did not intend to resume her work with me.

I never saw Ms. C again. Four months later, I was informed that Ms. C had thrown herself off the bridge. She had left no note.

Therapist's Reactions. When I was told of Ms. C's suicide by another patient who had been a friend of hers I felt immediate disbelief. I questioned the patient to seek verification and to make sure he was not delusional, then phoned Ms. C's new therapist who confirmed the suicide.

I then began to seek support. I phoned my husband; I considered, but decided against, calling my analyst. I discovered that telling others not only helped me to obtain support, but it also helped me to confirm the reality of the situation, to check my use of denial. I notified the staff at the inpatient unit where I worked and where Ms. C had been a patient.

Then I became aware of strong feelings of shame and embarrassment. What would the many staff and patients think who knew I had been Ms. C's therapist? Would people think I had not done a good job? Would they consider me responsible for the suicide? Was I responsible? What would people expect of me? Was I appropriately upset? Should I be continuing with my regular activities? I felt defensive and found myself telling people that I had not seen Ms. C for months, that for four months the patient had been seeing another therapist. Yet I kept thinking of something Ms. C's new therapist had told me, that Ms. C had often said I believed she would always be depressed. Had Ms. C killed herself because she thought I considered her hopeless? Had an interpretation of mine caused the suicide? Two months prior to the termination of treatment, I had switched supervisors. My new supervisor had suggested a different approach to the case. Had this new approach been responsible for the suicide? I was angry at the new supervisor and at myself for having listened to him.

That first evening, when I returned home, I once again felt the need to verify the news and to seek information. I phoned the coroner's office and asked many questions. I found myself curious about the specific details of the suicide, and, in keeping with Ms. C's intense preoccupation about her appearance, I found myself wondering how the patient's body must have looked after its impact with the water.

Throughout the first week I continued to be filled with disbelief. I had assumed that the patient's terminating therapy had been an acting-out behavior related to the vacation and that Ms. C would eventually resume therapy with me. Once before Ms. C had angrily broken off therapy, but that time she had returned. Why hadn't Ms. C phoned this time? Would things had gone differently had Ms. C done so?

One week after the suicide, I presented the case at a conference to an experienced analyst. The analyst remarked that the patient's death had in some ways been predictable, which caused me to become angry. Why hadn't I seen it? What should I have known that I didn't? Had I underestimated this patient's pathology?

Around the time of the conference, other feelings began to emerge. I became acutely aware of feelings of loss. I felt I had known the patient well and that the death was a tragedy. I decided to keep on my desk a paperclip holder which Ms. C had given me as a gift.

For several weeks after the suicide, I found myself being overly cautious with patients who were potentially suicidal. On the inpatient unit where I worked, I found that I was ordering suicide precautions more often than usual.

Eight weeks after the suicide, still experiencing intense feelings of sadness and loss, I began meeting with three other therapists, each of whom had had a patient commit suicide.

Mr. N

The Case. I was in my third year of clinical training when I began seeing Mr. N, a 42 year-old, white, homosexual male, once weekly, in psychodynamically oriented outpatient psychotherapy. Mr. N, diagnosed a psychotic character with severe depressive features, had sought treatment because of intense feelings of loneliness, depression and anxiety, and chronic suicidal ideation. He was alcoholic and diabetic and had suffered multiple early rejections and losses. His lengthy psychiatric history included many and varied treatments. His transfer to me was his second one within the clinic. One year earlier he had been transferred for the first time and shortly afterwards attempted suicide by taking a massive overdose of insulin. The second transfer appeared to take place more smoothly. The patient made no further suicide attempts until he succeeded in killing himself 19 months into treatment with me.

During the first six months I found working with the patient to be challenging and exciting, though very difficult. Mr. N seemed to attach himself quickly to me and the therapy process, to work hard, and to make good progress, both in his outside accomplishments and within the treatment. From the start Mr. N was graphic in describing his fantasies and feelings. I felt I understood the patient and was helping him to understand himself. All of this led me initially to believe I would succeed where the other therapists had not and to be hopeful, even though the patient was not.

After the first six months I found myself worrying a great deal about Mr. N. Occasionally letters would arrive from the patient, following a session, expressing despair not spoken of during sessions. I wondered whether he was imminently suicidal. Gradually the severity and chronicity of Mr. N's pathology became more apparent. Yet I still felt some hopefulness about treatment outcome. During the final six months of treatment Mr. N began to articulate most vividly his depression in terms of his overwhelming feelings of emptiness and deadness.

I last saw Mr. N before leaving on a vacation. The patient spoke at that time of his great concerns about being left alone and rejected, and of a fantasy of being taken along in my suitcase. He expressed concern about whether he would be able to continue to see me in private practice, although arrangements had already been made for Mr. N to do so.

Two weeks after this last appointment, Mr. N checked into a room at the YMCA under an assumed name. He left letters for his roommate and sister, placed his medications by his bedside, and took a lethal overdose of insulin.

Therapist's Reactions. Halfway through my vacation, I called the clinic for messages and was told that Mr. N had committed suicide. I thought, in rapid succession, about the role in the suicide of my vacation, about the last sessions with Mr. N, about what others would think, and about what might have happened to cause such a drastic course of action. I felt disbelief, that it was a mistake, and yet, never doubted that the patient had killed himself.

In the next few days I tried to put aside feelings of shame and guilt and attempted to talk with and comfort the patient's sister, as well as to find out about events leading up to and including the suicide. I felt a strong desire to discuss the last hours of the case with two senior supervisors and to discover what had happened and why. I did not feel that something I had said had caused the suicide, more that something I could have said or done would have prevented it at that time. My feeling that my error was possibly one of omission seemed closely connected to the feelings about having been away when Mr. N committed suicide. These feelings prevailed for the next few days, during which I very much wanted to have an experienced analyst say that no gross errors had been made, to be "exonerated" by senior staff.

I found from the start that it was very hard to speak to people at the clinic about the suicide. I felt the need for privacy and experienced a sense of shame about others knowing. When one staff member phoned me unexpectedly to offer solace, I felt angry and experienced the call as an intrusion into my grief and my vacation.

After three days I left on the second half of my vacation. I found that being away with a friend helped me to obtain some distance from my feelings about the suicide, the people at the clinic, and other patients. The pressure to discuss and explore what had happened was no longer externally applied. I could speak of it as I chose with my friend. During the vacation I experienced many "why me?" feelings, became aware of anger, and began to miss the patient. I continued to wonder what might have been done to prevent the suicide. I had one other seriously suicidal patient in my caseload at that time, and during the trip I found myself worrying about her.

When I returned to work, I found myself wanting to know what had happened to Mr. N and why he had killed himself at that particular time. I believed that the suicide would not have occurred, at least not then, had I, the therapist, been available.

I continued to have feelings of embarrassment and shame, of anger and helplessness for about two months. I was angry at and hurt by having had this "done" to me; but more, I felt regret that I had not been available to help this man of whom I had grown so fond. Over the two months following the suicide, I found myself, from time to time, continuing my discussion with my supervisors as new thoughts, memories, and feelings surfaced about this patient and his act of suicide.

As time passed, my feelings of loneliness and sadness increased. I found myself thinking about the patient and, at times, dreaming of him. One of my dreams, which I chose to discuss with a supervisor, illustrated, even two months after the suicide, both my identifications with the lost patient and some of the previously clouded feelings of responsibility for Mr. N's death. I realized how intensely involved I had been with Mr. N and with my other patients, as well. I continued to worry about the other suicidal patients in my caseload and was particularly aware of not wanting to go through such an experience again. It became easier with time to speak to

friends about these feelings for Mr. N and about having had a patient commit suicide. By the time the group of therapists began meeting, ten weeks
after the suicide, I felt a willingness to share some of my reactions with
the others.

Ms. Z

The Case. I was in my first year of clinical training when Ms. Z, a 31 year-
old mother of two, and former dental student, was referred to me from the
inpatient unit where she had been hospitalized following her first paranoid
schizophrenic decompensation. I was told she would be a "tough but
promising case."

Ms. Z's decompensation had come amidst stress over the breakup of her
marriage and soon after the birth of her second child. Despite florid presenting symptomatology, there was no prior history of either psychiatric
treatment or psychotic symptoms. I started seeing Ms. Z three times a week
while she was an inpatient and continued this frequency on an outpatient
basis for 15 months.

During the first four months of treatment Ms. Z performed several bizarre
suicidal acts (such as inhaling the fumes from a scorched Teflon pan) and
once required a four-day rehospitalization. Ms. Z seemed to improve, however, as a sense of alliance developed in therapy.

After the first 6 months of treatment therapy centered around her feelings
of emptiness and hopelessness. The earlier suicidal ideation and action
diminished. Ms. Z seemed to be highly invested in the therapy. She began
to reexperience strong feelings, starting with sadness and then anger,
which she feared would overwhelm both her and me.

I valued the sessions with Ms. Z and often felt exhilarated by understanding material which Ms. Z felt to be incomprehensible and disordered. It
troubled me, however, that seldom could I adequately convey to Ms. Z my
sense of understanding, and that it had little impact on her pervasive feelings of being doomed.

Throughout the treatment, I was aware of how intensely Ms. Z suffered.
I often caught myself viewing her as a helpless victim in need of rescue.
In supervision with a psychoanalyst, experienced in working with severely
disturbed patients, I became aware of my own feelings of helpless frustration as signs of my wishing to be an omnipotent rescuer.

The patient's child became seriously ill 13 months into therapy, and Ms.
Z became preoccupied with minor somatic complaints of her own. At this
time, I noted that I was experiencing difficulty telling Ms. Z that I would
be away for several days.

Upon my return, Ms. Z atypically cancelled several sessions to go on a
vacation. She returned, and the ramifications and meanings of her vacation
were explored; there was the sense of the sessions becoming increasingly
productive. I had no particular feeling of worry or concern during my last

session with the patient. Two days later she killed herself by cutting her throat in the bathroom of her home. She left no note.

Therapist's Reactions.   I was waiting for a seminar to begin when I received a phone call informing me of the suicide. I felt stunned and unaware of surroundings and experienced both the disbelief and the certainty that Ms. Z was dead. Then, remembering where I was, I wondered whether to stay or to leave the room. I remained and sat thinking that I would surely be sued for malpractice and that I had no business being a psychotherapist and should have gone into radiology instead.

After the seminar I went directly to my supervisor and was relieved to find him busy; my fears told me that he might have shown me some therapeutic error I had made which had killed the patient. I went to another supervisor, one unfamiliar with the case, and felt relieved not to be blamed for the suicide. It became important to go immediately to friends and tell them what had happened.

I went to the inpatient unit, where many people had previously been involved with the patient's care and made it my task to inform each one personally. I recognized feeling guilty and wanting both punishment and expiation, when I imagined going to the staff meeting and announcing her death, though I was not working on the inpatient unit. I also thought of calling the patient's ex-husband and her father, but I decided to wait until the next day to do so, by which time I was able to be supportive and reassuring.

Within a few days I became aware of feeling angry—at the supervisor who had encouraged me to work in psychodynamically-oriented therapy with so disturbed a patient, at the resident who had referred her to me, and at all psychiatry which felt it could help people. I was angry at the patient. How could she have "done it" to me? By about a week after the suicide, I worried that my reactions were "pathological" and "narcissistic."

In the beginning of the second week I met with my supervisor and, at the supervisor's urging, began reluctantly studying the case in detail to understand what had transpired in the therapy preceding the suicide. I was surprised over the next weeks that I could both see some warning signs had been missed and not feel guilty about it. I felt I could not have done this during the first week.

Toward the end of the second week I began to miss the patient. I would think of Ms. Z and tears would come to my eyes. I thought sadly of my own former therapist to whom I had never written and became aware of feeling new fondness for several of my patients. I thought of relatives of mine who had died and of concerns for my parents.

One month after Ms. Z's suicide it occurred to me that the four therapists who had experienced the suicide of a patient should meet as a group to discuss their reactions. The idea was that something productive should come out of the deaths of these patients. The group first met five weeks after Ms. Z's death.

The Group Meetings

The four therapists began meeting informally five weeks after the last patient had committed suicide. The meetings initially occurred every two weeks and after three or four sessions began to be held monthly. The group met at members' homes or offices. The meetings were leaderless, informal, and supportive. The commitment felt by each to these meetings was evident in that, despite very demanding schedules, each attended regularly for almost a year.

We discovered as soon as we started meeting that although all were in training and each had recently had a patient commit suicide, we were far from being a homogeneous group. Two of us were male and two were female, with each combination of sex of therapist and sex of patient represented. Two of us were residents in psychiatry, one was a postdoctoral psychology fellow, and one was a trainee in the Doctor of Mental Health program. One of us had seen her patient a total of five times over two-and-a-half weeks and one of us had seen his patient three times weekly for nearly one-and-a-half years. There were striking differences in the cases themselves. Transference and countertransference themes varied. Also, we were, at the start, in quite different stages of reaction to the suicides. The therapist whose patient had suicided first had presented him in a case conference and had had nearly 3 months to gain some sense of resolution. The therapist whose patient had died most recently was still experiencing acute feelings of loss.

Yet, from the start, our group found itself more focused on the similarities than on differences. After a brief, initial phase in which we variously asked ourselves—"Are these others competent?" "Will they accept me?" "Could they possibly feel this as intensely as I?"—we four seemed to work toward cohesiveness. In the first two meetings we presented our cases in some detail. As we were able to do so in a manner that was mutually supportive and nonjudgmental, we quickly experienced the forming of a sense of community. For all our differences, we had in common that a patient had committed suicide and at times this seemed almost to obscure the differences among us. Our unintentional emphasis on homogeneity may have blurred distinctions and led to oversimplification, but it helped to provide a safe atmosphere for exploration of reactions. As we began to feel safe, we shared with each other how isolated we had felt earlier in trying to deal with our loss.

During those initial sessions in which each of us presented his or her case, the others listened in silence and with marked empathy. Defenses were respected, which added to the sense of safety and trust. This seemed to allow us to experience or, in some cases, to reexperience those feelings which we had at the time of the suicides, and eventually it facilitated a more complete working through than had been attained previously. The denial, of which we spoke earlier and which Litman (1965) describes, was evident for each of us, but the safety we afforded one another seemed to reduce the need for that denial. The atmosphere generated by our group seemed also to permit the emergence and expression of feelings of guilt and shame.

After a time—two or three months into the existence of the group—we felt we had begun to work through these feelings. Next we found ourselves concerned with intellectual mastery. We wanted to understand what had happened to each of us and hoped that from such understanding something of value would emerge. We became task-oriented and began work on the present paper. Both the processes of intellectual and affective mastery proceeded concurrently over the next year.

Conclusions

The suicide of a patient in psychotherapy presents an undesired challenge to any therapist, a challenge to master and work through the complex reactions which follow a death by suicide. Through our experiences and discussions, we have arrived at a number of conclusions about this challenge and at some implications these conclusions have for training programs. Because we believe that the ways in which this challenge is met will in part determine the therapist's future ability to work with depressed and suicidal patients, we believe our conclusions and implications will be of interest, both to other psychotherapists in training and to those mental health professionals who plan, administer, and teach in clinical training programs.

We concluded that the process we went through was a process of mourning. It occurred over time and required time; we could not rush it, circumvent it, or avoid its various aspects. The usual elements of mourning were present, but because the people for whom we mourned were our patients and because their deaths were by suicide, some of the usual elements of mourning were intensified while others were attenuated. Like most people who undergo a loss, we experienced an initial state of denial and of disbelief. We also subsequently accepted the loss and experienced feelings of identification with the lost person. Intensified for us by these circumstances were our sense of threatened omnipotence and self-esteem and our feelings of shame, guilt, vulnerability, and self-doubt. Also intensified were our feelings of anger about the deaths, anger which was directed at our patients, their families, our supervisors and ourselves. Possibly attenuated were the more pervasive feelings of loss, as these people were part of our lives in circumscribed ways.

We recognized that, particularly at the beginning, we felt an intense need for support, understanding, and absolution, and yet we felt isolated.

We realize this was so, in part, because the process of mourning is and must inevitably be a lonely one. Just as we are convinced that no exercise of imagination or intellect can really prepare one for such an experience or inoculate one against its impact, so we are convinced that no support system or understanding on the part of colleagues or supervisors can entirely alleviate the pain and self-examination one must go through in the wake of a patient's suicide.

Nonetheless, we felt that in such situations the clinical community can prove helpful in very specific ways. We found it helpful when others recognized and respected our defenses. Not everyone was able to do so. It helped also to be given sufficient time to prepare ourselves for the painful but necessary task of the "psychological autopsy." How much time we needed varied. Those supervisors and teachers who prematurely wished us to discuss our cases or did not give us adequate opportunity to talk about them when we were ready were not helpful; nor were those who immediately barraged us with tales of their own patients who had committed suicide or who spoke of how lucky they were never to have been through it themselves.

We found that it helped to be in supervision and to work with our supervisors to understand the suicides in the context of the therapy. The relief that we found in talking with supervisors, and later in talking in our group, made us sensitive to the importance, during and after training, of consultation with colleagues. We found it helped to be able to talk openly with supervisors about our countertransference reactions during the treatment and about our reactions to the patients' deaths—not only because this helped with the mourning process, but also because it provided, albeit retrospectively, important clues to the patients' psychopathology and to their motivations for suicide. We felt that a greater exploration of and sensitivity to such clues would be useful in subsequent clinical practice.

A factor that contributed to our difficulty in feeling a climate of support was that even psychiatric communities seem to underestimate the duration and impact of the traumatic reaction process. Therefore, even though support had been offered some of us initially, we were struggling with intense feelings and in need of support and an avenue for working through the losses over many months. It was not until we met together, providing one another with a reasonably nonthreatening, nonjudgmental, supportive context within which to explore our feelings and thoughts, that some of us began to feel we were working through the experience. We believe that training programs should encourage staff and trainees to develop this sort of group in the event of a patient suicide.

We found that as we worked through our mourning, we felt we had been through a rite of passage. While we did not feel immunized against having to reexperience this painful process in the future, we felt we had undergone something which had transformed and matured us and increased our sense of what we could withstand. We became more able to give up magical expectations and fantasies of therapeutic omnipotence. We had undergone a process during which we had realized a profound sense of isolation, a painful sense of having betrayed our patients' and our institution's trust in us and having felt betrayed by them in kind. This had been followed by a sense of connectedness with one another in our group and with other therapists with similar experiences. Further, we became more willing to accept our own limitations and to forgive ourselves.

Incidentally, we discovered that it had *not* helped to have medical training, that the death through disease of a patient was quite a different experience from the death through suicide. The MD's among us, no less than the non-MD's, found themselves in need of peer and staff understanding and support.

We believe these conclusions have some further implications for clinical training. Training institutions might provide some forum at which particularly difficult patients can be discussed. An example would be "the impossible case conference." Such a forum would fulfill at least two important functions not always fulfilled in training settings. First, it would provide another forum in which ideas could be exchanged about the management of particularly difficult cases and about complex therapeutic issues, including suicide. Second, it could provide a setting in which experienced clinicians, who usually demonstrate only their successes and thus inadvertently contribute to the trainee's sense of failure in the event of lesser therapeutic disasters than suicide, would share with trainees their own questions and fallibility. It would also help to mitigate trainees' sense of isolation and helplessness when they work with such cases; and it would help trainees and staff to learn from each other's experiences.

A related implication has to do with the importance of recognizing and making explicit certain clinical and personal inevitabilities: therapists with depressed and dependent patients must nonetheless take vacations; patients sometimes have to be transferred or therapy terminated; patients will sometimes commit suicide. Cognizance of these realities and an open consideration of their impact can assist trainees in working through such issues, both with their patients and within themselves.

In conclusion, we believe that we cannot always prevent patients from committing suicide and therefore prevent therapists from having to undergo the process of mourning a patient who does kill himself. It is important, then, to know as much as we can about this process so it can be facilitated by a supportive environment when it does occur, an environment which recognizes that such an experience is both painful and lonely and an opportunity for mastery and growth.

References

Bloom, V. An Analysis of Suicide at a Training Center. *American Journal of Psychiatry,* 1967, 123, 918–925.

Havens, L. L. The Anatomy of a Suicide. *The New England Journal of Medicine,* 1965, 272, 401–406.

Litman, R. E. When Patients Commit Suicide. *American Journal of Psychotherapy,* 1965, 19, 570–576.

Rosen, D. H. Mental Stresses in Residency Training and Opportunities for Prevention. Paper presented at the 12th Annual Meeting of the American Psychiatric Association. May 1974, Detroit, Michigan.

Shneidman, E. S., and Farberow, N. S. (Eds). *The Cry for Help.* New York: McGraw-Hill, 1961.

Wheat, W. D. Motivational Aspects of Suicide in Patients During and After Psychiatric Treatment. *Southern Medical Journal,* 1960, 53, 273–278.

Questions and Activities

1. As you read the article on client suicides, what feelings did you experience? Who were they directed toward? What thoughts went through your mind as you read each therapist's account of his or her experience?

2. For the following professions, describe a death or grief situation commonly encountered: clergy (priests, rabbis, ministers, pastoral counselors), funeral home directors, rescue workers and paramedics, coroners, military medical personnel in combat zones, and veterinarians. Identify several stresses and supports that are unique to each profession.

3. How might the life stage of the professional affect his or her response to particular types of deaths? What developmental needs and issues of young adulthood, middle age, and late adulthood might be relevant?

4. Examine your own potential for working with dying or grieving individuals. What characteristics and life experiences do you have that would enhance your ability to work with these populations? What traits and personal concerns might interfere with your effectiveness? Consider your motivations for doing this type of work.

5. Explore your susceptibility to burnout. What are your expectations regarding your future work? How much realistic and reliable information do you have regarding the type of work you plan to do? Why do you think that it is appropriate for you? How do you currently handle stresses in your life? Do an inventory of your own internal resources, support systems, and life-style patterns.

6. Conduct an interview with a professional doing the type of work you think you would like to do. Inquire about the rewards and satisfactions of the job as well as the stresses and frustrations. What does the individual do on a day-to-day basis? In what ways does he or she work with professionals from other fields? What other similar positions are available, and what education and experience does one need to be considered for these positions?

Glossary

Bereavement Overload: Occurs when a griever must deal with several deaths in close succession, without time to cope with the first death before being confronted with another.

Burnout: A syndrome of mental and physical exhaustion, low morale, cynicism, and despair related to job stress.

Countertransference: An emotional reaction, usually unconscious and often distorted, on the part of the therapist to a patient or member of a family in treatment.

Death Saturation: The limits of personal tolerance for death-related work.

Internal Resources: Abilities, attitudes, values, beliefs, or techniques that help individuals handle difficult moments or periods of time.

Multidisciplinary Approach: Involves professionals from a variety of disciplines working together as a team to provide integrated optimum care for patients.

Psychological Autopsy: A formal review focusing on establishing events that led to a patient's suicide in order to identify causal factors.

Support Networks and Systems: Relationships with individuals, groups, or organizations that offer emotional or material support.

Surrogate Griever: One who grieves in the place of family members.

Transference: Term for distorted emotional reactions to present relationships based on unresolved, early family relations (for example, a patient may react toward a therapist as though he or she were a significant figure from the patient's family).

Suggested Readings

Givelber, F., & Simon, B. (1981). A death in the life of a therapist and its impact on the therapy. *Psychiatry, 44,* 141–149.

The authors discuss the work-related problems and opportunities that arise when therapists experience the death of a close family member. Givelber and Simon discuss how interactions with patients may be affected and how intended and unintended outcomes can occur as a result of telling patients about the loss.

Hilfiker, D. (1985). *Healing the wounds: A physician looks at his work.* New York: Pantheon Books.

Dr. Hilfiker gives an honest and moving account of his personal experiences as a physician. This book provides insight into the extraordinary pressures involved in practicing medicine today.

Raphael, B., Singh, B., Bradbury, L., & Lambert, F. (1983). Who helps the helpers? The effects of a disaster on the rescue workers. *Omega, 14*(1), 9–20.

This article reports the results of a survey conducted 1 month after a rail disaster on 95 of the personnel involved in the rescue work and a follow-up on 13 of them 1 year later. The effects of the experience as well as the value of debriefing sessions are discussed.

References

Benoliel, J. Q. (1988). Health care providers and dying patients: Critical issues in terminal care. *Omega, 18*(4), 341–363.

Bugen, L. A. (1980). Emotions: Their presence and impact upon the helping role. In E. S. Shneidman (Ed.), *Death: Current perspectives* (2d ed.) (pp. 241–251). Palo Alto, CA: Mayfield.

Cartwright, L. K. (1979). Sources and effects of stress in health careers. In G. C. Stone, F. Cohen, N. E. Alder, & Associates (Eds.), *Health psychology: A handbook* (pp. 419–445). San Francisco: Jossey-Bass.

Cobb, S. (1976). Social support as a moderator of life stress. *Psychosomatic Medicine, 38*, 300–314.

Daley, M. (1979). Burnout: Smoldering problem in protective services. *Social Casework, 24*(5), 375–379.

deVries, H. (1975). Physical education, adult fitness programs: Does physical activity promote relaxation? *Journal of Physical Education and Recreation, 46*, 53–54.

Dickinson, G. E. (1976). Death education in U.S. medical schools. *Journal of Medical Education, 51*, 134–136.

Dickinson, G. E. (1981). Death education in U.S. medical schools: 1975–1980. *Journal of Medical Education, 56*, 111–114.

Dickinson, G. E., Summer, E. D., & Durand, R. P. (1987). Death education in the U.S. professional colleges: Medical, nursing, and pharmacy. *Death Studies, 11*, 57–61.

Dunne, E. J. (1987). A response to suicide in a mental health setting. In E. J. Dunne, J. L. McIntosh, & K. Dunne-Maxim (Eds.), *Suicide and its aftermath: Understanding and counseling the survivors* (pp. 182–190). New York: Norton.

Edelwich, J. (1980). *Burn-out.* New York: Human Services Press.

Freudenberger, H. (1974). Staff burnout. *Journal of Social Issues, 30*(1), 159–165.

Friedman, G. R., Franciosi, R. A., & Drake, R. M. (1979). The effects of observed sudden infant death syndrome (SIDS) on hospital staff. *Pediatrics, 64,* 538–540.

Fulton, R. (1979). Anticipatory grief, stress, and the surrogate griever. In J. Tache, H. Selye, & S. Day (Eds.), *Cancer, stress, and death* (pp. 87–93). New York: Plenum Press.

Goldstein, L. S., & Buongiorno, P. A. (1984). Psychotherapists as suicide survivors. *American Journal of Psychotherapy, 38,* 392–398.

Gronseth, E. C., Martinson, I. M., Kersey, J. H., & Nesbit, M. E., Jr. (1981). Support system of health professionals as observed in the project of home care for the child with cancer. *Death Education, 5,* 32–51.

Hay, D., & Oken, D. (1977). The psychological stresses of intensive care unit nursing. In R. H. Moos (Ed.), *Coping with physical illness* (pp. 381–396). New York: Plenum Press.

Jacobson, S. P. (1978). Stressful situations for neonatal intensive care nurses. *American Journal of Maternal Child Nursing, 3,* 144–150.

Jones, F. A., Jr. (1987). Therapists as survivors of client suicide. In E. J. Dunne, J. L. McIntosh, & K. Dunne-Maxim (Eds.), *Suicide and its aftermath: Understanding and counseling the survivors* (pp.126–141). New York: Norton.

Kalish, R. A., & Dunn, L. (1976). Death and dying: A survey of credit offerings in theological schools and some possible implications. *Review of Religious Research, 17,* 122–130.

Kastenbaum, R. J. (1977). *Death, society and human experience.* St. Louis, MO: C. V. Mosby.

Kroes, W., Margolis, B., & Quinn, R. (1974). Job stress: An unlisted occupational hazard. *Journal of Occupational Medicine, 16*(10), 659–661.

Kübler-Ross, E. (1975). Death as part of my own personal experience. In E. Kübler-Ross (Ed.), *Death: The final stage of growth* (pp. 119–126). Englewood Cliffs, NJ: Prentice-Hall.

Lack, S. A. (1978). New Haven (1974)—Characteristics of a hospice program of care. *Death Education, 2,* 41–52.

LaGrand, L. E. (1980). Reducing burnout in the hospice and the death education movement. *Death Education, 4,* 61–75.

Lamers, W. M., Jr. (1978). Marin County (1976)—Development of a hospice in Marin. *Death Education, 2,* 53–62.

Lattanzi, M. E. (1983). Learning and caring: Education and training concerns. In C. A. Corr & D. M. Corr (Eds.), *Hospice care: Principles and practice* (pp. 223–236). New York: Springer.

Lazare, A. (1979). Unresolved grief. In A. Lazare (Ed.), *Outpatient psychiatry: Diagnosis and treatment.* Baltimore: Williams & Wilkins.

Lazarus, R. S., & Cohen, J. B. (1977). Environmental stress. In I. Altman & J. F. Wohlwill (Eds.), *Human behavior and the environment: Current theory and research.* New York: Plenum Press.

Lerea, E. L., & LiMauro, B. F. (1982). Grief among healthcare workers: A comparative study. *Journal of Gerontology, 37*(5), 604–608.

Marshall, K. A. (1980). When a patient commits suicide. *Suicide and Life-Threatening Behavior, 10*(1), 29–40.

Marshall, R. E., & Kasman, C. (1980). Burnout in the neonatal intensive care unit. *Pediatrics, 65*(6), 1161–1165.

Maslach, C. (1976). Burned-out. *Human Behavior, 5*, 16–22.

Maslach, C. (1982). *Burnout: The cost of caring.* Englewood Cliffs, NJ: Prentice-Hall.

Millen, L., & Roll, S. (1985). A case study in failure: On doing everything right in suicide prevention. *Death Studies, 9*(6), 483–492.

Moser, D. H., & Krikorian, D. A. (1982). *Nursing Leadership, 5*(4), 9–17.

Neimeyer, G. J., Behnke, M., & Reiss, J. (1983). Constructs and coping: Physicians' responses to patient death. *Death Education, 7*, 245–264.

Newlin, N. J., & Welisch, D. K. (1978). The oncology nurse: Life on a roller coaster. *Cancer nursing, 1*(6), 447–449.

Olin, H. S. (1972). A proposed model to teach medical students the care of the dying patient. *Journal of Medical Education, 47*, 564–567.

Paradis, L. F. (Ed.). (1987). Stress and burnout among providers caring for the terminally ill and their families. *The Hospice Journal* (special issue), *3*, 1–276.

Pattison, E. M. (1977). *The experience of dying.* Englewood Cliffs, NJ: Prentice-Hall.

Pearlin, L. I., & Schooler, C. (1978). The structure of coping. *Journal of Health and Social Behavior, 19*, 2–21.

Perez, E. L., Gosselin, J. Y., & Gagnon, A. (1980). Education on death and dying: A survey of Canadian medical schools. *Journal of Medical Education, 55*, 788–789.

Pines, A. M., Aronson, E., & Kafry, D. (1981). *Burnout: From tedium to personal growth.* New York: Free Press.

Pines, A., & Maslach, C. (1978). Characteristics of staff burnout in mental health settings. *Hospital and Community Psychiatry, 29*(4), 233–237.

Price, D. M., & Murphy, P. A. (1984). Staff burnout in the perspective of grief theory. *Death Education, 8*, 47–58.

Rando, T. A. (1984). *Grief, dying, and death: Clinical interventions for caregivers.* Champaign, IL: Research Press.

Sanders, C. M. (1984). Therapists, too, need to grieve. *Death Education, 8* (Suppl.—Suicide: Practical, developmental, and speculative issues), 27–35.

Schowalter, J. E. (1978). The reactions of caregivers dealing with fatally ill children and their families. In O. J. Z. Sahler (Ed.), *The child and death* (pp. 123–138). St. Louis, MO: C. V. Mosby.

Schulz, R., & Aderman, D. (1976). How medical staff copes with dying patients: A critical review. *Omega, 7*(1), 11–21.

Shady, G. (1976). Death anxiety and the terminally ill: A review of the clinical literature. *Canadian Psychological Review, 17*(2), 137–142.

Shanfield, S. B. (1981). The mourning of the health care professional: An important element in education about death and loss. *Death Education, 4,* 385–395.

Shneidman, E. (1969). Suicide, lethality, and the psychological autopsy. *International Psychiatry Clinics, 6,* 225–250.

Stephenson, J. S. (1981). The family therapist and death: A profile. *Family Relations, 30,* 459–462.

Sutterley, D. C. (1982). Stress and health: A survey of self-regulation modalities. In D. C. Donnelly & G. F. Donnelly (Eds.), *Coping with stress: A nursing perspective* (pp. 173–194). Rockville, MD: Aspen Systems.

Swanson, T. R., & Swanson, M. J. (1977). Acute uncertainty: The intensive care unit. In E. M. Pattison (Ed.), *The experience of dying* (pp. 245–251). Englewood Cliffs, NJ: Prentice-Hall.

Vachon, M. L. S. (1976). Enforced proximity to stress in the client environment. *Canadian Nurse, 72*(9), 40–43.

Vachon, M. L. S. (1978). Motivation and stress experienced by staff working with the terminally ill. *Death Education, 2,* 113–122.

Vachon, M. L. S. (1979, May). Staff stress in the case of the terminally ill. *Quality Review Bulletin,* pp. 13–17.

Vachon, M. L. S. (1986). Myths and realities in palliative/hospice care. *The Hospice Journal, 2*(1), 63–79.

Vachon, M. L., Lyall, W. A., & Freeman, S. J. (1978). Measurement and management of stress in health professionals working with advanced cancer patients. *Death Education, 6,* 365–375.

Weisman, A. D. (1970). Misgivings and misconceptions in the psychiatric care of the terminally ill patient. *Psychiatry, 33,* 67–81.

Yancik, R. (1984). Sources of work stress for hospice staff. *Journal of Psychosocial Oncology, 2*(1), 21–31.

Subject Index

Abortion, 290–291
Accidents, 26–27, 66–68, 217, 269
Acquired Immune Deficiency Syndrome (AIDS), 279–285
  AIDS-related complex, 280
  ethical issues, 284–285
  grief of AIDS survivors, 283–284
  grief of AIDS victims, 281–283
  incidence, 279–281
Adolescence, and
  adolescent egocentrism, 223–224
  causes of death, 217
  cognitive development, 24, 218–223
  coping with life-threatening illness, 239–241, 253–261
  coping with loss, 243–247
  death rates, 217
  experience with death, 216–218
  formal operational thought, 24, 218–223
  future plans, 231–232
  grief reactions, 241–243
  identity vs. role confusion (identity diffusion), 228–232

Adolescence, and (cont.)
  imaginary audience, 223
  moral reasoning, 222
  needs of the dying, 224–239
  peer groups, 236–239
  personal fable, 223–224
  physical development, 225–226
  psychosocial moratorium, 229
  relationships with parents, 232–235
  suicide in, 247–252
  understanding of death, 219–223
Advocacy, 159–160
Aged persons. *See* Late adulthood
Ageism, 388, 399
Alzheimer's disease, 400–401
Ambiguous loss, 400
Amyotrophic lateral sclerosis (ALS), 346–354, 366–372
Anger, 9, 52, 64, 65
Anniversary reaction, 55
Anticipatory grief, 11, 61
Arena of death, 26–27
Art therapy, 161–162
Attachment theory, 48–49
Autonomy vs. Shame and doubt, 24, 141–143
Awareness contexts, 14

Bereavement. *See also* Grief
  adolescence and, 241–246
  children and, 153–156, 165–175, 196–204
  definition, 47
  social support in, 68–69
Bereavement overload, 69, 109–110, 438
Bibliotherapy, 162–163
Bill of Rights, 34–35
Body Image, 7–8, 134–135, 226–228, 342–343
Bowlby's phases, 48–49
Burnout, 441–442, 450

Camp, for dying and grieving children, 203–204
Cancer
  coping with, 337–346
  incidence of, 26–27, 217, 328–329, 383
  survival, 218, 240–241, 344
  treatment and side effects, 227, 339–343
Cardiac care units, 334–336
Causes of death, 25–27, 217, 269–270, 328–329, 383–384
Chemotherapy, 341–342
Child life programs, 156–160

Child life specialist, 4, 156, 442, 454–455. *See also* Professional issue
Childbearing, 276–277
Childhood rituals, 142
Children
  bereavement and, 153–156, 165–175, 196–204
  books for, 178–179
  discussing death with, 144–155
  life-threatening illness and, 134–139, 185–196
  parent death and, 196–200
Child's death
  effects on siblings, 200–204
  parent mourning of, 150–152
Clergy, 4, 18–21, 453–455. *See also* Ethical issues; Professional issues
Cognitive development, 24, 135–138, 185–188
Combat death. *See* War
Communication
  styles of, 14–15
  with children, 155
  with dying persons, 14–15, 36–39
  within families, 107
Concept of death, 138–140, 188–189
Concept of illness, 140–141, 189
Concrete operational thought, 24, 185–188
Concurrent stressors, 97–99
Conspiracy of guilt, 202
Conspiracy of silence, 14

Control, 16–17, 32–33, 232–236, 386–387
Counseling. *See* Psychotherapy
Crib death. *See* Sudden Infant Death Syndrome
Crisis theory, 96–101
Cultural differences
  and effects on dying process, 24–25
  in grief, 58–59
Culture of childhood, 189–190

Death
  arena of, 26–27
  by suicide, 27, 247, 394–395
  influence of culture, 24–25
  influence of developmental stage, 23–24
  influence of dying trajectory, 21–22
  of an adult child, 406–408
  of an elderly parent, 362–365
  of a former spouse, 360–362
  of a grandchild, 408–410
  of an infant, 287–290, 303–319
  of a parent, 165–175, 196–200
  of a pet, 410–413
  of a sibling, 200–204
  of a spouse, 75–80, 354–360, 401–406
  of a young child, 134–139, 150–152, 185–196, 205–210
Death anxiety, 454
Death education, 33, 452–454
Death rates, 26–27, 217

Death saturation, 449
Death with dignity, 28–29
Dementia, 400
Denial, 9, 224, 352
Developmental counseling, 249
Developmental theory, 23–24
Developmental stages, 23–24. See also Erikson; Piaget
Diagnostic related groups (DRGs), 390
Dieticians, 4, 350, 454–455
Disclosure of diagnosis, 12–14
Disenfranchised grief, 361
Dissynchrony, 16, 103
Drugs, 6–7, 274. *See also* Chemotherapy
Duration of grief, 55
Dying persons
  body image, 7–8, 134–135, 226–228, 342–343
  communication patterns, 14–15, 36–39
  emotional needs, 9–12
  factors affecting, 21–25
  fears of, 11
  general needs of, 9–21
  grief, 11
  pain management, 6–7, 31, 193–194
  physical needs, 6–8
  positive emotions, 12
  psychological needs, 17–18
  social needs, 12–16
  spiritual needs, 18–21
Dying trajectories, 21–23

Early childhood, and autonomy vs. shame and doubt, 141–143

Early childhood, and
(*cont.*)
body integrity, 134–
135
cognitive
development, 24,
135–141
concept of death,
138–140
concept of illness,
140–141
grief of child, 153–
156, 165–175
grief of parent, 150–
152
initiative vs. guilt,
143–145
needs of the dying,
134–139
normalization, 147–
149
physical development,
134–135
psychosocial
development, 141–
145
separation issues,
146–147
skill development,
134
trust, 145–146
Erikson's stages, 23, 57,
134, 141–144, 163–
164, 191–192, 201,
228–232, 270–272,
331, 382
Ethical issues, 28–29,
284–285, 391–394,
414–421
Ethnicity. *See* Cultural
differences
Euthanasia
aged persons and,
392–393
and pets, 412
living wills, 29–30

Family
adaptation, 101–106

Family (*cont.*)
and ALS, 352–354
and cancer, 233–235,
272–277, 342–343
and heart disease,
336–337
coping, 96–97
crisis theory, 96
developmental stages,
93–96
discrepant coping
styles, 103
incremental grief,
103–106
intergenerational
issues, 110–112
intervention, 106–110
in hospice care, 31–34
perceptions, 101–102
positive outcomes, 98,
101–102
resources, 100
rituals, 112–114
roles, 107–108
secondary loss, 103
stressors, 97–99
systems, 91–93, 115–
121
therapy, 110–112
Family therapists, 4,
110–111, 275, 297–
298, 350, 453–455.
See also Ethical
issues; Professional
issues
Fears, 11, 52
Formal operational
thought, 24, 218–
223
Freud, 47–48, 53
Funerals, 113–114, 154

Genogram, 110–112
Generativity vs.
Stagnation, 24
Geriatrics, 389
Gerontocide, 393
Gerontology, 382
Grandparents, 408–410

Grief. *See also*
Pathological grief
after divorce, 47, 360–
362
and abortion, 290–291
and accidental death,
66–68
and age of the
bereaved, 57–58
and age of the
deceased, 60
and AIDS, 281–284
and cultural
background, 58–59
and families, 96–114,
115–121
and gender, 55–57,
151–152
and homicide, 63–64
and miscarriage, 286–
287
and perceived
similarity to the
deceased, 60–61
and personality
characteristics, 58
and pet loss, 410–413
and SIDS, 289–290
and suddenness of
death, 61–62
and suicide, 64–66
and preventability of
the death, 63
and relationship to
deceased, 59–60
and type of death, 61–
68
and war, 291–301
anticipatory, 11, 61
availability of social
support, 68–69,
109–110
definition, 47
delayed, 72
disenfranchised, 361
duration, 55
helping strategies, 69–
72
inhibited, 72

Grief (*cont.*)
  intensity of, 55
  normal manifestations
    of, 49–53, 153, 241–
    243
  of adolescents, 241–
    246
  of adults, 49–53, 75–
    80, 354–365
  of children, 153–156,
    165–175, 196–204
  of dying persons, 11
  of grandparents, 408–
    410
  of parents, 150–152,
    285–291, 303–319,
    253–261, 406–408
  of professionals, 434–
    441, 457–471
  overload, 69
  pathological, 72–74
  positive outcomes, 74,
    360
  secondary, 104
  variables affecting, 55–
    69
Grief work, 53–55
Guilt
  and children, 143–144
  and preventability of
    death, 63
  and SIDS, 290
  and suicide, 65
  and survival, 150–151,
    201–202, 294
  conspiracy of guilt,
    202
  parental, 150–151,
    290

Health care institutions.
    See Hospitals;
    Nursing homes
Heart disease, 26–27,
    328, 333–337, 383
Holistic perspective, 4–
    5, 30–31
Home care, 27, 32–34.
    See also Hospice

Homicide, 63–64
Hope, 19
Hospice, 30–34, 36–39,
    443–445, 449–451
Hospitals, 27, 156–160,
    230, 238–239, 275,
    303–319, 334–336,
    389–390, 435
Husband sanctification,
    358

Identity issues, 24, 228–
    232, 356, 385
Identity vs. Role
    confusion, 24, 228–
    232
Incremental grief, 103–
    106
Industry vs. Inferiority,
    24, 191–192
Infant death, 287–290,
    303–319
Initiative vs. Guilt, 24,
    143–144
Insurance, 278–279
Integrity vs. Despair,
    24
Intensive care units,
    435, 442–443, 451.
    See also Cardiac
    care units
Interdisciplinary
    approaches. *See*
    Multidisciplinary
    approaches
Intergenerational issues,
    110–112
Intimacy vs. Isolation,
    24, 270–272
Isolation, 15–16, 24,
    270–272

Journal writing, 301–
    302

Killing. *See* Homicide;
    War
Kübler-Ross's stages, 9–
    10, 456

Late adulthood, and
    ageism, 388, 399
  causes of death, 383–
    384
  disabilities during,
    400–401
  euthanasia, 392–393
  health care issues,
    389–390
  institutionalized
    elderly, 384–389
  integrity vs. despair,
    382
  life review, 382
  loss of a grandchild,
    408–410
  loss of an adult child,
    406–408
  loss of a pet, 410–
    413
  loss of a spouse, 401–
    406
  needs of the dying,
    384–390
  retirement, 396
  suicide in, 394–399
Life expectancy, 382
Life review, 17, 382
Literature, 162–163,
    178–179
Living will, 29–30
Long-term care. *See*
    Nursing homes
Loss
  ambiguous, 400
  and disabilities, 47,
    400–401
  secondary, 103

Magical thinking, 187
Malignancies. *See*
    Cancer
Marital bereavement.
    See Widowhood
Marriage, 275–276
Mastectomy, 339, 342–
    343
Medicaid, 390
Medicare, 390

Memorial services, 113–114

Middle adulthood, and ALS, 346–354
cancer, 337–346
causes of death, 328–329
generativity vs. stagnation, 331
heart disease, 333–337
loss of a former spouse, 360–362
loss of a parent, 362–365
loss of a spouse, 354–360
needs of the dying, 330–332

Mid-life review, 328

Ministers. *See* Clergy

Miscarriage, 286–287

Mourning, definition, 47. *See also* Bereavement; Grief

Multidisciplinary approaches, 4, 30–31, 454–455

Murder. *See* Homicide

Neonatal death. *See* Infant death

Normalization, 147–149

Nurses. *See also* Burnout; Ethical issues; Professional issues; Stress
education and training, 452–455
in critical care units, 435–437, 442–443
in hospices, 443–445

Nursing homes, 384–389, 436

Occupational therapy, 4, 350, 454–455

Older persons. *See* Late adulthood

Oncology. *See* Cancer

Organ transplantation, 29, 334

Pain, 6–7, 31, 193–194

Palliative measures, 4, 31

Parent death
and children, 165–175, 196–200
effect on adult child, 362–365

Parents
grief of, 150–152, 253–261, 285–291, 303–319, 406–408
relationships with dying children, 149–152

Pastoral counseling. *See* Clergy

Pathological grief, 72–74

Patients' Bill of Rights, 34–35

Peer group, 195–196, 203–204, 231, 236–239, 240

Perinatal death. *See* Infant death

Personal fable, 223–224

Pet death, 410–413

Pharmacists, 453. *See also* Drugs

Physical therapy, 4, 350, 454–455

Physicians, *See also* Burnout; Ethical issues; Professional issues; Stress
attitudes toward disclosure of diagnosis, 13
attitudes toward sexuality, 273
education and training, 4, 452–455
in hospices, 31

Piaget's stages, 23–24, 135–138, 218–223

Play therapy, 160–161

Positive outcomes, 12, 74, 101–102, 455–456

Post-traumatic stress disorder, 294–301

Postvention, 106, 249–252

Preoperational thought, 24, 136–138

Preschool. *See* Early childhood

Prevention, 249–252

Professional issues. *See also* Ethical issues
burnout, 441–442, 450
education and training, 389–390, 452–454
grief reactions, 434–441, 457–471
roles, 442

Prospective-payment system (PPS), 390

Psychic Numbing, 296

Psychologists, 4, 439–441, 452–455, 457–471. *See also* Ethical issues; Family therapists; Professional issues

Psychotherapy, 439–441, 457–471

Psychoanalytic theory. *See* Freud

Psychological autopsy, 440

Psychosocial crises. *See* Erikson

Quality of life, 391–394, 414–421. *See also* Ethical issues

Radiation therapy, 217, 341

Rational suicide. *See* Suicide

Replacement child syndrome, 203
Retirement, 386, 396
Right to die, 28–29. *See also* Quality of life; Ethical issues
Risk taking, 224
Rituals, 112–114. *See also* Childhood rituals
Roles, 60, 107, 230, 331
Role loss, 60

School-age child
  cognitive development, 24, 185–189
  concept of death, 188–189
  concept of illness, 189
  culture of childhood, 189–190
  death of a parent, 196–200
  death of a sibling, 200–204
  grief reactions, 196–204
  industry vs. inferiority, 191–192
  language, 189–190
  needs of the dying, 185–196
  pain management, 193–194
  peer group, 195–196, 204
  physical development, 185
  psychosocial development, 189–192
  school attendance, 194–195
Secondary grief, 104
Secondary loss, 103
Self-help groups, 109–110, 203–204, 405

Sensorimotor stage of cognitive development, 24, 135
Separation issues, 48–49, 146
Sexuality, 272–275
Sibling death, 200–204
Social Readjustment Rating Scale, 99
Social support
  in bereavement, 68–69, 109–110
  in life-threatening illness, 12–16
  in burnout, 448, 451–452
Social workers, 4, 439–441, 452–455. *See also* Ethical issues; Family therapists; Professional issues
Speech therapists, 4, 350, 454–455
Spiritual needs, 18–21
Spousal death. *See* Widowhood
Stage theory. *See also* Erikson; Piaget
  of dying, 9–11
  developmental, 23–24
Stillbirth, 287–289
Stress. *See also* Burnout and coping mechanisms, 445–452
  in hospices, 443–445
  in intensive care units, 442–443
Sudden Infant Death Syndrome (SIDS), 289–290, 435
Suicide
  causes of, 247–248
  contagion theory, 249
  effects on professionals, 439–441, 457–471

Suicide (*cont.*)
  intervention, 249–252
  in the elderly, 394–399
  grief reaction to, 64–66
  of psychotherapy clients, 439–441, 457–471
  prevention, 249–252
  postvention, 249–252
  psychological autopsy, 440
  rate of, 27, 247, 394–395
  rational, 396–399
  stigma and, 65
  warning signs, 250
  youth, 247–252
Support groups, 33, 68–69, 109–110, 203–204, 240, 344, 354, 451–452
Surrogate griever, 438
Survivor guilt, 150–151, 201–202, 294
Systems theory, 91–93

Teachers, 194–195, 205–210, 231
Technology, 28–29, 34, 391–392
Terminally ill persons. *See* Dying persons
Thanatology, 9
Toddlerhood. *See* Early childhood
Trust, 24, 145–147

Unfinished business, 6

Veterans, 292–301
Vietnam War, 292–301
Violence, 63–64, 291–301
Vocational issues, 277–279

War, 291–301
Widowhood
  age differences, 55–
    57, 403–404
  emotional adjustment,
    75–80, 354–355
  financial adjustment,
    358–359
  gender differences,
    402–403
  husband
    sanctification, 358
  interventions, 359–
    360, 405–406
  late adulthood, 401–
    406

Widowhood (*cont.*)
  middle adulthood,
    354–360
  mortality rates, 403
  role loss, 356–357
  self-help groups,
    405
  social adjustment,
    357–358
  statistics, 401–402
  remarriage, 358, 402
Wills, 358. *See also*
  Living will
Withdrawal, 15–16, 54
Work. *See* Vocational
  issues

Young Adulthood, and
  AIDS, 279–285
  causes of death, 269–
    270
  childbearing, 276–277
  education, 277–278
  intimacy vs. isolation,
    270–272
  loss of an infant, 285–
    291
  marriage, 275–276
  needs of the dying,
    270–279
  sexuality, 272–275
  war, 291–301
  work, 277–279

Name Index

Aadalen, S., 290
Abernathy, C. B., 65–67
Aderman, D., 454
Adler, Alfred, 232
Aiken, L. R., 73, 402
Aisenberg, R., 11–12, 15
Akers, S., 359
Aldous, J., 108
Alles, W. F., 244
Almquist, E., 387
Alston, J. P., 399
Altman, A. J., 217
Altman, D., 283
Amour, J. L., 239
Anderson, B. L., 343
Andrews, G., 68, 336
Annas, G., 13
Ansbacher, H. L., 232
Ansbacher, R. R., 232
Arkin, A., 52, 55, 61, 63
Arndt, H., 107, 109
Aronson, E., 449
Ashburn, S. S., 135
Atchley, R. C., 357, 364
Attig, T., 20
Aubrey, R. R., 244–245
Augustine, M. J., 19

Bader, M. A., 6
Baker, L. A., 284
Balk, D., 241, 246
Balkwell, C., 404
Ball, J. F., 53, 402–403
Baltz, T. M., 388
Banziger, G., 387
Barbarin, O. A., 146
Barbus, Amelia J., 35
Barnes, M. J., 60
Barrett, C. J., 359–360, 403

Barstow, L. F., 341
Batchelor, W. F., 279
Bates, M. S., 25
Battin, D., 52, 55, 61, 63
Baumrind, D., 233
Beck, J. C., 389–390
Beckwith, J. B., 290
Bedell, J. R., 239
Behnke, M., 454
Belsky, J. K., 400
Bendiksen, R., 289
Bengston, V. L., 383
Benjamin, A. H., 408
Bennetts, G., 222, 227, 229, 240
Benoliel, J. Q., 74, 434
Berardo, F. M., 402, 404
Berg, C., 155
Berger, K. S., 189
Bergman, A. B., 290
Berkman, L., 49
Berlinsky, E. B., 154, 196–200
Berman, A. L., 247, 249–251
Berman, L. C., 47
Berman, S. J., 231, 233–234
Bernasconi, M., 140
Bernstein, J. E., 163
Bertalanffy, Ludwig von, 91
Best, E., 289
Bibace, R., 140–141, 189
Bigner, J. J., 149
Biller, H. B., 154, 196–200
Binder, Renee L., 457–471
Binger, C. M., 201, 203

Blankenship, Jayne, 73–80
Blazer, D., 394
Block, A. R., 334
Bloom, V., 458
Bluebond-Langer, M., 145
Blum, R. W., 227, 240
Blumberg, B. D., 218, 224–225, 228, 231, 235, 237
Blumenfield, M., 12
Bok, S., 29
Boldt, M., 249
Boll, T., 239
Bolton, C., 113–114
Bolton, I., 65
Borg, S., 285–286
Borman, L., 405
Boss, P., 400
Bowen, M., 92–93, 110
Bowie, Wende Kernan, 303–319
Bowlby, J., 47, 48–49, 61, 72–73, 146–147, 404
Boyer, S. L., 334
Bozeman, M. F., 410
Brasted, W. S., 49, 68
Breme, E. J., 290
Brende, J. O., 292, 297
Brenner, A., 154
Brent, S. B., 57, 138, 188
Brittain, W. L., 161
Broderick, C., 91, 101
Bronstein, Abbot A., 457–471
Broome, M. E., 146
Brown, N. K., 415n
Brown, R. J., 55, 58

Brubaker, E., 407
Bufferd, R. K., 47
Bugen, L. A., 49, 60, 63, 447, 452, 454
Buksbazen, C., 65
Buongiorno, P. A., 440–441
Burgess, A. W., 64
Butler, Robert N., 328, 330, 382–384, 387–388, 394–395, 399

Cain, A. C., 201–203, 246
Cain, B., 203
Caine, Lynn, 357
Cairns, N., 194
Calhoun, L. G., 65–67
Callahan, E. J., 49, 69
Callari, E. S., 11
Calsyn, R. J., 388
Camerino, V. J., 346, 349
Cameron, P., 47
Camp, D., 113–114
Card, J. J., 292, 296
Carey, R. G., 357, 402–403
Carl, D., 283
Carr, A. C., 47
Carroll, J. F. X., 450
Carson, N. D., 251
Carson, R. A., 393–394
Carter, E. A., 93, 95
Cartwright, L. K., 455
Cassel, C., 350
Cassem, N. H., 334
Chaikin, A. L., 271
Chalmers, J., 61
Chang, P., 240
Charles, Ezzard, 372
Charles, K. A., 283
Charmaz, K., 12, 15–16, 58–59, 113
Charpentier, P., 49
Chesborough, S., 289
Chesler, M. A., 146
Chesser, B. J., 68
Chester, V. A., 61
Childers, P., 140
Chiriboga, D., 385

Chng, C. L., 290
Cho, S. A., 244
Chodoff, P., 410
Christ, G. H., 16, 103
Churchill, M. P., 97–98
Clark, Barney, 29
Clark, D. B., 67
Clark, P. G., 354, 357
Clayton, P. J., 52
Cleland, M., 97, 101, 109
Cobb, S., 448
Coddington, R. D., 245
Cohen, J. B., 445
Cohen, S., 290
Cole, E., 201
Collen, Michael, 281
Comstock, G. W., 403
Conley, B. H., 112
Conroy, S., 61
Cook, A. S., 220, 222
Cook, J. A., 56–57, 103, 151–152
Cooper, Gary, 366
Copper, M., 192, 194–195
Corless, I. B., 18, 34
Corr, C. A., 31
Corr, D. M., 31
Cowles, K. V., 412
Coyle, N., 7
Cozby, P. C., 271
Crosby, J. F., 97, 100, 109
Cuellar, J. B., 383

Daley, M., 442
Daniel, A., 334
Dash, J., 234, 239
Davidson, S. M., 389
Davies, B., 103, 153
Davies, E. B., 150
Davis, B. H., 47
Dawson, P. S., 21
Deasy-Spinetta, P., 195
DeFrain, J. D., 101, 109, 289
Demi, A. S., 52, 65, 72, 150–151
Denholm, C. L., 238

DePalma, D. J., 222
Derdeyn, A. P., 107
Derlega, V. J., 271
Desmarais, L., 52
DeVita, V. T., 337, 340
DeVries, H., 447
Dhooper, S. S., 337
Dickinson, G. E., 452–453
Dimond, M., 405
Dixon, P. N., 248, 250
Doane, B. K., 290–291
Doka, K. J., 18, 283, 361–362
Donlou, J., 283
Donnelly, W., 289
Dowd, J., 386
Doyle, P., 67
Drake, R. M., 435
Dunn, L., 453
Dunn, R. G., 66
Dunne, E. J., 440
Dupee, R. M., 6, 12
Durand, R. P., 453
Dustin, D., 13
Duvaul, R., 73

Earnshaw-Smith, E., 146
Eddy, J. M., 244
Edelstein, L., 150
Edelwich, J., 441, 449
Eggerman, S., 13
Eisenberg, M. G., 230
Eisenbruch, M., 59
Elizur, E., 153, 198
Elkind, D., 223
Ellenberg, L., 234, 239
Elsom, B., 139, 188
Englander, S., 108
Enlow, R. W., 280
Erickson, M., 201–202
Erikson, E. H., 23, 57, 134, 141, 144, 163–164, 191, 201, 228–229, 270, 331, 382
Erikson, J. M., 382
Ernst, L., 101, 289
Esbenson, M., 15–16
Evans, Beth J., 205–209

Evans, M. A., 15–16
Ewalt, P. L., 216

Fagan, M., 7, 347
Fairbanks, J. A., 293
Fairchild, R., 19
Fairchild, T. N., 248–250
Fairclough, D. L., 227, 277–278
Farberow, N. L., 250, 394
Farrell, F. A., 233, 235, 237–238
Farris, P., 61
Fassler, J., 163
Fast, I., 201–202
Fawzy, F. I., 282
Feigenberg, L., 12
Ferrell, B. R., 32
Figley, C., 292, 296–297
Fine, M., 150
Fink, S. L., 12
Fischer, A., 412
Fischman, S. E., 107
Fish, W. C., 105
Fisher, C. R., 390
Fitch, S. D., 399
Flavell, J. J., 135
Flesch, R., 60
Foeckler, M. M., 67
Fogel, C. I., 291
Foley, J. M., 222
Fong, M. L., 238
Forstein, M., 284
Foy, D. W., 296
Franciosi, R. A., 435
Frears, L. H., 70
Freedman-Leftofsky, K., 68
Freeman, E. M., 244
Freeman, S. J., 68
Freese, A., 60
Freiburg, K. L., 134
Freud, S., 47–48, 53
Freudenberger, H., 442
Freund, J., 20
Friedman, E. H., 113
Friedman, G. R., 435
Friedman, S. B., 150, 410

Friend, Robert L., 457–471
Froiland, D. J., 47
Fuller, R. L., 283–284
Fulton, R., 24, 60, 103, 113, 289, 382, 437–438
Furman, E., 154–155

Gagnon, A., 452
Galea, R. P., 284
Gallo, F. T., 340, 343
Gander, M. J., 225–226, 233
Ganz, P. A., 344
Ganzert, A., 110
Gardiner, H. W., 225–226, 233
Garfield, N. J., 294
Garrard, F. H., 67
Garry, K., 354
Gartley, W., 140
Gehrig, Lou, 366, 372
Geis, S. B., 283–284
Gerber, I., 52, 55, 61, 63
Gerson, R., 110–111
Getzel, G. S., 64, 280
Geyman, J. P., 103
Gideon, M. D., 272–276
Gilbert, Emily, 393
Gilbert, Roswell, 393
Gilchrist, L., 109
Gilson, G., 287
Ginn, P. D., 66
Giordan, B., 239
Glaser, B. G., 12, 14, 21–22
Glasser, L. N., 100
Glasser, P. H., 100
Glick, I. O., 52, 56, 355, 358
Golan, N., 360
Goldberg, S. B., 107–109
Golden, D. B., 157
Goldenberg, H., 92
Goldenberg, I., 92
Goldstein, L. S., 440–441
Gonyea, J., 97

Gordon, A. K., 95, 208
Gorer, G., 58
Gosselin, J. Y., 452
Gottlieb, M., 283
Gould, B. S., 332, 346–348, 350–352
Graham-Pole, J., 238
Graves, W., 287
Gray, P., 296–298
Grebstein, L. C., 106, 112
Green, Chad, 18
Green, M., 289, 357, 363
Greenberg, L. I., 153
Greenblatt, M., 71
Grobstein, R., 104, 107, 201
Grollman, E. A., 209
Gronseth, E. C., 452
Gruber, H. W., 389
Gruber, M., 107, 109
Gruman, G. J., 24
Gustafson, E., 388
Gut, E., 58, 73
Guzzino, M. H., 161
Gyulay, J. E., 409

Haas, A. P., 292–293
Hackett, T. P., 334
Hailey, B. J., 66
Hale, M. E., 70, 301
Haley, J., 135, 193–194
Hall, E., 384, 408
Hall, M. N., 67
Hallenbeck, C. E., 12
Hamburg, D., 410
Hamilton, J., 409–410
Hammett, V. L., 282
Haney, Patrick, 281
Hankoff, L. D., 220, 225
Hannon, N., 55, 61, 63
Hansen, D. A., 101
Hardgrove, C., 153
Hardt, D. V., 54
Harris, B. G., 291
Hart, N. A., 248
Harvey, B., 103
Hatton, C. L., 65, 248

Hauser, M. J., 65
Havener, R. M., 155
Havens, L. L., 458
Havighurst, R. J., 222, 232
Hay, D., 443, 451
Hay, Jean, 36–39, 71
Hearne, E., 194
Heikkinen, C. A., 69
Heinrich, R. L., 344
Helsing, K. J., 403
Hendin, H., 292–293
Herz, F., 106
Hewson, D. M., 68
Hilfiker, David, 414–421
Hill, Reuben, 96
Hiltz, S. R., 405
Hinton, J., 15
Hodges, M. H., 238
Hoffmans, M. A., 222, 227, 229, 240
Hogancamp, V., 292, 297
Holden, D., 353
Holland, J., 146, 193, 234
Holmes, T. H., 97, 99, 354
Holmes, W., 360
Holton, C. P., 224, 234, 239
Hooyman, N., 97
Horne, R., 7, 347
Horowitz, M. J., 363
Hoy, T., 20
Hoyer, W. J., 4
Hoyt, M. F., 52, 68, 73–74
Hozman, T. L., 47
Hultsch, K. F., 216, 219, 225, 229
Hurley, D., 47
Hutchins, S. H., 287–288
Hutter, J. J., 237–238

Iacono, C. U., 294–295
Ikeman, B., 198
Imes, C., 334
Inhelder, B., 185
Irwin, R., 201

Jackson, D. A., 245
Jackson, E. W., 208
Jacobs, S. C., 49, 403
Jacobson, S. P., 442
Jaffe, C., 15–16
Jansen, M. A., 230
Javits, Jacob, 372
Jerardi, N. C., 61
Jewett, C. L., 58
Jochimsen, P. R., 343
Johnson, A. I., 383
Johnson, D., 399
Johnson, P., 243
Johnson, R. E., 251
Johnson, V. A., 101
Johnston, L., 107
Jones, F. A., Jr., 440
Jones, T. J., 67
Jones, W. H., 47
Jose, N. L., 97, 100, 109
Joseph, S. M., 155–156
Joy, S. S., 291
Jubelt, Burk, 366, 368
Juergens, S. M., 347
Juretich, M., 405

Kaffman, M., 153, 198
Kafry, D., 449
Kalish, R. A., 14, 19, 24–25, 59, 216, 383, 392, 410, 453
Kalnins, I., 97–98
Kandal, K., 353
Kane, R. A., 389–390
Kane, R. L., 389–390
Kaplan, B., 59
Kaplan, D., 104, 107, 201
Kapust, L. R., 400–401
Karpel, M. A., 92
Kart, C. S., 382
Kasl, S. V., 49
Kasman, C., 442, 446, 448
Kastenbaum, R. J., 10–12, 15, 65, 69, 248, 454
Katz, E. B., 192, 227, 233
Kaufman, D., 12
Kavanaugh, R. E., 49

Keane, T. M., 293
Keeler, E., 389–390
Keidel, G. C., 248
Keill, S., 296–298
Kelemen, T., 346, 351
Kellerman, E., 192
Kellerman, J., 227, 233–234, 239
Kellner, K., 289
Kelly, J., 47
Kennedy, M., 282
Kennell, J. H., 285–286
Kerner, J., 103
Kersey, J. H., 452
Kinrade, L. C., 200
Kirschling, J. M., 33, 359
Kitson, G. C., 360
Kitto, J., 354
Klass, D., 102, 208
Klaus, M. H., 285–286
Kleck, R., 190
Klein, D., 160
Kleinman, A., 59
Kligfield, B., 59
Kliman, A. S., 206–208
Kliman, G. W., 205, 208
Kline, J., 238
Klopovich, P., 194
Knapp, R. J., 56, 285–286
Knorr, B., 101, 109
Koch, A., 100
Koch-Hattem, A., 200–201, 203
Kolodny, Susan, 457–471
Koocher, G. P., 139–140, 188–189
Kosten, T. R., 49
Kotch, J., 290
Krant, M. J., 107
Krell, R., 202–203
Krikorian, D. A., 445
Kroes, W., 441
Krupnick, J. L., 58
Krupp, G. R., 59
Kübler-Ross, Elisabeth, 6, 9–10, 19, 49, 145, 220, 456

Kulenkamp, E. J., 103, 150
Kupst, M. J., 97, 150
Kurland, L. T., 347

Lack, S. A., 449
LaGrand, L. E., 241, 448
Lamers, W. M., Jr., 449
Lamm, M., 21
Landon, Pam, 115–121
Landsverk, J., 282–283
Lange, N. F., 146, 160
Langer, E. J., 387
Langley, S., 25
Langlois, J., 190
Lansky, S., 194
Lapp, G. E., 439
Lardner, John, 367
Lasker, J., 285–286
Lattanzi, M. E., 70–71, 301, 447, 452
Lazare, A., 438
Lazarus, R. S., 100–101, 445
Leach, C. F., 346, 351
Lear, M. W., 333
LeBaron, S., 227, 233, 239–240
Leff, P., 286, 289
Leloudis, D., 32
Lerea, E. L., 436, 437
Lerner, J., 190
Lerner, M., 26–27
Lerner, R. M., 190, 216, 219, 225, 229
Lesher, E. L., 406–408
Levenson, P., 192, 194–195
Levinson, B. M., 410–411
Leviton, D., 273
Levy, M. H., 6
Levy, N. B., 12
Lewis, B. F., 284
Lewis, M. I., 328, 330, 383–384, 387, 394–395, 399
Lewis, M. J., 218, 224–225, 228, 231, 235, 237

Lewiston, N., 103
Ley, D. C., 18
Lezak, M. D., 401
Lieberman, M., 405
Lietar, E. F., 286
Lifton, R. J., 296
LiMauro, B. F., 436, 437
Lindemann, E., 50, 52–54
Lindsay, J., 78
Linn, E. L., 162, 164
Litman, R. E., 250, 457–458
Lonetto, R., 161
Lopata, H. Z., 356, 358–360, 402–404
Lopez, D., 280
Lord, J. H., 67
Louis, Joe, 372
Lowenfeld, V., 161
Lowenthal, M. F., 271, 385
Lowman, J., 290
Lund, D. A., 405
Lyall, W., 68

McClowry, S. G., 103, 150
Maccoby, E. E., 148
McCombs, M., 282
McCown, D. E., 153, 201
McCubbin, H. I., 96–97, 100
McGann, L. M., 390
McGoldrick, M., 93, 95, 110–111
McGrory, A., 11, 103
McIntosh, J. L., 396
McIntosh, W. A., 399
McKusick, L., 283
Maddison, D., 58, 63, 68, 355, 403
Mages, N. L., 102, 332, 337–340, 342, 344–345
Magno, J. B., 7
Maizler, J. S., 387
Malinak, D. P., 52, 68, 73–74

Malyon, A. K., 283
Manaster, G. J., 223, 226, 229
Maoz, B., 103
Margolis, B., 441
Maris, R., 247, 249
Markusen, E., 103, 289
Markush, R., 61
Marmor, T. R., 389
Marris, P., 54
Marshall, K. A., 440
Marshall, R. E., 442, 446, 448
Marshall, V. W., 392
Martin, B., 200
Martin, G. W., 224, 234, 239
Martin, N. K., 248, 250
Martinson, I. M., 103, 150, 452
Martocchio, B. C., 28
Maslach, C., 441–442, 448, 454
Mason, J. W., 410
Masters, R., 64
Matthews, S., 385–386
Mauritzen, J., 18
May, H. J., 290
May, K. A., 150
Mehr, M., 247, 251
Melear, J., 140
Mendelsohn, G. A., 102, 332, 337–340, 342, 344–345
Mercier, J., 412
Meyering, S., 360
Miles, M. S., 52, 72, 150–151
Millen, L., 439
Miller, D. B., 389
Miller, M., 394, 396
Miller, S., 357, 364
Millet, N., 32
Millison, M. B., 19–20
Mills, G., 163
Mingus, Charlie, 372
Mitchell, J. R., 226
Moglia, P., 353
Moller, H., 205

Montgomery, R., 97
Moody, H. R., 397–399
Moore, C., 224, 234, 239
Moos, R. H., 349
Moreland, J. R., 107–109
Morgan, J. D., 18
Morgan, L. B., 250
Morin, S. F., 283
Moriwaki, S. Y., 394
Morrish-Vidners, D., 66
Moser, D. H., 445
Moss, M. S., 363–364, 403–404, 406–408
Moss, S. Z., 363–364, 403–404, 406–408
Moustakas, C. E., 364
Moxley, R. T., 350
Moyer, J. A., 204
Mrgudic, K., 146–147
Mulder, D. W., 347, 351
Murphy, P. A., 456
Murray, R., 47
Myers, E., 363

Nagy, M., 138–140, 188
Nannis, E. D., 232, 236
Natapoff, J. N., 141
Neimark, E. D., 219
Neimeyer, G. J., 454
Nelson, F., 250
Nesbit, M. E., Jr., 452
Neth, Cecil, 366–372
Neugarten, B. L., 383
Newlin, N. J., 451
Newman, C., 47
Nichols, E., 284
Nichols, J. A., 287
Nieburg, H. A., 412
Nielson, P. E., 286
Niven, David, 372
Noble, D., 287
Nordlicht, S., 100
Norris, C., 7
Norris, F. H., 353
Nuckols, R., 358
Nye, F., 108

Ohlde, C. O., 294
Oken, D., 443, 451

Oldenburg, B., 336
Olin, H. S., 12, 453
Oltjenbruns, K. A., 104–105, 220, 222
O'Meara, Jim, 300–301
Omizo, M. M., 282
Orbach, C. E., 410
Orr, D. P., 222, 227, 229, 240
Osterweis, M., 357, 363
Ostfeld, A. M., 49, 403
Owen, G., 103, 289

Paine, W. S., 450
Palmer, C. E., 287
Paradis, L. F., 32, 444
Paris, C., 47
Paris, J., 146
Parkes, C. M., 52, 55–58, 68, 355, 358, 360, 404
Parks, R., 47
Parson, E. R., 292, 294, 296–297
Patterson, J. M., 96–97, 100
Patterson, S. L., 244
Patterson, T. W., 294
Patterson, V., 52, 68, 73–74
Pattison, E. M., 10–11, 22, 112, 240, 269, 328, 332, 438, 449
Pearce, K. A., 294
Pearlin, I., 100–101, 445–446
Peck, M. L., 250
Peppers, L. G., 56, 285–286, 291
Peretz, D., 68
Perez, E. L., 452
Perkes, A. C., 249
Perkins, L., 216
Perkins, R. J., 336
Perlmutter, M., 384, 408
Peteet, J. R., 20
Peterson, L., 157
Petrillo, M., 157, 159
Phillips, W., 155

Piaget, J., 23, 57, 135–138, 185, 218, 221–222
Picher, L., 110
Pine, V. R., 47
Pines, A. M., 442, 449, 455–456
Pizzo, P. A., 224, 227
Plumb, M. M., 234
Pohlman, J. C., 155, 160
Pole, L., 32
Pomeroy, M. R., 290
Poplack, D. G., 224, 227
Potter, P., 195
Powell, D. R., 109
Poznanski, E., 203
Pratt, C., 97, 101, 109
Pratt, D., 201
Prawat, B., 139, 188
Price, D. M., 456
Price, R. E., 282
Pumphrey, J., 20
Purisman, R., 103
Putnam, Nicholas, 166–175

Quackenbush, J., 412
Quigley, B. Q., 290–291
Quinlan, Karen Ann, 29
Quinn, R., 441

Rabkin, L., 202–203
Rachels, J., 393
Ragan, P. K., 383
Rager, P. M., 153
Rahe, R. H., 97, 99, 354
Rait, D. S., 146, 193
Rando, T. A., 18, 65, 69, 71, 103, 112, 151, 231, 269, 332, 407–408, 444
Range, L. M., 66
Raphael, B., 54, 57, 242–246, 355, 360–361
Rebok, G. W., 4
Redpath, C. C., 141
Reilly, D. M., 60
Reinharz, S., 286
Reiss, J., 454

Reister, R., 163
Reynolds, D. K., 24–25, 59, 383
Richards, V., 19
Richardson, S., 190
Richman, J., 251
Ridley-Johnson, R., 157
Rigler, D., 234, 239
Rinear, E. E., 71
Rink, A. 248
Roberts, C. L., 153
Roberts, L., 340, 344–345
Roberts, M., 195
Robinson, A., 163
Rodas, Hector, 29
Rodin, J., 387
Roelofs, G., 354
Rogers, C. S., 141
Rogers, J., 68
Roll, S., 439
Rolland, J. S., 93
Ronald, L., 190
Rosel, N., 7, 11, 14
Rosen, David H., 457n, 458
Rosen, H., 202
Rosenblatt, P. C., 243, 245
Rosenbloom, J., 187–188
Ross, C. P., 250–252
Ross, D. M., 194
Ross, J., 194
Ross, S. A., 194
Roush, S., 387
Rowe, G., 101, 109
Royal, M. E., 154
Rubin, S. S., 60
Rudolph, M., 207
Rusalem, R., 55, 61, 63
Rush, J., 283–284
Ryder, E. L., 412
Rynearson, E. K., 64

Sachs, M., 195
Salison, S., 296
Salladay, S. A., 154
Sanders, C. M., 55–56, 58, 61–62, 150, 364, 403, 406, 439, 441

Sanger, S., 157, 159
Satir, Virginia, 92
Saunders, Cicely, 6–7, 18
Saunders, J. M., 249–250, 252
Schag, C. C., 344
Schatz, B. D., 92, 101
Schatz, W. H., 152
Schauer, A. H., 294
Schiamberg, L. B., 216, 269, 328, 330, 408
Schiller, P., 286
Schilling, R. F., 109
Schinke, S. P., 109
Schlidt, R., 249
Schmal, V., 97, 101, 109
Schmidt, J. D., 64
Schmitt, B. B., 161
Schneider, J. M., 70
Schneweis, K. M., 403
Schoenberg, B., 7, 47
Schooler, C., 100–101, 445–446
Schowalter, J. E., 238, 442
Schroeder, William, 29
Schulman, J. L., 150
Schulz, R., 387, 454
Schuster, C. S., 135
Schuyler, D., 65
Schwab, J., 61
Schwartz, A. D., 217
Schwebel, A. I., 107–109
Schweitzer, Albert, 37
Scott, S., 390
Sebring, D. L., 353
Seibel, M., 287
Selby, J. W., 65–67
Seligman, M. E. P., 235–236, 387
Senescu, R. A., 7
Shaak, J., 163
Shady, G., 454
Shaffer, D. R., 219
Shanfield, S. B., 408, 438
Shaw, C. T., 287
Shearer, P., 283

Shehan, C. L., 292–293, 297–298
Sheposh, J., 201
Sheshkin, A., 66
Shirley, V., 412
Shneidman, E. S., 10, 12, 106, 249, 440
Shoor, 245
Sieburg, E., 95
Siegal, F. P., 279, 281
Siegal, M., 279, 281
Siegal, S., 192
Siegel, K., 397–399
Silver, S. M., 294–295
Silverman, Phyllis R., 108, 360, 405
Simos, B., 53
Simpson, M., 389
Sinaki, M., 346
Siviski, R. W., 354, 357
Slyter, H., 285–286
Smialek, Z., 290
Smith, A., 104, 107, 201
Smith, J., 91, 101
Smith, W. J., 391–393
Solkoff, N., 296–298
Solomon, D. H., 389–390
Solomon, F., 357, 363
Solomon, J. R., 387
Solomon, K., 386
Solomon, M. I., 65
Speece, M. W., 57, 138, 188
Speed, M. H., 245
Spinetta J., 103, 201
Stanford, G., 158
Stanley, E., 353
Stenback, A., 387, 395–396
Stephan, C., 190
Stephenson, J. S., 73, 93, 328, 453
Stevens-Long, J., 269, 277
Stinnett, N., 101, 109
Stolar, G. E., 339, 343
Strauss, A. L., 12, 14, 21–22

Strauss, E. S., 92
Sudnow, D., 389
Sulman, J., 336–337
Sumner, E. D., 453
Susman, E. J., 218, 224–225, 227–228, 231, 235, 237
Sussman, M. B., 410
Sutherland, A. M., 410
Sutkin, L. C., 230
Sutterley, D. C., 447–448
Swain, B. J., 408
Swanson, M. J., 434, 436–437, 451
Swanson, T. R., 434, 436–437, 451
Swarner, J., 201
Swoiskin, S., 289
Szklo, M., 403

Tarr, D., 195
Tavormina, J., 239
Taylor, P. B., 272–275
Tehan, C., 32
Tennant, C., 68
Terry, G., 97–98
Thomas, A. M., 67
Thompson, D. J., 415n
Thompson, E. I., 227, 240, 277–278
Thompson, L. M., 28
Thompson, R. H., 158
Tick, E., 296–297
Tobin, S., 385
Toynbee, A., 400–401
Trautmann, Carol, 253–261
Trautmann, Mary Winfrey, 253–261
Troll, L. E., 357, 364, 386
Tsu, V. D., 349
Tuckel, P., 397–399
Turner, J. G., 388

Unger, D. G., 109

Vachon, M. L. S., 68, 359, 406, 436, 442, 444–445, 449–450
Valente, S. M., 65, 248–250, 252
Valeriote, S., 150
Van der Hart, O., 112
Vander Zander, J. W., 23, 185
Van Eys, J., 192
Venters, M., 100–102
Verhaeghe, G., 336–337
Vermilye, G., 163
Verwoerdt, A., 385, 387
Vess, J. D., 107–109
Viney, L. L., 8
Viola, A., 58, 403
Vipperman, J. F., 153
Vollman, R., 107, 110

Walker, B. A., 247, 251
Walker, W., 63, 68
Wallace, S., 66
Wallerstein, J., 47
Walsh, M. E., 140–141, 189
Walsh, R. P., 245
Ward, R. A., 393
Warmbrod, M. E., 154
Warrick, L. H., 153
Wass, H., 145, 163
Wasserman, A. L., 227, 240, 277–278
Waters, D. B., 107
Wattenberg, S. H., 390
Weger, J. M., 61
Weiner, R., 354, 357
Weinshel, Edward, 457n
Weinstein, S., 91
Weisman, A. D., 14, 438
Weiss, L., 271

Weiss, R. S., 52, 56, 59, 68, 355, 358, 360
Weitzman, M., 195
Welisch, D. K., 451
Weston, D., 201
Wheat, W. D., 458
Wheeler, P. R., 146, 160
White, E., 139, 188
White, W. L., 450
Wiener, A., 52
Wilcoxon, S. A., 408
Wilimas, J. A., 227, 240, 277–278
Williams, C. C., 67
Williams, K., 192
Williams, W. V., 110
Williamson, P., 290
Wilner, P. J., 346, 349
Wimmer, M., 140
Winkler, D., 47
Winokur, G., 52
Wolcott, D. L., 282–283
Wolfelt, A., 58, 153
Wolff, B. B., 25
Wolff, J. R., 286
Worden, J. W., 54, 66, 112, 291
Wright, L. S., 47
Wright, S., 97, 101, 109

Yancik, R., 444–445
York, J. L., 388

Zarit, S. H., 394
Zborowski, M., 25
Zeligs, R., 145, 203
Zeltzer, L. K., 224, 227, 233–235, 239–240
Zeltzer, P., 227, 233, 239–240
Zimmerman, J., 203
Zinker, J. C., 12
Zisook, S., 73